The
Untold History
of
Japanese Gam[illegible]rs

Volume 1

By Szczepaniak

SMG SZCZEPANIAK

Published by SMG SZCZEPANIAK

In-game images, where not take by the author, are courtesy of: Hardcore Gaming 101 and MobyGames, used with permission.

All interviewee photographs are courtesy of Nicolas Datiche unless otherwise stated. **http://www.nicolasdatiche.com/**

First Edition: July 2014

Anyone wishing to contact the author can do so via his public email address:

szczepaniak@hardcoregaming101.net

ISBN: 978-0-9929260-0-7

To my mother,

for encouraging me to fight for truth and justice
in a world without any

~ SELECTED CONTENTS ~

~Foreword by GAMESIDE magazine's Editor in Chief~

山本 悠作

YAMAMOTO, Yusaku

ゲームは、ひとりで作られる芸術ではない。

出資者がいて、開発者がいて、作曲者がいて、営業職がいる。広報職がいる。
販売店がある。集団で創られて、売られて、プレイヤーの手に届く商品だ。
もちろん、本当に１人で創られたゲームもあるが、そのような例は、
世の中に存在する商業ゲームの中の、ごく一部だろう。

ゲームを遊ぶ人は、感動を得ることができる。
ゲームを努力する人は、達成感を得ることができる。
ゲームを鑑賞する人は、勇気を貰うことができる。
人の心を動かすからこそ、ゲームは商品でありながら同時に芸術品でありえるのだ。

ゲームは、ひとりで作られる芸術ではない。

ゲームクリエイターへのインタビューとは、
集団で創られた商品の課程にある、さまざまなメンバーの視点の中から、
取材対象となるクリエイターの視点に注視して、
創造の過程を探り、検証する、考古学的作業であると、私は考えている。

ゲームに関わったメンバーの数だけ、ゲームの真実がある。
人それぞれのドラマがあり、芸術的な発想がある。

取材をしてみると、メンバー同士の証言が、食い違うこともある。
その食い違いが、どちらかが間違っていることもあれば、どちらも正しい場合もある。

だから、クリエイターの証言を記事にしてゲームファンに届けるときは、
その証言が、大勢の視点の中の一つであることを、伝えなければならない。

クリエイターとゲームの関係はまるで、
地球上のあらゆる物質を構成する原子と分子の関係のようだ。

クリエイター１人１人が、ひとつの原子と考えると、
それらが複雑に結合した分子の全体像がゲームと言える。

だから、本書に掲載されているインタビュー記事の数々は、
過去のゲームの成り立ちを探り、研究するための、
歴史的発見となる貴重な原子のフルコースだ。

日本国内のゲーム専門誌の力では残念ながらたどり着けなかった証言と歴史的発見さえ、
本書には詰まっている。

さあ、新たな発見への期待を心に抱き、本書のページをめくろう。
探求の旅路へ、GAME START だ！

GAMESIDE 編集長　山本悠作　(Yusaku Yamamoto)

~ Foreword ~

Games are not made by people working alone.

There are investors, developers, composers, and salespeople. There are PR representatives. There are retail stores. Games are products, created and sold by groups of people, to be delivered into a player's hands. Of course, there are some games fully created by one person alone, but they make up just a tiny fraction of the commercial games in the world.

People who play games can be delighted by them.
People who strive at games can get a sense of accomplishment from them.
People who appreciate games artistically can be inspired by them.
Games move people. That is how games can be works of art as well as commercial products.

Games are not made by people working alone.

I believe that an interview with a game creator is a work of archaeology, a way of digging into and examining the process of creation from the perspective of the person being interviewed. That creator's perspective is just one glimpse from among a variety of perspectives that exist over the course of a product created by a group of people.

A game has as many truths as there are people who took a hand in its creation. Each person experiences their own dramas, and provides their own artistic ideas.

If you interview several people who worked together, they might contradict each other. Sometimes those contradictions are because one person is wrong. But sometimes, everyone is correct.

That is why a writer delivering a creator's own words to game fans must also tell them that those words are just one perspective out of many.

The relationship between creators and games is like the relationship between the atoms and the molecules making up all matter on Earth.

The individual creators are like single atoms, and they join together in complex ways to create an overall molecule we perceive as a game.

In that sense, the many interviews contained in this book are like a periodic table of rare elements, providing many historic discoveries regarding the origins of the games of the past.

This book is full of first-hand accounts and historic revelations that not even a Japanese specialty game magazine has been able to discover.

Now turn the page, and be ready to discover something new.
Your quest begins here. GAME START!

Yusaku Yamamoto (山本悠作)
Editor in Chief, GAMESIDE

[GAMESIDE was a regular Japanese magazine and is now a themed periodical which covers the history of games in Japan, and has developed an excellent reputation for quality. Several developers in this book, such as Kouichi Yotsui, have already been interviewed by GAMESIDE]

~ *Introduction* ~

Here it is. The book. I have walked through fire for this book. I hope it was worth it. For those who tried to stop me, I will see you in the 9th circle.

If you are holding this book in your hands and you find any value in it, please, I implore you to encourage others to buy a copy. Give it a positive review on Amazon. Tweet about it every day. Make a YouTube video. Post it on Facebook and spread the good word. I have no agent, I have no publicist. There is no one to spread the word of this book apart from you, the reader. A further two volumes are planned, but their creation rests on you, my dear reader, encouraging others to buy this first volume.

Now that it is published, if no one buys a copy then it would have all been for nothing.

~ *Acknowledgements* ~

Many helped. Without them it would never have been possible. Here they are in a semi-random order.

www.mobygames.com - this deserves a separate entry, since the circumstances are a bit unusual. Firstly, it's the most valuable resource for videogame related data I can think of. The ability to quickly cross-reference developer names against the games they worked on means I use it constantly. Every interview in this book was touched by MobyGames. While in Japan the site underwent a redesign by new owners, which removed certain search functionalities. I stopped using it. After many user complaints it eventually changed owners and returned to its former excellence. Simon Carless of MobyGames kindly gave me permission to use screenshots. Screenshots throughout the book, if not taken by me, come either from Hardcore Gaming 101, or MobyGames. If you've never visited the site, please do so. It's an enormous database of game titles, publishers, developers and screenshots. Its value with regards to videogame history is priceless. Equally as important: it's also really, really cool to browse. A wonderful site.

My dad - we should have bought that hotel in Africa! / **My brother** - who translated a French interview into English (and still charged me for it!) / **Matthew Fitsko** - a professional translator and a pillar of support while writing this. Matt not only acted as tour guide in Hokkaido, but provided high quality text translation and went through hours of audio correcting errors. I'll be honest, without Matt there would be no book. We all owe him thanks for his professional work / **Nicolas Datiche** - professional photographer with an excellent work ethic / **David Kalata** - editor of the accompanying DVD, making the entire process painless. I have nothing but praise for his professional work ethic / **Kurt Kalata** - founder of Hardcore Gaming 101, offered advice, took screenshots, captured in-game video, drove publicity, and allowed access to all screenshots on HG101 / **Ashley Day** - confidant, supporter, former editor, and my eternal professional rival / **Darran Jones** - editor on Retro Gamer. Had it not been for you encouraging me to become a writer, I'd probably have gone into art & design... / **Devin Monnens** - for proofing / **Carl Therrien** - for inviting me to give a keynote speech in Canada, along with, **Martin Picard**, who had faith and trusted me / **Kelly Boudreau** - for making the trip to Canada for my keynote speech extremely easy / **Andrea Babich** / **Ayako** - translations, emails, audio checking, and other invaluable help, thank you very much / **Ben** - founded and runs the Tokugawa forums / **Benjamin Peray** - did you ever end up eating that crocodile? / **Brady Hartel** and **Brandon Sheffield** - both gave me *Popful Mail* scans / **Bruno de Figueiredo** / **Charles Rodmell** / **Christian Nutt** / **CJ Iwakura** / **Dan Flannery** / **David East** of The Attic Bug / **Erik van Antwerpen** / **Frederic Zanchetta** / **Florent Gorges** / **GDRI** - the whole site, but also **CRV** and others / **George Bray** / **James Mielke** - for putting me in touch with **Josh Weatherford** of Active Gaming Media / also **Active Gaming Media**, for providing precisely what I requested at precisely the level of quality they promised without moving the goal posts / **James Kay** / **James Wragg** / **Jeremy Blaustein** - I should have taken your advice! / **Judy Garvey** - for providing the photo of *Crime Fighters* / **Kazuaki Yazawa** and family - thanks for letting me visit your home again, I'll study at *igo* for next time! / **Kevin Oke** / **Kosuke Iwakura** / **Lunar-net.com** for allowing use of certain *Lunar* screens / **Mangagamer.com** for translating questions for the Ryukishi07 interview / **Martyn Carroll** / **Matt Hawkins** - it only took 8 years, but here it is at last! / **Michael Doran** / **Michael Tedder** - for putting me in touch with Manabu Yamana and emails / **Mike Pavouris** - for being a huge Zainsoft fan and providing magazine scans / **Naoko Mori** - for arranging things with NudeMaker / **Oliver Clarke Smith** / **QC** at Bordersdown - for having the decency to stay away from my bins / **Rob Lowery** / **Robert Robichaud** / **Rory Milne** / **Ryota Akama** - thank you for the hospitality, and double-checking audio for mistakes / **Sam Roberts** / **Sam Derboo** - for providing a copy of *Oh!MZ* magazine to take to Japan, and helping with the *Haunted Castle* interview / **Sean Cadell** at Tech Bodz in Southampton, the bespoke laptop is fantastic / **Sergei Servianov** - we really shook the pillars of heaven, didn't we comrade? / **Sorrel Amadeus Tilley** - hurry up with that Game Boy book / **St Jude** - because the morning star takes many forms / **Takahiro Hori** / **Thomas Liebert** / **Tristan Donovan** / **Yuko Ogawara** - for writing a polite keigo letter for my interviewees, and buying me the best okonomiyaki in Osaka! / finally, **the language professor in Hokkaido**, for showing me the high standard that all interpreters should aim for - she was the best interpreter I hired / And anyone I forgot. You know who you are. Perhaps write your name in the following space: [________________________________]

Sorry I missed you off the list. Many thanks. In addition, I want to thank all my interviewees. This book was created by you, not just over 3 months during 2013, but over the last 35+ years.

All the backers who supported me and were patient. As for the ones who complained - I refunded some of you lot for a reason.

~About the author~

John Szczepaniak is a journalist, novelist, and copy editor.

He's written for Retro Gamer, GamesTM, Official PlayStation Magazine, Game Developer Magazine, Gamasutra, The Escapist, GameFAN MkII, nRevolution, 360 Magazine, Play UK, X360, Go>Play, Next3, The Gamer's Quarter, Retro Survival, NTSC-uk, Tom's Hardware Guide, Insomnia, GameSetWatch, Shenmue Dojo, Pixel Nation, plus others. He was also a keynote speaker at a Montreal University.

He frequently contributes to Hardcore Gaming 101, where he helped put together The Guide to Classic Graphic Adventures book, and was managing editor on Sega Arcade Classics Volume 1 book. He also once edited a 100'000 word fiction novel, bringing his book total to three.

John has been doing this for over 10 years, and has interviewed over 200 people. He also enjoyed a six month stint as Staff Writer on Retro Gamer and three years as sub-editor at Time Warner. He's licensed by the UK's Royal Yachting Association as a naval skipper, and also holds a Marine Radio Operator's license.

著者について

ジョン・シュチュパニアック

ジャーナリスト、小説家、コピーライター。数々のゲーム専門誌に寄稿し、過去 10 年間にわたりこの分野で様々な著作をおこすほか、200 人を超える人物へのインタビューを行ってきた。

寄稿誌は Retro Gamer, GamesTM, Official PlayStation Magazine, Game Developer Magazine, Gamasutra, The Escapist, GameFAN MkII, nRevolution, 360 Magazine, Play UK, X360, Go>Play, Next3, The Gamer's Quarter, Retro Survival, NTSC-uk, Tom's Hardware Guide, Insomnia, GameSetWatch など。

また、Hardcore Gaming101 では著述の他に、古いゲームブックの収集にも協力、Sega Arcade Classics Volume 1 では編集に携わっている。

一般購買誌では特に Retro Gamer 誌では６ヶ月間編集部のライターとして文才を振るった他、Time Warner では３年間コピーエディターとして活躍した。イギリス王室ヨット協会船長資格および海上無線通信士の資格を持ち、同人ゲームのプログラミングやワイン鋳造など行う多才な人物である。

The Untold History of Japanese Game Developers DVD

To buy the DVDs, please visit:
http://www.hardcoregaming101.net/japandvd/japandvd.htm

Between September and November 2013 I travelled around Japan interviewing developers for this book. I also produced an accompanying DVD, with segments of interview footage, game footage, and other visually interesting material. Find below a detailed summary of its contents with time stamps. Disc times are rounded, so there might be some slight discrepancy. All music on the DVD is by Yuzo Koshiro, used with permission, predominantly from his game *The Scheme*.

DISC 1

00:00 - Roy Ozaki & Kouichi Yotsui
An introduction, gift giving, various awards received by Mitchell Corp. I show Mr Yotsui photos from an anonymous source at Capcom, various design documents for games, including some which were never developed

00:21 - A mountain ryokan I stayed in

00:23 - Visiting Westone
Walk up to the company office, a look inside, plus interview introductions and gift giving with Ryuichi Nishizawa and Kouichi Yotsui

00:31 - *Cannon Dancer* director's commentary
Strider creator Kouichi Yotsui plays through the first level of *Cannon Dancer*, with commentary

00:38 - Tour of TGS 2013

00:43 - BEEP Shop with Takayuki Komabayashi
A visit to a high-end retro store located in Saitama, which is more like a museum. Rare Enix games, Japan's first RPGs, *Panorama Toh* by Yoshio Kiya, the man behind *Legacy of the Wizard*. A brief look at adult-only games

01:06 - Visiting Keigo Matsubara
Still in Saitama, I visit a collector with nearly 14'000 videogame related books

01:25 - Deco Cassette in action
Data East's DECO Cassette arcade system is an almost forgotten relic. I visit a tiny arcade in Akihabara to play the last known working unit available to the public - includes a history of the unit and its significance, plus a look inside it!

01:34 - *Flash Boy* and *Ninja*
Gameplay footage of two of the rarest DECO cassette games - possibly two of the rarest games in the world. Both are unemulated. This is direct video capture after the games were saved from destruction by Japan's Game Preservation Society. *Flash Boy* in particular is important, because it sets several arcade precedents. You'll never guess the date it came out

01:36 - Michitaka Tsuruta
Creator of *Bombjack* explains the development of *Solomon's Key*, with original concept artwork!

01:40 - Sony's Indies Stream Party

01:42 - Yuzo Koshiro
A visit to the legendary composer. We check out his studio and a couple of *doujin* games he made - one of which was never made public

01:46 - *Bare Knuckle 4*
A concept video for the never developed *Bare Knuckle 4* on Dreamcast, with a voice-over explaining what happened to it

01:49 - Professor Yoshihiro Kishimoto
Montage of the interview with Pr. Kishimoto, developer of *Pac-Land*, and programmer on Namco's *Star Wars* for Famicom

01:55:22 - END

BONUS: there are slideshows of photographs with music from Yuzo Koshiro, on both DVDs!

DISC 2

00:00 - **Human Entertainment**
Hifumi Kouno (*Clock Tower*), Masaki Higuchi (*Virtual Boy*), and Masatoshi Mitori (*Septentrion*) reminisce about Human Entertainment

00:05 - **Toru Hidaka**
Legendary Enix programmer. Created graphics, map, and audio utilities which in combination with his programming facilitated the creation of games. If you ever wondered how pixel art was made in the early 1980s, or how music ended up in games, this is for you

00:13 - **Yutaka Isokawa**
An introduction to the man behind the original *Pitman*, which became *Catrap* on the Game Boy. He was part of the NeGcon development team at Namco, and we dissect a NeGcon controller with his commentary

00:28 - **Kobe, Kyoto, and Osaka**

00:30 - **Unreleased MSX game**
Yuichi Toyama of Raizing/8ing sketches an unreleased MSX game he developed prior to joining TecnoSoft, called *Grand Slam*. Based on the *Area 88* manga and influenced by *Choplifter*, it would influence his creation of *Herzog*

00:32 - **PC Engine VS Famicom audio**
Takayuki Hirono of Compile explains the differences between the sound capabilities of the PC Engine and Famicom. Psh-psh-psh-BOOM!

00:33 ~ 00:35
Full design documents for *Guardian Legend*, *MUSHA*, and *Aleste 2*

00:35 - **Taito's art & pixel tools**
Masayuki Suzuki of Masaya/NCS describes a very unorthodox method of producing pixel art

00:40 - **Satoshi Nakai**
A look at some truly fantastic game art, from *Assault Suits Valken*, and *RE: Code Veronica*

00:42 - **PC Engine parallax and transparency**
Explanation by Masayuki Suzuki on how they achieved parallax-scrolling and transparencies on PCE, using *Shubibinman 3* as an example

00:48 - **Flying to Hokkaido**
00:50 - **Yasuhito Saito, his music on a wall**
00:50:30 - **Night driving around Sapporo!**
00:52 - **Night in a capsule hotel**

00:53 - **Hudson R&D**
Visiting the abandoned Hudson laboratory on the outskirts of Sapporo. Detailed information on the lab and Hudson

01:00 - **The Game Preservation Society**
The stuff these guys get up to is incredible. Thousands of games in storage, almost a hundred computers on hand, and more tech than you even knew existed.

01:14 - **The rarest PC Engine game on earth?**
A world exclusive. You were never meant to see this. No one was. Developed at the Hudson Computer Designers School, it allows players to meet and speak with Hudson staff

01:16 - **OutRun tapes**
Before making *OutRun*, Yu Suzuki and Yoji Ishii went on an epic cross-continent road trip with a video camera, for research. We didn't have a player to view the footage, but I shot video of the tapes themselves...

01:20 - **Famicom programming environment**
Manabu Yamana, programmer on multiple *Dragon Quest* games, describes in detail the development environment at Chunsoft.

01:22 - **Yoshiro Kimura**
A walkthrough of the Love-de-Lic offices, the bespoke board game *Potato Saga*, and an exclusive viewing of Mr Kimura's artwork

01:29 - **unreleased CBM game**
A detailed look at an unreleased game by Hiroshi Suzuki, titled *Dojin*, with added commentary by Masakuni Mitsuhashi of Game Arts

01:34 - **prototype model of MSX**

01:38 - **Rock, paper, scissors**
I play janken with the creator of *Alex Kidd*, Kotaro Hayashida. Can you guess who won?

01:40 - **Akihabara**
~ **Nakano Broadway**
01:55 - **Night photography**

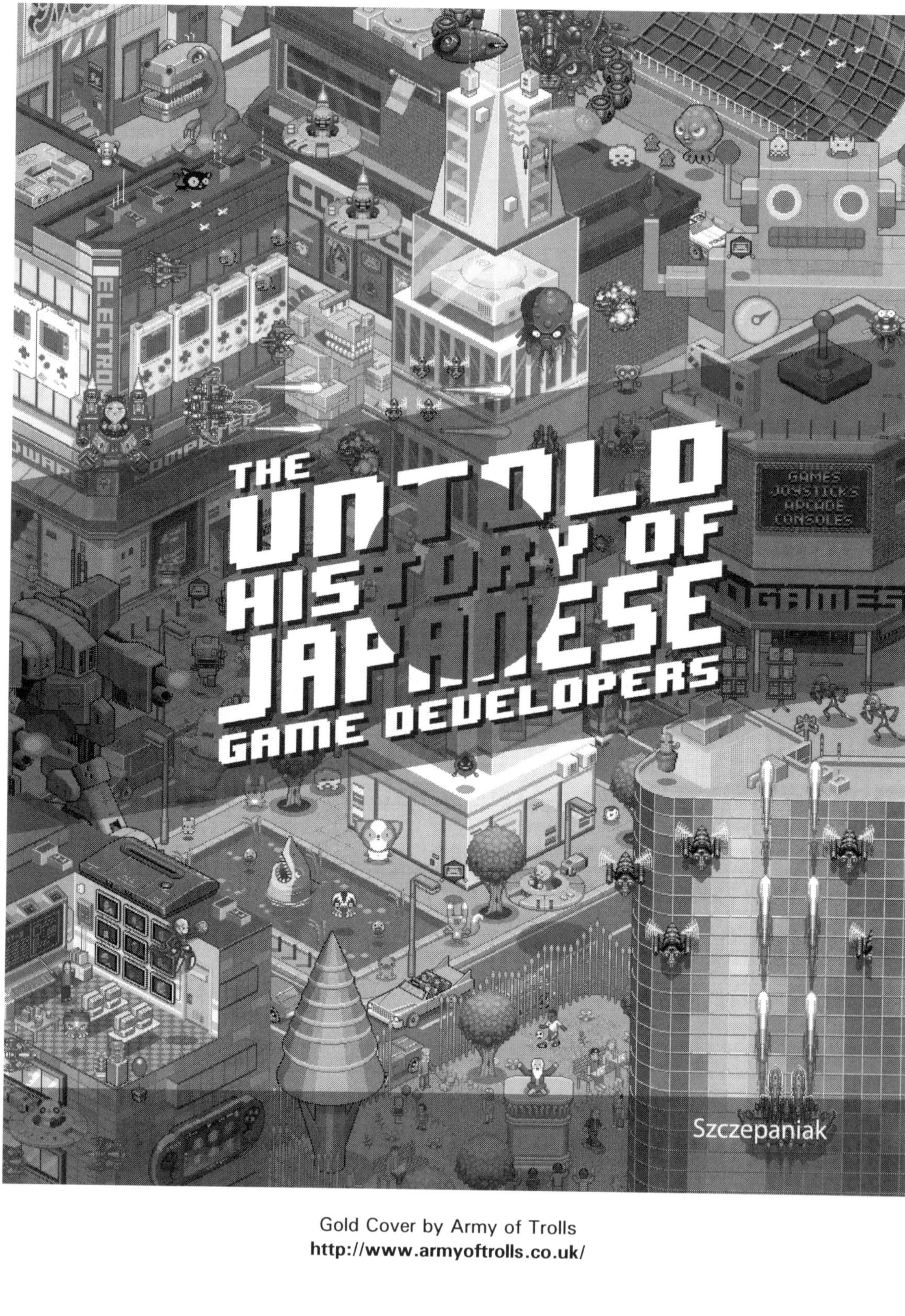

Gold Cover by Army of Trolls
http://www.armyoftrolls.co.uk/

Gold Cover by Jonathan "Persona" Kim
http://personasama.tumblr.com/

米田 仁士

YONEDA, Hitoshi

Birthplace: Nara

Interview with Hitoshi Yoneda
5 October 2013, Tokyo - Website: **http://members.jcom.home.ne.jp/zarathustra/**

It was a great honour to meet with and hire the services of Hitoshi Yoneda - legendary cover artist for various Falcom and Sega games, in addition to a multitude of work for books and magazines. If you've owned any of Falcom's original computer games you would have noticed his delicate watercolours. Mr Yoneda was also responsible for the Japanese Phantasy Star 2 cover, which adorned my Kickstarter page. The most poignant moment for me was when Mr Yoneda revealed that I was his first client from outside Japan. I hope that seeing Mr Yoneda's impressive artwork dotted around these pages, others outside of Japan will consider a commission, or perhaps even bringing over some of his - now quite rare - art book collections. Joseph Redon joined me, since he's quite the fan.

JS: Do you prefer sci-fi, or fantasy; do you have a particular theme you prefer?

Hitoshi Yoneda: I was raised on science-fiction, so for me it's very important. As an adult though, my preference is fantasy. Like Frank Frazetta, Moebius, *Heavy Metal* and so on.

Joseph Redon: The illustrations for *Sorcerian* at this time have strong colours from Moebius.[1]

HY: I was also influenced a lot by French *bandes dessinées.*[2]

JR: *Bandes dessinées* is from France *and* Belgium, and sometimes it's hard to know which country it's from.

JS: Can you recall your first professional piece?

HY: <*laughs*> It was a drawing for an article in a magazine. Very small. I'll have a look through my archive, maybe I have something from then. I keep everything, but I'm not sure where it is.

JS: Which magazine?

HY: This is the magazine, it's called *Spaceship*, or *Uchuusen*[3] in Japanese. This issue is from 1980 I think, Showa 55. It's the February issue.

JS: So this was the first ever magazine which ran your work?

HY: Yes, and it's also the first issue of this magazine. It's Volume 1. The illustration is on the very last page. My work. <*gestures to page*>

[Artwork at the back of magazine is a black-ink line drawing, showing a large room filled with cool sci-fi items on various shelves]

JS: Was this your office at the time?

HY: No, it was meant to be an idealistic place for science-fiction maniacs. So this place doesn't exist. <*laughs*>

JS: I love it when you can read titles on the books in an image.

JR: Ahh, this one says *Godzilla*. <*notes Japanese text on books*> There's one on *Godzilla*, *Gamera*, and *Ultraman*. Also foreign books, *Flights of Icarus*, Roger Dean, and a visual encyclopaedia of science-fiction. Tarzan... So it's a mix of Japanese science-fiction and foreign, mainly US or American, science-fiction.

JS: How long did this illustration take?

HY: I forgot. Hmm... One day? Perhaps.

JS: You wrote for issues 2 & 3?

HY: Two, and three.

JS: When were you interested in art?

HY: From elementary school. I was heavily inspired by sci-fi, including *Tetsuwan Atom*,[4] and other Japanese manga or comics.

JS: Were you sent copies of the magazines?

---

[1] Jean Giraud (1938-2012); French artist, produced the Japanese cover for *Panzer Dragoon* on the Saturn
[2] Popular variety of Franco-Belgian comics; ie: *The Adventures of Tintin*
[3] Kanji: 宇宙船
[4] *Astro Boy*

HY: Yes, this is a complimentary copy.

JS: How long did you illustrate for this magazine?

HY: I drew for about 40 issues. This magazine is still available today.

JS: And you drew for all the first 40?

HY: Yes, about that.

JS: So three years?

HY: No, it's not one issue per month. There's four issues per year. So it was a long time, about 10 years. So from 1980 until 1990.

JS: Did you only do the illustrations inside, or did you also do the external cover art?

HY: Not for this magazine - only the internal illustrations. But at this time already I had done cover and internal illustrations for novels.

JS: Every commercial product which included your art, did you keep a copy of that product?

HY: Yes, I have all of them.

JR: I wonder are there collectors of these items?

JS: Surely the art would have been featured in compilation books?

JR: Not all. I have his books, actually. But there's not so many illustrations from novels.

HY: These are comics I wrote by myself. [5] *<laughs>* I learned how to write comics because I loved *Doraemon,*[6] when I was younger. So I was drawing *Doraemon*, but as I grew up I changed my style to something more realistic.

JS: Was your first game cover for Falcom?

HY: I think so, yes. *Sorcerian*.

JS: Can you recall how that came about?

HY: It was someone from a publishing company called Takarajima. I think I did some work for Takarajima, and then a person from the company contacted me and presented me to Mr Kato[7] of Nihon Falcom, because they were looking for an illustrator. It's Mr Kato who wanted to get illustrations from me; so he asked me to draw illustrations for *Sorcerian*.

JS: Did you see the game before drawing these? Did Falcom give you material related to the game?

HY: Hmm... Yes, I got some documents from Falcom. I got pixel art, from the *Sorcerian* scenarios, and from that I did the illustrations.

JS: The pixel art was on paper? Or data files to load on a computer?

HY: Paper and video.

JS: Do you still have this video?

HY: Ahh... I'm not sure if I can remember! I'm not sure, but I think I first drew an illustration for *Xanadu*, for a mook[8] published by Takarajima.

<Mrs Yoneda enters the room with the mook containing the Xanadu illustration>

JR: It's not directly from Nihon Falcom, it was for Takarajima, and then I think Mr Kato saw this illustration and said, "We need him for *Sorcerian*!" *<laughs>*

HY: I think it's my first illustration related to videogames. This is an adventure book, like a choose-your-own-adventure.

JS: Seeing all this artwork makes me excited to see what you've created for my book. Illustrations for *Sorcerian* I would guess were strongly influenced by Mobius. You use colours the same way Mobius uses colours?

---

[5] These were yonkoma, or 4 cell manga; short strips consisting of 4 blocks

[6] Manga series about a time travelling robot cat

[7] Masayuki Kato, Falcom founder, 1981

[8] Magazine and book hybrid

Four of the five prototype sketches, before I made the final choice for the one to be finished

HY: Yes, yes, that's true.

JS: These are all watercolours?

HY: Yes, watercolours.

JS: Do you have a preferred medium - oils, watercolours, ink?

HY: Yes, watercolours are my favourite.

Mrs Yoneda: He uses paper from France, and pencils from England.

<*everyone laughs*>

HY: Indeed!

JS: Could you guess how much art you've done?

HY: It's hard to count!

JS: This book alone has over 100 pages of illustrations. So it must be thousands.

HY: <*laughs*> Not so much! But yes, it's hundreds of illustrations.

JS: Wow, this is from *Phantasy Star*. How did you come to work for Sega?

HY: Sega directly asked me to draw illustrations. In order to counter Nintendo, Sega put on the market the Mega Drive. But they didn't have enough power within the company to challenge Nintendo, so they decided to ask external people to help them. Such as myself, for illustrations.

JS: I have a difficult question. *Phantasy Star 2* had the cover changed when coming to the US market. Some of the worst art I've ever seen. Did you know that?

HY: <*laughs*> No, I had no idea!

JS: Were you ever hired by a company outside of Japan?

HY: No, I've never worked for a foreign company, or had any inquiry from one. Only Japan, unfortunately.

JS: So that means I'll be your first foreign client!

HY: <*laughs*> Yes! My first foreign client!

<*everyone laughs*>

JS: I'm honoured to be the first.

HY: It's my pleasure.

JS: <*to Joseph*> Perhaps we can use our smartphones to look up the US cover for *Phantasy Star 2* and ask what Yoneda-san thinks?

HY: I think that my illustration was perhaps not appropriate for the foreign market.

JR: I think the problem was not that. Maybe it was licensing, maybe it was cheaper to draw a new illustration?

The final version of the piece I chose, as it adorns the Platinum cover editions of this book. Interestingly, this image was not present when I visited Mr Yoneda's home and he showed me the art on the computer screen. But when he later emailed me the 5 options, this one was the most interesting.

JS: I don't think it's price, I think the foreign marketing departments were clueless and had no appreciation for good art. The new cover isn't appropriate for any market.

<everyone laughs>

JS: I'm sure anyone who saw the covers would be disappointed your cover was not used.

JR: We have different tastes in America and Europe.

HY: *<refers to PS2 over>* I think that this cover was intended for the American market, this style of oil painting.

HY: I was also influenced by Arthur Rackham,[1] *<shows book>* so for me this represents the traditional English culture of watercolours. I was also influenced by Edmund Dulac[2] and his method for blending colours. I used to read this book when I was a student at the Kyoto University of Art.

JS: Which area are you originally from?

HY: I'm from Nara prefecture.[3]

JR: And maybe in Europe we would have wanted Yoneda-san's illustration.

HY: England has a culture of water paintings.

JS: Sometimes, like with Famicom games, you would have entirely different artwork for Japan, America and Europe. They were all different.

JR: *<explaining artwork>* This is from an exhibition in Shiga, a fantasy illustration exhibition, with Amano-san and many illustrations for games, including this one from *Brandish*. And some nice illustrations from *Sorcerian* and *Warlock*. It's a pity Yoneda-san is not famous outside of Japan. The reason, for example regarding Amano-san, is his illustrations were also used outside of Japan. But in Yoneda-san's case, they were only used in Japan. He also thinks it's regrettable.

JS: Do you think it's because *Final Fantasy* gained a widespread international audience, whereas Falcom RPGs tended to be more niche?

JR: *Sorcerian* was only sold in America by Sierra Online. But a very limited production. So many don't even know about *Sorcerian*. For famous artwork, it would be *Phantasy Star*, mainly.

JS: Do you play the games and read the books which use your artwork?

HY: Not reading, usually just flicking through it if I'm doing the cover. However, when drawing illustrations within novels, in order to create the illustration I have to read the book through.

JS: The whole book, or just a section?

---

[1] 1867-1939, English book illustrator
[2] 1882-1953, French magazine illustrator
[3] Famous for the Nara deer park many UNESCO World heritage sites. Mr Yoneda spends a lot of time in Nara

HY: When I have to draw the inner illustrations I read the whole book.

JS: Commendable. Some artists just draw based off a brief.

HY: Ahh, is that right? In order to understand the colour of hair, and what clothes the people are wearing, I have to catch the details. So it's important to read the whole book.

<JR converses with Mrs Yoneda>

JR: I asked when Yoneda-san started to use computers. She said a long time ago, like 15 years ago, but specifically for his job, it was 10 years ago with card illustrations. He paints in here and computer work is done in the next room. He does hand drawings, then scans it and adds special effects.

JS: I notice on Twitter that you're often in Nara.

HY: I think it's safer to be in Kansai, because there are many earthquakes in the Kanto area. So usually I am in Nara, more than Tokyo. I love riding bicycles, so I prefer riding them in Nara rather than Tokyo.

<looks at books on a shelf>

JR: These are books for young girls, so a very different style. [4] [...] First Yoneda-san started using Mixi, which is like Facebook for Japan, and from Mixi he moved to Twitter.[5]

HY: This is a replica of my artwork which was used for an exhibition in Ginza, about 10 years before. Other exhibitions where I was involved, I was not alone. I was asked to participate in an exhibition in Turin, in Italy, but I didn't feel safe posting my artwork all the way abroad, so I didn't participate in that.

JR: Maybe in the future he will get another offer - I hope so. Maybe in Paris, or London. And then I hope he will accept!

<JR converses with Mrs Yoneda>

JR: This is Mrs Yoneda's artwork which went to that exhibit. The offer came just before the [problem with the banks in America], and then the offer changed, and it was just: "Please send us your artwork, but you cannot come to Italy."

JS: Presumably they returned it?

JR: Yes, she sent original artwork. He didn't make the replica by himself, someone else did.

[Lots of dialogue skipped]

HY: My best fan is my wife. We were together at university, and I was like a senior. She thought I was very good at drawing, so was my first fan.

<Conversation in Japanese - everyone laughs>

JR: We say that behind every exceptional man there is always an exceptional woman.

JS: What a wonderful story, and a nice situation to be in. Is there any message or comment you want printed in the book?

HY: From now I'm going to draw more and more illustrations. So I hope that with your book, I will be known by more people outside of Japan. So please encourage me.

JS: When I spoke with some gentlemen from Compile, and mentioned I was visiting Yoneda-san, they all went, "Wow! We wish we could come!"

HY: *<laughs>* I'm very happy to hear that.

JR: Yes, everyone who likes fantasy in Japan knows about Mr Yoneda.

---

4 The style is more light-hearted

5 https://twitter.com/Brise_Marine

野村 達雄

NOMURA, Tatsuo

Interview with Tatsuo Nomura of Google

After starting my Kickstarter project I was contacted by Tatsuo Nomura, who works for Google. He'd seen the project and liked the opening graphics I'd created. As it turns out, Mr Nomura had been an influence on the project. Although not a game developer, the opportunity for an interview was too good to pass up. Images on these pages taken from Google's explanatory video, and are Copyright of Google.

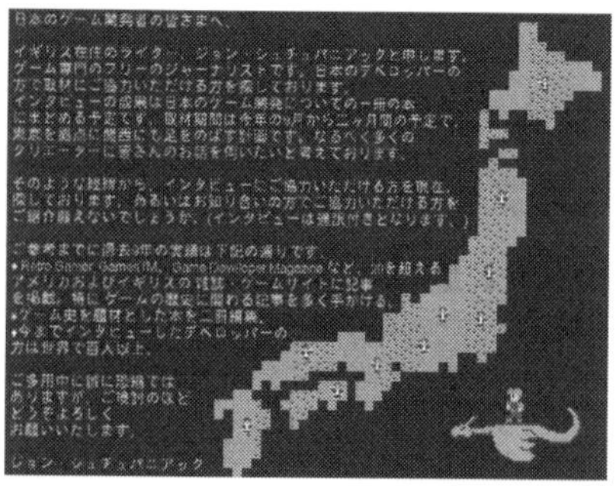

TN: I'm a software engineer working on Google Maps. I saw your project on Kickstarter by chance and am very excited about it. I was reading a book - *Super Mario: How Nintendo Conquered America* by Jeff Ryan - and was searching for related topics, and bumped into it. Your graphics reminds me of a project called 8-bit Maps I did a while ago. I did three April Fool projects for Google Maps; they weren't games per se, but I thought you might be interested in them. *<links to 8-bit Maps, Find Treasure with Google Maps, and Google's recent Pokémon Challenge project>*

JS: I was heavily influenced by 8-bit Maps! I wanted an image of Japan, so I shrunk down a map to around 25 x 25 pixels. Afterwards I

enlarged it, created a custom paint tile, and filled in the grass. Then I drew the sprites and pasted them in. Years of using *RPG Maker* paid off!

TN: Very cool! It's not very different from what I did for the 8-bit Maps, except that the 8-bit Maps was all computer generated.

JS: Were you a big fan of 8-bit RPGs?

TN: *Dragon Quest* (*Dragon Warrior* in US) is indeed the very first videogame I played. I could never finish it though. Since nowadays most games are super realistic, 3D rendered, with sophisticated shaders, I can't help feeling nostalgic about the pixel arts. They have some kind of softness which you can't simulate with 3D polygons. Apparently not only myself thought this, but also many colleagues did too. If you search for 8-bit Maps landmarks, you'll find tons screenshots of things like the Eiffel Tower, Forbidden City and so on so on. They were all hand drawn by over 100 of my colleagues, and they all enjoyed it very much.

JS: Where are you based - in Japan?

TN: I'm based in US. I was based in Japan when I made 8-bit Maps.

JS: Describe how 8-bit Maps started.

TN: It was in January 2011, my first year working at Google. I was having lunch with my teammates and chatting about what to do for the April Fool's prank. It was just one of the lunch time subjects and nothing too serious. I came up with this idea - what if we made the maps look like *Dragon Quest*? I grew up playing NES and SNES. I even created an NES emulator and a homemade FPGA NES[1] when I was in the college. So I think it was very natural for me to come up with this idea. After lunch, I went back to my desk and started to think about how I could make it. I quickly made a demo using Chrome extensions in a few hours and showed it to my team and posted it on the internal Google+. Although it was a really rough and quick demo, that was nowhere near the actual production quality, everyone that saw it laughed and shared their excitement. It didn't take too long before it became a project taking up 20% of my time. This soon turned into a 100% fulltime project, and expanded from a local to a global project. I was only going to make 8-bit Maps, but the Street View team joined us later and developed an 8-bit Street View version. It was a purely volunteer project, like most of the other April Fool's projects at Google. The goal of our April Fool's projects is to surprise users and make them laugh. I think because many Googlers loved 8-bit Maps and were willing to volunteer, the users could enjoy and share our excitement.

JS: Square-Enix told Game Informer: *"It was a collaborative effort between Sq-En and Google. Google came up with the idea, then we provided the assets and helped them to create the map."*

TN: As soon as we decided to launch this, I contacted our marketing team to get Sq-En involved. We showed them the demo I made and they were very happy and excited about it. They provided us with the assets that were once used in *Dragon Quest*, such as tile textures and monster illustrations and music for the video. All of the development was done in-house.

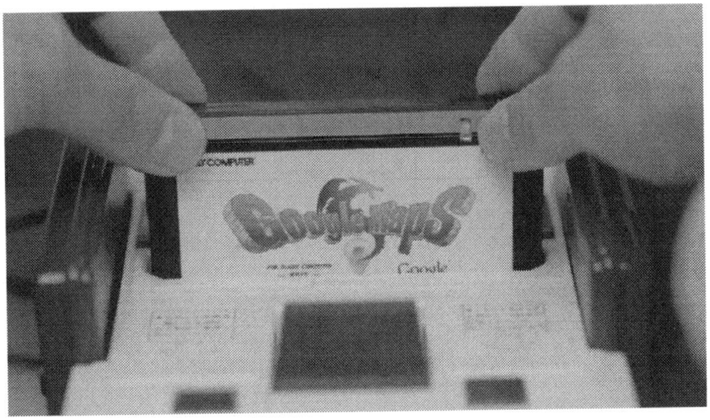

JS: Did you have to get permission from Nintendo to show images of the Famicom?

TN: Yes, we did ask Nintendo for permissions. In the promotion video, I said, "Blow on the cartridge to fix bugs." Even though that's officially not recommended, Nintendo thought that was a nice joke and gave us approval.

JS: Were you involved in the video filming of the family plugging the cartridge in?

TN: I was too busy developing the product when the creative team was shooting the video. I wish

---

[1] Field-programmable gate array; a homemade console

I could have met the actors in person, but unfortunately I couldn't; I barely had time to shoot my part.

JS: Is that your desk in the video? Whose FC cartridges are those piled up?

TN: The desk is not my desk, but the pile of FC cartridges is my personal collection. If you look closely, you can see *Dragon Quest III* is inserted to the homebrew NES I made when in college.

JS: How were the landmarks created?

TN: It was volunteers from worldwide Googlers. At Google, we have a culture where we first ask Googlers to use the product and test it before launching it to the public. This process is called "dogfooding". When we started dogfooding for the 8-bit Maps, I received tons of messages from Googlers in different divisions and different countries. Everyone seemed really excited about this project and many of them asked if there was anything they could help with. I remember that someone suggested the idea of having 8-bit style landmarks. I thought maybe I can ask everyone to help with creating those landmarks. I sent messages to a few different mailing lists and received great enthusiasm. I worked with a designer to create the spec and some rules. Anyone could draw any landmark or monsters or anything 8-bit-ish they wanted, and tell me where to put it. They were created by many Googlers and there was a wide variety, such as Tokyo Tower, Taj Mahal, a UFO at Area 51, Sasquatch in BC Canada and so on. One interesting example is the panda. A designer made the illustration and put it in all zoos in the world which have pandas. At the end, we had about 120 landmarks all over the world.

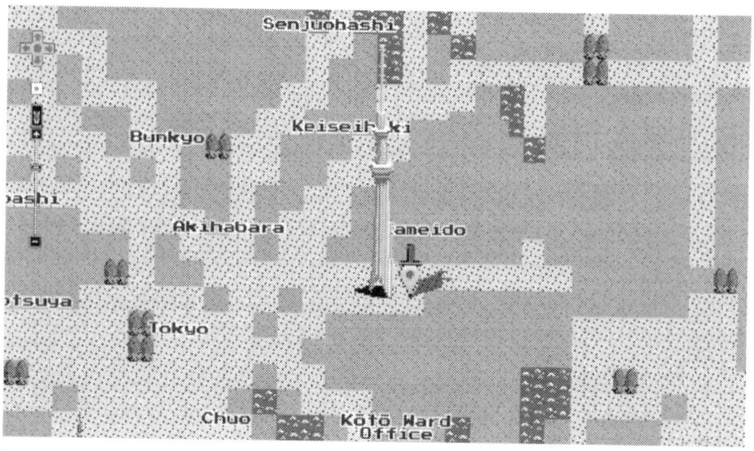

JS: Was there a Japanese language version of the video? The English version shows the Famicom, but refers to it as an NES.

TN: At Google, we always try to launch products globally. English was chosen because it's a global language. We used Famicom and a Japanese family in the video because the Famicom was invented in Japan and we felt it's natural to show that aspect.

JS: From conception to completion, how long did it all take to create?

TN: It took me more than a month in addition to about 20% of the volunteers' time.

JS: Can you describe the technical aspects - how much of the map layouts were done manually, versus being by computer algorithm?

TN: Besides where to put the landmarks, everything is done algorithmically. I'm proud of myself to be able to invent an algorithm that entirely changes how the world looks; at least on the map.

JS: From what I can tell, it's no longer accessible online. How do you feel about this? In a way it's a bit like ice sculptures - fleeting and only viewable for a time.

TN: It's truly like an art. Every year we spend so much effort and then it's gone forever after a day. But I guess the transitory nature is a part of its beauty.

JS: What's your favourite (non-*Dragon Quest*) Japanese RPG?

TN: It's a little bit old school, but I love *Mario RPG*, *The Legend of Zelda: A Link to the Past*, and *Final Fantasy VI ~ VIII*. If you can call it an RPG, I love *Pokémon* too - which became the basis for the 2014 April Fool's joke. Not only the games but I also love the music in these games. I don't play many games anymore, but I still love to listen to the music while I'm coding.

~In memory of~

With the passing of Kenji Eno in 2013, along with several others in the Japanese games industry that same year, I developed an increased awareness of the need to document games history while we still have time, and also the importance of remembering those who have moved on. Over the following pages I interview Katsutoshi Eguchi, friend and colleague of Kenji Eno. He reveals an incredible and as yet unknown side to the man. Throughout this book and the subsequent volumes are memorial pages for those in the games industry who have died. Where possible I have used quotes from their colleagues and friends.

The below list isn't even remotely comprehensive - it merely highlights the difficulty of keeping track. In many instances there isn't even a reliable source for the date of their passing. If anyone has information to contribute or knows of others who should be remembered here, or perhaps worked with someone who they want to reflect on, please feel free to contact me and I will try to do so for later volumes.

Kenji Eno	- Head of WARP (20 February 2013)
Hiro Isono	- Cover artist on *Secret of Mana* and others (20 May 2013)
Hiroyuki Kanno	- Visual novel scenario writer and designer (19 December 2011)
Masahiko "Patariro" Kurokawa	- Game design for *Strider* (NES), writer for *Tomba! 1&2* (2008)
Masato Masuda	- *Fire Pro Wrestling* creator (April 2014)
Mitsuhiro Matsuda	- Game Arts co-founder
Fukio Mitsuji	- Creator of *Bubble Bobble* (11 December 2008)
Takeshi Miyaji	- Game Arts co-founder (29 July 2011)
Kazurou Morita	- Renowned Enix programmer (27 July 2012)
Hideyuki Nakajima	- Tengen president (11 July 1994)
Shinya Nishigaki	- Climax Entertainment, *Landstalker*, *Illbleed* (July 2004)
Isao Okawa	- Former Chairman of Sega (16 March 2001)
Manabu Saito	- System Sacom composer (1992)
Tomoharu Saito	- *Streets of Rage 2* character designer (29 July 2006)
Akio Sakai	- Capcom employee, later producer on *FF: Spirits Within*
Tomoyuki Shimada	- Game Arts programmer (*Zeliard*)
Suu Urabe	- Character designer, also a famous indie comic artist (2001)
Ryu Umemoto	- Music composer (16 August 2011)
Gunpei Yokoi	- D-pad and Game Boy inventor (4 October 1997)
Hiroshi Yamauchi	- Former Nintendo president (19 September 2013)

江口 勝敏

EGUCHI, Katsutoshi

DOB: *secret* / Birthplace: *secret* / Blood Type: *secret*

Interview with Katsutoshi Eguchi
21 October 2013, Tokyo, From Yellow to Orange offices

One of the many reasons for starting this book was the death of Kenji Eno. I had long been a fan of his work - all of it, not just the horror games which were localised. Apart from the Japanese audio-only games he made, which fascinated me, I made every effort to source all of his titles, including obscure 3DO titles.

He was a maverick who played by his own rules, and his passing so young was a shock to me. I wrote the memorial page for him in Retro Gamer magazine. So it was a wonderful surprise while in Japan to be contacted by Mr Eguchi - a friend and colleague of Mr Eno. I interviewed him regarding their work together, and also his company's plans to keep the dreams of Mr Eno alive through crowdfunding.

At the time of editing this interview, 19 May 2014, Mr Eguchi's crowdfunding project, KAKEXUN, has reached its goal, making 5'486'300 yen (£32k / $54k). Reading this interview, and reflecting on Mr Eno's life and career, please check out KAKEXUN to see its progress: **http://www.kakexun.asia/**

NOTE: Some supplementary information was taken from 1UP.com's massively in-depth interview with Kenji Eno, titled "Japan's Wayward Son", by Shane Bettenhausen and James Mielke, circa 2008. Everyone should read this interview.

JS: Before we discuss Mr Eno, please tell me about yourself.

KE: I started as a punk musician at the age of 19! <*laughs*> I went to India for 6 months, in 1977. When I came back from India I got involved in the Tokyo Rockers movement, as a bass player. It was a collection of five bands. We used to play a lot of gigs together. After that the five bands were contacted as a group, by CBS Sony, who said, "We want you to record one album, between the five bands." So we did that and released it.

JS: What was the name of your band?

KE: S-KEN.[1] <*spells each letter out*> Then we did an album, called the *Tokyo Rockers Album*, which was the collection of those bands. Because it was the same time as the *Sex Pistols* arrived in the UK, punk was sprouting up in different cities at the same time all over the world. One of the other members from the Tokyo Rockers movement went to New York and worked with Brian Eno on an album called *No New York*. Then after this *[Tokyo Rockers Album]* release we did a tour throughout Japan. Then Columbia Records, which is a label in Japan, rereleased the album after the tour. After that I stopped - it was the end of my rock career. After that I was a manager for a handful of bands, and then at one point, a magazine publisher said they were going to found an independent music label. I was invited to join that label, and be involved. I wrote a bunch of letters to different labels and magazines in the UK, and eventually I went over there, met a lot of people, and I brought music of bands from England, to introduce to Japan. For example the music of Keith Levene[2] I brought over. The name of the indie label by the magazine publisher was Captain Records. We used to help bands that were coming up through the Japanese indie scene. Give them a foot up to get a big record deal. I was working in the indie scene around the mid-1980s. Then I got into music production, the production of albums and so on. So I had some relations or links to a lot of fans. I produced major records for about 20 artists or groups. Around 1990 I got five awards for my work, including the highest award from the Recording Industry Association of Japan.

In 1991 I already had an interest in Martin Heath of Rhythm King, who made music, but also game music in association with Bitmap Brothers and Renegade Software. When I went to meet him that's where the concept of making music for games - for me - came about. That's how I was introduced to it.

JS: I believe you published some games too?

KE: <*laughs*> You know the British game developer Bitmap Brothers, which made *Xenon 2* and *Gods*, and so on? Through Martin Heath I met the guys from the Bitmap Brothers. Even now I'm in contact with Eric Matthews[3] from the Bitmap Brothers, he's a friend of mine on Facebook. He works at Sony now. My company

[1] There's a Japanese Wikipedia page and YouTube vids

[2] Renowned musician; founding member of *The Clash*

[3] Designer on *Speedball 2*, *Gods* and *The Chaos Engine*

obtained the distribution rights and released *Xenon 2* and *Gods* in Japan through Nintendo and Sega, under the label PCM Complete. We localised them, as it were. Martin Heath was the one who said to me, "I've got this game contract. Do you want to take a look at it?" And it was with Renegade. That's why I got involved in the videogame industry. It started with Bitmap Brothers and, taking them as inspiration, that's how I later got involved with WARP and so on.

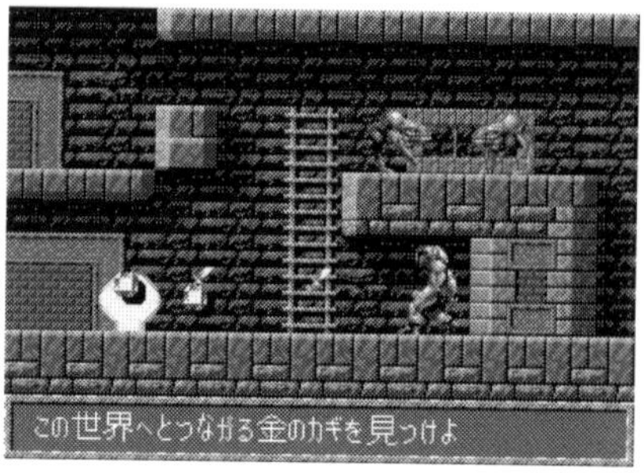

JS: Which version of *Gods* was this?

KE: The Mega Drive version. And *Xenon 2* was on... What was it? The first handheld, by Nintendo. Game Boy?

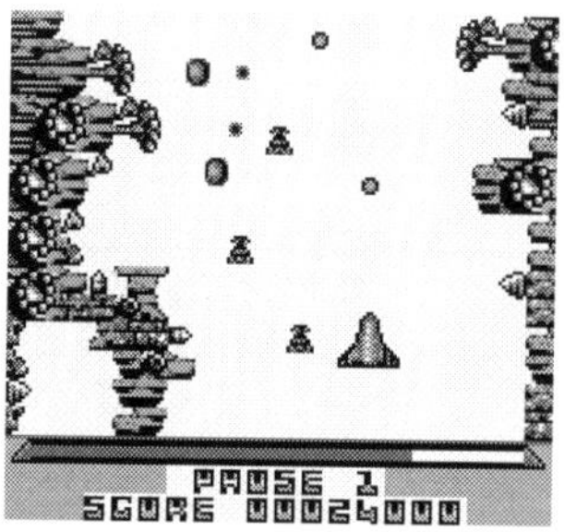

JS: Black and white?

KE: Yes, the black and white Game Boy.

JS: How did the Japanese market react to *Gods*? It feels distinctly European. I really liked it.

KE: I agree with you that it has a European style, and it feels as such, but when I went and played it, *Gods* was something that clicked with me instantly. It was something I immediately wanted to play more of. But it sold terribly. The PC-98 version and the Sega version, they did not sell. Essentially it was a loss. <*laughs*>

JS: I'm sorry to hear that.

KE: Even though it was a bit of a failure, that's how we all got to know each other in the industry. So Nintendo and Sega and so on, I met them through that process. Although it was a shame that it did not sell well, maybe overall it was worth it.

JS: What happened after that?

KE: In about 1992 or 1993 in Japan, they called it the "band boom", but the sort of diehard fanship of rock bands kind of fell away. So that's when I decided, I'm not going to work with music artists, I'm going to work on game music, and anime music as well. My job was that I took the music from games which had been developed by the game companies, and I would take them to record companies and work out how to get them released as albums.

JS: OSTs are wildly popular in Japan.

KE: Then I stopped doing that and formed my own record company. I made a label to release game soundtracks. First Smile Entertainment[4] was the name of the company I founded. I released some titles, including from *Gran Tourismo* and the *Zelda* series.

JS: Was it difficult getting the Nintendo license?

KE: Yes, it was difficult. I basically just kept going, down to Kyoto, until they gave me the license. <*laughs*>

JS: Tell me about *From Yellow To Orange*.

KE: When it was founded there was going to be a focus on web content, and online distribution. Our feeling was the web was quite... Cold might not be the right word, but an unfeeling place. It was founded with a view to communication, and we felt we wanted to make it more human, more warm. So, From Yellow to Orange.

JS: Let's talk about Mr Eno.

KE: First I'd like to talk about Eno-san's history, and where he came from. He was not really sure, after finishing the education he did,[5] what he wanted to do. He sort of headed around Japan, travelled, and wondered about what he wanted to do, what he wanted to become. He kept taking these jobs, and then he would leave after a day. He did that twice, two times he went in and on that day he realised it wasn't for him. So he definitely had strong views. A driven person.

When he was in primary school he entered a computer game programming contest, and he won a prize through that. He took the actual prize-winning game he made as an elementary school student to Interlink, and

[4] There's a profile on VGMdb

[5] 1UP: dropped out of high school aged 17

handed it to them, and they gave him a job. So yes, Eno-san was definitely very interesting, right from the beginning.

JS: I've read about that, amazing!

KE: He was given a computer by his father, an MSX I believe, when he was very young, and he used that to make the program. He left high school, and that's when he took the program that he'd made to Interlink. So when he actually applied he didn't really know anything about programming, because he hadn't done it in over 10 years! <*laughs*> He applied using a programmer's approach, but the company said to him, "You can't program." But he always had an interest in music, so he said, "I can probably give your music a go." That's what role he took on. He worked on the music for *Juuouki*, [6] and worked on *Ultraman Club 2*.[7]

Even though it wasn't really his job, he was not afraid to tell people when their projects were rubbish, and gave a lot of advice. He would say, "This game is not fun, and here's why..." By the time he finished with that company, he was considered a planner, not just a musician.

JS: He eventually developed *Sunman*, which was never released.

KE: Really? I'd never heard about this!

JS: It was leaked online, and someone asked him in a interview, and he was like, "How did you know about that?!"

KE: Ahh! That was not with Interlink though. It must have been between Interlink and WARP.

JS: It was the last game he worked on at EIM,[8] his first company start-up.

KE: When he was running EIM, what happened was they were doing games for other companies, like production house work, and all that ever came was requests for sequels of established titles. Especially from companies like Bandai and so on. Then he just stopped coming to work, his own company. Because he wasn't enjoying it, and it wasn't what he wanted to do. And that's why EIM closed, because they didn't have a leader, because he just didn't come in. He had no desire, no motivation to go in and work, because it was just the same routine: take our game, copy it, and change it a bit. Which was not what he wanted to do. He went to America to attend this software developers show in San Francisco, the Macworld Expo, and also the "Be-in" event that took place. [9] If you remember, he had been sort of bullied out of the industry because he was being forced to do sequels and so on. It was seeing these developers saying, "I'm going to make this game," and then just doing it. This showed him that it still could be done, and there was a place in the industry for innovators. That's why he came back to try to make WARP. Because this expo was evidence that it wasn't just sequels, or a factory floor, there was these people in America making whatever they wanted to. He wanted to do that as well. It was really that show that was the driving motivation for him to come back and form WARP. Apple were maybe the sponsors of the event he attended.

JS: Apparently *Sunman* started as *Superman*.

KE: He used to take his ideas for games to different companies, and I don't know whether this is also true of *Sunman*, but he would say that the company told him, "Hmm, we'll think about it," and then six months later or whenever he would spot a game that clearly used his idea.

Unfortunately I can't remember the names of any of the games that Eno-san thought had used his ideas, but back around 2001 he showed me a demo tape of a retail game. It was a kind of light-hearted action game with lots of cute characters coming together, I guess a kind of single player game, where you would have multiple protagonists, and you'd switch between them. Although I can't remember the title, I do remember Eno-san showed me this game and said, "This was my idea! This was my idea!"

He said it a lot. This is just one example. Of course, he used to say that he always had about 20 game ideas in his head...

JS: His ideas were original. On 3DO, his game *Short Warp*[10] contained minigames which seem to have influenced *Warioware* by Nintendo.

---

6 *Altered Beast*, specifically the Famicom port

7 1UP: planner on this, rewrote the document

8 Entertainment Imagination and Magnificence; a contract developer

9 1UP: in 1994; "Be-in" was described by Eno as a "counter-culture" event, the inverse of Macworld

10 Japan only, 1996, came packaged with a condom. The minigames are identical in style and humour to those found later in *Warioware*

KE: *Short Warp* is definitely one of the games where you had to have someone like Eno-san, who would just say, "I'm making this game!" It wasn't a game you could really sell to a developer. When the 3DO came... The big game they made on that was the first *D* title, but when they were given the specs from the 3DO developers they didn't really know if they were accurate. They also didn't really know what those specs implied, in terms of what they could make. That's why when the hardware came out they produced a handful of smaller games.[11] That was really just for the programming team to test the water with the 3DO. Once they'd sort of figured out what was possible, that's when they made *D*.

JS: Experiments to get a feel for the hardware.

KE: Yes, that's right. So there were two teams, and one was always working on *D*, and the other was making these smaller games. Then the smaller team would report back to the *D* team and say, "OK, look how well this worked, so whatever we've done with this, whatever code or graphics or sound, it works. So let's put that into *D*."

JS: When John Byrd[12] visited Japan Mr Eno treated him and other programmers to a night out, making sure everyone had a good time.

KE: That definitely sounds like him. It was a different time back then. It was much more of a done thing. For example Sakaguchi-san, the gentleman behind *Final Fantasy*, he used to take people to "lingerie pubs"[13] and spend 2'000'000 yen. It was right when Japan was in the economic bubble. Eno-san did it as well, it was not an unheard of thing.

JS: What an awesome era. I wish I was around back then to document the industry!

KE: Eno-san always had a desire to make customers and clients feel welcome and happy. It makes sense that he would do that, because I think he would spend as much as he needed, to make people feel welcome. That was definitely his style.

JS: Was WARP a strong supporter of 3DO because licensing agreements were easier?

KE: Whether or not it was simple to get contracts is not what's important. What is important is that Eno-san loved being at the forefront of new movements. It's more than what the 3DO was, or what it represented; it was really just the fact that its release lined up with the creation of WARP and his desire to come back into games. It was about timing. The 3DO started at around the same as WARP, or Eno's desire to come back into the industry, so it was more about getting on top of what he thought would be a big success.

JS: When did you meet Kenji Eno?

KE: I met him in 1996. I come from the music industry. When *D* came out I sent a message to Eno-san, asking, "Do you want to release the music for *D*, through our company?" As a music CD. That must have been in October 1996, and then after that everything else that came out, *D2* and so on, my company handled all the music. So that's when our relationship started.

The first time I called Eno and said I want to meet with you, he said sure. After that it took 6 months before anything happened, because that's just the way he was. I used to call again and again, and every time I'd get Eno's manager or assistant, and they said, "Sorry, he's currently busy." Then my company started developing 3D sound technology, and the concept of sound positioning. When I told Eno's manager that, the next day I got a phone call saying, "I want to meet today." Then I met him and we talked for hours and hours about it, and about his projects and what he was doing and so on. Then afterwards I called another record company's manager and said to him, I've just

---

[11] *Totsugeki Kikan Megadasu!!* (1994), *Flupon: Space Biology* (1994)

[12] Senior engineer at 3DO; posted this on Gamasutra: *"I spent many hours at the WARP offices, tried hard to make sure Eno-san and Hiro-san were comfortable when visiting 3DO. These guys were just a bunch of young random Japanese kids at the time. But they were so nice and so fun it was obvious that we had to do everything possible to help them. Once Eno-san took me and a couple programmers to a [hostess] bar in Shinjuku. Dude dropped like 100'000 yen on me in under an hour. I'll miss him a lot."*

[13] Hostess club, albeit with hostesses in lingerie

met a genius. This guy is where it's happening. I was definitely struck from the first minute I met him. Kenji Eno was a genius. When I met him he was 26 or so, but through that meeting I felt he was wise beyond his years. He was definitely far more mature and far more adult about it than you would expect of someone that age.

JS: Did you visit the WARP offices?

KE: Yes, they were in Ebisu, I went a few times.

JS: Perhaps I should photograph the old building?

KE: WARP moved within Ebisu, so its first location was in the south; out of the south gate, the south half of Ebisu. The second time was in the north of Ebisu. When I met him, Eno-san was in the north half, after they had moved. So I've never been to the original, south office. After that they went to a place called Gaiemmae in Aoyama, on the second floor of a building there. Then they went to Azabu-Juban, in front of the Columbian embassy! *<laughs>* Then they went back to Ebisu, right in front of the station. They moved all over Tokyo, basically. *<laughs>*

JS: Why did the company move so much?

KE: The simple reason is they kept adding more people. So things got crowded. They didn't move for any other reason. They just ran out of space, again and again.

JS: Mr Eno produced a game with no visuals.[14] That came with a bag of herb seeds?

KE: *<laughs>* That's right, yes. I'm not sure why, but it was definitely there. There's something interesting about *Real Sound*. Eno-san rented a recording studio for a week, to make this game for the blind. While he was doing that I went along to see what was going on - because it's an interesting thing. So I went there, and there was a recording room, and then a sound-mixer's room or booth, and they're connected but you can't hear one room from the other. Eno-san was standing in the engineer's room, watching it occur. I turn up and he sees me, and he says, "Just come over here, I'm going to go in there, and make them act, physical acting. They're going to act out what they're saying, even though there's no visuals. They're not acting and I want them to act. So you're going to take over and do the sound management." *<laughs>* So I then became the sort of impromptu sound manager for the project, and from then on I was in charge of the sound.

<laughs, then in English> I just came to look around there!

<in Japanese> I would stand in the recording room listening to them, to make sure the track was OK, while Eno-san would stand in the room. For example there's a scene where the two main characters kiss, and he actually made them kiss. *<laughs>* They were two really famous Japanese actors, and he really brought them together, because he felt it truly needed to be real, not just sound, but real. If they didn't really kiss, how were they supposed to make it believable? Every single scene in that game he would go into that room, and whatever happened he would make them do it properly. And he wouldn't settle for less. So the two actors who play the two main characters, there's a love story between them, and after the production of the game these famous actors started dating in real-life as well. The female actress was Miho Kanno,[15] and the male actor was Takashi Kashiwabara.

JS: What a beautiful story!

KE: I didn't know what the project was, and I didn't really know why I was there, and he didn't record the scenes in order, so the story didn't make any sense to me! *<laughs>* It was really a case of just watching a genius at work. I had no idea of the story, only a very brief outline. That project took an entire week, to read every single day.

Normally when you do that sort of thing you'd have like a catering service. But not this time - we had a sushi counter, because Eno-san had a friend who owned a sushi bar in Ginza. So we had sushi every day! *<laughs>*

JS: Were you with Mr Eno when he spoke with Michael Nyman in a hotel to arrange the *Enemy Zero* soundtrack?[16]

---

[14] *Real Sound*; Saturn (1997), no graphics, audio only

[15] Actress and J-Pop singer; was the Japanese voice of Rami in *Keio Flying Squadron*

[16] Michael Nyman visited Japan in 1995 following the Kobe earthquake. According to the 1UP interview Mr Eno visited Mr Nyman's hotel, invited him to his room, and spent 6 hours convincing him. Mr Eno said: "At the end, Michael was like, 'OK, I'll do it, I'll do it. Just let me go back to my room.'"

KE: Yes, I was there the whole time. In Kobe. I had spoken with Michael Nyman's coordinator. We told them that we were going to Kobe, and we met them there, explained the situation, and Nyman agreed. It wasn't actually in the hotel room, it was in the hotel bar. I was there the entire time. What Eno-san did for 6 hours was explain how he came up with *Enemy Zero* in the first place, and why it had to be Michael Nyman, over and over again.

JS: What were they drinking?

KE: It was a long time ago, but maybe Eno was probably drinking wine, and Nyman probably didn't drink anything.

JS: Was Nyman surprised? Reluctant?

KE: He wasn't reluctant, or uncomfortable or anything, he's just quite a quiet guy. So it was a case of warming him up to the concept. After talking a little we had dinner at the restaurant. We had Kobe beef. Then we moved to the bar, and spent the rest of the time there. [Prior to meeting in Kobe], Nyman-san had expressed a deep interest in game music itself, and said that it was an exciting time for videogames. So we brought up *Enemy Zero*, and Nyman showed some interest. We sent him a copy of *D no Shokutaku* while he was still in England, and he played it and thought it was good.

JS: The 1UP interview mentions the hotel room.

KE: Hmm... I feel like it wasn't. It was in the bar. I don't think Eno-san ever went into a hotel room. So that could be wrong.

JS: After Mr Nyman sent the first lot of music over, Mr Eno requested he redo all of it?

KE: I'm not so familiar with that point, but certainly that's what I think happened. The first thing I remember coming across was *Laura's Theme*. I seem to remember there was no problem with that. So whether or not that was in the first or second set, and whether or not other tracks were sent back or not, I don't know. Certainly the first thing I remember is Laura's theme coming, and Eno-san was happy with it.

JS: You were involved in producing the OST CD?

KE: The first thing released was a mini-CD of four tracks from the game. They were called the piano sketches, the four tracks, and I took those to Kitty Records, which is a record company in Japan. After that the other stuff we released came through First Smile Entertainment, which is my own company.

[118 words redacted - story regarding a character model in Enemy Zero being based on someone in the games industry]

JS: Have you played through *D2* until the end?

KE: I have not - it's too hard! I know the story, I know what happens.

JS: Was anything removed at CESA's request?

KE: That's not something I know, unfortunately. I know he switched the data on the original *D* to get around CESA.

JS: The original *D* he swapped the master disc.

KE: Hmm... I think he might have done that for *D2* as well. It's not something I can evidence, but... He hated CESA. They really got in his way all the time. One time he complained, and the head of CESA called Eno-san to his office. They basically said we're done with you now. But obviously he still had to follow the rules. So whether or not he tricked them with *D2* I don't know. But if he could, he probably did.

Cmode in drinks machines in Japan

<in a hushed voice>

[42 words redacted - OFF THE RECORD - side story not directly related to Kenji Eno]

JS: Hot damn! Is that off the record?!

KE: Let's just say, it's very difficult to complain to CESA successfully. I think that's what you can say.

JS: Yet Mr Eno always found a way!

KE: He always found a way. He always got what he wanted. So when it was coming up to the time for *D2* to go to CESA, they knew what he had done for the original *D*. So they were of the opinion they couldn't trust him, he'll probably break his contracts. So he had an uphill battle.

JS: *D2* was extreme. Full female nudity, gore, plus rather suggestive bosses (pictured).

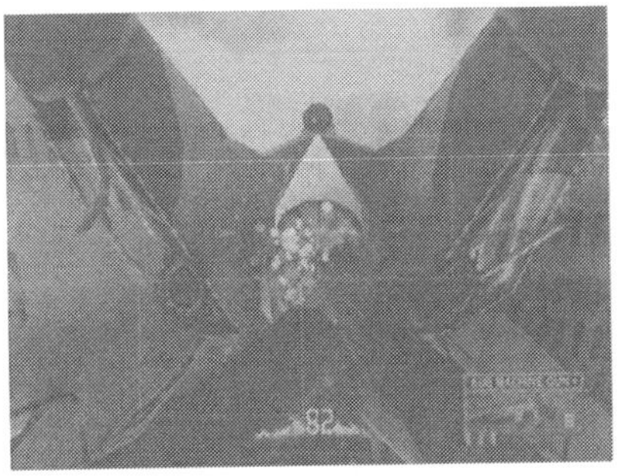

KE: I think now that's probably doable. But it does seem like something CESA would have almost definitely banned [at that time]. Which suggests to me that they never got that far in the game. Or they didn't know. He used to put the final FMVs and the final data in the disc the day before it went out. So it's possible that what CESA saw was not what everybody else saw.

JS: Do you know any other trivia?

KE: Kenji Eno actually came up with the name Dreamcast, and the spiral logo. He submitted the name and design anonymously.

JS: Really?! How did that happen?

KE: Sega accepted open submissions from the general public for their new console's name and logo. Eno-san posed as just a regular entrant, and he did it. He won it. Over a thousand entries and he won it. He said it. Whether or not it's true I don't know. But Eno-san said, "I came up with it," so it's probably true. I think it was open for everybody. I think anyone could enter... Maybe it was industry, I'm not exactly sure. But there was something like 1'000 ideas and if what he was saying was true, then Eno-san's entry was the winner.

JS: He came up with the warm orange spiral?

KE: The name and the spiral logo. Eno-san was also the one who said there should be a "turning on" sound for the Dreamcast, during the logo. So he got Ryuichi Sakamoto[17] to do it, just by asking him. He wanted something like what Brian Eno, the composer, did for Windows.[18]

JS: Mr Eno was obviously close with Sega.

KE: Eno-san was friends with Sega's president, and was kind of an advisor to the board of Sega. So he had the sway to do things like that.

JS: It's a shame Dreamcast didn't sell.

KE: He got to know Sega after the morphing logo incident, when "Welcome to Sega" was up on the screen. That's how he got to know the president of Sega. That's also how he got to meet all the board members. CSK was a company which controlled Sega, which was a child company of CSK, and Okawa-san[19] was the president of that controlling company. Obviously Eno-san got to know him as well. So that's how he knew a lot of players in the industry, especially Sega. After this he became a very big, important part of Sega, unofficially. He needed to talk to the president of Sega a lot, or the vice-president Irimajiri-san.[20] But he was always super busy, and it never really happened. So what Eno-san did is, the VP of Sega had to fly to America, so Eno-san just bought the first-class ticket next to him, had the meeting in the plane, got to America, said goodbye, turned around, and flew back to Japan. *<laughs - in English>* A very expensive meeting.

JS: Could you draw a sketch of the *D2* office?

KE: That's the Aoyama one. I'm not much of an artist. This was in Aoyama, on the 4th floor. There's three elevators in the entrance. There was a receptionist, or reception desk, and there was a TV on there. The WARP logo would loop

[17] Famed Japanese composer; *Yellow Magic Orchestra*
[18] He composed the 6 sec start-up music for Win95
[19] Isao Okawa; deceased
[20] Shoichirou Irimajiri

on that. In this next area there were five raised platforms made of silver, like large stepping stones, surrounded by gravel or pebbles. It resembled a zen temple. This is a lake, or like a pond, and this area had a shrine or garden-like design. They had one of those wooden temple ornaments. They're made of bamboo and slowly fill with water, and then go *clonk* when full.[21]

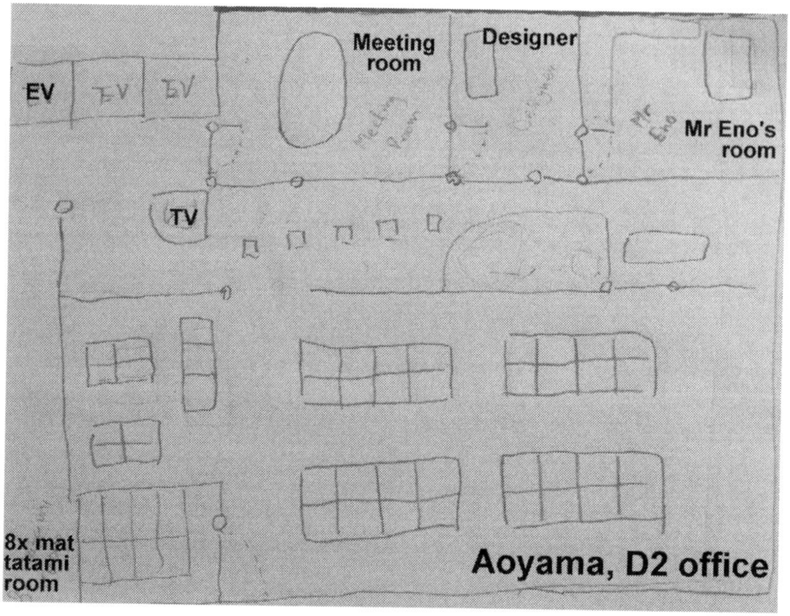

JS: These platforms were made of actual silver?

KE: Silver coloured metal, or silver plated. You would walk along these stepping stones, and it was like *Enemy Zero*, in that your steps would make a sound, like *kon-kon-kon*. While the water would make a sound like *chara-chara-chara*. Adjacent this area were three rooms. This was the entrance to the meeting room. Here was where the designers were, and this was Eno-san's office. To get to Eno-san's office you would go down all the stepping stones and then past the Japanese garden display, and that's how you pass through the office. He could hear the *kon-kon-kon* sound as you approached. It had a very Kyoto-style, zen garden feel to it. It cost twenty million yen.[22] Photographs of this office were shown in business magazines in America, as examples of office design. Works of design art.

JS: Do you have any photos?

KE: I don't have any, but WARP might have a video. This video was filmed by Japanese TV companies, for a look into the games industry. Programmes that ran a long time ago. Here in the corner they had a tatami mat room, about 8 tatami in size, that was designed so people could have a sleep. Because the programmers were working very late. But everybody would just sleep at their desks, put a jacket over their heads and just crash out.

JS: Were there long crunch times at WARP?

KE: There was always someone working at these desks, 24 hours a day. Essentially the people lived in the office. Eno-san would basically live in the office. They were not made to stay in the office, and I don't think the hours they had to work were that long, but because it was rendering video - especially back then it could take 20 plus hours - what you would do is, you would hit "render" for the bit you were working on and then just go to sleep. Then four hours later you'd wake up, go to the next one, hit render, and that's what a lot of people did.

JS: Sounds like an intense schedule.

KE: But it was a very relaxed atmosphere, and it didn't feel like pressure. Eno-san was never one to plan ahead meetings that much, so often when he wanted a meeting, he'd just yell, "Meeting time!" And you had to go. He used to do that at 3 or 4 in the morning sometimes. So it was a case of, if you weren't in the office at that point you didn't go to the meeting, so it would then be your prerogative to catch up later. So it made a lot of sense for at least a decent number of the developers to be in the room at any time. Because if they weren't, if only a handful of people went, it would slow down the development process.

JS: And throughout the day and night, there would be the gentle sound of tapping bamboo?

[21] *Shishi-odoshi*, lit. "scare the deer"
[22] Around £120k / $180k in 2000

KE: <*laughs*> Unfortunately they did not usually have it on. But if anybody visited the office, or it was open for meetings or business, it would be running. You could hear it sometimes.

JS: Like a metronome adjusting the pace of work?

KE: Maybe, but he didn't do that on purpose. It was just his style. One of his favourite things to do was to shock people, surprise people, in everything he did. So that's why he always went to the extreme, if you know what I mean.

Obviously, John, you're probably the most well read person in the West on this, but if there's anything you need. I know a lot, a lot more than there is maybe even on the internet, so if you want to ask questions, please feel free to take shots in the dark to bring up information.

JS: I always ask about unreleased games. Were there others besides *Sunman*?

KE: After *D2* was released, obviously we were all wondering about what would be our next title. Well, Eno-san went to *Famitsu* magazine and said to them, "Right, we're going to make a game that will sell 300'000 copies, it will be an RPG. No problem." <*laughs*> That RPG didn't even have a name, but they had a lot of meetings about it, and design specifications, or design ideas, were definitely cemented down. But unfortunately nothing ultimately happened.

JS: Incredible. Are there surviving documents?

KE: I don't have any, but I've been in contact with people from WARP, and I think there's a lot of old stuff knocking around. So maybe the original WARP members, before they were Superwarp, would have information on that RPG. The reason it's so easy for me to remember that title, and talk about it, is that ever since FYTO was founded, we've been... Pestered, I suppose? <*laughs*> Especially by people from 2chan, the forum. Who ask: what happened to that RPG? Where is it? Fans of his other works were very vocal in their desire for it. We've always been aaked about it. <*laughs*> In 2008 we released *You, Me, and the Cubes* **(top right)** for Wiiware, as a downloadable title. Obviously the reaction to that was fairly decent in Japan, but even then, people were saying on the forums, "This is great, but where's the RPG?" So wherever that RPG has gone, wherever it is, there was a big demand for it.

KE: Last year [2012], towards the end of Eno-san's life, we were talking about what we were going to do next. Eno-san's mind had been made up to go into some sort of education, to create a sort of learning institute. Eno-san also discussed the plan with Joichi Ito.[23] In January of this year [2013], Eno-san approached me with a project, an idea. It was his last idea. <*takes out leaflet*> This is ILCA.[24] The design of it was by Eno-san, <*points to page*> and the idea was to use these core concepts of **I**nnovation, **L**earning, **C**reativity and **A**rts, to produce workshops and media, symposiums, and types of classes I suppose. It was aimed at those who wanted to go into entertainment media; games, manga, anime, and so on. Something in line with the "Cool Japan" movement.[25] Basically anything to do with entertainment, that's what we wanted to teach. We held a party in Shibuya Hikarie to celebrate it. Then in April of this year [2013] that's when it started, with this school, and they're still doing it now. <*passes pamphlets*>

[23] Entrepreneur, and director of the MIT Media Lab

[24] http://ilca.asia/

[25] Used by gov. to further Japan's culture industry

KE: These are some of the pamphlets, and this is the sort of thing we do. Someone who is an expert in one of these industries or subjects, would come and teach or lecture. Obviously those attending could then give it a go in the workshops. Eno-san's plan was to develop a curriculum and be a regular teacher or speaker. The same student would come multiple times and it would be a sort of programme, kind of like a university programme. The idea was that Eno-san would be a sort of... The "dean of the university", as it were. He would develop these programmes and then students could take them. Unfortunately Eno-san passed away in February, but one of the things I am teaching at ILCA is a History of Kenji Eno, and what he produced. One of the things we did when we talked about the *D2* project, in this introduction of his history, is we got everyone who was in the original WARP to come back, and talk about the challenges they faced. They all discussed what they had done, and talked about and remembered Kenji Eno. Once all these people got together, they realised they wanted to work together. So on 1 October WARP2 was founded, which is a new company. <*laughs*> A good story, right?

JS: All those members discussing *D2*... I wish more teams would discuss old projects, maybe while someone plays through them.

KE: There's something more... What they're discussing right now is: what else did Eno-san want to do? They're going through his old notes, and trying to remember all the things he spoke to them about, years and years ago. They're going to try to produce other ideas of his that never really got any momentum going. If they can find evidence, or if they can find writing about them, the team will potentially push ahead with a project. Including that RPG everyone asks about. The reason WARP2 came together was because I think at this event they all sort of went, "Remember that RPG?" And that's how it was founded. So that's maybe one goal for WARP2, to make that RPG. Obviously they were all present in the discussion about the game, so they know what he was talking about.

JS: Was there any discussion about the unreleased *D2* for the scrapped M2 hardware?

KE: There's a promotional video for that, which was shown. That game video was codenamed "M". This unreleased *D2*, the only thing that was made was that promotional video.

JS: The M2 hardware was never released, but I've seen video footage of a prototype.

KE: With the daughter of Laura?

JS: Yes. Walking around a castle. I heard[26] that everything on the harddrives was destroyed.

KE: Yes, the programming, all the code is gone. They were all wiped. The video is the only thing which I know still exists. It's about five minutes long, right?

JS: I think so...

KE: You've seen it? Where did you see it?

JS: There's several videos. One clip was a bonus on one of the original *D* releases. Many clips were shared on an online forum community.[27]

KE: <*laughs*> Yes, if I recall correctly, she swings her sword and fire comes out the blade?

JS: There's a big knight in armour.

KE: Yes, yes. She slashes at an armoured man. <*laughs*> I can't believe how much you know!

JS: I recall discussion regarding the mirror reflections, because they seemed to be real-time.

KE: Yes it was. I see. Maybe a member of the development team uploaded it?

JS: I thought it was from trade show footage. People *love* information about unreleased games!

KE: <*laughs*> So talking about this RPG that nobody knows about, you must be quite happy? You can put the stuff about the RPG in the book. What WARP2 are doing... At the original WARP, they first started with the puzzle project and then moved toward the big *D* project. What

[26] Source: ASSEMblergames

[27] Google: "*D2 / M2 - Info dump and other musings*"

they're doing this time at WARP2 is similar. They will produce a smaller game first to get back into the original WARP mentality as it were. Then they'll make that RPG. Probably their timeframe is that they're going to start making the smaller game now. Then maybe from next summer, they'll begin development on other big projects.

JS: It's interesting WARP making an RPG, because I recall on the original logo, the letter "R" was a screenshot of an RPG.

KE: *<laughs>* Yes! The design for that was to make it look like *Dragon Quest*, which is the definitive RPG title in Japan, but it wasn't actually *Dragon Quest*. WARP made it. It wasn't a real game.

JS: Which platform will this RPG be for?

KE: Smart media, so probably iOS, Android, and so on. Up until now we've not discussed things like the 3DS.

JS: What about download services, like PSN?

KE: Maybe not. I guess it's something you decide later. I'm not in the WARP2 project, but from what I've understood, speaking with them, this RPG has multiplayer or social features, and so it makes a lot of sense to put it on iOS and so on, because maybe that's the easiest way to allow people to take advantage of those features.

JS: Social features? That sounds ahead of its time - when was this RPG first discussed?

KE: It was first discussed in 1999. It was intended to be released as a packaged game, like a store shelf game. But I can't tell you if there was talk of multiplayer functions or not, because I wasn't in the meetings. If the game is based on his original design documents it would suggest that he had thought of something like that. Even back in the late 1990s.

JS: Really thinking ahead. *<looks at KAKEXUN dossier>* And this is...?

KE: This is what was passed across in January, and the thing he said was, "I want to make it!" And now we're looking for partners. It's very important to build relationships and build a big network, not just supporters but also people who know what they're doing. I worked on a project for Campfire, which is a kind of Japanese Kickstarter, it's a crowdfunding service, and the project was related to movies. So I have experience in crowdfunding.

JS: Which building are we in now?

KE: The FYTO building.

JS: FYTO had staff from WARP, is that right?

KE: No, there's none from WARP in here now. Superwarp gave an announcement in April 2000, talking about what they were going to do and their projects. This included myself, and Eno-san, and the WARP team, which had all come across to Superwarp. We said OK, we're going to start making internet games, online games, and so on. But then a year later, October 2001, we decided not to do that. We decided to go into different areas, and so all of the programmers, those from WARP and the new ones who had come into Superwarp, were all let go in November 2001. Just before that, in August of 2001, that's when Superwarp became From Yellow To Orange. But because we got rid of all the programmers, there were no WARP members in FYTO. Only four people from Superwarp remained: myself, Eno, a gentleman who is the production manager, and then another one of the production team. So there was only four Superwarp members in FYTO when we changed over.

JS: Mr Eno also came up with Cmode.

KE: Have you ever used it? You would register your cellphone to the Cmode service, that's how they would bill you. The first thing you would do is put your money into a vending machine, and then that would link it to your phone. Then the next time you wanted to get drinks, you would just tap the phone on the machine. You couldn't pay through Docomo, it wasn't like your drinks appeared on your bill at the end of the month. It was kind of like a drinks debit card. Cmode functionality is still being used, even today, in Coca Cola vending machines. Even though the Cmode functionality is gone from a lot of machines, you can still see it, because they never replaced the machines.[28]

---

[28] At the time, visiting Japan, many vending machines adopted the Suica system, where a prepaid Suica card, which was swiped when entering the metro system, could also be used to pay a vending machine

JS: Can you recall how he came up with the idea?

KE: It wasn't really his idea, as it were. What happened was, when Superwarp ended, we were uncertain of where we wanted to go, and what we wanted to do, so we came up with 20 or more ideas and concepts. Then we spent our time going to different companies around Japan, asking, "Are you interested in this?" Trying to find someone who was willing to work with us. There's a company in Japan called Itochu Corporation, and one of them said to FYTO, "We don't want to do your project, but we are interested in doing something like this. What do you think?" And that's where Cmode came from, that's how it started.

JS: They suggested the idea?

KE: Japan Coca-Cola started this thing called iVending.[29] That just happens to be the time that we showed up, and [Itochu] said to us, at that point, well we want to do this, and this, and this, and it all sort of lined up. It wasn't a case of them picking us at random to do the vending machine. It was already a movement within their company and we fit the bill. The timing was right.

Of course all of our contracts were web related projects. There were no games, it was all internet services. The reason we didn't do anything with it is because the dot.com bubble had recently burst in America. So nobody was investing in internet services, around 2000. There was no funding going into web services, because everyone was reeling from the crash. All 20 of those ideas we drafted, but we never used any of them. Before we made those 20 projects, an "incubation company" called Neoteny funded us and said, "OK, make the projects, make the ideas, go to companies and find a sponsor, a company which wants to make it for you. Then our funding will be to make whatever project gets decided a reality." <*shows photo*> This is Joi Ito, he's one of the FYTO team. He was running an incubation company - like an angel investor for IT start-up companies. It was he who kept Superwarp alive in that time when they were deciding what they wanted to do. I'm not sure if I made this clear or not, the money from that was not used in Cmode - that was funded by Japan Coca Cola. The company Joi Ito invested in was Superwarp, but by the time this was being produced and everything was happening, we were called From Yellow to Orange. Cmode was the first thing FYTO ever worked on, to completion.

JS: What were some of these scrapped ideas?

KE: I don't have them personally, but they are still on Eno-san's computer. <*laughs*> One of the ideas was that we would produce a service, which was like a character - a fluffy character or something - who would live on your computer screen. As you got emails the program would read your email and work out if there was a happy thing, or a sad thing inside the email. If the email was happy the character would go *ping!* and would have a happy face. If it was a sad email, then it would have a sad face. If the majority of your emails had happy things, your character would sort of grow and evolve into a happier character. Whereas if you got a lot of sad emails, he would get sadder and weaker.

JS: I'd be nervous about it accessing my emails.

KE: Yes, definitely. But it's kind of like Facebook. The Facebook company definitely reads the content of your messages. The reason Eno-san wanted to make this project was he always said that reading your own emails and deleting the ones you don't like is not a pleasant experience. He believed this program would cause people to change themselves, the things they do, to try to only get good emails. Every time you saw that sad face you'd think, "Oh, I've done something - I need to improve myself."

JS: Is there anything else you can recall?

KE: Another idea he had, was like a character who was a mail messenger, who would live on your computer. You would put a message, or a picture on him, and he would go to different computers around the world that also had this installed, and they would receive whatever document or message you sent. They would then be able to attach their own stuff back. So you would make a link. It was kind of like a computer based pen-pal system I suppose.

JS: Or cloud service to trade information?

KE: But it was to people you didn't know. It wasn't a messaging service. More of a fun thing.

JS: Like a message in bottle thrown to sea?

[29] Interactive Vending, with a giant touchscreen

KE: Yes... I remember now, it was a dove! Why was it a dove? Because doves are the universal sign of peace. So whatever you sent, it was like an olive branch. But you would send a picture, or a document, or a little message. As with the other ideas though, Eno-san couldn't find someone interested enough to do it. Obviously nowadays there's plenty of services that can do both of these things. But in the 2000s, nobody was developing this sort of online concept.

JS: As well as being an innovator, Kenji Eno also found time to be a family man.

KE: Yes, he had two children. His eldest son reminded him of himself at that age. So they used to go, just the two of them, to Australia or abroad and so on. He was dedicated to his family, he loved his children. After the 2011 earthquake in Japan, and the Fukushima nuclear disaster, Eno-san wrote on his website. It was a column, of things he wanted to tell his children. "*Messages for my children*" you could call it. When the earthquake happened he wrote a lot about that, but to children. So that his child could understand it, what was happening, what he should think about it, that sort of thing. When these blog posts went live, they became a big talking point on the internet. A lot of people were reading them and saying they were impressed. Eventually a publishing company said they wanted to take his writings about the Fukushima disaster and publish them. So it became a book in Japan, called *To My Son*.[30] The book was released around mid-2011. It was like a collection of essays.

JS: When Mr Eno passed away, Kenichi Nishi wrote a long memorial. Did you know Mr Nishi?

KE: Yes, he's my friend. Are you interviewing Kenichi Nishi?

JS: I was going to, but unfortunately our schedules didn't match up.

KE: Nishi-kun was a very good friend of Eno. They worked together on the *Newtonica* game for the iPhone. I think it was the last product he produced. *Newtonica* is known as Nishi's product, but I had a chat with Nishi, and actually he said, "No, no, that was totally Eno's stuff."

JS: He was liked by developers and players alike.

KE: In Japan they have a thing called CEDEC,[31] which is like a convention, or event for the games industry. It was in August, and it's by CESA. We spoke about them earlier, they handle the ratings system in Japan. They never liked Eno-san, because of the cannibalism in *D*, and the violence and so on. So he used to fight with them all the time. Really wrestle with every point. When he died this year people wanted to nominate him for a variety of awards, and CEDEC wouldn't let them do it, because his history with them is so bad.

JS: Who wanted to nominate him?

KE: Masanobu Endou. The creator of *Xevious*. He was the guy saying, "Let's nominate him, let's nominate him." Obviously CEDEC were saying, "No we can't do that. He was a real thorn in our side." So in the end, there is one award, the game design award, that is voted for by the attendees or the public. So they put him up for that and of course he completely walked the competition, because he has a huge following. That was very nice to see.

Another thing which happened at this event, where these awards were given out. Eno-san had been nominated for the game developer award by the public, and I was there with his wife and two children. Masanobu Endou was giving the speech, but I wasn't really listening. He said, "This year's winner of the game design award is..." Then he sort of went silent. Then I looked up and noticed he was wearing a black tie, which is a sign of mourning, and he revealed, "by overwhelming majority, it's Kenji Eno." It was a very touching moment.

We weren't ready to go on stage of course, because the last game which Eno released which he was being considered for was 13 years old. So people were not expecting... I was not ready to go on stage at all. I was there with Eno-san's family, but of course they weren't ready either. Then Endou-san came out wearing the black tie, and as soon as he said the name a spotlight came down on us, and myself and the children and Eno-san's wife went up on stage, and Eno-san's wife gave a very tearful message to thank them for their support.

JS: What was the name of this award?

---

[30] 息子へ (*Musuko he*); ISBN: 4344019938 / 978-4344019935

[31] CEDEC = CESA Developers Conference

KE: The CEDEC Game Design Grand Prix. The award is given for the best designer of the year, so generally speaking it's for games released in the last year. It's given to whoever contributed the most, or someone who has really been outstanding in that field. For somebody who hasn't released a major game in 13 years to win is unbelievable.

JS: The voting is done only by attendees, or the general public too?

KE: It's voted for by a combination of the attendees of the event, and the judging panel. Obviously the judging panel didn't like Eno-san, but the reaction from the crowd, from the fans, was so overwhelming that he won anyway. He more than doubled second place in terms of votes and support.

JS: Was Mr Eno a friend of Mr Endou?

KE: Yes, they were friends.

JS: Is there any final message you want to give?

KE: This was the message that he really believed in: it's a message about making the future better for our children. When they were talking about the college Eno-san was going to do, and we talked about the book, *To My Son*, this was the under-riding message of all this stuff.

Even though he lived two minutes away from the FYTO offices, his office was on one of the upper floors, and he basically lived there, the whole time. That's all he ever did, was work on his current project - he's always been like that, for 20 years. Just sleeping at his desk.

JS: Dedicated.

KE: Absolutely dedicated, more than anything. That's maybe why he had the health complications that ultimately killed him.

JS: Also, he smoked clove cigarettes.[32]

KE: Yes, cigarettes with cloves. You really do know a lot about Eno!

<everyone laughs>

JS: Well, I'm one of his biggest fans. I also spoke with Justin Hall, who knew Mr Eno, and allowed me to use a photo of him. They used to socialise, hence how I know about the cloves.

KE: He went to America about two days before he died, and as soon as he touched back down in Japan he went to his office and went to work. He never rested. He didn't even go home on weekends, he just worked straight through. He had asthma, from sometime when he was an adult. He developed it. He went to the hospital a couple of times about it but the medicine, the treatment he was given, never took hold. So he always wrestled with asthma and poor respiration. Even on the day he died, he had an asthma attack, so he suffered from poor health.

JS: The flying would have exacerbated it.

KE: He used to fly a lot, as you said, but also the flight he did two days before he died, he had a 13 hour flight. He came back, didn't go home, straight to the office. So two days after the flight he was in the office, and around about lunch time, or in the afternoon, he said, "I don't feel very well, I'm going home." He went home, had an asthma attack in the house, and then the next thing that happened is that someone found him. He did not die on his own, his family were there at the end.

JS: His legacy will live on.

KE: He's still here, we can still feel him. *<laughs>* Every day. Definitely, the decisions he made and the person he was, you can't work in this industry in Japan without feeling that. Even if you don't know who he is, he shaped it.

[32] Containing tobacco and cloves, they produce an intensely sweet taste on the lips - though are regarded as more dangerous than standard cigarettes

~*In memory of*~

飯野 賢治

ENO, Kenji

5 May 1970 ~ 20 February 2013

~Selected Portfolio~

Parallel World	- NES, 1990	
Casino Kid 2	- NES, 1992	(Music)
Panic Restaurant	- NES, 1992	(Concept, music)
Sunman	- NES, unrel.	(Planner, director)
D	- Saturn/3DO, 1995	
Trip'd	- 3DO/PS1, 1995	
Short Warp	- 3DO, 1996	
Enemy Zero	- Saturn, 1996 / PC, 1998	
Real Sound: Kaze no Regret	- Saturn, 1997 / Dreamcast, 1999	
D2	- Dreamcast, 1999	
You, Me, and the Cubes	- Wii, 2009	
Newtonica	- iOS, 2008	

日高徹

HIDAKA, Toru

DOB: 11 July 1949 / Birthplace: Utsunomiya, Tochigi Pref / Blood Type: A

~ Selected Portfolio ~

Haunted Cave / ホーンテッドケイブ（幽霊洞窟）	- PC-8801 series, 1984	(Sole creator)
Magic Garden / マジックガーデン	- PC-8801 series, 1984	(Sole creator)
Eldorado Denki / エルドラド伝奇	- PC-8801 series, 1985	(Convert from FM-7)
Chikyuu Senshi Rayieza[1] / 地球戦士ライーザ	- PC-8801 series, 1985	(Convert from FM-7)
Hokuto no Ken / 北斗の拳	- PC-8801 series, 1986	(Programmer)
J.E.S.U.S / ジーザス	- PC-8801mkIISR, 1987	(Prog. tech. assist.)
Gandhara (Crusade of the Buddha) / ガンダーラ（仏陀の聖戦）	- PC-8801mkIISR, 1987 - later MSX2 conversion	(Programmer)
Ultima I / ウルティマ I	- PC-8801mkIISR, 1988	(Technical assistance)
Burning Point / バーニングポイント	- PC-8801mkIISR, 1989	(Technical assistance)
Cyber Space Action PRAJATOR - Image Ranger - / プラジェーター	- PC-8801FH, 1989	(Technical assistance)
AD&D Pool of Radiance	- PC-8801MR, 1990	(Technical assistance)
J.E.S.U.S II / ジーザス II	- PC-8801mkIISR, 1991	(Technical assistance)
Otasuke Nin-puu-den / おたすけ忍風伝	- Windows ME	(Creator)

In addition to various long running series of different books on programming, including:

Machine Language Game Programming
Machine Language Sound Programming
Machine Language Game Graphics
Quick C Game Programming
Turbo C Game Programming
QB/VB Game Programming
machine Language Master Bible
Machine Language for Beginners
Book of Machine Language Secrets
Burning Fighting Spirit: Legend of Machine Language I~IV **(right)**
Introduction to Assembly Language for Games
Making of a Computer RPG
Game Machine Language: Shooting
50 Cases of Applied Game Programming - Power Edition
Super Programming
The Essence of Game Programming

For a full list of all 33 books, please visit:
http://njprog.com/toruhidaka/books.htm

[1] In English *The Earth Fighter Rayieza*. An intriguing traditional RPG set in outer space, with the ability to travel through space. Later remade for the Famicom under the name *Ginga no Sannin* (銀河の三人); at the time of writing, the text has been dumped and translated into English, and a patch is awaiting completion

First interview with Toru Hidaka
28 September 2013, Shiki City

I actually interviewed Mr Hidaka twice, both times at his home - the second time with Game Preservation Society leader Joseph Redon. While technically none of the Enix games Mr Hidaka worked on were officially released outside of Japan, all of them in some way are linked to important aspects of game history or culture: from the formation of the computer scene in Japan and games which risk being banned, to technical innovations, and even competing against Enix's own Dragon Quest. His insights into the dealings of Enix are both fascinating and undocumented. More significantly, Mr Hidaka influenced a generation of programmers with his many excellent programming books. In fact, he was instrumental in setting up Enix-sponsored study workshops for budding programmers. He was akin to a magician at Enix, creating the utilities and tools which allowed others to make games. We also chatted about England, where Mr Hidaka had homestayed for two months. When discussing other developers the formal suffixes switched between -san and -kun. I've tried to keep these as is where possible.

JS: <shows *Comptiq* magazine> This is an old magazine from 1987, here's the Enix page.

TH: I have a significant collection of magazines from this time, in my other room. I contributed to many magazines back then, and also there were many advertisements within the magazines, so I've kept them all.

JS: You mean such as this? <*poster with Mr Hidaka, alongside four other Enix developers, including Kouichi Nakamura and Yuji Horii*>

TH: <*laughs*> Wow! Why do you have that?

JS: There's an archive online of various adverts and as part of my research I printed it off.

TH: I have the original copy as well, of that photo, back in my library. This photo shoot was my idea! I described my idea to the president of Enix, and he said, "Oh, that's interesting!"

JS: A group photo standing behind a computer.

TH: That's right. This is a room within the Enix offices from back then. And this gentleman... <*points to Kazuro Morita, far left*>

JS: Morita-san, he made *Shogi* and *Morita's Battlefield*. He passed away July 2012.

TH: Yes, that's right.

JS: This gentleman, 3rd from left, is Suzuki Takanari, who is now a medical doctor.[1]

TH: Yes! I'm surprised you didn't receive any answer from *Game Kyojin*.

JS: I contacted him via email, but I never heard back. I was wondering if the email got through. Several said my emails ended up in spam.

TH: It ended up in my spam folder too!

<*everyone laughs*>

TH: At first I couldn't believe it! Because, why would English people be interested in my games or my books? I thought it quite strange.

JS: Researching old games makes me feel like Indiana Jones discovering lost treasure. On the poster is Kouichi Nakamura of Chunsoft, and Yuji Horii of *Dragon Quest*. Did you all work together at the Enix office?

---

[1] 鈴木孝成 Suzuki Takanari; 芸夢狂人 *Geimu Kyoujin*

TH: Well, Enix didn't do in-house development.[2]

JS: At that time?

TH: Even as of today. The internal development is only being done by the Squaresoft teams.

JS: Yes, because Enix sub-contracted Chunsoft to create *Dragon Quest*.

TH: Well, Enix originally started out as an advertising company, to solicit tenants for a public housing complex. That's what Fukushima-san,[3] the then president, started out with as part of his business. So they did different business, and the name of the company wasn't Enix but "*Kodan Boshu Center*" or something like that.[4] Back then, slowly but surely, the recognition of computers was growing, but at the time not so much software was out. Back then most of the software was developed by individuals to be brought into shops in Akihabara, and they tried to publish them on their own. So they were not mass produced. So Fukushima-san, the president of Enix, came up with this idea of starting a "logistics business" for software. Another gentleman was cooking up a similar idea at the same time, which was Son-san,[5] the president of SoftBank. So that's why Son-san decided to name his company SoftBank - the name meaning "bank for software". So while SoftBank started out developing and manufacturing software internally, Enix was just thinking of distributing software. Unfortunately there was not much high quality software available at that time. <*shows magazine*> This is the oldest magazine that I have, back from 1983. Enix organised contests and they published those games which won as official products. These are the games which won the first contest from Enix in 1983 and were commercialised as a product.[6]

JS: <*notices Portopia Renzoku Satsujin Jiken in a second list*> Yes, I've played *Portopia*!

TH: <*laughs*> For Horii-san that was the second time around. The first time he won by submitting a game called *Love Match Tennis*.

JS: <*looking through magazines*> These old magazines are a great resource.

TH: I have more, way more, back in the other room if you want to see them.

JS: I'm fascinated by the Enix competitions, because it seems the company was keen to promote developers, with a photograph and biography on the back of the game box.

TH: That's because Enix didn't develop software in-house, there were no programmers who made games inside the company. But Enix still wanted to distribute software, wanted to create software somehow. So they decided to throw contests and competitions in order to attract prospective candidates, and would promote the software which won prizes. So they would select winners of the competitions, publish those games, and pay the authors royalties from that. Remember, these were the days of [solo] "game authors", [as opposed to big development studios]. Basically Enix wanted to nurture or raise game authors and creators by doing so.[7]

As I mentioned before, Enix started out as an advertiser for public housing, so they acted like they were risking the future of the company by holding these game competitions and awarding huge prizes.[8] But in fact, there was a kind of cheating or trick behind this contest - the contest was actually not so risky for the company. The prize was not really the prize. I mean, it was a kind of advance on the royalty! For example, suppose Enix proposed 1 million yen[9] as a prize, if it was really "a prize", after selling the software they should pay the royalties to the author separately from this award. But

[2] This conversation reveals an important but often overlooked fact with Enix - they were primarily a publisher. Software development was delegated to outside teams. *Dragon Quest* is not an Enix creation, they simply own the brand

[3] Yasuhiro Fukushima, formerly an architect

[4] Founded September 1975 as *Eidansha Boshu Service Centre*; machine translates as *Corporate Recruitment Service Centre*; Source: **www.jp.square-enix.com/company/en/history/**

[5] Masayoshi Son; a businessman of Korean descent

[6] The famous "*Enix Game Hobby Program Contest*"; Kazuro Morita, Yuji Horii and Kouichi Nakamura among the winners. Held in 1982 with a prize of 1 million yen, winners announced throughout 1983 (*Game Maestro*)

[7] Enix obtained publishing rights and paid royalties to the authors. The competitions were a way for Enix to get their pick of the litter, so to speak. The setup is very similar to the book industry. Term used was "*game sakka*" and *sakka* = author; the word "raise" is the same used for "raising children"

[8] To be clear: Mr Hidaka doesn't ever say the competitions and prizes were actually risky for Enix, rather Enix acted as though they were taking a risk

[9] In 1983, 1 million yen was roughly £2780 / $4210

Enix said this prize is a kind of advance on your royalty, so the company was essentially promising that you would earn at least 1 million yen of royalties and they would pay that, even if the software ends up not selling well. So for example, if the author receives 100 yen per unit sold, Enix would guarantee royalties equivalent to selling 10'000 copies. So Enix did not really pay 1 million yen, but would only guaranty 1 million yen of royalties. But if the software ultimately only earned 500'000 yen in royalties, Enix wouldn't pay more than 500'000 yen. Enix would just say, "We cannot pay." So it's not a prize actually, but a deposit or an advance on the royalty. Maybe creators were disadvantaged with this system, because they believed they would have the prize and thought they can earn royalties in addition to the prize. But they wouldn't get these royalties unless the software sold more than the initial award.[10]

JS: Sounds very calculated.

TH: Yes, exactly. But at the beginning most of the applicants did not know about this strategy which Enix had. If you take a look at the back of this magazine, you will see all the programs listed. Inside this copy of *I/O* magazine. There were many contributors who sent their programs for those magazines This is one for example *<points to type in listing>*. So Morita-san and Nakamura-kun [11] were popular contributors to these kinds of magazines. In order to successfully carry out their competitions Enix directly approached people like Morita-san or Nakamura-kun, asking them to come up with works on their own. Because such contributors were already popular in the world of programming and game creation at that time, Enix demanded they enter the contest. It was half forceful, so Enix were successful in having them come up with games. That way they could guarantee to a certain degree that the contest and competitions would be successful. So they kind of instigated the whole atmosphere, so that they would be involved, and that spurred the other programmers to enter as well.

JS: Some of the contestants, the people, were selected before hand...

TH: I have another interesting thing that I want to show you. There was this controversial advert in which Nakamura-kun was printed as part of the image in paper money. This was to show how much royalty-based income he had made, which kind of sparked a debate. His monthly income, just from royalties alone, was about more than 4 million yen.

Top text says third game hobby programming contest, while below it lists the prices, with the main prize being 5 million yen

JS: In 1986 he earned ~£12'500 a month![12]

TH: Since he was a best seller he was able to enjoy that high a level of royalties, at 4 million yen or more. Given that, other people might mistakenly think that it would be easy to earn 500'000 or 1 million yen, even if their software didn't sell very well. Because if a successful software title can make over 4 million yen, surely a mediocre or unsuccessful software title could get at least in the region of 500'000 to 1 million yen? Or so they thought...

JS: Mr Nakamura only made that much because his games sold more than the others, correct?

[10] This is called an "advance against royalties" - a standard practice in the book industry, though implying it to be a cash prize for the competition is a bit sneaky!

[11] Mr Morita isn't so well known outside Japan, but Mr Nakamura was programmer on *Dragon Quest*

[12] 4 million yen in 1984 was roughly $17'000

TH: Yes, that's right. But other applicants for the contest kind of came up with this idea that even if the games do not sell that well, they would still be able to generate at least one tenth of what Nakamura-san was making. I'm referring to "royalties", meaning that the authors or creators of the games would be receiving 10% of what the publisher had made. Myself, ever since I left the company, ever since I stopped being a salaryman, I have been living off my royalties. I get income from these publications as well. I receive royalties for my books.

JS: I noticed modern games on your shelves. Were you involved with those?

TH: Nakamura-kun sent me those. I'm not so close with him anymore, but every time he creates a product he would send me a copy. He used to send me whatever he came up with, until last year. I haven't received any this year.

JS: Oh, that's very nice of him.

TH: Many of the applicants or prospective candidates were misled to believe that they can make big money by leaving the company they worked for - maybe a nice software company - to become involved with Enix and its competitions. Many were lured by the image of being a millionaire, hoping to become one too. But many of them failed to do that, they couldn't earn anything, so it was kind of tragic...

JS: That's very unfortunate. So Enix approached skilled game developers, to bring them to the competition, to entice others to apply as well?

TH: It wasn't necessarily for the sake of enticing more participants. Enix basically wanted to be successful in holding their competition, so that they could capture or retain talented game developers. The most important thing for Enix was to be successful as a publisher, even if they didn't make products; a company which circulated games without developing. So to succeed in this business they needed to have nice products, they needed to have game developers who created "bestsellers" that would lead to strong sales.

There used to be a magazine called *Procon*,[13] which stands for *Program Contest*, which was rather short lived. They only published I think 8 issues altogether. But this magazine was basically for contest purposes. They went out of business after publishing only a few issues.

JS: Was this monthly?

TH: Yes, monthly. Even if the contests were quite popular back then, there were not so many of them going on. This is when I started thinking about applying for one of the game competitions, and I wanted to find out what kind are available. That's why I purchased these magazines.

JS: What was the first game you ever saw?

TH: It was the game that I was showing on the screen earlier, *Cosmic Soldier*.[14] This was also released by Enix. [...] The reason why is I went to England to homestay and study, because I took a year's leave when I was a university student. Meaning I was in my fifth year in university.[15] After returning to Japan I came up with this idea of becoming a trader, or working for a trading business, so I could go globetrotting. I did actually join a medium-sized trading firm, but the section I was assigned to was importing! So whatever we imported we had to sell of course, and so of course my customers would be within Japan! So I was basically locked within Japan, instead of flying around the world. *<laughs>* I spent six years working for that

[13] プロコン - Oct 1983 ~ May 1984

[14] 宇宙の戦士 by Yoshiyuki Okada, one of the winners of the first Enix game contest. Single-screen action game with free-form movement, a mecha attacking aliens. Not to be confused with the same named game by Kogado Soft. When I entered Mr Hidaka's home it was already loaded and running on an original PC-88

[15] Japanese universities are usually 4 years

trading firm, and after that I left the company and started working for a manufacturing company that dealt with automotive accessory products. In the hope of travelling all over the world, selling products worldwide.

So I entered a manufacturing company in the hope of travelling all over the world, but at the same time, the company headhunted another person for the position I wanted, and I was assigned to the indirect sales department. They had already found a replacement for the direct sales representative, which they were looking for just before I joined the company. Instead of being in international sales, I was assigned to a section where I was responsible for developing or nurturing new channels for the accessory products, such as clocks or car computers. Basically electronic products, and I had to be making rounds to Akihabara to cultivate new prospective clients. Basically, back then Akihabara only dealt with home electronic appliances, for the most part. The best selling products were sold and displayed on the ground floor, whereas minor products such as computer software were located on the 7th or 8th floors of the buildings. As I continued to make rounds to those electronic shops, the software products slowly but surely started coming down to lower levels. Meaning they were becoming popular.

JS: This manufacturer was Car Mate, right? The same name on *Haunted Cave*'s box?

TH: Well yes. The automotive accessory company, or manufacturer, that I started working for was called Car Mate. Seeing the computer software in Akihabara I described it to the company president, saying, "This stuff looks interesting." Then later the president of Car Mate came to me saying, "It sounds interesting, let's create software in our company too!" Then I asked him, "Who is going to be developing this software?" Because the company only handled car accessories. Since I was just a salesperson I thought there would be somebody else who would be responsible for developing the software. But then the president told me, "Of course it's you! You're the one who came up with this idea, so you should be making it!" I was stunned to hear this! But the company, or the president, bought a PC-88 for use in the office. And for this project I also spent my own money on a PC-88 for use at home. I had to invest 700'000 or 800'000 yen of savings, which I was saving in order to buy a new car. But instead I spent it all on purchasing the computer, the display, the cassette loader, and the disk drive, as well as the kanji ROM, because back then they were all sold separately. Computers were much more expensive than they are now. I had to spend a fortune to get it all.

JS: <*notices mint condition Haunted Cave box on desk*> Ahh, the original!

TH: Yes, this is the tape version. Do you know the medium of cassette tapes?

JS: Oh yes, of course. In England in the 1980s computer games also came on cassette.

TH: Yes, because floppy disks were very expensive back then.

JS: This looks mint. When did you open it?

TH: About 2 or 3 years ago. When I opened this package it came with a sponge, for preservation purposes, <*laughs*> but the sponge had become all worn out, so I threw it away.

JS: Seeing Car Mate on the *Haunted Cave* box seemed odd. But this car accessory company really did create and publish games.

TH: Yes, exactly.

JS: Did they publish quite a few games?

TH: No. Since Car Mate was a very small sized company, every decision was made by the president. So it was a fancy idea to create software. He had the say for everything. Since I had a degree for commerce, I had no knowledge of computers at all. But since I was engaged in the trading business before coming to this company, I was able to use a typewriter.[16] Since I had no knowledge whatsoever of games I had to start from scratch, and in order to enhance my understanding I purchased a couple. I bought a few games including *Cosmic Soldier*, and back then there used to be a message stating in which "language" the games were programmed in, on the back of the packages. So the categories were either BASIC or machine language.[17] Since BASIC is an interpreted language it tends to be slow. For a game novice like myself it was not that interesting. Whereas machine language had all kinda of characters moving around, which was quite amusing. So I became interested in machine language, but I had no idea what it was. Then in comes the president again, and I told him that I was more interested in machine language than BASIC, and the he was amazed because he knew I had no knowledge of it. The whole company was surprised at my remarks.

One day I had a lunch meeting with some colleagues, including the technicians, and I shared my idea of developing a game in machine language! They were shocked. They told me that they had spent so much time and effort in trying to understand machine language, but they had not yet been successful. The technicians said to me, "We studied machine language for a long time, for our dear lives! Whereas you, on the other hand, have a degree from a commerce course, and spent 10 years as a salary man. It will be impossible for you to develop a machine language game!"

But I resisted and counter-argued, saying I don't want my ability to be determined by others. I said, "Wait until I discover for myself if it's really impossible!" So I kind of committed myself to coming up with a machine language game, and I had to, because I had said so and made that declaration in front of the technicians. So I spent 6 months trying to analyse the game that I had purchased - *Cosmic Soldier*. **(below)**

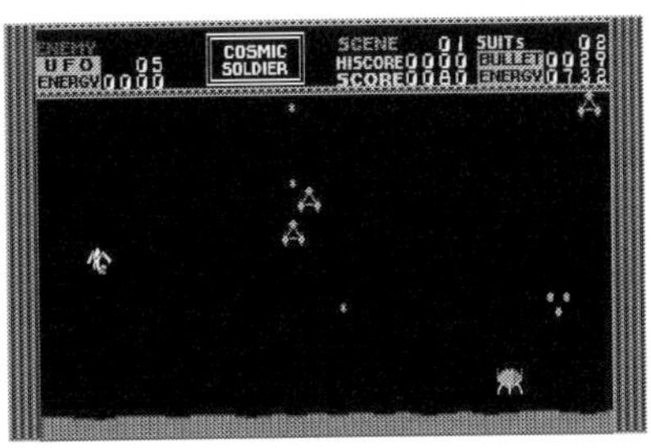

16 At this time few Japanese people would have had experience with an English alphabet keyboard

17 Low level prog. language; faster, more complex

<Hidaka-san shows detailed, annotated machine code print outs and flow charts relating to Cosmic Soldier - he reverse engineered the entire game manually, one line of code at a time>

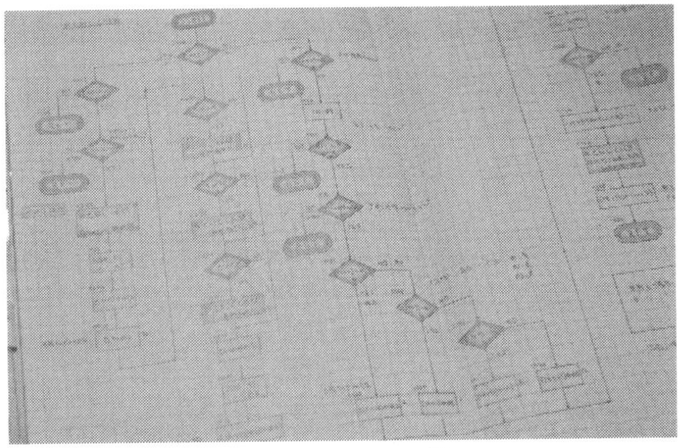

TH: This is all the research I did, and the methodologies that I had come up with by analysing *Cosmic Soldier*. Generally at that time games were not protected, and thanks to that, I could get all the lists like this, and trace the information in the game. I tried to define each sentence, each row, trying to figure out what they were doing. So I actually translated, or interpreted, each row. If the subroutine was being called I would bring it over here, *<shows flap of paper glued down into main code, detailing the subroutine>* and I just cut and pasted every subroutine that I came across. After I had done all this analysis, I compiled all the information into a flowchart. **(above)**

JS: An incredible historical record!

TH: *<laughs>* You can photograph all of them. I first touched a computer in February 1983, when I had no knowledge whatsoever. In one month I knew the limits of BASIC. To analyse *Cosmic Soldier* and create the flow chart took me 4 months; working in the evenings after I had done work as a domestic salesperson during the day. I have 100% of my analysis in this chart. I understood absolutely everything about *Cosmic Soldier*. I would stay up until 3 or 4 o'clock in the morning to work on this. I was always suffering from lack of sleep. But thanks to my hard work I was able to educate myself on the architecture and structure of a game. After that I spent about another 4 months to create *Haunted Cave*. By December that year, 10 months later, I had completed *Haunted Cave* in machine language. It was first sold April 1984.

JS: Your effort in machine language is staggering.

TH: The company basically was expecting its employees either to come up with results or not, so I just had to do it, so I could show them I can deliver. If I couldn't do it, I would be branded as a failure.

JS: You fell into it all by accident.

TH: Yes, exactly.

JS: These print-outs must be over 30 years old.

TH: Yes, that's right. I could never do this again! *<laughs>* Nor do I want to. Back then I used to have a close friend who was an engineer, and although he did not develop games, he was able to tweak around with the computer. So he gave me clues and hints about reverse-engineering, and how I should go about using computers. Do you know the word *mnemonic*?[18] This is a word to indicate how machine language is mapped to a computer; machine language entails numbers from 0 to 255, and this is the only language the computer can understand.[19] At first the machine doesn't understand words that we use, so it uses those numbers and a *mnemonic* is a word which corresponds to this those numbers.

JS: Ah, hexadecimal!

TH: *<in English, without interpreter>* Hexadecimal is the real machine language! It's 0 to 255. *<points to an opcode on the paper notes>* This word, in English, is an abbreviation for something. So these are the mnemonic codes.

JS: I see. And this is a conversion table?

TH: Yes. Maybe I can explain with... So for example 00, double zero, stands for NOP, meaning "no operation", which means the computer doesn't do anything. It passes through. So only the time lapses when this is there. So these are all mnemonics. Basically these are big letters matched with each number on the very left hand side. So when we actually do the programming, we use these mnemonics, and then the assembler is what converts these mnemonics into numerical values. *<referencing printouts>* So I thought that it would be a good idea for me to retain the memory of mnemonics, as a souvenir so to speak. Well, all my colleagues, including the president, thought that I would never be able to do this, but I wanted to do my best before I surrendered. I thought, even if I were to fail, I wanted to retain my memory of mnemonics. So I started out be memorising them. Once I had memorised all the mnemonics I only had to use the assembler for the conversion into numerical figures. So I did not have to memorise the assembler portion.

So with reverse assembling, we can get those mnemonics... After that the computer loads the program from those set of mnemonics into the memory, you see? The CPU scans this set of mnemonics, which is translated into a language for the machine - hexadecimal - and inputted in the computer. Then the computer starts working. So now, with reverse-assembly, we translate those hexadecimal numbers which were already installed in the memory back into mnemonics. This PC-88 already had that functionality embedded in it. There was a disassembly mode, which is the same as reverse assembly. What I printed out first was the disassembled portion. After I printed that out I tried to figure out what these figures stood for, or meant. What does the number 3 do for example, in this portion of memory, what does 1 do? And so on. For example I didn't know what this number 3 meant, exactly, but I hypothesised that this 3 may stand for the number of player lives at the onset. So assuming that was the case, I changed the number to 4, and found that the number of players when you start the game changed to 4. So my hypothesis was right! I tried out so many things, and after all this trial and error I figured out what happens when changing the numbers in memory. I was able to decipher what they stood for. Also, in a similar way, I tried to decipher what was happening with those numbers, for example, from point A to point B in this chart. *<shows section of flow chart>* And that is how I came to understand how computers work.

JS: The fact you showed such aptitude, it's almost like destiny that you became involved.

TH: Well, I liked mathematics. This must have been a coincidence, or destiny, or whatever. *<hands over book on Z80 machine code>* This is for you to keep, because I have a number of

[18] In computing: a symbolic name for a single executable machine language instruction

[19] aka: hexadecimal or base 16, represented by numerals 0-9 and letters A-F. The number 255 is represented by FF

copies. This is quite popular, even today. Sometimes people come to me and ask if I still have them. The publisher went bankrupt and no longer exist.

JS: Could you sign it?

TH: Yes, of course! This PC-8801 uses the Z80 programming language. The Zilog 80 CPU was developed by a Japanese developer called Shima-san.[20] Originally, the Z80 was a next generation version, or the evolved version, of Intel's 8080 CPU. Intel's 8080 and this Z80 use the same code... No, that's not the proper word... Machine languages - the hexadecimal is the same in those two CPUs, but the mnemonics are different. Even though this machine had a Z80 in it, for reverse-assembling we had to write the code with or in way of the 8080. So the reverse-assembled code that I showed you earlier... *<points to paper>* This is the machine language. But this is an early one, so it's kind of embarrassing to show you the way it's written out. You're supposed to have no spaces in-between, but I made a space on purpose so that it would be easy for me to read or decode. So these mnemonics differ between the two CPUs. So I had to memorise both. *<laughs>*

In addition, the PC-98 and other 16-bit machines came. In those days each manufacturer, like Fujitsu or others, used different CPUs. Fujitsu used their own CPU for example. So there was a job of "converting" between different machines. You've got a PC-88 game, written in a language specifically for the PC-88, but it doesn't work on Fujitsu's FM-7 or Sharp X1 as it is. For the game to run on these, we needed to reprogram it for each machine.

<Hidaka-san describes his interest in fitness>

JS: It's very different, programming and fitness.

TH: Different, but for me it's the same. Because programming needs not only a strong mind, but a strong body. Otherwise it's impossible to continue for a long time sitting and programming.

JS: It's a sedate profession, so you need to keep yourself in good condition.

<Mr Hidaka bends his arm and shows off a chiselled bicep that could break rocks>

TH: I'm trying to figure out when I started writing articles... I should have been writing them by this time... All of my articles were compiled and published as a book after I had completed writing articles for this magazine. *<shows magazine article>* This is me.

JS: Can you remember the date of your first magazine article?

TH: This is issue 19, so... *<goes through >*

JS: Can my photographer take some shots of the tape version of *Eldorado Denki*? It's quite rare.

TH: Sure. *<removes box from glass cabinet>* This is the tape version of *Eldorado Denki*.

JS: *<sees another box>* That's the disk version?

TH: Yes, the disk version cost 7800 yen, whereas the tape version cost 4800 yen.

JS: Considerably cheaper to buy the tape version.

TH: Yes. Although it's cheaper it's also very much more difficult to create the tape version compared to the disk version. I mean from the perspective of the developer.

JS: Plus the loading times are longer.

TH: Yes, of course. Whenever we had to make changes or amendments [to the program] it needed the same amount of time to save changes as to load. So it was quite cumbersome whenever there was a change to be made. We had a royalty that would come to us as 10% of the 4800 yen it sold for. That was how things worked back in those days.

JS: The disk version was better then?

TH: Well, the disks themselves were expensive, so that is why the prices were set higher. But the problem was that many users, including high school students and so on, did not have disk drives to use the disks. I tried to start my disk drive the other day, *<picks up disk drive>* but then smoke started to come out. So it broke down. This used to cost 168'000 yen back then.[21] Just for this alone.

---

[20] Masatoshi Shima

[21] About £550 / $700 in 1985

JS: Even without inflation that's a lot of money!

TH: I had to spend a fortune, all of my savings, to get this back then. This is the machine that I used for *Haunted Cave*. *<refers to bespoke tape player>* It was working a week ago, but I tried yesterday and found it broken, now it's not working. So the disk drive over there has gone down, and this recorder has also gone down. So that's why I've used the extension cord from my cassette player in order for us to play *Cosmic Soldier* today. *<a long cord trails from tape deck to PC-88>* At that time, even if you were able to obtain the computer, unless you were able to program on your own, you weren't able to play any games at all. You could do nothing with only NEC's machine and the display, so you needed to have a disk or tape drive. So if you bought the computer you would get this demonstration program *<shows demo tape>*, this came as a set, a package, back in those old days. Is there anything else you'd like to photograph?

JS: Technically, I'd like to photograph everything!

TH: These are the ones that I was involved with. *<shows impressive display case>* I have other games that were converted for other types of computer. But once a game was converted for this machine, I got rid of the other versions, to save some room, since they were bulky, and I just kept these.

JS: That's a shame.

TH: I didn't feel any sense of value or significance in them. Normally I just keep them on the shelves, because I can't play them and I don't have the opportunity to do that anyway.

<takes items off shelves, places them on floor>

JS: I played the Famicom conversion of *JESUS*.

TH: I should have the Famicom version of *JESUS* here somewhere.

JS: Were you involved with the conversion?

TH: No, I was involved with the data compression for this one, the original version.

JS: *<looking at items>* It's a nice collection.

TH: *<shows music CD>* NEC used to give these CDs whenever they launched a new product for the PC-88 series. As you can see there is a program on it for playing music, called "Sound driver". [22] Do you know Kouichi Sugiyama, the composer of *Dragon Quest*?

JS: Yes, I know of him.

TH: *<shows more CDs>* These are music CDs with his, Sugiyama-san's, soundtracks for *JESUS* and *Gandhara*. This was a transitional period for music media. We used to have tapes, vinyl records and CDs, all at the same time. Inside this you would have this insert, with photographs. I can open this. *<refers to factory sealed vinyl record>*

JS: No! It's factory sealed. I would feel very guilty if you opened that.

TH: Eh? *<laughs>* It's not a big deal. *<places record down, still sealed>* And these are all my personal books. *<laughs>* I like manga books, so you see a lot of them on the shelf.

JS: So do I!

TH: Do you know the manga called *Ninja*?

[22] NEC's *CD Takara Hako*, a pack-in item with a CD-ROM drive for PC-88

JS: No, I've not heard of it. <*mentions titles*>

TH: Those are the manga read nowadays? I'm an older generation, so I used to read older manga. <*takes two books off shelf*> This one is from Taiwan, actually. It's a book which I wrote, that was translated for the Taiwanese market, from my original Japanese book.

JS: Show me the original.

TH: *The Making of Computer RPG*. This is the original Japanese version. It talks about how to create an RPG for computers, and how they [RPGs] work. <*points to book cover*> This is actually a photograph from when they were developing software at Chunsoft. **(below)** I borrowed the photo for the book's cover.

JS: I love old office photos. They're so rare!

TH: <*shows inside the book*> I also drew all these illustrations and the characters, because I really love manga. Since I love manga so much I drew all these characters on my own. **(right)** I still have the original drawings, because these were done by myself. <*shows another booklet*> This is from the early days, when I first started working for Enix, and this was taken during a break. This is the original PC-88, or the first version of the PC-88, and this is myself.

(below) These are the scenes from a development meeting. **(not shown)**

JS: Such bulky computer monitors.

TH: Yes, these are the older ones.

JS: With scanlines!

TH: Yes! That's right. Now that you mention it, I guess you're right in that not many photographs are taken during the development phase, when we were at the office.

<Hidaka-san leaves room and returns>

TH: This is the vinyl record for *JESUS*. This is just the music. When we did the recording we produced the music using a computer, and that's what we used for *JESUS*. And also *Gandhara* and *Wingman*.

JS: Takashi Tokita from Square-Enix said *JESUS* on the PC-88 was one of his favourite games. He really liked the FM sound of the PC-88.

TH: *<shows photo from vinyl sleeve>* This is a gentleman, Taguchi-kun,[23] and he was very good at producing this kind of music.

JS: It's an important part of the game,

TH: Yes, yes that's right! The music is not merely an important component of the game. The game itself has a deep connection with music. In order to defeat the monster at the end, the player has to actually play a melody on the computer keyboard, like playing a piano.[24] So it was quite extraordinary.

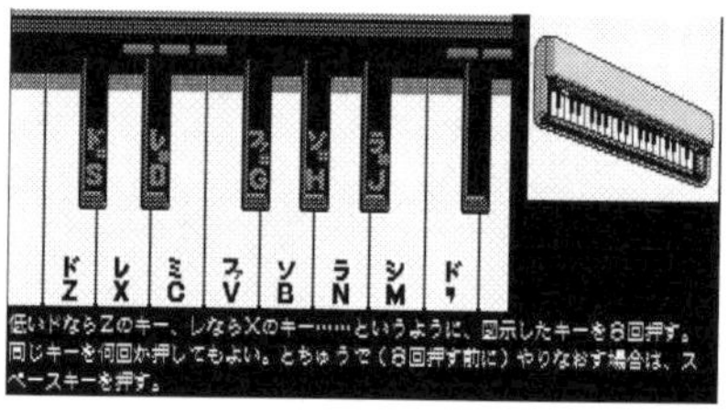

JS: I'm glad you've kept your collection.

TH: This is not a collection, so to speak. *<laughs>* I just kept whatever I have been involved in. So I don't see much value in them. You only have to spend a few thousand yen to purchase one of these games, used, in Akihabara.

JS: Some of them are rarer than that!

TH: Yes, you're right! *<laughs>* I'm keeping them as memorabilia, so to speak.

JS: There must be many memories in these.

TH: Yes. But my children were not interested in them in them at all. *<laughs>* Usually it's the other way around and the kids are more into computer technology and so on, so the fathers are the ones who are teased by their children, but in our case it's the other way around. *<laughs>* My two children, one is a medical doctor, and the other is a pharmacist. They both have a scientific background, but they have no knowledge of computers. So whenever they have to know something about computers they come to me. *<laughs>*

JS: You can show them your book interview.

TH: The older one is a son, and the younger one is a daughter. *<laughs>* I don't know how they would react! Even to this day both of them think I'm a weird dad.

<everyone laughs>

JS: As a writer I keep all of the magazines I write for as well.

TH: *<in English>* So in fifty years time you'll take part in such an interview?

JS: Would anyone want to interview someone who merely conducted other interviews? I'm just talking about the creations of other people.

TH: Well, you never know. It's hard to believe that you came all the way to Japan from the UK, to conduct these interviews. That's quite amazing. How did you find my homepage?

---

[23] Yasuhiro Taguchi

[24] This happens at the climax of the game, see image

JS: There's an internet forum I visit,[25] for fans of Japanese computers. On there I found the Enix advertising image. <*long explanation*>

TH: I was surprised that you were able to see my website, because usually you would have to have Japanese installed with Windows in order to read Japanese websites.

JS: I activated Japanese scripts on my computer. Would you like to look through a magazine I write for?

<*Mr Hidaka looks through Retro Gamer*>

JS: This magazine only covers old games.

TH: Wow! It's amazing you have this magazine in the UK. It's monthly. Incredible. In Japan you don't look back in the computer industry.

JS: A mixture of nostalgia and investigation.

TH: This is great! The same thing can be seen among anime and manga. They usually publish the retrospective versions, even today. So most of the manga that I have on my bookshelf are from the ones that were out in the 1950s, when I used to read them as a child. Many people look back on the old days, and like to reminisce about the music or the manga that they used to enjoy as children, back in the 1950s or 1960s. That kind of trend can be seen in the music or manga industry, but when it comes to computers, the Japanese never look back, they only see the future. I never thought there would be a magazine investigating past facts on computers.

JS: What do you feel led to the longevity of NEC's computers? Sharp upgraded the X1 to X68000, but NEC's models lasted longer.

TH: Well, PC-88 and PC-98 no longer exist...

JS: I believe they both came out around 1982.[26] People still used the PC-98 until the late-1990s.

TH: For PC-88 and PC-98, they used different CPUs, the PC-88 was 8-bit, and the PC-98 was 16-bit. Those two were categorised into different purposes. The PC-98 was for businesses, whereas the PC-88 was for hobbyists. Of course the PC-88 could be used in business situations, but it was considered to be a hobbyist computer.[27] You need to differentiate the two, we shouldn't mix those two machines. So the competing products for the PC-88 were Sharp's X1 or Fujitsu's FM-7. The reason why the PC-88 lasted so long on the market, I don't know... Why they were popular for a long time, I would guess was because NEC had strong sales and marketing capabilities, for one thing. I suppose the PC-88 gradually increased its market share versus the other 8-bit computers. Later the MSX, a different sort of computer, also came into the picture. But I think NEC was successful in growing their market share.

Another factor was NEC utilized an OS by Microsoft called N88-BASIC,[28] while Fujitsu used a unique dialect called F-BASIC. Meanwhile Sharp used Hu-BASIC, which was made by Hudson for Sharp. F-BASIC and Hu-BASIC were a little more idiosyncratic... But in terms of functionality, [the PC-88, FM-7, and X1 computers] weren't significantly different. On the other hand, Fujitsu and Sharp had sound from the beginning.[29] They used a programmable sound generator (PSG) sound source, which allowed them to create a Famicom-type sound. Meanwhile, the PC-8801 originally had only a simple beep, so the other computers offered better sound. But other than that, the computers

[25] http://fullmotionvideo.free.fr/phpBB3/index.php

[26] NEC's PC-8801 came out 1981; PC-98 in 1982; both received significant overhauls over the years

[27] PC-8801 was originally intended to be a business machine, a sort of top-of-the-line PC-8001, but then another division within NEC released the PC-9801, so the PC-8801 was repositioned as a hobbyist machine, which led to the extensive game-friendly overhaul in the form of the PC-8801mkIISR

[28] N88-Basic was based on M-BASIC 4.5

[29] Some context: From the start the Fujitsu FM-7 series and Sharp X1 series featured built-in sound using a General Instrument AY-3-8910 Programmable Sound Generator (PSG) chip, also found in many early arcade machines and other home computers. PSG produces an artificial "chippy" sound similar to a NES. Meanwhile, the original NEC PC-8801 and PC-8801mkII had even more primitive sound, just simple monotone beeps. Starting on the significantly upgraded PC-8801mkIISR in Jan 1985, all PC-8801 models featured built-in FM synthesis, which produces softer, richer tones than PSG. Although optional sound boards were available, the FM-7 series didn't actually offer built-in FM synth until late 1985, and the X1 didn't include FM synth until late 1986. So even though the PC-8801 started out with truly hideous sound, NEC was essentially the first computer maker to include FM synth as a guaranteed part of the hardware. Meaning developers were more likely to take advantage of the better audio, which in turn drew more users to the PC-8801

were pretty evenly matched. Under those circumstances I assume NEC was successful in gaining their market share, that is as far as I can think of, why NEC outlived its competitors. I have no idea why NEC won such a huge share at that time exactly.

Regarding the PC-98 it's a different story, since it started as a business machine. At first there were practically no games at all. But after a while, as the user base grew, games for the PC-98 started to appear. The reason why the PC-98 lasted for a long time was because of its kanji or Japanese display functionality. Back then IBM's MS-DOS[30] was common in the world, but in Japan there was the problem of displaying kanji, and IBM was not able to import them into Japan because of this language barrier. So IBM tried to solve the problem. For example, NEC used what is called a graphics plane or graphics mode, and thanks to that, they could have moving sprites like in a game. On top of the graphics plane NEC had another screen mode called a text plane, where they would show Japanese characters. What they would do is overlay the text plane onto the graphics plane. The PC-98 overlapped those two planes on one screen. What IBM did instead was display Japanese characters using the graphics plane itself, instead of overlaying a text plane onto it.

NEC used fixed-size characters of 32x32 pixels for displaying the Japanese text. So in other words the text was not scalable. If you zoomed them up or shrunk them, it would start looking blocky and would no longer appear readable. IBM used the graphics plane for Japanese text. But they created those Japanese characters not as a fixed combination of pixels like NEC did, but as vector graphics. So it was possible to recalculate the vectors as needed, making the text scalable. So that's how IBM was successful in entering the Japanese market - they adopted a vector methodology for Japanese characters. With this technique IBM could display text beautifully; even when changing the scale there is no distortion of pixels because it's created by vectors. But they weren't successful in acquiring a market share in Japan immediately, because they lacked software.

I think Windows came out sometime around 1993, starting out with version 3.0 or 3.1, and when they reached Windows 95 many users were able to make use of them. Japanese consumers started to switch over to Windows from NEC. [Meanwhile] NEC was still not totally in sync with the global standard. For example Windows used 640 x 480 pixels, whereas NEC only used 640 x 400, so it lacked 80 pixels on the bottom. So NEC had to compensate for that 80 pixel difference when releasing the PC-98 version of Windows. Before Windows 95, every time a new version of Windows was released in Japan it lagged behind the release in the US. Up until 95 every time Microsoft updated their version, NEC engineers had to go to Microsoft in order to consult with them as to how to compensate for the missing 80 pixels in the vertical resolution, at the bottom of the display. But it got harder and harder to catch up and continue with that. NEC acknowledged that would no longer work for them. So finally NEC switched the PC-98 over from 640x400 pixels to 640x480 pixels.[31] Once NEC switched over, the same software for Windows was able to run on the PC-98 without any changes. But on the other hand, that meant that the original merits of the PC-98 didn't matter anymore. So the PC-98 platform was ousted by DOS/V, since for customers, as long as the machine is capable of running Windows, there is no difference, and NEC started to release DOS/V machines and the history of PC-98 ended there.

I kind of side-tracked for a little bit from your original question! <*laughs*>

JS: That's OK! About *Gandhara*...[32] Enix's own *Dragon Quest* for Famicom was on sale and doing well, but Enix continued publishing high-quality games for computers, even though sales would have been lower than on Famicom. Why was this?

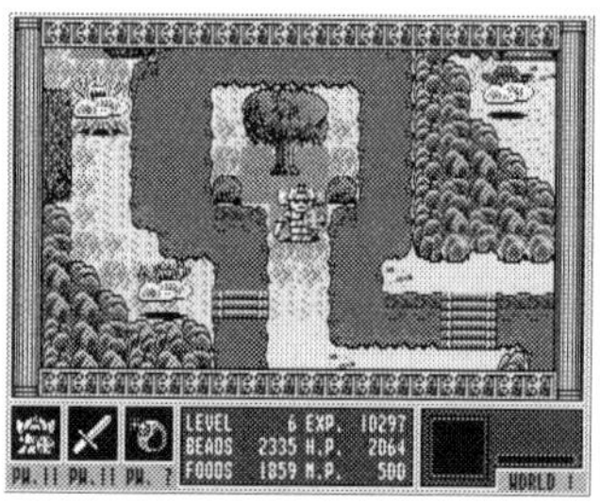

TH: The first reason would be that there was still a demand for computer games, and the second reason is although *Dragon Quest* was selling very well, it required a lot of time for development, because of its magnitude, it's size.

---

[30] Later on DOS/V, or Disk Operating System/VGA was released (1990); an attempt to allow IBM computers to display Japanese characters

[31] Marking the birth of the PC-9821 series, Oct 1992

[32] *Gandhara* (1987) for computers is *Zelda* but better in every respect: multidirectional scrolling, nicer colours, full screen portraits of NPCs, superior FM sound, richer more exotic story, levelling, food, and overall more depth to all the mechanics. Now fan-translated

It's a huge game and requires lots of time and money. So every time they launch a new version, of course it might be selling very well for maybe 6 months or so. But if it takes another 2 years to develop the next title, how can Enix earn money during the last 18 months? Their sales would go down to zero before the latest version came out. Enix always had trouble like this, it was a big headache. If you take a look at the stock price of Enix, the fluctuation was quite dramatic. When they're selling well the stock prices would go up, and if the sales started stagnating the stock prices would nosedive. So those computer games were a kind of a buffer product in order to mitigate this situation.

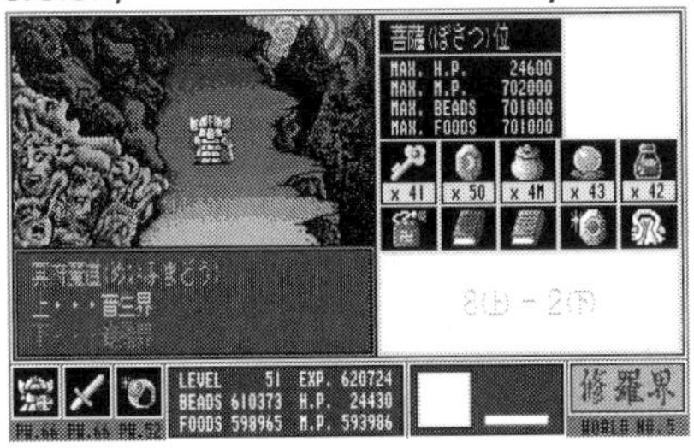

JS: Hence computer games such as *Gandhara*.

TH: But if you compare the scale of buying between console and computer games, there's a significant difference. The number of sales of those computer games was quite small compared to one game like *Dragon Quest*, so returns from computer games are very little...[33] So that's why Square and Enix decided to merge with each other, in order to minimise the time lag for new products to come out. Square had a very popular series, *Final Fantasy*, whereas Enix had *Dragon Quest*. So if they had both, they could kind of level out the timings for the launches of each.

JS: Why didn't Enix put *Gandhara* on the Famicom if console sales were higher?

TH: Well... They thought the game wouldn't be so popular.

JS: But if *Dragon Quest* is an RPG selling well on the Famicom, and *Gandhara* was an RPG, how come Enix didn't capitalise on *Dragon Quest*'s pre-existing popularity?

TH: There was talk of putting *Gandhara* on the Famicom. They had thought about it, but it's a totally different thing converting a game from one computer to another, compared to converting a computer game to a console. If they did so, it means we need to re-create the game from zero to the end. If they were to convert the graphics from one to the other they would have to start from scratch, and also include changes to the hardware, because they were totally different. Enix did not have enough manpower to do that. Yes, *Gandhara* and *JESUS* were launched at about the same time, and for *JESUS* there was a Famicom conversion which came out, so why not *Gandhara*? Maybe the capacity for developing it was not enough at the time? So yes, it would have been a good idea if *Gandhara* had been ported to the Famicom as well but... I think they did not have sufficient development capacity to do that. [34] There was a plan... However, ultimately it was not made.

JS: I believe *Gandhara* was only released on computers. I think there are games you simply could not make on consoles.

TH: I was actually asked to make the Famicom version of *Gandhara*, because at that time there wasn't the development staff at Enix, and so I was asked, but I didn't want to do it. I didn't feel like doing it at that time. Then at a different time I was also asked to convert *Dragon Quest* to the PC-88. But at that time *Dragon Quest*, or one characteristic of *Dragon Quest*, was that the character would only face forwards. As you can see compared to *Gandhara*, the character in *Dragon Quest* does not face to the right or left, the character does not face backwards, the character was constantly only facing the front.[35] After all the work I put into the character movement in *Gandhara*, where the character properly turns left and right as they move, I

[33] According to Tokihiro Naito, interviewed in a later volume, the sales of *Hydlide* across every computer platform (at least 8 formats), when added together only just matched the sales on Famicom alone

[34] This likely refers to the capacity of the FC and available mapper chips - *JESUS* was a graphic adventure with static images, technically easy to port, whereas *Gandhara* had multidirectional scrolling

[35] This is true for the Japanese original. The US version, *Dragon Warrior*, had improved graphics for the main character and he could face different directions

didn't want to work on something as simplistic as *Dragon Quest*. I rejected their request. An MSX version of *Dragon Quest* was made, however it was not me who made the MSX version. So there were a number of... how should I put it... circumstances for why we didn't make a Famicom version of *Gandhara*. Later on the MSX2 version of *Gandhara* was made, but that came about because the person who was requested to do the port came to me and said let's do it together. We spent a very long time on that version. It was not easy, it took a full year.

JS: Can you tell me about the PC-98 version of *Gandhara*? It wasn't published by Enix, but you've got a copy on your shelf.

TH: The person who was in charge of the PC-98 version was a gentleman called Aoyama-san, who knew me quite well. He was not the fastest worker. <*laughs*> It took him more than one-and-a-half years. So because he took such a long time finishing *Gandhara*, Enix sort of lost the chance to sell it. Then Enix told him, "We can't publish this through our company anymore." Then a different company found it and they said it was OK, so they sold it instead.

JS: I think the best version was the FM-77AV. I can't see it here. Do you know anything about it?

TH: I received a copy of every conversion for every game I worked on, but I couldn't keep everything, so I got rid of them. There was the X1 version, the FM-7 version, but I didn't have the machines here, so I threw them out.

JS: You kept only the version you directly worked on?

TH: Yes, the ones that I have I was actually in charge of, and as for the PC-98 version, I had a PC-98 back then, so I hung on to it.

JS: When you say got rid of them, did you literally put them in the bin?

TH: <*laughs*> No, actually, I went to sell them at Akihabara!

<*everyone laughs loudly*>

TH: Akihabara is one of the most famous districts in Tokyo, for electronics. I thought they would be worth something, so I sold them.

JS: Did you perhaps sneak a signature on the corner of the box?

TH: <*laughs*> No, no, I didn't even open it.

JS: Still factory sealed.

TH: Yes, but if I brought it into the store that way, people might think that I had stolen it. So before selling it I took off the plastic seal.

JS: Collector's would love those now.

TH: I don't think I was collecting as a "collector" - I was fine with it leaving my home at that time.

JS: Do you ever sell via online auctions?

TH: No, I've never put anything up for auction, but I have gone to Akihabara to sell stuff. I don't play them, so they just take up space for me. For me, games are something you make. I don't really like playing, to be honest. So even when I used to receive free games from Enix, it was only because they asked me in advance to write an evaluation.

JS: After years of excellent computer games in Japan, there was a shift towards consoles such as the Famicom. What are your thoughts on the decline of computer games?

TH: I think the biggest reason for that would be because those who played computer games would of course eventually grow up, become adults and stop playing games altogether. Then, the new generation started playing games, not on the computer but on Famicom. There was no incentive for those players who started out on the Famicom to switch over to computer games. [Computers were more expensive and complicated.] So computer games couldn't recover their popularity. So the changing generations of those who play games is the biggest reason, I think.[36]

[36] This was an insightful answer - the FC only became popular towards the later half of the 1980s, with few games of interest when launched. From before the

JS: Did you develop any games for yourself, which were never released?

TH: I hadn't gotten that far, where I would come up with another game, but I did come up with tools and utilities. There were many projects where they wanted to come up with new games, and the projects were launched, but they did not come to fruition; they ended midway through. So there were many cases of projects which fell through halfway.

JS: How many unreleased games did you witness? Can you remember their names?

TH: One product, *Prajator*, [37] was actually commercialised, but let me explain the background as to how it came into existence. In fact, the project was started by another guy and I wasn't included at first. My predecessor started developing the game before me, but then one of his programmers left the team. So he came to me asking me to develop the program for him. I was a replacement. But after that, when I actually started working on it, a person from the graphics section, who was on the team from the onset, came to me saying, "that is no good" or "you have to do it this way", and so on. This staff member who created the graphics started to work against me, because for him, he worked a long time on this game and he thought it was HIS game, so he often interfered in the programming. Then some of the staff developed the game without me, I was out of the circle! For some reason, somehow, I got kicked out of the team! The product was commercialised, but it was completed by a third party, myself being excluded. The end result was a very shallow, not very good game. The quality of the game itself was terrible. But the company wanted to release it as a product, so that is why *Prajator* ended up being released.

There are two or three other examples where the projects fell through. Basically, the pay structure of Enix is "payment as royalty" and it means, if developers couldn't finish their games, the company wouldn't have to pay those developers. Enix, or basically its project teams, were a kind of jumble of guys from everywhere, and you worked on some projects with people who didn't know each other well. So even if the project did not work, and was not completed, there's no damage to the company whatsoever. It's nothing if a project fails, because they don't pay for unfinished games, and there is no bond between people who work on the project. So there were a many number of cases, similar to *Prajator*, that weren't fully completed.

In spite of this, the fragility of the project teams, Enix did publicity in magazines often. There were many magazines featuring the latest information on software, and editors came to Enix saying that they wanted to feature a product of Enix's. Sometimes Enix announced "the new game coming soon" with some photograph which showed the game being played. But often those images were fake! It looked as if Enix had already finished programming the game halfway, and one could play the game like in the photo. But in fact, Enix only created the graphics with characters, as if it was finished, and then took a photo to give to magazines. Of course they hadn't finished these "games" at all, it was only a static image, you couldn't move the character, you couldn't play, it was totally motionless. So there were many games [that started] like that, and some games were never released.

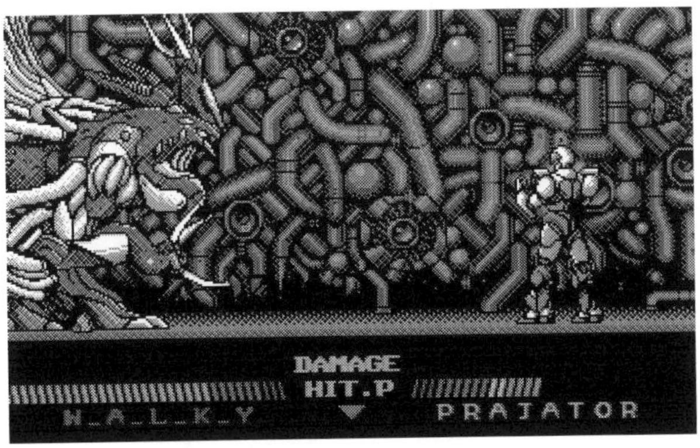

JS: They wanted to give the impression they had games, but these games weren't real?

TH: That's correct.

JS: Wow, that's unbelievable.

TH: There was a magazine called *PC Magazine*, and it would try to find gossip so that it could attract the readers. So at that time, in the

1980s, newcomers played in arcades or on computers. Diehards stuck with computers after the FC boom, but consoles became the platform of choice. A similar thing is happening now - those reading this book probably grew up with consoles, whereas today's youth are more interested in smartphone games

[37] Only playable on a rare higher end PC-88; a cross between *Rise of the Robots* and *Blackhole Assault*

magazine I showed you earlier, there was a section called *Maruchi Soft Tsuushin*.[38] It was a column for introducing those games "still in development" but with a taste for ridicule; they would try to collect information regarding software developers who were delayed in their production schedule, so that they could make fun of them.

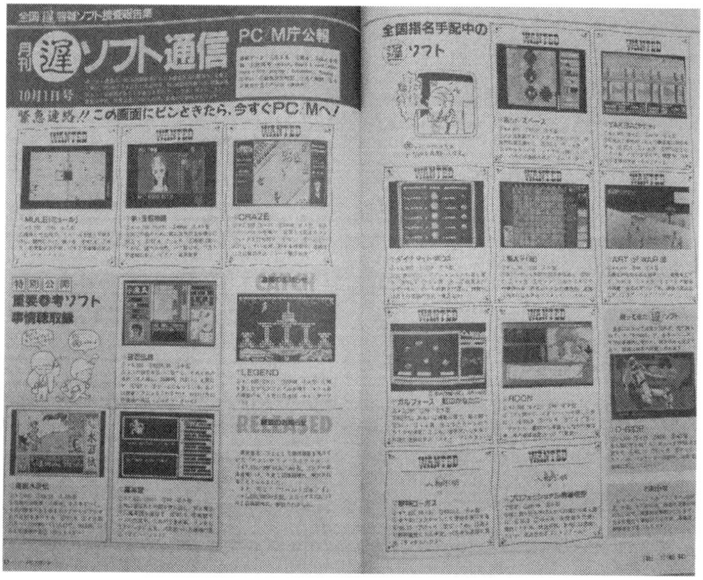

Additionally, back then magazines used to [run advertisements] to attract people's attention, but there were many unqualified or immature programmers who lacked insight. Sometimes they themselves couldn't tell where they were in the project concerned. So those young programmers often thought their project would finish soon, but it was not always true - they misunderstood the milestones of the project. They would talk big and boast about what their game would feature when completed, even though they're still at the start - they would reveal things that you'd only bring up when deep into a project [and the details were finalised]. So that created misleading information.

JS: I think that still happens today in magazines.

TH: In the past game producers used to be the person working behind the scenes, but little by little, they started to show up in public more and tried to promote themselves more. So they're actually showing themselves off in the front. But producers cannot know the things which are uncertain for programmers, of course, so their publicity became vague and irresponsible.

JS: Could you draw a sketch of the Enix offices?

TH: I used to visit Enix just once a week, even while I was working on a project. I would go there to have a meeting with them. Of course I was not a member of Enix itself, exactly. So I'm not well versed as to what the layout was.

<Hidaka-san shows copy of magazine with unreleased section>

TH: They made fun of delays in software development, and it's titled *Maruchi Soft Tsuushin*, which is kind of a pun, a play on words. The *maru* stands for the first half of "multi", and this *chi* is for the second half of *multi*, but at the same time they've used the kanji character meaning delay, which is also pronounced *chi*.[39] To make fun of the developers.

<looking through the article it reveals some fascinating Japanese games which were announced with screens but not released>

TH: So this type of article was quite popular, and you could find these articles in other magazines as well.

JS: If the game was never released, this would be the only record of it.

TH: Yes, you could say that. Looking back, I would say these articles contain valuable information. This was a monthly publication, so you could find this every month. This is also the issue where I first started writing articles.

JS: Let's take a photo of you holding it.

TH: All the articles that I had written for the magazine was compiled into books, and this was covered in volumes 1 through 4. *<shows compilation books>* I don't have the second book, but I still have the first, third and fourth books, if you want to keep them.

---

[38] Kanji 遅ソフト通信; Lit. *Delayed Software Report*

[39] Pun stems from fact the first word should be *multi* as in ***multi***media, but it's written in kanji to say *delayed*

TH: I want to expand my free space - I would appreciate it if you can take them. This publisher went out of business too. So I took up their stock, and I sell one or two books a year over the internet. A manga cartoonist, a Kurosawa-san, was making fun of me by drawing a picture of me like this. <*laughs - points to caricature*> This is me, yes. If you take a look at the "4 cell" comic strips at the back, he portrays me as a huge drinker. But actually I do not drink alcohol at all. So this is a misrepresentation. <*flips through*> This is not the one but... There's a comic where I am drinking too much in a pub. But this is not me! I don't drink. <*laughs*>

JS: Don't worry, I'll make sure to print the truth.

TH: He's just teasing me by coming up with a fake story.

JS: For *Magic Garden*, why did you choose Enix as the publisher? Did they influence it at all?

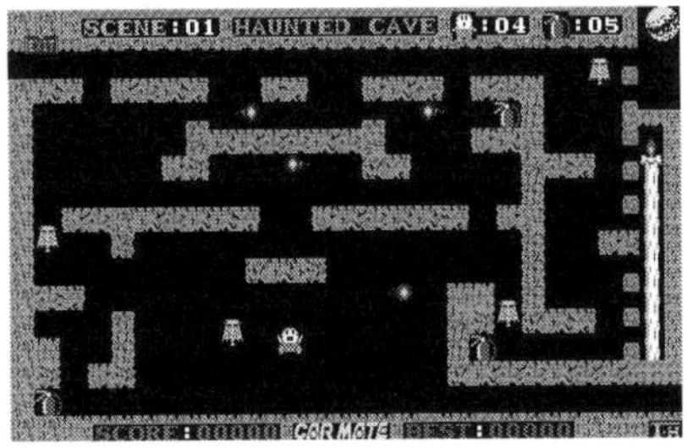

Haunted Cave for PC-88, Mr Hidaka's first game

TH: The game was already completed. Of course they requested some modifications. As I mentioned earlier, Car Mate was the one which released *Haunted Cave*, and I completed that game at the end of 1983, but the actual product was launched in April or May of the following year. Of course I was responsible as a sales representative of Car Mate, having the responsibility of selling the company's other products, and at the same time I was working on the development of *Magic Garden* **(below)**. I was also responsible for cultivating new sales channels for [*Haunted Cave*] at the same time. The end result was that [*Haunted Cave*] did not sell as much as we had expected. So the president, taking a look at the low sales, started saying, "Let's give this up now. We should not be working on this anymore." But since I had purchased this computer on my own for use at home, and I did not want to give up, I told the president that I'm going to leave the company.

About that time *Magic Garden* was 70-80% complete. But I developed this game secretly because I was not sure about how the company would react after. So after I quit the company I went over to Enix for a meeting, without making any appointments, with my copy of *Magic Garden* on me. I just decided I'd give it a shot, without making any appointment. To see what their response would be like. I was thinking, if Enix doesn't want it, I'll try other companies.

The reason why I visited Enix at first was because I knew they were throwing competitions. Enix was willing to commercialise it, so that's how I chose Enix.

JS: There was both a tape and disk version for *Magic Garden*. Were you responsible for both? What were the differences?

TH: Yes, I was responsible for both. The only difference between the tape version and the disk version was the functionality where the acquired score would be recorded. So the disk version would display a congratulations screen, and say you're the second or third highest scorer, or whatever, whereas the tape version did not have that ability.

JS: *Eldorado Denki* is a conversion of the FM-7 release. How hard was the conversion? It was designed by manga artist Tadashi Makimura.[40]

TH: Yes, it was a conversion. But no, the conversion from FM-7 to PC-88 was not difficult. I mean, normally I convert a game in 3 months after getting the request, but for this game it took only a month, because I was physically fit and I had the stamina to do that. So I was able to accelerate the process, reducing three months to one. It was a very lucrative job for me. It was a lucky opportunity, because that was when I became a freelancer and *Magic Garden* wasn't selling well at that time.

JS: You worked from home?

TH: Yes, this was my office. *<gestures around the room we're sitting in>* Well, this apartment itself is over 30 years old. We reformed the interior a few years ago, we used to have two rooms here. But we made it into one big room. Otherwise this was my office from back then.

JS: Did you ever meet Tadashi Makimura?

TH: Yes. Of course, because *Gandhara* was our collaboration, so yes. He was in charge of the graphics and the scenario, or the script, whereas I was in charge of the programming for *Gandhara*.

JS: Did you make the copy protection for *Eldorado Denki*, the disk version on PC-88?

TH: No, it was done at Enix, by a different person. Anyway, I have master disks of *Eldorado Denki*, without protection, so it's fine.

JS: But copy protection was also part of the games, a part of gaming culture. Some games were not fun to play, but removing the protection was like a game itself, for some. It's important to preserve the whole thing, including the protection.

TH: Nakamura-kun is an amazing person in the game industry, but unfortunately he added copy protection to his game *Newtron*. At the time, there were a number of different copy tools available, and what Nakamura-kun did was make the game appear to copy successfully, so people would think they had successfully made a copy. But he put in a message that would appear in the middle of the game, saying, "Sorry, too bad, you can't play any further." But this actually had the opposite effect, and some of the game crackers thought it was a funny prank. So Nakamura-kun inadvertently created a sort of metagame, a game of breaking the copy protection. After that, everyone started digging into *Newtron*, intent on breaking the protection, and ultimately the game was cracked.

JS: There are two kinds of protection: one, you can't copy the disk. Two, is a routine to check if the game being played is a copy or not.

TH: Basically, copy protection involved creating unformatted sectors. One technique involved intentionally damaging the media, like making a hole with a laser. By doing that, there was no way to create a full copy, because, unlike a regular disk, you're no longer able to read the bad sector and the data that comes after it. But if you skip that sector, there's no problem. But for the copy protection [in *Newtron*], it actually wasn't Nakamura-kun who did it. Enix retained the services of a copy protection specialist from outside the company, and when they were about to release a new game, they'd request copy protection. The specialist would then insert copy

[40] 槙村ただし; nickname *Doronpa*; worked on quite a few games for Enix

checks at various places on the media. So he was the one who actually put in the prank message. In other words, the copy protection specialist existed separately from the company. The *Newtron* message incident was quite famous, and various magazines ran articles on it and printed screenshots showing exactly when the message would appear.

JS: You did the PC-88 conversion of *Ultima*?

TH: Not all of them.

JS: I mean the first one.

TH: Part of the conversion, yes, I took part in. I think the original version was written for the most part in C language or BASIC... In order to convert the original version into Japanese we had to convert the sound effects as well as the graphics, which needed to use machine language. So that portion I was responsible for.

JS: It's said Lord British asked Falcom to convert and release *Ultima* in Japan. There are pictures of Lord British visiting Falcom. But in the end Pony Canyon did it. Do you know why?

TH: No, I don't know the reason why. At that time the job, like this game conversion for example, was often subcontracted from Pony Canyon to other little companies, but those subcontractors had no skill for doing the job either and so subcontracted the project again to other little companies. And those little companies often lack a professional level for developing. This would degrade the quality as well as the process. So this conversion of *Ultima* was also an example of this phenomenon... Some subcontractor of a subcontractor of Pony Canyon asked me, "There is no staff who can manage the machine language in our company, so please help us with it!"

JS: I would guess *Gandhara*, being an RPG, was the most challenging game to program?

TH: Up until this point PC-8801 had experienced a major change in terms of hardware. This is when the PC-8801SR came out. So the hardware performance changed dramatically. Hmm... *<pause>* It took me a year, but these are the files for the machine language for *Gandhara*. *<opens a cupboard on the floor>*

JS: You kept the source code for *everything*!

TH: Yes, I did. I typed all of these source codes manually. So I would first have to interpret and understand it before I could type it.

JS: Can I take some photos? It's very rare to find the source code for these older games.

TH: Is that right? At that time printers had ink ribbons. I ran out of black so often that I started to install other colours instead, as replacements. Because the ribbons came in groups of four different colours. Once I ran out of black ink I'd install a colour ribbon in its place. *<laughs>* So *Magic Garden* only contains this much information. *<shows a single blue folder>* In terms of volume, compared to *Gandhara*. *<points to three blue folders>*

JS: Today, this can help people understand how old computers functioned.

TH: You think so? I don't think I could ever print them out again, in terms of printer performance. But if I have to I think I can. I created the editor assembler on my own. Still today people occasionally contact me, saying they want to buy this editor assembler. I think it's the best program that I wrote in my life, much better, more impressive, than the games I created. I think I can boast about it being the best editor assembler in the world. *<boots computer>* This is the editor assembler, called *ROOT88*. For me, I am not so excited by the games, but this editor assembler... I created games because I loved to program, but sincerely I feel this assembler is much more valuable and great. This *ROOT88* excels more than the games I developed. What's amazing about this is the reverse assembler.

JS: You could put a commercial game in here, and it would disassemble it?

TH: Yes, for the most part, it would disassemble the program almost 100% perfectly. But of course most commercial games have copy protection. But if you understand those kinds of mechanisms [used in copy protection], and know how to utilise this, then you would be able to disassemble for the most part and can analyse the whole of the game with this editor assembler. It was available through shops.

As far as I know, this is the best reverse assembler that you will find; there is no assembler which can go as far as mine can in the world. I haven't seen one better than this. The other disassemblers are like toys compared to this. But unfortunately this only operates on the PC-88. *<laughs>*

JS: When did you become interested in wrestling?

TH: I don't when professional wrestling came to Japan, but back then when I was watching television, there were many famous pro wrestlers, like Rikidouzan.[41] So back then the broadcasting companies would show Disney programmes one night, starting from 8 o'clock on Friday, and the next week they would broadcast pro wrestling matches. It was broadcast on a bi-weekly basis, divided between wrestling and Disney. There came a time when Giant Baba and Antonio Inoki became the favoured wrestlers. Antonio Inoki was well known for his fighting spirit. I thought I would be able to catch up with Antonio Inoki's fighting spirit if I tried hard enough. That's why I would never let people judge me, and I decided to work my way through when I became interested in programming. The fighting spirit of this wrestler gave me the courage to keep fighting even though programming is very difficult.

My fitness interest started out when I was in fifth grade at elementary school. My parents let me keep a stray dog under the condition that I take the dog for a walk every morning and evening, and that's how I started training myself. I've been continuing to walk, or jog, ever since then. I do 500 sit-ups a day, and 200 push-ups a day as well. And I run for 6km.

JS: The lifestyle of a writer discourages fitness.

TH: This is my jog log. *<shows folder>* I started keeping records of my jogging, sometime in the beginning of the 1980s. Ever since then I've been recording it. Now it's 6km a day. But two years ago I used to run for 40km. Some years I would run a total of 4'300km. This year I ran this many. *<shows page - laughs>* That year, I came up with an idea like... "Let's defeat Mt Fuji!" But I had already run several kilometres and Mt Fuji's height is just 3776 metres. It's too easy! So I translated this height into 3776 ***kilo***metres and challenged that. *<laughs>* Often I come up with ideas like that. Last year, I even demolished my old house by myself - I had another house - and it took a year and a half. I keep myself busy, I really enjoy my life.

JS: Maybe you should program a new game?

TH: *<laughs>* I'm too busy for that! The times have changed. Enjoying game programming is not going to come back. It's a thing of the past. For me, what was most interesting about games was not to play them, but to create them. I liked working on my own. Up until *Magic Garden* I had the sole responsibility and discretion to create and develop everything, including the music. But little by little it shifted into the era of large projects, where there were multiple individuals involved, and where if one person had a delay or was behind schedule that would back us all up. It would delay our production process altogether. There was also a producer assigned to the project, who would give orders. I had no self discretion anymore. So that's why instead of working on programming, I thought it would be a good idea to work in books. So I can have full control over the entire process; I can work as I wish on my own.

[41] Mitsuhiro Momota; popularised wrestling in Japan

Second Interview with Toru Hidaka

12 November 2013

For this second interview I was joined by Joseph Redon of the Game Preservation Society, who was keen to meet Mr Hidaka. We were also joined by two Japanese TV producers, who were filming a documentary on crowdfunding in Japan and - given that my book on Japan was through crowdfunding - wanted to interview me and film some of my interviews. This second interview was extremely valuable, since it allowed me to film some of the utilities Mr Hidaka coded to allow others to create games for Enix.

<discussion about the UK - shows photo>

JS: When did you stay there?

TH: Forty years ago. The stone buildings are preserved in the UK, it's part of the culture.

JS: Did you visit England again after that?

TH: One time, 17 years after my first visit. But the family is not in this house anymore.

<film crew begins filming>

JS: Have you heard about new laws in Japan that would criminalise games such as *Eldorado Denki*?[1] Because it contains cat-girls who are nude and appear younger than 20. (right)

TH: I have never thought of it that way. I mean, even if you own the game now, it was legal back when it was released... But it's not that lewd I think. These are from the past, surely it's not a problem, because it's old and not exactly shocking. I think she's topless? Makimura-san continues to write manga like that, a sort of *doujin*. He used to belong to a company, called Dynamic Pro,[2] where they published the manga *Harenchi Gakuen* by Go Nagai.[3] That sort of naughty, sexualized manga was a common theme for Nagai. Makimura-san used to be Nagai-san's assistant. Makimura-san's first hit product was a rock-paper-scissors game, where if you win the female character in the game would start removing her clothes, one by one.[4] He wrote the game in BASIC, and that was his first successful product.

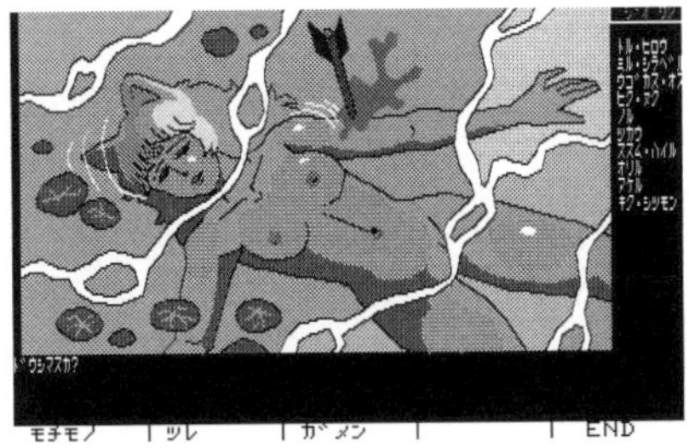

JS: The Japanese government is considering enacting a law where any representation of nudity of a minor is illegal.

JR: Yes, it would be illegal to possess such material even if it was released years ago, even a hundred years.

JS: Even though *Eldorado Denki* is quite innocent, it would still fall under this law. How do you feel about it? Would you send in your copy?

TH: *<laughs>* Well, no, I'm not planning to do so. I'm just joking, but as long as anyone, including you John-san, as long as you won't tell the Japanese government that I have this game with such content, I don't think anyone will know I have such a game at home. So I think I'll be OK.

<everyone laughs>

JS: I assure you, I won't be reporting you.

TH: *<laughs>* I don't really think about such things. If it happens, it will happen. There's nothing much I can do.

---

[1] The law is vaguely worded and would technically cover any drawn image containing nude minors (under 20), including games, manga, and presumably the paintings of Bouguereau. If passed anything breaching it would require handing over to the government for destruction; **apparently as of June 2014, both games and anime were removed from the legislation**

[2] Founded by Go Nagai with other illustrators, a kind of "Nagai school", the group created manga in his style

[3] *Harenchi Gakuen* was a pioneering ecchi manga, one of the first of its kind to be serialized in a mass-market magazine. Note that although the manga is sexually suggestive, it's not explicit. Incidentally, it was also made into a PC-98 game

[4] *Mari-chan Kikiippatsu* / マリちゃん危機一髪 (1983); one of 13 winning entries in Enix's game competition

JS: Enix now is quite a big company, they merged with Square to make Square-Enix, and maybe they will feel the need to control their image, and get rid of this history.

TH: In the computer magazines we discussed earlier there is a lot of awful content which could be called... How should I put it... Well, I guess today you might say "child porn". Back then it was called *bishoujo*[5] - back then there were much, much worse games, that could be considered pornographic today, but at that time the nudes of these girls, they were depicted not because of *lolicon* or a fixation with underage girls, but because adult nudity would be considered too sensitive. Whereas nudity of a girl was thought as being like a little doll. It's not as realistic, it was not as sensitive a topic as adult nudity, so it was actually one way of being less extreme. I do not think the *lolicon* notions were as prevalent back then as they are today.[6]

JR: I think we need to have rules. But this is a culture of that time, of that era, so it needs to be kept as is, in order to explain what was the culture at that time.

JS: If they enact the law for future media, that makes sense. But it seems strange to think you can whitewash the past. Presumably every game, every magazine containing a screen of such a game, would need destroying.

JR: The danger is that, for example, they will make a list of books, films, games, and they will send that to all archives or libraries, across the country, saying, "If you have this, you HAVE to destroy it." That really would be a problem.

JS: Mr Hidaka, on your website's front page you mention Shin Nihon Programming, can you describe what that was?

TH: Japanese people will acknowledge Shin Nihon Programming as something similar to Shin Nihon Pro Wrestling.[7] I like Antonio Inoki, who is a famous wrestler in Japan, famous for Shin Nihon Pro Wrestling. That's a picture of him with me. When I had a business trip I went to visit him actually, and got his business card and this photo. This was right after he fought Muhammad Ali,[8] and Antonio was also famous in New York. He was called Tony back then by Americans, so I thought I would like to be called Tony as well - purely and merely because my favourite wrestler was called Tony. However, Antonio is originally

---

[5] 美少女; literally "beautiful young girl"

[6] **Explanation by Matthew Fitsko:** The term "*bishoujo game*" itself was actually coined by the computer magazines in an attempt to legitimise the fledgling erotic game genre. *Lolicon* in the early 1980s was broadly applicable to girls even up to high school age (pretty much anyone in a school uniform). The Japanese *lolicon* phenomenon has many roots, but its modern form originated in the late 1960s, in the form of photographic art books featuring 12 year old girls in nude (but not really sexual) poses. This also coincided with the establishment of the teenage idol during the 1970s. These idols typically debuted around the age of 16, and weren't objects of sexual worship so much as living symbols of youth and beauty, a kind of celebration of *seishun* (青春), the springtime of life. *Lolicon* as a distinct theme in manga had emerged by 1980, and over time, a gradual process of intensification began, both in terms of a higher degree of sexualisation as well as younger and younger subjects. While the early photobooks might plausibly claim a purely aesthetic, artistic intent, over time that became a flimsier excuse. The early computer games landed right in the middle of this transition. The first *lolicon*-themed adult magazine appeared in October 1982, and things snowballed from there. However, keep in mind that, as often as not, erotic *lolicon* was not about adults preying on underage girls, but rather about young people mutually discovering sexuality and coming of age. Another way to think about it is in terms of what was considered pornography. Japan's obscenity laws, which date from the early 1900s, decree that pubic hair is obscene and must be censored, even in wholly artificial depictions such as manga and computer graphics. On the other hand, depictions of prepubescent genitalia didn't run afoul of the law, because there was no pubic hair! So the emergence of highly sexualised *lolicon* material may have been at least partially motivated by a desire to get around obscenity laws

[7] Major professional wrestling promotion in Japan, founded in June 1972 by Antonio Inoki

[8] 26 June 1976, in Tokyo

a Spanish name, as you may know, so I started to think maybe it would be strange if I started to call myself Tony. That's why I stopped that idea. But the reason why I created the name Shin Nihon Programming, is I sort of copied the image from Shin Nihon Pro Wrestling.

Also, on the back of *Haunted Cave*, I wrote about my favourite wrestler again, Antonio Inoki, saying that I really respect his challenging spirit. I actually wrote that I try to imitate this sense of spirit. The in-game character's kicking skill also comes from my favourite wrestler, the way he jumps and kicks his opponent. This copy is still sealed, in perfect condition. I have another copy which is open.

JS: There's rarely any makers who preserve their works in such perfect shape.

JR: Most programmers, usually after they make a game, think that it's not worth so much. After 10 years or so they tend to abandon their items. But you've preserved everything.

TH: I like to hang on to these things, these mementos and memories, and that's why I have all these pictures and everything else.

JS: I was impressed by all the source code you kept. Every line of code is preserved here?

TH: Not everything. The tools regarding the sound and graphics I have preserved on floppy disks, because it takes time to print them out. But otherwise it's all in that folder.

JR: There's barely any programmers in Japan who preserve their source code.

TH: <*laughs*> Oh, I'm not really preserving it, rather it's just that I haven't thrown it away. It's not like I had the intention to "preserve" it. <*shows graph paper with pixel art*> This is not exactly a program, but when I had just started my career I didn't know how to do everything correctly, so I had the graphics drawn out like this. I also made the music into data, as you can see on this page.

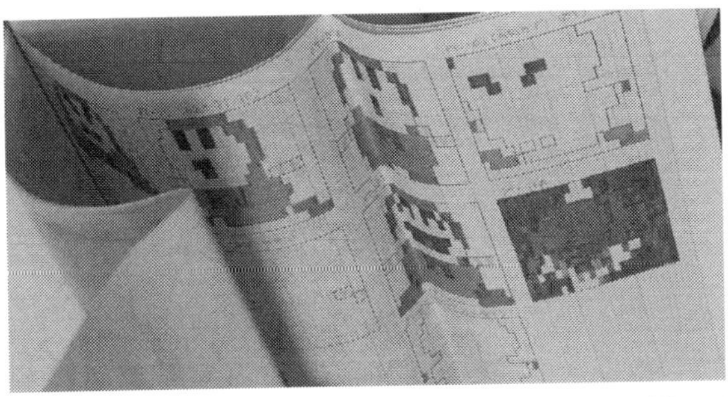

JS: Could someone take the source code, plus graphics and sound, and recreate the game?

TH: I think it would be hard for them to make an exact copy, because people back then needed a specific type of development environment, and there weren't so many who could control all the tools and equipment in order to make the game.

JR: What we have in front of us is the full process that was required to make a game at that time. This is maybe the most important thing, even more important than the game itself. At this time making a game was a huge challenge, because computers were more like word processors. They were not game machines - that's not how they were designed. So there is nothing like hardware scrolling, or sprites, the programmers had to invent everything from scratch. It was a challenge to create anything.

TH: <*Gandhara map tools are displayed*> As you can see on this screen now, it's moving and the movements of the screen are not so smooth, and people nowadays might complain. But they might not understand that we were using just one screen layer here, one picture, and nowadays there are sprites and scrolling, but back then there was just one screen so it's incredibly difficult even to move that one screen layer. So nowadays when people see this game, *Gandhara*, they might complain that the movements are awkward, and the scrolling isn't smooth enough.[9]

---

[9] Mr Hidaka is referring to how everything is being drawn on a single graphics plane, without any other scrolling registers or sprite layers and so on

JS: It's like art. You see an old picture, you think it's beautiful, but when you know what kind of techniques were used, when you know the details of the art, you understand its true value.

TH: Yes, that's right. <*pointing to map utility*> The numbers right there, shown on the screen around the map, are where the enemies will appear. In fact, without these numbers it would be impossible to make the game, because it would be impossible to see or know the entire view [of the land].

JS: In *Gandhara* the character always holds his sword in his right hand, whether facing left or right. With console games programmers cheated and used the hardware to mirror the sprite. Thereby making them ambidextrous![10] Was that kind of small detail discussed while making *Gandhara*? Did someone insist on it, or were you naturally inclined to program that way?

TH: It's not something I decided. When this was made the graphics designer, Makimura-san, was also a manga artist. So what I did was that I made a graphics tool for Makimura-san, and then he designed pictures of the character, where the character would be facing front, the character would be facing right, left, and back.

JS: I haven't seen credits for the game in English, online. Can you recall the other members of the team who made *Gandhara*?

TH: <*loads the game's opening*> There are all the staff credited, written here. I was the programmer. The graphic designer was Makimura-san. Music was by Kouichi Sugiyama, who is famous for *Dragon Quest*. The names are all in the opening.

JS: The programmer was behind everything. Today we have development tools, so it's easy, because an artist can concentrate on graphics. But at this time companies first had to create the tools to make the game.

TH: <*laughs - loads program*> This is the sound tool I was talking about earlier.

JS: After programming this sound tool, the musician would use it to produce music?

<*the excellent main theme plays*>

TH: The composer will give me the notes first, and then I will convert that into data for the computer. Like this. <*gestures to screen*> This was text music. Back then I thought that if I could do this, I will be able to adapt this into other things as well.

JS: When you say notes, you mean the composer handed you sheet music?

<*Hidaka-san takes out reams of sheet music from a folder*>

TH: Yes, yes! <*laughs*> And I could not read the music pieces, so I had someone tell me the notes, each note. It was professional music composers who made these music pieces, so their notes are not so accurately written on the lines. <*laughs*>

JS: This must have been incredibly time consuming. How long did it take for *Gandhara*?

TH: It didn't even take a week, actually. Because I couldn't read the notes there was someone else who would read me the notes, this is *DO*, this is *RE*, and then I would make the notes into data, and then after making the data version of the music I would ask for an ultimate check by the composer, in this case Kouichi Sugiyama.

JS: For these older projects, you were the enabler who facilitated the skills of everyone else coming together. It wasn't just programming, it allowed the abilities of others to work in unison.

TH: <*laughs*> Even before programmers were the central part or played a central role in making a game, in order for composers to make the music, the graphics artists to make the art, before that, programmers did everything. For

[10] *Super Metroid* used correct sprites, but you'd be hard pressed to find more than only a few others

example with *Haunted Cave* and *Magic Garden*, I made the music, I made the graphics, I made everything. But as time passed and as technology developed, despite that I wanted to be a creator, I wanted to do the creative things, I was feeling that I was becoming like a hammer, becoming like mere technology, just a tool or piece of equipment. When I started making games, when I started programming, I was the central part, I was the creator. Afterwards there started to be different producers and directors, who would tell me to make what kind of game, and what not to make. That's why I quit, because I wanted to do everything, I wanted to make everything on my own. To be a creator.

<loads a different program>

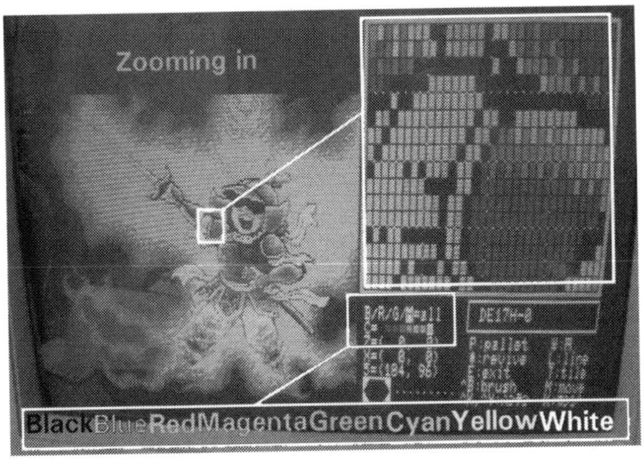

TH: This is actually the graphics utility I wrote for *Gandhara*.

[Author's note: the editor was astounding, allowing you to zoom in and out on an image and specify pixel by pixel the colours you wanted to use, before saving it as data for use in a game. This was basically like an in-house version of Photoshop for 1986]

JS: *<gesturing to image of swordsman>* How long would it take to create something so detailed? Was each pixel placed manually?

TH: I will show you how it's made from the beginning. *<takes out paper with hand-drawn picture>* So here's the base image, the basic picture for the image on the computer screen. Then I would scan this, and after scanning I would interpret it onto the screen in black and white. After putting it on the screen I would remove any residual image noise, or artefacting, and then I would add the colours.

JS: What's amazing is there were only 8 colours. You had to use techniques to convey a feeling of more than 8 colours. For example dithering.

TH: If you look at this part, for example, the scan colour, it's in RGB. If you look at it there's 8 colours. I would put the colours in a random order so that it would mimic skin colour. With the program there's options to see how it would look with a blue screen, and a green screen, and a red screen. *<flicks between colour modes, showing only those colours>* And for example this and this here, I could edit either the left or right half of the picture. *<the zoom function converts one half of the screen into a UI>*

JS: When zoomed in you can see the colours distinctly: blue, red, magenta, green, cyan, yellow, white and black.

TH: It's the 8 colours that it can make with RGB. They each have a numerical value. Zero is black, one is blue, two is red, three is... Magenta? Four is green, five is cyan, six is yellow, and seven is white. I would combine these, from 0 to 7.

JS: Ironically today, machines can produce more colours than the human eye can differentiate, yet so many games are brown and grey.

<everyone laughs>

JS: *Gandhara* was a transitional name, but used for the final product. They just added a subtitle. Were other names considered?

TH: First the graphics artist, Makimura-san, actually came up with the title *Gandhara Denki*,[11] in a similar style to his earlier game *Eldorado Denki*, but Enix told him that title was no good. So that's why it became *Gandhara*.

JS: How was the workflow structured?

TH: I would visit Enix once a week for a meeting.

JS: At these meetings you would be given content from the musician, artist, level designer and so on, then go home and input it?

TH: The music was put in last, usually. Initially I made a test program, checking that the main screen would be scrolling. First I would make

[11] *The Legend of Gandhara*

this main screen, then after we'd confirmed the screen moves, the artist Makimura-san would draw the characters using my tools. I would receive the character data from him and I would make sure they moved in the way they should.

JS: Who decided the layouts of the mazes?

TH: First I would create this tool called a map editor, for use with the entire game. Then I would give that Makimura-san so he could devise the layouts of the mazes and create computer data of them.

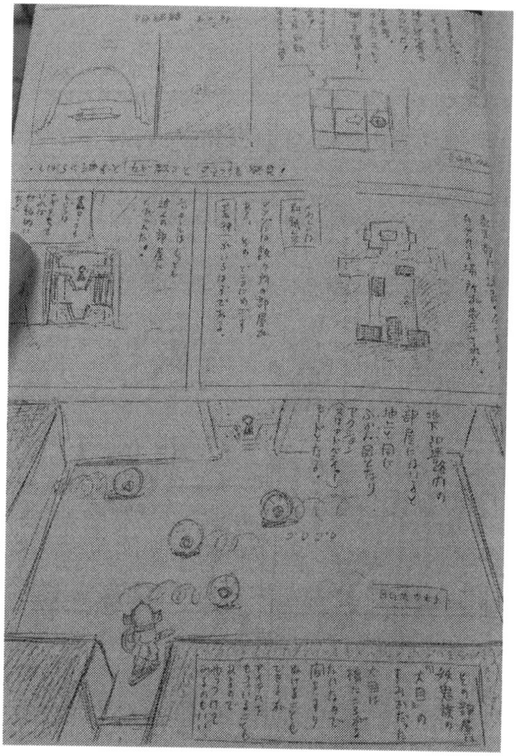

JS: Were you tempted to change anything he submitted? Maybe a maze to be more enjoyable?

TH: I've never edited the maps before. But I have edited some character animations before, because... For example, the characters were supposed to be walking, but because their legs weren't going high enough, it looked like they were shuffling or sliding, so in those cases I did edit the character graphics.

JS: I'm fascinated by its scenario, because it involves Buddhist mythology. Very different to *Dragon Quest*'s medieval Europe mythology.

TH: The original idea was made by Makimura-san, who as I mentioned was a manga artist. So he had this image made, this idea, and described to me the images, the story, the scenario, so that I could implement all this on the screen.

JS: Your PC-88 editor is quite sophisticated.

TH: Yes, I made this graphics editor. The reason why I made this was there is a game called *Hokuto no Ken*,[12] on PC-88, and the staff asked me to program something to compress the graphics data for it. In order to do this compression I needed a lot of things regarding how to use the colours, how to make the image look like it's supposed to be, so that's why I made this graphic data compression system. That's how I came up with this editor.

JS: Were you involved with the Sharp X1 version of *Hokuto no Ken*? I think it was the only version to be released on cassette tape.

TH: The Sharp X1 was exclusively on cassette tape. I think you can automatically rewind the tapes on that computer, whereas on the PC-88 you can't rewind tapes, it just goes forward. So I think that's the reason why it was only released on tape for the Sharp X1.

JR: Yes, the X1 was the only computer still to have tape releases at this time.

JS: <*noticing sketches of the map mazes on paper*> Can I get some shots of those?

TH: This was not actually made to begin with. In fact, as you can see on the screen, the one displayed on the screen was made first, and then I put it on paper afterwards.

JS: Anyone playing the game for the first time will find it easier with these.

TH: <*laughs*> Yes, I think so too.

[12] *Fist of the North Star* - PC-88 graphic adventure

JS: Usually when you want a map you must find a magazine with one. Some would photograph every screen then stitch them together.

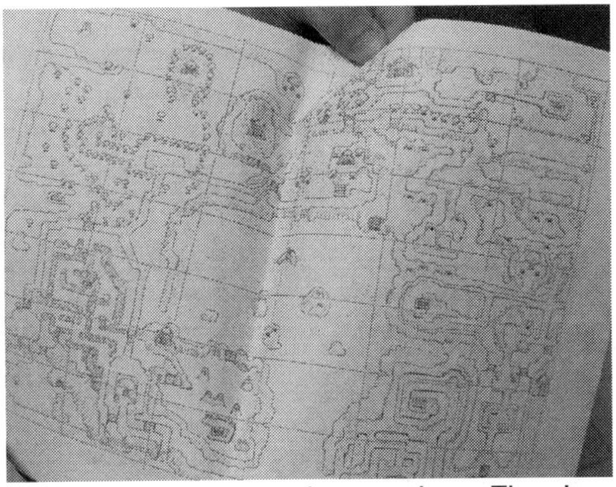

TH: Yes, there were such magazines. There's a magazine called *Popcorn*, which would take pictures of all the screens and connected them to make huge maps. Nowadays you can just find one on the internet.

JS: You can also find copies of these games, to be played via emulation. How do you feel about emulation of your older games?

TH: I never really thought about that either. <*laughs*> Not really. Regarding the copyright, it's definitely illegal, but it's not something I'd be furious about though.

JS: Are you happy that people still want to play your games today?

TH: <*laughs*> I never confirmed that before, with my own eyes. So if I could actually confirm it, I think I would be happy.

JS: Many outside Japan enjoy old Japanese computer games. *Dragon Quest* was not a hit abroad; contrastingly, a lot of Japanese computer games seem exotic and exciting.

TH: *Dragon Quest* was like a remixed version of *Wizardry*. But there's another reason it wasn't such a hit - in *Dragon Quest* there's a riddle, there's word riddles and rhymes, and word-plays which are funny for Japanese people. For example "*hyado*", the ice spell. There's a word *hiyakoi*[13] which means cold in Japanese, which Japanese people would understand. However, this sort of word play, the sound, the interesting thing about it would not be understood unless you really know Japanese. Another example is "*rariho*", the sleep spell. I think the Japanese sounds of RA-RI-RU-RE-RO give the impression of people going crazy, or getting sleepy, so people have this image for these sounds. But it's difficult to convey unless you're a native Japanese speaker who is understanding the sounds and the images they convey.

JR: *Gandhara* was not such a hit in Japan. But abroad it's exotic, and those who discovered it loved it. Now that people outside Japan know about [Japanese computers], they want to play *Gandhara*. Fans in the West translate games into English, so everyone can experience them.

TH: I'm touched by the fact there are people who are reassembling Japanese games.

JS: *Gandhara* has been fan-translated for the MSX2. With *JESUS*, fans took the Famicom game, extracted the Japanese text, translated it into English, and placed it back in the game.

TH: Ehhh... I don't think the graphics data is used from *JESUS* itself. I participated in the compression of big screen data, the large screen pictures. The compression was very, very difficult. I would think it's really difficult to put it all back into the file. So if there is such an English emulated version of it, I doubt that it is perfectly in its original shape.

JS: When fans translate games they decompress the data, redraw graphics tables... They have to modify and reverse engineer the game. It's a huge effort. People love these games, they share this work for free. Players outside of Japan have tremendous affection for games from Japan.

JR: Another solution is learn Japanese like I did!

<*everyone laughs*>

<*everyone enjoys a 10 minute break*>

JS: Tell me about *Rayieza*, the space RPG.

[13] *Hyado* is the ice spell in the *Dragon Quest*, first introduced in *DQ3*. *Hiyakoi* is a slang word to describe something cold, a derivative of the standard Japanese word *hieru/hiyasu* (to get cold/to cool something down). So the meaning of *hyado* is intuitively obvious to Japanese speakers, in the same way that blizzaga might be obvious to English speakers

TH: The conversion of *Rayieza*... It was in November, and they sort of joked that they wanted it by the end of the year. Then they actually managed to complete the conversion by the end of the year. Within less than a month, because it usually takes three months, and it was a joke, but they actually managed to do the conversion! The most important thing for Enix was physical power.

JS: Three months for conversions. I interviewed Zainsoft: They'd develop a game in three months then convert it in two weeks!

TH: Enix never made a retail game in three months. Everything took about a year to complete.

JS: Did you follow Zainsoft's work?

TH: No, I wasn't aware of Zainsoft. I knew the name, but I didn't follow them.

JS: Apparently the head of the company was quite a violent person towards staff.

JR: I think Enix was more like a normal company.

TH: The companies were fundamentally different. In Zainsoft the employees are making the game, so they're being paid a wage for their labour. Whereas Enix only pays out royalties for completed work, so they let you take as much time as you want. In fact, they would keep giving more suggestions and requests, because they're not really thinking about the developers' personal lives. The programmers at Enix were not officially employed, they were all unofficially employed. So for example the staff on *Dragon Quest* were all external staff. Now Enix is combined with Square, and they're making games with internal staff, but regarding *Dragon Quest* it's all external staff.

JS: At Chunsoft - a company hired by Enix to make *Dragon Quest*.

TH: They weren't an affiliate or subsidiary of Enix or anything like that. There was originally Horii-san, someone who participated in the Enix competitions when they started, and was earning royalties as a game author for his published titles, such as *Love Match Tennis*. He was only able to program in BASIC though. Whereas Nakamura-kun was good at programming in machine language, so they decided to cooperate and make a game together. Meanwhile, Horii-san also had connections with the publisher Shueisha, as he had done some work for the *Shonen Jump* manga magazine. So Horii-san asked Akira Toriyama, who is also a famous artist for *Dragon Ball*, to join them. I first heard about *Dragon Quest* when I was converting *Rayieza*, and I heard they would be making this *Dragon Quest* RPG for the Famicom. I was very shocked, because I didn't know how they would allow players to save their data. Most [Famicom] games up to that point were designed to end within a few hours of play, so I didn't understand how they would enable you to save your progress in a longer RPG on the Famicom. I didn't get it. So I was astounded when I learned they had made this special spell, in the game, for the saving of data. I thought that idea was very surprising and interesting![14]

JS: What kind of work environment was *DQ*?

[14] Unlike the NES version, the original Famicom *DQ* cartridges didn't include battery-backed memory for saving. Instead, the game used a password system, in which the entire game state was coded as a string of meaningless Japanese characters. It was called the *fukkatsu no jumon* (復活の呪文), the resurrection spell, and you would input the characters to "invoke" the spell from the main menu and recreate the game state where you last left off. A clever and immersive way of making saving an organic part of the game world. Strictly speaking, no data is ever recorded, because the game is entirely read-only. The password is simply an encoded definition of all the game variables

TH: I think there was a book about that. In this small building there was Enix, and at this time they would have meetings in this little room, right here. The development of the game was not held in the office, but a very personal room with the developer. So the actual procedure of developing the game I'm not sure of. But regarding the Famicom, there was apparently a development machine specifically for it.

JS: Manabu Yamana of Chunsoft drew a sketch of the programming set-up they used. It was an HP 9000UX computer with an Integrated Circuit Emulator, which was connected to a Famicom. They had a 500mb harddrive and he said it all cost around 60'000'000 yen.[15]

TH: Yes, there was an Integrated Circuit Emulator, and I heard they made it using that emulator. So sometimes I think I should have gone for the *Dragon Quest* project.

<everyone laughs>

TH: Maybe then I would have had a better life; maybe I still would have been making *Dragon Quest*. *<laughs>* Regardless of how fun or how interesting the activity is, maybe had I continued for my whole life, I would have just gotten sick, like Morita-san did.

JS: Did you know Morita-san personally? I believe he passed away not long ago.

TH: Last year [2012]. I'm actually much older than him. On the outside we were perfectly fine, it's not like we had any troubles or issues between us, but I was older than him, and yet I was his *kouhai,*[16] I was his junior at work. I do think that despite that I was his junior at work, I think that he was aware of and interested in my work, because I actually heard it from a common acquaintance that Morita-san commented on *Gandhara*'s scrolling. He told another producer that he wanted to look at the astonishing scrolling technique in *Gandhara*. Morita-san had a keen interest in the problem of scrolling, and in his own game, called *Riglas*, [17] he made a character in this game called Moritan, which is most likely named after him. And this character would break the fourth wall and brag about how smooth the scrolling was in the game. So I think that Morita-san was consciously aware of me and my own work.

JS: A friendly rivalry perhaps?

TH: I do not think he actually considered me as a rival, or anything, because Morita-san always mentioned how he would commit his life to shogi. So I don't think he considered me a rival.

JR: Morita-san made a great algorithm for the game *Morita no Battlefield*.

TH: But he was in a rush when he made that algorithm. He was trying to finish it in time for a contest, so it wasn't his best. Before that, he also made a number of computer versions of games like *Othello* and *Reversi*. He was already presenting those games in public back then.

JS: Thank you for sharing your memories.

TH: Have you seen this book before? *<shows book>* It's also from 1986.

TV PROD.: Joseph, do you collect these books?

JR: I don't have this one, but I have the one before this. I have about 3'000 magazines stored in my archive, right now.

TH: Do you have *ProCon*? I have all the *ProCon* issues, actually! Would you like to see?

<everyone moves to a different room>

TH: So this is my collection of *ProCon* magazines. The name standing for "programming contest". Back then there were so many competitions. So that's why they probably thought it would be good if they documented it like this.

---

15 Manabu Yamana's interview will be in a later volume; his diagram of this set-up is on the supplementary DVD
16 後輩; junior member
17 *Riglas: Tamashii no Kaiki* - large free roaming RPG exclusive to Japanese computers, worth checking out

JS: Does this contain every entry that was received for every competition? Not just the winners of them?

TH: Yes, I believe that it's a collection of most of the entries that were submitted to competitions back then.

JS: Were these entries all made available to the public, in some fashion?

TH: The entries that are actually documented here, were the ones that were presented to the public. There's an interview here writing about Nakamura-kun when founding his own company.

JS: *<gesturing to a spread of competition entries>* You would not believe how difficult it is to find such information outside of Japan. Yet all of these games, in one way or another, influenced games released outside of Japan. Unknown to Western players, the history in these magazines is significant to them.

TH: There's a ranking for competition winners, in fact. There was a game which was ranked in third place, actually, because the CEO of Enix wanted to publish the game, he wanted to sell it. But in the end it had no effect on sales. There was this game called *Light Flipper*,[18] which the CEO tried to sell as an official game.

JS: He placed it at rank 3 to boost sales - meaning the Enix rankings were fixed?

<everyone laughs>

TH: Maybe! I'm not sure too much about the details backstage. But Enix would have advertisements based on such rankings, for example. *<flips page>* So this game was placed in third, and it's even bigger and looks more significant than the one in second place! Then someone told me afterwards that they tried to sell *Light Flipper* by making it a higher rank, but it didn't work ultimately.

JS: *<looks at page>* Wow, *Portopia* only came in at rank 7.[19]

TH: The person who made *Light Flipper* is called Okada-san. I've reverse assembled the game, actually, so I could learn from it.

JS: *<noticing rank #1>* *Alphos* on PC-88 was really a revolution for scrolling, at this time.

TH: This was officially not scrolling, in fact. On the PC-88 back then they wrote a different set of code for it, so it's not really scrolling. So they tried to use straight lines as much as possible.

TV PROD.: The one at number 7 [*Portopia*] had more sales.

TH: However, the Enix CEO stated back then that *Portopia* would not have good sales. The reason being because these sort of adventure games were thought to be not interesting, because the result or conclusion was known from the beginning. Regardless of this hypothesis though, the game became quite popular and recorded a high number of sales. So the leader, the CEO of Enix, later commented how he cannot read what kind of games will sell and which will not.[20]

JS: That's incredible. Because the adventure genre became one of the strongest in Japan.

TH: This magazine didn't last for such a long time. Because no one was interested in buying it unless you were a programmer, or featured in the magazine. It wasn't officially announced that the magazine was going to close. I actually went to look for the magazine after the last month, but I eventually knew that it had become the last edition of *ProCon*.

[18] Maze game by Yoshiyuki Okada, PC-88 (June 1983)

[19] Kazurou Morita's *Alphos* in #1; ASCII's *AX-7* in #6 (see Akira Takiguchi chpt); Yuji Horii's *Portopia* #7

[20] Consider the ramifications of this: the head of one of Japan's biggest publishers wrongly dismissed one of his company's best selling titles in what would become Japan's leading genre: *the adventure game*

JS: Your webpage mentions confidence in your compression tools, and a competition?

TH: Oh, I actually held this competition myself. When I was at Enix, when I was working on compressing data... When data is compressed you are able to know to what percentage the original is compressed by, and then people started this little competition within the company. So for example, someone would say, "You compressed this original data into *something-something* percent, but using this tool I was able to compress the same data into *what-what* percent." So I thought this was quite interesting.

<Hidaka-san looks through shelf trying to find related materials>

TH: So I asked the editors of a magazine to hold a data compression competition, so they could prepare prizes and everything. I wanted to know if there were people who possibly had more technique than me. So that was why I decided to hold the competition, in order to know what kind of programmers are out there in the world. I think I held the competition twice, or three times, and once... *<laughs>* I used *Gandhara* for the competition. I provided the pictures so people could compress the images found in *Gandhara*. And once I was actually defeated! *<laughs>* I couldn't believe that I lost. There was this compression tool called PMAN11 back then, which had existed since version 0. I was using version 11 as a compression tool, and I updated it to versions 12 and 13, and then I defeated the winner again! *<laughs>* So I was personally very, very pleased. I did not want to lose.

JS: When the winner submitted the entry, what percentage was their additional compression?

TH: I don't remember so clearly, but I think it was about a 1% difference, it was a very, very subtle improvement.

JS: The magazine advert I brought last time, of everyone around a table, this was for a 3 day lecture on game development?

TH: Yes, that's right. *<referring to image>* At the bottom of the poster you can see my daily schedule for the school. But these others are guests. It was for three days. I told the CEO of Enix, if there isn't any interesting plan, how about we make a game school? A specialised game school like that did not exist back then. I wanted to found a very professional, quite serious game school. However, that was not possible, so we decided to make a "three day" game school.

JS: Please tell me about this.

TH: There's this book called *Machine Language Game Programming* I had written. So the school was after I published the book. I used this as a text book during the school for three days. Enix took care of all the expenses. The textbook was actually published by ASCII, but Enix bought some of these books at a discount from ASCII and they were provided to the participants. I had lectures based on this book, teaching up to the point of making characters move. The other teachers were just guests, so they had a lecture for an hour or two, maybe. It was not so much about the details, but it was more about their own personal stories. What kind of difficulties they overcame, and they would answer questions from the participants. I'm not sure about their lectures, or how they were conducted, because I was in a different classroom. I was only teaching the participants in my class. There were about 40 to maybe 50 people participating in a class. So about 40 to 50 participants coming each day, all the same members starting from the first day. I would use this machine language game programming book as the textbook and base my lectures on it.

JS: *<holding glossy brochure - pictured adjacent page>* Was this brochure produced as a result of that three day event?

TH: No, it was not made as a result. Rather, it was several years after the classes when that brochure was made. Because these game schools started to exist, for example Human Creative School, and the one from Hudson Soft... I actually went to that school on one occasion, just once, to hold a lecture there. After a year later Enix started to create its own game school. The Enix Game School was the initial name.

Above spread shows guest lecturers at the Enix game school, many involved with famous products. On the right page is Mr Hidaka, above him Kouichi Nakamura, to his right Yuji Horii, and above right Masaya Hashimoto of Quintet

JR: I think the 3 day session was around 1986. And I think maybe the Enix game school was created in 1991? [21] So it's 5 years.

TH: The first president of the school, when it was founded, was a producer on *Gandhara* - Takano-san was his name. <*flipping through brochure*> So there were teachers who would be special guests, special speakers. However, Enix did not have exclusive professors, exclusive teachers, so we started the game school from scratch.

JS: Do you remember the month in 1986 that the 3 day school took place?

TH: August, 1986.

JS: Was this the first ever event, of this sort?

JR: Yes, it's a programming school, but it was only a very short session. Not like a one year class. But yes, a very early attempt to teach game programming in Japan. You have to understand that everyone at this time who wanted to learn game programming used Hidaka-san's books. It was like a bible for them! He's not only a hero for game programming, I would say he's a hero for his books. I asked a lot of people around me who actually used his books, to learn game programming, and two of them told me the same thing: Hidaka-san kept the best techniques for himself. <*laughs*> Hidaka-san, was this maybe your decision, or did Enix say it would be better to teach just the basic stuff, and keep the best techniques for the company?

JS: That's a bit cheeky, Joseph!

[21] To clarify: the promotional advert in a magazine was for the 3 day event and detailed Hidaka-san's lecturing schedule; years later Enix started a proper school, with a glossy brochure promoting it, which is what I was looking through and is pictured above

TH: Oh, there was no such intention. However programming techniques are always, always developing, always evolving. So when I wrote the books, when I published the books I had written, it covered technology that was best at that time. Right after the book had been published there was already a newly existing technique. Technology keeps on progressing and developing. But I have no intentions of hiding secrets from anyone, or anything like that.

I had no intentions of hiding the techniques. There's a book called *Machine Language Game Graphics*, [22] the technique I wrote in there, for example on multiple scrolling, I revealed every single technique I had back then, which was capable of being used by anyone who read it. For example this is just normal scrolling <*referring to Gandhara on screen which had single scrolling*>, but *Ys III* had multi-layered scrolling, and people were thrilled by it! I was introducing these programming skills though, I was telling them that the scrolling itself is completely different, and I was revealing all my techniques and tricks.

JS: That's very commendable. Companies are so secretive today, and restrict the flow of knowledge by taking patents out on everything.

TH: The first time I touched a computer was when I was 33 years old. Back then people who were using computers were much, much younger than me. People would think I'm telling them some great thing, simply because I was older than them. Still now I receive emails, saying "thank you for teaching me this".

For example, sometimes I would get statements from middle school and high school students that were not quite logical, and then I would tell them to be logical. For example the copy protection on games. Some people would copy games, and laugh and feel superior to the game companies, without realising they were only damaging themselves [by hurting the market for new games]. But it was a matter of pride with them. So I would tell them, why couldn't you simply just say you want the software for free? That's what you really want, right? Why are you doing this knowing that you're doing something bad? Why can't you say, or think, I am poor now, but one day I will be rich enough to buy these at the official price? So I guess these things, which are not even related to technology at all, these sort of things which I said, young people, the younger generation, were touched by them. So it was quite an interesting experience to write articles in computer magazines during those days. I had a lot of reactions towards it.

JS: <*looks through brochure*> Did you ever meet Hashimoto-san of Quintet? The reason I ask is, he seems to have disappeared. Literally.

TH: That generation of programmers, who developed for computers back then, had a very difficult time in later years. Programming techniques were changing, and the hardware was evolving very quickly. On top of that, computer games weren't selling as well, and creating games became more difficult and involved. So a lot of the techniques and know-how that people had accumulated just wasn't useful anymore. People had trouble making ends meet. As a result, most people left the industry completely. Their books stopped selling. Their programs were no longer necessary. So they didn't know what to do.

Because of things like that picture of Nakamura-kun's face on the money bill, people left stable corporate jobs to join this industry, but found it difficult to create even a single title, and ultimately vanished. I have no idea where many of those people are now. There were a lot of people like that. The life promised in that advertisement did exist momentarily, but I think it sort of pulled people down the wrong path in their lives. I hate to say it, but there were quite a few people who ended up like that.

Even for Nakamura-kun of Chunsoft, he had a hard time afterwards, because with the money he got from Enix he made his own company, but even for him it was quite difficult to keep up to date on a technical level. As a result his games were not selling well, so even for him it was difficult. Nakamura-kun is the president of Chunsoft, so he succeeded in the end. But other people who entered games at this time, after looking at the "money picture" of Nakamura-kun, they did not succeed.

JR: So Nakamura-san was like an example for everybody. He was able to make his own company, but that was not the case for the people who came after him.

[22] マシン語ゲームグラフィックス, published in several editions in 1990 by Shogakukan

JS: I've heard that Nakamura-san felt quite depressed despite his success.

TH: That was because of his position as the manager of a business. He had the responsibility of paying other peoples' salaries. But in his case at least, he got a lot of royalty money from *Dragon Quest 1* through *4*, so in the end he managed to survive.

JS: Sad to think how fragile the industry is.

TH: I think the majority of people who were making games in those days lost their jobs or went out of business. I myself ended up doing something different. I'm retired now, but one of the last things I did in my career was publish programming books. I even made a Windows game, but I ended up having to sell it myself. It wasn't very successful. So times have been difficult for me, too. No matter what job you do, it's not something that is guaranteed to last forever. So when you look back over a long period of time, you see it as just a brief, shining moment. It doesn't last long. The same is true of the game industry. If a company cannot survive without assistance, sooner or later it's bound to fail, just like in any other industry. The software houses we discussed earlier, like Bothtec, and T&E Soft, and Falcom, they all faded away.

JR: On the other hand, Square-Enix is still around, and Falcom is still doing well.

TH: Falcom may be doing well, but they're a different company now. They're not thriving as a software house. I get the feeling that they're surviving on licensing deals and things like that. Kiya-san is no longer with them. Regardless, they're still using things like monetising schemes in social games to raise profits. It's a totally different way of making money. So now when you're talking about games you're talking about social games.

JS: There is hope from indie and *doujin*. Plus crowdfunding. People still want these games.

TH: I think it's a really great system. But I think I'm too busy - I don't have free time. There's too many things I want to do.

<*everyone laughs*>

JS: Tell me about your game for Windows.

TH: The game is like a dungeon crawler, a roguelike. Like *Torneko's Adventure*. It's called *Otasuke Nin-puu-den.*[23] There's a small animal called "Marimon" that lives in inside the player's pocket, helping them. The word "Otasuke" is a funny expression meaning "Help me!"

JS: Were the mazes randomly generated?

TH: Yes, yes.

JS: And it was commercially sold?

TH: No, because I was by myself. When I got a request, I would burn it to a CD-R and post it to whoever wanted it. I made a copy of this CD and included the key needed to activate the game. Of course it can no longer be ordered. It will not work on anything beyond Windows ME as it was made entirely in Visual Basic.

JS: How many requests did you receive?

TH: <*laughs*> Less than 100. No one knows this game! It's hard today even for game companies, because everyone is developing for smartphones. Maybe there is no market for traditional games like this. There are the few top selling games, which are selling well, but there is no place for anything else.

JS: The market used to accommodate more variety, all types of games. Now it's polarised. Sadly there is no middle tier anymore.

TH: <*melancholy*> Everything has its time. But I feel that for games, it was too short.

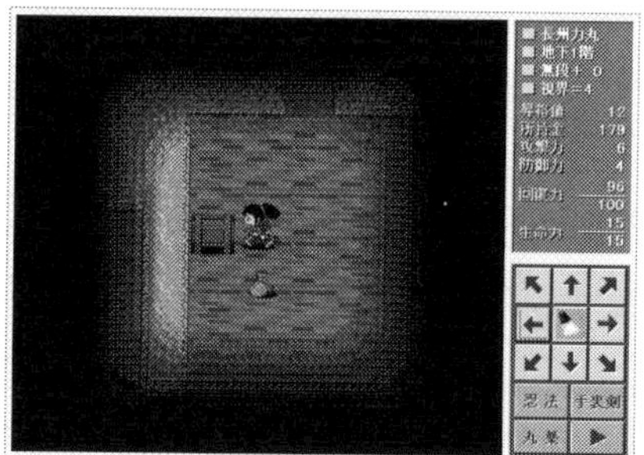

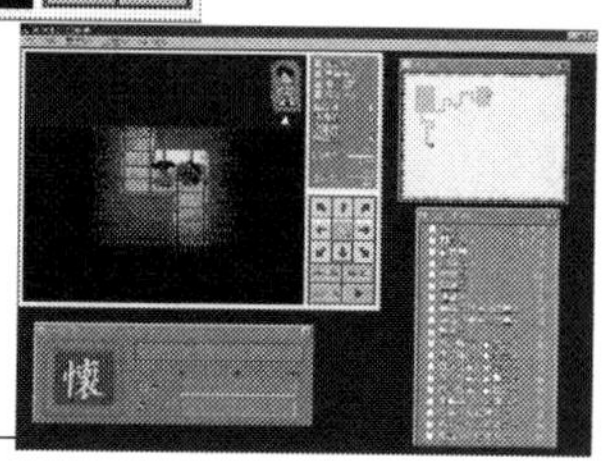

[23] おたすけ忍風伝

Left: Masanobu Endou, creator of *Xevious*, right: Kazurou Morita, creator of *Alphos*

~In memory of~

森田 和郎

MORITA, Kazurou

1955 ~ 27 July 2012

Morita-san always mentioned how he would commit his life to shogi.[1] Morita-san mentioned how he would commit his whole life to developing shogi, and developed a long line of shogi software called *Morita no Shogi*. He always had interesting things to say about programming shogi simulations. Shogi was what he had wanted to do from the very beginning. Those kinds of thinking games were his specialty. Morita-san also published a book, called *Shikou Game Programming*,[2] or *Thinking Game Programming*.

I don't think I was personally close with him. He was in this world a lot before me, from the *maicon* era. When I was still learning how to program computers, he was already announcing the release of *Alphos*.[3] I think it is a pity. I was shocked when I heard that he'd died, because we worked for and we were endeavouring for the same company.

- ***Toru Hidaka, colleague from Enix***

---

[1] It's like a traditional Japanese version of chess

[2] 思考ゲームプログラミング - ISBN 4-87148-186-7

[3] *Alphos* was an early but technically very impressive PC-8801 shooting game released in 1983, which strongly resembled *Xevious*; apparently, a licensing agreement was even made with Namco

中村 彰憲

Professor
NAKAMURA, Akinori

DOB: 20 August 1969 / Birthplace: Nagano / Blood Type: B

Interview with Professor Akinori (Aki) Nakamura
12 October 2013, Ritsumeikan University, Kyoto

I travelled to the Kansai region from Tokyo, on 11 October, to interview a gentleman from Xainsoft in Osaka. The company was known for shady business practices and rumoured to be yakuza funded. On 13 September I had an interview with Masaaki Kukino, formerly of Konami's arcade division. To save travelling back to Tokyo each day (the round trip is over seven hours on JR lines), I decided to sleep over two nights, staying with my comrade and fellow games journalist, Sergei Servianov. By fortunate circumstance, a gentleman on my Facebook friends list, Devin Monnens, introduced me to Professor Akinori Nakamura. The professor had recently written a book on the Famicom and, as it turned out, had been part of the translation team for Family Computer 1983-1994, by the Tokyo Metropolitan Museum of Photography. This being 2013, it was the Famicom's 30th anniversary - Hiroshi Yamauchi would pass away one week later, on the 19 September.

It cannot be overstated how important this Famicom book was in inspiring me. It featured nine interviews with industry figures, including Hiroshi Yamauchi. They were all candid and personal - as Professor Nakamura would explain, there was no PR filter involved. These were the kind of interviews I wanted to conduct. Given Professor Nakamura's proximity at Ritsumeikan University, I decided to meet and chat about the Famicom book(s). As it turns out, Ritsumeikan is also involved with game preservation. The journey there from comrade Servianov's house involved a walk, train, bus and then taxi. We skipped the taxi and had a delightful stroll accompanied by two young ladies who attended the university. Given the preservation work done by Ritsumeikan, head of the Japanese Game Preservation Society Joseph Redon was keen to join us too, along with Nico the photographer. The four of us crammed into the Professor's small office. The heat must have gotten to comrade Servianov, because he claimed light-headedness.

JS: Why did you decide to translate Family Computer 1983-1994?[1]

Akinori Nakamura: Well, in 1998 a professor at Ritsumeikan University, Koichi Hosoi, realised the importance of the Famicom as a cultural artefact. He convinced Kyoto Research Park as well as Kyoto Prefecture to form an industrial / academic / government collaborative organisation, focusing on developing a digital archive for videogames. This was how the **G**ame **A**rchive **P**roject was organized.[2] Shortly after this, Professor Hosoi visited various game companies, including Nintendo, to discuss the GAP. Nintendo decided to assist the project by lending all of the Famicom titles they kept. With the actual cassettes on hand, members of GAP, mostly students of Ritsumeikan University, began to create metadata as well as a digital record of each product. Professor Hosoi [at the time] focused just on the Famicom. Back then, the PlayStation and all these 32-bit videogame consoles were huge, and all the retro games were kind of being forgotten.

JS: So the book started off just as a database of titles and release dates?

AN: Right, back in 1998. Professor Hosoi saw that they were cultural artefacts of the era. Especially from the 1980s and 1990s. Even though a lot of people considered them merely as toys and started forgetting them, he regarded them as culturally valuable. Professor Hosoi and his colleagues at Ritsumeikan University were already working on archiving projects for other Japanese cultural artefacts. He thought that since Nintendo is in Kyoto, and since the Famicom is important, particularly with regards to computer culture, we should create a database for that. That's how it started. He talked with Nintendo, and Nintendo were really excited. He sometimes needed to convince them - but in the end, Nintendo decided they would lend all the Famicom titles to the school.

JS: Does Nintendo have a copy of every thing?

AN: They're supposed to have all of them, yeah. They missed some though.

JS: I noticed in the photographs in the book, some games such as *Pinball* were not shown with the main group; they were featured in a little circle in the upper corner. Were they...

AN: <*interrupts*> Right, were difficult to get, yes. The reason why games such as *Pinball* were

[1] ISBN: 4872338030 / 978-4872338034
[2] ritsumei.ac.jp/kic/~hosoik/project/GAP/index-e.html

not shown with the main group, I am not certain. But all the third parties were supposed to submit all of their titles, and Nintendo was the sole manufacturer to create the cassettes. [3] We should preserve everything, but back then there wasn't an understanding of preserving games for an extended period of time, like a century. Nintendo thought it was a product, and the way they preserved the product was not what we are doing now. Back then there wasn't any idea of how to put it into a database, but Professor Hosoi had been working on those kinds of projects for quite some time, so [Nintendo] decided to lend them, and then Professor Hosoi, and students, and the guys from Kyoto prefecture, all started working. GAP was the first research institute in Japan which considered the preservation of videogame titles from an academic perspective.

Right now we're celebrating the 30th anniversary of Famicom - in 2003 it was the 20th anniversary. The curators at the Tokyo Metropolitan Museum of Photography (TMMP) wanted to do something for it. One of the people who pushed this idea was Ms Yuki Denda. She was a curator at the TMMP and the wife of Akihiro Saito, a game director and producer who had worked with Toru Iwata, who at the time was an employee at HAL Laboratory. After getting approval from Nintendo, they found that all the Famicom titles Nintendo owned were over at Ritsumeikan University. So GAP agreed to collaborate and shipped all of the titles to Tokyo for the exhibition. So that book, created bilingually, was part of that entire project which celebrated the Famicom's 20th anniversary.

JS: This was Level X?

AN: That's right, Level X.

JS: The release dates are a tremendous resource. How easy were they to collate?

AN: Right, that's the data collected by the Game Archive Project - because they're putting them into a database. They confirmed the date by taking screenshots of the games or researching all these old magazines and stuff like that. *<gestures to bookshelves around room, filled with magazines>* The same method that they're still using now. So that's how all the information was provided in the book.

JS: Would you say it's 100% accurate?

AN: It's mostly accurate. Because all the Japanese periodicals on videogames were quite extensive. There were several magazines written about the Famicom, at the time the games were published. So mostly it's correct, I would say.

JS: No one, not even Nintendo, knows when *Super Mario Bros.* first came out in America.[4]

AN: Really?!

JS: A journalist, Frank Cifaldi, spent time investigating this. There is no conclusive evidence of the precise date it launched. Which is incredible, for such an important game...

AN: Yes, it is. Wow, that's amazing.

JS: The question hinged on when the NES was first sold in New York.

AN: That's interesting. Anyway, later Nintendo decided to bundle *Super Mario Bros.* with the NES, which was a great strategic decision. That's one of the most important decisions, making sure the NES became one of the most successful consoles. But in Japan the situation was different. In the States, back then, they did not have many magazines focused on videogames. Or rather, Nintendo of America thought that there was no one they could be partners with, so they came up with their own magazine [*Nintendo*

[3] In Japan, carts are sometimes called cassettes

[4] Google: "Cifaldi Gamasutra Mario" for article

Power]. That means they're controlling all the information, so if they didn't put the date on there, that's it. In Japan it was different, because there were already magazines dedicated to the Famicom being published. Nintendo had to decide exactly when those products would be manufactured and distributed. That information would go to several companies, so that's why it's really easy for us to cross-reference all the information and come up with solid dates.

Joseph Redon: Plus Nintendo had very tight control over the distribution. So no shop would put the games on shelves early. But it's a different story talking about computer games and arcade games.

AN: That's the issue now. We have references for arcade and computer games, but it's really difficult to nail down the particular date for anything. Especially for retro games, back in the 1970s and 1980s. But it's a different story for the Famicom. That's why it's quite accurate.

JS: How did you come on board the project?

AN: Well, I was a member of IGDA[5] Japan. Back then it was called IGDA Tokyo, and one of the members, Kiyoshi Shin, was involved in this museum project. As was the editor from *Game Critic* magazine, and he was also a member of IGDA Tokyo. They were working with the guys to create a book about Level X, and then in the middle of the project they realised there was nobody who could translate it. But they thought there might be some kind of cultural significance, so they decided: OK, we have to translate that! They asked IGDA Tokyo if they could come up with volunteers, and I raised my hand.

JS: The book was the first time I could read about the contextual significance of Japanese titles. For example *Takeshi no Chousenjou*.[6]

AN: <*laughs*> Oh yes, that crazy game!

JS: It detailed Japan's attitude to games. There was even an *intra-office politics simulator*.

AN: <*laughs*> Yeah, we have a lot of them!

JS: An adventure game about cooking food...

AN: That's from a manga, I think. Yes, yes.

JS: I wish there was a review for *every* game.

AN: Yeah! I guess back then the NES had quite a lot of titles published for it, but they were quite selective on what they published. A lot of games in the Famicom era were not released overseas. But we weren't concerned about that with the book; we cared only about which games had a cultural significance. Both the best games, and *kusoge*.[7] Because that's also memorable, right? If you're paying 50 bucks, and then don't enjoy the game, you'd get really ticked off. A lot of those involved in the project are magazine editors, and they thought these games have to be mentioned. There's even books dedicated to *kusoge* - the bad games! Or sucky games, or whatever you call them. <*laughs*> And they became popular. So the editors thought that's something we should put in, so *Takeshi no Chousenjou* was one of the titles, and others.

So we're working on it, and some guys at the museum thought we have to translate that into English, because there might be some guy from America, or overseas, who might be interested in coming to this museum. We'll need a guide. So they asked IGDA Tokyo and I came on board and started translating some of those.

JS: There's a lot of text in the book!

AN: Oh yes, back then I was just a research associate at Waseda University, so I had some time. I spent the entire summer translating a lot of text. But I was getting really concerned, because there's no time for native checks. So I know some of the stuff <*laughs*> is broken.

JS: It was fine. The book doesn't read like an academic book, more like a conversation.

AN: Casual, yes. Well that's something we intentionally did, as translators, because that's how it is in the original Japanese. It wasn't like an official or solid kind of interview, it was more like a casual interview, in a casual setting. Except for Yamauchi-san, obviously. <*laughs*>

JS: How did you get him on board?

---

[5] International Game Developer Association

[6] You must sing karaoke, leave the controller untouched for 1 hour, hit an enemy 20k times, etc.

[7] Lit. a portmanteau of *shitty game*

AN: Back then he was more outspoken. Well, Professor Saito worked with Iwata-san before, and he was involved in this project. Now he is a professor at the Ritsumeikan. But back then he was working at a game development studio in Tokyo - he was partnered with HAL Laboratory, having Toru Iwata as a producer, and they developed videogames like *Vegas Stakes* together. So he knew those guys, and was able to approach them directly through Iwata-san. That's how they were able to get Yamauchi-san on board for the project.

JS: I was amused, because he says Atari made games and they were "trash".

AH: <*laughs*> Yeah, quite outspoken and honest. Only he could do that. Anyway, I was surprised to see him on board. So there was a lot of contact with Nintendo back then.

JS: Recently you've written your own Famicom book?[8] But it's not in English?

AN: Oh yes, yes. It's all in Japanese.

JS: Do you have a copy I could look at?

AN: I should have brought it... But there's not one here. I'm sorry. But I am thinking about a way to create an English version of the book!

JS: I hope you're not going to remove information on distinctly Japanese games. That would be like the 1980s again.

AN: It's the same as with Japanese anime, right? We'll try to do it. I'm on board, for sure, when we do that. We'll tell them the significance of having local context in the text.

JS: Emphasise that! People outside Japan want this information.

AN: Yes, it's got academic value as well. Fortunately we didn't cover so much the software, which you'll be doing. So I think our project and your project could be companions. We're focusing on hardware, as it was being developed, and how it was distributed to US and UK, and other parts of the world, and how fragile the business model was back then, but was solidified after the Famicom. Plus all the social and cultural influence the Famicom had on its Japanese audience, and some for the US. I couldn't put too much about the US audience, but anyway, there's a lot of Japanese information associated with the hardware. For software, we didn't have time to do that because [hardware] already covered about 250 pages alone. It's really difficult approaching Nintendo; it's almost like a huge iron wall. <*laughs*> Fortunately we had Masayuki Uemura[9] as a professor, so that was the only way we could go through it. He disclosed so much information, but in a way that he could get it through PR. All the text was edited by PR.

JS: That's a terrible shame.

AN: But there's nothing you can do about that.

JS: You mentioned the USA. America acted like gatekeepers of what came out of Japan. For a large part, whatever Europe received tended to be the run-off from America, and we didn't even get everything America received. We got a few exclusive things, like *Terranigma*. But there was a filtering system, which I don't think was reflective of people's tastes.

JR: Yes, a good part of this, in France, is that they had a strong culture of playing the original - importing the games from Japan. For example in the US you had the TurboGrafx-16, but in France you had the original Japanese PC Engine from NEC, you could buy in supermarkets.[10]

JS: In the UK there was a strong grey import scene. Because in Europe we had PAL TVs, and the official PAL consoles were inferior - slower, with black bars at the top and bottom of the screen, so a lot of people imported an American SNES and cut the plastic tabs so they could fit Japanese SFC cartridges in it.

AN: Right, modifications - a mod culture already!

JR: Everything in 60Hz, RGB! Better than Japan.

AN: Yeah, you could play the Japanese and American versions.

JR: But there's also a hidden market of *doujin* games for the Famicom and Super Famicom.

---

8 ISBN: 4757170467 / 978-4757170469

9 上村 雅之; head of Nintendo's R&D2 team, responsible for developing NES and SNES

10 Distributed by SODIPENG, Google for info & fliers

This is unofficial, so today I think it's quite hard to preserve, because Nintendo is against it.

AN: Right, Tengen's games, and so on.

JR: To tell the truth, even some good games were released. Not really *doujin*, because some big companies were behind them. The sales figures were good for these games. But they're unofficial, not manufactured by Nintendo. They're quite expensive in Akihabara. Like collector's items.

AN: But it's difficult to approach those guys who developed those games.

JS: Do you know anything about *Snake's Revenge* for the NES? Amazing game. It was developed by Konami's Japanese department, by the same team behind *Castlevania III*. But it was only released in America and Europe.

AN: Not really. I've not even met those guys who developed *Castlevania*.

JS: You mentioned HAL Laboratory earlier. Iwata-san used to be a programmer.

AN: He was a super programmer back then, and that's why he was able to get a project from Nintendo to create a program for baseball and all that. Now he's head of the company - it's interesting how it works.

JS: Describe what you're doing at Ritsumeikan.

AN: Ritsumeikan has been working on game studies for years, having been headed by Professor Hosoi. He's the one who actually talked with Nintendo and ended up recruiting Uemura-sensei as a professor. When working on this project of game preservation, he approached Uemura-sensei and talked about the project. I guess they liked each other, and he was quite intelligent, so he decided to recruit Uemura-sensei to join the project.

JS: Your goal is a database of game names, the hardware it was released on, and release date?

AN: That's the initial step. Kyoto prefecture is also quite interested in this project, and so is the national library, which is established here in the western part of Japan. All these guys are interested. Right now, at this moment, we're just working on a database, but I don't think we'll stop with that.

JR: Ritsumeikan University made an official announcement, two or three weeks ago?

AN: Oh, in the newspaper, right?

JR: Yes, and they told the newspaper that they were starting a huge project and the goal was to preserve all Japanese games, including arcade games. There is no mention of computer games, but I assume they are included?

AN: That's a huge plan.

JS: Would that put you in conflict with Joseph's Game Preservation Society, or are you allies?

JR: No, there is no conflict, because my idea is that it's impossible to gather everything, even if there are 100 preservationists. So I think the key is cooperation. Well, this is my vision.

AN: Yes. I guess their strategy <*referring to Joseph*> is to keep their products or titles as is, right? Preserve them completely.

JR: Yes.

AN: So that's impossible, we understand that. But we've been to a lot of museums, like the Museum of Media in the UK, and all these guys who worked on GameCity. They have ways to do that. We also went to The Strong National Museum Of Play, and they're doing their own stuff, but they have their own way of doing it. I think the way The Strong is working is feasible, if the prefectures, or school, or the government could assist us. In fact, we have the International Manga Museum here, in Kyoto, and it's working. We know that The Strong is also working - that means operating and making profit even. So there must be ways we can do that. Generate some sort of necessary revenue, which allows the project to keep going. So that's something we have to calculate.

JS: You're funded by the government?

AN: Maybe the government, or prefectural government, either way. We know that Kyoto prefecture is getting big on this "cultural artefact" preservation. They want to make sure that this place is the capital for all the cultural stuff. So that means including all the videogame culture which emerged from Japan, especially with Nintendo. Because Kyoto is the capital for all the high culture, and even videogames are part of a sub-culture, or pop culture. But it emerged from Nintendo, that's for sure. I mean, yes, arcade games came from Tokyo, with developers like Taito. We created an entire culture and then exported it to the world. Sure, Atari created an entire culture, but the videogame crash erased all of that. Then after this wasteland, Nintendo built an entirely different culture, which comes up to now. So that's something we're proud of.

JR: You say it's impossible to preserve all packaging - what do you plan to preserve?

AN: Maybe some of the packaging is a little bit trashy, or has scars on them. We'll permit or allow them, as an artefact, or part of the collections. Unlike your project where you have to clean up everything as it is, and then send it up to France to preserve it, correct?

JR: No, no, we don't send anything to France! We have a laboratory in Tokyo. Everything is done locally. I don't know where you heard that we have to send anything to France. We are linked to a preservation society in France, which is MO5. We are working together to improve the skills and technology of preservation - the way of preserving old materials, such as cassette tapes and floppy disks. But Japanese materials stay in Japan, definitely.

AN: Oh, really? That's very good. <*laughs*>

JS: Regarding the need to preserve *everything*, have you heard about the planned change to laws in Japan, which would make certain old computer games illegal to possess, and they would have to be destroyed if passed?[11]

AN: Right. [...] In that article it says preserve ***everything***? <*laughs*>

JR: Yes.

JS: Wouldn't that be breaking the law then?

AN: I don't know about that. Oh, you mean if it's going to be preserved? It won't be preserved by an individual, it would be preserved by organisations, as a cultural artefact. That's probably a different story.

I think what happened is, Professor Hosoi talked to the journalist, and the journalist interpreted that this is his vision. But I don't think it's going to become reality, in a few years from now. It's not like it's a backed or funded project. I don't know how it worked out, but I guess he talked to the journalist about the history of this videogame archive, or whatever, and then the journalist probably misinterpreted it or something. Because if you were to preserve everything like he said, I don't know how much it's going to cost. It's not feasible.

JS: I've heard that there's about 75'000 games from Japan? Arcade, console and computers.

JR: Yes, that's it.

AN: That's a lot. You mean including all the... Did you include *doujinshi*, the *doujin* games?

JR: All the games to date. *Doujin*? No. It would be twice as many! <*laughs*> We don't know!

AN: <*laughs*> Right, right. It's something that he talked about, as a vision of this project. It's not necessarily going to become an actual reality - because it's backed up by the funding, and that's possible, but our funding is for digital archiving, not necessarily physical preservation.

JS: So you mean, like for emulation purposes? Digital back-ups of ROM data?

AN: For cultural affairs it's only for the database, a pure database. Information collecting. That's it at the moment. But for example Meiji University is working on actual physical preservation, and then of course over at Kyoto we have some physical preservation already. And then Sega has provided their titles for quite some time, so we do have physical preservation. The issue is the physical space. Where are we going to put all these? The university doesn't want us to put everything here. We've got all the arcade collections as well, but we don't know what to do with it. So it's really difficult, somebody needs to back this up, otherwise we're not going to be able to keep getting all these titles. So there's a lot of issues we have to work on.

[11] Changes in law would make material with someone under the age of consent, who is portrayed nude, as illegal and require being destroyed. This includes older computer titles, such as *Eldorado Denki*

JS: You also need to maintain the humidity and temperature at stable levels.

AN: That's what he says. <*refers to Joseph*>

JR: I think the biggest challenge today, more than money, is time. Because we're running out of time. We still have plenty of time, for example, for Famicom, Super Famicom. They're just EPROMS well protected in a plastic case. But it's a different story for magnetic materials. I'm sure Famicom games will still be playable in 30 years.

AN: Right now we already have a difficult time playing some of these games - sometimes we use them for our class, but sometimes they doesn't work. So we have to <*makes cartridge blowing motion*> a couple of times. <*laughs*>

JR: Well, maybe you need to change the resistors inside the cartridge. But the ROM data inside is quite reliable, for quite a long time.

JS: Do you have any personal thoughts or messages you want to convey?

AN: Yes. I think your project will work out, and when finished successfully, then our project, our book, and your project will work cooperatively. So I think that would be great. We have to translate this as early as possible, and hopefully by the time you are published, our English version will be available as well.

JS: Let's send each other complimentary copies!

AN: Yeah, that's a good idea! <*laughs*> There's similar books published in Japan, called *Cho Famicom*, that focused on software development and all the trivia about software. But that was published by a rival publisher. But we're friends because this market is small. We have to collaborate, otherwise it's not going to work. No one publisher could dominate another.

JS: In the UK there's only one magazine dedicated to old games.

AN: This one? <*gestures to Retro Gamer, sitting on the desk*>

JS: Yes, that's the one.

AN: That's good! The markets are limited. Very profitable; not extremely successful, but a good niche for a product. So *Retro Gamer* loves to understand about both hardware and software... <*glances through the Q*Bert issue*>

JS: Do you like *Castlevania* on the SNES?

AN: Yeah, yeah!

JS: I interview the director, here... <*flicks to page with Making of Super Castlevania IV*>

AN: That's good! You see, I used to write for *Game Critic* magazine in Japan, and I did similar things for companies like Valve, or Bioware.

JS: Wow! So do you like Western games?

AN: Yes, I loved it. That's how I got into this writing job. I explained all about first-person shooters, and all that stuff. When they were making *Half Life 2* I went to Seattle and spoke to Gabe and all those guys. That's how I was able to get into this game writing business, when I was a PhD candidate in Nagoya. That's how I was able to get into game research. Because it's difficult to get into the company and interview, unless you're a journalist of some kind.

JS: You mean in Japan?

AN: Yes, Japan, or even in the US or UK probably. It's really difficult for a researcher to talk to companies - they're quite secretive.

JS: If you go through PR departments. The trick is always bypassing PR. They don't do anything beneficial. They're simply gatekeepers.

AN: We could do that a lot back in 2000, but now it's getting so hard. They keep everyone out except for the media, and it's the same thing in the game business now.

JS: If PR is exerting so much control over what someone can say, it means companies will rewrite their history. For example, there was a *Mario Brothers* slot machine, officially licensed by Nintendo. But they never want to talk about it.

JR: It's revisionism.

AN: Right. Well, that's how they are now. So we have to follow that rule. Especially for us academic guys. So if you have a bad relationship with those guys [Nintendo], anybody in that company, you're not going to be able to do anything. So that's a side-effect of being in academia. We've got to survive, you know? So we have to live in both worlds.

JS: One final question, what do you think of Kickstarter, and Japan's acceptance of it?

AN: With the successful funding of Inafune's project, a lot of game developers are interested in that project. Wow, $3 million, that's quite a bit for an animation, or for a mid-sized videogame, so all the guys who created retro games back in the Famicom days are probably paying a lot of attention to it.

JS: This could set a precedent for old creators. Throwing away the old publishing model.

AN: Yeah, because in a lot of times, when those people developed these games, they were either... Not laid off, but left the company, because at a lot of companies they were no longer needed. Back in the polygon days they didn't need pixel artists so much, so they left the company. But now they have the opportunity.

JR: You were talking about The Strong Museum, which recently bought, I think, the biggest collection ever of Japanese games, from a French collector. Are you aware of it?

AN: A French collector? See, that's what we're scared about, because that's what happened to all the Japanese artefacts back in the Meiji era, like ukiyo-e. Back in the 1890s, all the Japanese artefacts went to the rest of the world, and there was nothing you could do about it.

JR: So history is...

AN: ...repeating itself!

JR: But what's your opinion today about games?

AN: Well, partly it's a Japanese problem, because maybe Japan thought all these artefacts are less important than its US or Western counterparts, and all the French people, who consider this as an important, valuable artefact. At least we could say in Japan, we or a couple of guys in Tokyo, are really the only ones who think it's really important. And we got funding, but the funding is only to create the database, not physical preservation. What we need is the physical preservation. We need to have space, but there's no space available at this point, and that's crazy.

JR: You think money is definitely the key?

AN: Money and a place. A couple of years ago...

JR: We don't have money at the Game Preservation Society. We're all volunteers.

AN: Well that's passion. And passion is also important, but the space is something we have to have. Passion is important, but it's ideal to have a place like The Strong Museum has. I know you're preserving it too, but it's not in a way that you could exhibit, right? Have exhibitions or whatever.

JR: Yeah, we could. Yes, sure.

AN: Oh really? That's good.

JR: Not ourselves, of course. But we could participate with any exhibition.

AN: People need to learn about why so many people in the world are so interested in these kinds of projects. A lot of people are thinking these things are historically valuable, not just a product. We have to be advocators of that, and I'm trying to do that.

~In memory of~

横井 軍平
YOKOI, Gunpei

10 September 1941 ~ 4 October 1997

What can you say about the man who invented the d-pad in 1982, to facilitate the controls in Nintendo's handheld *Game & Watch* series, later becoming ubiquitous in controllers for all home gaming systems? Or who then created the Game Boy, which sold over 100 million units and celebrated its 25th anniversary this year (2014)?

In 1999, as tribute to his name, *GunPey* was released as a launch title for the WonderSwan handheld system. A puzzle game, it went on to receive several sequels.

On March 6 2003, Gunpei Yokoi posthumously received the IGDA's Lifetime Achievement Award. It was presented to Mr Yokoi's family by the previous recipient, Yuji Naka, who said, "I am as deeply honoured to be presenting this award as I was to receive it."

GAME
PRESERVATION
SOCIETY

ゲーム保存協会

http://www.gamepres.org/

Although not a game developer, the Game Preservation Society is just as fascinating, given that it aims to create and maintain a permanent history of all the work done by Japanese developers. The GPS aided the production of this book at numerous stages, with setting up interviews, providing materials to show interviewees, scans, screenshots, translation help, and all manner of other things. The head of the GPS, Joseph Redon, was also the intermediary in arranging the limited edition platinum cover by Hitoshi Yoneda.

I visited the laboratory on a few occasions, filming video for the supplementary DVD, and speaking with its founder Mr Redon. Although originally from France, his passion and dedication to preserving Japanese gaming is as pure and intense as I have ever seen. His laboratory is the stuff that collectors' dreams are made of.

Join me as I document this unseen world...

Interview with the head of Japan's Game Preservation Society, Joseph Redon
16 October 2013, at an undisclosed location in Tokyo

JS: What was the first videogame you saw?

JR: I'm not really sure because I am the youngest of a big family. I have three older brothers and two older sisters and all my brothers used to play games. The first one I remember is an arcade game when I went with my family to Brittany, in a city called Carnac. This was the first time I entered an arcade and the first game I saw was *Moon Patrol* and an old lady was playing. I was very young, maybe four or five, and I thought wow, an old lady is playing! There were only young people around, and I think she was doing quite well because she played for a long time. I kept going to the same arcade every day, but I couldn't play because I had no money. The first game I played was *Moon Patrol* because when I went back to my hometown there was a very small arcade that opened, with *Moon Patrol*, so when I got some money I played it and was quite good.

JS: How old are you, may I ask? You preside over 40 years' worth of videogame history.

JR: *<laughs>* Yes, I was born in 1976, so I am thirty seven.

JS: Tell me about the Games Preservation Society. What is the Japanese name for it?

JR: In Japanese we say "*Game Hozon Kyoukai*" which means Game Preservation Society, and in Japan we don't use the word "video" game, we just say "game" which means the same thing. It was founded just two years ago, but has been involved in preservation for quite a long time, since the time I was in France, in Paris, so this would be around 15 years ago.

JS: When did you feel games need preserving?

JR: I think that 15 years ago it was not that we needed to preserve everything, but we wanted to know everything, because there are many, many games that were released but we didn't know about them. So for 15 years it was mostly collecting and attempting to know every game: Japanese games and also European or American games. For me personally I was mostly looking for Japanese games.

The first computer I had was a C64, and I kept it for quite a long time. Then one of my older brothers and I switched to the Amiga 500, which was maybe the best computer I had. One day we decided to sell it and from this time I completely moved to Japanese games. I bought a PC Engine, but I had some nostalgia about the Amiga and, like everyone, started playing on emulators. But to tell the truth we had a lot of original games on the Amiga and all the stuff I played on emulation was cracked. With some screens removed, many things changed in the game, and I couldn't have the same feeling as when I played on an original Amiga. So I told myself that if I want to play the Amiga again I need to buy an Amiga, and I need to search for all the old games I liked. But I didn't do that, because I moved to Japan and started to collect Japanese games for computers such as PC-88.

But then I had this wind of nostalgia and wanted to play Amiga again, and I discovered a group, the Classic Amiga Preservation Society, who are now known as the Software Preservation Society (SPS). [1] At that time I thought they were "pretending" to preserve the entire Amiga back-catalogue.

JS: You said "pretended"?

JR: I said "pretended" because at this time I thought: OK games are available on the internet, so in some way are already preserved. So what are they doing? Is it different; is it better? What is preservation? I discovered that they were ***not*** pretending at all, and so I contacted them. I said, I want to do something with you. I want to join, I want to help with the Amiga, but it will be very interesting to extend your knowledge to other machines such as Japanese computers. I mean, they had the technical knowledge to re-master an Amiga game.

JS: To produce a fresh, fully functioning disk?

JR: In theory. They couldn't do that at that time. Now they can, but at that time they had enough knowledge. When I say re-master, it's a script used at this time to produce original copies of the game, and they managed to achieve that

[1] http://www.softpres.org/

because the guy at the head of the SPS himself produced games for the Amiga.

The reason why he started to work on preservation is that he lost his own games and wanted to play them, and discovered that it wasn't the original that was available on the internet. He said, "It's not my game, and even if I buy the original, maybe in a few years it won't work, so all we'll have from game history is just a history about cracked games." Which is important. We need both, but keeping only cracked games is not a good thing for the future.

JS: The SPS is a non-profit organisation?

JR: There are many people across Europe, from England and Germany, and I think the Software Preservation Society is located in the United Kingdom, but it's not a registered group, so it's still informal.

JS: But your group in Japan, the *Game Hozon Kyoukai*, is formally registered.

JR: Yes. The story I was telling you would be seven or eight years ago; at this time the SPS was one hundred percent involved in Amiga only, and they still had a lot to do with the Amiga, but two years later they contacted me and said, "We're almost done with the Amiga, so we'd like to extend our effort to other computers. We have already tried the PC and Atari ST and an English computer called the Acorn Archimedes." They said, "We're interested in Japanese computers so let's do something together. Let's try; let's begin." After that I bought an Amiga and started preserving PC-88 games on it. But it was very difficult and a dead end. I was the only one in Japan with an expensive Amiga - a 1200 with some kind of extensions...

JS: You'd place the PC-88 disks directly into it?

JR: Yes, because fortunately the PC-88 uses 5in floppies and it's not HD, so the Amiga could handle this kind of disk. But the drive itself was very hard to find. It took me six months just to find the drive for the Amiga, and the 5in drive actually had no drivers for it. So one guy at the SPS made the driver and modified the application. It was quite a difficult job for everyone, but the quality we got wasn't as good as expected.

JS: Then you used Windows for preservation?

JR: Yes, yes. Then we started a new project and the SPS told me, "Join us. We really want to do something in Japan together, so we'll start a new project, and let's forget about the Amiga. The Amiga is good for preserving Amiga games, but we really need a hardware solution and software that could be used on any computer." So I'm using Windows, but this preservation work can be done on anything. Macintosh or Linux, anything you want.

So we spent one more year working on a piece of hardware called the Kryoflux.[2] It's quite simple; it's not unique. Other devices like the Kryoflux already existed at this time. I remember one called the Catweasel for the Amiga. It's just a digital sampler, and at the same time it's a floppy disk controller. So you give simple orders to the drive, you connect the drive directly to the Kryoflux, you read the tracks and you sample the direct output of the drive, and everything is sent by USB to your PC. Like sampling an audio tape. Then you have to analyse the result.

JS: And how much did it cost to prototype?

JR: The SPS in Germany and the UK did it, but the prototype was expensive. I paid for all expense regarding the prototype and the first lot, first batch, of this piece of hardware. The idea started, I think, because of the PC-88.

JS: This is specifically for PC-88 disks?

JR: Well, yes and no. The PC-88 is behind this. It started with the PC-88, but in the end the idea was to produce a piece of hardware that could sample any drive, so you could preserve any floppy disk.

JS: Famicom Disk System?

JR: FDS I would say yes and no, because it's a disk but it isn't really. It's not a disk, it's more like a tape. You have only one track on FDS and it's like a spiral. So you read the track from start to end. It takes 8 seconds. You don't have the same mechanisms. It's quite different from a floppy disk. We made our own hardware to analyse the FDS, to do the same as Kryoflux; we are using different hardware to sample the FDS because 8 seconds is too long for the Kryoflux, so we have a hardware limit here.

JS: It has to read the data in a shorter time?

JR: Yes, it's a problem of buffering and then speed of USB. But the FDS is not a complicated system to analyse. The Kryoflux was definitely released three years ago, and...

JS: Anyone can buy it?

JR: Today, yes of course. It's public and you can find all the schematics, so the hardware is open. The software to control the Kryoflux is open too, but the analyser isn't open. It's separate, so even if you don't have the analyser, you can use a Kryoflux for imaging floppy disks. I received the first Kryoflux and started to sample PC-88 disks. I started then to think that it was a huge task for just one person, so I contacted many game collectors around me. To tell the truth, I started this quite some years ago, but I had no technical solution. I just kept telling people, "We need to do something," and then I said, "We have the solution; let's do something!"

JS: That's why you formally began the Game Preservation Society?

JR: Yes. So at this time it was not called the Game Preservation Society; it was a longer name in Japanese, like *Computer and Videogame Culture Preservation Society*. I made publicity on forums and some home pages, and one guy contacted me, a guy on the west coast of Japan, and he said, "I didn't think that hardware like the Kryoflux existed, and I had the same idea about preserving software, so I was about to build something similar to it." So I visited him, and we talked about preserving Japanese games. We thought we had to do something official, not like private work or just geeks, something official

[2] http://www.kryoflux.com/

with a name, an organisation, with members. I came up with the idea of the Game Preservation Society right after that, and I started to fill in the papers, I started to look for members, but not just people who said it's important to preserve, but those who could be involved in preservation. I had to find 10 people to start, to fill in and send the documents to the government.

JS: Is that the minimum number for an NPO?

JR: Yes, it's the minimum.

JS: So who was this guy? What's his name?

JR: He is called Mr Fukuda. He's a heart surgeon. So like me he has a real, full-time job already. I'm an IT engineer. So it's 10 people including myself and Mr Fukuda. I could tell you about the other guys - they are all quite interesting. You've already met one of them, the book collector.

We are not all engineers, it's also a network of collectors. Some hardcore, heavy collectors joined our group. It took 7 months to get the approval from the Japanese government. A long time, quite a lot of money too. So officially the society started two years ago in 2011 at the end of September.

JS: You mentioned a number to me previously of how many games Japan has produced.

JR: To date it would be more than 75'000 games, but I do not include *doujin* games, and I do not include smart phone games.

JS: If you were to include *doujin* games?

JR: I don't know. We don't know. We really...

JS: Double as much, twice as many?

JR: Maybe... maybe.

JS: An unknown number, impossible to estimate?

JR: Yes, it's quite difficult, but for example, when we research old computers like PC-88 or MSX or PC-98, yes, roughly it [*doujin* games] doubles the figures. But only for computers, not for consoles. I would say 75'000; half of the 75'000 games are computer games. We have a database with almost everything in it, so we were able to use this figure since just one year ago. Until then we didn't know the exact number of games released in Japan.

JS: That database is commercial not *doujin*...

JR: Yes, commercially sold games. So it includes arcade games, console games, old computer games, and also Windows games, and so on. When I say 75'000 I'm including the games that were released this month, but at the GPS, usually we work only on old stuff and are not putting effort, for example, into preserving Windows games. We stop at PC-98. If we stop at PC-98 and if we deal only with the oldest console games...

JS: You mean like Famicom, Mega Drive?

JR: Yes. The exact figure for us would something like 28'000 games which need preserving *now*. Those are a priority.

JS: What are the dates this would occupy? Starting in the 1970s and...

JR: In the seventies we have only arcade games, the oldest arcade games, and a few computer games. Some released on vinyl records. It was BASIC stuff. When I say BASIC, I mean the OS. At this time the only available computer was a "*maikon*[3] kit". You didn't buy a computer, you bought pieces of the computer and made it yourself. There was still no software released at this time, so only record LPs, and most available programs were released in magazines. You had to type the list yourself. That's why magazines from the 1970s are very important. Magazines from this era are *I/O* and *ASCII*. They both started in 1976. And in 1979 *ASCII* released the very first games as a package. I think it was December, so in fact it's really starting in 1980. So if I said that I have material from the seventies, it's true, but let's say they're all from the eighties for computers, *<laughs>* because it's just one package.

We mostly concentrate on computer games today because they are the most difficult to find, they are the weakest, and most of them were never released out of Japan. For example, when you're dealing with the Famicom, the oldest games are 1983, and most of them were released outside of Japan. Even in 20 or 30 years I think you will still be able to preserve

[3] Micro computer

them. But for floppy disk, in some ways it's already too late...

JS: And audio cassette tapes.

JR: Yes, yes. But floppy disks are even weaker than cassette tapes.

JS: You mentioned 28'000 as a goal. How many games are owned or preserved by the society right now, what percentage are stored here?

JR: There's a huge collection of computer games on the second floor. They are almost all my private collection. We had to decide who is doing what; I'm the main collector of computer games today in the society. Today, I think I have around 10'000 computer games. But it's not unique titles, I have several copies of the same games. It's hard to define how many different games I have, I don't remember the figures. I have to look at my documents, but within the 28'000 [priority games] there is something like 3'000 arcade games, and no more than 9'000 console games. More than half the games are computer games, so it's a really difficult task. It's not like console games. With those you know what was released so you can make a list and collect everything. There are many console collectors around the world. Many people have a complete set of Famicom, PC Engine, or Mega Drive games, but no one in the world has a complete set of PC-88 or FM-7 or X1. It's impossible.

JS: Some were released in tiny quantities.

JR: Yes. So the first task is to compile a giant database of everything. Even today we discover games we've never heard about before, so we're adding to the database. Not everyday, but I would say we add one or two games every week.

JS: Do you have plans to make it public?

JR: In the end, yes. If it was possible I would make it available to everybody tomorrow, but unfortunately it's not possible because it's not a single database. We are three people working on three different databases. First, we'd have to merge everything. The other problem is that the database is mostly for managing our preservation work. So they're not something directly usable for the public. There is a lot of work to make it a public database, and the problem is we lack database engineers.

JS: And it's all in Japanese?

JR: Yes, you are right. There is not even English or romaji[4] readings of the games, so it's a lot of work. Every pronunciation and romaji equivalent has to be filled into the database.

JS: You mentioned three databases. How come it's fractured? What are the differences?

JR: My database deals with computer games and another guy is dealing with console games, and another one is dealing with game material such as magazines, books, CDs, hardware, and so on.

JS: If someone said we need a list of a company's games, would you...

JR: Yes sure, sure. As long as someone doesn't ask for a complete list of Famicom games or stuff like that. If it's not something already available online, I would be happy to help.

JS: You're French, in charge of a society in Japan. How did other members react to that?

JR: It is unusual, but if you look at Japanese history you'll often find that many important parts of Japanese culture was preserved by foreigners. So this happens. It's unusual, but there is no resistance. To tell the truth, Japanese people have quite a different view of what culture and preservation is. In France, in England, for quite a long time we've had museums, we have archives, we have libraries. But for Japanese people, I'd say this is something new in their history. They don't keep old stuff. For example, when you visit an old temple or something like that, it looks original, but in fact it's rebuilt every 20 or 30 years. But they are using the same techniques. They are going to look for the same wood, in the same place, so in some way they are preserving the "know how", they are preserving their culture, but it's not something widely available. You cannot easily become someone working in a temple. For games, people do not consider a game to be a cultural item.

JS: Professor Nakamura at the Ritsumeikan was talking about games being cultural artefacts.

[4] Roman script, used for phonetic spellings

JR: Yes, but that's quite recent. In some ways that's natural because it takes time for something to become a culture. For games, maybe it will take 10 or 20 years, but in 20 years the problem is they won't exist anymore. We have the Famicom, the Famicom will still exist whatever happens, but what about all the computer games, what about the arcade games? So this is something we definitely have to do today. We have to anticipate the fact that in the future it will be regarded as important culture. As I told you, it's already too late. We should have started this 10 or 20 years ago. But anyway, let's try to do as much as we can. So, how much time do we have left? I don't know. Maybe for some games it's too late. For some we still have 3, 5, 8, 10 years, I don't know. No one knows. Our first mission is to do whatever we can to increase the time we have left. To keep the games we gather in the best condition possible, so we keep everything at the best temperature and best humidity.

JS: What is the best temperature and humidity?

JR: Humidity, definitely it's around 40. Between 35 and 45 would be the best. So as you can see today we are just below 40 which is good.

JS: Is it possible that the humidity can be too low? What if we had zero humidity?

JR: No. This is not possible because this is relative humidity, but below 30 is not good. If it happens then we have to humidify the room.

JS: Because the boxes can dry out.

JR: Yes, the paper is a problem but also it's a problem for floppy disks. What is not good is to have the humidity changing. For example going from 30 to 50 and going back to 30 and so on. This will definitely damage anything. The same goes for temperature, but for temperature we have some problems. The best temperature would be below 15 degrees Celsius. [5] But keeping it below 15 degrees is a huge effort, we cannot afford it as a small society. And the other problem is that below 15 it's almost impossible to work in the same building. Also, when you take out a game from the archive and you want to work on it, you have to wait until you are at a temperature over 18 degrees. So in the end we decided to keep everything around 18 and 21 degrees Celsius.[6]

JS: How did you calculate these numbers?

JR: Well, we researched and we asked around, including universities in Japan and America. You

[5] 59 degree Fahrenheit

[6] 64.4 ~ 69.8 degrees F

can find quite a lot of documents and reports about that, so it's not magic numbers. The biggest problem in Japan is definitely humidity in summer. If you do nothing, if you are living in a typical Japanese house or apartment, you will have in the middle of summer more than 90 percent humidity, and temperatures between 24 and 28 degrees.[7] With humidity over 60, and temperatures in that range, it's the best match for your materials to rot - paper, floppy disks and cassette tapes. You will get a lot of mould in your materials in a very short amount of time. Almost all the material we've gathered here has not been cared for by people for 20 years. I would say that half, or more, needs cleaning before being preserved. Keeping them at low humidity will prevent the mould spreading over games, but we still need to spend a lot of time to clean every floppy disk.

JS: There's a natural disaster, you have to escape the lab, you can only save three items - WHAT DO YOU GRAB?!

JR: Wow! <*laughs*> Well, first I think it's quite heavy but I'll take the backup of everything we did here. So I'll take this server with me

JS: You've only got two items left.

JR: I think I'll take *Panorama Toh*[8] with me, from Falcom. Hmm... Yeah I don't see a further item.

JS: Really?

JR: Yes. *Panorama Toh*, because privately it's an important item for me. But then everything is important. I can't say it's more important than another. We need to preserve everything, so a third item would be everything. <*laughs*> What's important is that today, what we are trying to achieve is not to preserve all the games we have. This is the dream, the final goal. Today our task is to prove, to show that it can be done. Here it's mostly like a proof of concept. We are dealing with all kinds of different games, all different kinds of floppies, tapes. We are dealing with all the problems we could face during preservation. We can now say: "We can do that on a limited number of items, like a sample. Now let's do it for real, but we need a larger place, we need people, and in the end, unfortunately, I think we need money, because time is money."

If I have 40 years in front of me, maybe we can do it, but unfortunately I think in 10 years there is nothing more we can preserve because it's too late. If there is a huge movement for preserving computer games, this will have to start in a few years and it will have to be intense, with many people working every day. It cannot be just random people, because floppy disks are weak, they need cleaning, and if you don't handle floppy disks correctly you will kill it.

JS: What could kill a floppy disk?

JR: Well, when you remove the mould, you mustn't scratch the surface of the floppy disk. You use a kind of chamois. We need to use that just to remove the mould without scratching the surface, and it takes time. It's quite difficult and if you make even a small mistake, you lose some information on the disk, so then you need another exact copy to compare them, to make a recovery of it.

JS: When preserving floppy disks, specifically the disk for saving data, once used it's irrevocably changed and impossible to preserve?

JR: Yes, we have a policy - we have many policies - but one of them at the society is, as much as possible, we try to locate an unmodified copy of the game. Which means if you play the game, for example an adventure or RPG, and you save on the original disk, it's not original anymore. It's modified.

JS: Is this why the TOSEC[9] sets can sometimes have the same game duplicated multiple times, because if they find different versions with slight data variations, they include all of them?

JR: Yes, but TOSEC is just people gathering cracked images that are available on the internet. It's not a preservation job. So I don't think someone at TOSEC bought a game and tried to read the floppy disks, because even if he did that,

---

[7] 75.2 ~ 82.4 degrees F

[8] PC-88; action-RPG by the creator of *Legacy of the Wizard*, one of Falcom's earliest games

[9] *"The Old School Emulation Center (TOSEC) is a retrocomputing initiative dedicated to the cataloging and preservation of software, firmware and resources for arcade machines, microcomputers, minicomputers and videogame consoles. The main goal of the project is to catalog and audit various kinds of software and firmware images for these"* - **www.tosecdev.org**

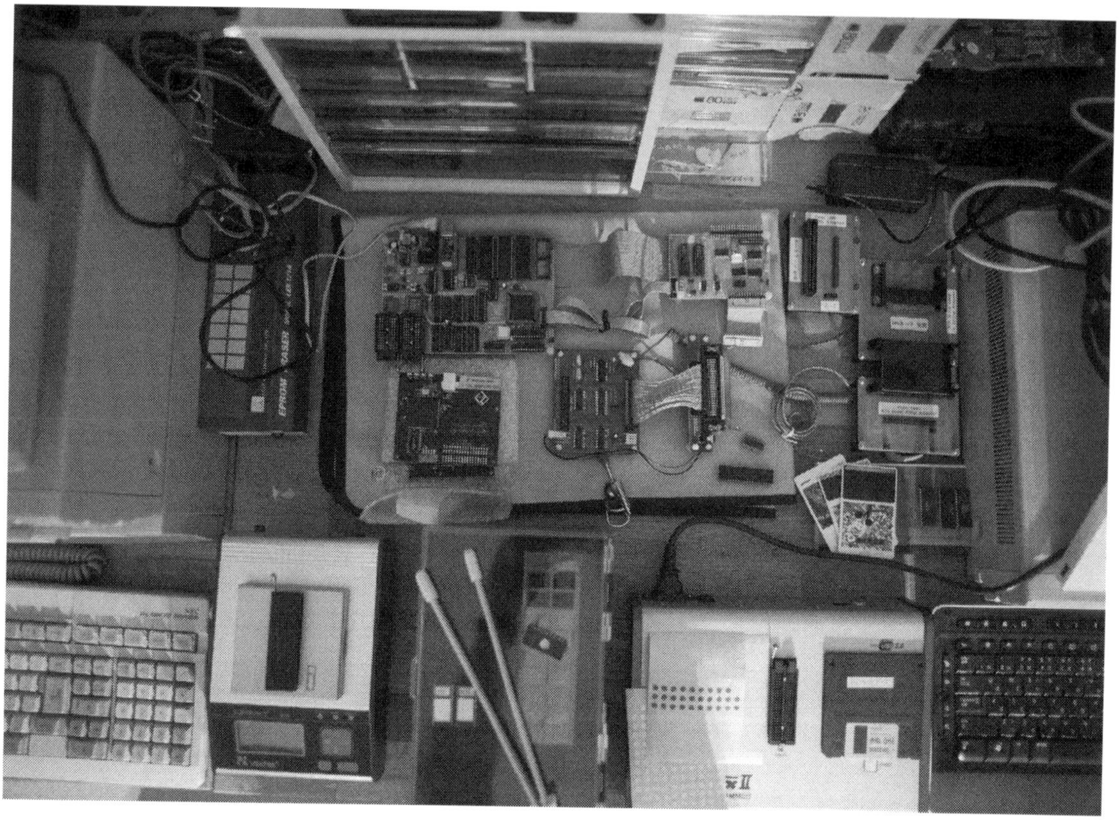

the dump cannot be played on the emulator because there is copy protection. So in the end you need to crack, you need to modify, you need to change the binary to make the games work on an emulator. But at the GPS, we are preserving the whole thing - we don't change anything. We keep the copy protection and, if possible, we want an unmodified copy of the game.

JS: Ultimately, what is this for? If you're preserving the entire thing, is this so people can play the originals on the original hardware?

JR: Every day I'm thinking about it, maybe next month I'll say different things about what we can do with what we're preserving. I think that it will be quite difficult to have a game museum where you can play everything. What could be done is like an archive. Not a museum, but a library where you know all materials are kept. Not only paper but digital copies of the games. So if you're doing research about games, if you are involved in game programming, if you are trying to write about history, this is definitely the kind of place you want to go.

JS: The important thing is to preserve it before it doesn't exist.

JR: Yes, and I think no-one has a good answer today, because no such archive, no such museum exists. So let's do it before it's too late and before it's needed. I'm doing preservation every day, but I don't know in the end how it will be used. Maybe I can show you some basic preservation with floppy disks.[10]

JS: Is this a standard PC-88 disk drive?

JR: No, no. We need to have the best resolution as possible, so we're using **H**igh **D**ensity drives. This drive was made 10 years ago.

JS: For use with a Windows operating system?

JR: Yes, yes. For Windows or DOS.

JS: What disk have you placed in there?

JR: Oh, it's a blank disk just for calibration or to remove anything on the head, if there is some random dust.

---

[10] After interviewing a gentleman from Zainsoft I was given an unused copy of *DIOS* on PC-88, which we preserved that day. This is on the supplemental DVD

JS: How much would all of this technical equipment cost?

JR: Wow. The drives definitely cost a lot because we need reliable drives, if possible new ones, and the production of floppy disk drives, I mean 5in, stopped 10 years ago.

JS: All this equipment is bought with donations from members of the society?

JR: Yes. We have some donations and we have around 15 supporters which are paying an annual fee, but of course it's not enough, so members actually buy materials for preservation.

JS: As a non-profit organisation you need to show, not only where the money comes from, but where it goes, down to the last yen?

JR: Yes, correct.

JS: You're about to back up these floppy disks?

JR: No, it's not a backup. We are sampling, that's quite different.

JS: You take all the data from the disk?

JR: No data. When you read the floppy disk, on the surface it's made of... Maybe ferrite?[11] It's magnetic. So you have north and south, and the head will go over it and you'll get something like that going up and down. So we are sampling this signal. We do not have data yet. Nothing, just signal. This is what is really on the surface of the disk, and from this sampled signal we will analyse it in place of the machine. So we can understand how the tracks and sectors are made, what is irregular, where is the copy protection, and so on. It's not a backup, because a backup would be, you put the disk in the PC, it reads what it can read. Then you get data and it works or it doesn't. If it doesn't, you need to modify it to make it work. It's quite a different process.

JS: Do you actually back up data for any game?

JR: Direct backup? No.

JS: The sampling that you take of this disk, what can you actually do with the results?

JR: Imagine that these drives are like a scanner, and the floppy is a paper document, so I'm scanning the floppy. But after, if you print it like that, maybe it's not good because you have to restore or modify. There are a lot of things you have to do after the scan before printing.

JS: Hypothetically: you sample these *DIOS* disks and then through some freak occurrence every *DIOS* disk on Earth is destroyed. All that is left is the sampled data. Would you be able to play the game again using that sampled data?

JR: If the sample is good, we will check it. It's like when you scan a document, you open it in Photoshop and check it. You have to check that physically the sample is good. If the sample is good, the answer to your question is yes.

We'll be able in 10, 20, or 100 years, you just need to spend time on it. It's just like the scanned document. If you want to make it clean and print it again, there is a lot of work. It's exactly the same with the floppy disks.

In some particular cases where the copy protection is... I mean if they did something very irregular on the floppy, for example, there are holes, they made holes with a laser on the floppy disk, and so on. For this type of unusual copy protection we need to do more. But for Japanese stuff there is only one game with holes.

JS: Which game is this?

JR: It's a game from Kogado. It's called... I think it's *Cosmic Soldier*. To tell the truth, the copy protection used by Japanese developers on their games is not high level like it was for the Amiga and Atari ST.

JS: What is your view on piracy and do you think it could be useful? There was a fascinating article[12] which said that because these floppy disks are dying, and nobody is preserving them, we might be in a situation where all that's left is a pirated copy.

JR: Yes, that's true. That's the case today. I think that 99.9 percent of available materials today are cracked copies of the games. All those copies were made like 25 or 30 years ago, so because of piracy we still have something. Even if we do not succeed in our mission... Well, it's

---

[11] Typical coatings include magnetic iron oxide, cobalt doped iron oxide, and barium ferrite

[12] "*Why History Needs Software Piracy*" by Benj Edwards, it should be mandatory reading for everyone

better than nothing of course. The question is this: "Is copyright a problem or is piracy useful?" It's quite a difficult question. I think that copyright is definitely important and needed, but if copyright stops you from preserving materials, there is a problem.

JS: Do you feel the GPS is restricted by any laws at the moment? Is there anything you'd like to do but cannot because of the law?

JR: No. We have the right to preserve the games we have. We are not making copies. It's just like scanning documents. We are not selling anything, we're not publicly releasing any materials - we are preserving. So we're okay with the law, but for example that unreleased Hudson game I showed you. I think this should be available, should be released so people can see it, can work on it, but unfortunately we cannot do that.

JS: Because that would break the law?

JR: Yes.

JS: You're sampling a PC-88 disk, how long does it take, from disk to disk?

JR: These disks are not of good quality, but they are in very good shape, so I'm making a quick read of them. I think that will be enough.

JS: They're not of good quality but they're in very good shape, what does that mean?

JR: It's like paper, you have paper of good quality, like in magazines.

JS: So it was cheaply manufactured but well looked after over the years?

JR: Yes. For example, companies like Nihon Falcom used very good disks to duplicate their games, but I think Zainsoft chose cheap disks.

JS: If some madman breaks in and says, "Tell me your three favourite games or I'm burning the laboratory down," what do you say?

JR: *<laughs>* It's very hard to answer. It's not enough to say three. It depends if it's a game I really like and want to play every day. So, if it's something I play every day, I would say that one of my favourite is *Super Street Fighter 2*. I still have it here. Not every day, but I'm sure that when I'm 70 I will still be playing this game. *<laughs>* And I love *Katamari Damashii*, the first one for the PlayStation 2.

<looks at results of disk sampling> So no fancy stuff, just regular sectors here, quite easy to read and understand. So the first floppy is okay. A normal image conversion is enough to play it on an emulator.

It's not a good thing though, because emulators for old computer games are really not accurate. I would like emulators to improve, to be more accurate, because a floppy disk is not only data. There is also some analogue stuff which is not emulated or supported by emulators. We need emulators in the future, but if we have no other choice than using an emulator, let's at least make a good one.

JS: There's that Super Famicom emulator...

JR: Yes, yes, like Higan I think![13] This is maybe the greatest emulator on Earth for videogames! So this is a good example to follow, but it's a little more difficult when you are dealing with floppy disks, because there is the drive, the drive response... So if you want to make something truly accurate, it's difficult.

JS: Talk us through some of the equipment that you've just switched on.

JR: Yes, this is a custom PC-88 I'm using for testing preserved materials. So we are playing back a re-mastered game on the real hardware.

JS: What are those two items at the back there?

JR: Oh, this is to replace disk drives. So the floppy is calculated on this computer and then the result is streamed through USB to this other computer, and then it will react like real floppy disk drives. So there will be no difference between the real disk and what is streamed from the computer.

JS: Are you the first person to have created this style of setup?

JR: I think this is done widely all over the world with a lot of PCs, but to be frank, not many

---

[13] Higan aims to emulate the SNES as accurately as possible through low-level emulation, and is apparently able to run every commercial SNES title through cycle-accurate emulation without any bugs

people are doing this in Japan. So me, Mr Fukuda and... anonymous people. <*laughs*>

JS: This is basically a floppy emulator...

JR: Yes, this is the HxC floppy emulator made by a French guy, a member of the MO5.COM game preservation group in France. We are working together on Japanese stuff.

JS: You said this was a PC-88, do you have a similar setup for PC-98 or Sharp X1 computers?

JR: Yes. We have all computers available here. We can do testing on almost any system.

JS: All of these computer models are unique. How many computers do you have?

JR: I don't know. I don't know... To be frank, it's not really a collection, it's really needed for preservation. They're all functioning.

JS: You mentioned there's some computers you don't have because they don't have any games for them. Which are they?

JR: Oh no, no. There are many computers which have no games. Since I'm not a hardware collector I don't buy them, but there is, on the contrary, very few computers which have games where I don't have that computer. If I don't have it, then they are very difficult to find.

JS: Which computers would these be?

JR: For example there is the Hitachi MB-S1. This one is quite difficult to get.

JS: How many members are there at the Game Preservation Society?

JR: At the moment the core members are 15, and we have something like 15 supporters, so it's 30 members. Which is not bad. I mean it's people really involved in preservation. Active at some point, with something in the process, and then we have people helping, so they are not members, but when I have some technical questions, when I need something. There are many people around the GPS who are not members, but are doing something for us. I would say in the end maybe 50 or 60 people around game preservation, which is quite a lot. But we are dealing with so many different things, many different machines, from arcades to consoles, cassette tapes, CDs, and so on. While books and magazines are another story.

<*DIOS boots up on PC-88*>

JS: This is from the disk that you sampled.

JR: Yes. So the protection used by *DIOS* is analogue protection. So the bits are not correctly aligned; you can read the disk, you can copy it, but the copy won't work. But because this is an analogue copy it works on the real hardware without removing the copy protection. It's quite simple protection, so it was possible to convert it for the floppy disk card emulator.

JS: The thing people won't notice if they emulate are the monitor scanlines.

JR: Yes. Very important for the PC-88. It's not square. It's like a panoramic screen and so the size between each line is very important for the PC-88. This is why you can never get the same result with emulation, because with emulation you have one line of pixels and you have one black line of scanlines. It's not far from the real thing, but in the end it's still different.

JS: I usually disable scanlines in the emulator. They make it look too dark.

JR: It's black lines. It's very, very hard to have the same result on an emulator. It's better to have some forced scanlines on an emulator than no scanlines at all, but yes, quite difficult to have the same results. But with very high resolutions, for example this is a 4K monitor, I think that we could simulate the same render as the original monitor, but no-one has done it yet. I am using 4K because I'm working a lot on the database, so it's very useful to have a large screen. And we are doing some video editing. All video capture is done at full HD, so when you edit full HD it's better to have a screen which is going higher than full HD.

JS: This is where you edited the video footage of the DECO cassette games?[14]

JR: Yes.

---

[14] Introduced in 1980 by Data East, the intention was to allow arcade owners to change games easily, via cassette. The DVD has footage of the unknown horizontally scrolling *Flash Boy* for DECO Cassette

JS: You thought the DECO cassette was lost?

JR: Yes. I told you we were doing proof of concept with computer games and console games, but with the DECO cassette we had to do everything from scratch and by ourselves. We could not afford doing so much research just for a sample, so we did the full project and it means that today we are able to repair Data East's DECO cassette, and we have re-mastered every single game for this system, so we are pretty sure that even in 10 or 20 years, we'll still be able to repair such a system.

JS: So if an old DECO cassette tape dies, you could put the data back on?

JR: Yes. We've done that for many titles already. They were already dead, you couldn't read them on the real hardware, but we used techniques to recover what we could from the tape, re-master them, and then write back the information as it was written.

JS: Which games did you revive?

JR: Well, quite a lot. There are over 40 games for the DECO cassette system, and I remember I had a very hard time with a few of them. Some were... I had just one copy of the game and it was in quite bad shape, so I spent a lot of time on it. But it was *not* worth the job. <*laughs*> Because in the end the game was horrible! But for preservation, even though I spent 15 hours on this game, and maybe just 2 or 3 hours on a better game, for me it doesn't matter. It has to be done even if the game is bad.

JS: Regardless of quality, all games are equal in the eyes of preservation?

JR: Yes. We don't make a selection. We don't say this is more important, so we'll do it before anything else. The priority is weak materials. Materials that are getting damaged by time every day, so the priority is floppy disks, especially those that are already damaged or of bad quality.

JS: Has anything been lost and you'll never be able to find it again?

JR: I would say that maybe at least between 20% or 30% of computer games are already lost. Maybe in 10 years you'll ask me the same question and I'll say, unfortunately, it's 40%. Or alternatively, because we found them and we had the opportunity, time, money, and so on, to preserve them, we only lost 15%. I don't know, but I would say at least 20% is already lost.

JS: Of that 20% that's lost, does that mean there's only cracks available, or is there nothing?

JR: Nothing.

JS: Nothing at all?

JR: Nothing. Because when you are looking for, say, PC-88 games online, you'll find only images of floppy disks, but half of the games released for this computer are tapes. Where are the tapes now? Where? Nowhere! <*laughs*>

JS: So we might go into someone's garage, find a tatty box for a game, and inside there'll be a tape which doesn't work. There won't be a pirate copy, there won't be a cracked image, there won't be anything, just a dead tape which you cannot recover information from. So there are games which existed at one point in time, but now nobody will ever be able to play again, or see them, or know anything about them?

JR: For some games it's even worse because there is nothing even in magazines. So someone will say, "I had this game," but there is no evidence of it existing. So if we cannot find a copy, then yes, it's lost forever. But most games that were released have some information in magazines, so at least you know the name.

JS: And maybe a small screenshot.

JR: Yes, maybe, maybe not! <*laughs*>

JS: I suppose a lot of the work when producing a database is going through magazines.

JR: Yes. Magazines are the first source to make a list, and to put dates and basic information, but then we need to look at a copy of the game to be sure it was actually released and to know that the information we have is correct. So all games where we don't have the package are in a grey zone. We're not sure. We pretend that it existed but actually we don't know.

JS: Like *DIOS* on CD?[15]

---

[15] There are adverts for it, but no one has seen a copy

JR: Yes, so *DIOS CD*, now we know that it was definitely released, but who kept a copy?

JS: The only difference in the packaging is the little sticker on the back?

JR: Yes. So maybe in some second-hand shop they have a lot of old *DIOS* boxes and they don't know one of them is on CD. It's possible.

JS: Didn't Mr [REDACTED] mention that NEC intended to give copies of *DIOS CD* to people who had bought that model of PC-88?[16]

JR: Yes, this was the deal but unfortunately it wasn't done. He said about 500 copies of *DIOS CD*. I know many, many game collectors, PC-88 collectors in Japan, and no-one has even seen *DIOS CD*, so it's really rare stuff.

JS: Tell me about unreleased games. Is that also something which the GPS tries to track down?

JR: Not really. We are tracking down the information. We are trying to understand why it wasn't released. Sometimes it's quite difficult, sometimes some computer games are said to be unreleased, but then we find a copy of it. But it was in such a small amount many people thought it was unreleased. But we are not collectors. It's interesting, for example, to get an unreleased game or unfinished game, but it's not a grail for us. I put much more time and effort to looking for stuff like cassette tapes, old Hudson games for example. For me this has more value than any unreleased game.

JS: Really?

JR: Yes. Usually games are not released for a reason. I could speak about this game. I think hundreds of people are looking for this game called *PC Cocoron* for the PC Engine. This is unreleased, but the game is finished and this is it. *<shows original>*

JS: May I take a photograph of this?

JR: No.

JS: Really?

JR: No.

JS: Okay.

JR: No. It's the same as the Famicom version but for the PC Engine.

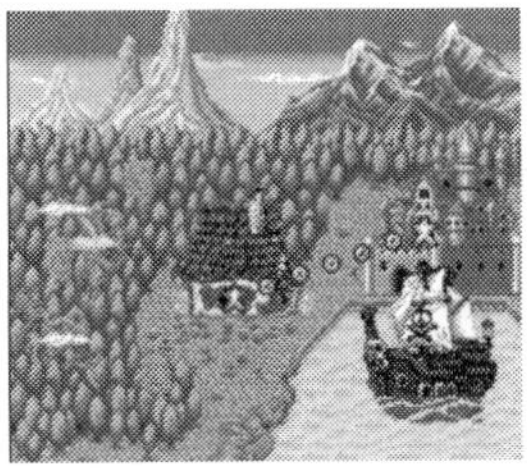

JS: How did you come to acquire it?

JR: It's not mine. It's from one of our collectors in the GPS, so my job is just to preserve it, that's all. *<laughs>*

JS: Have you heard of the ASSEMbler forums? It's a forum where American and European collectors trade rare items.

JR: They are collectors. They want unique items.

JS: Some will group together in order to fund the purchase of prototypes.

JR: Yes. I can understand that. It's like a treasure hunt. That's fine; I think it's cool, it's nice. But putting so much money on such bad games. I would say: let's use this money for more useful preservation work! *<laughs>*

JS: Frank Cifaldi in America paid $2'700 for *Bioforce Ape*. That game was amazing to play! Worth the effort I'd say. It's lot's of fun.

JR: In that case, yes. It's really interesting then to make it available, but that's another question that's quite difficult. In terms of the law.

JS: So why can't I photograph that? Is that because there's no image of it online?

JR: No, because it's not mine. I would need authorisation from the owner.

JS: So how many unreleased games would you say have come into your possession in the last two years since starting this society?

[16] The creator of *DIOS*, from ZAINSOFT, his interview is featured in a later volume

JR: Not so many, but mostly console games, Famicom, Sega MkIII, PC Engine. I would say between 20 and 30 titles. Not only unreleased materials, but works in progress. Or demos.

JS: Can you list ALL the names?

JR: Well...

JS: Simply knowing an unreleased game exists and knowing the name, is valuable in itself.

JR: Oh, but we all know about that because for console games, usually like 3 or 6 months before the release date there is a mention of it. So speaking about games that were unreleased and that are unknown, I don't have any.

JS: You haven't stumbled across any surprises?

JR: No. Not for console games.

JS: Apart from that Hudson game, that was quite a surprise for you.

JR: The contents were a surprise.

JS: Have you come across other, similarly rare items? With only a few copies?

JR: Yes. This one. There were only 15 copies of it, but in the end I think that Naxat Soft made more. It was *Super Real Mahjong PII&III Custom*.[17] And it's a special version. But what's different? The special version is not censored. So you have nudity, which was otherwise not normally permitted on the PC Engine.

JS: Isn't this illegal under Japanese law?

JR: No... How old are they? It depends, if they are only 15 years old it is. Let's check... <*opens manual*> Hmm, they look young! Right...

JS: You'll have to send that to the government, for summary combustion.

JR: Ahh... No, first I have to give it back to the owner. <*laughs*> So you had to complete the game, then you get a password, you send it to Naxat Soft, and the first 15 people to send the password could get this special version. And it's not pressed, it's home made. It's a CD-R.

JS: And this is numbered #8.

JR: Yes. But unfortunately there are also copies of this. So sometimes it's quite difficult... This is definitely an original copy. <*laughs*> A genuine burned copy.

JS: Is the cover for this the same as the retail?

JR: Yes, it's recycled. That's the problem!

JS: The only way to know it's the special, is because of the little red "not for sale" stamps?

JR: Yes. This one is expensive. But it's funny, because even if it's 15 copies, maybe more, it appears very often on auctions, or in shops in Akihabara. So people maybe buy it, play it, make a back-up, and then resell it. But I would say no less than 200'000 yen.

JS: That's £1'300 / $2'000!

JR: Yes. And because it's CD-R, it has a very short life. I think that in a few years you won't see it anymore. They will just be copies and it will be easy to spot them, because this CD-R was made in 1993, or 1994, before people could make CD-Rs at home.

JS: Do you compete with private collectors?

JR: Yes. It depends, because it happens every day. So I have my preservation responsibilities, and I have my private collection. That's two different things. For example there are some old tapes, I think these should be preserved, because we don't have them in our archive. So I'll buy them, of course. But if there are competitors, and they are bidding a large amount, of course I will give up. But if it's a very rare item I also want for my private collection, then I will compete. If possible, I will try to get it.

JS: What's the most expensive you've bought?

JR: Luckily I have never spent more than 100'000 yen[18] on a single game. I think it

[17] Long running series of erotic mahjong games

[18] About £660 / $1'000

wasn't even 100'000, so it was like 95k or 98k. I bought several at this price. One is an old Enix adventure game, called *High School Adventure*. Also, I bought very rare stuff from Koei. Just let me check the title, because some other games have a similar name. I think it's *My Lolita*.

JS: How many games are in your database?

JR: A lot! <*laughs*> Yes, it's *My Lolita*.

JS: *My Lolita* is illegal today?

JR: Oh, completely. Yes. Completely.

JS: Are those the rarest items you own?

JR: I told you about *Panorama Toh*, but of course it's rare, it's valuable because it's Falcom, and so on. A few people have it anyway. Images are available on the internet, and so on. So it's not lost. It's just a valuable item. Let me find something more interesting. <*scans computer*>

JS: Do you help private collectors back up rare items they own?

JR: Yes, of course. Because they have some rare stuff, but they cannot read it anymore on a normal computer, and usually they want a backup for emulation. So I say, OK, let's see what we can do. Usually I succeed. I give them enough information so they can play it on an emulator afterwards.

JS: Did you study technical work like this while at university?

JR: No, no, no. I learned everything which is related to preservation - computers, floppy disks, CDs, and so on - I learned everything from scratch when I started preservation. I'm a network engineer. So that's quite different. One of the rarest titles I would have in my collection is *Soft House Satsujin Jiken.*[19] You know for example *Portopia Satsujin Jiken?*[20] So that kind of *Satsujin Jiken* series were quite a trend, back in the day.

Oh, I forgot! I said it was less than 100'000 yen. But definitely the most expensive item I bought was 109'000 yen. It was not on auction. This usually happens. I have a message from a private collector. He says he needs money, and he knows about my project, about my collection, and he says, "I have some rare items, is there anything you would like to buy?" And he had this game, so we negotiated for quite a long time, and then...

JS: What game was this?

JR: This was *Soft House Satsujin Jiken*. It's a tape game, there's not much information about it. It's an adventure game and - as far as I know - it's not available anywhere. And it's for the MZ computer. Not many fans around for the MZ.[21]

JS: Were there ports for it to any other system?

JR: No, no.

JS: You have an item where there is absolutely no other way to experience?

JR: Yes, I have a lot like this. But this one is very valuable.

JS: Tell me about unique experiences. What interests me are games where it's impossible to get that experience other than with the original.

JR: Well, the Data East cassette system is the same. Because emulation is not very accurate. It's not good for this system. So this is definitely something you need to play on the real hardware. Happily, most of the stuff we've preserved for the Data East cassette system, you could play them at the Natsuge Museum. Not all, maybe half of the over 40 or so games were available in Akihabara. But it was only for a very short amount of time. Today, if you really, really want to play it, there is no possibility.

JS: It's not properly emulated?

JR: No, it is not. Like most games! <*laughs*> The people working on emulation, they're doing a good job, I think. But for example, for the DECO cassette system, they don't have a DECO cassette at home. They don't know the game, but they are making a driver for it. So you have to tell them, no, the speed is different, the colours are different. And here it's not a bug, so please don't fix it. And so on, and so on.

---

[19] ソフトハウス殺人事件 / *Soft House Murder Case*

[20] Adventure game by Yuji Horii, landmark release

[21] I did find one Japanese fan page with screens: **mio.servequake.com/~takky/emuz2000/seller/softhouse.html**

Because they are not emulating the hardware, they are just simulating the result. They pretend that the game in reality is running like that, so if you ask another guy to make a different driver for the same game, you'll have maybe a different result. Afterwards it's like tweaking or changing a few values for the speed, and so on. But it will never, never be the same. Because emulators have to be accurate, and you have to emulate every cycle of the hardware. But people are mostly concentrating on the software, and the final result on the screen. We had no choice with the technology of 10 or 15 years ago. But today it's a different story. If you say, for example, to the people who are working on the MAME drivers, "OK, let's do it again. Let's restart everything from zero." They'll say no, no way!

JS: Didn't they already restart MAME, a couple of times? Which is why old ROM sets don't work with the latest version of MAME...

JR: Well, ROM set is a different story. Usually people who are making the driver and people who are dumping PCBs are different. If we give up with MAME and another project is started, it would be good news for me. What has been done in terms of PCB preservation can be recycled any time. I mean: you read a ROM, your read is correct, or it is incorrect, so we still have bad dumps, but most of them are good, so it can be recycled in another project.

JS: I wanted to ask you about the Japanese government's statement that they can only preserve games from 2000 onwards.

JR: Well, I was told that, during a meeting with the government.

JS: You actually met the government?

JR: Yes, a few times. This is official, the government today is putting a lot of, I won't say effort, but a lot of money into... Their first step is to build a database of subcultures, including animation, manga and games. It's a 5 year project and now it's the 4th year. It's a government project so it's quite difficult to get the contract, but as an official group recognised by the government, the Game Preservation Society has the chance to try to get a contract. It's not just one contract for everything. For example, we could get a contract just to build a public database for computer games, and that was the idea. To tell the truth, the government came here to the Preservation Society and they told us, "We have no knowledge, we know nothing about computer games, and we tried to do that with universities but they have only knowledge of console games, not arcade and not computer games. So we heard about you, we came, show us."

<Joseph shows report>

JS: Wow. You got a report from them?

JR: Yes. This is a report of government activities for this 5 year project, but for last year. So there is a lot about who is doing what, and every single meeting is inside.

JS: Is there a report on meeting you?

JR: Yes. We had two huge meetings with them. One here, and another one with a collector of arcade games, and we were asked to do the job. So we applied to get the contract, but the university had the full contract for the project regarding games. So what you saw in Kyoto, one week ago. They are building a public database of Japanese videogames, and the government asked for a complete database of everything. Unfortunately this is not something we could be involved in.

JS: So there's a rivalry between your groups?

JR: Well, on this contract, yes. Because this would have been our first contract. Our mission is: we are an NPO, we are registered by the government, so we need to do something for everybody, for the public. It doesn't mean that we work for free. We don't get a salary from the NPO. We could, but we don't even have enough money for preservation, so we'll definitely never get a salary from what we are doing here. But talking about something that has to be done in a very short amount of time, a database is quite difficult, so we had this opportunity to spend the last one or two years hiring very skilled people. Database engineers, and also hiring people that are happy compiling all the data for the government. My project was to hire eight people. Everyone was okay, and I was involved myself, so I would spend one year just on the PC-88, because I have enough material. I know almost all the titles. For me the job would be to go after every package and add all the information to the

database, and this would have been done for every other system, every other computer, FM-7, X1, X68k, MZ, and so on. We told the government we would give accurate information for almost 15'000 games in two years.

JS: So where does the government's year 2000 date come from?

JR: This was someone from the government's Bureau of Cultural Affairs, so this is the top. It was right when a famous French guy put his whole collection of Japanese games on eBay for one million dollars. When collecting console games, if you have the money you can do it - but they're in such good condition, most of them were sealed. So you know when you open it you'll find everything that was in the box at the time. This is what is interesting, in terms of information for a database. So I told this representative of the Bureau of Cultural Affairs, the government has a chance to gather what they otherwise could not. Because the national diet library has almost nothing before 2000. I told them this, because for years they kept saying it's hard to get old games. I said, now it's your chance to get a full collection! That person said they already made a decision, which is to not look after games released before 2000, because it's too difficult, because it would take too much time, too much effort. So they just gave up on this idea. So I said fine, maybe for you it's impossible. You decided that it was impossible, but now there is a possibility, you just have to say yes. And they said no, it's already decided. That's the Japanese way of thinking. It was more than one year ago, I think it was in July 2012.

JS: Isn't it odd you're head of the GPS? When you collect PC-88 games, aren't you looking at them with a French perspective?

JR: Sometimes. Sometimes I do, sometimes I don't. Usually I don't, because I've known Japanese games for quite a long time now. I made the effort to buy the systems, and to play almost all games I had for the PC-88. So when I talk about games, usually I know these games. I can tell you why this game is important, and why it's technically impressive for that time, not only now. For example, when you play *Ys* for the PC-88, and you show the original *Ys* to someone, maybe they say, "Come on, there are more colours on PC Engine. So the PC Engine version is better." The context is really important. In art, it's the same. There is a context you need to understand: when, who, how. So you can start to criticise, you can start to talk about it as a cultural work. So even if a game is not so good, there might be some very interesting technical points. Talking about games, not just playing, is important, but you need to understand when the game was made, for which system, and what this system is. What are the difficulties when developing on this system? Who bought the game at this time, why, and so on? This is the interesting story, that you will never know, you will never understand if you are not in the country, if you do not understand the people or have the knowledge about that culture.

You cannot spend 5, 10 or 20 hours on each game to document it. We should, of course. I hope that there will be more and more game historians in the future. Those who take the time on just one game and try to tell you everything about this game. But if you want this kind of person in 10 or 20 years, or 100 or 200 years, to be able to do this job, you have to let them access the materials. So in my mind, when I started the preservation society, I was already thinking about a future when there are no copyright problems. When everything is freely available, so anyone can re-use any old materials, work on them, and so on.

JS: Do you think people will still be talking about videogames in 100 years?

JR: I don't know. Maybe. Maybe not. With music we always listen to Mozart, and so on. It's always the same, known stuff. But when you're talking with... For example, my girlfriend is a musician. She knows a lot about the history of music. She will start talking about people ***I have never heard of before!*** So I think this applies. In 100 years I'm sure *Mario*, *Zelda*, they will still be here. In some form. But what about *DIOS*? I don't know. But maybe you will find someone interested in old stuff, who will say, "Wow! They did that 100 years ago! Look!" Maybe if it's just one person, it's enough. It was worth the work to preserve *DIOS*. This is my thinking, I'm fairly sure there will be more and more people interested in old games. Not just because they played them, but because they don't know them. They will want to discover them. They will have fresh eyes. Even myself, I don't know how the future will judge our culture.

<we both take a break and enjoy a coffee>

JS: The highest you've ever seen a game, was *High School Adventure*, which went for over 200'000 yen. Is that right?

JR: 240'000 yen. But I would say it's a mistake. It's a mistake by two guys who were competing, because on Yahoo! Auctions it's not like eBay. When there is only five minutes left, if someone bids then it will go again for five more minutes, and many people are using software that will bid for them. So if two people are using this kind of software, it can go for 10 hours or one day, just bidding and bidding and bidding. I wanted this game. I think I stopped at around 100'000, and in the morning when I woke up I checked, it was still running and it was over 200'000. I woke up very early and it stopped soon after, but I'm pretty sure the two guys never wanted to bid such a high amount of money. It was like a bright surprise in the morning! *<laughs>*

Myself, for example, there is this game today I really want for my collection, *Game de Type*, a typing tutor. It's historically very interesting, but also I want it for my own collection because I'm trying to locate every single Enix game. It's for PC-88. It's floppy disk. So to be sure I get it, the money I've prepared for this game is 161'000 yen.[22] I think that it will end around 20'000 something, no more. But we never know. Maybe I will never have an occasion to see this game. The last time it was on auction was in 2002, so 11 years ago. I cannot afford waiting again!

Unfortunately this is the type of game I will put a lot of money on. Maybe I'm the only guy to do that. Everyone says, "Yeah, I got this *Dracula X* for the PC Engine!" and so on. But if I say I bought this game for 80'000 yen, no-one will understand me. *<laughs>* So anyway, the game has the price you give it. So for me it's both. Historical value, but also something I really want for my own private collection. There are only two Enix games for the PC-88 I don't have.

JS: Which are they?

JR: This one and the other one, it's called *Karakuri Ninpou*.[23] But this also a very rare game. I've never seen the package.

JS: You don't know what it looks like?

JR: No, I do not. But the game is... One image is available online, so the game is not lost, but I really want to see the package!

---

[22] About £1070 / $1610

[23] PC-88, Aug 1984, by Takeshi Nakazawa; action game, set in buildings in feudal Japan

JS: Is there a quantity of money that would fix everything, allow you to do it all? Someone says, "I'm going to write you one cheque..."

JR: Okay. Maybe. Maybe it's a lot, but maybe it's not so much. I think the best would be to build a place that is appropriate for game preservation. But the question is: do we build a place only for console and computer games, or do we also go for arcade preservation? And if you say yes to arcades, maybe we'll need five, six, seven times the amount of money.

JS: Purely because of the space they take up?

JR: Yes, yes. It's incredible! If you want to keep all cabinets, it's really, really hard. But let's stick with console and computer games. First we need a cheque for building such a place. Then we'll need money to run this place; huge electricity bills for several years. Then we'll need money to spend on research and hiring people to do the job. So if we need to do that in less than five years, I would say we need something like between 20 or 30 people paid fulltime to do the job. I cannot tell you how much that would cost, but maybe not so much compared to what the government has spent to make... Well, the project is not over, but I know how much the government spent. The figures are public.

JS: What are the figures?

JR: Two billion?[24] Yes. Two billion yen. It's a five year project, but in the end there is only one single database with animation, manga and games. So no archive. No place you can go to touch, to see the games. Just one list of released games, animation and manga. So it's quite a lot of money. I would say it's 10 times the money the Games Preservation Society would need to achieve preservation in five years.

Five years, so it's 400'000'000 per year,[25] right? And you have to divide this also among animation and manga. Then we have games, and we have something called digital art.

JS: There's all these internet millionaires. Wouldn't it be cool if the guy who invented Facebook was a game collector and he invested.

JR: <*laughs*> Yes. I think there is, anyway, a limit in game preservation. Too much money also wouldn't be a good thing, because... For example here, it's all private funds. I'm working in a company, I'm an employee, I have a salary. So I'm doing game preservation using my salary. It's not a hobby, because this is not what I would do for a hobby. It's something that someone has to do. This is something that no one is doing today. We have a short amount of time. No time to think, no time to play games like I would want to. Just a limited time, five years, 10 years. But if you have a huge amount of money, you tend to use money where it costs a lot of money. For example: buying expensive arcade games, and making a building for those arcade games. Then you would think that computer games are something small. Everyone thinks that actually it's small.

JS: But computer games are HUGE!

JR: Yes!

JS: Because there was no licensing required for it, and a lot of people could do it at home.

JR: There's no quality control, like Nintendo did for the Famicom. But it's full creativity. People just made what they wanted to make. It was quite easy to release something you would never see on consoles, or even arcades. It's different, but it's huge. And it's important because I think you would never find anyone... I mean you've interviewed a lot of people already, I think they all started on computers. Almost all of them.

JS: A lot of them bought a computer and made games which were published as boxed copies.

JR: Yes, yes! They played *Space Invaders*, or arcade games, and then they wanted to create something themselves. So they got a computer and they enjoyed computer games. The console market came later. So there is something special between 1980 and 1985, where the only way to release freely a game was to buy a computer and develop on that computer.

JS: You have a lot of passion for this project. But where this desire comes from?

JR: For me, being in Japan today, being almost like a Japanese citizen...

[24] £14 million / $20 million

[25] About £2'600'000 / $4'000'000

JS: But legally you ARE a Japanese citizen.[26]

JR: Well, yes... I spent a lot of time playing Japanese games, and making research about them, so in the end I decided to move to Japan to know more about Japanese games that were only available in Japan. Mainly PC-88 games. So I had a lot of fun, it was very interesting. I went to university in Paris to study Japanese. But I was already speaking Japanese when I went to university. I learned Japanese through games, so I spent my time in university looking for new games. But "old" new games. Or "new" old games? *<laughs>*

JS: Old games you had not discovered.

JR: Yes! Old games, but new to me. So I had a great time with Japanese games. My work around preservation is because I want to give something back, for all the fun I had with Japanese games. It's like a debt. Preservation is something that someone has to do, and I have a debt, so I'm paying my debt to this culture. Of course I enjoy this. It costs me money, time, which I could use for something else. But the most important effort has to be done NOW. I would not do this for the rest of my life.

JS: We're at a critical stage now.

JR: Yes, this is now, and only for the next few years. This is a difficult situation because it looks like I'm the only one in Japan taking care of this. Even if there would be another person, or two, it would be quite different. Maybe we could have preserved more and more games from now.

JS: You're looking for a likeminded person to take on some of the responsibility?

JR: I'd love to. But it's difficult. For example Mr Fukuda has responsibilities in the Preservation Society. He's spending a lot of time doing research. When he was young he loved cracking games. So he buys a game, he plays it, even if it wasn't fun - the fun thing was to crack the game and understand the copy protection. So he learned a lot about floppy disks; he is really skilled and has the knowledge needed for preservation. But he hasn't the time to spend on preserving every floppy. If you play with figures,

if it's a full time job, and if we're mainly spending our time on computer games, if there are five of us, I think it is doable.

JS: We spoke about the government earlier on, but they are also hampering you, with new laws, right? The law about the age of certain people in games, and having to destroy them?

JR: The law is decided, but it's not enacted yet.[27] But when this law becomes active, it will cover any material. Not just games, but illustrations, manga, animation, books, novels, anything. If the girl, or boy, looks younger than 20 years old, and there is nudity or something suggestive, then you shouldn't have it. You should destroy it, or send it back to the government to be destroyed. That's the law. Even for old materials. So it could be *ukiyo-e*. I don't know where the limit is. Maybe the government will say, OK, everything which is already in a museum is not touched. They would be saying this is important culture, but at that time even *ukiyo-e* was scandalous! Many works were destroyed. Many survived only because they were taken out of Japan. So now they're judging present culture and saying, these have to be destroyed. It's tragic. So there is nothing I

[26] Josep Redon officially has Japanese citizenship

[27] On 6 June 2014 I received a message from Mr Redon explaining the law had been enacted the previous day, **but games and anime were removed**

can today because the law is not enacted, but if it is, then we will have to see how it is applied.

JS: So you get a letter from the government saying you need to destroy *Eldorado Denki*...

JR: It's by a very famous *manga-ka*. The game was released by Enix. And the game... It's just an adventure game, with graphics of young girls. It's not suggestive. But it's nudity. You have young-ish looking girls, it's girls with cat's ears. <*laughs*> Yes, there is nudity in the game. But with the law we are talking about, it's already too much. So I think I would gather all sensible materials into one big box, and send it to another country! <*laughs*> Yes, definitely.

JS: *Eldorado Denki* seems quite innocent.

JR: What is innocent, what is not? That's the problem. The law at that time, and the culture at that time... For example when we talked about *177* with dB-SOFT. No one in the company thought it was strange to create such a game. Even the female staff were OK with it. So how should we judge it today? The problem is that it's a reflection of that time. So of course if you ask me, *177* is unbelievable. How could they make such a terrible game! In *177* you have to run, chase a girl, and rape her. Why? I hope no one after playing the game did that. But there is also some humour in the game.

JS: If you succeed, you marry the girl?

JR: Yes, this kind of humour. Let's take it as an example of what should not be done. Or just say, OK, the people have changed, this was before, and this is now. But you cannot destroy it, you cannot throw away your past. I think it's terrible.

JS: Is the law vaguely worded?

JR: Yes. You have to explain the law, in the text. You have to put words on the law, to say, this is the limit. What's innocent? What is not? It's impossible. If they want to prohibit such materials, they have to decide the rules. If it's under 20, if it's nudity or suggestive, then it 's not good, it's out. It applies to old materials. That's the contents of the law.

<I'm given a tour of the equipment in the lab. There's extensive footage of the Preservation Society Laboratory on the supplemental DVD>

JS: Are those standardised parts you can buy at any electronics store, or must they be ordered?

JR: No, they are not available anymore, so we had to redesign new ones and ask a company to manufacture them again. So this was quite expensive. This wasn't paid for by us anyway, it was paid for by people who wanted their system to be repaired. But now that we have all the information regarding those small parts, anyone who has the money can make new ones. So I think the important job is done.

JS: Do you often need things designed?

JR: No, usually you can find almost everything you want in Akihabara. Even for a single transistor, anything, just if you have the exact information, you go to Akihabara and you can find anything.

JS: What are these exposed circuit boards?

JR: This is the first PC-88, which had no disk drive. And this is an external disk drive. We had a project with... Not a company, it's a network of companies in Kyoto, which are making belts, or *obi*, for kimono, and also kimono themselves. They're using some ancient techniques - they decided in the 1990s to change the paper, because they had a huge amount of paper with holes in it, for the pattern of the kimono. And they changed it to a floppy disk drive system, with a computer. And they're still using this computer, but the floppy disk isn't working anymore. So we helped them to migrate from floppy to floppy disk emulator. So we made this for them.

JS: So if a company is in a situation where they need your expertise, they can hire you?

JR: No, no, this was a very special project, because at the same time, we were doing the same thing for the PC-98, and we said, OK, it's Kyoto, it's Japanese culture, so it's cultural preservation. So we did it for free for them.

JS: How many computers are in this room?

JR: I have no idea! I just know that I have all the computers I need to test, preserve games, or to make some research.

JS: Definitely over 50, maybe more.

JR: There are also some hidden ones. You have some MZ computers... *<walks to kitchen sink, opens cupboard underneath>*

JS: You see, you come to the game preservation laboratory and literally, under the kitchen sink, there's a computer.

JR: Yes, it's Japan. It's small, so we have to use every place we can to store materials.

JS: Isn't there a risk of damp in there?

JR: It should be OK. Again, it's not a collection. *<laughs>* These are working units. So from time to time we need to use them.

JS: This item is to pick up microchips...

JR: Yes! *<laughs>*

JS: It may seem conventional to you, but I'm sure viewers have no idea how this all works.

JR: Yes, the tool I'm using the most with microchips is this, it's an extractor, so when you need to remove a chip from a PCB, you use this kind of tool. I have many of them, because there are many kind of chips. Many sizes.

JS: This prevents static electricity and electrical shock? *<looks like wooden tongs>*

JR: If you don't use this, there's a chance of bending the connectors. It's quite hard to repair.

JS: So what are these units here?

JR: Well, it's mostly stuff to use to read - all you have here is stuff to read EPROMs, this kind of chip, also memory from console games. But anyway, it's EPROM.

JS: You've got an EPROM eraser here.

JR: Yes. So for example, when I come across this kind of EPROM, and if for some reason it's not readable anymore, I erase it and reprogram it. I have many blank EPROMs. But even blank EPROMs you sometimes have to erase completely. To be able to program it again.

JS: I noticed a PC Engine game on the shelf there. What were you using that for?

JR: This was just for testing. This is inside. *<pops the chip with connectors out>* It's interesting, because it's divided into two memories of different size. Usually you use the same size for both. If your PC Engine game doesn't work anymore, usually it has to do with this little thing - so if you manage to replace that, it should be OK. It's like... We say condenser in Japanese. In English it would be capacitor?

JS: Is there anything of note in this corner here?

JR: We're mostly dealing with tapes here, just reading tapes and also some pretty old records that contain data. Game data, or OS, like BASIC OS, for old computer boards.

JS: What is the most unusual item you have? Something the readership will never expect.

JR: Wow! *<laughs>* Yes, but our job is to preserve conventional stuff. So I have so many things, that sometimes I forget what is conventional and what is not. *<laughs>*

JS: That's not actually a clock, that's specifically to measure temperature and humidity.

JR: Yes. The archive is kept at 14 degrees Celsius.[28] 11 is the best, but it's impossible in summer. The work place is kept at 18 because people have to be able to work. I allow a variation of 2 degrees depending on the season. So now it's 12 - the most important thing is to avoid variation each day or within 1 day. In the middle of summer it's around 16 Celsius. The temperature changes slowly, not within one day. When I have a true place to keep things it will be 11 degrees for 365 days a year. Now I do my best, but it costs me a lot.

Most important is humidity level, NEVER above 60%. I try to keep relative humidity at 40-50% and it has a cost too.

JS: How much does this cost?

JR: A lot, a lot! It's electricity, running 24 hours a day 7 days a week. A dehumidifier, and air conditioning.

JS: Is that what part of the funds the GPS generates covers? The electricity bill?

JR: No, unfortunately I have to pay it myself.

<walks upstairs>

JS: What does this wall of boxes contain?

JR: I think it's 99% computer games.

JS: 10'000 games in this room?

JR: Not only this room... In this room I would say 7'000. Not enough room, so I'm also keeping at least 3'000 at home. I hope that in one year, because it's quite long, you won't see anymore boxes like this. Because we need to inventorise everything. Box by box, and separate floppy disks, tapes, from the box itself. So we keep everything separate.

JS: I notice some duplicates here.

JR: No... Yes. Some are duplicates, but some are just different versions of the same game.

JS: So for example these two MSX games...

JR: Version A and version B, but they're all different here.

JS: *<tries to take one out>* Oh, the plastic wrapping on the outside has stuck together.

JR: Yes, this is the problem. This is why we need to separate everything. For example, this kind of package is no good, because if we wait too long, we won't be able to pull out the paper.

JS: You separate the cover underneath the plastic, and put it inside special folders.

JR: Yes.

JS: This has some nice *omake* in the box.

JR: Yes, but some are missing for this. There is extra material. There should be an audio tape.

JS: With the soundtrack?

JR: Yes. Here it is.

JS: As we can see here, these are dehumidifiers.

JR: Yes. Many things, I had to use two of them. *<moves to new area>* These are all sealed Famicom Disk games.

---

[28] To convert Celsius to Fahrenheit, multiply by 9, then divide by 5, then add 32. So 14 C = 57.2 F

JS: How many folders like this do you have?

JR: Not so many. It's just that I have a pile of them here.

JS: I looked through a few of them, and I noticed a lot of RPGs, which I've never even heard of before, for Japanese computers. There could be thousands of unknown RPGs...

JR: Not only RPGs, also adventure games. Adventure games where you just have graphics and text. No animation or action.

JS: Basically there's a whole, untapped world of fascinating games, which never left Japan. But which people outside of Japan would really enjoy.

JS: Something like this must be difficult to get hold of. *<holds game in plastic bag, not box>*[29]

JR: For example, this cover has sun faded. But I don't mind. Because what we are trying to preserve is the content of the disk. We need to find unmodified copies. So if it's not a sealed game, maybe someone has played it, and saved.

JS: So how many games are in this box?

JR: I would say 150.

JS: You mainly have computer games. But FDS games are console...

JR: That's because everyone is talking about Famicom. But I never hear about Famicom Disk System games. They're quite difficult to preserve properly. So we had to do it.

JS: Let's have a look at the albums with the leaflets in them. Why do you remove the covers?

JR: Well, three reasons. First is it's not a good idea to let the paper stay in contact with that plastic. Second reason, is that it's easier to find materials according to the database. So we don't have to pull out every box. The third reason is that it's then easier to scan that way.

JR: This is *Mirai*, from Zainsoft.

JS: How many covers have you preserved?

JR: I would say 600.

JS: The manuals you keep separately as well?

JR: The manuals are over there. So in the end we will have separate boxes for the manuals, and this is not the final goal. I think even like this it's not so good to keep them for too many years. We still need to define what is the best method for keeping paper a long time.

JS: Do you have smoke alarms, or sprinklers, in case of fire? A fire breaks out - what do you do?

JR: Hmm.... Cry?

JS: There is a smoke alarm in the other room, on the wall. So if that detects smoke...

JR: I will get a phone call.

JS: Is this all insured? Is it even possible?

JR: I don't know. I don't know if it's possible. It's quite difficult because it has high cultural value for us, but it's just paper and plastic.

[29] Taito's *Replicart* for FDS came in a ZIP-lock bag

JS: You can't insure it for a monetary value, because it's irreplaceable. Here's another game, *Duel*, for the PC-88. I've never even heard of it.

JR: There is also a CD version, for the PC-88.

JS: There weren't many games for the PC-88 CD.

JR: Yes. I managed to get the CD version 3 months ago. I had been looking for a long time.

JS: How much did that set you back?

JR: It was not for a single game, I bought a huge collection of game, and it was in it.

JS: How many CD games are on the PC-88? There's *Mirrors*, which isn't a proper CD game.

JR: It's the same for *Duel*. It's just audio tracks, and then you have to boot from a floppy disk.

JS: So that means if the *DIOS CD* exists, it might be the only true CD-ROM game?

JR: It might be, yes. If there is no floppy disk with the CD.

JS: If you have to put all of these items on auction, what kind of figure would we have?

JR: <*pause...*> I don't think someone would be able to buy it. <*laughs*>

JS: Well, individually, sold one at a time.

JR: Wow. I don't know. I've never thought about that. We'd have to put a price on every single item.

JS: Millions and millions of yen.

JR: Hmm... No. Like, at least, 50 million yen.

JS: On the screen there that's *Panorama Toh*.

JR: Yes. This is a raw scan of *Panroama Toh*. So we used some tricks to recover the original colours, and I'm opening the result...

JS: Is that one of your goals, to provide materials such as that? Some covers are very difficult to find, and when they exist on Japanese websites, they're all watermarked.

JR: Yes, the problem is with paper. Packages made of paper.

JS: It's surprising that something as simple as an image would be lost forever. It's like when people restore old paintings to their former glory.

JR: Yes. So we did that for maybe 40 games. No more. It's just a sample, to say this can be done, this can be achieved.

JS: You want to prove to the government that this can be done, after the government said that it cannot be done for old games.

JR: Yes.

JS: The government are throwing away history because they don't want the hassle of it.

JR: This is the very first game made by Horii-san. This is a completely remastered version of the package. With accurate colours. So if we print this, on the same kind of paper, we would be able to rebuild the same package.

JS: You could remake the cassette tape, and reprint the packaging.

JR: Yes. It's not the goal, I mean we won't do that for every game. But I just want to say that this is possible if we try to do it.

JS: Is there anything you personally own, which you would be reluctant to share? There's no image of the cover online, someone asks for it...

JR: Yes, I'd be happy to provide it, of course. I think there is no problem to help with cover scans, or something like that. Providing data could be a problem for me, unfortunately.

JS: You mean game data?

JR: Yes.

JS: Some collectors watermark all over images.

JR: I never do that!

JS: You know *Tetris* on the Mega Drive is rare?

JR: Oh yes.

JS: One gentleman I knew, who had it, put a photograph that he owned it, but put like a 1'000 watermarks all over it.

JR: Maybe he put a huge amount of money on it.

JS: It cost a fortune. This here looks like a fascinating RPG, *Providence* on PC-88.[30] It's an action RPG?

JR: Yes, action.

JS: I have never heard of this - it appears to be by System Sacom. So this is a clone of Falcom's *Ys*?

JR: Yes. I would say so, yes.

JS: How many undiscovered action RPGs would you say there are? Hundreds? Maybe thousands?

JR: Not so many. I think that this kind of game, which was released after *Ys*, they were mostly floppy disks and it's for PC-88... I would say that almost all of them, maybe 95% of them, if you look for them on the internet, you can find them. It's not rare to find.

JS: When I visit the Tokugawa Forums, people trawl the games lists, but if all you have is a title, it can be difficult to guess: is this game worth playing? There's so many undiscovered games.

JR: Yes, that's why we need databases. So you can find them by yourself, the type of game you would like to play.

JS: Someone gave me an archive, with about 300 or 400 games in it. I randomly stumbled across one, and it was astounding.[31] An action RPG set on a vast island, with a kind of Greek legends theme. I discovered this purely by accident. For a non-Japanese person it's like finding buried treasure. Here's another, *Maidum*.

JR: This is NCS, the second game from NCS.

JS: You wouldn't be able to get away with this cover in America. Imagine if all of these covers were scanned and put online. Or shrunk down, 8 on a page, in a book of covers, and you could flick through and get a taste of what's available.

JR: Yes, that would be nice.

---

[30] Looks a lot like *Ys*

[31] *Courageous Perseus* - well worth reading up on

JS: Here's *Popful Mail* on PC-88! On the computer version, when facing left or right, the character holds the weapon in the correct hand. On consoles they're mirrored and ambidextrous.

JR: Yes, and the PC-88 version is compatible with CD-ROM. So you can buy music that was released on CD, and you can have CD quality while playing the PC-88 version. Unfortunately, while *Popful Mail* is CD compatible, there is no CD soundtrack - however, a CD soundtrack is available for *Eiyuu Densetsu*.

JS: What other weird, fascinating, and bizarre things can you show us, in this incredible house of mystery?

JR: As I told you, it's not a museum, it's mostly an archive. Even if I want to show you something, I would have to consult my database to know where the game is located.

JS: There's a plan eventually to make it public?

JR: Yes. At least the database, that should be made public. The problem is not enough room, not enough space to keep everything.

JS: So this house is rented by the GPS?

JR: Not exactly. This is the Game Preservation Society headquarters and laboratory. But the GPS is using a house I am renting.

JS: How many people have access to this house?

JR: All members. So 15 people. But on a regular basis I would say only 4 people are coming here every week.

JS: You're working here on your days off?

JR: Yes. Well, I work a lot here because I'm living near, so it's convenient for me.

JS: Do you have any scare stories? Did you ever purchase a rare game and you got it, and instead of a game, there was a dead pigeon in the box?

JR: Oh, a lot. No, no, no, it's even worse than that! Because I pay a lot of money, and when I read the disk I discover that the disk has been formatted. So there is nothing on it. If you buy something on auction, usually it's "no claim, no return". So you just have what is on the picture.

JS: Who would format a game disk?

JR: Even blank disks were expensive at the time, so I don't know why. Maybe someone would need a blank formatted disk for saving, or using with another game?

JS: Which game did you buy which was blank?

JR: It was *Night Life*, by Koei. Not really a game, it's something to... It's hard to explain.

JS: The erotic title?

JR: I wouldn't say erotic. It's a utility, a tool. To calculate when you can have sex. Then it suggests how you should have sex. <*laughs*> Well, after that I found another version. I would say that at least 30% or 40% of the games I purchase, when it's floppy disks, I need to clean them. But sometimes I really want to cry, because you see, a floppy disk is black. But in some cases it's white with mould! Just one uniform colour.

JS: Let's go through every box in this house!

JR: <*intense laughter*> I think I have something like 350 boxes. There's about 30 games per box. It depends. The database has records of the box numbers and contents. Almost everything is labelled. We have almost all CD game soundtracks released during the 1980s here.

JS: Really? How many?

JR: Not so much. I think 200 and something.

JS: Because CDs hadn't taken off yet?

JR: Yes.

JS: Is there anything else you wanted to show? Random box... Which do you choose?

JR: Random? Oh, that's nice. You know *Time Paradox*, from Hudson Soft? Oh, I like this one. This is the kind of stuff I do like - no one knows about it. But it's quite interesting. *Space Station Zulu*. But it's the Japanese version!

JS: What was the original on?

JR: This was released for the Apple II and Atari 8-bit systems.

JS: We're touching these with our hands. When you see documentaries, people wear gloves...

JR: Maybe it will be a concern in 50 years. It depends on the kind of materials. You have to take some precautions when handling the floppy disks. But boxes I think are still OK.

JS: You didn't lock the front door. What if someone snuck in while we were upstairs?

JR: Who would do that in Japan? *<laughs>*

JS: Europeans!

JR: Oh! What are they looking for? *Space Station Zulu*? *<laughs>* If I said I had a complete set of sealed NeoGeo games, yes, maybe French people would come here. But no, this is computer stuff. *<laughs>* I think only a few foreigners would have an interest in Japanese computer games. And most of them haven't even seen an image of the packaging for this. So maybe they don't imagine the cost of such games, or the cultural weight.

JS: Is there any question you wanted me to ask?

JR: I think preserving old games is a huge task, and as I told you, it's almost like a sample, what we are doing today. We need 5 or 6 people, like me, and 5 people like Mr Fukuda, and people working on the database and so on. Even though I do it, it's not enough. So everyone who has a passion to join the movement, they are welcome! *<laughs>* We are also looking for programmers - we don't have enough programmers in the group. The good thing about programmers is that they don't have to be in Japan. But it's a lot of time, and we are really looking for people who can join and be there for a long time.

JS: Do you feel games companies themselves should be helping you?

JR: How could those companies help us? I mean, they are the ones responsible for throwing away everything - games, source code, and so on.

JS: In some cases, something is only archived because someone went through their garbage.

JR: Yes, yes! And even worse. There are companies today who are saying, "Oh! We never made that game! So don't preserve it! We want to keep control of our history, and so on." So there is really nothing good about teaming up with game companies. Even if we have money from Sony. They will tell us: preserve Sony products as a priority. Not Microsoft, and so on. So no, definitely not, it's not a good option to deal with game companies. For me, anyway.

JS: In an ideal world you could go to Nintendo or Sega, and they'd open a secret vault and say, "Please help us preserve all this."

JR: I'd like to have people going around and meeting with old companies, or old people, so they can discuss about copyright, or maybe they can find lost materials, and so on. But this is time which I could not then spend here. So it's better for me to stay here and concentrate on preservation. I cannot spend 100 hours on just one game, while I could preserve 100 games in that time. There is no limit. I would love to, but in the end it's a problem of time and having enough people to do that. It's easy, but in the end when I ask someone, let's do it together, no one wants to do that.

The longer you let creators keep their own product with them, the higher the likelihood that it will be destroyed by its own creator. I mean, when something is released, on the market, this product belongs to everybody. It's our task to make sure it's preserved. If you ask the creator, maybe he says, "No, it's rubbish, and I don't want to be reminded about it! Let me just throw it away!" But sometimes you meet with creators, and they say yes, I remember that, it's my product. I'm proud of it. But not always. Not often.

JS: I wanted to ask about the box of game books you received. Presumably that's a bulk lot you purchased?

JR: It's a friend of mine. He knows you from Facebook. He is spending a lot of time translating stuff about *Metroid*.

JS: That *Metroid* game book looks interesting.

JR: I bought it for him, just two weeks ago. I should ship that to him tomorrow.

JS: It's choose-your-own-adventure book?

JR: Yes, exactly.

JS: I'd be interested in a fan-translation of it. I've never heard of fan-translations for a game book.

JR: Interesting. I've never heard of it either. I decided to concentrate on Japanese games, Japanese materials, for almost 20 years. The first thing I decided is, do not play translations. First learn Japanese. I think it's the best decision I took in my life! <*laughs*> So now I don't need to rely on translations. I can understand everything in the original language.

JS: As the creator envisioned.

JR: Yes. My message would be, if you like Japanese material so much, learn Japanese. <*laughs*> It's a good opportunity! <*laughs*> It's never too late. Learning Japanese was fun because it was like a game within a game. You're stuck somewhere, you don't know what to do, you think that someone has the key, so you're trying to understand what they are saying in Japanese. Looking at dictionaries, and so on. At this time there was nothing like the internet, or automatic translations. It was really like a game within a game. ***So the game is everywhere, even preservation is a game!*** <*wild laughter*>

JS: What is the holy grail of the GPS?

JR: Hmm... Personally, I'm looking for a Falcom game called *Bird Land*, for the PC-8001mkII. It's a tape game, quite difficult to find. I know it's not a good game, but as a Falcom collector, I would like to get it. From a preservation point of view, I think the most difficult one to find, again it's Falcom, is the 8in version of *Xanadu*. Maybe the contents of the floppy itself is not different from the 5in version, but the package has to be bigger to fit the 8in. I have a few 8in games already, like Koei games, Hudson games, and the

The stack of floppies in the central rear of this photo are the development disks from the original Thunderforce

package is always different. It's a custom version of the package. So I would love to see the custom package for *Xanadu*. That would be a really, really nice item to have in my collection.

But for preservation, there are so many items that we're looking for. Like early Hudson stuff, and also games that were only released for the Takeru vending machine.[32] Many of them are really, really hard to find. The vending machine system stopped suddenly. At this time, maybe many people did not have time to buy and keep copies of available games. So they just disappeared with the system.

JS: There's a collector on the Tokugawa Forums, who was saying there are a couple of rare Takeru System games which were only released via vending machine.

JR: Yes, this is true. I got one recently, it's an adventure game from Thinking Rabbit,[33] called *Madeleine*. It was only released on the Takeru system.

JS: He showed screenshots from a magazine, of a top-down action-RPG called *Elysium* for PC-98. Apparently there's no image of it floating around.

JR: Possibly, there are catalogues from Takeru. I have a lot of these. Not all, unfortunately. So if we could at least have all catalogues from Takeru, we could at least have screenshots. But sometimes the Takeru version of a known game is customised. It's a bit different from the retail version. That's interesting too.

<we leave the lab to go eat what Joseph described as the best pork cutlets in Akihabara>

[In restuarant]

JS: We were just theorising how much fun it would be to have a time machine and I pitched the question: "If you travel back in time for a week, what do you bring back, what do you look for, what mystery do you solve?"

JR: I think maybe I would... This is quite a personal interest. I would go to Falcom before they moved offices and try to save all the stuff they threw away.

JS: Did they throw a lot of stuff away?

JR: Yes, because they have almost nothing, no source code, not even packaging of old games.

JS: Presumably those computer hard drives they threw out are in a landfill somewhere...

JR: This should be done for every company, even Nintendo threw away a lot when they moved offices.

JS: The reason we have so many *Sonic* prototypes is because people would literally go through Sega's garbage and find that they'd thrown away. They would just chuck prototypes!

---

[32] As the name implies, a vending machine for buying games, as run by Takeru; some games were exclusive

[33] Creator of *Sokoban*

JR: But if it's not Falcom, then maybe I would go to 1985. One week should be enough to go around Japan and buy as many computer games as I can.

JS: Sounds like a good fiction novel.

JR: Yes, there is a game, a famous game called *Steins;Gate*. Where they travel in time to preserve an old IBM computer. Because this computer was used to develop the first Linux, and in the future Linux is still used, it's the main program used in everything, and a company has taken control of the world and is using this system. So guys are trying to enter into the system, but they have to decode some part of it, so they have to go back to the roots of how Linux was made. So they need this old computer. Interesting, because it's almost a true story. First it was a game for XBox 360 and then it became an anime. The PC version is good too. And when you complete the game you have access to an 8-bit version, made like on a PC-88.

JS: There was an internet legend a few years ago, about John Titor.[34]

JR: The game is based on this legend.

JS: Oh, it's actually based on that!

JR: Yes, yes. Everything he said is somewhere in the game.

JS: Oh, so you do know the legend, because he said he came back in time to retrieve the computer for the future.

JR: Yes, yes. There is speculation that maybe this guy had worked for IBM.

JS: Or perhaps really was a time traveller!

---

[34] Alleged time traveller from 2036 who posted on forums around the turn of the millennium

松原 圭吾

MATSUBARA, Keigo

DOB: 31 March 1979 / Birthplace: Takasaki, Gunma Prefecture / Blood Type: O

Interview with Keigo Matsubara
20 September 2013, Saitama

On 20 September there was an impromptu drive to Saitama by Joseph Redon, to introduce me to Beep Shop, which caters to collectors of rare items, and also Matsubara-san, a member of the Japanese Games Preservation Society who aims to collect every known Japanese book on videogames and document them in a publicly accessible database. He has over 14'000 books and around 4'000 magazines. Joseph owns around 3'500 magazines, but not so many books. The types of books cover everything from the earliest history books on games through every guidebook ever printed, and even a collection of rare choose-your-own-adventure books.

It was a surreal experience. Matsubara-san lives in a remote house surround by farm fields, yet inside it's like a museum, housing undoubtedly the largest private collection of game books in the world. I asked if he provides assistance to researchers who can't find a rare book. He does, but he says he hasn't had many requests. As Joseph put it, he's not that famous. Not yet anyway... For a detailed look through this museum, see the accompanying DVD.

Keigo Matsubara: There's two rooms full of game books. Dedicated only to game books. And there are several layers to the books you can see.

JS: Guide books, or also fiction books?

KM: It's almost all official guide books.

JS: How long have you been collecting for?

KM: I started when I was in high school. So it's taken me around 15 years to collect everything.

Can I touch the books? Should we wear gloves?

KM: No, it's fine.

<glances around the room>

JR: So it's a typical Japanese house.

KM: *<gesturing to bookshelf in one corner>* Only this space is magazines, not books.

JS: Which magazines?

KM: *<laughs>* These are *TECH GIAN* magazines. They cover eroge, or hentai games.

JS: Dedicated exclusively to erotic videogames?!

<Joseph flicks through while I film>

JR: It comes with bonus CDs too.

JS: Is this a recent magazine?

JR: It's from 2005. Not so old.

JS: Was it easy to buy these magazines, or were they sold only through mail order, or...?

JR: It's published by Enterbrain, so it's sold just like a normal magazine.

KM: There should be a message on it somewhere, saying, "Only for adults."

JR: It doesn't seem to be written anywhere. Anyway, it was easily available. Here's some older stuff, *Technopolis*. This is from 1994, about 20 years ago.

JS: Is this the biggest collection in Japan of books and magazines?

JR: The biggest collection of books, I think so. But magazines... For example myself, I have like 3'500 magazines. But only PC magazines, and I think Matsubara-san has console magazines. So we have different types of collections. But I have almost no books.

JS: So many books!

JR: I think the most difficult thing is knowing what exists. So he spends time not only buying the books, but also compiling a huge database of books. So he knows precisely, exactly how many books were released, and what is still missing today.

JS: *<noticing boxes around edge of room>* Are there books in these?

KM: No, just a small collection of games in those.

JS What are these books? <*gestures to what look like phonebooks with kanji on them*>

KM: These are called the *Daigirin* and *Kogien*, which are very famous books, covering tips and tricks in games.

JS: Does each book contain a variety of tips?

KM: It's tips for all systems at this time. <*gestures to listing on back of book*>[1]

JS: Any pictures or only text?

KM: No, no, only text. And the last edition came with a CD, a digital database. This was the last edition. And there is an online edition now, so no more paper.

JS: <*picking up Phantasy Star guidebook*> How exquisite Japanese guides are. Full colour, lovely imagery - as collectible as the games themselves.

JR: The game book market was a really huge market. For Famicom games, there is almost one book for every game.

JS: And for some games two books. How are all these organised? Are there specific categories?

KM: It's by publishing house. <*gestures to group of books*> So you'll have here a full collection from the same publisher.

---

[1] These are basically tip encyclopaedias - the one picked up stated 2056 PlayStation and 1127 Saturn games covered. In total it claimed to cover 4469 games across 7 hardware formats

JS: It might span different consoles and years?

KM: It's also by book size, so everything fits.

JS: It sounds like a complicated system.

KM: Regarding one guide book for every Famicom games, that's not quite true. There are more than 1'000 guide books, just for the Famicom, but they don't cover all titles since there are several books for the same game.[2]

<*everyone walks to adjacent room and glass cabinets of CDs*>

KM: This is my CD corner.

JR: I didn't mention it, but he has a huge collection of game soundtracks.

JS: How many CDs?

KM: Six thousand? <*picks CDs out of a drawer*> These are *omake*, so something you receive when buying a game. If you include everything, including *omake*, this extra stuff, and regular game soundtrack CDs, it's about 6'000.

JS: What's in the boxes atop the cupboards?

KM: It's manga related to games.

JR: Official. All official. Not *doujin*.

JS: Have you listened to every music CD?

---

[2] Numbers vary; low estimates are ~1'051 FC games

KM: Sure, sure. There's also a database for music CDs.

JS: If someone requires a piece of information - are you available as a reference source?

JR: He is, but he's not so... famous yet!

JS: Oh, he will be, after people see this.

JR: I hope so! Since he's a member of the Game Preservation Society, I think he's OK to make his collection available, if people need information.

JS: You could set up a library.

JR: We'd like to, we'd like to!

<I wander down another isle of cupboards>

JR: On your right are adventure books. These are books where you're the hero, the adventurer. And you have choices...

JS: Japanese choose-your-own-adventure books.

JR: Yes, yes. But these are not translations from English, these were created specifically for the Japanese market. They are mostly related to existing videogames. For example, you can see here *DAIVA*, *Super Starforce*, or *Final Fantasy*. Yes. These books are all quite hard to find today. This is a great collection of choose-your-own-adventure books.

JS: Do you have the *Metal Gear* adventure book?

KM: Yes, I do. *<moves to find it>*

JS Quite a while ago there was one on Yahoo Auctions, and forums were wondering what it was. *<receives book>* Yes! This is the one!

<Metal Gear book is flipped through>

JS: Ahh, it's asking you which decision you want to make.

JR: Yes, if you want to go East, or go West.

JS: Go East turn to page 23?

JR: It's not pages, but rather short chapters.

JS: Incredible. I wonder if things like this will ever be fan-translated?

JR: Well, maybe. If it's preserved, but maybe it will take 50 years.

KM: When I found the *Metal Gear* book, it was the first time that I'd seen it. I was amazed to discover it.

JS: The paging is interesting![3]

JR: Yes! It is interesting! You have information about companies on the top row. You have information about people in the middle. And then information about games at the bottom, here.

JS: Wow! What is the name of this book?

KM: The kanji says *Denshi Yuugi Taizen*. This is old style writing. *Denshi yuugi* is the Japanese way - no one uses it anymore - but it's the Japanese name to say videogames, simply put. We also used the phrase "*terebi game*", or TV game, but now we just say "game" in Japanese.

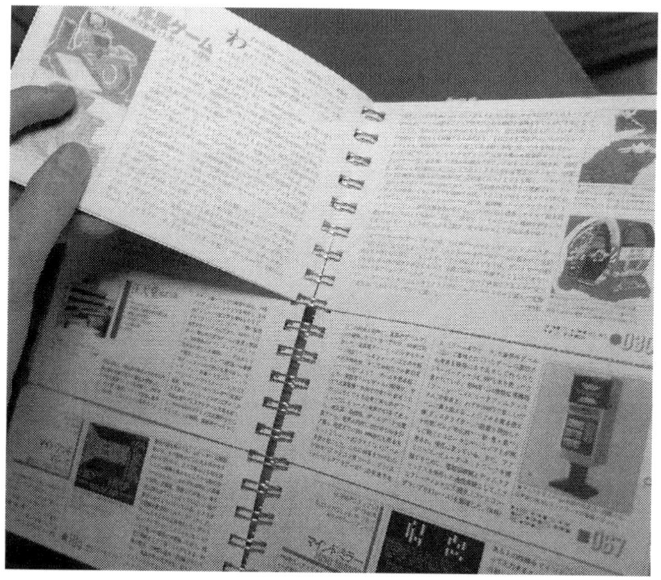

JS: Is it difficult to insure your house?

KM: *<laughs>* There's no insurance. Plus anyway, it's not something you could buy with money. You need time, not money.

JR: It's impossible to insure it.

JS: Do you do anything special to keep them in good condition? For example dehumidifiers?

JR: Because it's a typical Japanese house it's quite difficult; it's cold in winter, it's hot in summer. So this is not really a good place to keep books. We hope it's just a temporary situation. The value is not only the collection itself, it's a terrific collection, but the value is also the information inside the books.

JS: What's the rarest or most important book?

JR: We agree that this is the most... Not the rarest book, but the most important. It's a book about game history. It's fairly old actually; it was written in 1988. Although it was written in the 1980s, it really has a huge amount of content, about all the games released before this date. Not only in Japan, but also in the United States and England.

[Author's note: there's a section looking through this exquisite book on the accompanying DVD - photographs cannot convey its magnitude]

NAME: *Denshi Yuugi Taizen: TV Games* [4]
JAPANESE: テレビゲーム―電視遊戯大全
LIT: *"Electric Viewing Game Encyclopaedia"*
RELEASE: June, 1988
- ISBN-10: 4946432310
- ISBN-13: 978-4946432316

JR: It's quite an expensive book now, if you want to buy it. But you can still find it. Really, it's like a comprehensive database. We all agree

---

[3] I've never seen a book like this before. It is split into three horizontal sections (top, middle, bottom), and affixed like a series of file cards in a ring binder. Functionally it's like having three books simultaneously open, and you're able to read each independently. Printed on high-quality glossy paper with colour photos
[4] It sells for about £150 on Amazon Japan

that today we need this kind of book! Not just covering 10 years of history, but the last 40 years of gaming history. This isn't such a rare piece, but it's extremely important. Maybe the best example of what should be done regarding game history. Because it covers almost everything, from arcades to consoles, and of course computer games.

<takes out a second book>

KM: This is the very first game book in Japan. Released in Japan. About *Space Invaders*.[5]

JS: Most people I spoke to said *Space Invaders* was the first game they played.

KM: Hmm... I can't actually remember what the first game I played was. It must have been an arcade game though, for sure. The first console game I played was *Excitebike*, for the Famicom.

<moves to shelf to grab something>

KM: Let me show you one of my favourite items. A 100 yen guide.

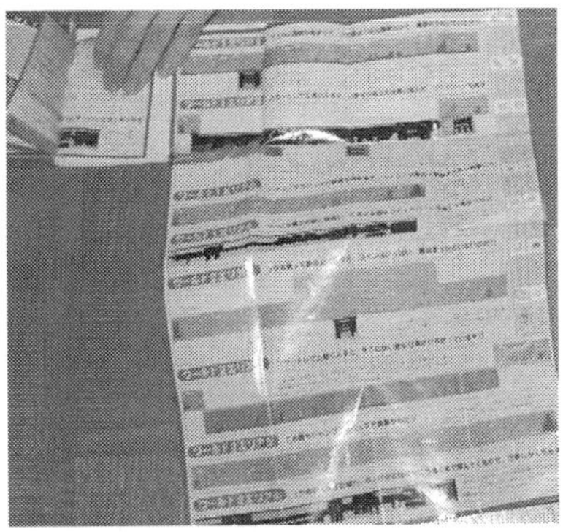

JR: A one dollar game book!

<Matsubara-san proceeds to unfold this mini-booklet, revealing glossy colour maps for the original Super Mario Bros. Ingenious!>

JR: Even kids, if they had money to buy candy, could buy it.

<A section on books related to the Mother series is on the accompanying DVD>

JS: That's a lot of books on just *Mother*.

JR: But usually, all the books are sharing almost all the same information, just with a different layout. Except for this one, which is an encyclopaedia on *Mother*, so there's a lot of original information. *<flips through>*

JS: Plus some amazing real-world photography!

KM: For a collector, one of the difficult things to know is whether a book originally came with an *obi* or not. An *obi* is what you'd call a spine card, wrapped around the book. Usually there is always one for normal books, but not always for game books. So for game books there is no definitive source of information on that. For example this one usually does not have an *obi*, *<holds Mother encyclopaedia with what seems to be a red obi>* but this is like a commercial message, for promoting the book when on the shelf. So for a book which usually does not have an *obi*, for example this one, there are different "commercial message" *obis* in existence.

JS: That would mean it's impossible to discover all the permutations.

JR: Yes, it's really a headache for maintaining a database and collecting. *<laughs>*

<we move to the next room>

JR: There's an impressive pile of posters here. *<gestures to what is likely over 1'000 posters>*

[The following interview section was conducted more formally, in Matsubara-san's office upstairs]

KM: My name is Keigo Matsubara. I am a game book collector. Not only books, but also magazines and also some other rare gaming pieces, such as posters.

JS: I believe there's 14'000 books?

KM: Only books, not including magazines - it's around 14'000 books. I'm maintaining a database, so I have some very precise figures. It's something like 13'800 for books only. There's around 4'000 magazines.

JS: Do you have any copies of *Retro Gamer*?

KM: *<laughs>* Oh, no! Only Japanese materials. I would be very surprised if I couldn't find any game book you're looking for... within seconds. *<laughs>* It's not just a huge collection, it's an almost complete collection.

JS: So we're in your office, where you maintain the database. Twenty-four hours a day?

---

[5] The book Matsubara-san is holding in his portrait shot

KM: <*laughs*> Yes, almost! I even dream about the database. It took me almost 15 years to collect all of this. But at the same time, I was compiling a huge database, and now I'm working on this database almost every day.

JS: Is it publicly available?

KM: Not yet. It's a database not only about games, but game books, magazines, CDs, game developers, it's enormous and comprehensive. There's something like... more than 100'000 entries in the database overall?

JS: Wow.

KM: Yes. So maybe it's one of the most complete databases in the world. With regards to Japanese games anyway.

JS: What is the highest price you've paid for any single book or magazine item?

KM: Hmm... I bought many game books when they were released, so they would have been bought when they were at the...

JS: The normal retail price?

KM: No, at the best possible price. I bought them not only as new books, but also older, second-hand books, when the price was lower. I don't think I've spent that much money on any single book. Probably the highest was a book of music scores - the music scores for certain games. There were three of them, and I bought them for 22'000 yen.

JS: Each?

KM: No, three books for that price. So it's not so expensive.[6]

JS: Not if it's for three books. Do you often end up with duplicates? Do you buy bulk lots? What do you do with them?

KM: I used to have a lot of duplicate books, but at that time - many years ago, maybe 14 years ago - I had a web page, and on this I wrote: "I've got duplicates, so let's exchange."

JS: A good idea.

KM: But today I'm not doing anything regarding duplicate materials. But I've got a lot.

JS: <*to Joseph Redon*> How did you two come into contact?

JR: Interesting question. When I had the idea to create a group of preservationists, I was in contact with the actual two directors of the Game Preservation Society, and one of them is a friend of Matsubara-san. So he introduced me. I was told, "This guy is crazy - he has so many books! He's also into databases." Because I am also maintaining my own database, the idea was to create a perfect database together.

JS: Containing everything?

JR: Everything!

JS: In addition to details related to each item.

JR: Yes, that's the difficult part.

JS: Does he have any non-Japanese books or magazines?

JR: No, I don't think so.

KM: No, I don't.

JS: What is the allure of printed material? A lot of people collect games, and buy a couple of books, but you do the inverse.

KM: Basically I was young, so I was buying second-hand books and games. But I realised that it was very easy to find games, and it was cheap, but even when books were cheap they were difficult to find. So I wanted to collect books and that's how I started.

JR: That's true. It's really, really difficult to find game books. There are not so many game book collectors either. So they are hard to find, even if they're not expensive.

JS: All of the older books you've read, but not so much the newer ones?

KM: Yes, I'm still buying game books, even recent ones. But only if I can find them cheaply.

---

[6] That's £150 / $220 for three books, or roughly £50 / $74 each

JS: How do you feel about the increasing discussion that print media is dead, while digital is proliferating? Everything today is online, on Kindle, or on a smartphone.

KM: Hearing that I feel... Well, in Japanese we would say *sabishii*, which means lonely. But what I mean is: it's too bad, it's a pity there are less and less printed books. But at the same time, as a collector, it's good news - because that means there's a definitive end goal for the collection! *<laughs>*

JS: Also, it makes your job even more important, because if print media ceases to exist, it's going to be you who preserves it.

JR: Good point!

JS: Crazy question time. Let's say a natural disaster befalls the world and there's no more electrical power, it's a nuclear winter, and you need to burn something to stay alive. What's the *first* thing that goes?

<everyone laughs>

JR: Maybe the erotic books? *<laughs>*

KM: Hmm, I'd start burning recent items, newer books, and going down to the older ones.

JS: Until we get to those top 3 special items, discussed earlier.

KM: I was thinking I should start with the hentai magazines, but they have plastic CDs inside, so it's not a good idea to burn them. *<laughs>*

JS: You can't burn the hentai, what are you going to read on cold winter nights?

<everyone laughs>

JS: Would you like to comment on the choose-your-own-adventure books? Because I find those fascinating. There are adventure books in English, but we never received the ones Japan had. To see *Final Fantasy*, *Metroid*, or *Metal Gear*...

JR: You have to know that Japan received ***all*** the foreign adventure books. These were printed only for the Japanese market.

JS: So the Ian Jackson adventure books...

JR: Yes, they have them here in Japan.

JS: Wow, those were translated?

JR: Yes, because the Japanese originals followed on from those translations. It's like the history of games. It started in America, but just a few years later Japan started to produce its own unique culture. It was a very, very short time period for adventure books. So a lot of books, but only within a short time. Sorry, your original question was to Matsubara-san...

JS: Let's switch the question. Of all the adventure books you have, are there any which are particularly special?

KM: It's the *Final Fantasy* book. It's because I was looking for it, and it was very hard to find. I think if for any reason I had to sell it, I am certain I would never find it again. Never. It's an important book for me. Priceless!

JS: I think a lot of things here are priceless! Thank you very much for allowing us to film inside your home. I hope you will accept a copy of my book for your collection.

[Discussion with Joseph in the car back home.]

JS: He also used to write *doujin* books you said? Does he collect *doujin*?

JR: I think it's 10 or 12 years ago that he used to write *doujin*. Those *doujin* were compilations covering guidebooks. So it's not a collection of books about *doujin* titles, but a collection of *doujin* books he wrote about guidebooks. He has not been collecting *doujin*. At this time there were no online databases, so the idea was to compile all the data on guidebooks into a collection of *doujin* books. I think he made a lot, like 8 or 9 books, at this time. I think he just kept one copy of each.

JS: So how does he pay rent?

JR: Today? It's a mystery! *<laughs>* I don't know. He just works on the database, and has done so since I first knew him. He's been doing that for years now.

JS: Maybe he's a secret millionaire.

JR: Maybe, maybe not!

QtQ

DOB: 2 April 1872 / Birthplace: Kanagawa Prefecture / Blood Type: B

Interview with QtQ (aka: Jun Kitamura)
21 September 2013, Akihabara, Natsuge Museum

Myself, Joseph Redon (stand-in interpreter), and Takayuki Komabayashi of Beep Shop, all travelled to Natsuge Museum in Akihabara, Tokyo, in order for me to film the last working DECO Cassette system available in an arcade. Detailed footage of the system, with an explanation of its history, and footage of two extremely rare games, is available on the supplementary DVD. Demonstrating the unit was QtQ, a long-time Scoreler. As was explained in the post-arcade interview, this is a part of Japanese gaming sub-culture which is fading as technology progresses. Our interview was aptly timed, since at TGS there was the announcement of a new TV drama series, No-Con Kid, which we discuss. As an aside, Natsuge Museum is a great retro arcade, and must be visited if you're in Akihabara. More information on their website: ***www.t-tax.net/natuge/index.html***

JS: The origin of QtQ's name is the third game from Namco, *CutieQ*?

JR: Yes.

JS: What were the first two?

JR: The first two games from Namco are *Gee Bee* and *Bomb Bee*. Both ball and paddle games.

JS: Of course, everyone has their 3 letter handle for arcade high scores.

<Joseph takes out magazines>

JR: So QtQ brought the very first issue of *Gamest* magazine, released in I think 1986.

QtQ: Yes, 1986.

JR: In May. It's been signed and annotated by many people, all over the cover. Also within the magazine. So it's been signed by game creators...

QtQ: ... and *scorelers*.[1]

JR: It's very difficult to pronounce. Because it's an English word, but it's not proper English. In Japan they say "*scoreler*" which is derived from score. It means someone who is playing in an arcade and aiming for the best score.

TK: Like this. *<points to magazine>* The number one high score. This is the guy who tries to get the highest score in this game.

JR: There are some very famous *scorelers* in Japan. They are famous, but at the same time they are anonymous. They only use their 3 letter name. It's like underground gaming.

QtQ: *Scorelers* are an important culture in Japan.

JR: In Europe we had groups of crackers who were in competition to be the first to crack a commercial game. It's kind of the same thing.

QtQ: When a new game is available in arcades, there is a competition to be the first to get the best score. There was no internet, nothing at this time. So they were communicating using magazines, such as *Gamest*. Or notebooks available within the game centre.

JR: Sometimes there is the best possible score for a game. So you have to be the first. If it's possible to decrease the time reaching that score, of course people will then try to decrease their personal time.

---

[1] スコアラー ; first time I heard this word I thought it sounded a little bit like "squalor"

QtQ: The word *scoreler* maybe began with this other magazine, called *Maicon Super Soft Magazine*. It was before *Gamest*. It was released January 1984. Through this magazine people started to show their high scores.

JS: How were the scores verified? A photograph?

QtQ: No, there were no photos, because it was all done in specific, known game centres. So the guy from the game centre would check the score and then send it to the magazine. Oh wait, here we have a magazine from 1983, and the word "high *scoreler*" is written, right there. So it's not only *scoreler*, it's *high scoreler*, from "high score". This magazine is called *Amusement Life*.

JS: What was your first game as a *high scoreler*?

QtQ: I think it was *Bosconian*, from Namco.

TK: But that's from 1981!

JS: You started chasing scores 33 years ago?

QtQ: I started going after high scores just before *Space Invaders*, so that would have been around, sometime in 1977.

JS: *Bosconian* was your first success, as a *scoreler*, then. Were you featured in magazines?

JR: I'm not sure. Usually *scorelers* are always in a group, but he's like a lone wolf *scoreler*. You have people making the game, you have the game itself, the PCB, and then you have people playing the game. I think all of them are important in Japan.

JS: The game we played today, *Zeroize*, have you played it before?

QtQ: No, I had never seen it before.

JR: Even at that time, Data East cassette games were a bit difficult to find. Not all of them, of course, but for *Zeroize* it was difficult.

JS: I noticed QtQ immediately did very well. Do you play games at home or only game centres?

QtQ: I mostly play arcade games. I also play arcade games at home. I have around 50 or 60 arcade PCBs.

JS: Are you worried that with the decreasing of game centres in Japan, that the days of the *scoreler* are numbered?

QtQ: Many, many *scorelers* today have no choice but to play on emulators. But I think that you cannot make a valid score if you don't play it on the real hardware. So yes, it's becoming difficult to be a *scoreler* today.

JS: Do you hold any world records?

QtQ: I have a website, and I'm sharing my high scores. Unfortunately that's done on emulator, for sharing. So maybe it's not recognised. Many people share their playing on NicoNico Douga.

JS: Have you heard of the American high-scoring society, Twin Galaxies? Have you considered sending your high-scores to them?

JR: It's like underground culture. So it's not like we have the world's highest score, it's not an open community. I know in America, for example, many people say that, "OK, I have the world record in *Pac-man*. I have the world record in *Burger Time*." But they don't even know the high-scores reached by Japanese people.

JS: So it's possible that a Japanese player has a higher score, but it's not publicised?

JR: Yes, I think so. Because they would have to read Japanese, they would have to research, they would have to read old magazines, and so on. In order to find the highest scores in Japan.

JS: So something like Twin Galaxies isn't actually world records?

TK: It is perhaps world records, just that sometimes they won't actually be ***world*** records.

JS: Is it possible to make money as a *scoreler*?

JR: No. It's just a hobby.

JS: Outside Japan people chase high-scores to brag. They want everyone to know who they are. What is the attraction of being unknown?

JR: They don't try to be famous, they just leave their name here and there. Basically they love playing, they love the game they are playing, and they want to do the best in it.

QtQ: I want to leave my name, but not my real name - not as a real person. Just the 3 letters.

JS: How many *scorelers* are in Japan now, compared to say 20 years ago, in 1993?

QtQ: Twenty years ago there really were a lot of *scorelers*. Everywhere in Japan. Some were what we called "almighty" - meaning they were playing any kind of game. They were good at all games. Some just focused on shooting games, and others just on action games, and so on. I think that today, maybe it's less than 100.

JS: What is your preferred genre?

QtQ: Hmm... I play everything. But my favourite is shooting games.

JS: And your favourite game? Just for fun.

QtQ: My favourite game is called *The Bounty*.[2]

JS: Modern arcade games are so different to classic arcade games. What's the most recent arcade game you've pursued a high-score in?

QtQ: The last game I played as a *scoreler* was in the middle of the 1990s. So nothing new.

JS: Are you officially retired?

JR: I wouldn't say that - because I often see him playing at the Natsuge Museum, and other retro corners. He still has his website, so he's still playing a lot. For example, at the end of the day, if you go to Natsuge Museum you will see SBY or DAN, and QtQ, and some others. So you know they're still around.

JS: Are they on Twitter?

QtQ: Some of them. There used to be a huge community with Mixi.[3] Do you know Mixi? It's kind of a social network. I would say it used to be the Japanese Facebook. Now it's not used so much. When it started, there were many *scorelers* on there. Today, yes, maybe a little on Twitter. Certainly it's just an underground community, again.

JS: So different *scorelers* from different cities knew about each other because arcade owners sent the scores to magazines?

JR: Yes, yes. But in some way I think this culture is dead now. So what we have today is old *scorelers*, still playing, but all the fuss about being a "*high scoreler*" has faded away. I think at the end of the 1990s. So we are here strictly talking about retro gaming. But back in those days, it was just when the game came out. People were running and getting the best scores.

JS: What I want to ascertain is, there are different cities in Japan with different *scorelers*. Would QtQ check the magazine to see, "Oh, there's a *scoreler* in Osaka, or Sapporo, who has a higher score than me. I need to pursue that."

JR: That's the idea! If you look at this magazine, there are several sections. For example, for one game you will have the first, second and third best scores. Along with the city and the name of the game centre, and then the *scoreler*'s name.

JS: Has QtQ ever travelled to a different city to compete? Do *scorelers* compete head-to-head?

JR: No, no. It's more like a local group of bikers. They are always playing the games in the same game centre. It's very local. It's not a huge game centre in Shinjuku or Akihabara, it's more a local activity. In the countryside, for example.

JS: Would you socialise with other *scorelers*?

JR: Most of them are creating a geographic group. After that it's a competition between groups. So I'm not sure *scorelers* are trying to

[2] Overhead arcade shooter, up a river. By Orca, 1982

[3] https://mixi.jp/

socialise with other groups. I think if they're in the same city, going to the same game centre, I think that naturally they will create a group.

JS: Do you have any closing thoughts, QtQ?

QtQ: *<laughs>* Play on the real hardware! *<takes out leaflet on "Nocon Kid">*

TK: That's a TV drama about *high scorelers*.

JS: *No Continue Kid*.[4]

JR: Yes, not continuing is part of the culture too.

TK: One coin clear, we say.

JS: Tell me about this TV drama.

QtQ: In the drama, the story starts in 1983. It's about people aiming for the best score. So *scorelers*. And it's covering a time period from 1983 to 2013.

TK: I think it's a playback of someone's game history. They're playing *Xevious*, *Pac-man, Dragon Quest II, Super Mario Brothers*... It lists the game names on the back of the flyer. It finishes by saying, "And many other games."

JS: But *Dragon Quest II* was not in game centres.

JR: I think they have to catch the interest of a lot of people, not only arcade fans. Unfortunately if you don't say the word Famicom, people won't even bother taking a look at the drama. So unfortunately I think this is a kind of obligation...

JS: Where did he get the flyer?

QtQ: At the Tokyo Game Show. Two days ago.

JR: The drama starts on 4 October 2013.

QtQ: They asked a real *scoreler* when recording a playthrough of *Pac-man*.

TK: Like a superplay video, for the TV drama.

JR: At the Game Preservation Society we were doing the same. We are calling in some famous *scorelers* to record videos of arcade games. Today we had a plan of recording some Data East games, using QtQ-san.

TK: The drama is on Channel 7, TV Tokyo. They're doing a lot of otaku cultural things, at night. This is on very late, around 00:55 in the morning. So in the middle of the night.

JS: Five minutes to one in the morning?!

JR: Yes. But in Japan it's not really a surprise. Most anime shows are on at this time. At midnight everyone is watching TV in Japan. It's Friday night, so I think many people will watch it. Children are sleeping, there's nothing to do at home, so they're watching TV dramas and anime.

JS: Nothing to do? What about sleeping!?

JR: I think the drama is covering a few people, and it's like a flashback. Their history, their connections to the games. So it's a drama, but the idea is to show old games and old game culture. The importance is not only to show games, but also playing those games. For them it's not only playing good games, but doing good while playing those games. It's like a sport. This is a culture.

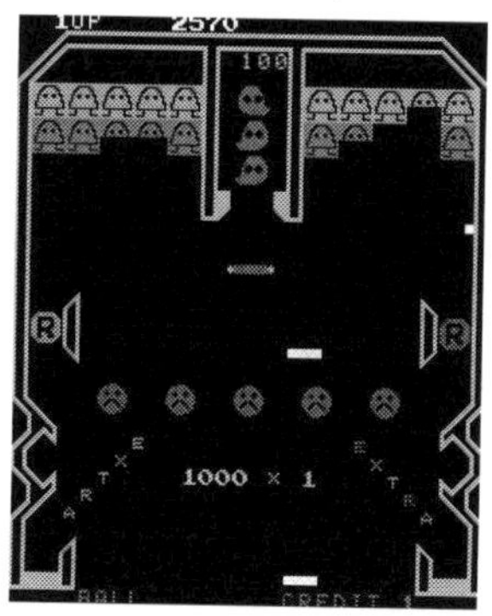

CutieQ by Namco

---
[4] http://wiki.d-addicts.com/No_Con_Kid ; 12 episodes

~*Appearing in a later volume*~

The other side of Japanese games are the players and traders who keep it alive.

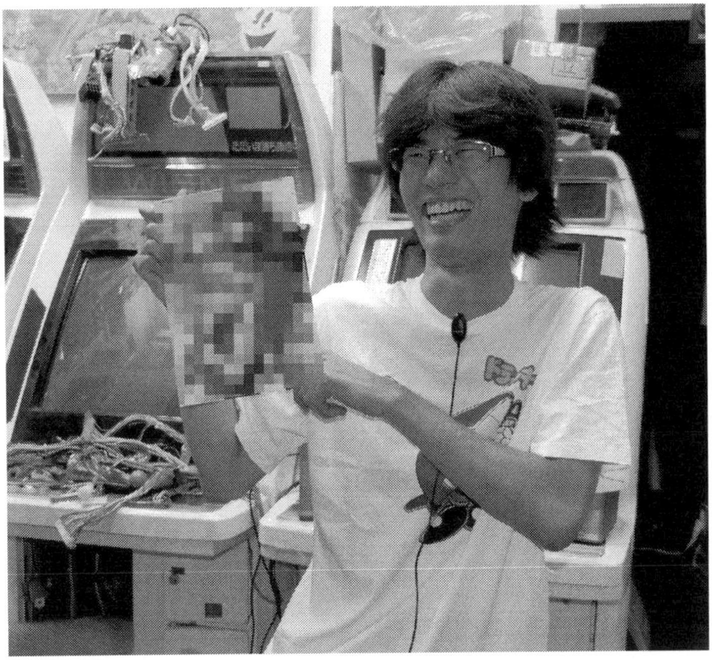

Takayuki Komabayashi
Those who ordered the DVD will recognise Mr Komabayashi from Beep Shop in Saitama. Not only is he an expert on classic videogames, with a truly unbelievable encyclopaedic knowledge of arcade games, but he designed Japan's green variety of bubble wrap, now used on arcade PCBs. He's also a games journalist, writing for *GAMESIDE* magazine, and producing *doujinshi* (pictured). Oh, and he really likes developer ZOOM.

Ryota Akama
Most outside of Japan who read this book probably fall into the category of being fans of Japanese games: we import software and systems, we prefer the original Japanese cover art to Western localisations, we even learn a foreign language to facilitate our hobby. The fascinating inverse of this are Japanese players who prefer American and European games - there was even once a store in Akihabara dedicated solely to non-Japanese games. As a lifelong FPS fan, citing *System Shock 2*, *Deus Ex*, and *S.T.A.L.K.E.R* as personal favourites, Mr Akama offers a unique insight into why these games appeal to a certain hardcore niche in Japan. Is there a quantifiable difference in how different countries approach design? And is there any truth to the phrase *yoge kusoge*?[1] How better to understand your own games, than through the eyes of another...

[1] *Western games are crap games*

尾崎　ロイ

OZAKI, Roy

The official Mitchell Corp website
（株）ミッチェルホームページ
http://www.mitchell.jp/index.htm

Formerly at arcade developers Data East and TAD, Roy Ozaki owns Mitchell Corp, distributor of arcade games for Capcom and developer of many original titles. The following are some of the company's known games. However, there are many title conversions handled by Mitchell Corp (ie: *Street Fighter ZERO 3* for the Saturn), and games they assisted with but were not credited on. Mr Ozaki showed me his games shelf, which he said contained only titles Mitchell Corp were involved in, since publishers would send him copies. Several mysterious items were on this shelf, including *Rockman X2: Soul Eraser* for GBC. Then there's the secret work they did for Nintendo... Sadly, since Nov 2012, the company has been dormant.

"***Mitchell is currently looking for a licensee for our arcade titles. For use on mobile phones, computers, and other devices. The terms would be a limited-time license on ports and sales. We would want to receive royalties as well as advance payment. The following bolded Mitchell arcade games are currently available for licensing. For the titles listed, the arcade PCB, source code, and instruction manual are available. If anyone is interested, we would be happy to discuss matters further.***" **- Roy Ozaki**

Titles in BOLD, prefaced by (*) are available for licensing

* **Funky Jet** / ファンキージェット	- **Arcade, 1992**
* **The Karate Tournament** / チャタンヤラクーシャンク	- **Arcade, 1992**
* **Double Wings** / 雙翼	- **Arcade, 1993**
* **Lady Killer** / 燃えよゴンタ!!	- **Arcade, 1993**
* **Demon Mirage Mahjong** / 妖獣麻雀伝	- **Arcade, 1994**
* **Party Time: Gonta the Diver II** / がんばれゴンタ!!2	- **Arcade, 1995**
* **Diploma** / 卒業証書	- **Arcade, 1995**
* **Charlie Ninja** / チャーリー忍者	- **Arcade, 1995**
* **Osman / Cannon Dancer** / キャノンダンサー	- **Arcade, 1996**
* **Three Engraved Intentions** / 三刻志	- **Arcade, 1996**
* **Gamshara** / 銃武者羅	- **Arcade, 2002**
* **This Good Octopus** / **E**タコ	- **Arcade, 2003**

Rest of the Mitchell portfolio (NOT part of the licensing list)

Mad Motor	- Arcade, 1989
Poker Ladies	- Arcade, 1989
Pang (aka: *Pomping World, Buster Bros*)	- Arcade, 1989
Super Pang (aka: *Super Buster Bros*)	- Arcade, 1990
Super Pang (aka: *Super Buster Bros.*)	- SNES, 1992
Super-X	- Arcade, 1994
Pang! 3	- Arcade, 1995
Buster Bros. Collection	- PlayStation, 1997
Puzz Loop	- Arcade, 1998
Ballistic	- Nuon, PlayStation, GBC; all 2000 / NGPC (unreleased)
Mighty! Pang	- Arcade, 2000
Puzz Loop 2	- Arcade, 2001
Polarium (aka: *Chokkan Hitofude*)	- Nintendo DS, 2004
Polarium Advance (aka: *Tsuukin Hitofude*)	- Game Boy Advance, 2005
Magnetica (aka: *Shunkan Puzzloop, Actionloop*)	- Nintendo DS, 2006
Pang: Magical Michael	- Nintendo DS
Tokyo Crash Mobs (aka: *Gyoretsu Nageloop*)	- Nintendo 3DS eShop, 2012

四井 浩一

YOTSUI, Kouichi

(aka: Isuke - 伊助**)**

DOB: 7 February 1963 / Birthplace: Osaka / Blood Type: B

~ Portfolio ~

The Speed Rumbler (aka: *Rush & Crash*) - Arcade, 1986 (Background artist)

Bionic Commando (aka: *Top Secret*) - Arcade, 1987 (Background artist)

Ghouls 'n Ghosts (aka: *Daimakaimura*) - Arcade, 1988 (Background artist)

Strider Hiryu - Arcade, 1989 (Designer)

Nostalgia 1907 (pictured) - X6800, 1991 (Designer, writer)

The Karate Tournament (aka: *Chatanyarakushank*) - Arcade, 1992 (Designer)

Lady Killer - Arcade, 1993 (Designer)

Cannon Dancer (aka: *Osman*) - Arcade, 1996 (Designer)

Submarine Hunter Shachi - PlayStation, 1999

Suzuki Bakuhatsu - PlayStation, 2000 (Designer)

Drakengard 2 - PlayStation 2, 2005 (Assistant planner)

Otoshi Deka - Nintendo DS, 2008 (Scenario)

Moon Diver - PS3 / X360, 2010 (Designer)

Tokyo Crash Mobs - Nintendo 3DS, 2012

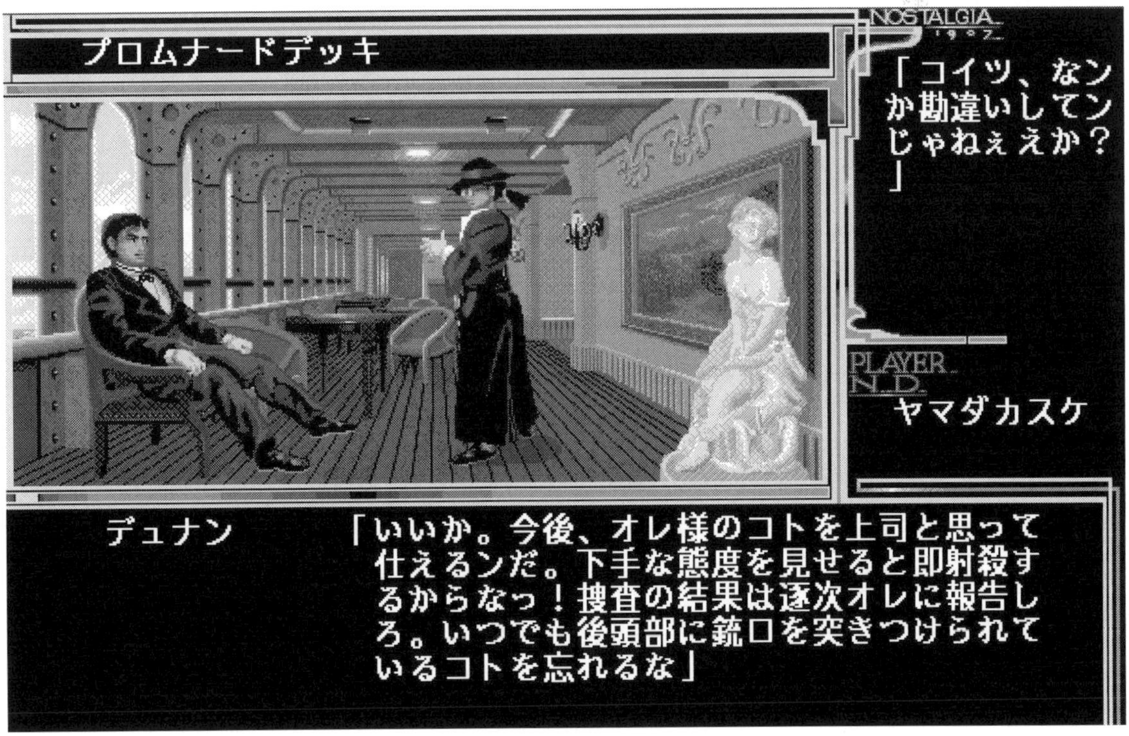

Interview with Roy OZAKI and Kouichi YOTSUI
15 and 16 September 2013, Mt Takao area outside Tokyo

Due to the typhoon approaching Tokyo that day, the stairs at my apartment were wet. I fell down the stairs, slammed my elbow, landed in the gutter so water flowed inside the makeshift coat I'd fashioned out of trash bags, and I smashed my camera stand. So when I met Mr Ozaki I was soaked, dirty, and my equipment didn't work. The plan was to buy a new stand. I also burned my fingers on the stove that morning.

The Roy Ozaki interview took place over two days, using a mixture of video and audio, culminating in around 7 hours of material to transcribe. Conversations took place in the car, at restaurants, at a mountainside inn, and at Mr Ozaki's home. Mr Kouichi Yotsui, creator of Strider, was with us. Mr Ozaki said he would act as interpreter, though I would be interviewing Mr Yotsui again a couple of days later, with a professional interpreter. I regarded the evening as a warm up.

**text with stars* denotes garbled audio and a best guess at what was being said. Mr Ozaki had a stroke several years ago, and admitted he'd lost the ability to enunciate. In some instances I've placed [inaudible], or edited it to remove sections. The roughly 7 hours of audio and video took four days to transcribe.*

The original interview was over 21'400 words, spread over more than 40 pages. To save space, anything unrelated to games or Mr Ozaki's background has been trimmed. The interview no longer runs in chronological fashion either - sections have been moved around.

[Eating inside a soba restaurant at Mt Takao]

John Szczepaniak: You were saying, about your graduate course that you took?

Roy Ozaki: Education of philosophy. I used to be a school teacher, teaching children in high school. I came to Tokyo to go to this school, I didn't have money, and a buddy of mine worked at Data East. At that time Data East was like, compared to Namco's salary, Data East was number one.

JS: What was your role at Data East?

RO: At that time Data East just started making... What do you call it - LaserDisc games? *Cobra Command*, those kinds of games. They paid me pretty well; I wrote the scenario and the voice scenario. I was a voice director. I had no money at all then, and they paid me so well that I quit going to school. Because I speak English, and I can read and write English... Have you heard of Mori Ogai? He's a Japanese writer. He wrote *Takasebune* - it's about this ship that goes up the Kyoto river, and takes criminals to an island off Kyoto. I'm the first one that translated that to English. When I was 19. That was the first time that I got paid for translation - $150. It's only a short story. This is when I learned that if you're in the higher echelons of society you can screw anyone. That's how it is in the USA, that's how it is in Japan. Anywhere is the same! UK is the same.

JS: Where did you learn English?

RO: At international school - I'm bilingual. So I don't know how to translate, but I can switch from English to Japanese to English. That's why I had been an interpreter. You know, one time there was a conference, of USA game machine manufacturers and JAMMA. They used Simul International, who are the best interpreters. They paid something like the price you're paying for your interpreters, but 20 years ago. They had me, in the middle, checking out both English and Japanese. Since I was making so many complaints at the rehearsal, all the interpreters said, "Why don't you do it!"

JS: So did they walk out?

RO: Of course not, it's money. They don't walk out! But there were a lot of problems.

JS: You've also met Nolan Bushnell, I believe? Tell me about this.

RO: Yes! This was five or six years ago. I've had dinner with him a couple of times. He's crazy!

JS: Why?

RO: He's just into *Pong*, and that's all. He doesn't realise that the world has changed. One of my teachers for coin-op sales was *[inaudible - sounds like Joe Turner]* of Bally. He was a sales rep there for a long time. He taught me a lot of things. There's a lot of people who taught me a lot of things. And Nolan Bushnell is not one of them. Did you know that he owned a castle, in France? He used to have parties for all the rich coin-op guys, in this castle. He had a plane - what do you call those planes that land on water?

JS: A seaplane?

RO: And he had two pilots on standby. He'll have a weekend party, and then Sunday lunchtime he'd say, let's go have spaghetti! And they'd fly to Rome, on Sunday, and it's like an hour or two hours, and they'd land in Rome, have lunch and fly back.

JS: Oh yeah, that's the way to live!

[152 words redacted on request]

RO: That's something, you can't find anywhere. And I will deny it!

JS: I can print it, but you'll deny it?

RO: Don't say Roy Ozaki said it!

[Discussion regarding where to take photos - in the restaurant or outside]

RO: Oh, tell them you're a gaijin and they'll let you do it.

[Time passes, we all eat soba]

JS: Please ask Mr Yotsui what he thinks of the new *Strider* game announced recently. Capcom are letting Double-Helix do it.

RO: *<interprets>* He says he hasn't seen it.

JS: They've put videos online.

KY: *<Japanese>* Demo video?

JS: *Hai, so desu, demo video. (Yes, that's right, a demo video.)*

RO: *<interpreting>* A Western fan asked his opinion on it too. At that time, seeing the gravity stage - Yotsui said he wanted to make it!

JS: Is this just hot water? *<points to little kettle placed on table>*

RO: Yes, to water it down to become soup. *<gestures to dipping sauce>* It's not just hot water, they boiled the soba in this water, so it has a soba taste.

<interpreting for KY> He says he doesn't understand why the company that made it - who made *Strider* - [are doing it]. Because *Strider* is not the kind of game where you sell a lot.

JS: Oh, *Strider* was very popular on the Sega Mega Drive, so maybe...

RO: *<interrupts>* But it wasn't a big hit!

JS: In England it was a big hit.

RO: The British are crazy anyway.

JS to KY: *Igirisu-jin ha Strider ga dai suki desu yo. (British people love Strider!)*
In Britain, *Strider* was popular in arcades and when converted to the Mega Drive. It was also ported to computers and sold a lot.

[Brief chat between RO and KY]

RO: *<interpreting>* You know the title *Strider*? That's taken from Tolkein's book.

KY: *Lord of the Rings!*

JS: Oh, *Lord of the Rings!* Yes, the Strider character. Which reminds me, I emailed Mr Yotsui with an idea. In an interview about *Chatan Yara Kuushank*, known as *The Karate Tournament* in English, he came up with the name because: *"I like titles that make absolutely no sense (laughs)."*[1] **Perhaps Mr Yotsui and you could suggest a name for my book, and I'll ask all of my interviewees and then I'll make a decision on it.**

RO: *<interpreting>*

---

[1] Kouichi Yotsui Interview from *GAMESIDE* magazine 2009.02 Vol. 16

KY: *<laughs>*

RO: Titles for games, that's a big headache. The last couple of years I was on a lot of projects with Nintendo. They used a whole legal department, right? Fifty lawyers to check all the names [for games].

JS: Wait, 50 lawyers to check names?

RO: Well, just to show how rich they are. All the lawyers are from Kyoto University. Tokyo University lawyers are the same rank. It's a national university, like Oxford or Cambridge. People don't need 50 lawyers from Kyoto or Tokyo University.

JS: So these lawyers are earning a salary for doing nothing?

RO: Really, that's what I think. To come up with a name, they'd check it. That's why I came up with all these names that were never tested, because I can't afford 50 lawyers checking up on all these things.

JS: So you'd come up with names that are...

RO: Crazy names!

JS: I like crazy names. We should come up with some for my book.

[We finish eating and leave to travel to Roy's home; transcribed using video and audio. Discussion regarding book content]

JS: [...] plus I'm interviewing someone from TecnoSoft.[2]

RO: Technos[3] was not a good company.

JS: I said TecnoSoft, they were different to Technos.

RO: *[inaudible due to rain outside]*... Hoods were mainly involved, money wise.

JS: Funny you say that, I'm travelling to Osaka to interview a guy who from a company apparently funded by gangsters.

RO: All the companies were funded by gangsters.

JS: All of them - including Mitchell Corp?

RO: No.

JS: Because you inherited it from your dad?

RO: No, I started out from scratch.

JS: At Data East?

RO: Right. And I had money, I earned a lot. I was a copywriter, and I had a knack for money. Then there's this guy, *<points>* Yotsui. He made me lose a lot of money. Na?

KY: Eh?

[RO and KY converse in Japanese]

JS: Oh, you mean with *Cannon Dancer*? [4] ***<To Mr Yotsui in Japanese> Don't worry, I really liked Cannon Dancer.***

KY: *Ah, arigatou gozaimasu. <laughs>*

JS: Do you have a *Cannon Dancer* arcade board? I thought we could film it.

RO: I probably do, but I don't have the machine to play it on.

JS: We could emulate it on my laptop. What are your views on emulation of old games?

[2] Also spelled Technosoft

[3] Makers of the Kunio-kun series

[4] Known as *Osman* outside Japan; arcade game similar in mechanics to *Strider*; 100% awesome

RO: You know, I would have owned this whole town, if the [software pirates] didn't copy my games. If they hadn't copied, I would have owned everything, even this steak house *<gestures>*. Everything I made they copied.

KY: *<Japanese> What about beer?*

JS: I thought we'd be on sake all evening.

RO: Well, he wants to start with beer. I got everything you want, whiskey, sake. We'll get to my house and I'll get stuff ready. We're going to cross the dam. I can tell you the whole history of this area.

JS: Have you lived here your whole life?

RO: No, my ancestors. 700 years. Our family must have been really, really rich.

KY: *Ima ha? (Now?)*

RO: Really, really poor.
<Both laugh>

[230 words redacted on request]

JS: I'll publish anything you like.

RO: *<interrupts>* If I say I what I like, I'm gonna get killed!

JS: Is it really that dangerous?

RO: Yes! I could probably get the whole game industry into a lot of trouble.

JS: Maybe things need to be shaken up?

RO: No, not really. This is either the police, or the *<whispers>*. This is very, very dangerous ground. You see, I know all... *<gestures to building>* This shop, most days I'm drunk on the third floor, in the Paradise Cafe.

JS: What's it like in there?

RO: Paradise. [...] From this area onward, it used to be owned by my parents. Socialists took over the government after World War II, and we weren't farmers, but we owned a lot of the land. That's why we had to sell it *dirt cheap* to the farmers! My great uncle was the first mayor of Tokyo, he was in parliament for 63 years. My great cousin, he was a Supreme Court Judge. So I'm the only odd one in my family.

This is the Ozaki Museum *<gesturing to nearby historical building>*. We donated most of the stuff. My family is famous for making democratic movements in Japan. This is what we owned, my family owned. My uncle owned most of it. This is my house.

[Inside I give him Pang for the ZX Spectrum]

JS: The ZX Spectrum is an old British computer, and this version of *Pang* comes on cassette tape. While I researching this I discovered another Spectrum game by Hudson, called *Bubble Buster*, which was a port of a Japanese computer game called *Cannon Ball*. [5] Apparently Mitchell Corp licensed *Cannon Ball* from Hudson?

RO: Hmm? We did pay money, but we did all this hush-hush.

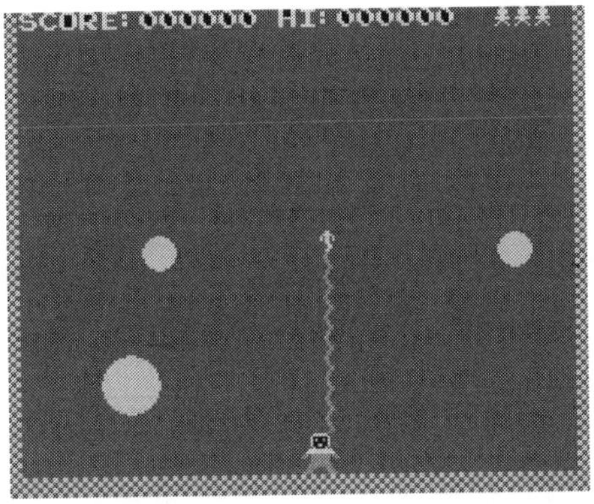

JS: Under the table?

RO: Not under the table. We paid for it legitimately, but there's a company involved in-between, which I don't want to say too much about. Mainly because this is all old time [people]. Either they're gone from the industry or dead now.

[5] Prototype for *Pang*. Spectrum version released 1983. Original Japanese version probably for PC-6001. Also bonus game in *Susanou Densetsu* for PC Engine

JS: Surely then it's important to document it before it's lost?

RO: *<gesturing to shelf of games>* That's all the games that Mitchell Corporation worked on. Most of the games, if you think of *Polarium* or *Magnetica*, they were released by Nintendo. *[inaudible]* ... second party company we used to make games for.

JS: Is that *Rockman X*?

RO: We did the conversion to whatever format that is.

JS: So *Street Fighter Zero 3*, how was Mitchell Corporation connected?

RO: That's for Sega, no?

JS: It was by Capcom, this is for the Saturn.

RO: We just did the conversion for it, the program conversion.

JS: So these games, did you have to buy them, or did the companies send you copies?

RO: These are all complimentary, I don't think I bought anything. I don't play games anyway. If they're open, that means it's my son's, and that I bought it. But I don't think they're open, so... Anyway, most of them were given to us. For instance the European version, and the Japanese version, they sent to us.

JS: That's nice. Speaking to programmers from Konami, they said they had to buy copies of games they worked on.

RO: That's Konami.

JS: Yeah, that IS Konami!

RO: The arcade boards are somewhere else. Actually, I have the boards in the next room. But I also have Nintendo development tools in there, which are top secret. Nintendo will sue me forever if you see that...

JS: Are you still doing work for Nintendo?

RO: No, I told you, my R&D is gone. I can always contact them and get a team together. You give me a day and I'll get everybody together. We're just looking for sponsors.

JS: These British home computer ports of your games, you never received copies?

RO: Oh no, I've never even heard of them.

JS: OK, can we add it to your collection?

RO: Yes, please.

JS: We'll slide it in here, between *Polarium* and *Street Fighter Zero 3*. A nice addition.

[After slotting the gift into Mr Ozaki's collection, he showed two sales awards he received, starting with one from Nova]

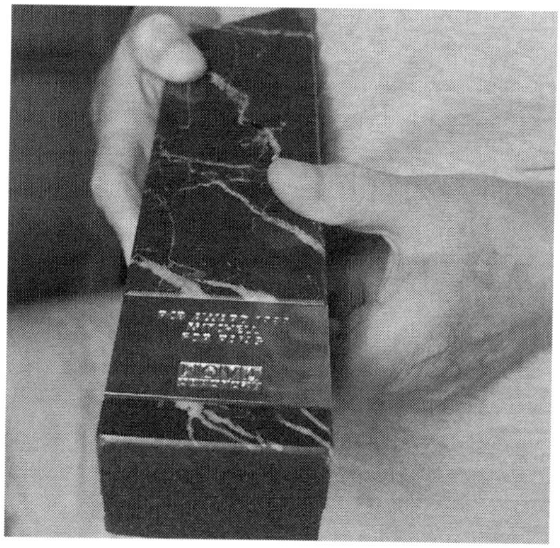

RO: Nova was the biggest importer in Germany. And they sold a lot of *Pang!*

JS: May I see? This says: *"For Award, 1989, Mitchell, for Pang."* That's amazing!

RO: Nova doesn't exist anymore. I'm on the sales side of things, and Nova's vice president before they went bust was the same age as me. So when I was at Data East, I was way at the bottom of the line for sales, and he was at the bottom. So as he went up the ladder, and became a manager and all that, I went up the ladder and then I started my own company. And he was vice president of Nova. That's why sales were very easy. You know, people grow up the same as you.

JS: So his company published *Pang*?

RO: Well, they sold *Pang*. <*gestures*> And this plaque is from Capcom for selling... We were also a distributor for coin-ops for Capcom, and this is... We sold a lot of *Street Fighter* boards and they gave us this.

When Koichi Niida and I started [Mitchell], and we didn't have money, there were six distributors of Capcom games, for coin-ops in Japan. And we were one of the six. Niida and I, we didn't have anything. One month's credit was 50 million yen,[6] right? That's how we started. Then the next year it would be like, 1 million US dollars. After a couple of years it would be 2 million US dollars. ***A month***. In credit. So I can order Capcom products and sell them, 2 million [dollars worth]. Then with *Street Fighter*, we made a lot of money.

JS: You distributed *Street Fighter II*?

RO: And I sold some to the USA. I sold all over the world. Capcom had their own... What was his department? One guy I met, he says, "Roy, you keep doing this, you're going to have the North and South Pole, that's it!" Which meant nowhere. And I said, "You should have known I was selling to all these places I wasn't supposed to!" <*laughs*> And what he told me was, "I knew you were selling to Chile, Los Angeles, and all over the place!"

JS: You were selling to South America when you were not supposed to?

RO: I was selling all over the place!

JS: How did that work? Did you...

RO: <*interrupts*> I had a customer list from all over the world, and one company in Osaka was willing to pay 20 million yen, for the list of my customers. They wanted to - but I didn't it give it to them. So that's why I was offered a place at Capcom.

[I take photo of Mr Ozaki holding Pang. The cat takes a keen interest in the new camera stand; Mr Yotsui tries to coax it over, but the cat ignores him. Mr Yotsui takes out a collection of unused game ideas. He also produces a variety of sketchbooks and other materials. An impressive collection. In addition, I brought out a surprising collection of my own!]

[Mr Yotsui removes from a paper wrapping his original Strider oil painting]

RO: He's good at painting. He painted it at the end of making the game. When making adjustments. He painted it in his office.

JS: Do you still paint today, for recreation?

RO: <*interpreting*> When he takes scripting plans to different companies. He has to put in paintings, and maybe more.

<*Mr Yotsui passes along the script for the Strider manga, along with the manga*>

[6] about $350k / £200k in 1991 (fxtop.com)

RO: *<interpreting>* He and **Masahiko Kurokawa**[7] wrote one each - one script each. This one is Yotsui's script.

JS: And then the two stories were placed inside the manga?

RO: *<interpreting>* Motomiya Productions' scenario writer did the final one.

[Shows original early script documents for Strider - implication is it's different to what's in the final game]

RO: For *Strider*, the real script, I think it's at Capcom. That's his very original version.

JS: His first draft?

RO: Right.

[I show Mr Yotsui some Capcom related photos I was given by another interviewee]

KY: Where did you get those?!

JS: One of my other interviewees gave me copies, after I told him I was interviewing you. *<name removed>* passes on his regards.

RO: *<interpreting>* He says he very surprised to see these - they're very nostalgic for him.

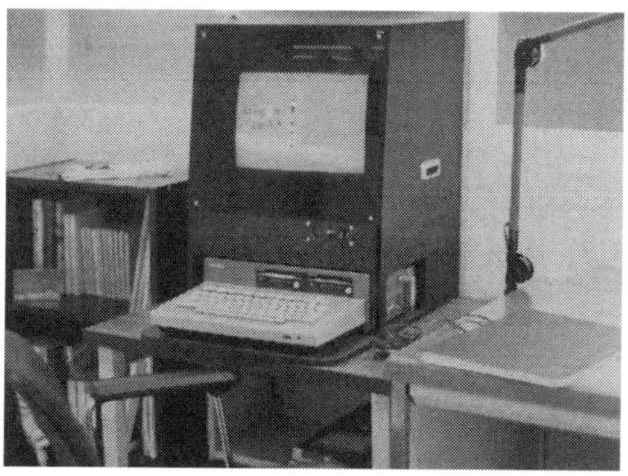

Capcom's hardware for making pixel art.

KY: There was one, one, one. *<gestures how they were lined up in rows>*. This is from *Rush & Crash.* (*The Speed Rumbler*)

JS: It has Sony written on it.

KY: *Sony? Honto da ne.*
(Sony? Yeah, so it does.)

JS: Does Mr Yotsui recognise everyone in the photos I brought with me?

From left: Akira Kitamura *(Megaman)* / Kouichi Yotsui / Tokuro Fujiwara *(Ghosts 'n' Goblins)* / Hiroshi Matsumoto *(Art of Fighting)* / Tomoshi Sadamoto *(Magic Sword)* / Takashi Nishiyama *(Street Fighter*, SNK, DIMPS). 18 January 1987

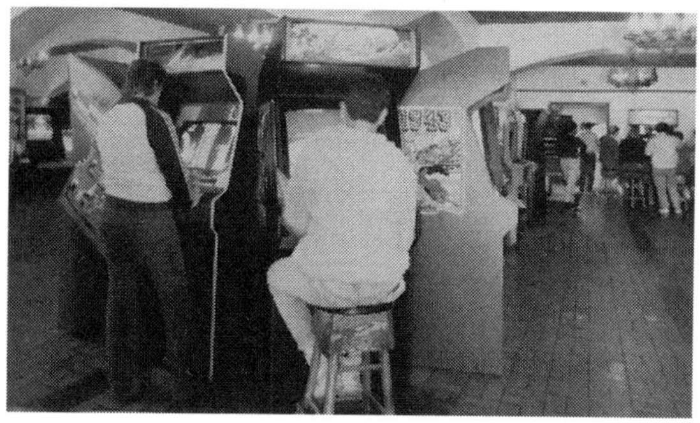

KY: The first location test for *Strider*. This is Nishitani-kun, planner for *Street Fighter II* *<seated man: Akira Nishitani>*

From left: Tokuro Fujiwara / Kento Hasegawa *(Bionic Commando)* / Kouichi Yotsui / Kenshi Naruse (Ukiyotei[8] founder) / Akira Yasuda *(Street Fighter II)*

---

[7] AKA Patariro; designed FC version of *Strider*, lots of other games; since passed away

[8] Development company behind *Hook* and *Skyblazer*, plus *Metal Slug* on NGPC

KY: On the far right is Inafune-kun when he was younger. He was our junior.

<Author shows photos of a woman - request made not to print these>

KY: That's Inafune-kun's wife, who did the graphics on *Strider*.

JS: Is this a Capcom company vacation?

KY: This is now the Capcom president. *<points to man circled>*

JS: I contacted Capcom, but they didn't want anyone visiting. They're very reclusive.

RO: The president is like that. That guy there. *<points to photo>*

JS: Who's this man smoking a cigarette?

KY: Shinichi Yoshimoto.[9]

JS: And the story behind this photo of everyone practicing martial arts in the water?

KY: *<laughs loudly>* I have no idea!

<Mr Yotsui takes out his own photo, from his days as a student>

JS: Does Mr Yotsui (circled) still have his original films, that he made as a student?

RO: *<interpreting>* Yes he does. But he's too embarrassed to show anybody.

KY: *<laughs>*

JS: *<with Suzuki Bakuhatsu sketch book>* Friends and I would import Japanese games on eBay. This was popular among friends because it was so unusual. [10]

RO: *<interpreting>* You don't need Japanese to play it.

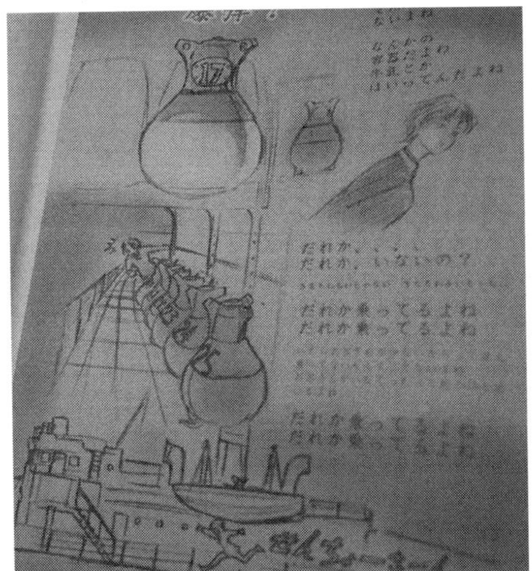

JS: Exactly. Is this the original story design?

RO: *<interpreting>* He brought *Suzuki Bakuhatsu*, when he wanted to sell the game, to Enix. That's what he brought as a presentation.

---

9 Credited on: *Ghouls 'n' Ghosts, Little Samson,* photo not shown due to lack of space

10 Puzzler where a woman defuses bombs found in everyday objects; first level is an orange

JS: This is the original concept document! Am I noticing a trend? There were also explosives hidden away in *Nostalgia 1907*.[11]

RO: *<interpreting>* *Nostalgia 1907* was more story oriented, that's why he wanted more action in this one. So he took the diffusing the bomb part, and put all of that into *Suzuki Bakuhatsu*. In the end Enix liked the main thing he brought, and then he was talking to the producers and then it became that. *<gestures>*

JS: It's amusing that when saving your data a sign flashes towards the screen and says to push either left or right, but it moves so quickly you're not able to see it in time.

RO: *<interpreting>* He said, I thought it was fun too - that's why I put it in! *<laughs>* He liked that feature, but Sony has all these...

JS: Regulations?

KY: *Regulations, right, right, right.*

RO: Sony has regulations, but even so he passed.

JS: He managed to sneak it through?

RO: Sneak it through!

KY: *<Japanese - mentions sekaikan>*

JS: Ah, *sekaikan*! The feeling of atmosphere!

RO: That's all contained in the writing.

JS: What are these? *<picks up dossiers>*

RO: Designs for games nobody bought.

JS: Unreleased games! We have to film them! Was this an action or a puzzle game?

KY: An action game. Actually, it was an action-puzzle game.

JS to RO: Has Mr Yotsui ever considered creating these games independently, for example on an iOS device?

RO: *<personal view, not interpretation>* Look, either way, you need money to make it, right? So if nobody backs it, he doesn't have the money to make it.

JS: Have you heard of Kickstarter?

RO: I know about it. A lot of people suggest it, but that's no good. As a businessman, I would say no. *<interprets question to KY>*

JS: Because Keiji Inafune's *Mighty No. 9* project got a lot of support.

KY: *<laughs - speaks Japanese>*

RO: He's laughing because he says that when translating what you're saying, I also gave him my opinion on Kickstarter, and I don't like it. That's what he's telling me, "You're not translating properly."

JS to RO: Have you heard of *Mighty No. 9*? Inafune wanted to make another *Megaman* game, and Capcom wouldn't let him, so he left and started Comcept. He put his idea on Kickstarter, and he received a lot of funding.

RO: But Capcom has the rights, how can he pitch an idea?

JS: Oh, he's not pitching *Megaman*, he's pitching a game which is only similar.

RO: That, he can get screwed for!

JS: It's different enough to be OK.

RO: Capcom is probably getting ready. Capcom's chairman loves to do that.

[11] Adventure game set in 1907 on a luxury liner

JS: <*gesturing at folders*> People will be excited to see these concept documents.

<*RO and KY converse*>

RO: He says, "Is this interesting?" He's got ***millions*** of them at home.

JS: Millions of unreleased games?

<*everyone laughs*>

KY: No, many are saved on PC.

JS: Cool. If you can't use them, perhaps put them into a book and sell it on Amazon: *The Unused Ideas of Kouichi Yotsui*.

RO: Who is going to buy it?

JS: I'd buy it! I would buy a copy of that.

RO: One is not enough.

JS: My editor, Darran Jones, would buy it.

RO: You fools!

KY: <*laughs*>

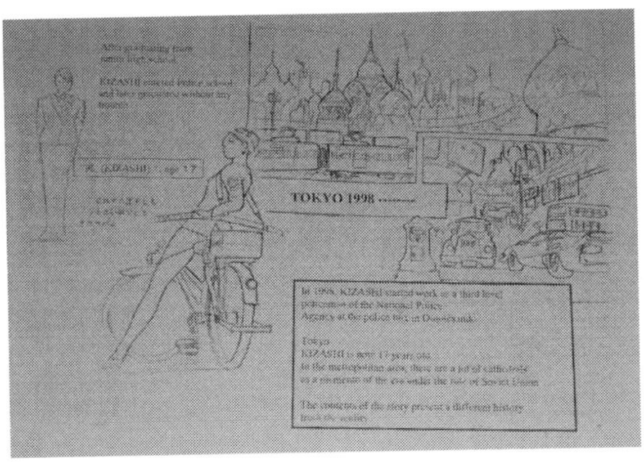

JS: This game, *Subway 20*, is from 2001? [12]

KY: Yes, 2001, but I probably wrote it two years before that.

JS: It looks incredible, like a Treasure game! It's all about very precise timing for attacks.

RO: <*phones ryokan*> He'll be here soon.

JS: I'll pack up my gear. <*notices another dossier*> Is this another unreleased game?

RO: <*interpreting*> Another unsold game.

KY: Car action!

JS: Ahh, two jets hurtling towards a car?[13]

RO: <*interpreting*> You don't use a steering wheel to control the car.

KY: For PlayStation 2. <*Japanese*> *Right analogue stick, danger; left stick, safety.* <*makes sound effects: don don don*>

JS to RO: What was that?

RO: How to operate the game. If you keep turning the left one around, you'll be speeding into the danger zone. And if you keep turning the right one you get into the safe zone.

JS: Is this Godzilla?

KY: It's not Godzilla, it's Jaws!

JS: Oh, he's being chased by a shark!

[12] Fantastic looking action game with a female samurai

[13] This game also looked insanely awesome. There should be images on the accompanying DVD.

Further discussion took place at the ryokan, enjoying a meal of fresh river fish and sake - Mr Ozaki interpreted for Mr Yotsui, though I suspect he mixed in his own views on topics. Consider him more of an unpredictable narrator. The word consumer is sometimes replaced with console

KY: *<Japanese - explanation regarding Capcom, Akira Kitamura, Famicom>*

RO: Almost three sections were making arcade and console stuff. Later on it was divided between arcades and console. Kitamura was in section two. And he did *Megaman* for consoles because he wasn't liked by his bosses. He's a strange guy - real strange. He screwed me a lot of times. And I thought I saw through him, but I didn't I guess. Basically he has a weak personality. He has talent, but he's weak. He doesn't know how to use the people who do graphics or... He just can't get on with people. So while he was at Capcom, and they had console and arcade staff, they made him do console, because nobody wanted him.

KY: *<Japanese - arcade/console sections>*

RO: Right around that time, Capcom stopped the sections one, two and three, and divided it into coin-op and console.

KY: *<Fujiwara-san, console, Okamoto-san, coin-op, Nishiyama-san, Sakai-san>*

RO: Tokuro Fujiwara became the chief of the console division - Fujiwara used to be chief of section one. And Yoshiki Okamoto became chief of coin-ops. And Takashi Nishiyama from DIMPS became chief of all the sections... Chief of R&D. You know Akio Sakai?

JS: No, what did he work on?

RO: He didn't work on anything!

KY: *FF no eiga producer. (Final Fantasy movie producer)*

RO: Later on I think he quit Capcom and joined...

KY: Square.

RO: Square! And he was a producer for the [*Final Fantasy*] movie, which was a flop. He died though.

JS: He died?!

KY: Mm... *<confirms>*

JS: Oh right... When was this?

RO: Yotsui killed him.

KY: Iya, iya. *<dismissing the statement>* -

<Long talk on Nishiyama-san, SNK>

RO: And Nishiyama, he wasn't having it. He wasn't having a good time at Capcom. Then SNK told him to come over, and he went.

KY: *<Japanese - Akira Kitamura, new console division, Fujiwara-san, Rockman>*

RO: Kitamura wanted to make *Rockman 2*, but Fujiwara wouldn't allow it. They weren't getting along. That's why he left.

KY: *<Fujiwara-san, Sakai-san, giri giri de>*

[RO and KY converse]

RO: Kitamura wanted to make *Rockman 2*, Fujiwara always said no. But Sakai said: "You know, Kitamura got a pretty good hit with *Rockman 1*, so let him make it." So Kitamura started making it, and then he got pulled into *[inaudible]* Nishiyama-san. Then he went to SNK, then he went to Takeru.

JS: Oh yeah, together they all worked on *Little Samson / Serei Densetsu Lickle*.

[RO and KY have long conversation]

RO: I know only the business side of this story. All this stuff is from the R&D side, I only know the business side.

JS: I wanted to ask about R&D. One of my Guest Editor's is a fan of *Pang*, and when he got married he and his wife were considering going on a holiday, visiting all the locations featured in *Pang*. He sent questions about Mitchell.

RO: Mitchell Corp is a big question. *<laughs>* - *<interprets for KY >*

JS: I've got a lapel microphone, would you like to wear it when speaking?

RO: Some things you don't need to hear!

JS: OK... Your most enduring game series is *Pang*, or *Buster Brothers / Pomping World*. Did you have any idea when you created the first version in 1989 that new versions would still be released some 20 years later.

RO: No. Games, it's the times. Nobody has the *[inaudible]*. *<points to KY>* He made a game. It's luck, it's all luck. There's a mixture of a lot of factors, when we got a hit. Like *Strider*, I think it's a pretty good game. It's a bit of a tragedy, it should have done better. He just didn't have the luck.

JS: I think it did well in home conversions.

RO: No, not too much. I don't think so.

JS: How did the *Bubble Buster / Cannon Ball* connection come about with *Pang*?

RO: No, that's got a whole bunch of people involved. *Cannon Ball*, that's not Hudson, that's Namco...

JS: Oh, so Namco made the original?

RO: It's a whole bunch of people involved. I really don't want to talk about it!

JS: Let's discuss *Puzz Loop / Ballistic*, which spawned numerous versions. Not just impostors like *Zuma* from PopCap Games, and *Luxor* from Mumbo Jumbo, but also your own *Minna de Puzzloop / Magnetica* and *Tokyo Crash Mobs*. How did you add new elements to the gameplay with each version while also keeping the simplicity of the concept, and making it feel new?

RO: *<coughs>* I'm not the one who makes it. I just play it - is it fun, or no fun? That's all, for me. For *Tokyo Crash Mobs*, Yotsui got involved. This is the last one of our games. It's *Puzz Loop*, people version. It uses real people. All the photography direction was done by Yotsui. So that's for 3DS. It's a download, pay 700 yen and you can buy it.

JS: I haven't bought a 3DS, because Nintendo put region locking on it. What do you think?

RO: That's to get more sales. You see, Nintendo is a hardware company. They want more people to buy their hardware.

JS: So you think it's deliberate, to encourage people to buy multiple machines?

RO: Yes. Nintendo has a lot of Kyoto University graduates. So you've got the best brains in there. As a matter of fact, I'm on pretty good terms with the guy that comes out with those kind of ideas for Nintendo.

JS: Really? Who is the guy?

RO: Higashiyama? I don't know, they're like banks. Every three years or so they move. Anyway, Higashiyama really helped us a lot. With a lot of things. Really nice guy.

JS: So Higashiyama came up with the idea to region-lock the 3DS?

RO: Probably, it's all on consensus.

JS: Regarding Mitchell's games, do you leave the finer details to R&D?

RO: I'm not a gamer; I'm not a creator. For instance, this guy's got more talent than me, for sure. *<points to KY>* He looks at one thing... Let's say he looks at a cup, *<places cup in central position on table>* or he looks at a drawing from a totally different angle from me. I look at it from the business side. If I left it up to him, it would be a good game but we won't have money.

JS: So what do you feel are one of the aspects which allow you to make money?

RO: I have a feeling for the market, that's all. I didn't study marketing, I didn't study pricing. I didn't major in all that at college, I majored in history. That's life. That's a game also. Like Kitamura's *Rockman*, all the sales guys said, "No, it won't sell!" And he begged the Capcom vice president at that time *[inaudible]*. And he said, "OK, we'll try and sell it." And it sold! Much more than they thought. That's what the French say - *ce la vie*.

JS: That's life.

RO: With games, you don't even know *[inaudible]*. Like *Puzz Loop*, if you're in the game business, you ***know***. It's very simple, it's the basic logic of a puzzle game. Can I tell you this story? I was introduced to a Hong Kong distributor, this guy has a market into China. Which I was told was very big. But I didn't have a market into China. So this guy introduces me at the Japanese show, to this Chinese guy. So I sit down and talk to the guy, and I've got photographs of *Puzz Loop*. I show it to him. The guy says, "I know this game! I sold 10'000." But I hadn't sold a single board to Hong Kong!

JS: So they copied it?

RO: No, no. It was a copy from Korea. He bought copies from Korea. We already had a Korean company fitted out. So the guy sold 10'000, whereas I didn't sell one.

There were more bootleg copies of *Pang* sold than the legitimate version. With *Puzz Loop*,

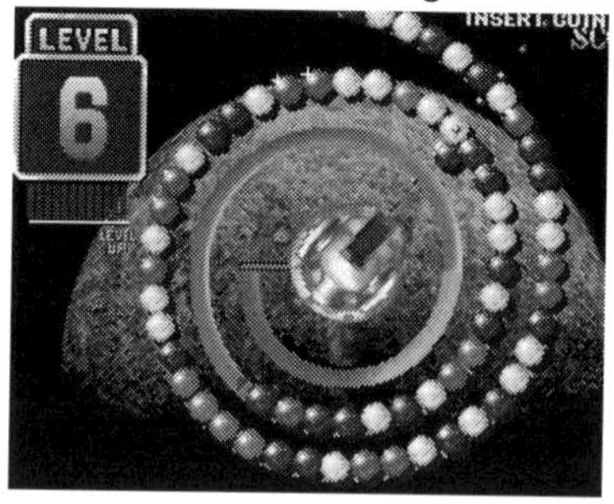

(left) there were more copies sold than the original. I can't believe the Americans, with *Zuma* and, what do you call it?

JS: *Zuma* and *Luxor*. There was a court case, wasn't there?

RO: No, I didn't bring it to court. But in the end, that's Americans for you. That's what I said in interviews. If I bring it to court? I have to spend all the money on lawyers in the USA, to bring them. All those *Zuma* (below) guys and everybody to court. And you know what? *Zuma*

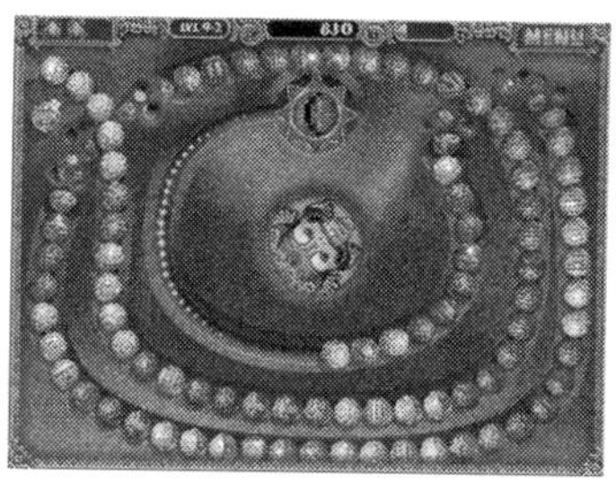

is out on Nintendo DS. Why? Because PopCap games was bought by Electronic Arts. So, Electronic Arts brings *Zuma* on DS to Nintendo USA, and they put it right out. That pisses right on me! You may quote me on that!

JS: Nintendo screwed you over.

RO: But they won't fuck EA, because EA is big. It has games. And I asked them, "Why are you doing this to me?" *And then I got a reply from *[inaudible]*.* I couldn't post it to people on the Japanese side, because they know it's the same company tied up with *[inaudible]*. I'm pissed off at that!

JS: I thought you had a successful relationship with Nintendo. In an interview, you said you liked the way Nintendo Japan...

RO: But are they Nintendo USA? I told them, this is morally wrong, what they're doing. So they can screw me, but this is morally wrong. Ethics!

So you still want me to quote Nietzsche or anything, I can do that. This is business! Anything in life, it concerns ethics! You don't cheat people and then keep making money. That's not fair. And you can quote me on that. I'm pretty pissed off at all this. Especially with the Americans.

JS: The question is, if *Puzz Loop* was published by Capcom, or Infogrames, how come they didn't help with the legal process against PopCap games? Surely Capcom would have had your back, if not Nintendo?

RO: I'd like to remain independent. I'd like Mitchell Corp to be independent. That's why I don't borrow money from banks.

JS: So if you'd relied on Capcom's help, it would have compromised your freedom?

RO: What was that well known saying? "Nothing comes free."

JS: They would have retained the rights or...

RO: *<interrupts>* They would for sure! But Mr Tsujimoto Snr, the founder and chairman, he liked me. He was real nice to me when I started out. And Capcom wanted me. I remember that time, I was an ace salesman in coin-op. But nothing comes for free.

JS: When your R&D department is developing these puzzle games, do you have an influence on the difficulty?

RO: Before I had a stroke I could... But you know, it's just an oh-point-one (0.1) second difference that makes it. So I watch a lot of people play, but I don't play it myself. These past couple of... Five or six years?

JS: Do you tell your staff to make it easy, to attract more people? Or do you let them do as they see fit?

RO: For consumer games, I don't... Well, they know that if you want to sell, it has to be really good. We have a lot of people try it out and see if it's fun or not.

JS: Oh, like focus testing?

RO: As a matter of fact, one section of Nintendo are in charge of us. They bring it inside Nintendo... They don't usually tell who developed it, but they let people try it out. What was it, *Polarium*? It's a completely different business section of Nintendo. There was a big push. So Nintendo's R&D section that's in charge of us, brought it to the business section. Nintendo is a big company, there's about 100 people in that section, and they just left it in there for people to play. A lot of girls were playing the game. That's when they decided to make a lot of it.

JS: It appealed to the female market.

RO: And then once it was out on the market - BOOM. It went.

JS: How many sales did it have?

RO: I won't tell you, but it was big. Much more than what people think. A lot of interviewers ask "did it sell this much" and I say no, usually it's much, much more than people think. It really is a good game.

<speaks Japanese to KY>

KY: *So desu ne! <laughs> (That's right!)*

RO: I asked him - don't you think that *Polarium* was a good game? And he said that's right! He would never say no to me.

JS: *<laughs>* Over the years you were closely affiliated with both Capcom and Nintendo, how did the relationships vary? Any interesting stories?

RO: When I dropped out of TAD[1] and all that, Capcom's chairman, president and chairman, was very good to me. The present president, he doesn't like me.

JS: The current president? That's the gentleman in the skiing photo.

RO: Yotsui's friends are all [wiseguys].

<RO and KY converse - KY laughs>

[1] Arcade developer, known for *Toki*

RO: He said I'm a big liar. He said to me, are you a liar? I said yes. I said, I will never tell the truth to a writer.

JS: <*raucous laughter*> Are you telling me the truth when you tell me that?

[RO and KY converse - pachinko is mentioned]

JS: Did you say pachinko?

RO: I used to make a lot of money - the pachinko business is not good these days.

JS: Because it's become pachislots instead?

RO: That's not good either.

JS: I always wanted to try pachinko.

RO: It's no good. I used to make money, before. Gangsters used to run it. Now it's the police. It became legal, then it's the police who run it.

JS: Your final arcade game was *Kono e-Tako* in 2003, shortly before you transitioned to being a Nintendo third-party developer. Were these two events related? Was the arcade scene winding down, and you had to shift your business?

RO: Right! Basically what you're saying is right. Arcades are down all over the world. And Nintendo wanted to tie up with us. So we went along with them.

JS: And it was more profitable than...

RO: Arcade games were not selling.

JS: Was your source of profit purely the selling of machines to distributors. Because any money made in the machines goes to the owners of those machines.

RO: Yes, when you put it that way. Yeah.

JS: Is that why Taito started up arcade centres, to cut out the middle-man and profit directly from their games?

RO: One time, running an arcade was very profitable. That's why Taito had a lot of arcades. So did Namco. So did Sega. So when Square-Enix tied up with Taito, it was the wrong time.

JS: Do you know Taito was working on a home console, called the Taito WoWoW?[2]

RO: No.

JS: Yes. You know the WoWoW satellite company? Taito partnered with them and prototyped the WoWoW console.

RO: In the arcade business, the platform always changes. When I got into arcade games it was *Taito over Sega*. And then Sega took the top, and then Namco took the top, and Data East was getting there but the president wasn't interested in games. That's why Data East screwed up. Data East had good people but the president didn't want to put money into games. He wanted to do something else.

[RO and KY converse a lot about Taito - from an adjacent room a string instrument can be heard playing]

RO: That's the innkeeper playing. I think he went to school to play music. That's how I know him.

JS: This is a big house, isn't it?

KY: It's a good house.

JS: It's got a good atmosphere.

KY: Yes, a good atmosphere! In Osaka, the house I was born in, was like this.

RO: Did you like this? <*gestures to food*> I've never seen these in any other countries outside of Japan. These are like scallions.[3]

JS: So, over the years, has the R&D department at Mitchell Corp developed anything which was never released?

RO: Many!

JS: Could you tell me about some of them?

RO: I don't remember.

---

[2] 16-bit CD-ROM system with satellite connectivity; joint venture between JSB, Taito and ASCII, shown at 1992 Tokyo Game Show

[3] The small onion-like vegetable had a strong pungent flavour, partly countering the effects of the alcohol, if only temporarily

JS: Do you still have the prototypes?

RO: Maybe, or maybe not, I don't know.

JS: We should go through and film all of them, for historical posterity.

RO: I'm supposed to have the scenarios, with the graphics and stuff. I'm supposed to have all that, but I didn't go through it. It's in the box somewhere in my closet.

JS: Can you recall even one title?

RO: I don't remember anything.

JS: It must be expensive to invest in R&D and then not release it.

RO: Alright, alright! Let me tell you the process. The main process is, the guys that are game designers, they come up with new ideas, maybe more graphics, and then there are some programmers in my company that are good at producing games. *<coughs>* My VP and a couple of other people, we have like six people in a meeting, and if we think it's worth brushing it up, we'll tell them to come next week again. Don't do other stuff - keep concentrating on this. Some people *may have better ideas than others, and we'll say, go around designing whatever you want.* We'll try to help them then. When they come back a week later or so, we'll really think it's good. We'll do the presentation to Nintendo, that's when we want to get the money. Because we have to... Just to make the first demonstration, that's going to take us a couple of months.

JS: What kind of demonstration?

RO: Demos. For the DS. That will take us three months or so. We need to survive on that. We want to ask for money. Most companies try to borrow money from banks, I don't. I don't believe in that. Actually, more times than not, it's like pay a buck... Right now, there's a story on [Japanese TV], a drama, about how corrupt the banks are. Right now it's on Channel 6. It's a big hit.

[RO talks to KY about the TV series, and whether it comes on at 8 or 9pm]

JS: You were saying about interpreters, earlier. What was the going rate?

RO: No, I don't know. I've never used an interpreter - but for anything I say in English I need an interpreter. Nobody understands me. I speak in Japanese, and nobody understands me. I guess I lost the power to enunciate things. Let me tell you this story! *<laughs>* You know Niida, my partner?

JS: Yes, Koichi Niida.

RO: We are supposed to be the only company that... In Japanese there is "*O hyaku-do mairi*", it means go to the temple 100 times to get what you want. So, in the game business you go to Nintendo 100 times, to beg for help. Everybody does that. I never did that. They came to us, for *Puzz Loop*. That's how we started all this. Then they saw *Polarium* when they were checking it out. They came and said let's join together. Because we come up with hits once in a while. So anyway, we started doing business together, and there was one point that we weren't going along with Nintendo, so this is business, strictly not the games, but business, OK?

So my partner and I, we went to Nintendo in Kyoto. We were talking, so I'm the president of Mitchell, right? So Nintendo, they have like a hundred meeting rooms you go to. With the level of the room, like if there was just a desk and a chair, then you're not that important to them. So Niida and I went in, and we got this fluffy armchair. *<laughs>* So we're like this, *<describes their posture by sitting back comfortably in his chair>* right? And you know how I can't get up, so... I was just out of the hospital and I wasn't talking like this, it was much worse. I was spitting a lot. So Nintendo people are very, very polite. So these three business people are in front of me, right? They're all in suits like this, and we're in suits like this, Niida and I. So I get up and I start talking. They're very polite, you gotta realise that. They actually listen to what I'm saying, they had to report it to the chairman or whatever. But I'm mumbling and all that, and they can't hear me. So they're on that side, and they go like this, *<leans forward and moves to edge of seat>* to listen to me. They go like this and I'm spitting like hell. *<laughs>* So they go like this. *<leans back in chair>* For two hours it was like this! *<laughs>*

JS: <*laughs*> Back and forth!

RO: And Niida was laughing all the way through! So that's the whole story.

JS: And you got the deal?

RO: I knew we'd get it. I spent train fare, bullet train fare, to Kyoto, and taxi from Kyoto station to Nintendo office. And I showed them how sick I was.

JS: And this was for *Polarium*?

RO: No, no. That's completely different. The game deals like that I don't... I'm not *a bastard*. I'm pretty fair with business. So we just disagreed on a point we wanted to do in business - this is strictly business. Nintendo's R&D side were very helpful to us. Whereas Capcom's business side, was very, ***very*** helpful to me. But the R&D side, his bosses, <*gestures to KY*> they were all [jokers].

JS: He won't know if I publish it in English.

RO: He'll know. All the people I hang out with, whatever I say about them, they would understand. <*laughs*>. So whatever I say to you in English, he understands. <*gestures to KY*> He doesn't need an interpreter. Like my partner Niida, he's been with me for years, he went around Europe, he went around the USA, he went to a lot of places with me. He used to have meetings with Americans, or British, or whatever. He's with me all the time, he knows what I say. I just pretend that I'm translating. I say, give me a minute I have to explain to him. I don't have to explain to Niida! <*laughs*> He knows what I'm thinking - I need time to think, but I don't want the opponent to know that. So the best way is to say, let me translate, I can't make a decision on my own. My partner doesn't give a shit. <*laughs*>

JS: So what kind of role does Mr Niida play at Mitchell Corp?

RO: Fifty, fifty.

JS: He was VP - Vice President and...

RO: No. That's just a matter of... See, a company can have two managing directors. It doesn't matter. So long as you're independent it doesn't matter. You just have to go to two people to get the seals and signatures and all that bullshit. So we just made him... I happen to be a year or two older than him, so he said, "Why don't you be the president?" I said I don't want to be. He said, "I won't run away," so I became the president.

JS: You inherited Mitchell from your dad?

RO: We didn't want the company, both of us. But my father was already dead. He didn't leave any money to run the company. My mom said, "Do you want to run the company?" No! It was involved in the shipping business, and that wasn't for me.

Ship building, I should say. Do you know a wood called *Lignum Vitae*? It's the heaviest wood. It contains oil, and it only grows about this high. <*gestures with hand*> It grows in central America. Guatemala, Cuba, that area. What my father was doing was, he brought in all that from Guatemala, and he had a factory, in Kobe. *[... Long explanation on wooden ball bearings, and how the oil in the wood prevents corrosion ...]* All ships, from small sized fishing boats to big tankers, they used these *Lignum Vitae* ball bearings. Then the shipping industry moved out and went to Sweden or somewhere. Anyway, that's when my father quit, and he died anyway. That's when I started out as a business major. I realised the first year I wasn't meant for business. But I ***was***! That, I would find out much later. I didn't think I was good at business, and I was more interested in other stuff, so I got into history. But anyway, I studied business. Then when I found myself at Data East I could sell more than anybody in the company.

JS: What did that process involve? You were selling manufactured arcade boards?

RO: My biggest customer in the UK was John Stergides, Electrocoin, in London. Brent Leisure. They were my big customers.

JS: And they'd order a thousand units?

RO: No, arcade units are in hundreds. And John Stergides happened to be the same age as me. Do you know Electrocoin? They built the biggest outfit. John started out as an engineering student in the UK. He emigrated from Greece.

JS: So, the doors of Mitchell Corp were closed on 20 November 2012. Will they ever re-open? What's going to happen to your back catalogue of games?

RO: Mitchell ***is*** open, it's never closed. It's just the R&D is closed. If Yotsui comes out with a good idea, we'll start. It's up to me to look for money, and when he's not greedy we'll start developing again.

[Mr Ozaki's phone rings, it's his son]

RO: ***The typhoon is coming!***

[Wind and rain outside builds up tremendously. Everyone moves to have a group photo taken]

RO: I think we're going to float down the river![4]

[Some opening dialogue was lost before a new recording was started. We were discussing Mitchell's Lady Killer[5]]

RO: <*Referring to KY*> He's better than most graphics people. And you should see the original graphics for *Lady Killer!* It's so embarrassing now, you couldn't see it done.

JS: Lot's of beautiful, naked women?

RO: No. They were all good looking but... Ugh... It was too dirty. You couldn't sell it on 42nd Street. So he put in, just for example, an extra stage. You complete all the stages and then you get an extra stage. There was a girl, sitting on a speaker - you know, a sound speaker - tits bouncing around! And! On top of that, a snake going around her.

JS: Well, nothing wrong with that, if that's what you like.

RO: No, no, for a game company to do that... I mean you gotta have pretty big balls to do that. And that was his idea for a good game. No wonder I...

[Everyone is served warm sake]

[KY explains his game, Subway 20, in Japanese - only partially understood - it features a parallel history with samurai]

RO: <*interpreting*> In foreign countries, the samurai have a certain identity that foreigners put to... What Yotsui wants to say is, in Japan the samurai, during different periods, it's a different rank. During the Edo period it's... <*trails off*>

[RO and KY converse - long discussion about samurai left uninterrupted]

RO: <*laughs*> That's why I don't get paid as an interpreter!

JS: We're doing OK. We just need a few more drinks!

[RO and KY discuss the plan for Tuesday - Mr Yotsui's second interview would take place at Westone, with Ryuichi Nishizawa]

JS: I wanted to ask, how Mr Yotsui first met Mr Nishizawa?

RO: <*interpreting*> Kogure[6] introduced him to Nishizawa. How old is Nishizawa? Yotsui is 48. He said he's probably one year higher or lower.

KY: *Eh?* <*Speaks in Japanese*>

RO: <*laughs*> He's already 50, I didn't know that. He says, I'm more or less the same age as him. <*to the author*> You're not drinking at all.

JS: I am![7] [...] Anyway, throughout your years in the industry, have you ever looked at somebody else's game and thought to yourself: "I wish we had made that."

RO: *[inaudible]* We didn't come out with good things. We didn't have that many good things.

JS: I thought Mitchell Corp had quite a few high quality games. What about *Gamshara*?[8]

RO: *Gamshara* was not good.

---

[4] Although we were close to the river, this was said somewhat jokingly

[5] An interesting twist on the nude "pin-up" genre, you need to dive underwater and flip panels

[6] Takashi Kogure, former Capcom pixel artist

[7] Actually, I was not drinking - I stuck to the small sake cups to stay sober

[8] An arcade 3D shoot-em-up

JS: It interests me, because it hasn't been emulated. You can only play it in arcades. I also like the pseudo-feudal Japan setting. It has a mysterious allure. And what about *The Karate Tournament*?

RO: *Chatan Yara Kuushank.*

JS: I love the name, what does it mean?

RO: *<interpreting - barely audible>* Karate has a style like *katan*. It's the opening of the name.

JS: Did Mr Yotsui practise this style?

KY: *[Japanese] Dekinai. Muzukashii.*
(I didn't, it's very difficult.)
[English] It's high grade.

RO: All he did was, when he couldn't come up with good ideas, he'd punch holes in the wall. And I had to pay a lot of money when he was working.

JS: Really?! Holes in the...

RO: ...wall. Better than punching the graphics people.

KY: *<waves hands to dismiss allegations> Nai, nai, nai. (No, no, no.) <laughs>*

RO: You know what he [Mr Yotsui] used to do? Well, I'd call up a meeting, right? He'd always say, "I want this kind of graphic done." He'd come in two weeks later and the graphic guys didn't do it. He'd just tell them, it's no good, move! And then he'd sit there for 15 minutes and just do the graphics, saying, "I want this kind of graphics!" And you're expecting the graphics people to hang on to Mitchell? He threw out a couple of people.

JS: Is Mr Yotsui a strict boss?

RO: He can draw, himself. We had a couple of good graphics people, but these were guys straight out of school. He couldn't *[inaudible]* them, because he knew they were lousy, and ***he's*** the one who hired them.

KY: *<glances away from the TV>* Hm?

[RO and KY converse]

RO: He says the company can go bankrupt, he wants to make a good game. So I'm saying, he *sat there needing six more months, then six months go by*, I lost like 60 million yen.[9]

JS: Wow! Because of...

RO: *<interrupts - gestures to KY>* him!

JS: On one game, or every game together?

RO: *Cannon Dancer*. To run a company for one month, you have to pay all the salaries. Each person probably has five people in his family. A wife, kids, grandparents, all that.

JS: How come *Cannon Dancer* was never converted to a home system?

RO: Because it didn't sell, as a coin-op.

JS: You said *Strider* didn't sell well, but when it was ported it made money. It's money for nothing, because the game already exists. Converting to a home system can be done quickly and cheaply.

RO: OK, let's say we do a conversion, you need money for that! I have two cats and one kid to support - I need money.

JS: Do you still own *Cannon Dancer*'s rights?

RO: Yes! You want to buy them?

JS: Perhaps, how much?

RO: The money you need is not to pay me. It's to pay Sony or Nintendo, if you want to make it.

JS: You mean to have it run on Wii or PS3?

RO: You have to make the *[inaudible]* or whatever, right? For that you need money.

JS: What about on PC, there are companies like Good Old Games. The PS3 or Wii is a locked system, which Sony and Nintendo controls, but a computer is an open platform. You could sell it without any extra publisher or middleman.

RO: But how much money can you make?

---

[9] About £400'000 / $600'000 at today's rates

JS: Probably... Possibly... I have no idea. I don't know figures. But people have made money selling their back catalogue through places like GOG. How much money could you lose selling it? Probably nothing.

RO: But you need to get a programmer to convert it to PC.

JS: Well, really all you need is someone to program an emulator.

RO: Well, if somebody wants to do that, I'm willing to license it.

JS: So if someone was interested in producing an emulator for you to sell *Cannon Dancer* online, through GOG, you would be open to negotiating with them?

RO: I don't know. I licensed to Real Arcade, and there was nothing. I mean, what they paid me was probably what we drank tonight. They were using a Chinese guy that spoke English, Japanese and Chinese, perfectly. He was an agent in Japan, he came to my office so many times. He was such a nice guy. The Real Arcade vice president came. But we were getting like 20'000 yen (£130 / $200) or something. Anyway, I don't know the PC people so well. I do business with people who I think I try to drink with. I mean, it's not the paperwork. We drink three cups of this and I'm *[inaudible]*. I mean, that's what this whole world is. I've done different businesses, and worked with companies. I realised that if you drink, you can get along with anybody in the world.

JS: What I've found is, Japanese developers seem reluctant to embrace the Western PC market, even though a lot of developers make a lot of money.

RO: *Cannon Dancer* - nobody else was involved. It was ***my*** game.

JS: They wouldn't own the rights, it's just a distribution platform...

RO: It's a license?

JS: Not really. For example, with GOG, a lot of other companies put their games on there. They're a shop. You're not licensing to them, you're selling it yourself, in their shop, and they take a percentage, and the rest of it goes to you.

RO: I don't have people to do that kind of thing for me.

JS: Plus there's other games in your back catalogue that you can make use of.

RO: I'm willing to go along with it...

JS: Do you still own all the rights to all the other games developed at Mitchell?

RO: Coin-op, yes. Consumer, erm... Because of the patents... See, with *Zuma* I realised that videogame copyright is *[inaudible]*. So that's why I hooked up with Nintendo. We have patents, registered patents for DS and stuff. So if we get copied, we can really screw them. To have Nintendo as backup for that is not the money part. People are pretty scared to copy Nintendo.

JS: So with *Pang*, you own the coin-op rights, while the console rights belong to...

RO: It's complicated. Maybe... Leave it alone.

JS: Leave it alone?

RO: I don't want to talk about it.

JS: Oh, sorry. [...] What did you think of the fact that someone liked *Pang* so much, he wanted to go on a holiday with his wife, to all the locations in the game?

RO: He can give me the money, and then I'll give him a signed copy of my game.

JS: <*laughs*> I'll tell him.

RO: Actually, there's a *Pang*, from Rising Star Games, who released the game, called *Pang: Magical Michael*. For Nintendo DS. And it didn't sell. One reason I think is that Rising Star Games didn't try hard enough.

JS: Yeah, Rising Star is more of a small budget label. They release games, but...

RO: They didn't promote it enough. I think the license is up in a couple of months. I'm going to try to sell it again, to somebody.

JS: Sell it again? Oh excellent, so we will see *Pang* in the future.

RO: It's a good game. It's *Magical Michael* because, the *[inaudible]* name in the title, and Michael Jackson had just died then.

JS: Do you remember an interview with Chaz Seydoux in 2006?[10]

RO: Yes. He sent me an email, and I replied. *[110 words redacted]*
You should make games. Get involved. If you're writing, and you don't have any money, you don't care. You just told me all these things, and this will take a couple of weeks of hard thinking, to make a decision, to put it on PC or not, to find the right people. You said it's easy.

JS: On PC, hmm, yes, I'd say so.

RO: No, no, it doesn't work that way. Because you're not a business man. Look, if you had 40 people working for you, and each guy had five people in his family, you'd be thinking seriously about making money. This is not about if I drive a Bentley or not. Look at the car I have! It's probably smaller than all the other guys' in my company. That's not the point though. If you want to make money, you work for Credit Swiss, or Morgan Stanley, or whatever. That's not making money. That's ripping off people. Working through labour, that's how you make real money. I really don't like bankers, that's why I'm watching this programme. *<gestures to TV - laughs>* I hate bankers! You have an MBA, what is that? It's nothing. They can't start a game company. I just happen to be in the gaming business. I got stuck with a guy like him. *<gestures to KY>*

JS: He's a great guy!

RO to KY: You are?

KY: Eh?

JS: The British companies which converted, for example, *Pang* to the ZX Spectrum, did you deal with them directly?

RO: No, I didn't. Ocean did that. But so many people in the UK were from Ocean.

JS: Yes, Ocean was huge in the UK.

RO: Yeah, but they disappeared. Look at Rising Star Games... The guy I used to supply games to, he used to work under me at Data East. I interviewed the guy! Japanese, but supposedly he graduated from an American university.

JS: Do you know *Cannon Ball* was also published in the UK, on the ZX Spectrum, under the name *Bubble Buster*?

RO: So probably Hudson thought logically. I can't say anything right now.

JS: I spoke to a Hudson programmer. He said that every new programmer, as a test, had to program *Cannon Ball* from scratch.

RO: One of the reasons, because you're wondering, Hudson is not Hudson anymore.

JS: They were bought by Konami.

[262 words redacted on request - When Mr Ozaki noticed that the recording device was capturing the following dialogue, he exclaimed: ***"Wait, this thing is on?!"*** *Mr Ozaki was concerned the material might physically endanger me]*

RO: Anyway, business is heavy stuff! It's not easy making games. Yotsui doesn't realise it. But that's why you need a tough guy like me, to stand around.

JS: Well, I'd like to print everything.

RO: No, don't!

JS: Are you worried you might get into trouble? Or are you worried I might get into trouble?

RO: Both, both.

JS: Well, if you're worried you'll get into trouble I won't print it.

RO: I'll get into trouble for sure!

JS: Well, I'd better remove some stuff.

[10] www.insertcredit.com feature, Shokkingu Hitofude, 16 January - no longer available online

RO: Yotsui doesn't understand all this.

[Mr Yotsui is moving around the room, taking photos of us conversing]

JS: I might ask him about gangsters on Tuesday.

RO: Don't get involved with that!

JS: I want to find out the true story.

RO: Gangsters usually use front companies. There's a couple of big ones that disappeared - physically. I ain't kidding. You know, one story I can tell you is, my partner Niida... OK, he's my best friend, alright? I trust him with my life. He was the youngest branch office manager at Data East, in Osaka. He was the office manager at the sales office. He's very straightforward. He doesn't know it, but his nickname was "Niida Square". He dislikes gangsters. When you're selling coin-op stuff, gangsters were always coming, because people would buy their calendar. Who wants such a calendar? One that costs like 100'000 yen![11]

JS: What are they for?

RO: For the money. And Niida, right... The gangsters came in, and Data East had 11 employees in Osaka. They were scared, because you know... Niida sat with those two in front of him, in the office, for 10 hours!

JS: Ten hours?!

RO: He didn't do anything. He said, "No! I'm not going to buy this calendar!" And he sat there for 10 hours. They gave up and went back home. And he's a legend for that. Most companies would buy the calendar.

JS: Is that like a protection type thing? You buy the calendar and they won't bother you?

RO: Right! Niida is a legend for that kind of thing. One time, with [redacted], he's our buddy, we went to a cabaret in Shinjuku, and this is expensive. One portion is 50'000 yen.[12] Niida paid for all of us to be let in. So, we went in, and you know how the system is in Japan. The girls come around, saying *irashaimase*, *irashaimase*. And we saw a pair of bad guys looking by us, and Niida says, let's leave! We just sat there for three minutes, and he paid 150'000[13] for three of us, and we left because he didn't like them. He didn't want to sit on the same floor as criminals.

JS: Why did he feel so strongly?

RO: Probably he had a lot of trouble with them. [...] Niida and I started the company. We were in TAD, I was in *[inaudible]* and Niida was number three. And I travelled with the president. He took my money, and Niida's money.

JS: Which company was this? TAD?

RO: Yes. All ex-Data East people.

JS: And the president just ran off with everyone's money?

RO: No, no, no. *[inaudible]* I was like 30 or 31, and he ripped me off. It's complicated. Anyway, we developed a game, which I created with ***my*** money. Not the president's money. And Niida and I, were supposed to get 80 million yen,[14] but we didn't. *Toki* was one of the games.

JS: Oh, *Toki*! The coin-op platform game.

RO: When I had a fight with the president, Niida walked in, right? We're in the conference room, we're talking. And Niida walked in and says, *<Japanese phrase>*, which is basically like the Latin phrase, "*Et tu, Brutus?*" You see, I didn't know what was going on behind my back - I had been in Europe for a month. When I came back Niida had told me how the president was running off with the money and everything. So I told Niida, I can't stay here anymore.

Then Niida and I went out to a takoyaki place, and we got pretty drunk. We decided to start our company together, because he had all the Japanese companies to distribute with. And I had all the American and European distributors. So together we can do anything. That's how Niida is - Niida gets pissed off when somebody is playing dirty. I've been with him for 30 years. I was a teacher before, and he was a history teacher before.

---

[11] About £660 / $1k

[12] About £330 / $500

[13] About (£1'000 / $1'500)

[14] About £500k / $800k

JS: You were both teachers? How long did each of you teach for?

RO: He taught for a couple of years. I taught for three and half years. Our tax accountant was a math teacher. One thing Niida and I promised each other was, not to be dirty with money. Not just with each other, but to other people. So he got paid all along. *<gesturing to KY>* Anyway, Niida is not dirty with money. I don't have many friends, but I trust him. This guy, *<gesturing to KY>* he's crazy but you can trust him. With money, yes. He'll make you lose money, but he won't screw you. I think that for most people, it's important to have a good family. Like this guy. *<gesturing to KY>* He comes from a very good family.

JS: Did Mitchell work on anything other than games, for example UFO catchers, pushers, or...

RO: Yes, yes, pushers! I don't want this mentioned, but we did all the pushers for Capcom. The Capcom chairman, he really took good care of me. I probably would not be here today, with the Capcom chairman. He was a really nice guy. But his son...

JS: You mentioned in the interview with Chaz, that *Gamshara* used System 10, Namco's arcade board, because Namco had surplus stock. How many units were made?

RO: I don't remember, not much. See, at Namco it's not really called System 10. It's called 264. Why? Because 264 is Route 264 - very slow. Traffic jams. A real slow board to use. That's why it was called 264 within Namco. So I didn't know this System 10 name until now.

JS: But the quote, attributed directly to you, says: "We used Namco's System 10..."

RO: I don't remember that! I don't remember most of my interviews.

JS: So I can print everything you said tonight, and you won't remember?

RO: OK, but it will go through me! I would really prefer if you don't use that story. Because it will topple the whole game industry in Japan.

JS: You think so?

RO: Yes. Let's say you write that bit, and somebody gets wind of it - if I get any pressure, I'm really going to blow the whole top! I'm a really crazy person, you just don't realise it!

JS: Excellent. Let's just see what happens.

RO: But again, I got a wife and kid. And two strays. So I'm stuck with two cats, and Yotsui cleans the house! *<laughs>*

JS: Your company used "standard" hardware made by Capcom or Data East, but sometimes Mitchell arcade games were based on custom hardware. Was it worth the risk to develop this custom hardware?

RO: No, no. We just used Data East hardware because I used to work for them. The Capcom hardware never... It wasn't too good. You gotta remember, we're not a rich company. So I just see a little chance to make money, and I can run it. I don't care which system it is. So, if I hear Namco has stock, I'll go to Namco.

JS: Didn't *Puzz Loop* use the CPS-II hardware from Capcom?

RO: Alright, alright. Capcom's number two at that time, he's our buddy. Especially Niida's buddy. So we order Capcom's stuff. When they want to get rid of stuff, we hear about it.

JS: And then you buy up the stock to manufacture arcade games?

RO: No, no. So we'll go to Mr Tsujimoto (Snr) and make a deal. We'll say we have a game, we want to sell 1'500 boards. Will they support us for that? Usually they want to get rid of the board, so they'll say yes. Namco likewise. That's why I'm not drunk enough, because I'm fat. *<slaps belly>* John, when I was about your age, my uncle, he's rich, he said, "Roy, you're getting fat. You started working?" His idea was that if you're fat, you take customers to restaurants, start drinking and eating, that's working for sales. He says, "Roy, I'm glad you're getting fat." You can't take a person to a steak dinner and eat salad. If the guy loves to drink whiskey, you stay with the guy until four o' clock and drink whiskey. You can't say, "I can't drink." That's why I'm a good salesman. *[... lots inaudible ...]* That's the risk of the game business, not all games are a hit. Coin-op is like this. That's why I like the coin-op division. Consumer division isn't my type of people. You now know how crazy I can be.

JS: There's more fun in coin-op?

RO: They're crazy! Look at him, <*gestures*> he's crazy! Who brings a yukata to a ryokan?[15]

<u>**16 September 2013**</u>

I awoke in the ryokan, and called Mr Ozaki to pick me up. The innkeeper gave me the bill for the previous night, but accidentally misplaced the point in the numbers, thereby adding an additional zero to the price. Instead of 20'000 yen (£130 / $200), it was 200'000 yen (£1'300 / $2'000). Ten times as much. I said to Mr Ozaki: "It's a bit high, isn't it?" To which Mr Ozaki replied: "Well, he probably added all the drink on to the bill." Without a calculator it was difficult to work out the GBP equivalent, but I knew something was odd, because it would have cleared out my entire living budget for the trip, and some of the interpreter budget. I dug out my envelope of money and nervously handed over the requested amount. The innkeeper's reaction was priceless. He immediately gave me back the wad of cash. I showed him the bill and he apologised. Mr Ozaki and I laughed. As way of apology, the innkeeper gave me a book about the ryokan. Apparently it featured prominently as the filming location for a popular TV drama from the 1960s.

The typhoon was still blowing, which meant no trains were running from Mt Takao back into Tokyo. I enjoyed lunch at Mr Ozaki's house, along with Mr Yotsui. I was also given access to his cupboard of development materials, including the original PC-98 developmental floppies for several arcade titles.

Audio files were recorded sporadically that morning. Given the unstructured nature of these, a lot has been edited out.

JS: You were saying the calendar on the DS, you were hired to do the localising on the different languages?

RO: <*long pause*> Right. <*long pause*>

JS: So how many staff did you have at...

RO: About 30. More or less.

JS: Can you talk about any of the 3DS games you were working on?

RO: I don't know. They're out already.

JS: Ahh, here's *Puzz Loop* on a CPS board. So, when did *Puzz Loop 2* come out?

RO: Don't ask me difficult questions, I don't know. I just ran the company.

JS: Did you personally interview everyone you hired for R&D?

RO: For graphics, there's a graphics chief. When he can't make the final decision... I don't know who was good or not. He was the all round chief for graphics, right? So I can't tell.

JS: But you can tell what looks good.

RO: Alright, but I'm not going to pay 300'000[16] yen a month for a *[inaudible]*.

JS: Who designed the original *Pang*?

RO: I forgot his name, it's so long ago. <*laughs*> It's not just one designer. The names are almost coming up, but it's on the tip of my tongue. <*long pause*> You see, *Pang* is another one of these games, where we didn't think it was going to be a big hit. Well, it did sell.

---

[15] Mr Yotsui brought his own yukata to wear during the meal that evening

[16] About £2'000 / $3'000

JS: In arcades and home adaptations?

RO: Mainly arcades.

JS: Capcom handled the Super Famicom port - did they take a larger cut than you received on the arcade version?

RO: We didn't get anything...

JS: Oh... You didn't get *anything*?

RO: We just had the rights for the coin-op. See, it's not just a one by one thing, everything is all inter-related. I cannot tell you we get this for this and that for that.

JS: So it's like a package deal?

RO: Usually it turns out to be a package deal later. The situation changes... Same with Nintendo. We did some educational software for... Nintendo introduced us to, that uh... Well, I'll say it's a big educational book company. They were looking for good programming companies, and they asked us to do it. The graphics and programming. But my staff didn't want me around - I'd only end up saying the wrong thing.

JS: Regarding...?

RO: Any kind of deal. When I get involved I always cause problems. Everyone thinks I'm crazy. Probably Yotsui's apartment is in shambles. The window was open. Eighth floor.

JS: Isn't his family there to close it?

RO: He has a daughter. I think his daughter went to the grammar school holidays - so I think until Tuesday or something he's alone. The cat isn't even there. His daughter took the cat on the train to Osaka.

JS: So he's free to hang with us. He's a freelancer - what does he do day-to-day?

RO: Just mess around. He climbs mountains a lot, like Takao. There's a lot of places he... Come to the window here, see the top of the mountain there? That side is Tokyo. This side of the mountain, it's Kanagawa-ken. Right over the mountain is the road we took, to Takao. Right across the mountain, next to the bottom of the mountain there, that's route 20 that goes to Takao. And the Takao mountain range is all on that side. I think he was in the mountains in August. He went up pretty high. He takes his motorcycle. He rides a big one!

JS: What's in here? *<moves to open box>*

RO: A dead rat? *<laughs>* My employees could have packed a dead rat.

JS: As a joke?

RO: When I worked for Data East, my bosses said to me, "Roy, you're a real good salesman. You're bright, and everything, but the trouble with you is you think the whole of life is a joke."

JS: Why'd they say that?

RO: Because I think in business, I think it's a fucking joke.

JS: Because people screw each other over?

RO: Right!

[Author's note: While unpacking Mr Ozaki's cupboard I came across a mysterious box without markings. Lifting the flap I froze in horror - there were six human heads inside, with neat, long black hair. My immediate thought was: would I be next? No one would find my headless corpse, buried on Mt Takao. Just as my heart was about to explode...]

RO: Oh, my wife's a hairdresser. Those are her practising heads.

JS: Oh... Under this box... Awesome, you've got PC-98 floppy disks!

RO: That's got a lot of the old games on it.

JS: Amazing, I'm going to take photos. How long did Mitchell use the PC-98 for?

RO: Don't ask me this question! You're asking the wrong guy.

JS: *<mumbling to self> Double Wings, Charlie Ninja, Street Fighter Collection...*

[Author moves to take photos of items]

JS: If you had to put a reason on why Mitchell's R&D department had to close?

RO: Because we didn't come up with anything good. A lot of ideas came up, but they weren't good. With games, you have to come up with something good, if you want to make money. Many ideas happen and they're all shit. I'm not going to put a million dollars in a game that's not... You see, I'm not the only one that makes decisions. There's other people in my company. We sit down and hear the presentation and decide to do it or not. I think it's the same with all other companies.

JS: Surely successful games like *Polarium* provided you with a surplus of money?

RO: No, not enough. Look, I told you, one guy has five people to support at home. And you have 30 people. Plus the rent in Tokyo is phenomenal. Office space. We had a lot of space. Plus insurance money for each individual, social security and all of that. It takes a lot of money to make a game. If you go one year without making a game, that's a lot of money. Plus Sony, Nintendo, they always go from one system to the next. You need tools for that. You need computers. For instance, Nintendo went up to what... They used Windows 7, and now 8? I forgot. So if they start using Windows 8 for everything, we had to change everything in our office also to Windows 8, and that costs money.

JS: You mean to use custom dev tools?

RO: Right. So like with Sony, their development tools are ***so*** expensive. That's one of the reasons why I didn't do a Sony. Look at a company like Square-Enix, they joined together and they're both public companies, big companies. They joined together, why? Because they weren't making enough. They're not going to last. You know how many game companies like us, who are on 30 or 50 people, went out of the game business in the last two years?

JS: There's been a lot of closures recently.

RO: A couple of hundred of them went out. It's a tough world. People are a lot more interested in other stuff than just games. For instance the Paradise Cafe I visit, other customers that are there, they're people in their late 20s, early 30s. Only one or two like playing games. Another phenomenon is, car sales went down because young people... When I was right out of university, I wanted to get a car and drive it. Look at my son, he's 21 and he doesn't even have a driver's license. My son isn't interested. I think that's a phenomenon that's happening all over the world. Everything has its time, and the car was before. Then games. The game age is gone now, I think.

JS: In Akihabara, 12 years ago there hundreds of game stores, but not anymore.

RO: Because they can't sell that much. I don't want to invest in something that I know won't make money. Puzzle games are the easiest and cheapest things. I know what I'm doing!

[This next audio file starts suddenly]

RO: Iwata was the president of HAL. But even he's not the final decision maker. In Japan everything works on consensus. It's not one guy.

JS: I'm surprised Yamauchi didn't make his son-in-law head of the company.

RO: No, no, the guy that married his daughter was the president of Nintendo USA. I had dinner with him a couple of times. He's the one who started Nintendo USA. And I remember him telling us about when he started the company in Seattle. I would think that Texas or Chicago would be more in the middle. So Seattle, he gave me his reasons, but I forgot. Probably because Microsoft is next door, that's why.

JS: Should we discuss *Cannon Ball*?

RO: Why? No.

JS: So how did you first see it?

RO: Hmm... The Hudson one, before? When I saw, I didn't realise it until *Pang* was made. You're really hung up on that, aren't you?

JS: I'm not hung up! I'm just fascinated.

RO: Well, I told you I don't want to talk about it.

JS: I thought I could wear you down slowly.

RO: No, you're talking to a tough negotiator. I really don't want... I'm not interested. I don't see how it's going to help me. It's going to help you, but it's not going to... <*refers to payment made at the ryokan*> You pay me all the cash I saw you had earlier today, I might talk.

JS: <*loud laughing*> I need that to live on!

RO: Well, I need my secrecy to live on. [...] It's not a secret, but it's too complicated. If I start saying something there's going to be a lot of people who *won't want me to say it*. I don't want needless complexity, right now in my life. I have my troubles, and my cats breaking up the tissue box.[17] That's enough trouble.

JS: Would an official license cause trouble?

RO: No, no. It's the people that are involved - a lot of difficult people are involved.

JS: I thought you said a lot had died?

RO: There's somebody that used to work for them and stuff. When things that involve people *[inaudible]*. If you keep making me open my mouth, there's going to be lots of trouble.

JS: For you?

RO: Everybody! You should not let me talk. You're going to have trouble. We're not going to talk about Hudson.

JS: I'm meeting some people from Hudson.

RO: OK. Katsuki[18] was alright. Katsuki was like a vice president. He's OK. I had a big fight with him, but we got along after that. In the end he left Hudson. When Konami took over, everybody left Hudson! But the people at Hudson, they only know things on paper. So I don't want to get involved with those kinds of people. That's why I don't want to talk about Hudson. I'm a negotiator, I talk my ass off. What's written on paper is paper. I make back deals. That's why I survived. That's why I don't have any sponsors, that's why I don't have anybody telling me shit. I don't care now because I don't have employees.

JS: So you're free to say what you like?

RO: But I don't want any hassle. That's why nobody knows my phone number.

JS: I know your phone number.

RO: Well I hope you don't let me think I made a mistake. I only tell it to people that I feel necessary, that's all.

JS: I hope you feel you can trust me.

RO: I hope so! Then again, you're British. Don't trust the British!

ミッチェルがアーケードタイトルのライセンス先を探しています。携帯電話、コンピューターや他のデバイスでの使用。条件としては、移植と販売ライセンスの期間限定発行。ロイヤリティの他に、先渡金希望。今回案件としているミッチェルのアーケードゲームタイトルには下記のものがあります。リストにあるものには、基盤、ソースコード、取り扱い説明書があります。

ファンキージェット
チャタンヤラクーシャンク
雙翼
燃えよゴンタ!!
妖獣麻雀伝
がんばれゴンタ!!2
卒業証書
キャノンダンサー
三刻志
銃武者羅
Eタコ
チャーリー忍者

（株）ミッチェルホームページ
http://www.mitchell.jp/index.htm

[17] The previous day there was shredded tissues from a full box spread around the lounge
[18] Likely Kunji Katsuki, who has been Vice President, Executive Officer and Director

~*Appearing in a later volume*~

LEFT: **Kouichi Yotsui** pictured with the author. A second interview took place after the Mt Takao interview, at the Westone offices. While there, Mr Yotsui gave a running commentary while playing the first level of his arcade game *Cannon Dancer*, and revealed which version of *Nostalgia 1907* is his favourite.

While at the Westone offices I also met those behind Japan's beloved *Wonderboy* series. In particular I interviewed Ryuichi Nishizawa (third from the left), and Maki Ohzora (second from the left).

Meet the team, from left: Jun Watanabe, Maki Ohzora, Ryuichi Nishizawa, Masatsugu Murakami, Yuji Yoshino, Tatsunobu Usui, Takanori Kurihara

Tokyo Game Show group interview - Thompson and Bangs
Thursday, 19 September 2013

This was my first time visiting TGS. I don't really see the need to attend again. Queues are so ridiculously long you'll end up experiencing more games by sitting at home and browsing websites. I played nothing on the day, and saw very little. Whereas that evening English websites such as SiliconEra had detailed coverage with videos. My main reason for attending TGS was to interview game developers, and see if I could find the SNK booth to request an interview. SNK didn't even bother with a proper stand, though I did find their cubicle. It was locked. A highlight was meeting two magazine journalists from America - though due to their contracts they can't have their real names printed. Our conversation conveys a slice of the gaming zeitgeist. For a video tour of TGS, check out the supplementary DVD.

JS: So chaps, getting any scoops?

Thompson: Nope, no point. Have you seen the queues? *<shows smarphone>* I've already got the press releases and screenshots in my inbox.

Bangs: TGS is only good when someone like Keiji Inafune gives a speech. Print is so slow we might as well just get our stuff online.

JS: He's centre of attention with *Mighty No.9*. Does Kickstarter offer developers a new avenue?

Bangs: Like maybe, not Activision... But for companies like Take Two, Acclaim. Are they gone now? *<laughs>*

JS: What does Capcom think, seeing *Mighty*'s success? How many have bought into *MN9*?

Thompson: Well, the thing is, the mechanism between the officer class in the company, and their ability to make a decision... You know, you could have the R&D guys, and they want to make another *Mega Man* game. Then they have to ask the bosses, and the bosses are white collar salary men.

Bangs: But they're going to say yes, right? I mean, for the main man.

Thompson: But I think they already would have, if it were that easy. So I think the answer is no. It's a question of, to me, the officers of the company not necessarily being able to read the market correctly, because they're so out of touch. So Kickstarter is a direct access into...

Bangs: Especially, you know this is only the case for Capcom, but lately I see them as becoming more of a vendor. Because the one reason they decided to do *Monster Hunter 4*, on 3DS, is because they were paid ***a lot*** of money from Nintendo. So basically the management, in my opinion, stopped thinking about what is the right market for which game. Now it's more like, do they pay for the game?

JS: *Monster Hunter* sells the console. The 3DS doesn't even have a second joystick - the PS Vita has, yet *Monster Hunter* is on 3DS.

Bangs: So if Microsoft pays, they say, "OK, *Dead Rising* for you guys." If Nintendo pays, "OK, *Monster Hunter* for you guys." Anyway, I'm rather surprised Inafune is not still sued by Capcom, to be honest.

JS: It's probably just different enough. *<notices Thompson's jetlag>* You want Redbull? *<pulls one from jacket pocket - everyone laughs>*

Bangs: Yes, maybe he does.

Thompson: No! I need something *stronger!*

Bangs: Do you think Keiji Inafune will be sued?

JS: No. Over the years other games have been even more blatant copies of others.

Bangs: I still think he was a board member of Capcom, once. He has trade secrets, of course.

JS: Which maybe are subtly helping him?

Bangs: Yeah, yeah, yeah. And trade secrets, meaning he knows ***all*** the staff, who did the *Mega Man* series. You know, he's got people...

JS: *<interrupts>* He's got some on board.

Bangs: Yes. So that kind of stuff is very risky, I think. I'm rather surprised he's not been sued yet.

JS: I like the fact that it's shaking the industry up. Obviously Capcom is aware of this.

Bangs: Yeah, yeah, of course!

Thompson: Yeah, I'm sure that's quite a conversation around the water cooler at Capcom!

Bangs: The only possibility that I can really think of, if he can get away from this, is actually that he already made a deal with Capcom.

JS: Interesting conspiracy theory! Maybe some kind of profit sharing deal.

Bangs: Maybe he does actually have some deal with Capcom, already, that he's going to give some 10% or 5% of the profits.

JS: Or maybe Capcom sues them later, only after seeing how big a success it becomes? OK, 50 million, now we're going to sue you!

<everyone laughs>

Bangs: And that's the actual damage that he receives, after he actually sells the game.

JS: But if he doesn't get sued, it's a precedent.

Bangs: True.

JS: I think Kickstarter is exciting, because it feels like developers are held back by publishers.

Bangs: I still think the developers, they're fine. But the board members... Hmm... Inafune was a board member once!

JS: I bring Kickstarter up with everyone. A lot don't realise it exists. Some say they're worried they won't be able to pay the money back. I tell them: "You just need to make the game!"

Bangs: As long as you ship the game.

JS: I hate to cut and run, but I must dash.

Thompson: Oh yeah, it's OK. You'll be at Sony's Indie Stream? All us journos are going.

Bangs: We're tired too, so let's head off.

JS: I'll have to buy you sake. Get you liquored up and see what stories come out.

Bangs: *<laughs>* In that case I will never go drinking with you!

<everyone laughs>

JS: You guys know where SNK is?

Thompson: There's no display for them. They've just got a little cubicle in a small hall separate from the main one.

~Appearing in a later volume~

While at TGS I interviewed three people, for publication in a later volume.

Pictured on the page to the left is **Rica Matsumura**, General Manager at Agatsuma Entertainment. We had a deeply philosophical interview on the role of women in the work place in Japan, and her hopes for the future. In addition, Ms Matsumara discusses her early years as a programmer on the Apple II computer, Studio Saizensen, *Code of Princess*, and her translation work on *Operation Darkness* for the Xbox 360. During my trip I also met Ken Ogura, who made the strategy title, so plenty of good coverage coming up.

Alongside (on the left page) I also interviewed programmer **Yasuo Nakajima**, who discusses his role on *Kamaitachi no Yoru* for Super Famicom, Japan's early and much beloved Sound Novel. He also programmed *Fushigi no Dungeon - Fuurai no Shiren GB - Tsukikage Mura no Kaibutsu*, which was the GB port for the original *Mystery Dungeon*. He discusses some of the technical difficulties. In addition, he reveals an unprecedented game which went unreleased...

Yoshihide Kobayashi

Also while at TGS, I spoke with Yoshihide Kobayashi, formerly of Sega, now with Sony. He spearheaded the drive to update *Ico* from a PlayStation title to a PlayStation 2 title. He also handled *Gravity Daze*'s shift from PS3 to PS Vita. Before all this he was also producer on cult-classics like *Sky Odyssey* and *Mister Mosquito* - two of my personal favourites.

Toshinobu Kondo

Although I did not interview him at TGS, Ms Matsumara arranged for a later interview with Toshinobu Kondo, creator of *Umihara Kawase*, the fantastic (and fantastically cute) series of bungee cord physics-based platformers. Mr Kondo also reveals some fascinating information on the background to Fill-in-Café, the small developer he used to work at.

久木野 雅昭

KUKINO, Masaaki

DOB: 2 February 1964 / Birthplace: Kurashiki / Blood Type: A

~ Selected Portfolio ~

Konami, 1986 ~ 2003

Unnamed educational game	- MSX1, unreleased	(Artist)
Full Throttle (aka: *Super Bikers*)	- Arcade, unreleased	(Game design, artist)
Fast Lane	- Arcade, 1987	(Game design, lead artist)
Rack'em Up	- Arcade, 1987	(Artist)
Haunted Castle	- Arcade, 1988	(Game design, artist)
Hot Chase	- Arcade, 1988	(Game design, lead artist)
Crime Fighters	- Arcade, 1989	(Game design, lead artist)
Surprise Attack	- Arcade, 1990	(Director, game design, lead artist)
Asterix	- Arcade, 1992	(Game design, lead artist)
Unnamed fighting game with monsters	- Arcade, unreleased	(Director, game design, lead artist)
Run and Gun (aka: *Slamdunk*)	- Arcade, 1993	(Director, game design, lead artist)
Speed King	- Arcade, 1995	(Game design, artist)
Midnight Run	- Arcade, 1996	(Artist)
Winding Heat	- Arcade, 1996	(Director, game design, lead artist)
Racing Jam	- Arcade, 1997	(Director, game design, lead artist)
Racing Jam Chapter 2	- Arcade, 1998	(Director, game design, lead artist)
Silent Scope	- Arcade, 1999	(Director, game design, lead artist)
Dark Silhouette - Silent Scope 2	- Arcade, 2000	(Director, game design, lead artist)
Silent Scop EX	- Arcade, 2001	(Director, game design, lead artist)
Xtrial Racing	- Arcade, 2002	(Director, game design, lead artist)
Silent Scope Fortune Hunter	- Gambling mchn, 2002	(Director, game design, lead artist)

Gamewax, 2003 ~ 2007

Valve Limit	- Arcade, 2003	(Director, game des., ld artist, cab design)
AKUMA	- Arcade, 2005	(Director, game des., ld artist, cab design)
Chase HQ 2	- Arcade, 2007	(Director, game design, lead artist)

SNK-Playmore, 2007 ~ 2010

King of Fighters XII	- Arcade/PS3/X360, 2009	(Director, producer)
King of Fighters XIII	- Arcade, 2010	(Producer)
A game for Chinese market (NDA)	- Windows, Unreleased	(Producer, lead artist)
SNK Game, new version (NDA)	- XBLA/PSP, Unreleased	(Producer, director)

Wahlep Tec, 2011 ~ 2013

Steel Revolt	- Arcade, Unreleased	(Producer, director)

Fast Lane, for arcades in 1987, was a car-themed action-puzzle maze game

Interview with Masaaki Kukino
13 November 2013, Kyoto

I visited the Kansai region for three days, from 11 until 13 November. It was a wild ride. On the final day, just before my departure, I interviewed Mr Kukino at a coffee shop by the train station. I had actually interviewed him via email before, for an unpublished Haunted Castle interview. This would be a follow-up. Mr Kukino is a true arcade veteran, starting at Konami and now working at SNK, having produced a variety of arcade titles over the years, several of them arcade exclusives. He reveals a lot of things about the nature of arcade development, technological progress, and a few things no one knows about.

JS: Which company are you with now?

MK: As of November this year [2013], actually, I'm going back to SNK. The chairman, Kawasaki-san, he talked to me about his new vision.

JS: Directly?

MK: Yes. He asked me to come back.

JS: You know him personally?

MK: Correct, yes. Exactly. I think you know these guys, <*gestures to paper*> one American guy and two French guys, they're working at SNK at the moment, and I'm close to them.

JS: Yes, I do. SNK seems reluctant to talk with journalists. I could not get interviews...

MK: Here's what I think. After the reinstatement of Kawasaki-san in SNK as a top person, the company is now trying to shift its position back to games. Kawasaki-san has a long career in games, and now that he is back he is gearing the company more toward the gaming business again. In other words, it's in kind of a transition at the moment. In this sensitive period, probably they do not want to speak to the media or give interviews.

JS: I think it's good they're shifting back to games, because when I started the book there were a lot of requests for SNK. A lot of people wish SNK produced more games.

MK: You know, I left SNK back in 2010, so it has been almost three years since I left. At that time the company was undergoing a big change in its organisation, and at that time I felt the company was not feeling that much attraction to the games business, at all. That was the reason why I decided to leave the company. But now we have Kawasaki-san reinstated at the top position, as the chairman, and he is willing to focus on games again, and so that's why I'm going back. I'm really looking forward to working on games at SNK. Likewise, you know, I'm determined to do my best in order to provide fun content for fans of our games. I hope our fans continue to look forward to new releases from us.

JS: Which company are you leaving currently?

MK: A Chinese company, but they stopped developing.

JS: I wanted to ask about your work in China. How long did you spend there?

MK: One year and eight months.

JS: I'd like to discuss your life, the games you worked on, and so on. I spoke to you via email about *Haunted Castle*, but it was never published. I'll include it within this main interview.

MK: <*laughs*> Well, I'm not sure whether it's much fun, or not, but it's... Yeah, I don't mind talking about it.

JS: It's significant, it's the first *Castlevania* for arcades. I also discovered that the Golem boss first appeared in *Haunted Castle*.

MK: Yes, that's correct.

JS: So *Haunted Castle* influenced the series.

MK: <*laughs*> I'm not that worried about it. So you don't have to be that mindful for me. <*laughs*> It was a long time ago!

JS: I have two signature books, which I'm hoping you would sign.

MK: *<laughs>* Just a normal signature? *<laughs, signs>* Actually, I lived in London for four years. So even during that time I provided my autograph in kanji characters, because nobody would be able to mimic my writing. This is in the Kyoto dialect.[1]

JS: Excellent! [...] **What is the first videogame you can ever remember seeing, or playing?**

MK: The very first game for me was *Pong*. The tennis game. When I was small a friend of mine had this game, so I played it with him at his place, all the time.

JS: As someone who has mostly worked on arcade games, what was the first arcade game?

MK: *<laughs>* The first game was *Space Invaders*! But it kind of generated a social issue; it was seen as something very problematic later on. So school students were not supposed to play the game. So I didn't get to play it all that often. I didn't play the invader games all that much, and instead I played more *Pac-man*, or *Galaxian*. All those old games.

JS: When did you want to work on games?

MK: First of all I majored in art, in my college. I went to an arts school, and at that time I majored in textile design, like interior design or apparel design, and so on. But I came to know that there was a company called Konami. A friend of mine talked about the company and then we went there together, and it was so much fun for me. Right away I decided that this was what I wanted to do.

JS: I read online about your textiles background.

MK: *<laughs>* I didn't know that was online! When I was in high school I liked painting, and at that time there were not really games yet. I came to Kyoto during my summer vacation, as a high school student, though I'm not originally from Kyoto. But when I came to Kyoto I saw a lot of traditional arts and customs, and all these old traditional Japanese things in town - small handicrafts, kimono, and so on. I felt so comfortable in this environment. So I fell in love with the city of Kyoto, full of traditional artefacts, and then I decided I wanted to come and live in Kyoto. First of all my interest was drawn to traditional Japanese art in Kyoto, and later on I narrowed down the direction towards textiles.

JS: Kyoto is the cultural capital of Japan.

MK: Yes. Kyoto is somewhat different to any other city in Japan.

JS: Yesterday I was speaking with a Ritsumeikan University professor; the local government wants to preserve videogames as a cultural artefact. Nintendo is in Kyoto, and Japanese videogames play an important cultural role in the world.

MK: Well, I'm happy about that! *<laughs>* My college was so interesting. The name is Seika College of Arts, and it has a manga museum. They put a lot of emphasis on manga culture, and other sub-cultures, and in that context the college has many visitors from overseas.

JS: Konami was your first choice?

MK: Yes, indeed, in the games industry Konami was my first choice. Because I was in Kyoto, the other option I thought about was Nintendo. I actually visited Nintendo, and at that time Nintendo had just launched the first generation of Famicom. So the company was not putting that much emphasis on the Famicom or the video gaming business, at all.[2] I don't know whether I should say this to you or not, but when I visited the company, what I saw was... I was applying for a job as a designer, at that time, and I felt that my job might be designing playing cards and hanafuda games - which are Japanese card games. So it did not look that interesting to me. So I thought, well, this is what I will have to do if I join this company. All day long, all year long, and I don't know whether it's interesting enough for me. On the other hand, Konami's job looked much more interesting. But soon after I joined Konami, Nintendo's performance skyrocketed with the success of the Famicom! So I regretted that a little bit. *<laughs>*

JS: Nintendo's pre-Famicom work: everybody thinks it made arcade games, like *Donkey Kong* (1981), but that was actually outsourced to Tokyo-based company Ikegami Tsushinki.

---

[1] Message said, "Welcome to Kyoto"

[2] FC launched July 1983; that year only 9 games were released (*FC1983-1994*, Ohta Pub.). Nintendo still focused on producing a diverse range of toys

MK: Yes, I know the story.

JS: Have you heard any interesting rumours?

MK: I'm sorry, I don't have any. Yes, Nintendo launched a variety of arcade games as well, a long time ago, but they shifted their focus on to the Famicom home-console business. So after I joined Konami I didn't hear many industry anecdotes or rumours about their arcade games.

JS: You joined Konami the same year as Toshinari Oka[3] and Hideo Kojima?

MK: Ah, yes, yes, I know Hideo. He was my colleague, we joined Konami in 1986. Kojima-san is a friend of mine, and he was a planner. I worked as a graphics designer, an artist for arcade games, when he started *Metal Gear* 25 years ago. He talked a lot about his new plans, and what he wanted to do, and his representative title is *Metal Gear*. I wasn't involved with the development of *Metal Gear*, but I still remember how he told me his exciting plan for the first game. It's great that it's not faded, even after 25 years have passed. I remember hearing about that first version's planning, and what he wanted to do, and that's one of my best memories, from back in the day. *<laughs>* I think that he is a true creator.

JS: Did Mr Kojima ever mention *Lost Warld* [sic] to you?[4] The spelling of *Warld* is unusual.

MK: I don't know. I'm not cognisant of that title. But I think he probably planned the title, but it never got through for some reason. I think the title was formed in that way intentionally, because at that time there was a game for MSX called *Knightmare*.[5] So literally nightmare, but with a K at the beginning, denoting a knight. So it has a double meaning. So he probably wanted his to have a double meaning.

JS: When I interviewed Mr Oka he asked me to pass on his regards.

MK: Oh! I haven't seen him for the past 10 or more years...

JS: We visited the old Konami building.

MK: Oh, is that so! You know, inside that building, Konami was the only game developer. Around the building there were so many other businesses, like apparel companies. Big ones, like World and Tasaki.[6] There was also a ladies lingerie manufacturer, and so on. So the people working for those companies were really highly fashionable. *<laughs>* On the other hand, Konami's employees were all kind of... Well, they didn't dress up quite as well. So, you know, sometimes Konami got complaints from employees of surrounding companies. *<laughs>*

JS: Computer geeks definitely have their own style. Plus it's more relaxed at a game company.

MK: *<laughs>* Well, we were a little dirty because - you know - we were so busy we didn't take as many baths as we should have, perhaps. So that's why.

<everyone laughs>

JS: I've heard similar stories from developers.

MK: We were sleeping on the floor in the office. We were not relaxed, but we passed out. It's the same as at any time in the games industry.

JS: Long hours, very intense development.

MK: That's right. Well, it was not anything that the company imposed on us. In game program development, there really is no end to it. You can keep improving the program forever - literally speaking. It should be ourselves, knowing when to stop. But being in the development section we tended to pursue a better level for any program, so it was hard for us to stop ourselves. So we ended up working until late at night, and working throughout the night. That's something which was self-imposed by the employees, in a way.

JS: Konami had a reputation for high technical quality, in the 1980s and 1990s.

MK: Yes. In the arcade game division we worked on both - hardware as well as software. Those two departments, hardware and software, competed and collaborated with each other,

[3] Mr Oka's interview will feature in a later volume
[4] Unreleased game by Kojima, prior to *Metal Gear* - few sources (one is the silver book that came with the ltd edition of *MGS* on PS1). Sometimes spelled *Last Warld*. Second half allegedly a portmanteau of *war* and *world*
[5] MSX1 (1986), vertical shooter with a knight

[6] World is a fashionable clothing company based in Kobe, Tasaki Japan deals in high-end jewellery

making each other even better, and it applies to other game development companies. So the situation at that time was somewhat different to what we have today.

JS: Speaking of hardware... Konami, around 1994, wanted to develop its own home console.

MK: I'm not an insider with regards to the home division, so I don't find myself in any position to comment on that. But here is what I think - and this is speculation. I think probably technology-wise, developing hardware for a home console was no problem for Konami. But when it comes to costs, in terms of developing a console that is - technologically speaking - really capable and high-capacity, and then having it make money while maintaining that high-capacity, was maybe a challenge for Konami. The other possible challenge is distribution. So probably the company had to make a comprehensive analysis of business feasibility, and opted out.

JS: Your portfolio lists *Full Throttle* (1986) as your first game.[7] Did you help out on titles prior?

MK: Yes, I worked as an assistant before that. I joined Konami in April, back in 1986, but even before that the company wanted to have me as a part-timer. The program I helped the company with was some MSX educational software. That was my very first work at Konami. At that time the original MSX was already a kind of obsolete computer.[8] It was very hard to program anything on it. In terms of pixels, I was only able to use two colours horizontally. Given the constraints I still had to design attractive animal characters, and so on. I remember that as a tough project.

JS: What was the name of it?

MK: Maybe it was never released in the end... It was a kind of educational software, teaching math or something.[9] I'm not sure what happened to that, because this educational software division was relocated to the Tokyo office soon after I joined Konami. Then I was assigned to the arcade division. So I don't know what happened.

JS: Was the arcade division a lot more fun?

MK: Right! I was happy to work in the arcade division, rather than the MSX division, because at that time the performance capacity of arcade machines was so much higher. I'm a graphics designer, so I like to express myself artistically. I was able to use 16 colours when I designed arcade games. On the other hand, with the MSX, I was much more limited in terms of colour and what I could express in those programs. Also, in addition to that, because I played arcade games myself, it was so much fun to be able to work on arcade games.

JS: With *Full Throttle / Super Bikers* you were both a planner and an artist?

MK: That's my first game, but when I joined the arcade game division as a new hire, the project had already been started, and so my role was limited to an artist. Designing the player's mount on the motorbike, and the animation and the actions taken by the player. But the development of this title was stopped before release. It was not released. Typically when we design any title, there are artists and there are programmers, and there is a planner - known in English as a game designer - who plans out all of the design for the title. They have clear boundaries among their roles, but at Konami, when I worked in the arcade division, we only had artists and programmers, and then so-called directors. So between the parties, all the game designs were brainstormed and planned in detail. So I learned a lot from the experience. I think this was a good virtue of Konami's development environment.

JS: Your first two projects were unreleased?

MK: Hmm. *<confirms>*

JS: Were there many other unreleased games?

MK: There are so many, actually! *<laughs>* The numbers are countless! It's hard to remember all of them.

JS: How many were you involved in?

MK: I was so disappointed when I came to hear that my first ever title was not going to be released, because I worked on the game day and night, and throughout the night. So it was very disappointing. Having said that, let me explain how arcade titles are developed. We have repeated SATs - Site Acceptance Tests - or

[7] Unreleased; *Full Throttle* (US title), *Super Bikers* (Japanese title). *Full Throttle* is also a 1987 Taito game
[8] The enhanced MSX2 model launched in 1986
[9] *Monkey Academy* fits the description, but it was released 1984

location tests, and when we cannot get the presumed results, for example there's a bad response from the players, or something technical, we keep amending the program. Then based on that we have to determine whether we should go on, or terminate the project. It's a hard decision to make. So when any title is not released, that is the responsibility of the development team. Nobody else's. I had that keen awareness too. It applies to any time period.

JS: Between 1986 and 2002 at Konami, could you give an estimate?

MK: <*laughs*> I have to wonder!

JS: More than 50? More than 100?

MK: Not that many... I don't think the number is in multiples of 10 or anything, because in the case of arcade titles, the development period tended to be much longer than that for consoles or home games. Typically in the case of console games the development period for the prototype was more like two months. As opposed to the development of arcade games, which was between six months and one year, because we had to make something that is acceptable on-site at game centres. So from there we keep amending what needs to be addressed and so on. One team had to work between six months and one year - given that fact, the number [of unreleased arcade games] cannot be that many. So even when we did not get what we wanted, in terms of player responses and so on, sometimes we drastically had to change the development direction. So it could be acceptable for players. So it's not that we started to work on a project, and then aborted right away, and then repeated the process. On the other hand, there are so many projects that were aborted even before getting started. So it's not something we would let outsiders know about. We had in-house evaluations of a specific project, which provided only the bare bones of the new title. We might as well get that project examined internally, in the company. So many of them came and went. The number is much higher if I include those projects.

JS: Do you want to describe any? I like to read descriptions and play the game inside my mind.

MK: Ah, yes, yes! There were so many projects that had to be stopped. Or we had to shift our direction, to do something else. I have lots of experiences like that. Let me explain the most impressive or most memorable project that was terminated - for me personally. We were thinking about a fighting game, around 1992, and we had already formed a team to work on the project. Inside the team we were planning the game, and we were making progress. But that title was very innovative for the time. It had really breakthrough ideas in terms of art style, and also the [mechanical] game system, and we found the idea really interesting. So we wanted to do it. The reason why we could not proceed on that project was that it required really high manpower, and it was so time consuming. Also the capacity required for the hardware was too high. So those challenges were not something we were able to overcome. That's why we had to terminate it. The entire team had to shift its focus on to something else, which was this basketball game *Run and Gun*. We worked on this instead.

JS: What was your role on the fighting game? Was it like *Street Fighter*?

MK: Well, rather than *Street Fighter* which had sporting rivals, probably another title which is closer to the one I worked on is *Mortal Kombat*. In the sense that the characters are more like monsters, abnormal characters. So in that sense it was closer to *Mortal Kombat*. My job was planning, basically the director. Also art direction. So I was working on the title completely.

JS: The monster aspect sounds fascinating.

MK: <*laughs*> I still hold on to the old business plans for that project. The documents I still have in storage are hand written, because at that time it was not standard to have Word documents, or Excel spreadsheets, or Powerpoint presentations. So I still have my handwritten plans.

JS: You should scan it and put it online!

MK: <*laughs*> It's all in cardboard boxes right now, at my place! <*laughs*> I don't see any legal issue with that, I can upload them on to the internet. Because those are unreleased ideas, I can treat the business plan as my personal drawings, and so on.

JS: If you can, I'd love to include an image of artwork, in your chapter.

MK: If I can find it, sure.

JS: How many characters could you select from?

MK: I'd say there were 8 characters. That was really an extraordinary program I was thinking about. You know, let me explain why I say that. Those characters were really extraordinary - for example I took some characters from horror movies. Like Medusa, whose hair is made of snakes, and also a Centaur, which is part human and part horse. Also, do you know Kannon?[10] The bodhisattva?[11]

JS: The Buddhist deity?

MK: Yes, with a thousand hands behind her. And all of these creatures are supposed to be robots. In order to feel satisfied when destroying those monsters, part of the Centaur, and Medusa, and the Buddhist deity of mercy... Parts of them would fall off, after one hit, or two hits. We were trying to do that using 2D images, not even 3D. So the manpower required to create and program that was really beyond imagination. <*laughs*> It happened more than 20 years ago, so would have been difficult at the time.

JS: This game sounds AMAZING.

MK: <*laughs*> The team members who worked on the project, and later also on the basketball game, we're still close friends. All of them went to and are now working for other companies, but we're all still friends.

JS: Lots of people will be interested. Put it online!

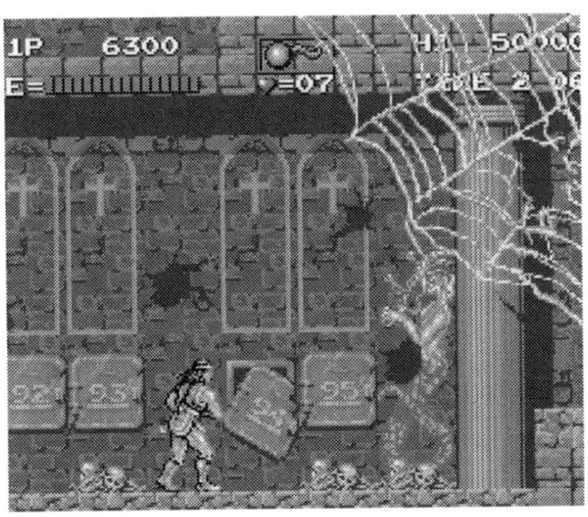

MK: I see. I'm going to think about it! But I think if we were to make the game using modern 3D technology, the result would be just an ordinary title. The way we worked 20 years ago, drawing all the images by hand and developing the *sekaikan*, I think that may still hold interest. But making the game with today's technology would just yield an ordinary, run-of-the-mill game.

[10] Also known as Guanyin, the Goddess of Mercy

[11] A being of enlightenment

JS: *Sekaikan*! There's been discussion in English circles on the importance of that word. It has deep layers of meaning; the atmosphere, world lore, world view, the background behind things.

MK: Yes. The word *sekaikan* includes everything, it's the magic that attracts players into the world of that arcade game. How can we get players immersed in the world, using the surroundings? So probably it's very hard to explain that in English. The *sekaikan* is the most essential part of any game. Because that represents the entire attraction the title might have. When people play games, they only have a limited space and time. For example if you think about films, if you go to a movie theatre you are there sharing the same thing with other people, all present in that space. You are surrounded by a certain world in your imagination. That way people can be attracted to something more easily, and become absorbed much more easily. But when it comes to home console games, and arcade games, all we have is just the screen. The world we would like to express to the players, is represented by the limited space of that screen. It might be small, tiny even. By moving one's eyes [to the side] the player might suddenly be faced with day-to-day life. On the screen we're trying to express non-daily life. *Sekaikan* is the key to attract the player, get them absorbed, totally immersed in the new environment and value system, the surroundings represented in the world of that game by that screen.

JS: This fighting game, did it have a name?

MK: I have to think... I forgot! I'm sorry. <*laughs*> It might come back to me after a while. <*laughs*>

JS: You worked on *Haunted Castle*. Why wasn't it called *Castlevania*? In Japan it was still known as *Akumajou Dracula*.

MK: The original Famicom and arcade version differ in mechanics and gameplay. In the arcades, complicated mechanics pose a problem, so it became a very different game. It is an *Akumajou Dracula* game, but very specifically made for the arcades and not a port. I think that's why the *Castlevania* title was not used in favour of an original title. The marketing plan for the Japanese market was probably built on the name recognition value of *Akumajou Dracula*.

JS: Many series started in arcades then went to consoles. *Akumajou Dracula* was the reverse...

MK: When the [arcade] development team planned a horror action game, they needed a taste for gothic horror, and thus imitated the concept of the Famicom hit. So a unique *Akumajou Dracula* for arcades was planned and made. So it's not quite a reverse conversion from home consoles to the arcades.

JS: Can you remember the moment you were asked to work on it? One of my favourite ideas is the last stage, with the collapsing bridge.

MK: I was not an original member of the development team. At that time the game was in a bad shape, quality- and schedule-wise. So the then boss [of Konami] ordered me to help out the team. I was developing an entirely different game, but for a single month all the artists of that team joined the project. We crunched the whole month to complete the unfinished stages and characters, and to improve all the player and enemy sprites, effects and attacks, which were not so good. The schedule left no room for any bigger considerations or changes, but the player attacks and gameplay were changed and improved. I think the crumbling bridge was an idea during that phase.

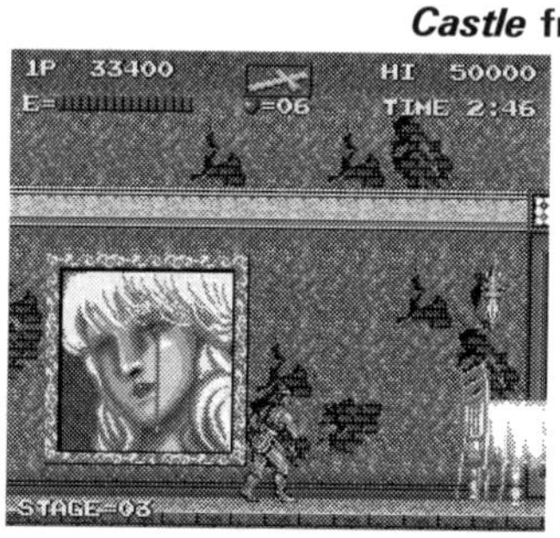

JS: What do you think are the important characteristics of the *Akumajou Dracula* series?

MK: Of course I consider the setting, which is not simple horror but gothic horror, and also a refreshing feeling, most important.

JS: How much contact did you have with the Famicom/MSX teams during development?

MK: Since it was not a port but an original game, there wasn't any frequent contact.

JS: Your composer, Kenichi Matsubara,[12] was also composer for *Castlevania II: Simon's Quest*. Did *Haunted Castle* share other staff members?

MK: No. Matsubara-san was working for arcade games at that time. He later moved to the consumer R&D department.

JS: Did you know any of the team from the first *Akumajou Dracula*? They're not credited.

MK: Yes. I also know the sound composer of *Castlevania*, she joined the company the same year as I did. Now she lives in the United States. Ms Kinuyo Yamashita[13] was the composer of the original score. Ms Muramatsu[14] was the lead artist. Mr Akamatsu[15] was the lead programmer. The other guys I don't remember. There was another person who did the sound programming, he now lives in Osaka. He became independent. I sometimes work with him.

JS: Is that Masahiro Ikariko?[16]

MK: I know him too! The gentleman I'm talking about, the sound programmer, is Mizutani-san.[17] Right now we're on the same project.

JS: Do you know anything about *Snake's Revenge*, which shared staff with *Castlevania III*?

MK: I don't know the details about *Snake's Revenge*. I know the game was developed by the same staff as the original *Castlevania* for NES. So you can find their names.

JS: You mentioned you were moved to *Haunted Castle* from another title. Please tell me more.

MK: Please do not misunderstand what I am going to tell you next. I am not criticising the company! OK? <*laughs*> Simply because of development policies, that was what I had to do. In essence the team that was developing *Haunted Castle* needed extra hands. Like hired guns. That's what it is. First of all, the title I was working on at that time was called *Hot Chase*, which is a driving game. So the other team was working on the development of *Haunted Castle*. But they were shorthanded. We needed to finish

[12] 松原 健一 ; also did the sound for *Crisis Force* (FC)

[13] 山下絹代 ; huge portfolio, incl. *Arumana no Kiseki*
[14] First name unknown
[15] Hitoshi Akamatsu - likely the father of the CV series. Worked on *Time Pilot*. I found his partial home address via an arcade patent, but the letters were undeliverable
[16] Composer on *SD Snatcher* and *MG2:SS*
[17] Possibly Iku Mizutani, *Konami Kukeiha Club* member

Haunted Castle, so my boss ordered the entire team [on *Hot Chase*] to provide helping hands to the team of *Haunted Castle*, for a limited time only. For two months. In order to make the game better they needed more manpower, external help. That's what we did, working on ROM graphics, and planning, and so on.

JS: Why did the game end up being so difficult?

MK: The project was short-staffed. Time for debugging was needed, but we couldn't make any more changes to the balancing. At that time I had already returned to my original project. That was the most regrettable part. I think the development time was about 6 months.

JS: Some arcade games you can put infinite coins in, but *Haunted Castle* has a max limit.

MK: I didn't touch upon all the details of the programming of that title. But I remember, depending on the game developer, there were different policies. In terms of insertion of coins, or tokens, the manufacturer can make it infinite, as you mentioned. Or they can make it where once a game has ended, then Game Over. There is no restart even if the player wants to insert another coin. What was important for arcade game development was the fine tuning of the difficulty. For example if the player is good, or skilful, then the player can reach the second level, and third level, and on and on forever. Using just a few coins. In order to avoid that, what we needed to do was adjust the difficulty level so that as the levels go up, the game becomes more difficult to complete. So even skilled and really experienced players have a hard time going on to the next stage and continuing forever. But the truth is, we didn't have enough time to refine the game to that level, and also a different programmer was working as a director on *Haunted Castle*, which was not myself, and that director's intent behind the scenes probably played a role in making the decision.

JS: Was it considered a success in arcades?

MK: No. We would have liked to make it a better game if we had the time.

JS: Did you see the Oretachi Game Center Zoku release of *Akumajou Dracula* on PlayStation 2?[18]

[18] No-frills arcade port, sold as a standalone PS2 game

MK: No. By the time it was released I had left Konami and was living in London, so I didn't know about it.

JS: Tell me about Hitoshi Akamatsu.

MK: Akamatsu-san is the original Famicom game programmer. He didn't have anything to do with the arcade version.

JS: Did Mr Akamatsu work on *Time Pilot*?

MK: I don't think so, actually.

JS: After you mentioned Mr Akamatsu was head of the FC version, I wanted to find him. There were no clues apart from a patent registration for *Time Pilot*, on a Canadian patents website. It listed his partial home address. I looked at the city and street name, and found five possibilities. Unfortunately all my letters were undeliverable.

MK: Ahh.

JS: Do have any interesting anecdotes from working on *Haunted Castle*?

MK: When I joined the team to provide some help, the project was ongoing already. The planning for the game itself was already far along; the release date had been fixed, and the title in particular was also already decided to be *Akumajou Dracula* in keeping with the home versions. But on the other hand, the actual game content was not up to speed.[19] So the mission that I was given was rewriting all the players and graphics and so on. What was missing in these graphics was a sense of presence. They were not formidable enough, and that's what I wanted to do. <*laughs*> So I started to work on a variety of things and we had other team artists, and many of them were really capable. I still keep in touch with them today. We brainstormed what we were going to do about the bosses, and so on. So the game itself, I find it's too difficult to be successful. Regrettably. But graphics, I am confident about those characters that we created. For example the rock character, the

[19] Chronologically in Japan: *CVII*, Aug 87; *HC*, Feb 88; *CVIII*, Dec 89. The time constraint was due to the fixed arcade release date. Meanwhile, the theme and the title had already been decided based on the earlier home versions (the first Famicom and MSX2 games). The time constraint is due to the arcade release schedule only, and not any of the home versions

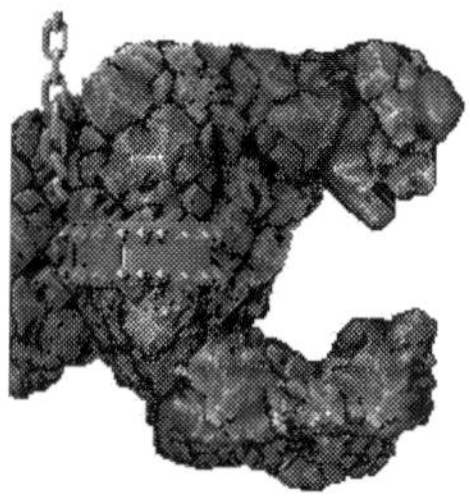

Golem boss you referred to, or the skeleton characters, I think we put a lot of energy and spirit into those characters. So we were really confident about the visuals. But the other side of the coin is that I only had a limited time to work on the game. And only for two months. Given the time frame, I couldn't do even one half of what I wanted to do on the game. We might have been able to polish the program, so it was a little better. We could have done many things on the program, but we couldn't due to time constraints. That's one regret I have about that game.

[55 words redacted regarding Haunted Castle]

JS: I'll keep that off the record. Is it true that Mr Isao Akada,[20] producer on the *Jikkyou Powerful Pro Yakyuu* baseball series, is the grandchild of the landlord at the flat you lived in 22 years ago?

MK: <*laughs*> That's right! <*laughs*> Well, before I got married I wanted to save on rent so that I could save money. The person who introduced me to that building, which was not an apartment, it was an old building. I had a female senior, one year senior to me, and her husband was producer on *Pro Yakyuu*. His wife's grandmother was the owner of that old building. So I remember visiting her, this old lady, and having a nice little chat, when I paid the monthly rent. Unfortunately the landlady passed away in the Great Hanshin earthquake back in 1995.[21]

JS: Mr Oka mentioned the 1995 earthquake. I think that's when Konami changed buildings.

MK: Correct. Because the office was located on the artificial island of Kobe, Port Island, and the ground was liquidated. That's why.

JS: You also mentioned that the illustrator for *Metal Gear 2* was Mr Yoshiyuki Takani, one of the most famous illustrators for TAMIYA?

MK: Yes. We outsourced the illustration to this gentleman, an illustrator, who mainly did work on TAMIYA military plastic models, for the design of *Metal Gear 2*. It was his first piece of work for videogames.

JS: Do you have any anecdotes?

MK: That's a game for home computers. But this applies to arcade games as well. When it comes to posters or catalogues, Konami used external contracted illustrators for those purposes. So I think you can do a little interesting analysis... Because Konami, and this applies to any other game developer, they tended to use a couple of the same illustrators, when it comes to posters and catalogues and so on. So depending on the time period, you might find some similarities in the artistic styles. But it depends on the region. What I mentioned only applies to the Japanese market. In the USA and Europe, typically those games were sold through distributors or sales companies, and the cabinet design, posters, catalogues, publicity materials, and so on, were created by those sales companies. In Japan we used illustrators, to provide those publicity materials. But in the case of the USA and Europe they might hire some actors, and provide a photo shoot with the actor playing the game. Those photos would be applied to the cabinet, as a seal, or maybe used in the catalogues.

For example with *Crime Fighters,* that title is very interesting. In Japan we used an illustration, but in the US they used a photo shoot and, for example, the final boss looked like a mafia boss. He doesn't have any hair. In the US they brought in an actor, who wasn't actually quite as bald, <*laughs*> and then the actor had to shave off his hair. So the hairline was kind of visible in the picture. We also had in the different stages punks with Mohawk hair, a red haired boss, and that one also was

[20] Programmer on *Vampire Killer, SD Snatcher, Metal Gear 2, Hyperstone Heist* et al
[21] 17 January 1995, in Kobe

expressed by an actor having that hairdo, in a photo shoot in the US, for the side of the cabinet. Rather than an illustration.

Photo by Judy Garvey of www.judygarvey.ca

MK: For the promotional image on the basketball game's cabinet, we actually used photos both in the United States and in Japan. We did the photo shoot in Chicago, in the US, and because it's Chicago, you have to use the Bulls. Am I right? The basketball player, a black gentleman, was lower down in the hierarchy of the team, so you wouldn't recognise his name - but we took some photos of him doing dunks, shooting the ball, and so on. That was used both in the US and in Japan.

JS: Let's talk about *Crime Fighters*. It allowed up to 4 players.

MK: That's right. For the Japanese and European versions only two players were able to play. Given the difference in game playing cultures, between Japan and America, we decided on the number of players. Let me explain why we decided on the number 4.[22] In terms of the US version, at that time Atari's *Gauntlet* was a big hit in the United States. That enabled 4 players to play simultaneously. That style of play was not really the mainstream, but it was kind of trendy at that time. So based on that we decided to create a fighting game (beat-em-up) enabling 4 players to play at once.

In the United States, at that time at least, people who were total strangers played arcade games together. As long as there was an opening in the slots. So one person might have a Game Over, and then another steps in and all that. That's why we decided we should enable 4 players to play simultaneously. But quite separate from that, in Japan and Europe, the main demographic of players in arcades was friends who played together, or maybe individual solo players. So we decided the maximum number of players who can play at once should be limited to 2.

JS: Did it reduce the cost of the hardware, limiting it to 2 players?

MK: In terms of hardware, it didn't make that much difference. It originates from the arcade game sales distribution channel. In the US we had to provide so-called "turn key" solutions. As soon as the unit's power is turned on, it's immediately usable. In the case of the US we sold the entire cabinet, with 4 controllers, to be played by 4 people. But in Japan we had all those "universal purpose" cabinets, in which only a PCB was replaced.[23] So the cost for the sale was totally different. But the hardware itself, specification wise, was identical.

JS: *Crime Fighters* had some amusing in-game adverts - were they your idea?

MK: <*laughs*> Yes, I thought about those. There is a specific stage which I really worked on a lot, by myself. The subway stage. I drew the characters and the background, mainly I was

---

[22] Konami developed an excellent rep for 4 player arcade games, including: *TMNT2*, *Bucky O'Hare*, *X-Men*, and *The Simpsons*, among many others

[23] It's worth noting a cultural difference for arcades: in Japan little emphasis is placed on the cabinet, marquee, or artwork, it's the original PCB which is important. Conversely in the US, much more emphasis is placed on restoring and maintaining the bespoke cabinet itself

working on the characters but for the stage, I also did the backgrounds. I also worked on the billboards and I thought about ideas for the adverts, along with my team members.

JS: Some of them were quite amusing - and racy!

MK: <*laughs*> Yes, yes, I came up with some of them. You know, some of my team members donated or contributed some of their ideas, and so on. When we started to do game launches outside of Japan, we had one guy who came fresh out of LA university.[24] His parents came from Hong Kong. He came to Japan and worked with us, and I brainstormed with him. So we came up with phrases that were edgy, but not quite edgy enough to be arrested for. <*laughs*> One I remember is, a billboard for an insurance company, illustrating a young lady covering her breasts with her hands. The logo says "Are you covered?" The assumption is it means covered by insurance. But as the player gets close to the billboard, it collapses over the player and they take damage.

In the game, what I wanted to do was create interesting enemies, rather than making the player really exquisite. So in each stage there was a boss, and those bosses were created to be more human than in other games. We gave some directions towards that end, and probably you don't know about this... Actually the Japanese version of the game is different from the English versions. We removed some problematic scenes from the US version, and the ones that were cut included a so-called "hard gay" boss, wearing a leather jacket, really tight, and with a moustache. He enters the scene dancing, and tries to get close to the player. Once close, he kind of hugs the player and starts shaking his hips. <*laughs*>

Another character we created was an S&M Queen with a whip. She comes to the player and tries to use her whip to attack the player. Also, for an enemy we created a dog character as well. So some of them are just normal dogs, but some of them, other dogs, might be... in the mating season. <*laughs*> Those dogs which are in mating season, as soon as they come to the player they start shaking their hips as well. So some of those things had to be eliminated from the English versions.

JS: I know an arcade expert with the PCB. He says he invented the green wrap for PCBs.[25]

MK: I see! <*laughs*> I have the PCB myself. I bought one for myself. I had the experience of helping out with the shipment of PCBs, or replacing ROM chips when they've a problem with bugs, and so on.

JS: Have you seen the green bubble wrap?

MK: In the case of Konami the wrap typically used was either pink or transparent. The pink wrap was supposed to eliminate the static charge. Because PCBs are a precision piece of equipment, you had to eliminate the static.

JS: Were you influenced by other games?

MK: Hmm, other companies' creations? We were constantly studying other game developers' programs. Of course all the companies boasted about high technology - high technology in everything - software, hardware, game design, and everything. So we were constantly studying competitors' products. Capcom, for example. They were using unusual techniques, not common in the industry at that time.

JS: For example?

MK: In *Daimakaimura*. I learned a lot from Capcom's techniques. To give you an example, in terms of the background, at that time we painted everything in detail. Even in the background. But what Capcom did was, they might black out some parts of it, so it's supposed to be the shadow portion of something. So that made a really strong contrast between those blacked out areas, as opposed to detailed areas, thereby creating more depth in the picture. Also, for example, they might shake the trees in

[24] MobyGames lists a "C. Lee" who might be him

[25] Takayuki Komabayashi of Beep Shop - interviewed in later volumes

the background. So those things were new to me. I learned from their techniques in *Daimakaimura*. I mention the title just because it stimulated me, and at that time it was a really sophisticated title. I learned a lot from that game. So given the standards of the time, Capcom's game was really sophisticated. You know, nowadays, the industry's technology level has become pretty much standardised. All the game companies have about the same capacity as each other. But at that time, hardware and programming skills varied from one company to another quite a bit! So depending on a person's programming skills, what could be expressed in a game differed a great deal. At that time it was not technology driven, it was more like craftsmanship driven. So one team member's good sense could change the outcome quite a bit. It was a large factor in doing the programming.

JS: On your biography you listed *Surprise Attack*. I haven't played this, please describe it.

MK: That was an experimental development title. In terms of the content of the game, it was fairly standard in one sense. It's like a horizontally scrolling timing-action game. Meaning it's like a puzzle, and the stage is set in outer space. But it's horizontally scrolling, so you have to wait and see when is the right moment to fire your gun, and then the enemy could be falling from the ceiling, from further in outer space. You have to aim at that and shoot them down. So it's not that you keep shooting everywhere no matter what, it's more like you time your firing and aim at specific enemies. Put simply, it's close to Namco's *Rolling Thunder*.

JS: I know the game.

MK: And Sega's arcade *Shinobi* title. It was experimental in that apart for myself, all the other development members - artists and programmers and hardware designers - were new people at the company. We formed a team and I worked as a director of the team, and then of course because everyone else was new, we couldn't quite convey a nice outcome in the end. But it was experimental as a development initiative. From here this is off the record please.

Originally the new title was meant to be a kind of homage to, or licensed title of ***[REDACTED]***. Back in the 1980s there was ***[REDACTED]***. We were creating the characters in line with that. We became, in the end, unable to create the title due to licensing issues. At that time ***[REDACTED-A]*** was having exchanges with ***[REDACTED-B]***, but ***[REDACTED-C]*** came in, and they offered a higher bid. Then ***[REDACTED-B]*** started to realise how much value that license might have. So rather than contracting with another company, ***[REDACTED-B]*** decided to use their ***[REDACTED]*** to do the development. But in the end that flopped, it didn't come through. But ***[REDACTED-A]*** had already been making a great deal of progress when it flopped. We licensed ***[REDACTED]*** music, and also we were creating a demo trailer, and so on. Because the project was terminated we shifted direction into something entirely different, into this horizontally scrolling timing-action game, using space as a theme.

JS: What percentage of *Surprise Attack*, as it is now, is still recognisable as that cancelled prototype?

MK: I would say 60% in terms of game system. We kind of transplanted 60% of the main game system, but of course it was a ***[REDACTED]*** featured title, then we should have a ***[vehicle]*** stage, and so on. So that had to go. Also, originally, we assumed there would be physical fights, using knuckles and knees, and kicking and so on. But as soon as the project shifted its direction to something different, it became a shooting game rather than a physical fighting game. But nonetheless 60% of the main game system came from that ***[REDACTED]*** title.

[63 words redacted entirely]

JS: Is it OK if I put *[REDACTED]* in the book?

MK: <*laughs*> That sounds funny.

JS: If you ever feel comfortable about it being revealed, let me know.

MK: OK, I will let you know. Even though it's about the past, I don't think the information is going to become available for disclosure, at any time in the future. Because there is an issue between myself and many other companies. So I don't think it's going to happen.

JS: I'll put it in my secret memoirs, to be published after my death.[26]

<everyone laughs>

MK: Well, I had a lot of challenges in developing that game, *Surprise Attack*.

JS: We're on the record now, right?

MK: Yes, that's fine. But it was a good experience for me. Well, you can say we were trying to license a movie, or something like that.

JS: OK. Keep it ambiguous.

MK: I'm a big fan of ***[REDACTED]***, I'm a ***[REDACTED]***, so that whole idea of creating a game out of the film was my idea. So I was the one who contacted ***[REDACTED]***, asking for permission. So at that time, I had to wait for another 6 months before the release of the film in Japan. I remember going to the United States just to see the film!

JS: Wow! That's incredible. Let's talk about *Silent Scope*. You were the director, planner and lead artist. How did the concept come about?

MK: That was an interesting game. There were other gun games, but this is the first ever sniper gun game. At that time the cost of small, colour LCD screens, such as those used in mobile phones, was coming down - because of the increasing proliferation of mobile phones in society. The idea wasn't only limited to myself, many others were thinking about possible applications for those small-sized LCDs at that time. What I wanted to do was not use the small LCD screen as an input device, I wanted to give more depth to the game using those small screens. So in terms of the rifle game, the player can aim at something using the smaller sized LCD, in which the image of certain parts can be magnified. So I was very happy to be able to express my concept of giving more spatial depth to the game.

JS: It was rare in the UK. I only saw it once, in London. But the concept was amazing. Was there resistance from colleagues?

MK: We didn't have too many opposing opinions to start with. Including myself, all the team members had a firm conviction that it was going to be an interesting title, and a success. So I rejected all the opposing comments. Because this was an unprecedented new system, two months after we started on the project we provided a prototype cabinet. Program wise, we completed it up to the second stage. We started early testing, on site in game centres. Because it was an innovative new system we had to do the site testing early on. We wanted to see how players might respond, and whether the system could be easily understood by the players or not. We were repeating the process over and over. I'll give you an interesting anecdote about what happened during the on-site testing.

In the area where the game arcade was located, there were so many students - college students, and high school students, and so on. The arcade was open until late at night. One of the guys who played the game, he was so absorbed in watching what can be seen in the scope, that when there was a physical system short-circuit, a shortage in the prototype, there was smoke coming out of the screen, all over and around his head. But he didn't even notice it! Afterwards I had to profusely apologise to the guy, for the breakdown.

JS: There were several sequels, plus conversions to consoles. I enjoyed the Dreamcast release. Magazines speculated it would never see a home conversion. Did you follow the conversions?

MK: Well, including myself, arcade program development staff had a strong sense of pride. At that time, the hardware specifications of home consoles was higher than the specifications for arcade games. What we thought was, we should do whatever cannot be done inside any home. Something only arcade game centres can offer to players. In the case of *Silent Scope* it's not a game where a controller should be used to provide the input. It's a game designed to use a smaller-sized LCD to take aim at the target. So technologically speaking, the

---

[26] True fact: I have a big dossier of "off the record" knowledge, all of which will become public upon my death. All journalists should do the same

conversion was 100% complete I think. But in terms of the objective of the game, that was lost I feel. I didn't work on the home conversions myself, other staff did. I had some exchanges with this independent team which worked on the console versions. But in terms of how to "season" the game, the taste is completely different between the home versions and arcade version. They were two separate things, I think.

At present, for example, the iOS devices have an application called *Silent Scope*, it's a converted version which can be run on iOS. But the data input device is different from the arcade version. Only the software was converted and transplanted into iOS. So here is my idea - if they would like to recreate the world of *Silent Scope*, then they should create something new, as an original project. For example, these days AR technology[27] is available. So if you're trying to take a picture, the enemy pops up in the display, or something. What I think is, it's not enough just to convert the program so it can run on a new device. It's such a waste to do that, considering the great innovation and intentions of the original program. They should create something brand new incorporating new technology that is the best fit for the new device.

27 Augmented Reality

JS: An AR version sounds ingenious.

MK: You know, honestly speaking, I feel like I should reboot the program myself. I left Konami, so I can't do that anymore, but if I could, I wish I could work on that. <*laughs*>

JS: Out of your career which game holds the most meaning? Would it be *Silent Scope*?

MK: I love all of them! <*laughs*> I say that because I put more than 100% of myself into development of any game I worked on in the past. But if I had to choose, for example *Silent Scope* is one. Also *Crime Fighters*, because of my affection for my dear team members who I worked with at that time. It was an experience for me. Also, the basketball game - we had so many challenges in the development, but nonetheless it was interesting. Also, in Europe, there was a game I worked on called *Asterix*, and this experience was somewhat new to me; the style of development was unprecedented for me. One thing that pleased me a lot was a comment from the French media people. This game was based on a manga in France, and those French media guys asked me whether the game was made in France or not. That pleased me! <*laughs*> Because the entire team that developed *Asterix* was Japanese. All of them.

JS: How did the *Asterix* project start? Had you read all the comics?

MK: At that time, Konami was trying to have greater emphasis in the overseas market. At that time the largest market was the United States, and development was skewed towards that large market, naturally. But around that time we also started to think about putting more emphasis on Europe. So we were trying to find comics that might be helpful in development, and were considering licensing options, and so on. We wanted to utilise the fighting game expertise that we had cultivated from past titles. At that time the overseas business unit happened to bring about the proposal of *Asterix*.

By that point in Japan *Asterix* was still unknown. There was no Japanese language edition, so almost nobody knew about it; even now I think it is still not commonly known. So we imported the comic books - the entire collection, every volume. And I read all of them in Japan. Also, in contracting the license agreement with the licensor, I went to the US,

France, and Germany, to gather information. In France there is this license company, to which the original author entrusted the rights. So we did market surveys, and we had many meetings, and there is a theme park dedicated to the *Asterix* comic, in a suburb of Paris. So I went there in order to study the comic. I gathered a lot of information about it.

JS: Sounds like a lot of fun, travelling the world to make games!

MK: Well, nowadays it's kind of standard, to have this kind of information gathering tour in the area, when doing the planning, and prior to game development. In modern games, we need to take pictures of materials to use as reference for stage design and for fine details, such as textures when creating 3D objects. So now it's common to go on research tours and take photos, which we then process and paste onto 3D models as textures to create a realistic scene. But back in the day, when I did the development of *Asterix*, the hardware was not yet so developed to accommodate 3D images. So maybe it was a kind of a rare experience, for me, at that time. I had such a good experience in doing the tour all over the world, that it helped me to remain motivated.

That comic book, *Asterix*, is a kind of caricature. It's not designated only for children, but adults can also enjoy reading it. So the stage is set to be in a variety of countries: Italy, England, America, India, Egypt, and so on. So depending on the country, the perception of the comic or things in it are different. We found out that *Asterix* is an old, long-standing character, that is loved by many people in many places. I came to understand that I cannot work on the game with an easy going mindset, I had to get serious about it.

JS: Your last *Silent Scope* game, *Fortune Hunter*, was a gambling game for the UK. The next year you left Konami to join Gamewax in the UK. Is there a connection between *Fortune Hunter* and moving to the UK?

MK: <*laughs*> Yes, there is a connection! You know, my wife and I, we were always interested in living in the UK. We really wanted to live there. So I was talking to Konami management about the possibility of opening up a development office in the UK, but it didn't come easily. So at that time the company asked me to develop *Silent Scope Fortune Hunter* for the UK market, a gambling videogame version. From which cash can be refunded if the player can achieve a high score. Only under UK law was that doable. So I did. I stayed in the UK for 2 months, as the director of that version, along with another person as a programmer. We did market surveys and we made necessary adjustments on the spot, and those two months were very enjoyable for me. I loved it! So I wanted to keep living in the UK. At that time, seizing the momentum of the moment, a French arcade game distributor came up with an idea to establish a game development company. That information came to me via an acquaintance. I was invited to participate in that new company. And I said yes, because I really wanted to live in the UK, and that seemed like a good opportunity. So that's why I left Konami.

JS: Was it a fruit machine type game? [28]

MK: Hmm, not quite. It was an SWP game - Skill With Prizes. A fruit machine is AWP. [29] In the case of AWP, what mainly drives the game's outcome is sheer luck. Whereas with SWP, what matters is the player's skill and capacity to play the game well. Of course we have some internal program adjustments, so that it's not the case that a skilful player can always win a prize. But nonetheless it's skill dependant. In terms of input device, we used exactly the same rifle, with the small LCD to aim at the target. In terms of the game system, it's similar to the arcade version - not all of it, but part of it. I don't think you can find them anymore, but at the time they were available in London, in the Soho area, or Leicester Square, in places with gambling games. This was back in 2002 or 2003.

---

[28] Almost like a one-arm bandit without the arm

[29] Amusement With Prizes; interaction but not dependant on skill

JS: A decade ago! What did you think of the UK?

MK: I would return to the UK if I could! *<laughs>* My wife and I, we're actually planning a trip to the UK, after my current project is over. I loved everything - the food, the cloudy weather, *<laughs>* and the National Trust.[30] Plus the scenery in downtown London. I know a good fish & chip restaurant as well. *<laughs>* Paul Weller and Noel Gallagher, the musicians, they frequent some fish & chip restaurants, and that's what I like. The food served at those places is excellent! *<laughs>*

JS: Do you like black pudding?

MK: *<laughs>* Maybe a little. I don't like marmite so much. Actually, Noel Gallagher, I happened to meet him on the way back to Japan. While I lived in China I had to change flights in Hong Kong, to return to Japan. And Noel Gallagher was in front of me, going through immigration. I was so happy.

JS: You should have tapped him on the shoulder and said, "I made *Silent Scope*!"

<everyone laughs>

MK: Well, maybe he doesn't know it.

JS: You'd be surprised who plays videogames.

MK: Actually, you know, there are so many sheik in the United Arab Emirates, and one of the princes - presumably the most powerful one - he has a game arcade inside his palace. He has a *Silent Scope* unit inside the arcade.

JS: Hopefully after the book is out, someone standing behind you will tap your shoulder and say: "Hey! You made some great games!"

MK: *<laughs>* I'm looking forward to having that experience.

JS: Can you sketch the SNK layout?

MK: In terms of the number of people, a headcount, I cannot be so precise because there is an issue in terms of non-disclosure.

JS: I understand. Can I use this image?

MK: Fine, you can go ahead.

JS: Tell me about joining SNK-Playmore. You worked on *KOF XII*, and then *KOF XIII* was when they made the big jump to high-resolution.

MK: We wanted to keep living in the UK forever. But at that time I had some family issues, my mother was hospitalised, and although I love everything about the UK, maybe there were some policy changes in the company for which I worked at that time. So we decided to come back to Japan. But once back home I couldn't stay idle, without earning any pay. I had to look for a job. At that time SNK was recruiting, so we had a little chat and then I decided to work for the company. At that time, as you mentioned, *The King of Fighters* was undergoing a great technological change between version *XI* and *XII*. The art style changed, everything changed. Up to version *XI* the series succeeded and capitalised on its legacy artwork. But everything had to go when shifting to a new style. That was the intent of the development team, as well as the corporation. I did not work on the title

[30] A charity that protects historic places

before, so I had to go with the decision of the other guys. But that kind of drastic change always entails a lot of challenges. That's what I experienced. It was really an "across the board" kind of change. Starting from the development method, and hardware, everything had to be changed. In terms of hardcore fans of *The King of Fighters*, we found divided opinions.

JS: After that you worked on *[REDACTED]*, for the Chinese market. Then a few years later you go to China. Is there a connection?

MK: <*laughs*> No, no, there's no connection to that. From here, it's off the record.

[114 words redacted]

JS: Why did you leave SNK?

MK: As I explained earlier, SNK had a lot of policy changes, and those policies did not fit with my ideas about games. I was interested in the Chinese arcade game market, because it's a big business, and so that's what I wanted to try. Hence why I went to China.

JS: What was China like?

MK: <*laughs*> Every day I had many culture shocks. Good and bad. I learned a lot from that experience. I came to understand how nice a country Japan and also the UK is. I don't mean to criticise China, but it was a tough place to live. Of course there is the issue of language, but it was also a tough place in terms of the environment and the food, and so on.

JS: Is this why you returned to Japan?

MK: One is a personal reason. I used to always live with my wife, ever since we got married. But for the first time we were separated, because I had to work in China. I didn't feel like bringing my wife with me to China. Also, my mother-in-law eventually passed away. So I needed to support my wife because of the loss. I wanted to be with her in that hard time.

Also, there was a change in the state head of China. A new guy assumed the state head position. So there was a great change in the arcade game market, and it was driven down to almost zero. Because the top guy was changed, everything had to change, many industries had to undergo great changes. The arcade game business was almost frozen, and that great tide of change made me think that perhaps I should also change jobs as well. Then I decided to head back to Japan.

JS: And now you're planning to return to SNK?

MK: The company, in terms of SNK, the company was changing again, with the reinstatement of Mr Kawasaki, as chairperson. Even before I came back to Japan I had some talks with acquaintances, but the nature of the talks was not anything serious at that time. But when I came back to Japan for good, that's when Mr Kawasaki made a personal call to me, to come back and join SNK again. In the arcade gaming business Mr Kawasaki is one of the most charismatic people in the industry. I always had the desire to work with him. This time Mr Kawasaki has come back to the field, and I'm so happy to be able to work with him.

JS: Is there any final message you have?

MK: I've spent my entire career on arcade game development. I love my work, and going forward I continue to love my work. From now on I will continue to work on developing games that I truly love. I shouldn't limit myself to arcade game development, because in any country the market for arcade games is declining, in a way. So I don't mean to limit myself to the platform of arcade games, I'm open to other platforms.

~Appearing in a later volume~

Toshinari Oka
Continuing the Konami coverage is an interview with one of the company's MSX programmers, revealing the inside story on games such as the original *Parodious* (including content so risqué it had to be cut!), and humorous stories of late night food runs for meat buns.

Manabu Yamana
The programmer behind the original *Dragon Quest* series discusses working at Chunsoft, and the time he met the then-president of Nintendo, Hiroshi Yamauchi, in a traditional tea house. He also gives a detailed explanation on the expensive programming environment used during Famicom development.

村山 吉隆

MURAYAMA, Yoshitaka

DOB: *secret* / Birthplace: *secret* / Blood Type: *secret

~ Selected Portfolio ~

Suikoden	- PlayStation, 1995 (Producer, writer, director)
Suikoden II	- PlayStation, 1998 (Producer, writer, director)
Genso Suikogaiden Vol. 1: Harmonia no Kenshi	- PlayStation, 2000 (Writer)
Genso Suikogaiden Vol. 2: Crystal Valley no Kettou	- PlayStation, 2001 (Writer)
Suikoden III	- PlayStation 2, 2002 (Producer, writer, director)
10'000 Bullets	- PlayStation 2, 2005 (Producer, writer, director)
Tensho Gakuen Gekkoroku	- PlayStation 2, 2006 (Writer)
Unnamed Action-RPG (某社アクションRPG)	- Not yet released (In charge of scenario)

Interview with Yoshitaka Murayama ***(Contains mild plot spoilers)***
Conducted via email, translated by Harry Inaba and Jeremy Blaustein

"When one of my Guest Editors requested a chapter on the *Suikoden* series I was extremely pleased. It's an all-time favourite, both for the story and the mechanics. Reading the histories and epilogues of each of the recruitable 108 characters gave the world greater melancholy and gravitas than anything Square-Enix ever put out. The series tackled difficult issues of war and patricide with more heartfelt realism than any game of the time. It also innovated mechanically, allowing you to bribe enemies, or let them go if you were of a high level. It also introduced cooking minigames, squirrels, and a satisfying sense of progression as you accumulated resources, troops and fortified your castle. The first two are timeless masterpieces."
- John Szczepaniak, Author

"When I was young I imagined that making videogames was the best job in the world. I thought that making these works of art would be like pouring my soul directly into the characters that inhabit them. When I played games I wasn't just a lonely kid anymore. I was the hero that everyone depended on. I was living a life so much greater than I dreamed of. Games influenced me profoundly, and helped set a path that would eventually turn into a career. None more so, than *Suikoden*. Friends become enemies, and enemies into friends. The political nature of the story and diversity of the 108 characters that can join your cause created a unique and wonderful experience. *Suikoden* influenced the course of my life so strongly, I wanted to share it with as many people as possible."
- Jared Neal, Guest Editor

Unfortunately, prior to leaving for Japan I was unable to contact Mr Murayama. However, once I arrived, I met and spoke with Harry Inaba, formerly of Konami, and he revealed that he was again in contact with Mr Murayama. I provided him with translated Japanese questions, and Mr Inaba, along with Jeremy Blaustein, very kindly translated these into English for me. Given that both gentlemen were involved in the localisation of Suikoden and Suikoden II respectively, it seems rather appropriate. A lot of my questions were influenced by an interview Mr Murayama did for Swedish games magazine LEVEL, specifically #41, the August 2009 issue. You don't need to have read the LEVEL interview to appreciate these, but it explains why I focused on certain topics - notably the Konami console.[1]

When Mr Murayama started, he was assigned to create an RPG for Konami's planned system. It was an RPG about two countries at war, with childhood friends on opposing sides. Two other games were in development, a fighting and a racing game. Ultimately all were scrapped and Mr Murayama was assigned to create a game for Sony's PlayStation; he was given the choice between an RPG, a baseball game, or a racer. He chose to make an RPG, posing it as a prequel to the game previously worked on. Alongside the original Suikoden were two other RPGs being developed for PlayStation, which were later scrapped so all three teams could focus on completing Suikoden.

JS: Describe when and how you joined Konami.

YM: I joined Konami as a new graduate in 1992, in the role of programmer. In my second year after joining the department I was in was put in charge of creating games for Konami's game machine, and that's when I got involved in game design. Since it was an extremely secret project inside of Konami, there were very few people involved. So even though I was close to being a new recruit, I was expected to play a very large role. The plan at first was for Konami's game machine to be a console type, and it was suggested that it have a card reader function to allow players to exchange data. The plan changed midway from a console type to a portable type game machine, and it was going to have 3D (polygon) functionality that was not common at the time.

JS: What medium were the games to be on?

YM: Since it was going to be a portable game system, the plan was to use ROM cartridges.

JS: Had the outer design and control layout been finalised? Can you draw a sketch?

YM: The designs are all lost and I'm afraid that, with my poor memory, it would be difficult. It gave the impression of a Game Boy with a somewhat high-class feel.

JS: What kind of tech specs did it have?

YM: I don't have the details, so I really can't answer, but as I mentioned before, it was a portable game machine with 3D capability.

JS: Why was the console cancelled?

YM: While it was in development, it seems that we got word of the Sony PlayStation (first generation) and we shifted our direction into providing games for it.

JS: In addition to the RPG you were working on, there was a racing and a fighting game by other teams. How far along were these, and did they evolve into other titles which were released?

YM: When the development for the game machine was cancelled, those titles were completely abandoned. Actually, at the time, I was involved in the development of an RPG and a fighting game. The fighting game had about two characters that could be operated to a degree, and the RPG had a playable opening. Since the racing game was being done by another team, my recollection is a bit vague, but I think it was about 20% along in development. None of those titles went on to completion, but

[1] Partial translation of interview on Suikosource forums. Search for "Murayama's Reasons For Leaving"

the name of the hero's best friend in the RPG I was working on was later reused in *Suikoden*. That name was "Ted".[2]

JS: Please describe meeting and working alongside Junko Kawano.[3]

YM: We were contemporaries who entered the company at the same time and we were put into the same department. In our early years at the company, we often went out drinking with our contemporaries (those who entered in the same year) and we were very close.

Miss Kawano wasn't merely a designer, she had very strong ideas about games, and though we sometimes had disagreements about the contents of the games, it was fun and beneficial to work with her.

JS: Why did you create a prequel to the game originally planned for Konami's new console, rather than just carry on with the original?

YM: The RPG we were planning for Konami's game machine was designed for the purposes of a portable game machine, and had a strong emphasis placed on the element of raising characters. More concretely, we had planned for many classes and the players were going to strengthen their characters through repeated class changes. But when we changed to planning for an RPG on the PlayStation, since we were designing for a home console, we decided to place a greater emphasis on the game world and so we just decided to start over.

JS: What other RPGs did you play through before creating *Suikoden*? I read that you examined the source code to *Dragon Quest V*?

YM: Back then, I played RPGs that existed at the time like *Dragon Quest* and *Final Fantasy*, but I never got their source code. *Dragon Quest* was a particularly useful reference for me and I studied the fighting balance and the data information as I played through it.

JS: Please describe how the *Genso Suikoden* setting came about. I believe it was accidental, as a result of your desire to have strong secondary characters?

YM: I think you are correct in saying that I was trying to create strong supporting roles. There are many Japanese comics in which the characters, other than the main hero, are attractive and become close friends. Some examples of that at the time were *Captain Tsubasa*, *Saint Seiya*, and *Dragon Ball*. In American comics, you might say that *X-Men* is something like that. I wanted to create a dramatic story with many characters like that, so that during the game players could find the characters they liked - that was the starting point for *Suikoden*. The reason that this became "*Suikoden*" is because when we did an in-house presentation for our game idea, the higher-class executives were able to grasp easily what we were going for when we used the image of *Suikoden* as an example of what we meant.

JS: Were you a fan of the *Shui Hu Zhuan* novel?[4] The game's story seems like a departure from the written material.

YM: From an early age, I was a fan of old fables like "*Suikoden*" and "*Romance of the Three Kingdoms*" (*Sangokushi*), and I was strongly influenced by them to do a multi-character story. However, I decided that a pure Chinese style worldview was not a good choice for a Japanese RPG with a major fantasy focus, and so it became a half-fantasy and half-Chinese style worldview. For *Suikoden I*, I designed some story episodes based to some degree on "*Suikoden*" [the novel],

---

[2] In the original *Suikoden*, Ted is also the hero's friend

[3] Writer, director, and character designer on *Shadow of Memories*; I contacted Konami repeatedly to interview Junko Kawano, and while the US branch was keen, Konami's Japanese head office declined

[4] Chinese pronunciation for the novel known as *The Water Margin*, which *Suikoden* is loosely based on. The original deals with 108 outlaws who form an army, are pardoned, and then face foreign invaders
Traditional Chinese characters for the book: 水滸傳
Japanese Kanji for *Suikoden* the game: 水滸伝

but since *Suikoden II* was based on the story "*Kouu and Ryuuhou*",[5] it got rather far away from *Suikoden*.

JS: Before they were cancelled, what were the other two RPGs being developed alongside *Suikoden* like?

YM: One of them was cancelled while it was still in the planning stage, so I don't remember the details. The other, I think, was an action RPG. I really don't remember much about that either.

JS: Other RPGs allow players to run away from battle, but the *Suikoden* series introduced the option of bribing enemies and - if at a high enough level - letting enemies go free.

YM: In *Suikoden*, I was trying to focus on dramatically reducing the player's stress. As an example, for the enemy encounter determination, it's set up so that if you continue in one direction for a certain amount of time, the chances of an enemy encounter go down.

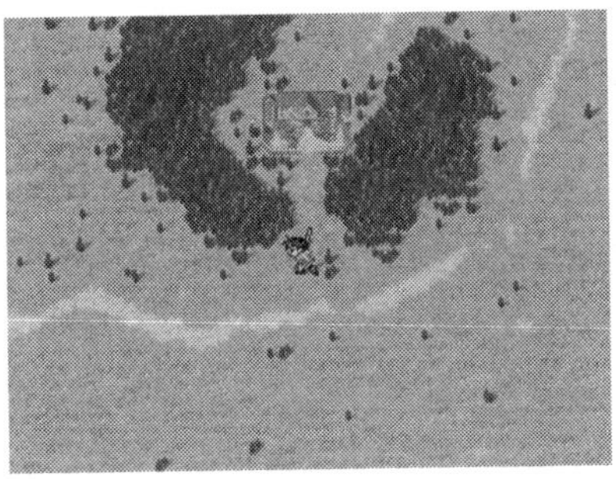

This is so that if you are heading for a certain destination, it will be less likely that you encounter an enemy, but if you are wandering around in order to level up, it will be easier for you to find an enemy.

The idea behind "Let Go" was so that you wouldn't have to fight enemies that would be easy to beat, and it works 100% of the time, or it's supposed to. "Bribe" is an extension of this and is designed to let you choose to avoid battle while paying for it with a financial penalty.

JS: The *Suikoden* games feature A LOT of content which is easy to permanently miss - for example the quest for the character Clive and Gremio's recipe #39. How did the team feel about this? Were you concerned some players would never see elements of your work?

YM: In fact, we designed the game so that clearing it without gathering all 108 members was normal and, conversely, gathering all members would be a special challenge. We also were thinking of Gremio's resurrection as a special "bonus". With regards to the contents, the thinking was that we just wanted the players to enjoy what they chose to enjoy. We're extremely grateful to those players that went so far as to play all those parts as well.

JS: Did any material have to be left out of the first two *Suikoden* titles, due to time? Please describe anything which did not make it.

YM: I don't remember very well since there were so many changes that happened during the development process, but just before the deadline for *Suikoden I*, there was one episode featuring a village that went over in terms of data memory, and so we were forced to cut out the second floor of a building by placing an NPC at the first floor stairs, who barred you from going upstairs. This was such a last minute measure that after *Suikoden* went on sale, some fans wondered whether or not there was some kind of "secret" up on the second floor that could be found. As a sort of apology for that, in *Suikoden 2* I put in a secret room that could only be found if there was a failure in the teleport mechanism. <*laughs*> I think that place also had a second floor that was impossible to get to.

JS: The first two *Suikoden* titles deal with very adult topics, including: patricide, terrorism / freedom fighters, chemical weapons, genocide, the execution of war criminals, the killing of civilians, racial prejudice, and other things. Was there any resistance from management over these? Did you feel like you were forging new ground in videogames?

YM: Since the story was left up to me, I never directly received any criticism. Since I myself decided to make the theme of it "war", although there were aspects that I put in to make it more game-like, I created a story that wouldn't allow

[5] 項羽と劉邦; *Kouu* is the Japanese translation of Chinese warlord Xiang Ji, while *Ryuuhou* is the Han Dynasty founder Liu Bang; there seems to be manga and board games based on this premise

people simply to close their eyes to the realities that exist in war. With regards to the existence of acts such as "war" and "death" in the game, I did not intend to force my own personal views on players. If players felt anything regarding such issues, I'd like them to decide for themselves how they feel about them. If players see something of value in there, nothing could possibly make me happier.

JS: One of my favourite parts in *Suikoden 2* was the cooking minigame and collecting recipes - how did this come about?

YM: At the time, there was a popular manga that showed off the beauty of food in a competition format. I think we were strongly influenced by that in making this minigame. At first, it was a little simpler, but at some point the designer increased the number of food graphics and we began to add a lot to match them. <*laughs*>

JS: The first two *Suikoden* games are loved outside of Japan. Do you have a message for your fans?

YM: Even now, I receive mail from inside Japan as well as from overseas, and I am extremely grateful to those fans out there that love *Suikoden*. The characters in *Suikoden* are not just large in number, but each one of them was born as an individual with their own unique characteristics and backgrounds. If people can find, among them, a character that they can empathise with, then I am very happy.

JS: At the start of *Suikoden III*, was there any consideration of making it 2D?

YM: Naturally there was a discussion of whether or not we should do it in 2D or 3D. At the time, there was no settled decision regarding the transition period from 2D to 3D, nor was the method for doing it decided. Part of the reason for choosing 3D was because of the sense of us looking for an internal challenge.

JS: I've heard rumours there was to be a chapter in *Suikoden III* where Sasarai[6] was controllable. Is this true? Was anything left out of *Suikoden III*?

YM: As a result of internal company issues at the time, the amount of time for the development of *Suikoden III* was extremely restricted. The original intention was that there were going to be a lot of events after the heroes gathered and one of them was the "Sasarai version" viewed from the perspective of the enemy's side. However, due to the conditions I just mentioned, I can't deny that we had to move very quickly and a large number of events had to be cut.

JS: Why did you leave Konami - was it during or after *Suikoden III*?

YM: From the time we started development of *Suikoden III*, it was my plan to quit when it was completed. Much of it has to do with the tough conditions for an employee doing game development within a large Japanese corporation. I was extremely attracted to the idea of doing freelance development work. I told Konami about my intentions from an early stage and, to a certain extent, my resignation period was decided. With that schedule set already, and due to the complications of the *Suikoden III* development schedule going this way and that way, the result was that I left the company when the game was in its final stages of development. *Suikoden* was not created by myself alone, but by the entire R&D team involved. From *Suikoden I~III*, there were many people involved who also moved away from the project midway in the development, and I'm nothing more than one of them. However, that

[6] Bishop of Harmonia, first appears in *Suikoden II*

doesn't change the fact that *Suikoden* is extremely precious to me and even though I moved away from it, I never "threw it away".

JS: What are your plans for the future?

YM: It's a secret. <*laughs*>

JS: What can you tell me about the below image, which shows *Suikoden I* in the lower left corner? It appears to be a cinematic scene, showing the hero facing off against someone.

YM: This was a video of a game event that took place for the game information magazine "*V Jump*". This is the event where *Suikoden* was first unveiled. I was sitting in the participants area during this event and, when the *Suikoden* announcement video showed that there would be 108 characters, I remember that there was a Capcom guy from the *Breath of Fire 2* team sitting next to me and he said something like, "Are you seriously going to do that!?" <*laughs*> Also, since we were still in the middle of development then, the one-on-one combat scene was different than the one that eventually made it into the finished version. The screen shown was a visualization that Ms Kawano hurriedly drew and put into the video.

JS: Do you perhaps have an anecdote no one has heard before?

YM: Hmmmm, that's a tough one. <*laughs*> The voice of the flying squirrel, Mukumuku, from *Suikoden 2*, was done by me! <*laughs*>

稲葉 治彦

INABA, Haruhiko

DOB: *secret* / Birthplace: *secret* / Blood Type: *secret

~ Selected portfolio ~

TMNT: Tournament Fighters	- SNES, 1993	(Thanks)
Suikoden	- PS1, 1995	(Translation management)
Vandal Hearts	- PS1, 1996	(Localisation)
Castlevania: SOTN	- PS1, 1997	(Localisation)
Azure Dreams	- PS1, 1997	(Assistant director)
Suikoden II	- PS1, 1998	(Special thanks)
Silent Hill	- PS1, 1999	(Recording director)
Silent Hill 2	- PS2, 2001	(Casting coordinator)
Battlefield 2: SF	- PC, 2005	(Translator)
Star Ocean: FD	- PSP, 2008	(Localisation supervisor)
Halo 4	- X360, 2012	(East Asia Localisation)

Interview with Haruhiko "Harry" Inaba

I met Mr Inaba briefly during my trip to Japan, along with his long time colleague Jeremy Blaustein. Not only did Mr Inaba kindly agree to answer my questions regarding his role as translation manager for the original Suikoden, but he also put me in touch with Yoshitaka Murayama, the original creator of Suikoden. Mr Murayama had been out of the public eye for a while, and tracking him down proved difficult. Mr Inaba is currently working with Mr Blaustein, and other industry veterans, on a series of exciting game development projects, including the adventure game ***Blackmore****.*

JS: How did you join Konami?

HI: I joined Konami as a fresh grad - I was very excited to join the company which made games I had played on Famicom and in arcades. Great games like *Goonies*, *Road Fighter*, *Gradius*, *Castlevania* and so on. Konami was part of my youth and it felt great joining them.

JS: Did you hear about Konami's game console?

HI: I never heard about any games console when I was working inside Konami.

JS: Describe receiving the *Suikoden I* project.

HI: At that time I was working in the HQ office, mainly dealing with special tasks which didn't belong to other divisions. So *Suikoden* was given to me as a special task and I organised a task force under my given authority. I don't remember how long it took since it was so long ago!

JS: Was it always officially a PlayStation title?

HI: Yes, it was officially a PlayStation title.

JS: Did you regularly interact with Murayama-san and the *Suikoden* team?

HI: Yes. I was transferred to Konami Computer Entertainment Tokyo, a subsidiary R&D company of Konami, after working on *Suikoden*, and interacted a lot with Murayama-san and the team on a daily basis.

JS: Was there a lot riding on *Suikoden*?

HI: I don't think so. At that time nobody knew PlayStation would be a success. But maybe it's just because I was staff. Maybe the higher management was pushing hard. The most interesting thing for *Suikoden* is it's actually the first game released by Konami on the PlayStation outside of Japan.[1] And a JRPG. It was also the first JRPG Konami released in English.[2]

JS: Had you read the Chinese novel *The Water Margin*, which *Suikoden* is loosely based on?

HI: It's a very popular story, so yes I did know and read *The Water Margin*. However, I never considered *The Water Margin* during the game localisation process, and I personally don't think there's a legitimate connection between the two. I like *Suikoden* better, to be honest.

JS: What kind of team did you have?

HI: It was a pretty small team. At that time, game localisation was not handled in the way it is today. We didn't split the work between 10 translators and 5 editors or something like that. It was one translator who played the game from start to finish. And one editor who played the game from start to finish, and that was it. And our overseas counterpart checked the game before launch a couple of times and fixed errors.

JS: How difficult was the localisation?

HI: Like I said, we didn't have to rush the localisation process, so the translator and the editor and the final checkers could spend enough time to make sure the translation was good.

JS: Were there major changes or censorship?

HI: I don't recall any major change. Sony didn't have a strict censorship policy, at least at that time, and it was much, much easier to get content approval compared to getting approval from Nintendo of America.

---

[1] *Gokujou Parodius Da! Deluxe Pack* seems to be the first Japanese PlayStation title by Konami

[2] Despite Konami producing several traditional JRPGs, like *Lagrange Point* and *SD Snatcher*, it would seem *Suikoden* was indeed the first released in English

BLAUSTEIN, Jeremy

DOB: 7 June 1966 / Birthplace: Long Island, New York / Blood Type: *secret*

~Selected Portfolio~

Snatcher	- Sega CD, 1994	(Localisation supervisor, trans. by Scott Hards)
Vandal Hearts	- PlayStation, 1996	(Translator)
Castlevania: SOTN	- PlayStation, 1997	(Translator)
Metal Gear Solid	- PlayStation, 1998	(Translator, asstitant-directed Eng VO)
Suikoden II	- PlayStation, 1998	(Translator and coordinator)
Alundra 2	- PlayStation, 1999	(Translator and scriptwriter)
Valkyrie Profile	- PlayStation, 1999	(Translator and English VO director)
Dragon Quest VI	- PlayStation, 2000	(Translator and coordinator)
Shadow Hearts	- PlayStation 2, 2001	(Translator, scriptwriter, English VO director)
Silent Hill 2~4	- PS2/Xbox/PC, 2001~2004	(Translator, English VO director, mo-cap director)
Phoenix Wright - T&T	- NDS, 2007	(Translator (with Nanica Co., Ltd., edited by Capcom)
Banshee's Last Cry (aka: *Kamaitachi no Yoru*)	- iOS, Android, 2014	(Writing and adaptation)

Interviewed with:

LOE, Casey & DES BARRES, Nick

Jeremy BLAUSTEIN, Casey LOE, Nick DES BARRES

Interview with Jeremy Blaustein, Casey Loe, and Nick Des Barres

This interview is actually a combination of real-life conversations had with Mr Blaustein, email correspondence with Mr Loe, and public forum posts made by Mr Des Barres. Through the use of space magic (and clever editing), it appears as if we're having a round-table conversation. ***There are massive plot spoilers throughout this interview.*** *You have been warned.*

JS: Both *Suikoden* games were exquisite in their storytelling. You see good people die, and it's emotionally moving.

JB: Right! Regarding the deaths of the characters, I just rewatched the death of Nanami. That was pretty good stuff! Great music. Nice, smooth dialogue. Many translators were on this project and they were divided up by character instead of just doing chunks of text. This was to maintain consistency of voice. And yet when you consider *Suikoden*, graphically it was quite cartoonish. Isn't that amazing?

JS: With 2D art rather than 3D.

JB: Right, and yet that did not prevent you from experiencing the emotion of that particular scene. Because you knew that those hand-drawn images were representative of characters, they didn't need to look like your next door neighbour in order for you to feel they were human. It's a suspension of disbelief, and games these days, it's as if the idea of suspension of disbelief, or the idea of actually engaging people to use their own imaginations - it's almost like it's become a bad word.

NDB: <*sighs*> Yoshitaka Murayama - he built one of the most expansive fictional worlds in gaming history, then left Konami under semi-mysterious circumstances prior to the completion of *Suikoden III*.

JS: Curious localisation point: I recall a forest village of Amazon women in *Suikoden III*. That area specifically had some bizarre, out-of-place dialogue. There was references to graffiti tagging, and an NPC in an inn who said that a blanket was made from the donkey of a recently checked-in guest - without their knowing!

CL: It's funny, I never played *Suikoden III* in English and while I vaguely remember the Amazon village, I don't recall any dialogue like that in the Japanese version. Hopefully you can track that down for [a screenshot]!

JB: If you break it up by chapters and you have one person doing an entire chapter, then you're going get a cross-section. The translator is going to do multiple characters, and then another translator is going to do chapter 2. How do they approach dealing with the same voice? How do you achieve the same voice with different people translating it? If you slice it up so that one translator does 10 different characters, then they won't know what the hell is going on with the story unless they read every other person's line as it goes up against their own lines, in the context of everything. You're worrying about a million things when you're localising stuff.

NDB: I only know I was honoured to interpret Murayama-san's grand vision. I faithfully played and adored *Suikoden I* and *II*, both *Suikogaidens*, *Suikoden III*, and I saw it as a crime the man was unable to unleash his expansive mythos. Murayama-san was the victim of the way our industry works. But so business goes. Murayama-san resigned from Konami. They tinkered around, *Suikoden IV*, distant prequel, *Suikoden V*, distant (geographical) sequel, hoping he might come back. He didn't. Hence the DS and PSP games.

JS: He made that cryptic Rubicon post on his blog I recall.[1]

CL: Unfortunately I don't know anything about Murayama-san or his motivations, beyond what I read on his blog. [2] Personally, I see him as another victim of a broken Japanese system that can only reward success with a "promotion" to a managerial role, driving more ego-driven creators to outsource companies and small studios where they lack the resources to make an impact.

---

[1] Yoshitaka Murayama: "*A decision. I received an offer from a certain company. Although I'm extremely thankful, the idea left me very troubled, personally. Should I accept it or not? Even now, it still concerns me. What's to be done about this...? They say the Rubicon is a very small river. I wonder what it felt like to cross? That's my current mood.*"
[2] www.bm.ai/modules/wordpress/

JS: Do you gents have any amusing stories from working on *Suikoden II*?

CL: I was only hired to help with the raw translation of *Suikoden II*, so I wasn't privy to Jeremy's instructions from the [development] team or how the editing process proceeded after I turned my files in. But I'll answer what I can! Incidentally, I had left *GameFan* magazine at that point and did the work between strategy guide projects. I believe everyone was working at their individual homes.

JB: <*laughs*> Well, I don't know how entertaining my recollections are. It takes a pretty determined person to find out who translated something, and then get hold of them and give a piece of their mind. You end up getting a wide disparity of messages, as you'd imagine. If someone likes it that much that they would track you down to give you a message, it's a really nice message and they say the greatest things. On the other hand, I've got a couple of skeletons in my closet too. Not necessarily through any fault of my own.

JS: You've had feedback from fans?

JB: I guess the worst for me was this website. <*laughs*> They wanted to... There's a community for everything on the internet, and this little community, they've been talking for years, about how they got "double-dealed" with *Suikoden II*, because some character or another wasn't right. So there's this little, fomenting rebellion going on.

JS: Wait, people didn't like the translation?

CL: The changing reception to *Suikoden II* has been kind of interesting. Back in the day, everyone was like, "You worked on that? That was awesome!" And then over time I get the sense it's transitioned into something we should be ashamed of. It IS a little embarrassing seeing some of the text I wrote now... My inexperience definitely shows through at times, and I can't blame all of that on the circumstances. It certainly wasn't any worse than the other games of its era, but I guess the disappointment comes from it being one of the few games from those days with a good enough story to deserve a better localisation than it got. Maybe one day we'll get a second chance at it... When it's licensed to a Chinese developer and converted into a mobile phone social game. <*sobs*>

JB: You know, the thing is, I don't even really remember it. The biggest thing that I would want people to understand is... Well, somebody contacted me to do an interview. But when I began to look at the website that I was being interviewed for, I saw that they weren't that happy with *Suikoden II*. Then finally I asked them to pre-send some questions, and he sent them over, and it kind of amounted to a fancier version of, "Can you tell me why your work sucked so badly?" I know *Suikoden II* is regarded as a very moving thing, but the localisation was definitely troublesome.

NR: I struggled with my compatriots, Casey and Jeremy, to make some sense of the mess that was *Suikoden II*'s script - in the format Konami delivered it. I had already played the game for 90+ hours, and was confused.

JS: So there were technical difficulties?

JB: It's my recollection that the assets came to us in a rather, erm... Disorganised way. Things wound up being kind of disorganised. When you have like, I think with *Suikoden*, with its 14 characters, right?

JS: It was 108 characters.

JB: Oh wow, pardon me! A hundred and eight. Thank you. So, 108 characters, right? What you want to do, obviously, is you'd like each character to have a unique voice. What most people don't understand is that Japanese offers you the opportunity to have an extremely wide range of voices in written material. Because it's a manga culture, the history of manga, or the fact that Japanese can be written in two or three different writing styles, there's so many different dialects, plus the high literacy rate. Whatever you want to say. In Japanese you can make a lot of things clear in the way that you write dialogue. The reader can read it and say, "This is an 80 year old person from the north-eastern region of Japan, who has a lower class education, and a bad sense of humour, and watches a lot of cop dramas." You can get all that out just by how you write down the written word. Now in English, you don't have that. So now you've got 108 characters, and you've got two months to translate something...

JS: You only had two months?

JB: Well, I'm just making that up. For the most part, with only a few exceptions, companies don't give you more than a few months. They say, "Just get it done." You can get it done, it can be done, by throwing more translators at it. But here's the thing about *Suikoden*: 108 voices that are difficult to get down as being as unique as they come off in Japanese, and us not being the writers of the story, and being under the time gun, unless you have the assets organised in a very easy to manage way...

NDB: We were delivered the script among code, with no indication as to who was speaking. Text was bunched together based on location. The solution? Play the game multiple times, searching as we did so for strings to gather context. We did our best. We were actually provided with Murayama-san's personal encyclopaedia and log of *Suikoden*'s world... It rivalled [*Game of Thrones*] and beyond in complexity.

JB: Nick's recollections about *Suikoden* are correct, 100%. But I really can't add anything to it I'm afraid. I vaguely recall that there was a "*Suikoden* encyclopaedia".

CL: I don't remember too much about Murayama-san's encyclopedia... It was a digital Word document, and I don't recall the page count. Probably a fairly standard world-building document by today's standards, but in that day and age it was pretty shocking to see a videogame with a depth of background comparable to a fantasy novel series or tabletop RPG. I believe it was all text, although there may have been a map included...?

JS: Hold on, they sent you the source code?

CL: I'm not tech savvy enough to know if the files we were working on were source code or what, but I recall it as strings of English text in files full of gibberish, probably the instructions regarding the text and character portrait display. I believe we were eventually able to figure out which character was speaking by matching hexadecimal strings or something.

JS: That's beyond the role of a localiser...

CL: Fortunately Nick and I were big *Suikoden* fans who had already played the game and were able to recognize much of the out-of-context content - which was why Jeremy gave us a chance, instead of working with more experienced translators who wouldn't be willing to spend so much time navigating through a game as they worked.

JS: Later on in the game there's this minor NPC and the graphic is for a woman, and she comments on how she's smitten with this female teacher. At the time I thought, "Oh, an openly lesbian character?"

JB: *<laughs>*

CL: I always tried to load up a file so I could use in-game event scenes and such as a reference, but it wasn't feasible to hunt down every NPC in the game and confirm their age or gender, if it was not already clear from their manner of speech, or confirm at what point in the game those NPCs were speaking their dialogue - so I doubt the lesbian thing was intentional

JS: So the dialogue box was assigned to the wrong character?

JB: Perhaps. It's the fact that in Japanese it's not clear, because you don't use pronouns much in Japanese. So you don't know a person's sex. You cannot tell all the time. Especially if you've got characters named Jowy - a Japanese Katakana name, where it isn't clear what the sex is. You have six different translators, and mistakes crop up. Because in Japanese, like I said, you don't generally say he or she drank something. You just say, "drank something", or more specifically, "something was drank". Which brings up a whole other bunch of things going against you in a localisation.

JS: Were there any other difficulties? Do you have any regrets?

CL: The main thing I would note is that we had no ability to add text boxes, and our English text had to fill the same size text boxes as in the Japanese version. The released version ended up using a non-fixed length English font that seemed to allow for more text than the Japanese font, and at some points in the game (like the endings) they did manage to increase the size of the text windows, but - if I recall correctly - at the point at which I was working on the project, we didn't know that would happen, and our marching orders were to stick to the original Japanese character limits.

JB: I remember being unhappy about a lot of these names. I was so unhappy about those names. I struggled with all those names. I mean, in Japanese you have "Appuru" for example. Now is that "Apple" or is it "Appulu"? You tell me! Also, the developers would tend to put in a name like "Victor" or "Edward" or "Ted" and to me that sounds SO conventional. So I would make it "Viktor" for example. But that still left me somewhat dissatisfied. I was trying to satisfy the demands of keeping it close to the Japanese, but still interesting enough.

JS: While still sticking within the size limits...

CL: Writing the same line in English usually takes at least twice as many characters, so if the original Japanese line filled up all four lines of the text box, then the English text would need to be cut to the bone to make it fit. That meant going over every line dozens of times, replacing every word with its shortest possible synonym, cutting every bit of flavour and information that wasn't absolutely essential, deleting any idiom that wasn't more space-efficient than what it represented, and so on, until lines I had once been proud of were reduced to elementary-school primer text. And then since the final game did end up having a thinner font that often didn't fill up the text boxes, it often ended up looking look like we made those cuts for no reason at all.

JS: Thank you for your time gentlemen. On a positive note, at the time of writing this, it's been reported that *Suikoden II* has been rated by the ESRB, implying an imminent PSN re-release. No more paying $400 for a used copy off eBay!

~Appearing in a later volume~

Kazuma Kujo

Always cool in his sunglasses, Mr Kujo discusses his early days developing Irem arcade games, including the nicknames they all used. He was the gentlemen behind the phenomenal original *Metal Slug*.

In later years he moved from arcade games to consoles, creating the beloved cult classics of *Steambot Chronicles* and the *Disaster Report* series. He shares a few secrets no one knows, and sketches the Irem office layout from during his time there.

Today he works at Granzella.

Mayumi Nishimura

Ms Nishimura is a long time colleague of Mr Kujo, from his days at Irem, and she explains her role at Granzella and some of her favourite moments in games. We also discuss the future plans for Granzella, which has been expanding into the online space.

A Brief Introduction to Visual Novels

Visual novels. Sound novels. Adventure games. Graphic adventures. Text adventures. Interactive fiction. Dating-sims. In addition to these umbrella terms there are also many sub-genres. What I became acutely aware of when investigating this genre bouillabaisse, is that there are a myriad of interconnected terms, meaning different things for different people. From *Portopia Renzoku Satsujin Jiken* (below), through *Snatcher* and *Policenauts*, to *EVE* and *Disgaea Infinite*. All distinct, yet all sharing similar DNA. There are even games developed in the West which could be described as being akin to visual novels, such as certain FMV games from the past, and more recently *The Walking Dead* by Telltale Games. You move an avatar, but it's all about decisions and narrative choice.

The Guest Editor for the visual novel chapter is Nathan Treichel, who explains his views below. The majority of VN interview questions were by him. On the final page are the musings from a colleague of mine who assisted with the trip.

Nathan Treichel – Guest Editor

What do you value in your games most? Do you love the visuals that the next-generation gives us? Do you love the characters and see them almost like a friend or someone you wish you were more like? Is it the sweeping and epic storylines, or maybe the more personal stories which say something about us as humans? Is it the feeling of blasting away your opponent with a *hadouken*? Maybe you like the puzzle box of riddles that is trying to get through a *Professor Layton* game? Visual novels/adventure games are not for everyone as a genre, however, almost every person is likely to find at least one title they will enjoy.

While many people first think of dating simulators, porn, or logic puzzles when you first mention visual novels, the genre can be much more then just these things. Many popular game series, from *Persona* to *Mass Effect* contain elements of visual novels in them. There are also many visual novels with strategic role playing battles, stat raising mechanics, logic puzzles, and point-and-click investigation. Contrary to popular belief it's actually rather fun to play visual novels with another person, especially if the game involves love, as you come to understand the logic of the other person in why they make the choices they do. The best way to think of a visual novel is to imagine that you are watching a play that you have the power to control where it goes.

The reason for this comparison is simple: in most visual novels you have the background art, the actors providing the voice of the characters, the costumes, the music, the story, and then of course your choices that guide the story. There is not much in Western gaming that tries to do what many visual novels do. Something similar in style would be the old fashioned choose-your-own-adventure books. However, not only are visual novels unique in their execution, but also in their themes. Visual novels, unlike most videogames, are more romantic and sentimental than the gritty and realistic titles that constitute the majority of the work from most Western developers. To put it another way, most Western developers try to replicate the reality of what they think our world is, or would be in X situation, and draw us into this world via the feeling of reality they create. Many Japanese developers who make visual novels go about creating the pull of their games via the creation of emotions and reflections on what is going on in the game, making us slowly realise that, despite how unlike our reality it might be, it is reality to the characters and is not as different from ours as first appears.

How do you create a game where the player can lose to the computer/author, when there is nowhere for the user to control the game except moving forward or back through the text? Ryukishi07 actually accomplishes this in his golden-age murder-mystery throwback, *Umineko When They Cry*. If it takes a seed of truth to sell a lie, then how do you best convince someone that they are on a boat when they are in the middle of the desert? There are many ways you could do that, but doing so successfully and in such a way that a majority of readers are completely fooled is another matter. There is always the idea of having your protagonist not realise what is going on in the story, but if that is all you did you would never get the fans to come up with the name of the ocean the boat is on, right?

While there is a lot more to visual novels then just plot twists and falling in love with fictional characters, what is wrong with an art form which focuses on these things? Perhaps you played *Bioshock*

Infinite just to see what everyone was talking about, and in particular see the story and its final twist? Perhaps you were brought into its beautiful world but wanted more out of the characters and that final twist everyone spoke about? Go read *999* or *Ever 17* by Uchikoshi and you can see how well sci-fi endings can be handled, ones that are not an entry level to Physics 101.

Part of the reason why *Ever 17* and *999* have such tremendous depth to their stories is thanks to the fact that the Japanese have a strong ability of taking items that they like from other cultures and making them their own distinct art forms. Japanese visual novels have over the years become strongly character focused with most blending sentimentalism, historical fantasy, supernatural, and sci-fi elements. Most of the games are actually a combination of various stories that are reached via the choices made by the player. These unique stories are normally one per major character, and commonly one more "true route" which is unlocked after you complete the other routes. Many visual novels and adventure games will require you to play through multiple stories in order to understand those you've previously read and to unlock further stories, in a similar way to *Virtue's Last Reward*.

The term visual novel was created for Leaf's new line of games, however the name ended up having tremendous staying power. So much so, that despite never being an official name for the majority of games popularly called visual novels, they are commonly associated as visual novels and are the term used when describing these games.

The popularity of visual novels and adventure titles focusing on romance exploded with the release of Konami's *Tokimeki Memorial* (left). Originally released for the PC Engine in 1994, *Tokimeki Memorial*, or *TokiMemo* as it is affectionately called by fans, saw enhanced remakes on many other platforms, including the PlayStation, Sega Saturn, and PC. The game focused on the player building their stats over the course of 3 years in high school and going on many dates with their character of choice, in order to win her heart. It jump-started the popularity of "dating-sim" games not only by capturing a large male audience, but also by attracting a large female demographic.

The franchise's light-hearted tone and heavy emphasis on romance became a hit with female gamers in Japan as well. This paved the way for the eventual spin-off series, *Tokimeki Memorial Girl's Side*, which has become a notable series in the "*otome game*" subgenre, which features a female protagonist romancing male characters. In a reflection of much of the visual novel and anime market, even after the original series effectively ended, the *Girl's Side* spin-off has continued on and is still ongoing. And while there has been sales of *yuri*[1] games aimed mainly at guys for many years, it has never been as strong as the sales are for *yaoi*[2] games aimed mainly at girls. These games have had such strong sales that some of the biggest names in the industry, like Nitro Plus, have devoted their best people and some big budgets to these games. The writer of *Madoka Magica* and *Fate/Zero* (two of the best selling anime series of all time) helmed one of the best selling *yaoi* visual novel series, *Dramatical Murder*, for the company.

Given the wide fan-base of the genre, many other developers began creating visual novels and adventure games focusing on romance - both for users of all ages, as well as games designed for the over 18 crowd, who wanted to go a little further with their love interest. In many cases developers will release an 18+ version of the game on PC, followed by an all ages release for the PC, consoles, and even Andriod/IOS devices. The term *eroge* applies to all games that have a sex scene. These scenes are commonly referred to as H-scenes, the "H" standing for hentai. While there are many examples of H-scenes being thrown out for no other purpose than to generate sales, there are also many instances of them actually being key to the point of the game. In quite a few cases, sex scenes are actually used to elicit horror from the reader, such as in *Song of Saya* or *Over the Rainbow*. Titles like this have started to be called *darkige* for their dark themes and horror, which borderline on *guro*.[3] Games where the purpose is purely titillation are called *nukige* (it's a vulgar pun based on the root verb *nukeru*, meaning for something "to escape").

---

[1] Girls pursuing girls
[2] Guys pursuing guys
[3] Wikipedia has a long explanation; basically grotesque pornography

The 18+ rating for a game commonly changes from T to 18+ based on what release it is. For example, when Key originally released the game *Little Busters* for the PC it was all ages. The edition that came out one year later, subtitled *Ecstasy*, added H-scenes for each character's route and then added three new character routes. This made the new edition an *eroge*. This was followed shortly by a version for the PSP, Vita, PS2 and PS3, which was the same as *Ecstasy* version, albeit minus the H-scenes and earning a "Teen" rating. Then, upon announcement of the 48 episode TV adaptation, the game received another release for the PC that did not have any H-scenes.

With the dawn of the internet boom and people coming, working, and learning together outside of Japan, many anime fans came together to create English translations for Key's first visual novel, *Kanon*, which had just had its first sub par TV adaptation. While this was somewhat questionable, legally, it lead to a strong rise in interest and appreciation for visual novels outside of Japan and more translations, for what ended up being called "visual novels" by a new generation of foreigners. Many foreigners were also being introduced to Japanese adventure games through the English release of Capcom's *Phoenix Wright*.

This lead to a creation of a group of customers who were underserved and, in many cases, took it upon themselves to bring English copies of the games they wanted to the English speaking world. This led to the eventual, official English releases of many such "visual novel" games. This also lead to a surprising amount of cooperation between the fans of these game and the publishers. In many cases publishers, instead of telling fans they will be sued for what they put online, will work with fan-translators to officially release games being translated. Recent releases like *Steins;Gate* and *Ef: A Fairy Tale of the Two* had the fan-translations officially released, after some negotiation with the developers. Also, in the case of Ryukishi07's *Umineko: When They Cry* series, and other games, the fan-translators have his approval and gratitude for translating his games and are now considered the official English translations.

Part of the reason why it is easier for certain publishers to work with fans like Ryukishi07, is because he is *doujin*. *Doujin* means that the game is self-published, or to use an inaccurate but more familiar term: indie. The major difference between indie and *doujin* is that while many *doujin* games are original works, a large percentage are fan works of existing properties.
[See the ZUN chapter for a detailed explanation on doujin - ed.]

Matt Fitsko - Hokkaido based consultant

So just what are visual novels exactly? Where did they come from? If you're looking for answers to these questions, the Ryukishi07 interview is a goldmine, especially in conjunction with Uchikoshi-san's comments about the term "visual novel" itself. The striking thing to note is that while we in the English-speaking world tend to refer to all Japanese adventure games as visual novels, in Japan, it's actually a very narrow category, and generally refers to an adventure game in which the text is laid directly on top of the art and fills up the entire screen instead of a little window on the bottom. A broader term would be simply "novel game", which is gaining currency in Japan. But games with significant puzzle elements, like *Phoenix Wright* or *Virtue's Last Reward*, would not be considered "novel games". Still, just calling these text-heavy titles "adventure games" doesn't quite fit, and the term "visual novel" makes intuitive sense.

So why the difference? Japanese and Western adventure games certainly started from the same place. Like their Western counterparts, Japanese adventure games are one of the oldest videogame genres, and have existed since the dawn of the 1980s. (The genre really came to life after a Japanese company called Microcabin released an unauthorized, heavily revised version of the classic Western adventure *Mystery House* by Roberta and Ken Williams.) But unlike the Western tendencies that led to kleptomaniac MacGyver simulators (and I use that term lovingly), Japanese adventures very quickly started to emphasize story and characterization over puzzles and inventories. In this way, Japanese adventures are closer to modern interactive fiction, except with the addition of lush, expertly drawn 2D artwork.

Early on, most Japanese adventure games scrapped the item gathering and logical puzzle solving while still retaining the same verb-noun interface, like OPEN MAILBOX or TAKE ENVELOPE, that was originally established by the first text adventures. In the influential Japanese adventure *The Portopia Serial Murder Case*, you hardly collect any items at all. Instead, you collect *information* that helps you solve the case. The downside to this approach is that instead of being blocked by some kind of concrete obstacle, like a locked door, the player's progress becomes hampered by a lack of information that cannot always be deduced. As a result, even into the early 2000s many Japanese adventures featured great artwork and storytelling, but were hobbled by brute-force gameplay. You had to keep selecting the same commands, like "Look at shrubbery" or "Talk to Misako", often getting stuck on the same repeating responses, until all the text is exhausted and the game engine sets a flag that unlocks new text somewhere else and allows you to progress.

The first major breakthrough came when Chunsoft released *Otogirisou* and *Kamaitachi no Yoru* on the SNES in 1992 and 1994, respectively. Dubbed "sound novels", these games introduced a new, full-screen text interface, and replaced the repetitive verb-noun menu with "a series of interesting choices", to borrow Sid Meier's phrase. Instead of making hundreds of micro-decisions, like "TAKE KEY", "UNLOCK DOOR", and "OPEN DOOR", Chunsoft's sound novels focused on macro-decisions, in the form of explicit choices: Quick! Someone's coming up the stairs! Do you try to unlock the door, or just jump out the window? Now it was impossible to get stuck, because the player's decisions always lead to some kind of ending (even if it's a bad end). This also enabled truly multi-ending games. Most prior Japanese adventures just had a single ending, or a simple parallel structure like in most romantic *bishoujo* games (if there are five girls you can date, there are going to be five endings, mostly identical except for the choice of girl). In contrast, the stories in *Otogirisou* and *Kamaitachi no Yoru* branch out in exciting and unpredictable ways, and depending on the player's path through the game, even the genre can mutate from murder mystery to ghost story, spy thriller, or slapstick comedy.

In 1996, a Japanese computer game developer called Leaf took the sound novel template and combined it with the erotic adventure game genre on the PC, calling the result a "visual novel". These games, *Shizuku* and *Kizuato*, were a huge success, blending the suspense/horror and choose-your-own-adventure style of the Chunsoft sound novels with a *bishoujo* experience. After two very dark and harrowing games, Leaf then surprised everybody and released the much lighter and comical *To Heart*. Building off from that, as well as earlier dating games like *Doukyuusei* (Elf, 1992), another computer game developer named Key replaced the physical and psychological trauma of *Shizuku* and *Kizuato* with a purely emotional trauma, resulting in the *nakige* (泣きゲー) or "crying game" genre, which is less about sex or even romance, and more about building an intense emotional bond between the player and heroine. Together, these developments revolutionized the Japanese adventure genre, and established the defining elements of the modern visual novel.

In the following interviews, Ryukishi07 explicitly lays out this lineage and how it inspired his own work. At first glance, games like Key's tender-hearted *Clannad* and Ryukishi07's dark and disturbing *Higurashi* seem to have nothing in common, but they're drawing on the same ideas and tensions. It's interesting to consider the parallels between the anxiety of a good horror story, and the anxiety of a good love story. In either case, the readier is anticipating a moment that will change everything - death in one case, a kiss in the other.

This kind of emotional intensity simply would not have been possible with the traditional Western adventure game format, where you might need to distract the barber to grab the scissors, cut the flowers, and perhaps do something involving a moustache made of cat hair in order to make a bouquet for your love interest. In contrast, the visual novel's emphasis on making meaningful choices - such as whether to admit your secret love for your best friend's girlfriend, and then deal with the consequences - is what emotionally involves the player, and makes visual novels a worthwhile experience.

This style of choice-based storytelling has also been present in some Western adventures and role-playing games for years, and is becoming ever more important as players demand more sophisticated and emotionally resonant storytelling in their games. *The Walking Dead* by Telltale Games is a good example. Like a Japanese adventure game, *The Walking Dead* focuses on characters rather than items, and choices rather than puzzles. As a result, *The Walking Dead* has more in common with *Ever 17* than *Monkey Island*, and proves that the visual novel template still has plenty of untapped potential.

It's unfortunately true that the majority of Japanese visual novels have focused on sex and romance at the expense of other themes, but the diversity and inclusiveness of the genre continues to grow thanks to the pioneers featured in this section. Even though Japanese visual novels have provided many potent erotic explorations and heart-moving love stories, there are many other possible choices to make, and many other paths to explore. Ryukishi07 and Uchikoshi can help show us the way.

竜騎士 07

Ryukishi07

DOB: 19 November 1973 / Birthplace: Chiba-ken / Blood Type: AB

~ Selected Portfolio ~

Higurashi When They Cry **(series)**	- Win/PS2/DS/iOS/Android, first release 2002	(screenplay, illust.)
Higurashi Daybreak	- Win/PSP, 2006	(screenplay)
Umineko: When They Cry **(series)**	- Win/PS3/PSP, 2007	(screenplay, illust.)
Rewrite	- Win/PSP/PS VIta, 2011	(partial screenplay)
Ookami Kakushi	- PSP, 2009	(original plan/director)
Higanbana no Saku Yoru ni	- Manga, 2010～2012 / Win, 2011	(Writer)
Rose Guns Days **(series)**	- Win/iOS/Android, 2012	(screenplay, partial chara design)

Interview with Ryukishi07
28 October 2013, outskirts of Tokyo

Working under a pseudonym, Ryukishi07 is a rising star of doujin visual novels, now branching out into mainstream commercial titles, including Ookami Kakushi for Konami. He is perhaps to visual novels what ZUN is to shmups, and in fact when handing him the signature book, he immediately recognised ZUN's penmanship, showing that the world of doujin games is one where creators are aware of each other. What was fascinating with this interview, was how acutely Ryukishi07 understood the paradigms of narrative within games, the shift in attitudes to visual novels over the years, and the dichotomy between doujin and mainstream commercial success. It is little wonder that he was able to grow his followers so successfully from simple Comiket beginnings.

Japanese text translation of questions prior to interviewing provided by MangaGamer, a visual novel localisation company which handles Western publishing of Ryukishi07's works. **www.mangagamer.com** *Interview arranged through Atsushi Seto of Hobibox. Screenshots taken from the Visual Novel Database.* **http://vndb.org/** *Check them out for all things VN. Many thanks to the above for their assistance.*

JS: What is the first game you remember playing?

R7: If you go back to the very first game, I was about 7 years old, and it was a Nintendo Game & Watch, with a ball bouncing. In fact it was called *Ball*. This was released when I was about 6 or 7, and then when I was 9 the Famicom was released, and this is the time in Japan when videogames were just coming out. I'm part of that first generation of people playing games.

JS: Did you play Famicom or PC games?

R7: Actually it was both! My father was also quite interested in computers, so we had at home both a computer and a Famicom. On the Famicom I would play games, and on the computer there was this game called *The Black Onyx*[1] - this was when I was in primary school.

JS: Did you play *Portopia*?[2]

<Group laughs with surprise>

R7: I knew about it, but actually I didn't play it until much later. The first visual novel I played was *Otogirisou*[3] on the Super Family Computer.

JS: I interviewed a programmer of *Otogirisou* - it was by Chunsoft.

R7: *[Without waiting for interpretation] So desu, so desu, so desu, Chunsoft! (Right, right right!) [After interpretation] - <laughs> So desu ka! (Is that so!)*

JS: When did you want to create visual novels?

R7: This was actually much later, I was almost 28 at this time, when I thought about making my own visual novel. At this time I was actively involved with the *doujin* community at Comic Market (Comiket). At this time there was this card game called *Magic: The Gathering*, which I liked very much, so I was participating in the *Magic: The Gathering* **doujin** scene. Right around

[1] Henk Rogers, 1984, one of the earliest and most popular RPGs in Japan
[2] *Portopia Renzoku Satsujin Jiken* - one of Japan's earliest domestically made adventure games, by Yuji Horii. First computers, later Famicom

[3] March 1992, popular horror sound novel

this time, a sound novel called *Tsukihime*[4] was released by the circle Type-Moon, and became a huge hit among the *doujin* community. So then my younger brother said that we should create our own sound novel, and that's how it started.[5]

JS: Your family was involved with your games over the years. What are some of the challenges to making games with your family?

R7: Actually, I'm the eldest of three brothers in total. I have two little brothers. It was mainly me and my second *[the middle, i.e. 2nd eldest]* brother, who would do most of the work. We were young, we had a lot of energy and a lot of enthusiasm at this time, and my parents were very supportive, especially when we were not that known. At that stage they were very supportive. At the beginning, when we were not that famous yet, it was just the three of us, me and my brothers, and when the copies being sold were 50, then 100, we would create these on our computer. We eventually reached the limit of how many copies we could produce ourselves, and started reaching out to friends and family members for help. For example, when the first instalment of *Higurashi* debuted at Comiket, we prepared 100 copies. For the next Comiket, we brought 200. Next, 300. Then 500. And then 2'000. We reached the limit of what we could do ourselves when the number of copies reached 10'000 and then over 20'000. I don't remember the exact number, but somewhere around that point we started outsourcing to a factory.

JS: You mean copies being sold at Comiket?

R7: Yes, that's right. The sales volume.

JS: Mr Seto explained that your current set-up has changed. Could you describe it?

R7: Actually my parents are running the office part of the company, and my youngest brother is in charge of accounting. It was right when my second youngest brother said let's make our own game, that's when I left 07th Expansion[6] and went independent to make my own office. That's as far as the family goes, and then it's friends and close friends, who are now cooperating with us. And of course we are using this apartment, and we have the people you see here,[7] but besides this there are people who are helping us out and we're just communicating via the internet. These guys are in charge of, let's say, making the imagery or the music. In total I think, it would be about 10 people, at least, involved in the production process.

JS: Those who you communicate with via the internet, are they based in Tokyo?

R7: Mostly in Tokyo, but even if they're further afield, it would still be in the Kanto area. [8]

***AaQ* backer: We read the words of a story and process them in our heads. For a videogame, we interact with what's created. There's debate on if games should be a medium for stories or whether they should create their own language. What are your thoughts?**

Mr Seto: Are you asking for a definition of visual novels, from Ryukishi07-san, or are you asking what elements should be in a game?

JS: Visual novels are interactive stories. They're distinct from purely linear fiction, like manga. Does this give games an edge, or is it more challenging competing with linear stories?

R7: *<draws sketches of classifications>* With visual novels, I think of it as being between manga, anime, and an actual novel. Also, it would be somewhere in-between an action game and a novel. So I believe that because it has this, let's say, central position - at the centre between all these different genres - depending on which elements are stressed it could become closer to action games, or get closer to an actual novel. This central position gives you a lot of freedom. You know for us, the otaku culture, people who are passionate about something, I think about visual novels as being the middle position between manga, games, animation and novels. So there are these four classifications, and we're getting something from each of them, and we can integrate them into one type, which stands by itself. So this is the expectation I have toward visual novels. It occupies this middle position.

[4] Lit. *Moon Princess*; adult VN (2000) by Type-Moon, same group behind fighter *Melty Blood* (PC/Arc/PS2)

[5] Ryukishi07 doesn't mention belonging to any particular *doujin* group, and refers to *Tsukihime* as a "sound novel", not a "visual novel"

[6] 07th Exp. is the name of Ryukishi07's *doujin* circle

[7] There was a man and a woman at computers, in addition to Ryukishi07, a female assistant, and Mr Seto

[8] East side of Japan, island of Honshu

JS: It contains the strengths from all of them?

R7: It's as you say, it combines them. From the novel you can take the text; from the manga you can take the illustrations or the character expressions; from the anime you can take the music, and more recently even the voices. It can really bring together all of these elements.

Right: Higurashi When They Cry (PC original)

JS: I believe *Higurashi When They Cry* was going to be a stage play. What changes had to be made for it to become a visual novel?

R7: At this time my friends were actually studying playwriting, and we went to see a play and there was this poster that said: "Play script wanted - the winner will get a prize of 100'000 yen."[9] So since my friends were on the stage, and they're playing, I'm just sitting in the audience and I thought, I want to become involved myself. I thought the best way to do so, one thing I can do myself, is to write a script as a scenario writer. This actually became the script for *Higurashi When They Cry*. This first script was supposed to be written for a small cast, and it was supposed to last about one hour in total, so it was quite limited in scope.

At this time it was my younger brother who was influenced by *Tsukihime*, and he said let's do a visual novel. Of course this is where your question comes in, of what changes were necessary to make it into visual novel. At this time the popular brands in the visual novel genre were Key[10] and Leaf.[11] John, you are probably already quite familiar with these, but there were games like *Shizuku*, *Kizuato*, *To Heart*, *One*, *Kanon*, and *Air*,[12] which we regarded as the cutting-edge at that time. I was a great fan of these and I researched them, because I thought these were the latest in the visual novel genre, and so I rewrote my script to fit that *sekaikan*.[13] More concretely, when you have a stage play the characters have to be quite realistic. But once you change it into a visual novel, characters can be portrayed closer to manga or anime characters.

JS: With *Umineko: When They Cry* (below), what were the challenges of writing in the theatrical style? Were you worried about people's reactions to the *estrangement effect*?[14] In German it's Verfremdungseffekt, and in Japanese it's *ikakouka*.[15]

R7: This is going to be complicated, but with *Higurashi When They Cry* we had included a sub-scenario called "*otsukaresama no kai*",[16] and after the play, what happens is the characters get together, and while still maintaining their characters, they talk about the story. So you'll have a guy who gets killed during the play, and saying, "OK, who killed me, I wonder?" What happens here is that you can have the characters draw the attention of the reader to the mystery - to one part of the mystery - and get them to wonder about this particular part. When I introduce this discussion point, where the characters give some hints to the readers, it was actually very much appreciated in the reviews as being easy to understand, and it received quite positive feedback. So when I made the next one, *Umineko*, I thought we're not going to have this as a separate part, as we did in *Higurashi*, we will have it integrated into one story, to make it clear what the points are that will be discussed.

---

[9] About £660 / $1'000 at today's rate

[10] Popular Osaka-based dev. Co-founded by Jun Maeda in 1998. Games are more adventures than pure VNs

[11] Competitor to Key, popular, founded Osaka, 1995

[12] *Shizuku*, *Kizuato*, and *To Heart* form the Leaf Visual Novel trilogy that originally catapulted Leaf to fame, and also established the term "visual novel" itself. *Kanon* and *Air* were the first two works by Key. "*One - Kagayaku Kisetsu e*" was made by a company named Tactics, and the upper management dictated the game design largely in response to the success of *To Heart* by Leaf. The core members of Tactics then left to form Key, so *One* is often considered to be Key's 0th work

[13] Complex term; world view, or world canon

[14] Theatrical technique designed to alienate viewers from the characters

[15] 異化効果 / いかこうか

[16] Roughly: Job well done, let's have a small party

JS: Players interpret stories in different ways. Do you find it frustrating when they misinterpret a particular message?

R7: Something that happens with my fans is that they sort of... There's a Japanese expression called "*meisou*", which means to start running confused, basically to run amok, with an idea. In order to correct these feelings of anxiety, and correct misunderstandings so that players could better enjoy deducing the mystery, I introduced what we discussed previously, regarding characters explaining the story.

JS: When readers misinterpreted something, it affected how you wrote further instalments?

R7: This is exactly the case. Actually, with *Umineko* in particular, we received some comments and thoughts from some of the players, and we made great efforts to reflect this in the next instalment. Personally, I like people to deduce what's going on, but a frequent misunderstanding I had with readers was that when people were trying to guess who the real killer is, they started to imagine: "Ryukishi07 is following everybody's reasoning, and when somebody works out who the real killer is supposed to be, he secretly changes the story to make the killer somebody else." And I got irritated with this, and I said publicly, no, I would not do something like that. The killer stays the same as originally planned.

JS: Speaking of the murders, and you don't have to answer this... <*Ryukishi07 laughs*> In *Umineko* episodes 1 to 5, were the murders that occurred on Rokkenjima done by Yasu? Or is there another in the Ushiromiya family who committed them?

Mr Seto: Who is your book's target readership?

JS: My book is aimed at a diverse range of people - not just visual novel fans.

R7: So that means it's those who are familiar with Japanese games? [...] In *Umineko*, what you have is this bottle with a note in it - "bottle mail" basically. This message is like a confession, it seems to be a confession by Yasu, and this represents one answer which is right now considered a very persuasive, very likely possibility. But this is just ***one*** interpretation, and I will stop at that. <*laughs*>

JS: For many *doujinshi* authors, the start of their work can be difficult to get into, but sticking with it you're rewarded and it makes sense why the opening was like that - such as with *Higabana the First Night*. Do you consider this a trait of *doujinshi* writing?

R7: I understand the question is basically whether the *doujinshi* style is to have an ambiguous start, not very clear, and thus interest the player in finding out what's going on. This actually is right now one of the most popular methods of capturing a player's interest. First you have [a situation in which they're] completely clueless, and the player is actually attracted by this feeling of not being able to understand. This is becoming the standard and also the most popular method of writing in Japan right now.

This is one item that I'm now a bit concerned by, because this is a really good question. Right now in Japan, I'm not sure if you know, the Japanese narrative style is defined as the four elements: *Ki*, *Sho*, *Ten*, *Ketsu*.[17] ***Ki*** is the beginning, the starting point. ***Sho*** is the development. ***Ten*** is the switch, the surprise element. And ***Ketsu*** is the summing up, the concluding element. Right now, as I said, this style of: "I don't understand the beginning, but because I want to know more, then it becomes interesting to follow." This would correspond to number three, the *Ten*, the switch, the surprise part. Now everybody in Japan, it's so tough, it's like a tidal movement, where everybody is concentrating only on this, too much on this surprise element. Of course the Japanese idea is that even if you have something that's well written, if you don't have a surprise element, then it's kind of boring. Right now it seems to be that everybody is concentrating so much on the surprise element that it doesn't matter how the beginning is, just make it a big surprise. It seems that it's not just games, but also animation, manga and books, which all seem to be carried by this tidal movement, to make this surprise the central element in narrative style.

JS: It seems different to the English narrative style which follows a "3 act structure": the setup, the confrontation, and the resolution. What fascinates me is the distinction between Japanese and English narrative styles.

---

[17] Kanji: 起承転結

R7: <*sketches the two different styles*> This is the Japanese style. This is the English style. This seems to be the element which is particular to Japan, <*taps sketch*> number two. *Ki* is the setup, *Ten* is the confrontation, and *Ketsu* is the resolution. So the second element, *Sho*, is the everyday, the average, ordinary - in Japanese - "the daily occurrences".

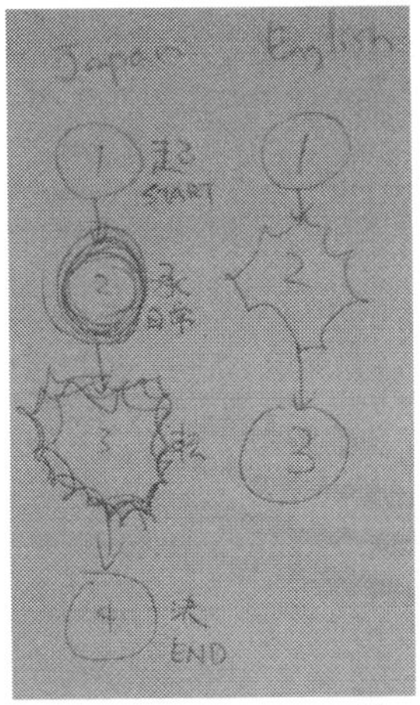

Mr Seto: <*searches web on phone*> In Japanese they're translated as introduction, development, turn, and conclusion.

R7: These elements with the one, two, three and four, as I mentioned it's number two and number three which are now the main focus in Japanese narrative style. Especially number three, the turn or surprise element, is really focused on. So now players are so used to this trend that when they start reading from the first one, the introduction, they are already starting to imagine what number three, the surprise, will be. In their head it's something this big, like this, <*gestures with hands*> and then finally they prepare for number three in a certain way, because of this tendency, and then they get to number three and it's not, it's something a bit different, smaller let's say. Then because of this preconception the reader says, "Oh, this is boring," and ends up being very disappointed because of this.

My conclusion is that the otaku culture right now has caught on a [problem] which is this tendency to jump at number three. The most important part of my argument is that the Japanese culture has produced a lot of novels and visual novels which are really great, and because of this, the otaku culture has become familiar with a great number of twists - number three - which are really excellent. So they've created this image that, because they're acquainted with all of these fantastic examples, now they expect the next one, whatever comes up, it's going to have to overcome this. It's going to have to be better than the experiences so far. And of course if it's not, then they're saying, "Oh, this is not as great as we expected, the old games, the old novels were so much better, it's all going downhill right now."

JS: Indeed, fan expectations can make the job of creating a game much more difficult.

R7: Yes, that's right. There's an expression in Japanese that says the hurdles become higher. Because of these hurdles becoming higher and higher, and this is even more so with popular writers, because the demands from the fans are so much above what this person can now produce, at some point he seems to fall below expectations and not meet those of his readers.

It's actually like if you have a famous novelist, a famous writer, and he becomes so famous that his level is let's say a 10. And he produced a novel that's only an 11, then the acclaim, the reviews that he gets, is that OK he's managed an 11 minus 10, meaning he only gets the accolades for 1. Whereas if somebody who was completely unknown produces something that is let's say a 6 or a 7, his score is 6 minus 0, because he's completely unknown. He gets a 6 and everybody is like wow, it's great. For the popular writer who is a 10, if he actually just makes a small mistake and he only ends up with a 9 novel, then he already gets booed for it and receives a bad review.

JS: I think it's the same in Europe and America as well, with game developers.

R7: Is that right? By the way, I'm a great fan of the *Call of Duty* series, and I really enjoy it. But apparently every time the new instalment comes up, it gets quite sharp reviews from the fans, because it always seems not to meet their expectations. I feel very bad for these guys, because they make this great series and every time there is a new instalment, a new game coming out in the *Call of Duty* series, all that the fans seem to concentrate on is what's gotten worse? "This is bad now, it was better before." This is bad, because I feel they've made such a great game, people should not just complain about it.

JS: Yes, it's hundreds of people spending several years to produce. Do you play it online?

R7: *[In English]* Yes, yes! <*laughs*>
[Interpreted] Yes, of course, of course!

JS: Is your online nickname publicly known?

R7: <*laughs*> Well, probably it's not known, but when I was playing *Call of Duty: Black Ops II* online, I actually used the illustration of Beatrice, from *Umineko*. It was shown on the pistol; a sticker. *<laughs>*

Above: Have you seen Beatrice in Call of Duty?

JS: You mentioned the trend of focusing on the surprise - do you ever speak with other visual novel authors, about your ideas and the industry?

R7: No, basically no. It may be a bit unexpected, but not really. So actually, no, there's not much exchange going on between visual novel authors. There would be two reasons. One is that if you're a professional then you work in a company, and you don't have many contact points with the other guys. Whereas if you're like me, an amateur, this is the problem with the culture in Japan, sometimes people are really close minded and they might decide, "I'm not interested in other developers."

JS: We're up to an hour, should we take a break?

R7: I'm completely flexible - it depends more on you, and how your schedule is.
[turns off recorder - lost audio][18]
Japanese journalists, once they start they just don't let you go! *<laughs>*

[After returning from photographs Ryukishi07 signs the two signature books, draws a picture of a tiny creature, and notices another doujin signature from the day prior]

R7: This is my character, Namekuchi! *<laughs - notices ZUN's signature>* Oh, it's ZUN-san! If it's ZUN-san you need to be drinking while interviewing.

JS: Yes, we enjoyed some beers!

<everyone laughs>

R7: If you don't provide some alcohol he won't respond to your requests. *<laughs>*

JS: Well, at the end of the interview he did have a coffee. It wasn't all beer.

<everyone laughs>

R7: *<referring to sketch by signature>* I gave up on doing humans, so I'm only doing Namekuchi.

JS: These little creatures?

R7: Creatures! *<laughs loudly>*

JS: What is Namekuchi?

R7: *<contemplates to self>* Hmm, what is Namekuchi? Like in *Metal Slug*... It's a slug!

JS: One of my interests is the *doujin* scene in Japan. It's not well documented in English. What does *doujin* mean to you?

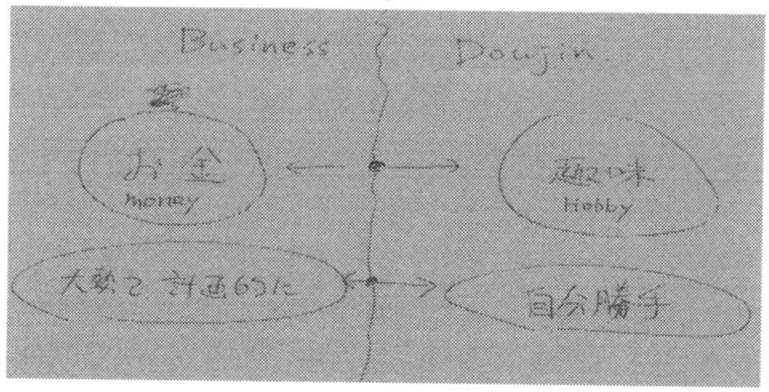

R7: Let me get some paper. About *doujin*, this is actually a question I've been asked by Japanese media as well, and it's been debated, what is the definition of *doujin*? What is not *doujin*? Sometimes it depends on the person. *<sketches>* So, money and then hobby. And this is business, and here is *doujin*.

JS: Can I get a photograph?

R7: *<laughs>* I'm going to get killed!

JS: A lot of *doujin* devs make a living off it.

R7: Yes, that's right.

[18] Lost piece of conversation from Ryukishi07 and Mr Seto, expressing surprise and gratitude that I insist on having a break every hour during interviews

JS: I believe when you started your parents were against it? What was your motivation to carry on?

R7: <*laughs*> Regarding my parents, they weren't against me doing this. But one thing they probably asked me... At the time I was a public servant, and right now the job market in Japan is not in the best condition, so being a public servant is considered one of the best jobs to have. But I quit and wanted to become a scenario writer, and this was one thing which my parents said, "No, stop and think very well about what you want to do." This is one of the things, but they were not opposed to it.

JS: Well, it worked out well for you, because the popularity and sales have grown.

R7: Thanks to all of you, yes.

JS: A lot of *doujin* producers tend to gravitate towards eroge, [19] **perhaps because it means easier sales. You've avoided that...**

R7: If I can be very blunt, it's just because I'm on this side, <*gestures to sketch*> on the hobby side, not on the... I was completely ignoring the money, the business aspect. When I wrote *Higurashi When They Cry*, at this time in America there was this movie that came out, called *The Blair Witch Project*, in which you have three students, university students, who get lost in the woods, and they get caught up in this witch legend. But this feeling of horror is only perceived by an American audience. This would not be immediately perceived by a Japanese audience. So I thought to make a Japanese version, a Japanese horror story, and that's how *Higurashi* came about.

JS: Many consider *Higurashi* to be one of the first dark games, or *darkige*,[20] and that it paved the way for titles like *Song of Saya*.[21] Do you feel this description fits your work?

R7: <*laughs*> Let me talk about this. In Japan today, most people think of visual novel games as being love stories, with an adult theme, and there's a huge number of "pink" (erotically-themed) games. So most people imagine games with some cute girls coming in. But for me personally, that's not it.[22] For me it's *Otogirisou* and *Kamaitachi no Yoru* which I consider the starting point of the visual novel genre - this kind of dark horror, where somebody gets stabbed and dies, and it's like a mystery. So when I started creating visual novels, from the very beginning I decided that my visual novels would be murder mysteries.

JS: There's a lot of sub-genres or classifications. Visual novels, sound novels, adventure games, *nukige*,[23] *eroge*, *darkige*, *nakige*, and so on. Do you feel some aren't given enough attention?

R7: I actually think about, not these sub-genres in particular, but I think about visual novels in general as one, let's say, comprehensive genre. When people now say visual novels, they now just concentrate almost... The whole field is concentrated on *nukige* or *eroge*. I think we should expand the definition to include more - there's more to it than this. I have my own personal desire to see that this genre, visual novels, becomes more established. When you have a popular novel like *Harry Potter* it then becomes a movie, or even a TV series, a sitcom or drama, or a manga. Before in America it was *Superman*, which started out as a comic, and then it was movies and a TV series and so on. My personal dream is that to these three types of media - movies, TV series, and manga - I would like to see visual novels added, as another option when transforming a written novel into other types of medium.

JS: I'm actually dedicating an entire chapter to the broad classification that is "visual novels". It needs more exposure outside of Japan.

R7: That's right. The situation is probably similar to the initial period when manga came out, where it was perceived as being aimed at children. There's some action, it's targeting children, it's a bit silly. But this has now changed, and through manga we can explain some difficult content, or even art books, or they can even be used for studying something. I think that the

---

[19] Erotic Games

[20] Dark or horror novels

[21] Body-horror VN for Win, by Nitroplus (2003). After brain surgery a man's senses are inverted. The normal world is a flesh covered nightmare, amidst this he sees and befriends a normal young girl - except in reality...

[22] It's important to note that Ryukishi07 doesn't say bishoujo-type visual novels are "wrong", only that he is drawing on a different lineage

[23] A VN where the sole focus is sex, different from *eroge* which is a VN that happens to have sex; not to be confused with *nakige*, which is a "crying game"

visual novel, right now, is too stuck on this *nukige*, *eroge* type, and that it should aim to reach a wider audience.

JS: A good point regarding difficult topics. In *Umineko*, some feel the character Maria (below, character on left) shows signs of having Asperger Syndrome. Was this your intention?

R7: Regarding Maria, who appears in *Umineko*, I think about her as sort of like a Joker character. When you think about a child you don't think that they're capable of killing somebody, you don't expect that they would have tricks up their sleeve. But Maria is portrayed as somebody who is not a typical child - someone who is a bit strange, a bit mysterious - so she can do these things. So this was the background to creating the character Maria, as a different type of child, with some characteristics that make her different from everybody else.

JS: Your work seems to be historical fiction. *Umineko* is set in 1986, *Higurashi* in 1983, and *Rose Guns Days*[24] in post-war Japan. How come?

R7: That's right. I will answer these individually. About *Higurashi*, when it was released the readers would be university students, so they would be born around 1983. All of the *catch copy*[25] for *Higurashi*, it was "*Human, Occult, or Just a Coincidence?*" If you think about stuff happening, if it's 100 or 200 years ago, it's a long, long time ago and it cannot be known. But if it's something that's 20 years ago, or about the time that you were born, it feels a bit more familiar. It feels like you don't know, but you could find out more. It feels a bit more everyday.

For *Umineko*, it's set in a time when there's no mobile phone, because of this simple fact that there can be no mobile phone, it has a lot of impact on the potential killer and the relationships in the novel. That's why we decided on 1986. This can be said for *Higurashi* as well; it's a time in 1983, it's a time in 1986, where you cannot speak on a mobile phone, when there is no such thing as a mobile phone. Before mobile phones become popular. This is why the setting was chosen.

For *Rose Guns Days*, why the past, right? It's a bit difficult to explain to a foreign audience. But for Japanese people we think about post-war Japan as, "How should we define Japan? How should we think about Japan?" This is a sort of universal thing, it was very relevant in 1947, which is the setting of *Rose Guns Days*, but even now it's still a relevant topic of concern for Japanese people. The thing that resonates throughout the 20th century is, how should foreigners and Japanese people interact? There's one more item, it's that right before I wrote *Rose Guns Days* I went to France. There was a university festival about animation, and during this event I had a talk with someone there, and it was interesting for me to find out how foreigners think about Japan. It motivated me to write *Rose Guns Days* (pictured below) and offer a perspective to foreigners on how to think about Japan.

JS: It's very different to your other works. Did you have to prepare for it differently, perhaps with regards to your writing methods?

R7: I think about *Higurashi* and *Umineko* as games. You try to find out who the criminal is, find out the tricks he or she uses, whereas with *Rose Guns Days*, it's not a game for me. Its purpose is to raise a topic, to submit an idea to an audience. So basically it's a message.

JS: *Rose Guns Days* feels closer to an anime. There's been adaptations of your work into anime, but generally people feel they don't match the quality of your originals. What are the difficulties faced with adapting games to anime?

R7: This is a distinction that's made only in Japan, between novels and light novels.[26] This distinction is very clear to the otaku culture in

---

[24] Manga on *Rose Guns Days* was pub. by Square-Enix
[25] Japanese term for advertising text meant to "catch" your interest, like a catchphrase

[26] Novel targeting middle and high school students, no more than 50k words; perhaps akin to a novella?

Japan. The first type is a type of novel that does not envision adaptations to anime. So of course this means that when it's going to be adapted to an animated medium, there's going to be some problems coming out. But as a light novel, from the beginning the author is aware that there will be an animation made of this same material. In my case [my games are] not written with the idea that they will be turned into animation, so it's very normal for problems to appear in the process. This is what I wanted to say.

JS: Did you start *Rose Guns Days* to rekindle your love or writing?

R7: First of all, for *Higurashi* and *Umineko* I had a story, and this was the main focus. Whereas the characters were secondary, and they were just there to support or scaffold the story. Whereas with *Rose Guns Days* I had the characters as the main aspect, and they would develop into a story.

JS: What parts of the writing process do you like and dislike? Do you have a favourite part?

R7: This is a difficult question! What I really enjoy is when you have a character who has an opinion, and another character has another opinion, and these opinions bounce off each other. And of course feelings also bounce off each other. So what I really like is when we can put this in: <*draws*>[27] For me, what's really more difficult to write is the scenes that are really ordinary, really common occurrences, which feel a bit more average. From that point of view I am more challenged by these daily events. It's easier for me to write a visual novel like *Umineko* where roughly every hour some character dies or is killed.

JS: On that note, in ep. 6 the reader gets an indication of what the detective thinks happened on the island.[28] However, there seems to be reasons not to trust his conclusions. Should the reader work on their own to deduce events?

R7: This is exactly why I'm saying it's like a game. There's a part where you can trust this guy's reasoning, or you can doubt it and come up with your own theories.

JS: In English we call that the "unreliable narrator" - the viewer is encouraged to question the person conveying events.

R7: Ahh. In *Umineko* the catch copy was, "If you challenge the view, then it's a mystery. If you submit to the prevailing view, it's a fantasy." So that you could choose your approach.

JS: You said that when writing *Higurashi* you made reference to work by Key, but put your own twist on the pattern. What else has influenced you?

R7: <*laughs*> I said before that I took characters that were real and made them more like manga, and my approach was strongly modelled on the characters in Key's works. You know, up to that point in Japanese *moe*[29] games, the heroines were all just lovable and cute young girls, but Key made their girls just thoroughly bizarre. In that vein, I decided that from now on the heroines can't be just cute, they have to be a bit crazy, a bit perverse or strange.

JS: Leading on from Key, I believe you worked with Jun Maeda[30] previously. What was that like?

R7: I helped Mr Jun Maeda with a title called *Rewrite.*[31] Mr Jun Maeda is a person with a great sense of responsibility, and this of course puts a lot of pressure on me. So for him being a top class scenario writer, it's thanks to him that I also became a scenario writer. For me, working together with him, I felt greatly honoured, but also a lot of pressure because I'm standing next to such an important person.

JS: As this interview proves, your work is also highly regarded, alongside Jun Maeda's.

R7: Thank you, but I'm much lower than him. <*laughs*> Thank you for that comment, but it's not... For me, he is like a god.[32]

---

[27] Sketch showed the alphabet characters: !!?
[28] A series of murders take place

[29] Multiple meanings - basically a style of "cuteness"
[30] Co-founder of Key - read VN intro for explanation
[31] Win/PSP/PS Vita, 2011
[32] Kami-sama

JS: Have you followed the work of Mr Kotaro Uchikoshi? *[lists games]* Now he's at Chunsoft. I was just curious if you'd heard his name...

R7: *<looks at Mr Seto's phone>* Wow. I'm looking at the Wikipedia page for Mr Uchikoshi, and I didn't know his name, but he's a really prolific writer! Many of his visual novels I've played and I greatly appreciate them. I just didn't recognise the name.

JS: I'm dedicating a chapter to visual novels - I specifically wanted you for this section, and I'm interviewing Mr Uchikoshi later. I also interviewed two guys connected with *Otogirisou*.

R7: I feel a bit... Wow... The other guys are so big, I'm feeling overshadowed. *<laughs>*

JS: Oh, not at all! [...] How did you meet and start working with people such as Dai, who provided the amazing music for your work?

R7: How I came to meet Dai-san is, as I said before, my brother and I were making these games, but we didn't have any music - we couldn't create music. So what we did is, we used all this free music that's available on the internet. Of course this presents a problem because these have different sound volumes, which means that we couldn't balance them properly. So we used this free software which allows you to adjust the volume to make it all the same. Unfortunately, because we're not very good at this, we made a really bad job and it was really full of noise. At this point Dai-san actually contacted me by email and said, "Shall I help you guys with this? Because you obviously need help."

JS: Your game *Ookami Kakushi* [33] was for Konami. What must you do differently when working for a company like Konami?

R7: There are two important things when we work with a company that's developing the game. First, it's the schedule: they have a schedule to keep and they give you this really detailed plan. You must have the scenario written by this date, you must have the heroine coming up by this point, and you have to have this revelation by this point. So there's actually a really broken up schedule which you need to follow. But [when writing for myself], it's the opposite. I just go by motivation, I just go by inspiration, it's what I want to do. So this is where the conflict comes in - the schedule conflict, which is decided by commercial interests, which comes into conflict with my personal inclinations, when I want to be free to follow my inspiration.

Secondly... *<laughs>* When you work with a company of course you have a schedule, and then this means that everything has to be done by the deadline. Whereas when I do this by myself I like to be able to change things, and sometimes it's even a couple of days before - even the last day before - the master has to be uploaded, that I change some character, or change some part. Which I really like. Of course this is a nightmare for the staff I employ.

<adds more to the previous sketch> This is the difference between... On the *doujin* side you can do it all by yourself, you can be selfish. Whereas on the commercial side many people work together, according to a plan.

JS: I believe you were quite open to fans translating *Umineko* - tell me about this. Also, I heard a rumour you secretly worked with fans on translating *Rose Guns Days*.

R7: To begin with, it was a group called Witch Hunt[34] and they were doing this as part of their fan activities. In the *doujin* world it's kind of considered natural, or the right thing to do, to support your fans in their activities. So that's why I was open to the translation project.

Mr Seto: One reason that we worked with these guys is that some other groups of fans would just say, "Go to this server and you can download a free English version." Whereas with Witch Hunt, what they did is, they said, "Buy the product and using our patch, you can play it in English." So this is why we cooperated with them.

JS: Yes! Fan-translations can encourage official sales of the product in Japanese!

R7: That's right. Of course, when fans were translating this for native English speakers I was very happy to get their support in producing an English version. But also - linking back to the previous question about if it's only a hobby how

---

[33] Commercial release on PSP

[34] The Witch Hunt Translation Project - *witch-hunt.com*

can you live on this - to continue writing we need a certain amount of money. We're here drinking this <*gestures to chilled green tea*> because of the support of our fans. So obviously this kind of support, which encourages other people to buy our product, there is no better support than this that somebody can hope for.

JS: Have you been surprised by the support your work has gotten outside of Japan?

R7: Yes, of course I was very surprised. When I wrote this I wrote it for the Japanese comic market, and Japanese audience, so I was very surprised when I got mail with some comments from one of my fans overseas.

JS: You visited a convention in France - any chance of visiting the US or Europe?

R7: Ah, yes! If I would be invited, I would be more than glad to participate. Of course once I go overseas, then my motivation will also be increased to write more, and there's also more I can learn. This was the inspiration for *Rose Guns Days*, it came when I was in France. This is already widely known, but there are many pictures, many photos from my time in France, in *Rose Guns Days*.

JS: Do you have any unreleased games? Did any content have to be removed due to space or time limits before release?

R7: Most of them, no, not that I can think of. Most of the content ends up in the game.

Mr Seto: Yes, because you're doing it as a hobby - without deadlines. <*smiles*>

R7: There is one item, however, and this is before *Higurashi*. The title is *Flowers*, and it didn't get released. I was not part of 07th Expansion at that time, I was part of a *doujin* circle, and the scenario was actually completed, but the circle disbanded so it just ended, tragically, without getting published.

JS: Did you keep the material you created?

R7: What I wrote on the computer is on my harddrive here, but some of the related materials are not at this location. I was thinking about restarting the work on this one, and publishing it eventually, unfortunately it's a *moe* game. <*laughs*> It's not a mystery murder detective story, so I think my fans right now would be quite disappointed. It's not what they expect.

JS: People are always interested in the unpublished chapters of someone's work. Perhaps you can include it as a small bonus in your next game?

R7: <*laughs*> Thank you for your kind advice - yes, it's a good idea that maybe I could put it in something in the future. So that all the effort doesn't go to waste.

JS: Do you have any thoughts or message you want to put across?

R7: For foreign people? <*laughs*> One thing I could say to fans is take a photo of your surroundings, because as you saw in my games, there's a murder happening and there's a photographic background. So if you sent me photos of your neighbourhood, or your house, or your family, if it gets picked up I will make a murder happen in that place. <*laughs*>

JS: Excellent! I'll definitely put that down!

R7: <*laughs*> Thank you very much. Any place in the world is OK. Actually, I'm more in trouble when I don't have the background. So any photos would be more than welcome. But please, I'd rather not have ***[commercially recognised mascot]*** in these photos. <*laughs*> Maybe I'm going to get killed for saying this now. <*laughs*> Maybe cut that from the interview.

JS: One final question. Your game boxes are in the DVD slim cases. Is there a particular reason you choose those?

R7: DVD box? Ah! These are called "tall cases" in Japanese. There's a very simple reason. In *doujin* shops in Japan it stands out more when on display, compared to the smaller CD cases often used. Most of the famous titles in Japan are published in tall cases actually.

JS: Thank you for your time. It's been a pleasure.

<We take a farewell photo and say goodbye>

If you're interested in buying Ryukishi07's titles in Europe, check out **www.mangagamer.com**

打越 鋼太郎

UCHIKOSHI, Kotaro

DOB: 17 November 1973 / Birthplace: Tokyo / Blood Type: O

~ Selected Portfolio ~

Joined KID in 1998

Pepsiman	- PlayStation, 1999	(Modelling)
Memories Off	- PlayStation, 1999	(Planning, scenario)
Never 7: The End of Infinity	- Dreamcast, 2000	(Planning, scenario)
Memories Off 2nd	- PlayStation/Dreamcast, 2001	(Planning, scenario)

<leaves KID>

Ever 17: The Out of Infinity	- PS2/DC, 2002	(Planning, scenario)
Secret work	- 2003	
Remember 11: The Age of Infinity	- PS2, 2004	(Planning, scenario)
EVE: New Generation	- Win/PS2, 2006	(Planning, scenario)
Kamaitachino Yoru: Niwango Version	- mobile phones, 2006	(Scenario)

Joined Chunsoft in 2007

12Riven - the Ψcliminal of integral	- PS2, 2008	(Planning, scenario)
999: Nine Hours, Nine Persons, Nine Doors	- NDS, 2009	(Planning, direction, scenario)
Virtue's Last Reward	- 3DS/PS Vita, 2012	(Planning, direction, scenario)
STEINS;GATE: Senkei Kousokuno Phenogram	- PS3, 2013	(Contributed one scenario)

Interview with Kotaro Uchikoshi
28 October 2013, Tokyo

Mr Uchikoshi is the mainstream, commercial analogue to Ryukishi07, and represents a fascinating intersection of Japanese and Western perspectives, given that his narrative-focused games are extremely popular outside of Japan, perhaps even more so than within Japan. At the time of editing this interview, in 2014, Mr Uchikoshi had been tweeting regarding the difficulty of getting permission to continue his Zero Escape series. Given the desire of Japanese developers to appeal to Western audiences, Mr Uchikoshi's work deserves further examination.

JS: Thank you for meeting us tonight, especially at this time. Would you like something to eat? Do you mind if I order us some coffees?

KU: *<laughs> Zenzen! (Not at all!)*

JS: What was the first game you played?

KU: To tell you the truth, I'm not sure at all, because I had a Famicom at home, when I was a kid, and there was *Excite Bike*, *Baseball*, and *Mario*. I'm actually not sure what the first game was that I played. But basically what my generation were playing, those sorts of games, I was playing as well.

JS: Your first job was at KID, correct?[1]

KU: Actually I dropped out of college, and in Japan there is a specific name for this, called "*freeter*" - which means that you're without a job, you dropped out of university, basically the people who fall through the cracks. I spent about one year like this, then I joined a technical school for games, a vocational school. Then I joined KID, and at this time the company was doing visual novels, but they were also doing board games for the Super Famicom.[2] When I started work for KID I was supposed to be a planner on the board games, but my supervisor said, "Well, Uchikoshi-san, you could do scenarios, you could write scenarios as well, probably." He really asked me

[1] Kindle Imagine Develop (1988-2006); NES *G.I. Joe*

[2] This would be *Super Jinsei Game*, an adaptation of a Japanese board game version of *The Game of Life*. Instalments *2* and *3* are credited to KID, released in 1995 and 1996

lightly, but I ended up being a visual novel planner and writing scenarios.

JS: I did not realise KID developed board games. How long did you work on them?

KU: The board games were actually videogame board games.[3] I didn't work on them, I actually got in with *Pepsiman*, an action game, and I was in charge of 3D models. There was no break-up between divisions at KID. Basically there was one division, and we did board games for computers. There was this game called *Jinsei Game*, which we had to make upon request from a company called Takara, which outsourced the development to us, for the Super Famicom. This is what our company was supposed to make at that time, when I joined KID.

JS: How did *Pepsiman* start?

KU: You know, about *Pepsiman*, I'm not very clear about it, because I was just a new guy, I wasn't somebody big. So I wouldn't know about the contract and so on. When I joined the company the *Pepsiman* project had already started. Probably somebody from a higher up position negotiated this with Pepsi. For me as well I was a bit surprised - how did they do it, how did they manage it?

JS: Had you been trained in 3D modelling at the vocational school?

KU: At the vocational school I did planning, I did 3D modelling, I covered all the basic stuff of games; 2D, sound, art, programming, I just covered all the basics.

JS: Which vocational school?

KU: Vantan. *<spells it, V-A-N-T-A-N>*[4]

JS: There weren't many videogame vocational schools. Human Entertainment had one, and Hudson had one in Hokkaido. Where was Vantan?

KU: You're quite knowledgeable about this! Before that it was 1997. In Ikebukuro. Actually Vantan was not... It started out as a famous vocational school for clothes design, and later on they kind of also branched into game development. So it's not really well known, for this reason.

JS: Tell me about the school.

KU: One interesting thing is that, because they were basically just a vocational school centred on clothes, and they just started in the game business, the level of their teachers was not that high. This meant that the courses were not that interesting, so a lot of the students started boycotting classes and not going to school. And actually, many people dropped out because they were not happy with the level of teaching. In the end it was basically me and about five or six other guys who still kept on attending classes. Perhaps, due to this reason, the teachers could really focus on and take good care of us. I attribute the reason for our achieving a higher level of proficiency due to the fact that we were a very small group taught by the teachers.

JS: What were you studying at university when you dropped out?

KU: Management engineering.[5]

JS: Did you not enjoy it?

KU: No! It was not enjoyable. *<laughs>* It was one of these majors that would treat humans from a mechanical point of view, like a machine. That humans are just tools - how do you increase efficiency? How do you raise productivity? These were the topics. I did not feel that they matched my style.

JS: Being a writer on visual novels is very different to 3D graphics modelling on *Pepsiman*.

KU: *So desu neee... (Yeeeah, that's right...)*

JS: Just building polys in a 3D shape?

KU: Yes, that's it exactly, as you said. It was just creating shapes with polygons. The texturing was done by somebody else. Even this, making the polygons, was not a very

[3] lit: "*computer game no board game*"

[4] Vantan Design Institute (http://www.vantan.jp)

[5] Lit: 経営工学

important part. I was just in charge of the event scenes, which are between the game sections. Something like the helicopter scene, or you'd have the biking Pepsiman, or the rolling barrels. Stuff like that.

JS: The game is quite wacky. *<does the game voice> PEPSIMAAAAN!* There's video of a fat guy drinking Pepsi, and a lot of jokes. It feels like the team had a lot of fun. Was this the case?

KU: *<laughs>* Ehh... First of all, I really commend you for your good knowledge of *Pepsiman*, because it didn't sell that well. These video scenes, like that one with the American drinking Pepsi, actually this was because we just didn't have a lot of money, and we just had to create these low cost scenes. This is the one comment that I would make.

JS: I love *Pepsiman*! Can you sketch the KID office layout?

KU: *<laughs>* There might be some mistakes in the way I remember things... *<draws office>* I was sitting in this, *<gestures to star>* it's called a writer's booth. This area was known as the area for people who could be booted at any time. It had the nickname of "The Edge of the Cliff." So, these guys could always be disposed of. There was a piece of paper here, like a poster, which said "Edge of the Cliff".

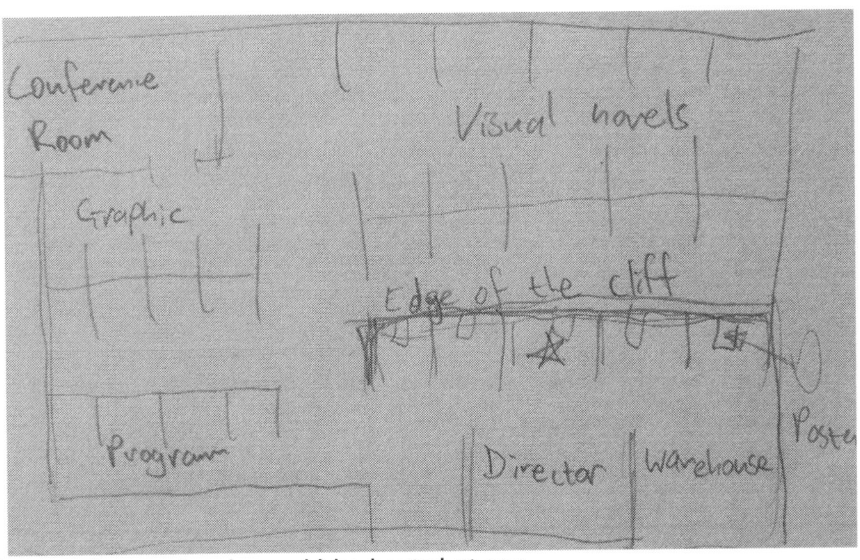

JS: Well, that's one way to motivate your staff!

KU: There's also more. This is where the director was, the division director. This is the warehouse. This is graphics, and I think this was programming. The conference room, meeting room. And this area I think it was not *Pepsiman*, but the visual novels area. The same here, basically the whole area.

JS: Your first visual novel was *Memories Off*.[6] What was the first you recall playing? Did you play *Portopia Renzoku Satsujin Jiken*?

KU: Yes, I did play it, of course. When I was a primary school student, I think.

JS: Would you say *Portopia* is a visual novel, or would you say the genre started with *Otogorisou* and *Kamaitachi no Yoru*? How do you define the boundaries of the genre?

KU: I think this depends a lot on the person you ask, but the visual novel, it's generally accepted that they started with *Otogorisou* and *Kamaitachi no Yoru*, these are the first to be called visual novels. Whereas *Portopia* is more like an adventure game.

JS: How would you define the difference between adventure games and visual novels?

KU: First of all, the visual novel term does not really represent the genre in Japan. This is accepted as the genre and regarded as the genre outside of Japan, overseas. In Japan people basically think about it as... We have the adventure game, we have the sound novel, and we have the *bishoujo* [7] genre. But there is no visual novel genre per say. With me

---

[6] Long-running series of romantic visual novels

[7] Lit. "beautiful young girl". AKA "gal game" or *galge*; interaction with young women in a particular art style

personally, when I made *999*, and *Virtue's Last Reward*, these are not referred to as visual novels, they're referred to as actual adventure games. Whereas overseas they're referred to as visual novels. But in Japan, we don't really make that distinction [between visual novels and adventure games]. Hmm... I think it's quite a difficult question. As far as I can tell, with visual novels and adventure games the main difference is if there's a lot of text or not. How much text will be there.

JS: I'm a little worried now. I'm dedicating an entire chapter to visual novels.

KU: <*laughs*> You should probably ask other Japanese developers about visual novels, but I don't really hear much about the "*visual novel*". We think about it as sound novels or adventure games, which includes the *bishoujo* genre.

JS: After *Memories Off* you worked on *Never 7* (above), the first in the *Infinity* series.[8] This focused on being a dating-sim[9] with a slight sci-fi twist. The second game, *Ever 17*, had a strong balance between dating-sim and sci-fi action. The third game, *Remember 11*, ditched the dating-sim in favour of pure sci-fi adventure. What brought about these changes?

KU: <*nods in agreement while question is being asked*> It's a very simple reason, actually. Basically it was right after *Memories Off*, where you had it centred on a girl, and I could not put heavy sci-fi content in the next game. The reason I couldn't do this immediately was because I was told from above, my superiors, that if you don't have a cute girl showing up in the game it would not sell - not without introducing stronger dating game elements and designing it so that developing a relationship with a girl was the main focus of the game. So in the first one, *Never 7*, I couldn't really put too much sci-fi content. So I kept it quite light. The thing is, *Never 7* came out and the sci-fi aspects actually got rather good reviews. So then, gradually, I could increase the sci-fi content, and it just grew from that.

JS: Sounds like you were trying to break out, in order to create the story you really wanted. Did you feel restricted with *Memories Off* (pictured adjacent) and the type of scenario needed?

KU: Not really. In terms of *Memories Off*, I knew from the beginning it's a love game, a romance. I did not feel that I wanted to put some sci-fi in it, or that I was limited in some way. However, I really felt that I was good at this genre, the sci-fi genre, so I thought that at some point in the future I would like to write sci-fi. The problem was that at this time, even if there were some sci-fi elements in the *bishoujo* genre, it was not the main trend. I planned the next game, and overall it got accepted, but I was aware the whole time that it had to fit in to the "dating-sim" genre, the *bishoujo* genre. So there would be some girl, there would be some dating involved. I knew that even with my sci-fi themed next game, the structure would be there for a *bishoujo* game, and I would have to fit my sci-fi profile into it.

JS: Have you been influenced by any particular sci-fi creators?

KU: I did read some sci-fi books, but not that many. It's strange, but many people ask me this question, and to tell you the truth, not really. Of course I know *Back to the Future*, but I wouldn't say I was very influenced by it. Like, I'm not ***really*** into *Back to the Future*, for example. In the 1980s a lot of sci-fi movies came out, and of course Hollywood movies that I saw in this period, so up to a certain point I might have been influenced by these. <*laughs*> I'm sorry, actually, there is one person who influenced me. Hoshi Shinichi.[10] An author of sci-fi. He produced these sort of short volumes, and when I was a

---

[8] Series: *Never 7*, *Ever 17*, *Remember 11*, *12 Riven*, and *Code 18*. Complex time travel storylines

[9] Dating-sim is not a familiar term in Japanese, more commonly it's *bishoujo*, *ren'ai sim*, *gal game*, etc.

[10] 星新一, 1926-1997, novelist and sci-fi writer

junior high school student, I really read a lot of his work, and I probably was influenced by him.

JS: In the list you sent me, it says that after *Memories Off 2nd* you left KID. Why was this?

KU: *<laughs>* With *Never 7* and *Ever 17* (pictured below), they got really good reviews, but on the other hand, I felt now I've got the confidence to go off by myself and become a freelance writer. It's not that the company was bad in some way, I just wanted to become independent, and I had the confidence now. Also, another point was that as long as I worked for KID, I could only produce the work that KID gave me to do. Whereas if I became freelance, if I became independent, I could do work for other companies by myself too.

JS: It says here in 2003 you did "secret work" - is this an unreleased game?

KU: I can talk about it - there's a very simple reason. It was an adult game! *<laughs>* It was published, but not with my name.

JS: What was this adult game?

KU: What was the title... *<laughs>* Honestly, I'm not really hiding it, I just can't remember it. The title... What was it? As soon as I remember I'll tell you! *<laughs>*

JS: You wrote the scenario to an erotic visual novel?

KU: Yes, that's right.

JS: Freelance?

KU: Yes, that's correct.

JS: The fact your name was not on it, was that at your request?

KU: Yes, it was my request!

<everyone laughs>

JS: The first *EVE*[11] game on computers, that was also erotic.

KU: Yes, yes it was.

JS: Because in 2006 you were scenario writer and planner on *EVE: New Generation*, for the PlayStation 2, correct?

KU: Yes, that's the correct. But there was also a PC version. I worked on both.

JS: I've played the original *EVE*, but not this one. Did it retain the adult themes?

KU: *<laughs>* Yes, that's so. For the computer version anyway, yes.

JS: Did your work on the earlier 2003 erotic game make it easier to write *EVE*?

KU: *<laughs>* Yes, that's right!

JS: You only worked on two adult games in your career then?

KU: Yes, that's correct. *<laughs>* It's a completely different story, but can I say something on a different track?

JS: Yes, please.

KU: *<laughs>* One thing that I wanted to say is, you know, when you write these adult games, something I get very tired of when writing these is... I apologise that I'm going into the gutter with this one, but, you're writing and your

[11] *EVE Burst Error*, 1995, renowned erotic visual novel also released in English for Windows

imagination is concentrating on writing these adult scenes, and you have all of these desires that you're creating and you're imagining in your head, but you're also at work, so you can't really resolve them and... you know... satisfy your cravings. So you have to just hold it in and keep on writing and writing and writing... in that sense, it's a very difficult job!

<everyone laughs>

JS: After the secret work, you worked on *Remember 11* (pictured below), correct? Were there plans to have extra content added, or a different ending?

KU: Yes, there were many things around this, I don't know how to put it... At that time the director was Mr Nakazawa,[12] and for myself, I was in charge of scenario writing and I had an ending in mind. But this ending was not something he was happy with. He had another, different ending in mind, which we had differing opinions about. Also, we didn't have enough time to write it ***all***. So it kind of came up as a halfway, half done job, the ending. Because of this difference in opinion. As far as I'm concerned I think I put my ending into the story, but as a result of this difference in opinion it sort of felt half finished.

JS: Regarding this game, and all your games, if you could go back in time and make any changes, would you?

KU: I don't really feel that I need to go back and change much, but in terms of the ending, for example, I'm happy with the ending. However, because a long time ago, at the beginning of my career as a scenario writer, I didn't have that much skill - I don't feel I have great skills right now - but at that time it was really not good. I would like to go back and revisit some scenario portions. The ones that were a bit boring or where development of the story was not that greatly achieved. I would like to rewrite these or maybe cut off some boring scenes. I would like to do that. But in terms of content, I wouldn't change anything or add anything.

JS: With regards to this disagreement you had with Mr Nakazawa, have you often had to change your work before release? Perhaps at the request of a publisher?

KU: Well, not really, actually. *Remember 11* was the worst, as it were. But for other games I was both director and scenario writer, so there wasn't really the anticipation that I would come into conflict with somebody. On the other hand, of course, at the company there were these disagreements about the schedule, about money, and so on.

JS: With all these different projects, do you approach the writing in different ways?

KU: Hmm... A difficult question. You know, it's a difficult question, because basically I have the same approach when writing, even if they're different things.

JS: What about something like *Steins;Gate* and *999*? What about branching pathways? Do you have a methodical system?

KU: Hmm, it's a difficult question, because it's not really sequential, the way I write. It's more like in parallel, and even if for example I decide the characters, then we have the stage or the setting beside them, then I decide the time, then I decide the ending, which may include some trick or... Let's say, like a punchline. Even if this is a typical approach, if at some point in the writing process I feel I want to give priority to this ending, to this trick, to this punchline, then I will have to go back and change the characters, or change the time, or change the setting. So basically it's going back and working in parallel, that's why it's a more disordered process or style of writing.

JS: Do you have an enormous white board, with all the cast written down?

[12] Takumi Nakazawa, 中澤 工

KU: No, not really. For *Virtue's Last Reward* (pictured above) I did assign a number to each character, and I managed this using an Excel file. However, mostly it's done using notes, and on these notes I'd have some diagram with the branching lines, or branching stories, and I think about it. But mostly the way it's done, if you ask me how do I integrate all this, it's by using text files. These files are, let's say, in my thoughts, and that's how I manage them. The reason I use these text files is because it's easy to search. So for example if I want to see where was this particular word used, it's something which is easy to find.

JS: Something in this list caught my attention.[13] What did you mean "degenerate life" in 2005?

KU: <*laughs*> Ehh... I did say that, didn't I...

JS: If you don't want to comment, that's OK. We don't have to talk about it.

KU: The reason is, simply, this year I was really into an online RPG game for personal computers - a network game. There's this Japanese word, *hai-jin*,[14] where *hai* means going to waste, and *jin* is person. So it's basically a person that goes to pieces.

JS: What was the online game?

KU: It's not very famous, but *Belle Isle*.[15] I don't think it's available anymore.

JS: I've heard how people can get really addicted. So this was an MMORPG?

KU: You know, in this game, you can have a male character or a female character. I don't know if this is particular to *Belle Isle*, but you can get married in the game as well. I wasn't married at the time, I am married now [in real life], but at that time I had a girl I liked, and this girl said let's play *Belle Isle*. So we started playing together, and we got married in the game. Then later on she dumped me, so that didn't go anywhere. But once she dumped me, my life sort of degenerated.

JS: I played the original *Kamaitachi no Yoru* on Super Famicom; you worked on the *Niwango Version*, was this some kind of sequel?

KU: This was a long time ago. The thing is, do you know about NicoNico Douga? [16] The company that makes NicoNico Douga is Niwango. So this company, now it's famous for this, but at that time there was a company called Dwango, so the same as Ni but with "Do" in front. The subsidiary company would be Niwango. Now Dwango, what these guys did, is they made content for mobile phones and they would distribute it. So for example, if you sent a message to the server, the company server, then they would send an automatic reply stating that today's weather is sunny, or Akasaka has great water. It's kind of like Siri[17] right now. So in 2006 this is happening, and they were doing this automatically via emails. So they said OK, now let's do an email game, an email and game combination, and the basis of this would be *Kamaitachi no Yoru*.

As I said, this was sent by email to the users. The basis would be *Kamaitachi no Yoru*, but they gave us permission to modify [the original story as we needed]. So what we did, we came up with this idea of a main character who would actually be a woman, or a girl, and she's secluded on this snowy mountain, in a cabin, and she can't escape this area. And she sends this email to the player: "I am in this cabin all by myself, there is a body, what do I do?" And then you have choices. These choices are sent to the player, and the player can choose to search the body, go outside, get help, or something like that. Then, based on this development, whatever you choose as a player, and you send this email, the scenario develops further. Searching the body brings up some other

[13] Mr Uchikoshi provided a list of his career; the only entry for 2005 was: (Degenerate life)
[14] Lit: 廃人 - can also mean disabled person
[15] Obscure MMORPG by Headlock
[16] Japan's equivalent to YouTube
[17] iOS app that answers questions, requests

options, going outside has other options, and so on. Finally you get to the point where, at the end, she escapes - this character, the woman, escapes the criminal and gets out of this situation on the mountain.

JS: Ingenious! How did they generate money from this? Fees, adverts?

KU: Just at the beginning you pay a fixed amount, at the very beginning, and "buy" the game. No adverts.

JS: This sounds like a clever modification. Were you a fan of the original on Super Famicom?

KU: *<laughs>* No, when I played it the game was on PlayStation.

JS: Were you surprised at the tremendous success that *999* (pictured below) had when released outside of Japan?

KU: Yes, I was really surprised. Because with visual novels they really seem to be particular to Japan, and overseas I didn't think they would be accepted very easily. So I was very surprised.

JS: Did the strong sales in America turn it from a one-off project into the *Zero Escape* series?

KU: Yes, that's correct.

JS: I heard it sells more internationally, than in Japan. Why do you feel that is?

KU: No, that's a question I want to ask you! Why do you think it is?

JS: I'm not sure... There's this big debate, and some Japanese developers say, "We have to appeal to America and Europe more." And these developers try to make a game that arbitrarily appeals to foreigners more. I feel that with *Zero Escape* being distinctly Japanese, and selling well outside Japan, shows that it's best to be true to your own vision.

KU: Yes, that is best.

JS: Developers should simply try to make a good game, not arbitrarily do things in the hope it appeals to some specific demographic.

KU: Yes, I think you may be right.

JS: When writing the *Zero Escape* series, how conscious are you of foreign markets?

KU: Ehh... Of course the game is made for a world audience, but if you ask me what's foremost in front of my eyes, what's foremost in my mind, it's actually the Japanese audience, or players. So I think about what's... The lines are designed with a Japanese audience in mind, the funny scenes, the humour, the jokes are all tailored for the Japanese audience. Of course I'm creating for the global market, but it's kind of tailored for Japan. What's funny about this, is that despite this effort I make to tailor it to Japan, in Japan it doesn't sell so well. Let's just say it has a kind of average result. Whereas overseas it seems to be much more appreciated, which is kind of ironic.

SUBSEQUENT TEXT CONTAINS A SPOILER FOR VIRTUE'S LAST REWARD LATER ON

JS: It seems you've managed to tap into the American and European psyche. Do your bosses at Chunsoft try to analyse how this happened? Do they want to replicate the formula?

KU: Sorry, I'm going to drift on this one. But, there's no discussion or analysis about why this occurred. I think, honestly, nobody really knows. I received many prizes for this [*Zero Escape*], and I'm mentioned on many websites, but nobody really knows why. ***[90 words redacted on request]*** Right now there is a game called ***[REDACTED]***, which sold about ***[REDACTED]*** copies, and they're saying we should make a game like this.

[Off the record discussion - several minutes]

JS: Can you describe entering Chunsoft in 2007? Why did you stop freelancing? Have you met Kouichi Nakamura?

KU: As for joining Chunsoft, it's a very simple reason, actually there's two. I had a child, and wanted to get a stable income, and also my wife's mother and father would insist on me getting some stability in my life. <*laughs*> Also, I liked Chunsoft and I knew that they're famous for adventure games and visual novels, so I was quite eager to join the company. About Nakamura-san, he's the chairman.[18]

JS: Yes, they have a long heritage of creating popular sound or visual novels.

KU: Yes, but you know, right now the company is not selling very well, and in terms of the visual novel team, we're almost completely non-existent right now. We actually had a merger between Spike and Chunsoft, and we're now Spike-Chunsoft. Right now Chunsoft produces this game called *Mystery Dungeon*, and the team that is producing this are the only members still remaining from the visual novel team. So for visual novels per say, it's just me.

JS: Wow! That's rough. [...] Going back to *999*, I've heard rumours it was supposed to have a different ending. What was different and why was it changed?

KU: <*to self*> *999*... Was it like this... Did I say in an interview it was supposed to have a different ending?

JS: I've heard rumours, but couldn't find a direct source. Who better to ask then?

KU: <*laughs*>

JS: If the ending is as you wanted it, then these are just rumours.

KU: I really forget quickly about the things I write, and regarding *999* I think it was as it is. There was no other ending. However, for *Virtue's Last Reward*, the game was completed when the earthquake struck, in March 2011. It was completed, but with that ending we felt that it's a bit... Not cool to go with it. So we did change it a bit, and added something.

JS: I've not actually seen this ending. Could you describe the changes? *SPOILER ALERT!*

KU: The ending was really crisp. You might want to put a ***SPOILER ALERT***. What happens is that human kind is all destroyed, nobody survives. At this point somebody goes back into the past, and the original ending was to go back to the past, change a little bit so that the future is saved, and then it finishes. However, this felt a bit crisp and sudden. So what we did is, we added a lot of content to say that you, by going back and working in the past to change the future, thanks to your efforts there is some hope. To give it a more positive nuance.

JS: Do you have any funny stories from development that you'd like to share with your fans outside of Japan?

KU: Hmmm... I do have some! On one occasion when we did overtime work, I have this problem, where I talk in my sleep quite frequently. I act on what happens in my dream, so that I actually scream - I woke up screaming, and people came to me and said, "Uchikoshi-san, are you OK?" Sometimes we work too much and we sleep in the office, and this was one episode, when I woke up screaming.

JS: Were you having a nightmare?

KU: Yes, that's right. Basically the only dreams I have are nightmares, as far as I know. In this particular nightmare there was a ghost-like person, who was pulling with a lot of force on my legs. You know the incubus phenomenon? You know when you wake up from a dream, but you can't move at all? In Japanese it's called "*kanashibari*". I was really frozen, and couldn't move, and this guy was pulling on my legs, and I started screaming, and that's how I woke up.

JS: You only ever have nightmares?! Isn't that a bit worrying?

KU: <*laughs*> Uh, no, because now I'm quite used to this.

JS: How long has this been going on for?

[18] Word used: *kaicho*

KU: From when I was a teenager. Now actually I'm quite enjoying it. Right now, even studying how to solve this incubus phenomenon, I don't seem to be able to find a solution.

JS: Do you draw inspirations from your dreams?

KU: Yeah, quite a lot actually! I really think hard about stuff before going to sleep, and then when I wake up I'm really drawing inspiration from the dreams. *<laughs>*

JS: Is there anything else you'd like say?

KU: Since in overseas countries my works - *999, Virtue's Last Reward* - have been much appreciated, there's just one thing I want to say: have great expectations for my next work.

JS: When will it be out?

KU: It comes out after your book.

JS: Oh! Is there any hint you can give?

KU: *<laughs>* I think it will be out on PlayStation 4.

JS: Excellent. I look forward to it. Do you like working on PlayStation 4?

KU: I haven't actually touched the PlayStation 4 machine. We first write the scenario, then we develop it.

JS: Do you feel that other visual novel developers should put more effort into releasing their games outside of Japan? It feels like we're missing out on a lot of titles.

KU: With visual novels I feel that there are many titles out there that are really interesting. But the big answer there would be that they should definitely be translated, to try the overseas market. But the biggest problem here is that for these visual novels, the volume of text is really huge, and this becomes a serious obstacle towards localising them for overseas.

JS: Thank you very much.

KU: Thank you!

~Appearing in a later volume~

If you like 2D shmups

Naosuke Arai
One of the longest serving employees from TecnoSoft, Mr Arai describes the origin of and changes in the company over the years, working with the creator of the original *Thunder Force*, his role in sound production and music composition, and also an almost unknown telephone service that TecnoSoft provided, where he voice-acted the role of a videogame playing demon.

Below, from left: **Takayuki Hirono**, Compile veteran, details the technical differences between the PCE and FC, the complexities of the *Aleste* series, and also why there were two different *Power Strike II* titles. **Satoshi Fujishima**, Compile and later Fujipac, creator of action-RPG *Golvellius*, the only shmup for the PC-FX, plus puzzle-platformer *Lupop*. **Yuichi Toyama**, TecnoSoft, Compile, now head of Raizing / 8ing, early computer game programmer, involved in many great shmups, including one unreleased. **Mitsuakira Tatsuta**, now 8ing, reveals some interesting trivia from his days at TecnoSoft. **Kenichi Yokoo**, Compile and now 8ing, another shmup veteran, including *Soukyuugurentai*.

ZUN

DOB: 18 March 1977 / Birthplace: Nagano prefecture / Blood Type: A

~ Selected Portfolio ~

Touhou games up until Mystic Square were on PC-98, subsequent games are on Windows

TOUHOU

東方靈異伝 ~ *Highly Responsive to Prayers* - 1996
東方封魔録 ~ *Story of Eastern Wonderland* - 1997
東方夢時空 ~ *Phantasmagoria of Dim.Dream* - 1997
東方幻想郷 ~ *Lotus Land Story* - 1998
東方怪綺談 ~ *Mystic Square* - 1998
東方紅魔郷 ~ *Embodiment of Scarlet Devil* - 2002
東方妖々夢 ~ *Perfect Cherry Blossom* - 2003
東方萃夢想 ~ *Immaterial and Missing Power* - 2004 (Collab. with Twilight Frontier)
東方永夜抄 ~ *Imperishable Night* - 2004
東方花映塚 ~ *Phantasmagoria of Flower View* - 2005
東方文花帖 ~ *Shoot the Bullet* - 2005
東方風神録 ~ *Mountain of Faith* - 2007
東方緋想天 ~ *Scarlet Weather Rhapsody* - 2007 (Collab. with Twilight Frontier)
東方地霊殿 ~ *Subterranean Animism* - 2008
東方星蓮船 ~ *Undefined Fantastic Object* - 2009
東方非想天則 ~ *Choudokyuu Ginyoru no Nazo wo Oe* - 2009 (Collab. with Twilight Frontier)
東方文花帖 ~ *Double Spoiler* - 2010
東方三月精 ~ *Fairy Wars* - 2010
東方神霊廟 ~ *Ten Desires* - 2011
東方心綺楼 ~ *Hopeless Masquerade* - 2013 (Collab. with Twilight Frontier)
東方輝針城 ~ *Double Dealing Character* - 2013
弾幕アマノジャク ~ *Impossible Spell Card* - 2014

TAITO

International League Soccer (aka: *Greatest Striker*) - PS2, 2000
Magic Pengel - PS2, 2002
Bujingai - PS2, 2003
Graffiti Kingdom - PS2, 2004
EXIT - PSP, 2005

In addition, various musical soundtracks, printed works, manga, and other related creations. Too many to list comprehensively, please see one of the various Touhou related Wikia sites online.

Interview with ZUN, aka Junya Ota
25 October 2013, Tokyo

When I was first asked to interview ZUN, the challenge intrigued me. The doujin scene was something I definitely wanted to cover, given that it's even less well documented in English than mainstream Japanese games, and certainly ZUN is as iconic a doujin figure as any. However, he's also very difficult to get hold of. Fortuitously, I met him at Sony's Indie Stream event, when I was chatting with Yoshiro Kimura. We were discussing our planned interview when ZUN walks up, along with a collection of fans and well wishers - he and Mr Kimura had long been friends. After this Mr Kimura acted as my liaison, arranging our interview. I was to meet ZUN at the Shinjuku blood bank, where we would then retire to a coffee shop for refreshment and talk. Later that day I would interview Mr Kimura, the facilitator of the day. Below is a word from our Guest Editor, who requested the interview and wrote many of the questions.

"Touhou Project games are a great example of no longer needing the support of a publisher to be successful in the games industry. Many people turn to *Braid* when they think of early indie success, the incredibly well-received platformer from Jonathan Blow released in 2008, but it was far from the first. The Japanese *doujin* market was already filled with quality releases, unbeknownst to many gamers in the West.

"Although ZUN has been releasing games under the Touhou Project name since 1995, its success isn't driven by the games alone. *Doujin* artists, musicians, cosplayers, animators and more, continue to release their own original content based on the characters and settings seen in the Touhou Project games, and it's this fandom that makes the series so fascinating.

"As much as I personally enjoy the games and the community, it's ZUN that I find most fascinating. Videogames are frequently reported on in Western media, with many developers being pulled into the limelight, whether it's to promote an upcoming title or to defend one from criticism. In stark contrast, ZUN keeps to himself, rarely venturing into the public eye. So little is known about him and the motivations behind Touhou Project, I'm sure I'm not the only one that wanted to know more.

"I hope you find this interview with one of the most secretive game developers of today to be intriguing, perhaps enough to try out some of the best shoot 'em ups available!"
- ***Chris Walden, Guest Editor***

The dual columns of character art featured in this interview are courtesy of artist: フウザサ / **Fuuzasa**

*****

<we order beverages, coffee for myself and beer for ZUN>

JS: Maybe I should ask the last question first. Have you ever tried British real ale?

ZUN: *<smiles>* Yes, yes, I have!

JS: What do you think of it?

ZUN: I like real ale style beers. I think it's best suited for when it's cold in the winter. So I think it's maybe a winter ale. But in the summer, when it's hot, you've got to drink Japanese beer.

JS: What was the first game you played?

ZUN: Well, we used to have these game cafes[1] in Japan, and there was *Space Invaders*, or classic games like that. I can't remember exactly which one was the first I played. But the ones where they had a table, and the game would be in the middle of the table. Maybe that, or another old style arcade game.

JS: When did you want to create your own?

ZUN: It wasn't a matter of looking at a game and thinking, "I want to make something like that." I really played games my whole childhood, it was my main interest and I was super into them. Doing something with my life other than games never crossed my mind. When I came to university in Tokyo that's when I lived on my own, and that's when I had the opportunity and the time to start making games. I wasn't even thinking about entering the game industry. I just started making games; it sort of happened naturally. But in terms of when did I want to

[1] *kissa* (喫茶) usu. refers to a tea/coffee lounge

start making games, I think that desire has always, from a very young age, been in me.

JS: What did you study at university?

ZUN: My major was mathematics.

JS: Did you teach yourself programming?

ZUN: Indeed. Making games was much more of an interest to me than programming, so yes, you have to learn programming to make games, so I taught myself that. In terms of how I did it, this wasn't really the age of the internet in those days, so much. There was some stuff out there, but it was much more about trial and error, and reading, and so on.

JS: Which coding language did you start with?

ZUN: The first thing I learnt was C.

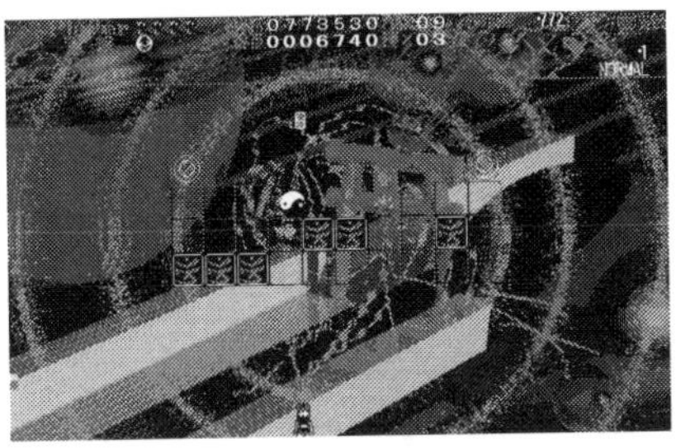

JS: Before *Highly Responsive to Prayers*, (above),[2] did you make any other games?

ZUN: I made a handful of games before the first Touhou, but I never released them. Some of them I showed to my friends, but they weren't official releases. The first game I ever made was a copy of *Puyo Puyo*. <*laughs*>

JS: Awesome. Do you still have this game?

ZUN: <*laughs*> I don't know if I still have the data! The computer I made that one on is gone, so I don't know.

JS: I'm sure a lot of people would be interested in seeing these pre-Touhou titles.

ZUN: I'm sure they would be. I don't know where the other games are. I'm sure if I hunted for them I might be able to find them, but...

JS: Well, keep an eye out.

ZUN: It's very nostalgic, thinking about them.

JS: You started with a PC-98, but in 1996 it was on the way out, being replaced by Windows computers in Japan. Why start on PC-98?

ZUN: The simple fact is that I didn't think games would run on Windows. I honestly didn't really consider Windows computers when I made the first Touhou games. Windows didn't have things like DirectX back then.[3] I just didn't see it as a platform for game development. Certainly the games that I knew, and the games that I was interested in, had all been done on different systems. Some people owned a computer, like a PC-98 or an X68000, exclusively for games. So the concept of using Windows for games was one that I never really considered. Making them on the PC-98 seemed very logical and very natural to me. So that's why I chose it.

JS: What was the first computer you owned? Was it a PC-88?

ZUN: No, it was the PC-98. That's the very first computer I bought, and it's the one I developed the Touhou games on.

JS: Do you still have this Touhou computer?

ZUN: I still have it, yes.

JS: Does it still work?

ZUN: <*laughs*> I don't know, and I'm not sure if I can remember how to use it. It was a long time ago.

JS: Old hardware slowly breaks down over time.

ZUN: Absolutely, and also floppy disks get mould on them, or fall apart.

JS: Someone showed me the original dev disks for *Thunder Force*, which went white with mould.

ZUN: It happens, that's the way it is.

JS: Your first Touhou game, *Highly Responsive to Prayers*, had a *Breakout* feel to it, and then

[2] First game in the Touhou series, for PC-98 (1996), sort of like a cross between *Arkanoid* and a shmup

[3] DirectX was not widely adopted until the retail release of Windows 98 in the summer of 1998

the formula changed for the second game. What motivated this?

ZUN: Obviously, *danmaku* as it exists now wasn't really around back then, in 1996,[4] and even before I made the first game, I did have an image in my head, of that being kind of what I wanted to make. It may not have been what the second game became, but that was the idea, and although I didn't have the word *danmaku* to describe it, that sort of wall of bullets was definitely there. But I needed to practise as it were, I needed to learn how to produce that. So the first game was, really, a training exercise for me in a way. So I learned a lot about game production, engine development, through the creation of *Highly Responsive to Prayers*. Then from the second game onwards, that was when I made the game that was in my mind.

JS: Between each game in the Touhou series, do you re-use parts of the source code and engine?

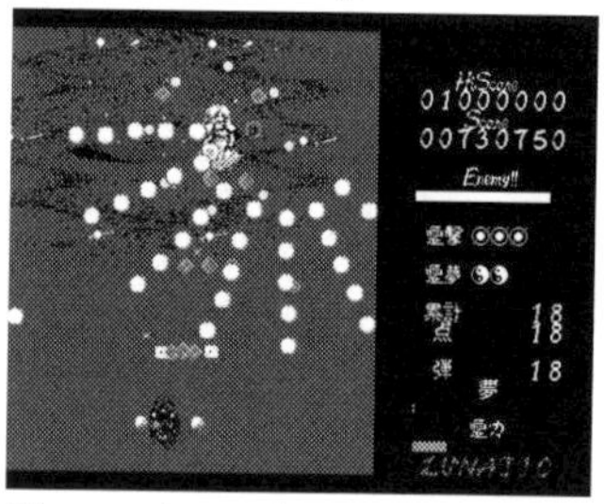

ZUN: There's a break for the code, and it's when I switched to Windows development from the PC-98. So that was between *Mystic Square* (right) in 1998 and *The Embodiment of Scarlet Devil* (below) in 2002. Those two have no similar code, and it was completely from scratch again. But since then the mechanics, the very core engine, is the same. So I change it, and I improve it, but there is some code which I wrote in 2002 that still exists in recent Touhou entries as well.

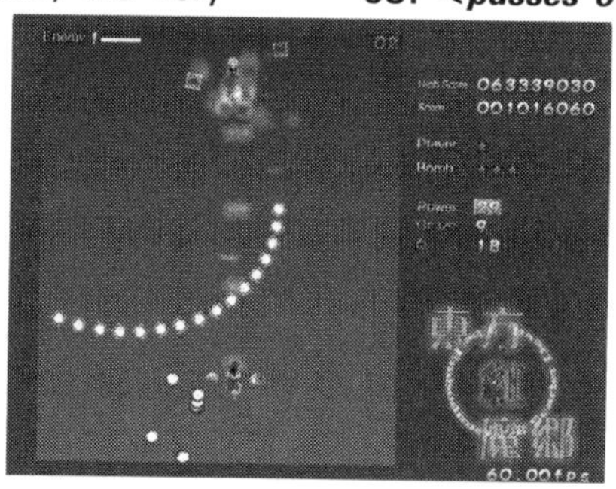

JS: One of my favourites is *Shoot the Bullet* (second column), with the photography mechanic. Ingenious! What inspired you?

ZUN: This goes back to the reason why I started making *danmaku* games. The shooting game genre was stagnating. The typical arcade shooting games had fallen into a pattern. I think Touhou as a series, and as an idea, is quite original. But obviously as the popularity grew, and the genre grew, a lot of Touhou style games

were being made by a lot of different developers. As a result, standards for judging what makes a good *danmaku* game had evolved, which was more or less a good thing overall. And when you think about the standards for games like this, something that has to stand out for the games to be successful, is the way it looks. So I thought that the best way to show everybody what a game looks like is obviously to take photos, so to speak, and I thought if *danmaku* fans have an interest in images and the way things look, I should make a game where they can control that. So I created the "screenshot feature" if you will, because I thought that would be a very interesting way to interact with the fans in a way that I knew they were already interested in.

JS: As a journalist I take snapshots of games using a capture card, so this really resonated with me. Waiting for that perfect moment.

ZUN: It's all about timing, which is fun.

JS: <*passes over Retro Gamer*> It only covers old games. I interviewed the director of *Akumajou Dracula*.

ZUN: Ahh, *Castlevania*![5] Which system?

JS: The Super Famicom.

ZUN: What do you define as retro gaming? In terms of time frame?

JS: Everyone debates it. I think we've reached a point where, because classic games are being re-released, and that older style of 2D is being used again, it's less about old and new, and more about ethos. Today I can play new games in a style I've not seen for 20 years.

---

[4] The genre is generally regarded as starting with *DonPachi* in arcades, November 1995

[5] Amusingly, I used the Japanese name while ZUN used the English name

ZUN: No one knows what "retro" is exactly, do they? In Japan, too, they use terms like this one here, <*points to author's business card*> "retro classic reporter", but I'm not sure whether the stuff they talk about is truly "retro".

JS: This magazine covers everything from the origin of games all the way up until around the Dreamcast. It's the cut-off point at the moment.

ZUN: So it's not to do with 3D or 2D?

JS: No. There were also 3D games in the 1980s. What are some of your favourite older games?

ZUN: <*laughs*> There's a huge amount of games that I really like from the old days, so this may get out of hand! It's very hard to choose. But I have an answer that I always give in this situation. Of course, it's *Super Mario Bros*. That's what I tell people, but really choosing my favourite game from that era is essentially impossible. I really can't do it.

JS: Touhou's popularity has exploded. Do you feel some fans take what Touhou means too far? Do you feel you might lose control over it?

ZUN: It's not something I have a problem with. Generally speaking, there are a lot of fans out there who are very driven, and every interested in my series, but in terms of creative control, it's not really something I am that worried about, or concerned by, to be honest. A lot of fans are very good at getting permission, or asking me, I'm going to do this or that, and that's fine. There are plenty of things out there as well that I was never asked about, that were made using characters of mine, or whatever. But it's not something that troubles me so much. At times I've thought that it would be terrible if I stopped liking games because of a fan-related issue. But that's never happened. I have the freedom to make the games I want, and that's enough.

JS: It's a nice attitude to have. Some large companies have clamped down on fans.

ZUN: Well, it definitely can be a problem, and I can understand why companies do that, but it's not how I deal with it.

JS: Fans create their own stories for characters - do you have a canonical story planned out? Do you conceive of it beforehand, or as you need it?

ZUN: In terms of development, whenever I start working on a new game one of the first things I do is decide what the story will be. I don't do it at the same time as programming the game, I do it beforehand. In terms of taking influence from the fan stuff, I don't really pay much attention to it. I don't really read them or play them, so I don't really think there's much influence from the fans on the actual Touhou series. I make the stories I want to make, basically. I don't incorporate ideas from the fan works, so they're not really an influence on me.

JS: I know some fan creations tend to veer towards, shall we say, *amorous themes* between certain characters.

ZUN: It's not something I particularly like, and sometimes it's a bit too much. The fans are free to do what they want, but it's not something I like. I have no plans to put something like that into one of my games. <*laughs*>

JS: You're a one-man creator, you create all the games in your house?

ZUN: Yes, I do it in my house.

JS: Can I have a layout sketch?

ZUN: Ah, OK! That's fine, sure. <*laughs*> Just my office?

JS: Sure, or the whole house, whatever you like.

ZUN: It really all happens in one room.

JS: What kind of games have you been into recently? Play anything interesting?

ZUN: *Dragon's Crown* just came out. That's a cool game, I'm enjoying that.

JS: Do you play many games from computer download services, such as GOG or Steam?

ZUN: I'm not a big FPS player, but just about any other genre I can get into. So I've been playing some *Sim City*, some *Civilisation*, that kind of stuff. In terms of digital distribution services, I think they're great. I'm thinking about Touhou and those kinds of systems, and it's something that maybe I'll go into, in the future.

JS: There's a lot of characters in the Touhou series. One estimate I heard is there are over 150 characters. Is that true? The majority also appear to be cute girls.

ZUN: I don't know how many characters there in the series. <*laughs*> I've never counted. I'm fairly confident that the fans' counting of them on the internet is probably accurate. So, sure, 150 perhaps. In terms of why there are more girls in the series than men, that's definitely a conscious design decision that I made. I believe that the play style of *danmaku* games has a feminine aspect to it. It's not a toe-to-toe contest of strength; you don't simply run up and pummel the enemy.

JS: Right, in an action game with soldiers, or people carrying guns, the image is one of men.

ZUN: With *danmaku*, I'm trying to make games that are beautiful. The way the bullets move, the way the game is played, it's a visual spectacle, and I think it has beauty in it. When you think of beauty as a general thing, you tend to think of women rather than men, so it's more a case of... I think *danmaku* and the games I create are more about aesthetics than they are about action. Although they feature bullets, they're not about guns. So that's the kind of game reason, but also I just think it's easier to make pretty looking girls, to make it appealing, than it is with men.

JS: A very eloquent answer.

ZUN: Yes, it's definitely to do with that, and I certainly think it's okay to feature both male and female characters in games, but I do feel like if I put a lot of male characters in the game, it will make the game seem like a more aggressive, toe-to-toe contest. Also, something that I think maybe people assume, is that I put a lot of girls in because it's what my fans want, but that's not the case. That has nothing to do with it.

JS: I know from planning the book's cover, there seems to be a growing aversion to the feminine form. It's an excellent policy to focus on your own vision. Many creators today are worried about trying to appeal to everyone, and companies have focus groups to increase sales.

ZUN: I definitely think that is an issue, although I would say if they do it well, I don't really have a problem with it. But I can see where you're coming from with that. I would say that in terms of Touhou, one of the things that I'm doing, and one of things I'm aware of, is I try to invent or use characters that I believe link to the style of the level.

JS: So a tricky level might have a mysterious looking character, compared to an easy level where a character would appear friendly?

ZUN: I think that putting in characters - certainly in terms of Touhou - it's not just to sell titles or to appeal, I think it absolutely has an effect on the gameplay and on the game's design. They're not arbitrary at all, they're part of the design of the game.

JS: I think fans notice. Something which is scary to hear in the West is, "Oh yeah, we went to a focus group to make decisions for us." Which then dilutes the vision of the creator.

ZUN: I think most companies in Japan do it as well. For example, a company might look at Touhou and think, "That's pretty successful, so let's stick a load of pretty girls in our game, it's bound to work." That kind of thinking is pervasive now, but it's an attitude that doesn't come from the actual game developers.

JS: I wanted to ask about Comiket. Can you describe your memories of it?

ZUN: Well the reason I chose Comiket, obviously, is because as a one-man development team, it was the only way that I knew of, the only place I could think of, which would give me the opportunity to sell my games. I wasn't comparing it to anything. Also now, obviously, through these services you can upload games to be downloaded at any gigabyte size. But back when I was making the original Touhou stuff, people could not get hold of games that were so big. So it had to be physical distribution. It had to be hand to hand. When I thought about what kind of environment I can do that in, Comiket was the only one that I knew about. Even now, Comiket is the only place I can really think of where I can distribute physical copies, with actual game packaging. I get enjoyment from handing the product over to the customer, and seeing them face to face. It's part of what I enjoy with this whole process. So I think even if I do go digital, I will always do boxed distribution as well.

JS: Can you remember the first time you sold something at Comiket? Do you have photos?[6]

ZUN: <*laughs*> The first time was 1997, and I do remember it, since it was obviously the first one for me, and it was a big deal. I would say one thing that definitely struck me... I took about 30 copies of the first Touhou game, and 50 copies of the second, so about 80 copies together, to sell. And I really thought to myself, there's no way I'm going to sell these, no one is going to be interested. But I sold them all, and I sold them rather quickly. So that was surprising for me. That's something that definitely sticks out in my memory about Comiket.

JS: Did you number each copy?

ZUN: <*laughs*> I did not, no.

JS: I wonder where those first copies are...

ZUN: I don't know where they all are, obviously, but I assume the people who bought them still have them. Some of them went on to become my friends, so I have friends who still have my original 1997 Comiket games, somewhere. One thing is that the people who really like these kind of *doujin* games, it's the same people each year. So the fans I was selling to in 1997 and 1998, it's still the same people who like the games today, they've just gotten a little bit older. Both the people who make *doujin* games and those who buy them, it's often the same people each year. It's like a community.

JS: These first few games, they were on PC-98 floppy disks? They've got a limited memory size; did you have to omit content to make them fit?

ZUN: If you look at it now, it's hard to imagine fitting a game into that size of space. But to be honest with you, the games weren't really that memory intensive. I think, generally, I got everything I wanted on to each disk, each time.

JS: Some developers put long cinemas in early computer games. In one instance I recall the opening took up two disks needing switching![7]

ZUN: You don't need those movies. <*laughs*>

[6] It's worth looking online for photos, the huge mass of people cannot be imagined without seeing it first...
[7] Several PC-88 games had multiple "opening" disks

JS: Did you attend Comiket before you started selling games?

ZUN: No, I did not. The first time I ever went to Comiket was to start selling the Touhou series.

JS: There's nothing quite like Comiket outside of Japan.[8] For me it has this mysterious allure. Has it changed over the years?

ZUN: I think the fundamental, underlying idea and the design of Comiket has not really changed much. I would say the scale has gotten bigger, in terms of fans attending and also vendors. In addition, the number of foreign people who visit is going up. I think it's become more open. But I think that the concept of Comiket has remained more or less the same since I started going in 1997. Back when Comiket was a more underground phenomenon, *doujin* material was more likely to be considered questionable in terms of copyright and legality. People would make *doujin* stuff, and while it wasn't exactly illegal, it existed in a sort of grey area of copyright. So Comiket used to have a more secretive, underground kind of feel. But now Comiket is much more open, and people don't worry about that as much.

JS: Is this because illegal content was banned?

ZUN: No, it's because it's NOT banned, so *doujin* creators don't have to be... [so secretive and cautious anymore]. Now that *doujin* games are an established genre, there's a lot of original content, so that's not a problem. In fact, I think that *doujin* game creators can afford to be a little more bold. Hmm... How should I put this? Obviously illegal content should not be distributed, but I don't think there are enough *secondary games*[9] in the *doujin* game world. It's a delicate issue.

[8] I know there's many conventions outside Japan, such as PAX and so on, but the enormous scale of Comiket, its long-running history, and the diverse nature of its homegrown products, makes it unmatched
[9] 二次創作 (*niji sousaku*), lit. a secondary creative work, is a Japanese term for a new creative work, usu. in manga or novel form, borrowing characters or elements from an existing commercial work, perhaps akin to fanfiction

A word from expert Matt Fitsko

When Comiket began in the 1970s, the attendees were overwhelmingly women buying and selling secondary manga works as well as original creations (including quite a bit of yaoi, or Boy's Love). Perhaps this shouldn't be so surprising, given that women have always played a leading role in fanfiction communities in the West too. When it comes to risqué content, women invented "slash fiction" pretty much single-handedly. Contrary to popular conceptions, even today the majority of doujin creators selling work at Comiket are women, around 60% as of Comiket #84 (summer 2013). Historically speaking, female doujin creators at Comiket have generally outnumbered their male counterparts by more than 2:1. The demographics likely skew towards men for doujin games and software in particular, but it's important to note that a huge chunk of overall doujin output, even the really hardcore stuff, is actually created and consumed by women.

Comiket is much more open now, and doujin circles are much less afraid of falling afoul of copyright law, so there's more secondary work than ever. Some people on the commercial side of things are openly embracing the doujin community. For example, there's the manga artist and former doujin Ken Akamatsu, who designed a special "doujin-allowed" watermark for commercial artists to print on their works, similar to the Creative Commons license. For manga with this mark, doujin circles are free to create any secondary works they want, for free or for sale, without fear of reprisal from the copyright owner.

ZUN remarks that there aren't many secondary doujin games, which is certainly true compared to the plentiful secondary doujinshi (magazines and comics). Perhaps it's because companies like Nintendo are so trigger-happy with C&D letters when it comes to fan-made games. The two Chrono Trigger fan games that were shuttered are famous examples in the West, but this has happened within Japan, too. EG: There was a Power Stone-esque Haruhi Suzumiya doujin game. It wasn't pornographic, but for some reason Kadokawa shut it down.[10] Touhou has by far the single largest collection of secondary doujin games. Touhou is unique in that whereas most secondary doujin works are based off a mainstream commercial property, such as a popular anime, with Touhou the original work is itself doujin. Touhou has flourished because of ZUN's lenient attitude towards derivative material based on his work. As he indicates, he would like to see more secondary doujin games based on commercial works.

[10] *Suzumiya Haruhi no Gekitou:* youtube.com/watch?v=bu4WHsxHG64

JS: I came to Japan last time in 2001. I've noticed an increase in mobile phone gaming, which is changing the industry. Does this concern you? Would you put Touhou on phones?

ZUN: I think it will continue going into the future. I myself play a lot of games on mobile phones. The problem I think with smartphones is a lot of games get ported straight over, and they get ported from a system where there are actual controls - like a physical controller, or built-in to the machine. On a smartphone these can be quite irritating to play, and I think it can have a negative impact on the game. I think Touhou is definitely a game that needs a controller, or would be difficult to play on the screen alone. If I ever come up with a fun game idea that's suited to a smartphone, something that couldn't be done except on a smartphone, then I might make a smartphone game.

JS: Would your fans be upset?

ZUN: <*laughs*> I don't think they'd get upset at all. If I come up with an idea, maybe I'll do it.

JS: Hypothetical situation: Microsoft comes to you with a generous contract to make a Kinect-only Touhou game. What do you say?

ZUN: <*laughs*> If that happened, it would not be a Touhou game as any of us know it. I think trying to force a game like Touhou on to a Kinect system would make a really, really bad game, and it would not be fun. <*laughs*> If I could think of something that I think would work well with the Kinect, and was designed specifically for the Kinect, then yes. If I could think of a good concept, I might do it.

JS: Microsoft insisted the next *Steel Battalion* should use Kinect, and it was universally regarded as unplayable.

ZUN: Absolutely. I think the best thing to do is to take the game idea first, and then make or find the right controller for that. Not to look at the controller or system, and then try to force a game to work with that controller. That's why I think arcade games are excellent. Because every single idea has the possibility of a custom controller for it, and it's exactly what it needs - nothing more, nothing less.

JS: Do you consider your audience outside Japan, when making Touhou games? To what extent do you interact with fans outside Japan?

ZUN: Well, to be honest with you, I don't really communicate with my Japanese fans, so of course I don't really communicate with my foreign fans either. In September [2013] I went to an event in Atlanta, in America, I sort of made an appearance. I was shocked at how many Touhou fans there are in America. I couldn't believe it! [As for creating a Touhou game aimed at a Western audience], it's not something I've ever considered.

JS: You're a tricky man to get hold of. I only managed through Mr Kimura. How did you first meet and become friends with him?

ZUN: I met him last year. Kimura-san does a sort of broadcast, a live broadcast on Ustream, called Poripori Club,[11] where he talks about games and has guest speakers. And he invited me along, and that's how we got to know each other, and now I do it sometimes too. We became friends through that. We've never worked together on a title, or anything like that, though.

JS: Have you considered working alongside Mr Kimura on a game?

ZUN: It's possible but unlikely. I like to keep my business partners and my friends separate.

JS: When business is involved, friendships can go up in flames.

ZUN: *<laughs>* If I worked with my friends, we'd probably just get into arguments.

JS: You worked at Taito for a while?

ZUN: That's right. For about 10 years, yes.

JS: For 10 years?

ZUN: At Taito, yes. From 1998 until around 2008 or 2007.

JS: There's little info online regarding that.

ZUN: There's not much in Japanese either! *<laughs>*

JS: Are you happy to talk about it?

ZUN: Yes, it's fine.

JS: Perhaps you can solve a mystery for me.

ZUN: A mystery! *<laughs>*

JS: In the early 1990s Taito was working with a company called WoWoW, to develop the Taito WoWoW game system. It was a CD-based console, meant to have online capabilities and play arcade perfect ports. It was shown at trade shows, but never released...

ZUN: *<cuts in>*... I don't think it was something I was involved with at all I'm afraid. *<laughs>*

JS: But did anyone at Taito ever talk about it?

ZUN: It was cancelled before I joined Taito, so unfortunately it wasn't really something people were talking about when I was there. I'm afraid I really don't know anything about it.

JS: I thought perhaps a colleague lamented: "I worked on a machine, but it never came out!"

ZUN: There was this one machine that Taito released. It was a console that worked as a home karaoke machine, but it also had games. It was basically a game console. It was a game console that you could also use as a karaoke machine. The Taito X-55.[12] It was meant to be a karaoke machine, but games got released for it. But it barely sold any units. *<laughs>*

JS: Now Taito's been absorbed by Square-Enix.

ZUN: Well, they still exist. They're a child company of Square-Enix, but they are still around in a sense. They're not developing games anymore. They predominantly work in the field of game centres in Japan.

JS: The way I understand it, Taito was your day job to pay the bills, whereas Team Shanghai Alice was the way you expressed yourself?

---

[11] http://poriporiclub.blogspot.com

[12] According to adverts on YouTube it could play early Taito games and cost around 65'000 yen. Images and information online are almost non-existent. While there's a few interesting looking X-55 brochures online, they're all thumbnails and too small to print

ZUN: That's exactly how I felt as well.

JS: Where were you before Taito? Studying?

ZUN: I was at university. I went straight from university and did job hunting, and the first place I went was Taito. I joined as a programmer.

JS: Can you recall the process of joining?

ZUN: I went to a *setsumeikai*; it was like an explanatory meeting. That time, in 1998, when I was looking for work, it was called the "ice age of job hunting"[13] in Japan. It was a really rough time, so you would go to every interview you could, you would attend everything. Getting that offer from Taito was a relief for me, and that's why I took it immediately. *<laughs>* At the Taito *setsumeikai* I went to, there was about 10'000 applicants who went, from lots of different universities. They hired five people. That's the kind of ratio. It was a tough time to be looking for work.

JS: That's almost like winning a small lottery.

ZUN: Actually, the reason I got my placement was because I'd already made some games while at university. I just showed them the games I had made, and was hired immediately. Thinking about it now, the Touhou games I made while in university were only profitable in that they helped me get a job. *<laughs>* I didn't make them specifically to get a job, but they opened many doors for me.

JS: Did Taito know that you continued to make *doujin* games? Did they approve of it? Is that why you developed under a pseudonym?

ZUN: When I first started I did hide it. There were some co-workers of mine who were making *doujin* games as well. Taito did have a rule that you were not really supposed to do it. But I think the people who did it, just did it anyway. **But that's not the reason I left Taito at all.** It was unrelated, just to make that clear. *<laughs>* Taito didn't forbid me to work on Touhou. In fact, they asked me if I would be willing to release Touhou as a regular arcade game, under Taito's brand. I flat-out refused. "NO!" *<laughs>* But even after that, they didn't explicitly say that I couldn't produce *doujin* games. We weren't really supposed to work on personal projects, but most people at the company looked the other way. The other thing to consider is, from Taito's perspective, those of us making *doujin* games on the side, it was really good practise for us. It helped us to improve at our jobs.

JS: It's interesting they wanted to put their name on it. They would own the property.

ZUN: Absolutely. I feel that, not only could they then control it, but also I would lose my autonomy. I didn't like that. Hypothetically, if that had happened, and Taito had gotten hold of the Touhou name, I'd probably have worked on whatever game I agreed to do it with, but that would have been the end of Touhou from me. I like making games where I am in control. I don't want to be beholden to someone.

JS: Could you sketch a layout of Taito's office?

ZUN: *<laughs>* Taito kept redesigning its layout. So it might be a bit difficult. I don't know if I can remember them all.

JS: Maybe your favourite layout? Or the oldest?

ZUN: If you can think of a Taito game that you would like the office layout for, I might be able to do that.

JS: Can you recall the first game you worked on?

ZUN: The first game was for the PS2... It was *Greatest Striker,*[14] a soccer game.

JS: But if you joined in 1998...

ZUN: The game came out in early 2000, immediately after the release of the PS2, so the development period was prior to that. The PS2 devkits were already available in 1998.[15] I was assigned to work on initial research into the system. I did that for a long time, exploring what could be achieved with the PS2.

JS: Benchmarking the hardware?

ZUN: That's right. I wrote software libraries for Taito to use in PS2 game development.

---

[13] 就職氷河期時代, *shuushoku hyougaki jidai*

[14] Released February 2000 according to GameFAQs

[15] The PlayStation 2 launched March 2000 in Japan

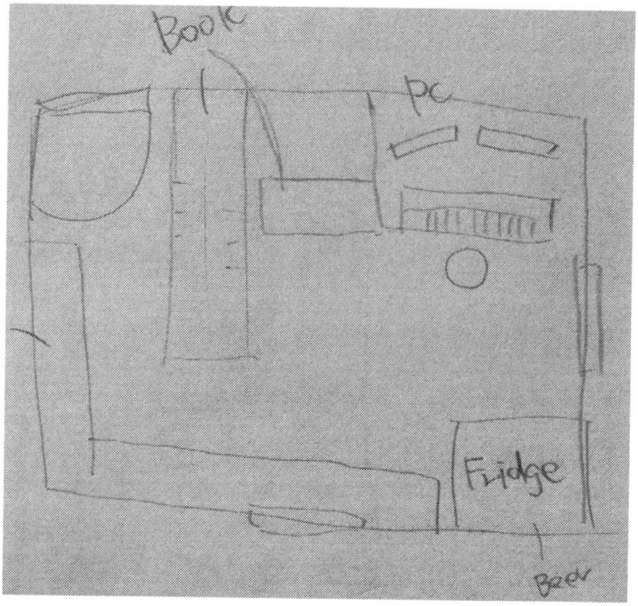

ZUN: There is a computer, some bookcases, a chair, and a fridge.

JS: What's in the fridge?

ZUN: Beer! <*laughs*> It's my beer fridge.

JS: Any particular brand?

ZUN: At the moment, I'm really into premium malts. It changes from time to time, but right now it's premium malts. There's a lot of bookshelves, and it's mostly things to do with programming, games, stuff like that. There's two computers and two screens. I have one computer for development, and one computer for debugging. I have a musical keyboard here for making game music... and that's it. It's just a 6 tatami mat room. That's Kantouma mats, which are different from the size of the mats in Kyoto. Anyway... 6 tatami mats.[16]

JS: How long does it take to make a game?

ZUN: It takes about 4 months to go from original planning and deciding to start, to finishing.

JS: How has your development process changed from when you first started?

ZUN: My method, my approach, hasn't really changed. I think the only thing that's really changed is that I do it in a nicer place now. <*laughs*>

JS: How about the Taito offices?

ZUN: The Taito offices are not so interesting - are you sure you want them? They're literally just an office.

JS: Well, that in itself is interesting.

ZUN: OK, I'll draw the office layout for *Graffiti Kingdom*.[17]

JS: You worked on the soccer game for PS2, *Magic Pengel*, *Bujingai*, *Graffiti Kingdom*, and *Exit*. Are those the only games from Taito?

ZUN: That's right, I worked on those games. And then after we did *Exit* I also worked on a bunch of different games, which I don't really recall. Some of them for PS3, some of them for the Wii, but none of them got released.

JS: Did that happen a lot at Taito?

ZUN: Hm, for the most part. It happened a lot.

JS: Tell me more! If a game is unreleased, the words you say now could be the only record.

ZUN: Eh... There are a lot of things that I can't tell you. For various reasons. <*nervous laughter*> *Bujingai 2* was in development and looked really good, but never got released. <*nervous laughter*> So that game existed...[18]

JS: I bought *Bujingai* (pictured below) the other day, in Akihabara.

[16] 6 tatami mats is a standard room size in Japan, approximately 9.3m² (100 sq. ft.). Add a kitchenette and a bathroom, and it's basically your typical "single twentysomething living in Tokyo" apartment

[17] Good game where you create your own characters

[18] ZUN seemed uncomfortable about this question, so I dropped it. *Bujingai* is a 3D action fighting game with a Japanese pop celebrity modelling the main character

ZUN: Was it released in the West?

JS: Yes. It was released in America and Europe.

ZUN: Actually, I worked on the localisation a little bit! I helped with the process of allowing fonts and sizing, and so on.

JS: 505 Street Games was the publisher in Europe. It's a small Italian company. They would bring over unusual Japanese games and release them in miniscule quantities.

ZUN: *<laughs>*

JS: I have no idea how they made money.

ZUN: I see, indeed. *<slightly melancholy>* We worked really hard on them... *<hands over Taito office sketch>* Is it OK if it just looks a bit like this? I've written in Japanese. This is the server room. These are the titles of the games being worked on in different places around the office.

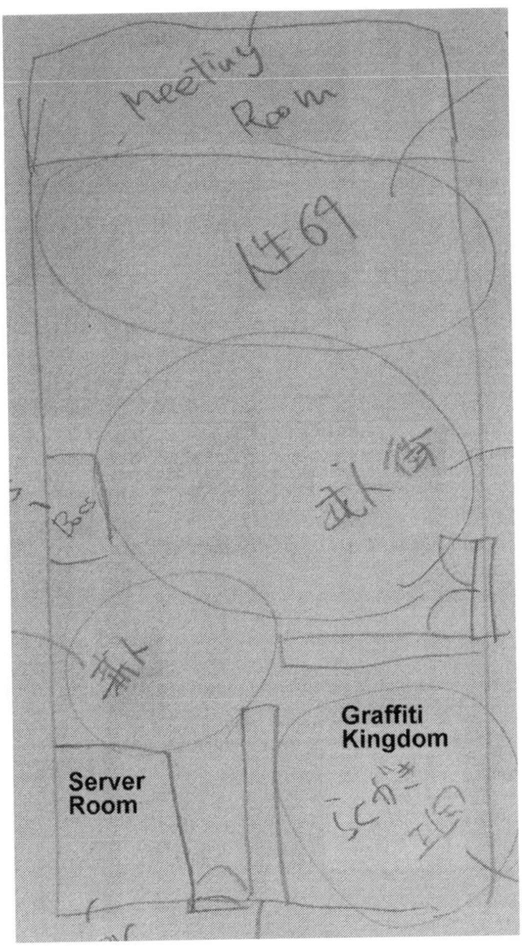

JS: I know some people imported *Bujingai* direct from Japan, to get it earlier.

ZUN: Honestly though, it wasn't that great a game, I think. *<laughs>* I think the sequel was going to be better! It's a shame.

JS: What can you tell us about *Bujingai 2*? Can you draw some sketches showing it?

ZUN: *<laughs>* I don't think I can tell you very much about it! I don't want to get in trouble. But I think the people who were working on it, were really enthusiastic about it. They were making it sillier and more tongue-in-cheek than the original.

JS: If you had to guess a number, how many unreleased games have you seen?

ZUN: *<long pause>* I can think of about six titles that were in development, or had work done on them, that never got released.

JS: If you ever want to talk about these games - you've got my email address.

ZUN: *<laughs>* It hasn't yet been 10 years since I left Taito. If Taito ever does get shut down, then it's open season. Until then, it's a little difficult.

JS: Have you ever started a Touhou game and didn't finish it? Are there unreleased Touhou?

ZUN: Because I'm making them on my own, obviously I'm not really beholden to other people. So the only time it happens is when I play it and then I go, "Oh, this isn't much fun." So I've had games in the series, or I've had times, where I've gone back and made changes. That happens and it's a process of improvement. I don't think I've ever cancelled a Touhou game. Every Touhou game that I've set out to make has been released or come out.

In terms of story there are some parts that I was developing into games, and then I thought, "Ah, this part of the story is boring. I'm not going to put it in." So the story of Touhou as a whole series, it's not exactly complete. It has an overarching story, but there are some parts that are not in any game.

JS: Were there any new mechanics which you experimented with, but were scrapped? Could you describe these mechanics?

ZUN: Yes, absolutely. There have been some things that I wanted to put in. One was something which I named the "net gallery" - and the idea was to have a system where, when you were playing, you were connected to the internet and then other players could watch you play. It would also have a very basic messaging system, so that if you got hit the viewers could send a message saying "unlucky" or something. I was thinking about that back in, maybe 2005 or so? There are games that have that functionality now, but I think I was considering it a few years ago. It did not happen in the end, but it was something I thought could be interesting.

JS: I'm picturing something like NicoNico Douga, where messages stream across the screen.

ZUN: Actually, the reason I didn't do it, is because while I was thinking about it and working on the game, that's when the age of online streaming or online video began, and I saw NicoNico and thought, "Well, this is fine. I don't need to do it." Why bother putting it in the game when someone already provides the service? I guess the necessity disappeared so I didn't do it. <*laughs*>

JS: This interview will say you had the idea first.

ZUN: I don't know. I think maybe quite a lot of people were working on that process at once, and maybe it's just that NicoNico were the fastest in Japan. Certainly I was thinking about doing it for my game, but I had never thought of the concept of having a website where loads of different games could be streamed. So maybe I was not the first. It was an idea of mine that didn't come to fruition.

The reason I thought about doing that was because... If you ever go to an arcade in Japan, and you see there's a really good player on a shooting game, someone really skilled, they will have a crowd of people watching them. And I thought the people in Japan who would go to watch skilled players, they must have the internet now. So I'm sure they'd want to do it online as well. I thought there would be people interested in this.

JS: Indeed, superplay DVDs are very popular.[19]

ZUN: Yes, they are popular. It's definitely evidence that people like watching excellent players. From my experience with the chat messages on NicoNico and so on, I think one thing that people really love is watching live streams, because they get a chance to see even the expert players mess up. <*laughs*>

JS: Do you consider yourself *doujin* or indie? Is there a difference?

ZUN: I'm getting asked that a lot recently. I would say that indies, the indie boom if you will, came from the West. A few years ago, I started hearing stories about how popular indie games were becoming in the West. And I thought to myself that the content of indie and *doujin* games is quite similar. They're similar, but I feel that... I feel that *doujin* games are a broader category. *Doujin* encompasses a lot of non-commercial activity, whereas I believe that indies need to succeed. I feel that indie developers, their dream is to make it their job. They aim at being a game developer, while *doujin* developers, if no one ever buys their game, or never plays their game, maybe they won't really care?

A word from expert Matt Fitsko

The line between indie and doujin is blurring in Japan, but there's still a recognizable distinction between indie games (インディーズ), which are treated as a relatively new phenomenon mostly occurring in the West, and the traditional doujin scene, which has been continuously churning behind the scenes since the 1970s. Indies are seen as an exciting new commercial phenomenon, a reaction to overstuffed AAA game development, and a harkening back to small and medium-sized development studios that have been disappearing for the last decade. This manner of thinking leads Inafune to say that the original Mega Man games were essentially "indie" games, for example. They were created in a small-scale, creativity-first development environment that rarely exists today. On the other hand, doujin suggests a truly amateur style of creative activity (in the literal sense of amateur; "for the love of the art"), one that is closer to the label "fandom" in English. Doujin material is sold among fans, but in tiny quantities, and rarely in the expectation of actual profit (according to a 2010 report, only around 10% of doujin creators make over 20'000 yen (~$2'000) in profit by selling goods at Comiket, while about 70% actually lose money). Success and recognition is not really a factor, and the doujin games that have broken out to mainstream success (Higurashi, Corpse Party, Yatagarasu) are the rarest exceptions.

---

[19] A superplay DVD has footage of an extremely skilled player going through a game showcasing this skill

JS: Would you continue making Touhou games if nobody bought the next one?

ZUN: Well, it would certainly be depressing if nobody bought my games! On the other hand, I believe that if I make something good, it will sell. You could say that I've become more like an indie developer as opposed to a *doujin* developer. Among *doujin* creators at Comiket, even those who have released commercial products like an indie developer, I think many of them aren't necessarily concerned with being successful.

JS: Until what time are you free?

ZUN: <*laughs*> I don't mind, I really don't mind.

JS: I think this is great content we're covering.

ZUN: <*laughs*> As long as there's beer, I can answer questions all night.

JS: Which Touhou game sold the most?

ZUN: *The Embodiment of Scarlet Devil,*[20] in 2002, was the most sold. I like to bring back old characters in the new games, so there's a loop with the character appearances. Often, when I make a new game, the old ones sell a little bit more, so they have an advantage.

JS: Which do you feel is most popular with fans?

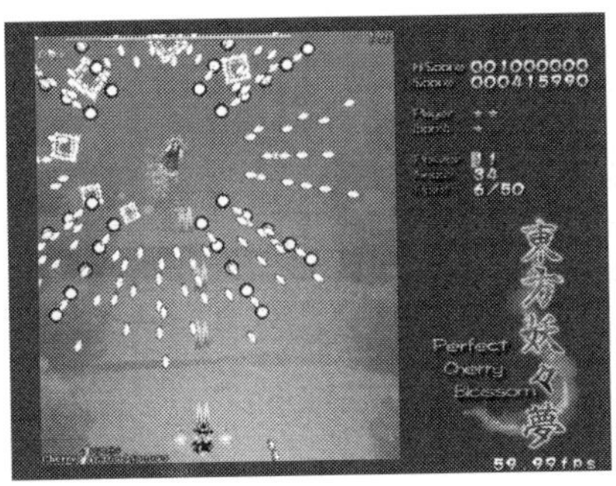

ZUN: That's difficult... I think *Perfect Cherry Blossom*, 2003 (right), might be the most. And also *Mountain of Faith*, from 2007 was also quite popular. Also, the one I released this year, the most recent one,[21] was also very popular. So maybe those three. You'll have to check the English name.

JS: I love the English titles. Do you choose them by yourself?[22]

ZUN: That's right, I do. But generally speaking it's not the same as the kanji, for the title. I look at the story and then I try to find words which link to the story.

JS: I was interviewing the creator of the arcade game *Strider*, who said he liked names which didn't make sense. I asked if he had any suggestions for the name of my book. If you have any ideas, please suggest them.

ZUN: Are you going to release it in Japanese and in English?

JS: Just English at the moment. The current title is a little dry.

ZUN: I don't have any ideas, but I'll think about! <*laughs*>

JS: Your titles in English are very poetic.

ZUN: <*laughs - waves hand as if to decline*> They're original, but I think the reason is because I cannot do English, so I don't know how good they are.

JS: As a native English speaker... <*notices second signature book*> There's two books...

ZUN: Can I write a different thing in each one?

JS: Oh, sure. Anything you like... As a native English speaker, for me the titles resonate with a kind of poetry.

ZUN: <*laughs*> I really didn't think about them too hard! The way I choose them, it's the same with both the Japanese and the English. I choose words that sound nice when you say them aloud.

JS: It's a system that works.

ZUN: <*laughs*> Thank you very much. I've always wondered.

JS: I think it's preferable to Hideo Kojima, who just invents words which make no sense. *REVENGEANCE!*

ZUN: <*perplexed*> He does that on purpose?

---

[20] The first Windows release; two characters with distinct attacks; features Touhou Spell Card system

[21] *Double Dealing Character*, 2013

[22] The English text in Touhou titles doesn't quite match the accompanying Japanese text, for example: *Hopeless Masquerade*'s kanji reads *Touhou Shinkirou*, which literally means *Eastern Tower of Heart Fabric*

JS: Kojima is really popular, so he can get away with whatever he wants.

ZUN: That must be nice.

JS: Do you own a PS3 or Xbox 360?

ZUN: Yes, I have a Wii, a WiiU, a 360 and a PS3.

JS: Are you going to buy the new ones?

ZUN: I probably will. But I don't even know if the Xbox One is going to come Japan. It does not seem so popular. But I'll probably buy a PS4.

JS: It might be the reverse situation with the Xbox One. Where Japanese fans have to import a machine, similar to how Europeans imported the PC Engine and so on, back in the day.

ZUN: The PC Engine didn't come out abroad?

JS: It came out in America, as the TG-16, and there was a *tiny* amount sold in PAL territories.

ZUN: And the PC-FX?

JS: It wasn't sold outside Japan at all.

ZUN: It didn't sell inside of Japan!

<*everyone laughs intensely*>

JS: How do you feel about foreign fans creating patches to translate your games into English?

ZUN: I don't have a problem with it at all. Obviously, since I can't speak English, I can't make the games in English. It's great, it lets more people play the games. I'm very grateful.

JS: Are you worried about the quality?

ZUN: I can't tell but I think that, actually, the people who are willing to put in the time and effort to translate it, would do their best. It shows a lot of dedication.

JS: If a Western publisher of Japanese PC games approached you to officially translate and publish outside Japan, what would you say?

ZUN: I think if I was approached by something like that, obviously I'd think about it. I'd feel like it would probably be a bit of a bother, and I honestly think I'd probably get sick of the whole process rather quickly. I think it would probably just be a hassle. I would say though, that in terms of would I rather have fan-translations, or a company translate it, I think because Touhou has such a dedicated fan-base, I feel like the fan translations are going to be better than a professional one. I think some of the content of Touhou's stories and so on, it might be quite difficult even for Japanese speakers to understand, so I feel like, even if it's translated directly, it won't make any sense to a lot of people. So I feel like it's not... I've been thinking, I might just sell it in the West, in Japanese. I don't think it's necessary to speak Japanese to be able to enjoy the game, the artwork, the playing, and so on. Translating stuff takes a long time and can be very difficult.

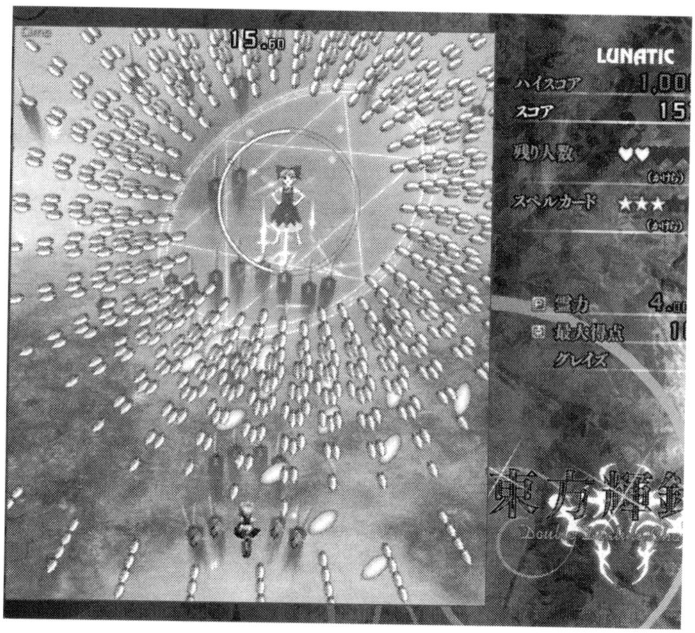

JS: It's interesting mentioning the difficulty of dealing with Western publishers. Because Treasure was tweeting about the immense difficulty of bringing *Ikaruga* to the West.

ZUN: It seems like there's not much to translate for *Ikaruga*...

JS: It wasn't the translation, but things like the contract with Steam.

ZUN: Treasure are not *doujin*, but it's definitely something I think a lot of *doujin* developers feel. I think most *doujin* developers would like to release their games on Steam if they could.

JS: Do you have any advice for someone who wants to make *doujin* or indie games?

ZUN: My advice for people who want to make games, *doujin* in particular, is *make them*. Don't worry about it, just make them. Just do it. That's all the advice I can honestly give. You've just got to make them. I think it's getting easier and easier as well, for people to make games on their own. Because the technology you have available, and the documentation you have available for free, is leagues ahead of what was available in the past. I think the support and the network is there.

JS: There's also tools like GameMaker.

ZUN: I think when it comes to developing your own games, there's not really anything you have to avoid. As long as you do whatever you want for your development. I think after you've made the game, learning about what to do next, that is something you should do. But I think you should make the game first, and then when it comes to the release aspect, and publishing, that's when you need to read up. In terms of making the game, just do it.

JS: Do you want to comment on leaving Taito?

ZUN: First of all, I no longer had a real need to stay at Taito, thanks to Touhou. I decided that I would quit after the completion of the games I was currently working on at Taito. One of those games was for the PS3, I worked on it for over a year and then it was just cancelled. That was kind of a blow. And then the next one was meant to be for the WiiU. I was already thinking about quitting at that point, but for the WiiU title, one of my colleagues working under my supervision had proposed the game design, and it was the first time a game proposal by that person had ever been accepted. So I decided I would continue on for my colleague, and then bail out as soon as the game was completed. But ultimately that game was cancelled too, and I realized there was no longer any reason for me to stay at the company.

JS: You became disenchanted?

ZUN: Yes, I was not enjoying it in the end. For the last two years nothing I was working on was getting released. I wasn't moving up the company. I thought to myself, this just isn't any fun anymore.

JS: Can you say the name of the PS3 game?

ZUN: No, I cannot tell you that! <*laughs*>

JS: You said Touhou has become popular. There's even conventions dedicated to it. You've seen it grow over the last 17 years. It must almost be like a watching a child grow up...

ZUN: <*laughs*> I don't consider it so much my child, I consider it my life's work. Obviously I'm overjoyed. To have the thing that you base your life around be this successful is wonderful. It's a fantastic feeling. I'm very happy that the fans get so much joy from it.

JS: <*noticing name on ZUN's business card*> After leaving Taito you formed Korindo?[23]

ZUN: Yes, that's right. It's just me, my company.

JS: Like Shanghai Alice?

ZUN: I had to form a company, because if you don't it's hard to keep selling things in Japan. <*laughs*> So I created Korindo. Shanghai Alice is more like a brand, it's not a company. Shanghai Alice is what I do, but Korindo facilitates that, it's the name I put it under.

JS: You have to deal with taxes and logistics?

ZUN: Yes, taxes have been a problem in the past.

JS: Have you ever felt the urge to work in genres other than shooting games? Perhaps RPGs? You've collaborated on other projects.

ZUN: Are you asking would I like to do that? Yes, absolutely, of course I would. I think everybody would. But, honestly, I want to make *danmaku* shooting games even more. That's what I love. I want to try lots of things, but one of them will always be shooting games.

JS: I believe you got married in 2012?

[23] ZUN's blog, *Invisible Games and Japanese*, has a similar URL: http://kourindou.exblog.jp/

ZUN: Yes, I got married.

JS: To another programmer?

ZUN: Yes, she's a game programmer, at a games company.

JS: Do you discuss programming techniques?

ZUN: We don't really talk about Touhou, but we do talk about programming. The area of games she programs is unrelated. They're smartphone games.

JS: Perhaps she could give some advice on bringing your games to smartphones?

ZUN: <*laughs*> Yes, maybe! But I'll still do it on my own, because you keep your friends separate from your co-workers.

<*everyone laughs*>

JS: Exactly! If you could have made any game which was made by someone else, what would it be? You can't say *Super Mario Bros.*

ZUN: There's a whole bunch. <*laughs*> It's difficult. I think if I give a specific answer, I'll change my mind later. To be absolutely honest with you, whenever I play a game that's really fun, I have that feeling. <*with strong emotion*> Every time I play a game that I enjoy I always have this feeling of, "I wish I'd thought of that!" So every game I enjoy, I guess is the answer.

JS: The book is coming out the middle of next year. So technically this question will be out of date. But do you have ideas for the next Touhou?

ZUN: I actually just finished the last game. So I really don't know what I'm doing for the next one yet. It came out in August, so only a few weeks ago.

JS: How long a break do you usually take between each title?

ZUN: I take regular breaks. It takes me about four months to produce the game, which means the other eight months of the year are... I don't know if you could call them a holiday, but the pace I go at is about one title a year. Obviously I use that time, I'm not just relaxing. I really do spend a lot of time thinking and making preliminary designs for the next title. That process is always ongoing.

JS: According to this list in English, there was no game released in 2006.[24]

ZUN: Indeed. Well, it was a time obviously when I was still working at Taito, so my time was less my own. I had to balance Touhou development with my job. The other thing is, you'll notice sometimes there are certain years where I did two, and some years where I only did one. It's because it was unpredictable for me in terms of how much time and energy I would have to spend on the games. So there's no real reason 2006 didn't have a game. It's just the way it happened. I guess you could say, although I can't remember why, I guess 2006 was a particularly busy year for me at Taito, and as a result Touhou had to be sort of put on the backburner for a while.

Above: Mountain of Faith

JS: Something I ask every interviewee about is pseudonyms, or nicknames. Tell me about ZUN.

ZUN: In terms of why I don't use my real name, it's a cultural thing. In *doujin* culture, I think most developers do the same. That's why I chose to use a pseudonym. In terms of why I chose ZUN, well my real name is Junya, and ZUN sounds like the Jun part. Another reason for ZUN is, with old arcade games you could only put three characters in the high score list. I think that most arcade goers, who grew up playing games in the arcade, have a three letter name that they use.

---

[24] *Shoot the Bullet* (2005); *Mountain of Faith* (2007)

JS: A lot of people outside Japan use their three initials. Am I correct that in Japan no-one has a middle name, so you have to get creative?

ZUN: There are also a lot of people who just put a full stop in the middle of the two letters.

JS: We've spoken about your games. But it's more than that. A lot of people love the music. Tell me about that, since I believe you have no formal training in music?

ZUN: Originally I belonged to the concert band, or orchestra club, while in school. The ultimate reason why I created Touhou is because I wanted to make game music at first. I was more interested in making music for games rather than the games themselves. So I made all this music, and I thought great, I'll find someone's game and put it in. But I didn't know anybody who was actually making games. So the next thing I thought was, right, I better make a game for this music to be used in.

JS: I've never heard this before... Touhou was born from your desire to create a game that matched the music you had already made?

ZUN: Yes, to start with, that's right. The reason that there's no releases between 1998 and 2002, that's when I started at Taito... When I decided I wanted to do *doujin* at that point, I was actually planning to make a *doujin* music group. The name of the group, *Shanhai Arisu Gengakudan* or "*Shanghai Alice Ensemble*", actually has a musical theme.[25]

So about 6 months to a year prior to this [around 2001], I applied to Comiket as a music circle, and I got rejected! So I thought to myself, I guess I gotta make another game... <*laughs*> Even now when I make the games, I consider the programming of them as my job. Whereas I consider making the music for them, making music in general, to be my hobby.

JS: Is Touhou now your sole work, or business?

ZUN: Yes, absolutely, Touhou is my life's work. It doesn't really matter if I did a different job, people are always going to think about Touhou, or think maybe it's related to Touhou. I actually make my own beer, and some of the fans call it Touhou beer. I actually do some reviews of alcohol, beer reviews and so on, for a magazine.

JS: In Comptiq?

ZUN: That's right. I think my fans, even if they have no interest in alcohol, they'll still buy the magazine because it's by the creator of Touhou.

JS: Regarding other shmups, what do you like?

ZUN: I guess I mainly like... Well, they're all fairly old games.

JS: That's great.

ZUN: My number favourite would be... *Darius Gaiden*.

JS: *Sakana no boss! (fish bosses!)*

ZUN: <*laughs*> Yes, I really like those. I think my favourite shooting games are all from the 1980s and 1990s.

JS: Ironically, that's before *danmaku*.

ZUN: I think *danmaku* took off with *Battle Garegga*, from around 1996 or 1997?[26] Which is around the same time I was doing it. Anything before then may have some elements, but it's not a *danmaku* title I feel. It's roundabout the same time Touhou started, so it was really at the dawn of the genre.

JS: CAVE was also influential on the genre.[27]

ZUN: I really liked *Pro Gear no Arashi* by Cave. I love that game.

JS: I must make time to play it. Could you fill in this form, for sending out complimentary copies? Would you prefer your real name, or pseudonym.

---

25 The name of the *doujin* circle is 上海アリス幻樂団, lit. "*Shanghai Alice Ensemble*". The name is stylized. A 弦楽団 (*gengakudan*) refers to a string ensemble, such as a string quartet, but the name of the *doujin* circle uses the character 幻 (phantasm, illusion) instead of 弦 (string), and an older version of the "music" character (樂), so the overall effect in Japanese is more like "Shanghai Alice Phantom Ensemble". The official English name is "Team Shanghai Alice"

26 Battle Garegga (バトルガレッガ) by 8ing/Raizing, for arcades (1996); designer Kazuyuki Nakashima

27 *DonPachi* (1995) is regarded as another early influence. According to Guinness World Records (2011), CAVE is the most prolific developer of *danmaku* shooters with, at the time, 48 releases

ZUN: You'll write the kanji with English underneath?

JS: Yes. I could put both your name and ZUN.

ZUN: I think just ZUN would be good. There are probably some fans out there who might not recognise my real name.

JS: I believe you make a guest appearance in *Touhou Soccer Moushuuden* at the end?[28]

ZUN: <*laughs*> I've never seen that. Am I a character in the game?

An example of fanart of ZUN taken from http://en.touhouwiki.net (artist not credited)

JS: Apparently, you appear at the end announcing the next tournament. Have you played any of the fan games?

ZUN: I've played a handful, but obviously I'd be rather busy if I played them all.

JS: What kind of challenges did you encounter when shifting from PC-98 to Windows?

ZUN: Obviously changing across was difficult, in general. But now that I look back, the PC-98 was a massive headache to work with. DirectX is amazing, and it will do whatever you tell it to. It makes worrying about hardware not so important anymore. I guess the hardest thing dealing with Windows is that there's no standardised hardware. Everyone is using different variations. It's frustrating when certain players can't enjoy the new game because the hardware requirements don't quite match.

JS: According to the Touhou Wiki pages,[29] your name is related to Taito's Zuntata?[30] Is that true?

ZUN: No, there's no connection. The Wiki page is wrong.

JS: Yes, they are often wrong.

ZUN: <*laughs*>

JS: One of my motivations with this book is to correct misinformation. There's a lot of mistranslation, or missing information.

ZUN: Definitely. I think it's something that happens a lot, and it can be a problem.

JS: One of the strangest things I've seen, is I'll write an article, then a Wikipedia editor will use the article as a reference for something which isn't related. And I think: "I didn't imply that!"

ZUN: It happens in Japan a lot too. <*finishes writing address*> I'm not sure if it will get delivered or not.

JS: If it doesn't, please email me! I'll send a second copy to Mr Kimura.

ZUN: Thank you.

JS: Apart from Touhou do you have another job?

ZUN: Well, besides programming, I also work on things like manga projects. It's all related to Touhou though, I don't really have any other job.

JS: According to Twitter, apparently you started a new job in September 2009 and turned up an hour early.

ZUN: I'm not sure what that would have been! Everything I'm doing right now is related

[28] I couldn't find a picture of this. Source taken from: http://en.touhouwiki.net/wiki/ZUN

[29] http://touhou.wikia.com/wiki/ZUN (seen June 2014)

[30] Zuntata was Taito's in-house band, analogous to Konami's Kukeiha Club. According to the *Darius* Wikia, band members include(d): Hisayoshi Ogura (OGR), Masahiko Takaki, Norihiro Furukawa, Yasuhisa Watanabe (Yack), Shuichiro Nakazawa (SHU), Kazuko Umino (karn.), Tomohito Takahashi, Munehiro Nakanishi, Katsuhisa Ishikawa and Tamayo Kawamoto

somehow to the Touhou project. I don't have another job.

JS: Living the dream!

ZUN: <*laughs*> Yes, I get to do what I enjoy as my job.

JS: Is there any final message you'd like to give?

ZUN: What I'd like to say is, Touhou is currently not being released overseas. It's a shame, because I know there are a lot of fans out there, I know that it's a name that has a following. It is something I'm thinking about, it is something I want to do. If it does happen, please, I hope you enjoy the titles that come out in the West as well.

JS: I would love to see them officially come out. Maybe with Sony's recent drive for indies, they'll want to put a compilation on PS4 or something.

ZUN: As I said before, it's to do with how much work it requires. I'm quite busy with the work right now. I would definitely think about.

JS: I'm looking forward to some good developments. Thank you for your time today.

ZUN: How long will this be?

JS: Maybe 20 or more pages.

ZUN: How many others in the book?

JS: I've interviewed over 80 developers. I'll have to split the volumes, but you'll be part of the core group in Volume 1.

ZUN: In general, who have you been interviewing around Japan?

JS: Everyone, actually. Japanese developers from all sections of the industry. An eclectic A-Z of everyone.

ZUN: I don't how much I'm involved in the industry as a whole though.

JS: You're a well known figure. It's not only about the industry, the *doujin* scene is also important. My regret is that I don't have enough time to cover the *doujin* scene more.

[...]

JS: Have you followed crowdfunding, such as Kickstarter? Will Touhou ever be on Kickstarter?

ZUN: I've been following it. I'll be honest with you though, there's no need for Touhou ever to do a Kickstarter. It doesn't really cost anything to produce. I'm making it all by myself. If it's just one person developing it, you don't need money to make the project work. I don't see any reason that I would do it. One thing I worry about, I guess, is that if you successfully get all

ZUN

the money, and you have to make the game, and if mid-production there's a problem... Your book was done through Kickstarter?

JS: Yes, it was.

ZUN: Isn't it possible you could run off with the money or something?

JS: Any creator can run off. There's no real accountability. Just my reputation to back me up.

ZUN: If that starts happening, people are not going to want to use Kickstarter anymore.

JS: It's funny, because a couple of high profile projects hit the rocks. Tim Schaeffer received 3.5 million dollars, and then ran out of money.

ZUN: I know the story. It was the end of last year, wasn't it? Kickstarter is kind of scary! You're really against your own clock at that point. You have to make the game - if you run out of money, then you're out of money.

JS: My question is, how do you spend 3 million dollars so easily?

ZUN: Did he use it effectively? Or did something go wrong? I don't have any plans to use crowdfunding now, and I don't think I ever will. *<laughs>* It might be a case that I want to buy some more alcohol, so maybe I could run a Kickstarter for that!

<everyone laughs>

ZUN: But nobody would give me money for that.

JS: I don't know. Maybe. It's keeping it old school - physical packaging, money for direct goods, one man and his computer...

ZUN: Yes, but it's not like I'm trying to keep that process alive. It's just more that it's the way I do it. I'm used to it.

JS: Can we get a photo together.

<photo is taken>

ZUN: Can I put these on Twitter?

JS: Sure! That would be great!

Below and left, as explained via the Touhou Wiki: "A figure creator called Moge Koubou made an action figure of ZUN. With his permission, it was sold at the 2009 Winter Comiket."

Images taken from a random forum...

~ Appearing in a later volume ~

Mikito Ichikawa / Mickey Albert

Continuing the coverage of indie / *doujin* game developers is an interview with Mr Ichikawa, veteran developer who recently created a horizontal shmup with the longest play area ever - *Super Chain Crusher Horizon*, running at a stunning 3200 x 800 pixels.

More significantly though, Mr Ichikawa is a real-life action-hero. When gangsters grabbed his sister to intimidate him during a court case, he took matters into his own hands, smashed an arcade, and faced them head on. No one messed with him again. His English nickname is Mr Albert, though Mr Arnie would work just as well.

Professor Hiroshi Ishikawa

In the 1980s Professor Ishikawa was a hobbyist game maker who won Enix's game programming contests, and had his entries published. He only developed two games, but even today they're something special. He recalls with fondness attending the parties Enix held for the winners, and seeing gaming celebrities like Kouichi Nakamura. Today Professor Ishikawa works to create Artificial Intelligence which can visually discern items the same way the human eye and brain can. Could this lead to the creation of a real-life Skynet situation?

木村 祥朗

KIMURA, Yoshiro

DOB: 7 November 1969 / Birthplace: *secret* / Blood Type: *secret*

~ Selected portfolio ~

Romancing SaGa 2 - Super Famicom, 1993 (Map creation, map checking)

Romancing SaGa 3 - Super Famicom, 1995 (Combat design)

Moon: Remix RPG Adventure - PlayStation 1, 1997 (Game design)

L.O.L.: Lack of Love - Dreamcast, 2000 (Assistant game designer)

Chulip - PlayStation 2, 2002 (Director, scenario writer)

Rule of Rose - PlayStation 2, 2006 (Planning draft, CG movie director, storyboard design)

No More Heroes - Wii, 2007 (Producer)

Little King's Story - Wii, 2009 (Producer and Director)

No More Heroes 2: Desperate Struggle -
Wii, 2010 (Producer)

Shadows of the Damned -
PS3 / X360, 2011 (Exec. producer)

Sine Mora -
Xbox 360, 2012 (Special thanks)

Million Onion Hotel -
iOS, TBA (Director, game designer)

http://www.oniongames.jp/

Interview with Yoshiro Kimura
13 October 2013, Tokyo

I first met Mr Kimura at the Sony Indie Stream event - he was surrounded by well wishers and fans, but he kindly took the time to introduce himself and discuss my book. He also introduced me to ZUN, who he was friends with. I was keen to interview Mr Kimura, given his rich portfolio, notably Love-de-Lic.

The day I met Mr Kimura for an interview I was late. I'd interviewed ZUN in the afternoon, and then promptly got lost. Myself and my crew spent a long time navigating a confusing section of night-time Tokyo. The original plan was to visit 8-BIT CAFE, but the map on their website was so minimalist it was impossible to find, despite asking multiple people for directions. When I met Mr Kimura he'd been waiting for some time, in the rain. Ever the gentleman, he ignored my lack of etiquette and invited me to his home to start the interview. He supplied the beer, I ordered everyone pizza. He discussed games, Love-de-Lic, Rule of Rose, his personal artwork (very impressive), and a board game he built called Potato Saga. We discussed a lot of non-game related topics, which I have left in. Mr Kimura gave a fascinating cultural insight into NicoNico Douga in Japan, highlighting the worldwide trend of developing media where anyone can have a voice.

More than five hours later I made my way home. It was a good evening. That night a typhoon would hit Japan again. Luckily I was home by then.

[The interview starts suddenly in a taxi, which is en route to Mr Kimura's home - it turns out he had been a keen MMORPG player]

Yoshiro Kimura: How is *Ultima Online*, are they still going?

JS: They're not running it anymore. But I think fans have made servers, so you can still play it. *World of Warcraft* took a lot of players away.

YK: Yeah, yeah, yeah!

JS: But that's more focused on combat. In *Ultima* you could just be a baker if you wanted.

YK: <*laughs*> How many people have you interviewed?

JS: In total? Over 40 so far?

YK: Forty! How are you going to write them?

JS: I'm going to transcribe the spoken English. Maybe I can complete it in three months?

YK: Amazing! I don't know if there is a promise between you and Kickstarter, like a time limit?

JS: I had to give an estimated release date, but with so much content I need to take longer. What have you worked on today?

YK: Today I was discussing my next game with my planner. And what else was I doing...? Waiting for you! <*laughs*>

JS: I am so, so, so sorry about that!

<*everyone laughs*>

YK: And also, ZUN-san was afraid, asking, "Is he coming or not?" And I said, it seems he is coming. I was talking to you both on the phone, and you were both going to the Shinjuku blood bank.[1] <*laughs*> It was funny!

JS: I am very sorry I kept you waiting in the rain.

YK: No, no... It is not that ZUN does it on purpose. I am often [in a situation] like this.[2] ZUN doesn't contact others a lot. <*laughs*>

JS: You organise his interviews. <*laughs*>

YK: Yes, but this is recently. Before I was doing this, maybe someone else was there? <*laughs*> ZUN really doesn't want to read English. Not only English emails, but also he doesn't want to read Japanese emails.

JS: He was quite talkative today.

---

[1] Many interviewees were met outside the Shinjuku blood bank, due its location and easily recognised front
[2] ZUN is difficult to get hold of for interviews - it's thanks only to Kimura-san I was able to interview him

YK: Once you meet me he cannot stop talking.

JS: He enjoyed some beer too.

YK: It's very famous. He's a beer maniac.[3]

JS: He makes his own beer too, Touhou Beer.

YK: He did, at NicoNico Chokaigi.

JS: Did you try it?

YK: No, I didn't go. I don't like that kind of festival. NicoNico Chokaigi, the festival of NicoNico Douga.[4] You know NicoNico Douga?

JS: Japan's equivalent of YouTube.

YK: I didn't know that culture, but recently... ZUN, and Yoshi Naga-kun, and Doguma-san,[5] appeared in front of me, and they are kind of living in the NicoNico world. <*laughs*>

JS: The comments go across the screen.

YK: Isn't there the same system in...?

JS: NicoNico has an English site, but I think YouTube is the only popular one. Also, to watch NicoNico video you need an account.

YK: In Japan, NicoNico Douga is much bigger than the people who watch YouTube, really. You might think it's only maniacs who are watching it. I thought so, but recently changed my mind.

JS: YouTube in Japan shows things like bands, I thought maybe companies use YouTube...

YK: For the companies, yes. They use YouTube. But for younger people, they watch NicoNico. It's like the culture of radio, from my era. Did you listen to the radio at midnight? A long, long time ago? When I was younger, like 13 years old, I was listening to disc jockeys talking about ridiculous things at midnight. And then I could speak about it the next morning, with my friends. It was a happy time.

JS: I guess for me it was TV?

YK: Maybe radio is something... The radio guys seemed like older friends of mine.

JS: Everyone listens to radio in the car.

YK: But a young person doesn't want to listen to your usual radio - only the radio shows at around midnight. When older people are talking about erotic things, and stupid things, and making ridiculous jokes a lot.

JS: Crazy stuff they can't say during the day!

YK: And now NicoNico Douga is used instead of this. It's not conventional companies talking about straight and happy things only, but <*laughs*> NicoNico Douga users can talk about ridiculous and stupid things, and no one can stop it! <*laughs*>

JS: You lived in London?

YK: Yes, but only for around 3 months. My English comes from my travelling. Did I talk about my travels?

JS: No, please tell me about it.

YK: I travelled ***a lot***. I went to Kenya, London, and Peru. All over Europe, Russia, Alaska...

JS: How long did you spend in each country?

YK: Sometimes short, sometimes long. And I often go to Switzerland. There is a... They are not my family, but they are really good friends. I could live there! If I don't have a job then I can go to Switzerland. So they are not native speakers, but one of them is an artist, an older friend, now he is 80 years old. He is like my mentor of the arts. We often speak in English, like over the telephone.

JS: I read on your blog that you were worried about being homeless when older?

[3] In Japanese the word "maniac" is used affectionately for anyone passionate about something
[4] A mass fan convention; attendance tops 100'000
[5] Famous blogger: www.dfnt.net / famous game player

YK: <*intense laughter*>

JS: Were you serious?

YK: Sometimes I am thinking about it, yes. Recently I've not been working at a proper job. It's like... I don't know! <*laughs*> Ridiculous.

JS: But you're head of Onion Games.

YK: Yes, but Onion Games is not gaining money without my doing proper work. So if I cannot find success with games development, I don't know what will happen. And if I tell this story to my parents, maybe they will be worried.

JS: Which story?

YK: You know, they don't really know what I'm doing. Not only now, but also before. While I'm working hard in the videogame industry, they don't understand anything about it. So now they're thinking I am living in the same situation as before. But if I explain about recent events in my life, to my parents, maybe...

JS: Feel free to say it in Japanese.

YK: If I don't drink, I can't do it.

JS: Just like ZUN.

<*everyone laughs*>

YK: Myself and ZUN, every time we meet we go for a drink. When somebody from France interviewed me, we drank beer. It's not really comfortable [without a drink], maybe?

JS: The words flow more easily.

YK: There was an interviewer from France who came over, but in France there's a law that you can't show alcohol on television. So we went to 8-bit cafe and had to drink tea, oolong tea. As soon as the interview was over we hit the beer!

JS: The image of France is they all drink wine. They also love manga and anime.

YK: I often go to Switzerland, so I also go to Paris a lot. I found other people who love Japanese animation and games a lot. That's why I have a lot of friends over there.

JS: France has *bandes dessinées*. So they're more receptive to the visual style.

YK: Yes, yes! *Bandes dessinées*!

JS: You're planning a title with Onion Games?

YK: Yes, yes, I'm making and planning games.

JS: Is it a secret? Does it feature little onions?

YK: Ahh! From the website! Yes, I will put onions in the whole of my game. <*laughs*>

JS: Why onions?

YK: Why onions? There are no strong reasons; we were discussing our company name, between Kurashima-san[6] and Ikeda-san,[7] the first two guys who joined me. After GDC I often talked about having cried while in front of indie games, when seeing them at IGF.[8] So then my colleagues were saying, "Oh, it must be because of onions!" <*laughs*> But actually, what I was trying to say is, my teardrops came from me, my thoughts and feelings. It was the same as when seeing nature in its true, wild form. Like going to see the Rocky Mountains or Grand Canyon. Don't you feel something?

JS: Emotionally moved, yes. This was at GDC?

YK: Yes, when standing in front of a lot of indie games - suddenly there were so many in front of me. Then, and I remember, I was like this... <*gestures to eyes*> It moved me.

JS: You're making games as you want to.

YK: Yes, but actually, I was very free even when I was in the mainstream games industry. So I don't know if it's really due to indie games being more free or not. I don't know. Was I not free before? Maybe I like wild things. Like wild art, wild sound... A lot of people make art, right? But some can only express their emotions with a very raw technique. And we call this *art brut*. Do you know the phrase *art brut*? It's French, but in English you say *outsider art*.[9]

---

[6] Kazuyuki Kurashima (倉島一幸); artist at Love-de-Lic, also worked on *Super Mario RPG*

[7] Tom Ikeda; planner and writer on *Rule of Rose*

[8] Independent Games Festival

[9] Art created outside the boundaries of official culture

JS: Indie games are more about exploring a wilder side to creativity? A stylistic choice.

INT: Wild art... You'd maybe call it fringe art? Stuff that's not for the mass populous.

[Taxi arrives at Mr Kimura's house - we all get out. Requiring refreshments, Mr Kimura heads to a convenience store, but insists we wait at his home until he returns. Upon his return we crack open some beers]

YK: When I am in Switzerland I can only speak English, and other people can speak English and other languages. Two or three languages. *Kanpai!*

<the four of us all say kanpai!>

JS: What did you think of the Indie Steam event?

YK: Unfortunately, when I was there, I was exhausted - **a lot** - after being on stage at TGS. I was talking 6 hours a day! So when I was at Indie Stream, all I could do was go like this... *<gives a look of exhaustion>* Ahh...

JS: We spoke a bit - you were very popular.

YK: But I did have some purpose in going there. Because I wanted to see Milky again,[10] and I wanted to talk to the Playism people again, because they came from Marvellous...

JS: Didn't Yoshida-san from Sony travel with a lot of indie developers on an aeroplane, to entice them to Sony?

YK: Ehh! That's nice, that's the dream. I heard Sony wants to get the indie developers on board. But, I don't know, is that something that's good for me? *<laughs>*

JS: Your other options are Microsoft or Nintendo. But Microsoft are difficult to work with.

YK: Really? So why is that?

JS: I've read accounts from developers, like Brian Provinciano of *Retro City Rampage*.

YK: *<laughs>* Fundamentally I should not talk about or criticise them. Also, I cannot criticise them, because I do not know what they're doing. Maybe I should be a good friend of theirs?

JS: Are you working on PC games now?

YK: Now I'm working for iOS systems. But actually I'm thinking I should make games for PC, as my next target. I don't like dealing with big business game developers and companies. I'm interested in them, but what bothers me is that I feel tired talking with big companies. This is the only problem. Maybe I'm not ready to stand in front of the business people. *<laughs>* I have worked and experienced this a lot. From a young age, 26 or 27, I was going to show my ideas and give presentations. Sometimes people are interested in them - and I was calculating the whole of the project's required money. I'm used to doing this. But now, really, I don't want to have that responsibility. *<laughs>*

JS: Would you say you want to focus on creating games, and not the business?

YK: If I could say so, it would sound very cool. *<laughs>* But maybe, in truth, my fatigue is really just tiredness. *<laughs>* Also, when I am thinking about games, when I am talking about game ideas, then I feel happy in front of my colleagues. So maybe I can say yes to that question, but when I am explaining my feelings to people in Japanese, I do not say so. Only that I feel tired existing in the games industry. But I still love making games. I want to invent new games. I should talk about my situation first. I was working as an officer, you know?

JS: An officer?

YK: Until the end of Marvellous I was a freelance producer; I was a freelance developer. But after Marvellous I went to Grasshopper. They called me "chief creative officer". When I talk about the past, it is easy for me. But the recent past is difficult, because I cannot analyse myself. I am not used to speaking about it. But sometimes I need to talk about these things to my friends, to explain my situation. So for this book, I am trying to say as much as I can.

JS: Thank you. Let's start with an easy question: what was the first game you ever played?

YK: First game? The first, in my life! Hmm... Maybe *Missile Command*? At a friend's house.

[10] James Mielke, former EGM editor and now Director of BitSummit; helped me find replacement interpreters

JS: Oh, the console version?

YK: On the Atari, or something. In Japan, if someone had an Atari, it was very special. Maybe he was a rich kid. I don't know why, but he had it... No, before that, when I was very, very young, I played *Block Kuzushi*. Do you know it?

JS: *Breakout* in English, yes.

YK: It was the first, *Block Kuzushi*. Thinking back, the game which made me feel especially happy when I was playing it, was *Lode Runner*.

JS: On the Famicom?

YK: No, the computer version. Before it was ported to the Famicom, it was by Douglas Smith. I was so happy when playing *Lode Runner*, and I read the newspaper, and it spoke about how this one man who made *Lode Runner* had a house and two cars, all thanks to developing *Lode Runner*. <*laughs*> It was so fabulous for me, because I thought, "Oh, is it worth this much? I can make games like this!" Then I started making games. Before *Lode Runner* I was already programming, with BASIC.

JS: Do you still have the games?

YK: <*laughs*> No, no. I don't have a computer which will... It was during the first age of the 8-bit computers in Japan, so it's a very rare machine. I cannot get this rare machine again.

JS: What was the name? PC-6001, or PC-88?

YK: No, it was a JR-200. It was made by Panasonic. [11] Very rare. No one knows it. Anyway, it was Douglas Smith! When I turned 23 I was at Square, and I went to Seattle, for Square's... For some reason or another. And I met Doug Smith! At that moment Doug Smith was working for Square Seattle! And I was so happy! "Oh, you are Doug Smith! What are you doing here?" Then he said... I don't remember exactly. He didn't say he's happy working there, just that he moved from somewhere to somewhere... For me, he is like a super idol. Like *The Beatles* or something. <*laughs*> But when we were talking about the past, it seems he didn't want to talk! <*laughs*>

JS: Anyway, you travelled to Seattle? [12]

YK: Yes, for... I remember going to Los Angeles to see the Consumer Electronics Show, then we moved from Los Angeles to Seattle. At that point Square had made Square Seattle, and we were going there to talk with foreign developers, about what they were doing, to learn about things. One of them was Doug Smith! I don't know how many years Square Seattle existed. A long, long time ago! So when I was 23 years old, that was 20 years ago.

JS: Your first game was *Romancing SaGa*?

YK: *Romancing SaGa 2*.

JS: Hackers looked at the code behind the *Romancing SaGa* games, the series, and discovered lots of unused data.[13]

YK: <*laughs*> I think that's the era - people were not thinking hackers would search the ROM. Now we are seriously thinking about it. We don't want to leave any kind of dust there.

I cannot answer regarding *Romancing SaGa 2*, because I was just one small planner there. It was my first job. So I was a beginner. What I remember is like this: the leader of *Romancing SaGa* was very strong and clever; a wiser man I have never seen![14] <*laughs*> At Square, I had come straight out of university, where I felt that the ideas I had, the things I wanted to do, were good. I felt my ideas were unique, or strong. But then meeting these people who worked in the industry, I realised that no,

---

[11] Obscure 8-bit computer with a chiclet keyboard and bespoke BASIC dialect (1983)

[12] Kimura-san was born November 1969, so this would have been around the time Doug Smith was executive producer on *Secret of Mana*

[13] As explained to me by journalist Derrick Sobodash: "The games (especially from *Romancing SaGa* onward) make use of a very advanced, very high level scripting system. As a result, they're littered with unused event code that, when disassembled, reveals all kinds of actions and quests that were planned, and sometimes even associated dialogue and storyline forks, that were lost. The advanced scripting even extends to the battle engine, and is how Japanese hackers have been able to do some amazing things with *Romancing SaGa 3*, creating all new attacks and spells, and porting new characters and bosses from other *SaGa* games into it."

[14] This would be Akitoshi Kawazu; ironically, Tim Rogers described him as gaming's Ed Wood

they're further along than I am. Their ideas were better. We have a word in Japanese, *shakaijin*,[15] which is like a full, working member of society. And I felt like I wasn't there yet. But this realisation was a good thing, because I had someone to look up to, like a role model to aim for. But at the same time, knowing that and how far ahead I still needed to travel, made me realise that I won't get to make my own game for a while. It wasn't going to happen, because there were people having much better ideas than me. It was a happy and a sad thing at the same time. <*laughs*> When I met the project leader of *Romancing SaGa 2*, and the director of the battle system, the designer, it really put everything in context. It made me realise how, actually, I wasn't such a maverick.

JS: Were you able to leave a mark on the game?

YK: I did only one good thing for *Romancing SaGa 2*. For the battle scenes there's a feature where when the characters learn a new attack, a light bulb will pop up above their heads.[16] Originally it was an exclamation mark. But I saw that and thought, no, that's boring, don't do that. Even at my young age, when I was doing *Romancing SaGa 2*, I said to the designer, this should be a light bulb! And they changed it, and they kept that all the way through the series. So I had an effect on the entire series of *Romancing SaGa*. <*laughs*> You know, I don't want to say I made that system, because of course the battle game designer made it. But I did just a little bit, and now the whole *Romancing SaGa* series has that light bulb.

JS: The entire series has your signature.

YK: That's right! <*laughs*> So every time in any *Romancing SaGa*, when I see the light bulb, I'm reminded that I had a part in that series. Even if it was a small part. But at the same time, I was coming to that realisation that I won't be making my own game any time soon. When I have a good idea my body starts trembling a lot. It feels very good. Sometimes someone will ask me: "When do you want to die?" Then I say, "Ah... Maybe the moment when I get a new idea and feel good! Then it will be nice!" <*laughs*>

JS: <*laughs*> Go out on a high note! Did you meet Kenichi Nishi while at Square?

YK: But Kenichi Nishi is not the one who invited me to Love-de-Lic. It was Taro Kudo.[17] There were two key people, Nishi and Kudo, and Kudo isn't so well known among foreigners. But Love-de-Lic, the idea for it, 70% of it I think comes from Kudo.

JS: Really?

YK: And me! <*laughs*>

JS: Maybe Kenichi Nishi gets too much credit?

YK: You know, I respect him [Nishi]. We made *Moon*, me and Kudo, and Nishi. And Nishi is like a "conceptor"[18] - talking to the outside world very well. And Kudo, really, doesn't want to talk to people. He wants to talk to his colleagues, to work together. Because he loves to invent games, to invent stories. The music part, really, was his idea.[19]

JS: How did you meet Kudo-san?

YK: In Square. We worked a lot, and we played a lot. While we were working there, we went outside at night and went on adventures, to find out what Tokyo city at midnight is like...

There are a lot of interesting stories. But I cannot talk about them because it is too dangerous to explain. I don't know, maybe when I am 70 years old I can talk about them. But not now. Is that enough to explain it? <*laughs*>

---

[15] 社会人, lit. member of society, but with deeper meaning, applied to people after graduating

[16] Called a Glimmer, or colloquially Tech Sparking

[17] 工藤太郎; formerly of Konami and Square; according to MobyGames, composer on *Axelay* and designer on *Mario RPG*; the Japanese honorific for Mr Kudo switched between -kun and -san, and was sometimes omitted entirely

[18] Otakumode.com attributes creation of this word to Keiji Inafune, but I came across it regularly in Japan - usually refering to an "ideas man" who isn't hands on

[19] The game is often silent unless you find magic discs, which can be played in the MD (Moon Disc) player

JS: Oh, I understand precisely. *<wink, nudge>*

YK: Regarding Kudo-san, when he wanted me to join Love-de-Lic, when it started, I declined because I did not want to make games anymore. I often do this.

JS: What would you do if not make games?

YK: At that moment I was like a lost child of the world. I mean, I'm like a lost child now, again, because I don't know what I will do. But at that moment I wanted to travel, a lot. I created this one character, who is always walking around somewhere, like this. What do you call it?

JS: Rambling? Wandering?

YK: Ah, yes, wandering. I think it was a miracle that I stayed there for three years, in Square. From childhood I can say I was a wanderer. Suddenly I would feel, "I should not go to school today! I will go to the shrine." *<laughs>*

JS: So you'd skip school?

YK: Sometimes. Often I did not want to go to school. I liked school, I did like school, but sometimes I needed to escape from that... You know, too many people. I was sleeping at night, when I was a child, at the shrine.

JS: Did you go on any interesting adventures?

YK: Yes, when I am sleeping in the shrine a strange woman would appear, and she wanted to talk to me. And I felt I was in a lot of danger - what did she want from me?

<everyone laughs>

YK: So, this is the kind of person I am. After three years of Square I left the company and I said to the boss, "I need to go back to the western side of Japan, and I will never make games again. I am too busy helping my family." Or something. It was an excuse. *<laughs>* It was a lie! Also, I said to Kudo, "I like you, and I like your idea, and if I have the motivation to make games, I will immediately join Love-de-Lic." But then I also said, "No thank you."

He replied, "What do you want to do?"

I said, "I will go travelling." Of course, I could speak honestly with a friend, so I didn't need to use an excuse.

Then Kudo says, "When will you go?"

I reply, "In one month's time?"

Then he says, "We are starting Love-de-Lic now. So I don't need your promise of joining Love-de-Lic. But come along for one month only, and discuss games and listen to our ideas."

So I joined him for one month and I discussed the first part of *Moon*.

JS: It's incredible how things turn out.

YK: But I promised I would go travelling, so I said goodbye to Kudo and Kurashima-san. Bye bye! I left the games industry. Then I went to Peru... No, not Peru. At that moment I went to... New York first, I've got some friends there. Then I went to... I can't remember. But anyway, the last part of my travels was Peru. I remember before going to Machupicchu, there is a station village called Aguas Calientes and I saw the children were playing videogames outside, at some kind of vending stall. It's a stand, like a small house? *<draws>*

YK: There was a TV here, and they had games, with a Famicom, Super Famicom, Mega Drive. It was a game stall. The children would line up, it was outside, there was perhaps a corrugated iron roof or something on top of it, maybe a tent, basically a shack. Next to it was a cinema. There was *Mario*, *Zelda*, and also *Final Fantasy IV*, that kind of thing. The kids would line up and pay just one cent, or a small amount of money, to play for 10 minutes. Then the kids would go to the back of the line and wait again. Obviously if it was *Super Mario* or an action game, that was fine, you can enjoy that in 10 minutes. But they were playing *Final Fantasy IV*, for 10 minutes a time. But obviously because they watch from the queue, they would understand the story. It was team play. When I witnessed this scene, I realised I wanted to make games again.

JS: That pivotal moment, which brought you back, were these Peruvian children. Amazing.

YK: After I had spent 2 or 3 months wandering, I went back to Japan, and I met Kudo-san again, and Kurashima-san again. But at that moment I did not say I want to join them, because I didn't have to say, "I want to join *your* place." I felt I should choose a place. But they were watching me, very seriously. I remember they also did not ask me, "Are you coming to Love-de-Lic?" They just said we were going to watch a film at the cinema. What was it - do you know this animation about a dog?

<doodles on paper>

JS: *Wowser*?[20]

YK: No, not *Wowser*. A better looking animation. It's very famous. This dog likes *pants*.

<everyone laughs>

YK: Not Goofy, not Snoopy... Ahhh... Why can't I remember the name?! Very famous... Anyway... This animated dog was being shown in the cinema, and it's a puppet based animation, because I love puppet animation and my friends knew this. We went to Shibuya and watched the movie, then they started to say, "So, are you coming to Love-de-Lic tomorrow?"

To which I replied, "Tomorrow? What are you talking about?"

They said, "We can prepare for tomorrow." Suddenly they started talking about how I would do my job the next day. They just kind of decided it, and what they said was, "We've got a box in the office. So if we stick a computer on the box, your office is ready! You can do your job."

So I felt they really want me to go to their place, very much. I said, "Yes, OK, I can go." Then I went there and I saw their situation again. I think after they started to develop *Moon*, four months later, or six months later... In my eyes, they did not make any progress.

Only Kurashima-san's character part is OK. Akira-kun,[21] his background part is OK, the environment is OK. But the game part - they were still considering "opening doors" instead of battles. An "open door" system, I don't know... A system of "opening the door" to the monsters' minds? *<laughs>* It turned out there was nothing in *Moon* at all. They were still discussing and talking about the story... At that point I felt I was in a lot of danger with this project. Because they're happy just to talk, talk, talk. I was considering: should I run away from this place now, or should I work hard for them?

JS: The full names of these gentleman are...?

YK: Taro Kudo. Kazuyuki Kurashima. He still works with me. I remember they asked me, do you need more details? At that moment I decided I should not talk with all of them at the same time. For the story part, I spoke with Nishi-san, and said we should make it compact. Smaller than what he was imagining, and I had an idea. Like this, like this. *<doodles on paper>* So I went to Kudo and asked how he wanted to make this new game system, opening doors into the mind, instead of battles. I suggested that he shouldn't think up too complicated a system instead of battles, and please could he just make it simpler, like catching monsters. *<doodles>* This is an easy way to think about and complete it. Then he agreed, and he agreed, *<referencing colleagues>* and I gathered all the people and I explained my ideas. The whole team agreed.

JS: You saved the project.

YK: Yes. *<laughs>* But I don't want to say I didn't help. A strange phenomenon is, if you do this suddenly in a team, usually if there is a tyrant or strong personality, or some kind of genius there, then they will retaliate. They [the Love-de-Lic team] never did that. What I mean is, they just helped me with my idea. Kurashima-san is the best, and once I started talking about the story he drew some characters. Kudo-san is also good, and when I asked what should the catching of monsters be like, he asked, "What is clay like? Don't you want to make things out of clay together?" *He knew I loved clay!*

JS: Like claymation?

YK: Clay models. We started to... When I say "we", it means not only the character designer, but also the engineers, the planners, and the management people. Everyone started to make things out of clay one day. Then suddenly there were 50 monsters! *<laughs>* It was very

---

[20] Belgium comic adapted into a Japanese anime series
[21] Akira Ueda (上田 晃), director, designer, and artist; *Secret of Mana, Mario RPG, Shining Soul, Michigan*

enjoyable. Everyone got into making the clay models, and suddenly we had 40, 50, 60 monsters! Then we said, right, these are the monsters of our game. Isn't this a game? Usually, if someone wants to make a new game system... <*laughs*> You know, usually a lot of characters appear after you make the *alpha* version of the game's system. Right? But we started making characters without thinking about a proper game system. <*laughs*>

JS: Just creating them...

YK: Yes. Of course we had the idea to capture the monsters, but we were thinking we would keep it simple. That's why any kind of character would work, and fit the system. We were going to make a system called "monster catch", and it would complete the game. It's not such a good game system, like *Dragon Quest* or *Final Fantasy*, but it was fun and looked nice, so that's OK. The story. <*sighs*> The storyline *was so hard.*

JS: Because it was a game within a game? Who came up with that?

YK: The game within a game was... First of all, when they started the project they had the idea of a *Dragon Quest*-styled game within a game. But there wasn't such a good story in there. Meaning, there was a map constructed, but there was no story. <*very softly*> It was very tender and natural, like a movie story, and the main character was with a girl. I cannot remember because... *It was ridiculous!*

JS: <*intense laughter*>

YK: And silly. Yeah, really, I don't know why the main character and the girl character existed. After I joined Love-de-Lic, I wrote the story again.

JS: So it was completely different before?

YK: Yes! <*laughs*> This is the first time I've spoken about this!

JS: I'm very excited to document this!

YK: However, I think I should not talk about this.

JS: People love the games. Do you know the website Lovedelic Life, run by my friend?[22]

YK: Oh really, is that so? I know him!

JS: Fans really want to know.

YK: What I feel is this: Kudo-san is a good musician, and he had a good idea. He wanted to make a game based on or involving music. He has these kind of ideas a lot, and his details are so beautiful. The idea which Kudo-san came up with, it involved a small monkey... No, no, no, I cannot explain, that's why it's so difficult. It's not your usual game. But anyway, his musical game idea was so good, and maybe if he was not in Love-de-Lic, then *Moon* would not be the way it was. I made the story part. Meaning the main story, like this. <*doodles*>

Kudo-san's idea was that in *Moon* there would be a music shop, if you will, that players could go to and find a song that they liked, which had been made by various indie artists, and they could then choose which songs would play when they played the game.

Or he had another idea where there was a, sort of, new-age guru in the game, who would dance, and the way he communicated with you was to a beat.[23] And that was another of Kudo-san's ideas, the kind of things he was presenting.

Kudo-kun's best skill is taking each small thing, each small idea or action, and polishing it beautifully, with music. These small elements are very important for *Moon*, because *Moon*'s concept is each character has their own life. That's why his details are very important. Then I wrote the story, the main flow of it.

JS: After ditching the boy and girl story?

YK: <*laughs*> Boy and girl, yeah, yeah! The first one was a boy and girl.

JS: Was the original a love story?

YK: Ahh, the original... Really, it was not my type of thing, that's why I didn't... I cannot remember, it was too long ago. But what I changed was Yoshida, the small bird like this. <*doodles*> He is the main character for telling the story.[24]

JS: The narrator?

---

[22] http://lovedelicgames.wordpress.com

[23] Referring to the character of Adder - named after *Moon*'s composer Masanori Adachi, who often sang and danced during development

[24] An intellectual bird afraid to attend university, speaks with Kansai accent

YK: Yes, of this *Moon* world. He navigates or guides the player, on how to live and whether his heroic efforts are going well or not.

JS: He tells the player what to do.

YK: Not only what to do, but also he can talk about the scenes in the story. This character is very inventive for me, he's not an explanation character. He's not just an instruction manual, but a real character, with a real story. An actual living character. This bird is called Yoshida-san, and he speaks very well. This invention was good for *Moon*, really. *<doodles>* The *Moon* world... *<doodles>*

<I order pizza to be delivered to Mr Kimura's>

JS: Your company is called Onion Games. What's your favourite dish with onions?

YK: Onion rings. *<laughs>* No. Usually I like sushi. *<laughs>* I came up with the reason behind *Moon*'s existence, and why people are moving within this world. The whole of the game was programmed by somebody, but this storytelling is by me. It looks like the characters are alive, and each character has a good atmosphere. More so than other games. Then at the end of the story it says this is also a game, just like the others, so please go outside and stop playing. This is my storytelling.

JS: It sounds like Plato's allegory of the cave.

YK: Yes, yes, I know, yeah! The reason why I used this idea is I love underground theatre.[25]

JS: Really?

YK: Oh yeah. Do you know this, it's like a circus tent? *<doodles>* I often visit and see the famous underground theatre, and [at the end of the play] they say, "Get out of here!" Suddenly, at the last moment, the wall opens and I can see the Shinjuku area. Until the end of the story we're all sitting down, like this, *<hunches over>* these people watching a play. But suddenly **BAH!** Behind the actors the wall opens, and we're surprised, because fresh air flows in from outside. This kind of fresh feeling, I loved it, and I remember wondering, can I create this same atmosphere in a game?

JS: The message of *Moon* is that it's a game?

YK: The message of *Moon* is - have you thought about going outside, instead of playing games? I cannot remember the name of this director, but someone made a movie within a movie.

JS: Like Shakespeare's play within a play?

YK: Yes, Shakespeare did a play within a play, and a European artist, ahh... Fellini![26] Or the same age as Fellini. I loved those old movies, and I thought, can I create the same atmosphere of a revolution like they did? So I made *Moon*. That's why if someone asks me, "What do you think about making *Moon 2*?", then I say no, no, no, because with *Moon*, the story is about the player stopping the playing of games. So I cannot make *Moon 2*!

---

[25] A little Googling reveals the term "*sho-gekijo*" meaning "little theatre", also referred to as the Underground Theatre Movement; plays often occur in tents, focusing on fantasy rather than reality

[26] Frederico Fellini, Italian film director and scriptwriter (1920 - 1993)

JS: It's got the perfect ending; it is as it is.

YK: During the ending scroll there are a lot of real pictures of Tokyo city. I remember we went outside and took photos everywhere, like Tokyo tower, then we added *Moon*'s monster characters, like this. <*doodles*> No, not Tokyo tower, like Shinjuku building! The skyscraper.

JS: It's a beautiful game. Shame it was never officially released in English.

YK: <*laughs*> It seems the people, foreigners, are playing it still. Even in Japanese.

JS: Someone is making a fan-translation.

YK: <*laughs*> That's amazing! In that case, you know there's also a lot of strange things in the *Moon* CD, right? Some hackers extracted the data from *Moon*...

JS: I wasn't aware of this. What did they find?

YK: Test text, plus a TV idol's name from that time, and old characters, and event scenes which were not implemented.[27]

JS: One of the fan-translators posted about it.

YK: There are several guys? One of them is a follower on my Twitter, and he introduced me to what he is doing. I didn't want to say anything critical to him, and I said, "When you make the Android version, please give me a copy."

JS: His nickname is GhaleonQ.

YK: Ah, yes, yes, this one! He brought me the test version they were working on, for emulation on a PC, but I only have a Mac. So it was not possible for me to emulate it. But it seems they can already play it on a PC.

JS: How do you feel about that?

YK: It's OK, for me. Maybe if I was one of the publishers, then I would not say yes. If someone can read my story, it's OK. It is so difficult for people to play old games, so if this is the only way that someone can understand what I was doing... What should I say? No thank you? I should say, "Yes please!"

JS: When the English patch is released you'll have a whole new collection of fans. Do you have any message for them?

YK: Have fun. <*laughs*> Have fun, and find out the philosophy that I was trying to convey. I don't know if people will understand it or not though, because at that moment in time there were two very famous role-playing games, *Dragon Quest* and *Final Fantasy*. That's why we could show our idea of a game within a game. At that moment people were obsessed with role-playing games. That's why I wanted to say, what do you think about stopping playing games and going outside? Find a real adventure, like going to Peru. But I don't know if now, people will feel the same or not.

JS: I think the message is timeless.

YK: But this experience was the first time for me to express myself, really. When I was at Square it was impossible for me to show my storyline. There were a lot of people who were geniuses when it came to role-playing games. Maybe Kudo and Kurashima-san gave me a chance to show my skill. <*laughs*> While I was making *Moon* ideas came automatically, non-stop, like this, like this... <*mimes ideas entering his mind*> At that moment I was not the director. There was no director. Me, and Kudo, and Nishi, we were game designers. There was no leader. We just decided on things suddenly. <*laughs*>

JS: A wild free team.

YK: Yeah, yeah. No one stopped me from adding ideas, no one stopped me from cutting ideas when I said "cut here". Then sometimes Nishi-san would say, <*whispers softly*> "Ohhh... Is it OK or...?" <*pauses*>

[27] **http://tcrf.net/Moon** covers this content extensively

JS: Real design freedom.

YK: Design freedom, yes! Speaking honestly, regarding inventive ideas, I respect Kudo-san. But I was not feeling Nishi-san's part well. *<laughs>* But Nishi-san inspired me a lot, because after I became the producer, I had to show my ideas to the people. I remember Nishi-san was a very important person for expressing and conveying our game to the public. The question is this: is he pretending that he wrote the story?

YK: I don't remember. One of the producers on *Moon* was working on it, but he left Love-de-Lic. That's why suddenly it was pending.

<finishes sketch - see accompanying DVD>

YK: Here was the music composer's room, with keyboard and computer. Where was the living room? With two sofas... We were discussing things or eating lunch here. *<gestures to upper left of sketch>* Oh, and there was a TV, which we played games on. Nintendo...

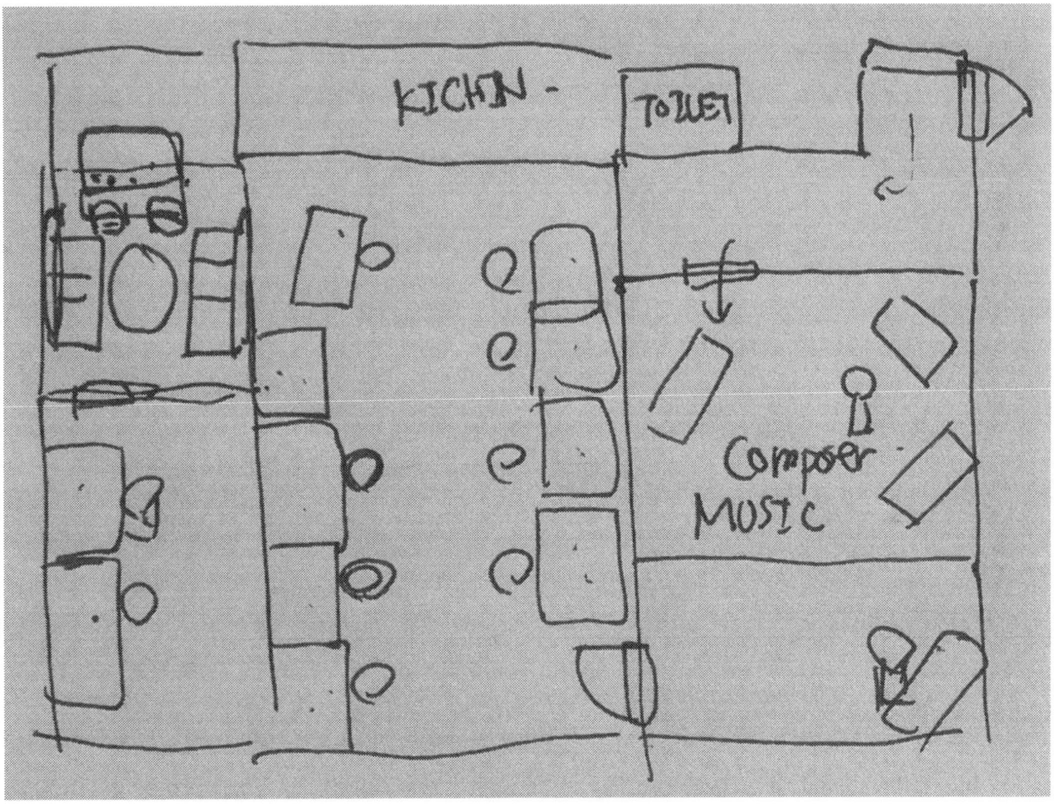

JS: Can you draw the office layout?

YK: What?! [...] I am trying. Let me do a practise version. Ahh...

JS: I don't think any of Love-de-Lic's games were released outside of Japan.

YK: *<laughs>* I remember we were making the English version of *Moon*. We were doing it. But I don't know what happened in the end. I think maybe somewhere there is a hard-disc, but...

JS: Why wasn't it completed?

JS: *Roku-jyu-yon? (64)*

YK: Eh, was it *roku-jyu-yon*? We played *Starfox*, four players.

JS: Yes, that's the N64.

YK: And *Goldeneye*! Here was the boss, the manager. *<points to beneath the lounge room>* But there were two company presidents. *<points to second president's room beneath the music room>*

JS: Are these desks? *<points to central room>*

YK: Yes, desks, desks. *<counts the desks>* Here was the kitchen. During our Love-de-Lic era, the manager, a woman, made lunch or dinner quite often. Almost every day. We were all eating together, like we're a big family.

JS: How many people were there?

YK: I'm counting... *<counts to self>* About 12 or 13 people?

JS: Did you often have to sleep at the office?

YK: No, I didn't do that. Some of the people, yes, but I loved to go back home and sleep.

JS: Did you normally go home late? A lot of people in the West think there's always overtime.

YK: Of course I was working 12 hours every day, but this was for our artistic creation, so I didn't mind at all. To maintain a high quality though, I would not stay up all night. So I was sleeping properly every night. That moment at Love-de-Lic was a very special time, because the whole of our team was young, and we could work 12 hours every day, no problem. The graphics were done by just two guys - one person was drawing all of the characters, and one person was drawing the whole map. So it was very special. It's impossible for them now, to do it like that.

JS: Only one person does all the onion sprites on your website, right? Who is that?

YK: Oh, Kurashima-san! The same guy from *Moon*. Kurashima-san and me have a very good, strong friendship, because even when I did my private stage work - I was an actor, sometimes I did acting on the stage alone - and I wanted to make a flier, he drew them for free. From an early age he was like this. Still, now, he is working with me. It is a miracle.

JS: You first met him at Square. On *Romancing SaGa 2*?

YK: No, he was on another team. He was on *Hanjuku Hero*.

JS: Ah, with Takashi Tokita![28]

YK: Yes, Tokita-san. I remember Kurashima-san did not know anything about computers, and he couldn't even type his name on the computer. For Japanese people, really, this was not so strange. Because I typed English from childhood, it was OK for me to use a keyboard on computers suddenly. When I was 20 years old it was not so popular for Japanese people to type in front of a computer. Now for young people it's OK, but Kurashima-san would say, "How should I do this?" *<laughs>* So he touches K. Then U. Ahhh! Then R, then A!

JS: So he was a beginner with computers when joining the company, while also developing computer games.

YK: Yeah, but now it is natural for us to use the PC or Mac for development. But at that time we were using not only computers, but also Nintendo's special "dot drawing machine".

JS: Tell me about this hardware that drew pixel art. Did it have a light pen, or a mouse?

YK: It was not a mouse, and not a light pen. It was like... A stylus ball? Stylus mouse? Until the PlayStation, we were using this Nintendo machine. It was very strange, we had to use a big machine called NEWS. *<writes name on paper - all capitals>* Do you know NEWS?

JS: No.

YK: No one knows about this. It was made by Sony, but the [Nintendo] development kit would only work on this. It was very hard for us to develop games using a computer.

JS: Could I trouble you for a signature?

<Mr Kimura looks through books>

YK: Ah, ZUN-san!

JS: Of course! I said draw anything, and he drew a cute girl with beer.

YK: It's a nice signature.

JS: On your blog, did you draw all those sketches of you; as the naked man of Shinjuku?

YK: Yeah, yeah, yeah. *<laughs>* I did, I did. When I feel something, I will add it. Recently, I

---

[28] Takashi Tokita, perhaps best known for *Final Fantasy IV*, *Live-a-Live* and *Parasite Eve*, also helmed the *Hanjuku Hero* titles - literally "*Hardboiled Hero*"

am not so easygoing. I've always felt like I'm very easygoing, going with the flow, but maybe recently I'm not feeling that so much. I'm not sure, you start to wonder if things in the past were just easier to go with? <*sighs*>

<*speaks in Japanese - uninterpreted*>

YK: <*laughs*> I'm wondering now if we should translate that or not, because what I said was actually kind of miserable and depressing. My life now is OK, but maybe I'm feeling that someday I will wither, or fade away. A feeling of sadness is OK. I'm under pressure but I can talk about these things to people, as I'm doing now, and maybe my circumstances are still alright. Around me I have friends, and still I am able to stand. It is up to my strength of mind, my spirit, to endure. Recently people, especially younger people, don't want to talk about unhappy things with their friends. They only like the happy ending stories of the cinema. It is terrible for me.

JS: I agree. Life is melancholy by default.

YK: Yes. Stand in front of a melancholy mind.[29] <*laughs*> You know, I like both happy endings and bad in the cinema. Usually though I love bad endings. Did you recently see the movie *Mood Indigo*?[30] Directed by Michel Gondry.

JS: No, I've not seen it.

YK: Wonderful. It's a French movie, they speak French. Very good. Do you know Michel Gondry? I like his films very much. Please watch it.

JS: I'll keep an eye out. You talk about sad endings, and I watched *Junko*...[31]

YK: <*laughs*>

JS: And that had a very sad ending.

YK: Yeah, yeah. Is that sad?

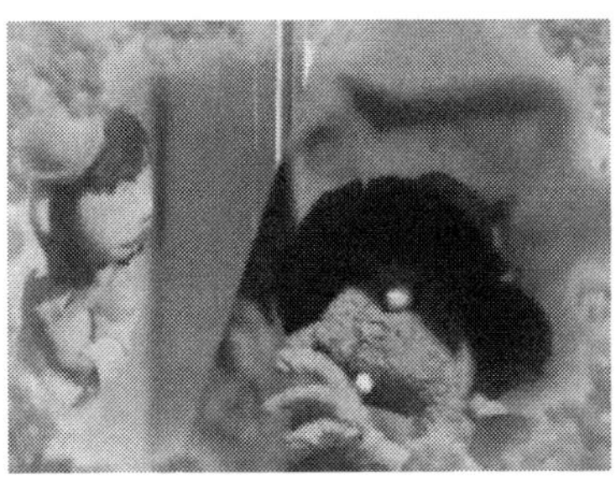

JS: Well, the woman in the well kisses the disfigured beggar, but then she realises what he is, and goes back down the well.

YK: Yes. You know *Junko*.

JS: You made it over two years, in your bedroom, using stop motion? If you're a claymation fan, you must know Nick Park. Of *Wallace and Gromit*?

YK: Ah, yes! What I was saying earlier on, it was *Wallace and Gromit*!

JS: Oh, the film about the dog, who liked pants!

<*everybody cheers and exclaims loudly at our belated epiphany - it goes on for some time*>

YK: After going to Peru I came back to Japan to watch *Wallace and Gromit*.

<*everyone hums the theme tune*>

YK: At that moment *Wallace and Gromit* was not as big as they are now.

JS: Did it influence *Moon*, because *Wallace and Gromit* go to the moon?

YK: <*laughs*> No, there's no relationship between them, but after Peru Kudo-san and Kurashima-san wanted me to go to the *Wallace and Gromit* movie.

JS: You joined Love-de-Lic because of *Wallace and Gromit*.

<*everyone laughs*>

YK: No, no, no. But I liked *Wallace and Gromit*, and it gave them a chance to talk with me. Kudo-san is living near here. Three hundred metres.

JS: Perhaps we should have some more beers and pay him a midnight visit?

YK: <*laughs*> And after Love-de-Lic, hmm...

JS: You worked on *Lack of Love*.

YK: A little. This part is very sensitive. Before joining the *Lack of Love* project, between *UFO* and *Lack of Love*, I stopped making games

---

[29] Said in English - my interpretation is that you must face sad things rather than pretend they do not exist

[30] 2013 French drama about a man & terminally ill wife

[31] *Junko* is a 2004 short stop-motion puppet film created by Mr Kimura, in French and Japanese. It should still be available on: http://dagaya-films.com/junko/index.html

because I was ill. My heart was enlarged. *<gives technical explanation>* It is really a dangerous situation. It's really difficult to explain in English. But anyway, my heart condition was very serious.

JS: Bloody hell!

YK: I'm OK now. At that time I did not know why it was happening and I felt very sad. Also, before this heart-pump problem, I was saying goodbye to Love-de-Lic. I left Love-de-Lic, but it was not because of my heart condition. First of all, it was impossible for me to stay there. I don't know why, but my temperament made me feel I should go.

JS: Like, your gut feeling?

YK: Yes, and I went to Alaska, and I went to other places. But I came back to Japan and suddenly I had this strange feeling a lot. I spent 6 months living in my house alone, but my body did not recover. I felt there was something wrong, so I went to the hospital. There the doctor discovered my heart was enlarged.

JS: You're OK now though, right?

YK: Yes, I am OK. See, while I was making *Rule of Rose*, I was having too much sex. *<laughs>* Well, then I went to the doctor again and this doctor found a problem with something else. It's difficult to explain in English. This part of the body produces adrenaline and dopamine a lot, and this made my heart bigger. So the doctor suggested removing it.

JS: An overactive gland?

YK: So the doctor operated on it, and then my heart became normal again.

<pizza has been delivered and we all tuck in - everyone says itadakimasu!>

YK: *<looks through E-J dictionary>* It was a tumour! A tumour... This pizza is good, thank you very much!

JS: *Douitashimashite! (You're welcome!)* Can I film a short message for your fans, for a DVD?

YK: You are producing a DVD also?!

JS: Yes, to go alongside the book. Do you have any message for English fans?

YK: Yes. Hmm... Hi, hello! I'm still making games, even though I don't know what will happen next. But, maybe, in one year I can show something. Please look forward to seeing my game in the future.

JS: I'm very much looking forward to it. *Ganbatte kudasai! (Please do your best!)* So between *UFO* and *Lack of Love*, it was difficult?

YK: Oh yes. But I got medicine and even though I had a heart problem, I wanted to make one more game. After I left Love-de-Lic there were no people around me. But I started to gather people who wanted to make a game with me.

JS: Is that when you formed *Punchline*?[32]

YK: Yes, but Punchline was after that. We called the name of my company Punchline. But at that moment I just said, do you want to come to my... What? My game discussion? *<laughs>* And we were discussing it in my house - not here, my old house, which was much bigger and cheaper. It was very dusty, an old building, in the old Japanese style. We discussed once a week and some of the people liked to hear my ideas. So I suggested to them, wouldn't you like to present our idea to a publisher? I went to Suzuki-san,[33] who was the producer on *Moon*, and even he didn't know what I was doing. He knew I was ill, and had a heart problem, and he helped me a lot. He said he wanted to bring my idea to the publishers, and helped me. After going to show my idea to more than 10 companies, the publisher Victor appeared. But I spent one and a half years before the project went ahead, to get the money for it.

JS: Was this game *Chulip*?[34]

YK: Yes. While I was recovering my body, taking medicine for my heart, I was going to present the game to publishers and also I was working on *Lack of Love*, helping them as an assistant. At that moment I lost all of my energy and a lot of weight. I was very light, around 60kg.

---

[32] Developed *Chulip* and *Rule of Rose*; one of three companies derived from Love-de-Lic, incl. VANPOOL and Skip (which made *Giftpia* and *Chibi-Robo*)
[33] Hiroshi Suzuki, huge portfolio incl. *Captain Rainbow*
[34] *Chulip* was published by Victor in Japan (PS2, 2002)

JS: It sounds like you were under a lot of stress. Doing at least two jobs while ill.

YK: No, no, it was not two jobs. My weight was the result of my heart pump problem. I could not eat, I could not walk, that's why I became slimmer and slimmer. I wanted to recover more, so I asked Suzuki-san, how can I recover? He wanted me to work a little bit, on *Lack of Love*. I was really only helping as an assistant.

JS: Like an advisor?

YK: No, no, I made just two maps of sequence data. Do you understand the term sequence data? Of the game's events, of characters.

JS: The order things happen, and so on?

YK: At that time in *Lack of Love* there was a lot of creatures, strange creatures, so I was working on the creatures. I was making an ant, a bear... <*laughs*> While I was waiting for the results from the publishers, whether they will give us some money, I was making *Lack of Love*. At the end of *Lack of Love*, finally, I had news - the publisher Victor! Wada-san,[35] the producer of *Harvest Moon*, he appeared in front of me, and he loved *Moon*. He knew I made Yoshida, who I mentioned earlier, and we talked a lot about *Moon*. Because he was a fan of *Moon*, he wanted to work with me. It was great. If Wada-san had not appeared, I could not have made *Chulip,* I could not have made *Little King's Story,* so Wada-san's existence was a miracle in my life.

JS: I was going to interview Wada-san, but our schedules didn't match. It's strange, after *Lack of Love,* Love-de-Lic closed down. Why was this?

YK: If I talk about the timing of the dissolving of Love-de-Lic... Before *Lack of Love* Nishi-san wanted to make a game with ASCII and... How to explain this? Nishi-san wanted to make *Lack of Love*, and Kudo-kun wanted to make *UFO*, so before Love-de-Lic closed already they were...

JS: So the team was fragmenting, and when you left it all collapsed?

YK: <*laughs*> Right, right. And I was ill, and I couldn't work, and so now I cannot talk about the dissolving of Love-de-Lic. <*laughs*>

[35] Yasuhiro Wada

JS: You were the glue that held them together.

YK: No, no, I don't think so. No. Each one had such a strong character, even Kurashima-san, and not only the planners but also the graphics people, they have good skills, and each one had maybe the ability of a director. So the Love-de-Lic era was a miracle of timing. Extremely clever people, talented people, were all gathering at the same time together. It was incredible. <*laughs*>

JS: Would you say it was never meant to last?

YK: Each person wanted to make something, clearly, by themselves, for themselves, of themselves. But how can they come together again? I don't know. After that, several times we talked about a sequel to *Moon*. Sometimes from me, or from others. But often it came down to...

JS: Somebody saying no?

YK: Right. Someone says no, someone says yes.

JS: As you said, *Moon* had the perfect ending.

YK: For me, *Moon 2* is *Chulip*. This is a very correct answer. *Moon* showed the possibility of going outside, into the world. *Chulip* is the next step, really. To find out about your neighbours; to find out who your neighbour is, and that feeling of community...

JS: And getting the girl?

YK: Ah... No, no. There is a very strong theme: happiness is not the same thing for everyone. People, each person, has a different kind of happiness. If you have a good eye to see your neighbours, you'll find there are a lot of strange people in the real world. The *Chulip* story was very much influenced by my phase of ill health. While I was recovering from my heart condition, I was able to walk only around my house. One man, and one old woman, appeared in front of me - all of them were my neighbours. At that moment I had a good relationship with these people in my town. Do you know *Igo*?[36]

JS: Yes, the board game, I play it.

[36] Japanese board game using black and white stones; more complex than chess; goal is to capture territory by encircling the other player's stones

YK: When I could walk 40 metres from my house, then 100 metres, there was an *Igo* house, which was run by an old man. He started at around that time and I was one of his first visitors. He said, "If you don't know it, I can teach you." Then I went there everyday. I didn't have any work, I only went to the hospital once a week. So I walked to his place, played *Igo*, and came back to my house to eat vegetables again.

JS: How good are you at *Igo*?

YK: Hmm... Not so much! <*laughs*> But, you know, it was ***good***. I had a reason to go out. At that moment my personality had become really negative. I did not want to talk to anyone, Kurashima-san was far away, and I was under a lot of pressure in my life. I was thinking, "I'm going to die in 5 years! What will I do? I want to make one last game, but my body can't recover, what do I do?" Naturally, I did not want to go out. But this old man appeared and I often went to his place to play *Igo*. There were only old men there; only old men were coming to see him, and only old men play *Igo*. These old men were all happily talking about illness, and dying, and death. Even if someone had a serious problem, they were happy and smiling, and talking about it. One person started talking about an ache in their leg, then another person would say, "Me too! Me too!" They would all start saying I have it like this, and I have it like that. He has cancer, he has something else. Then they start to play! <*laughs*> It was a happy atmosphere, and I changed my mind. I realised, it is OK to live with illness. If they had not appeared, I would not have started to gather people in my house and discuss game ideas again.

JS: That old guy saved you.

YK: Until I met him, I never went out. After I met him, then I could go to a bar nearby, and I drank *a little bit* of sake with him. He wanted me to sing a song, because I like singing songs. Then I started to think, I could work a little bit. I can go out on the train, a little bit. I had a part-time job, and then I gathered the people again. I could not go a lot, so I said to them, wouldn't you like to come to my house to discuss games, every weekend or something?

Then we started talking about *Chulip*, and while I was discussing ideas for the game, I recovered more quickly. I left my house and went to the house of Suzuki-san, the *Love-de-Lic* boss, and asked if he could help with my idea and introduce it to publishers. Then he said, "Yes! Of course!" He really doesn't talk about negative things, and he just said, "Good! Come on! Do it!" At that moment my idea's name was not *Chulip*, it was *Happy Birthday*. <*laughs*>

JS: The working title was *Happy Birthday*?

YK: Yes, *Happy Birthday*. Maybe there is still a planning document somewhere. The player can kiss the people, and people can follow the player, and the player makes a big parade for the world. The player makes love with others and makes babies a lot, so a big parading tribe would form. This was my gaming idea. <*laughs*> And Wada-san wanted to make *Happy Birthday*, but *Happy Birthday* was too big a project. I wanted to make a world encompassing game. ***A big world*** for the parade! But Wada-san said we don't have enough money for it. Then I said I could make a smaller world, a smaller game. So *Happy Birthday* became *Chulip*.

JS: The world became a small Japanese town.

YK: But it's good, because I have good memories of people in my town, when I was ill.

JS: Is there a character in *Chulip* who represents this old man who helped you?

YK: Unfortunately, <*laughs*> he doesn't appear, but the people who he introduced me to, do appear in *Chulip*.

JS: Characters are based on those you knew?

YK: Half of them are real, and half are original.

JS: Were there any games at Love-de-Lic which were in development, but not released?

YK: At Love-de-Lic? Half completed games? No, while I was at Love-de-Lic I did not see any cancelled games. Until the end of Love-de-Lic, there was no work that was cancelled.

JS: You released everything?

YK: Yes, if something was started. Of course there were a lot of planning documents which I made, and Taro-chan made, but these are just for planning. They're just ideas. If something was started with money, then it was completed.

JS: Can you describe any of these unused ideas?

YK: No! It's too old! <*laughs*> Many of my leftover ideas went into *Happy Birthday*, which became *Chulip.* So it's not worth discussing.

JS: How many unreleased games have you seen?

YK: In my life? For others as well? Then, I don't know really. Maybe I cannot recall them. There are some, but for me... *Rule of Rose* was a bit of a crisis project, but it was eventually completed. Over the whole of my life, actually, I did not start a lot of games, but once I started I completed them.

JS: Even at Square, you were never on a project which got cancelled?

YK: Cancelled by publishers? <*long pause*>

JS: No *Romancing SaGa 4*?

YK: No, no. *Romancing SaGa 4* never existed.

JS: ZUN mentioned that he worked on a lot of games that were cancelled at Taito.

YK: Ah, yes, yes! He was very sorry about that, being a programmer... At Taito, yes, maybe. But around me, no. Maybe it's because I've not belonged to the games industry continuously. You understand? I start, and finish, but for some reason I then go travelling, or I became ill. I think that's why I've not experienced the unhappiness of a cancellation. <*laughs*>

JS: That makes sense. It must be devastating to see all your work thrown away.

YK: Yeah, I'm a lucky guy. I only did some work, and none were cancelled. It is wonderful.

JS: So why did you say *Rule of Rose* was a crisis project?

YK: Because of... <*laughs*> You know, I've experienced a lot of problems in my life, because I went for an operation, for my heart pump, and... I went to London, as the director of *Rule of Rose*. The voice recording was OK. But when I arrived at the studio, they were preparing another script. We were also preparing a script, and the recording time which was booked was too short to accommodate everyone. So we were rushing. Luckily the sound engineer was wonderful, which helped. [This was a learning experience for me.] When I prepared the *No More Heroes* voice recording, we did very well I think. You know, the important thing with voice recording is you ***must*** prepare well the day before the recording. You must prepare yourself 120%! But *Rule of Rose* was my first experience, that's why I could not judge how good it was.

[450 words redacted, off the record]

JS: Did you hear about the controversy? *Rule of Rose* was released in France but not England.

YK: <*laughs*> It's strange. Do you remember the governor of Italy saying bad things about it?[37] This is a well known story. <*laughs*> Then a Twitter follower said, "This guy doesn't want your game sold in Italy. But we can buy the French version." So I was surprised. In Germany they said they could not buy it, and my friend in London said there was no *Rule of Rose*. Only French people could buy it. My friend lives in Paris, and they know my game. Not only *Little King's Story*. They know *Rule of Rose*. Maybe French and Americans only know it?

JS: The French version has an English language option, so I bought that one.

YK: But I understand that some people, you know, the "proper people", don't like it. <*laughs*> Proper people, how would you say it, *square people* don't like it!

[37] Two Italians in fact: mayor of Rome, Walter Veltroni, called for its banning, as did European Union justice minister Franco Frattini

JS: The weird thing is, they'll sell *Grand Theft Auto*, where you can murder prostitutes.

YK: I think each game has a theme, like *Moon*, like *Chulip*, and *Rule of Rose* has a theme. Love is binding. So if someone says I love you, for example. Even if they are teenagers, 15 or 14, they love each other, and they don't love others. I think I would call it a "binding love".

When I was in high school, or junior high school, when I saw the girls in a group, I felt fear. Are they really enjoying a friendship? Are they saying "we are friends" to each other? I wanted to make a game about bullying. An accurate one, especially about the kind of bullying that goes on between girls. The one girl says, "We're the Red Crayon Aristocrats." They are imitating the aristocratic system; there are higher people and lower people.

JS: A hierarchy of social status. But it's also a horror because there are actual monsters.

YK: It's a reflection of what children witness or feel as being the system of society. And it also asks, what is the love that develops between girls and girls? Each girl has a different character; I love you, she loves her.

JS: It's like a web of this girl likes her, who likes her, but this one doesn't like her? *<gestures to different invisible characters>*

YK: Yeah, but they don't show this directly to each other. If they want to maintain the group they won't talk about it directly. It's a secret between them.

JS: It sounds like it has a strong Japanese ethos, protect the harmony of the group.

YK: Yes, but it's not only Japanese. Also, it's a cold type of harmony. Actually, it's not really harmony at all.

JS: Hidden behind that is anger, or sorrow?

YK: Right, right! To me, girls had a fundamental scariness to them. I always wanted to express that in a game somehow. I always wanted to have a certain scariness to a set of female characters. The people who liked it, they really liked it. The fans of it are very dedicated. Even now, on Facebook and so on, I get messages saying, "I really liked *Rule of Rose*, it's a great game, thank you!" Obviously I was not involved in a lot of the development, because of various issues. But I feel the final game was what I wanted. I'm happy with the release. It changed a lot in development. The cut-scenes were already complete, having been decided and controlled by me, so all of the cut-scenes were still the same as before.

JS: What changed then, from your original?

YK: Hmm... I didn't play all of it, so I don't know. The last part was the same.

JS: Did you come up with the idea for the dog?[38]

YK: *<laughs>* Yeah, yeah, yeah. But, you know, *Rule of Rose* has a long history from before development. Before I started to write the "girls" story, I was writing a "boy and a big man" story. But it was refused by producers.

JS: A prototype version featured a boy and...?

YK: The planned draft was a boy and a big man. The big man is a kidnapper, and the main character is a boy, his victim. But the producer didn't like this, so I changed it into a story which examines the fear between girls. Then he said yes and I worked on it.

JS: The publisher thought the kidnapping story was too dangerous a topic?

YK: Yes. *<laughs>* I still have the concept paintings. Do you want to see them?

[38] Throughout the game you're accompanied by Brown, a small dog who helps you

JS: Yes! Can I photograph them?

YK: I don't want you to take a photo, because I'm still thinking I'd like to make this. You can talk about it in the book, but describe it vaguely.

JS: You painted these?

YK: No, the art director.

[Author's note: There were about six paintings. Acrylic on hard board, maybe 75cm x 40cm. They featured a variety of scenes detailing the game. In some scenes the boy appears to be pursued by hostile ghosts. The kidnapper stands facing the audience in one. They attempt to convey the atmosphere, rather than the game mechanics. While the brushwork could be described as beautifully rendered, the scenes themselves were all quite disturbing]

JS: He's kidnapped a few boys?

YK: No, this is the boy, and these are the ghosts of boys. The boy wants to run away from the big man, but these small, old looking men appear, but these are really the ghosts of the boys kidnapped by the man.

JS: This is quite sinister.

YK: So this is a boy's story, about running away from this big guy. And the boy meets another boy, like a *kodomo no tengoku.*[39] Limbo, the space between heaven and hell. Like a spirit.

JS: So this scene in a filthy bathroom, showing a boy with a knife. Is he a ghost, or a real boy?

YK: A ghost. This is the main character here, and these are spirits in limbo.

JS: It's so dark.

YK: Yes, dark! *<laughs>* I wanted to make something very dark.

JS: Would you call it a horror game?

YK: Dark fantasy. I'd call it dark fantasy.

JS: *<reads text aloud>* "Kidnapping, imprisonment, children, bullying, dwarfs, airship, escape." Are these key words?

YK: Yeah, yeah.

JS: This is like *Silent Hill* turned up to 11. I think it was a bit too strong for publishers to accept.

YK: I know, I know, I know. Of course I explained it all, but at that moment... I think with *Rule of Rose*, there were three or four producers. The producers changed, and changed, until I was wondering, who is the producer? This is very prevalent. If I decide and agree on something with the first producer, then that producer changes, the next producer will say, "Oh, that was because of Kimura-san." So there is no responsibility or accountability.

JS: What's going on here? Who are these two adults in the background, fornicating?

YK: Ahh, this was not really my idea. This was only for expressing how we might do it. *<laughs>* And I wanted to show what the limit of sexual expression is.

JS: Do you feel that videogames, as an expressive medium, need to cover difficult topics?

YK: At that moment, for me, I was thinking it is possible for the audience to understand a kidnapping story. But everybody else said no, so!

JS: Books, films, theatre, all cover such topics.

YK: I know, I know. I understand what you are saying. That cinema and books are so exciting, and they can push sexual boundaries, and be risky. With books it's OK, because there are no visuals. While cinema is doing it even though you can see everything. Like Tarantino's films. Of course I want to create a more adult themed story, but it's not only producers, also my friends didn't want me to do a game like this. *<gestures to paintings>*

JS: You'd like to cover mature topics, but it's difficult to convince people?

YK: I wanted to do it. But now I'm so exhausted from fighting against it, against enemies on the outside. Recently I decided, if it's pretty, if it's a pixel character, I can express an adult story.

---

39 子供の天国 - lit. children of heaven

JS: You're going to be expressing a mature and adult story with tiny onions?

YK: <*laughs*> Not now, in the future. So this is my other idea, but I don't know if I'll be able to do it.

JS: Producers are worried that players won't accept sad endings. Do you know *Ico*? The happy ending in that is because the marketing department insisted it had to be added.

YK: *Ico* is OK. After I put a lot of effort into playing that game, I wanted to see the happy ending! It was so hard! <*laughs*>

JS: Have you played *Panzer Dragoon Saga*? That had such a beautifully sad ending.

YK: I don't want to deny players a happy ending, but I want to make an interesting story, an interesting ending. So after you've spent a lot of time playing the game, what you feel is happiness. Games are fundamentally about making humans feel ecstasy. From the first moment when game culture started, the games were about winners and losers; cleared or not cleared. Erased or not. Shoot or not. Make enemies vanish or not. It's all for the ecstasy of your brain. But! I want to say that other media, such as movies, have the same issue, though some of them are good at showing new philosophies. Some animated films show a new horizon for the world. But how can games do this? From my view, smartphone games and big Hollywood-style triple-A games, all are aiming to create ecstasy. I don't want to say joy... It's like that instant, that moment in sex.

JS: The climax?

YK: Yes, climax! People want to feel an immediate climax. I don't want to say it's wrong, because it's part of being human. But another part of being human is seeking and thinking about another world, another philosophy. I'm making a game for this now. But I don't know if it will succeed or not. I use the ecstasy analogy, and also I want to convey my story using this. While you are playing it feels good, but after playing the game that extra layer of story stays with you. There are a lot of different kinds of satisfaction in life. It's not only sex!

JS: You want to create a game with depth?

YK: <*laughs*> At first it looks like something light, but afterwards feels deeper. These are some of the thoughts in my mind, but I am unsure of how to express them fully.

JS: Like the *Mother*[40] series by Shigesato Itoi. It looks light-hearted but covers serious issues.

YK: I liked the *Mother* games. *Mother 1* and *Mother 2* are good.

JS: *Mother* 1 had no kanji. On Twitter you suggested we should all write like that?[41]

YK: No, I was just playing around. There is no philosophy behind it. It's just that someone used only hiragana on Twitter, so I was playing along. You know, using only hiragana and katakana without kanji, it's hard to read for the Japanese. But I like it, since it controls my timing of how quickly I read a story. It's done more slowly. <*pretends to read some text, each word is distinctly separate*> You - are - stupid. - Yes - I - am. <*laughs*>

JS: You put everything into *Little King's Story*. Are you upset that Marvellous owns the series?

YK: <*laughs*> This is very simple to answer. I feel good. I don't want to say I'm upset. From the first moment there was a contract, right? Of course this can be a problem. But I made promises, and they made promises, so it's OK. If I have any criticism regarding the rights I should talk about the whole games industry in Japan, because they don't want to give the IP to individual artists. But this is OK, because with *Little King's Story*, I made a promise by signing the contract. So as a man, I should not complain. And also, this was the first time for me where a "part 2" appeared.

JS: The first sequel to something you created?

YK: A sequel appeared! So I should say thank you very much. I can say that if people are playing the Vita version, and someone knows the Wii version, I have confidence that the Wii version is much better. <*laughs*> So it's OK, people know what is Kimura-san's work, what is not Kimura-san's work. <*laughs*>

---

[40] *Earthbound* in English

[41] Using only hiragana and katakana can be difficult to read; omitting kanji can imbue a child-like tone

JS: How does it feel to play a continuation of your vision, through the interpretation of another?

YK: Ooh... <*pause*> Like *Chulip*, *Little King's Story* has a lot of characters who are very personal to me. Like Howser,[42] who comes from Switzerland, really. When I see a different Howser, I feel strange! But it's just a very small thing. <*laughs*> I don't feel any disrespect. I can only say thanks to Marvellous. When I play it on Vita, I have just one request. I want to play *Little King's Story*, the same as the Wii version, but on the Vita. Then I can walk around with it on me and show people.

JS: I see!

YK: No, no, it's OK. Sometimes people want me to say, "I'm angry", or something like that. But really, I don't feel anything like that. Of course I feel a little sadness, but a lot of happiness too, that a sequel appeared. I don't mind. It's their job, and they noticed that if they made a Vita version, they could gain a little bit of money. I'm very glad, because the original *Little King's Story* cost a lot of money to develop, but maybe it wasn't so profitable. Of course it did well, but I think they anticipated more.

JS: When it came out, my colleagues said it was one of the few games worth owning a Wii for.

YK: <*laughs*> That's right, but... Also, when Metacritic or EDGE gave *Little King's Story* good scores, I was surprised! I had a lot of confidence and was I waiting to hear people say good things, but not to such a large degree! <*laughs*>

JS: EDGE isn't a good barometer to judge games - they've given great games low scores.

YK: I know how difficult it can be to get points in EDGE, that's why I was reading again and again the review. <*whispers*> Oooohhhhh... This guy is playing my game!

JS: Do you have many notes on planning games?

YK: Do you want to see something? This is my board game. <*Mr Kimura brings out **Potato Saga**, his home-made board game, involving little potato knights - some footage is on the accompanying DVD*>

JS: Tell me about this board game. It's just with dice, and it's a race to the top of the tower?

YK: Yes, like this. <*rolls dice*> One, two, three. In Japanese it's called *Jaga Saga*.[43] And *jaga* is potatoes, so in English *Potato Saga*. These characters are potatoes.

JS: When did you make this?

YK: This year? I started to recover my creativity. This was one of my creations.

JS: Do these characters have names?

YK: Yes, yes. There are four. This is Baron, Red Baron! This is the Doctor. And this is father, Daddy, and his son.

JS: Are they a family?

YK: No, each one is called a "potato knight", and each one is competing to reach the top of the castle, to help the Queen of the Potatoes. The father and the boy, and the Doctor, or this Baron, each one is fighting each other. So there is no relationship. These two are family, but the other two are not related.

JS: The Red Baron looks a little bit like the main character in your film *Junko*.

[42] The king's adviser who encourages world conquest

[43] In Japanese, Irish potatoes are called "*jagaimo*"

YK: Ahh! It's because I made them, so they have a similar design. *<laughs>* You noticed! You know, this is very good, because if you do this... *<pushes a character over>* Automatically it goes like this. *<character rights itself >*

JS: The base is weighted so they stand back up.

<we spend time knocking over the knights to watch them then get back up - we both laugh>

YK: Of course if I do like this, he won't get up. *<moves a knight into an awkward position>*

JS: Look at the little one, he's really good at it.

YK: For testing my creativity I am trying to experiment a lot. For example, with this, it's only for four people to play. Four people can play in front of me, with this. This is a very important ritual. For example, a videogame goes out to the world, and now everybody can download it without needing to get a physical version. So without my knowing it people can play the game, but I cannot feel if they're happy or not. What I'm trying to find, or understand, is what is my purpose? What do I want to feel? Maybe I like it when someone is smiling when playing my game, so in that case I will feel satisfied with making smaller games like this, where there's only one copy of it. If four people play it in front of me, and they are happy, I will be very glad. If I can succeed, then I can verify what I was originally thinking. Not only with this, but other things. This year, in April [2013], I was on a live stage with Poripori Club.[44] The club members with me wanted to make games in front of a live audience. It was really... Ridiculous!

No, it's impossible to play. In front of the audience we tried to talk about the start of a game, making the plans, through to the end when completing the game, and it was then played by the audience. We only had three hours, and yet still we made a game.

<shows the game on iPad - it features what looks like a frog, moving around a field; seems to be four areas, one in each corner>

YK: See? Terrible! *<laughs>* Four engineers were working on each area. If you push like this, the character moves like this. If I push like this, then they move like this.

JS: Who was programming this on stage?

YK: My friends, called App Bank Games. A company which develops games using Unity. I would draw, and we would discuss, and there was a leader who relayed instructions to his juniors. And they churned it out. Of course, this is not a complete game, but I wanted to entertain the audience instead of simply making games. We were making the game together. So while myself and the team were making this game, we were also asking the audience, what should we make? What should I do?

JS: It's dangerous to ask the public - because they often give unfeasible ideas.

YK: Yeah, but so what! People are afraid of this, and I am afraid of this too. Sometime I am still thinking like this: I should not listen to the opinions of others, at least until the beta version. But this year, after Grasshopper, I wanted to experiment with something new.

The idea is not a game idea or a game story. My idea relates to how we make games. What is the purpose? Regarding this game, I was working for an audience of 200 people, who were all in front of me. That's 200 people who were watching and talking, *<claps>* and clapping, or booing, and things like that. Meanwhile, we are talking about how hard it is to make games, and we must show our creation to the audience. It's like live music, it was all improvisation. This was very experimental and I was not thinking "success is good". An experiment is... Well, it's an experiment! So I don't need to achieve success, because an experiment is an experiment! *<laughs>*

This was also an experiment. *<gestures to Potato Saga>* But this was a success, I think, for me.

JS: All by hand. What's this made from?

YK: *<laughs>* Clay which has dried. These stones were taken from a river. These are all the same material. It was really cheap. 5'000 yen maybe?[45] Next week, in November, the game board market is coming. It's for amateurs and fans. So I'll bring this and have people play it.

Right now I don't know what my future holds. But I'm thinking about what I love and what I want to be. Without thinking about

---

[44] http://poriporiclub.blogspot.com

[45] About £33 / $50

videogames, I often love to create something. Like toys. What can I show you...?

<Mr Kimura wanders into adjacent room>

YK: I often go to Switzerland, as I mentioned before. I had an exhibition in Switzerland, and these are some of my drawings. This is Japan.

<the artwork itself was stunning - ink on paper, depicting various fantastical vistas>

JS: It's submerged. Was this after the tsunami?

YK: No, I drew these a long, long time ago. This is Hokkaido. This is Kyushu. My idea is, a long, long time ago, the islands were big creatures. They died and turned into bones, a skeleton, and lot of other smaller creatures started to live on the bones. Then it becomes Japan. Mt Fuji would be a big bone sticking up.

JS: This could make an amazing game.

YK: Yes, yes, maybe. I like to create worlds.

JS: It's a good *sekaikan*?

YK: Hmm... *Sekaikan* is a word related to storytelling. But what I want to say is, creating a world... How do you know the word *sekaikan*?

JS: *<explains>*

YK: *Sekaikan*, this word is like a curse of Japanese games. Yeah, a curse. *Sekaikan*... Terrible! *<laughs>* It's funny, of course, but when someone starts to say that *sekaikan* is very important for videogames, or role-playing games... The JRPG was born from these discussions, maybe! *<laughs>* I dislike JRPGs.

JS: I really like this one with the eggs.

YK: These are the first... You know, first of all, one big man became an egg, and from the egg hatched a dragon baby. Ah, I feel nostalgic looking at these. They're numbered, but I can't remember the order. The dragon flew like this...

JS: There's factories on its back! Is this an onion?

YK: Yes, this is an onion, but it's also a time machine! The time machine is checking what happened in the past.

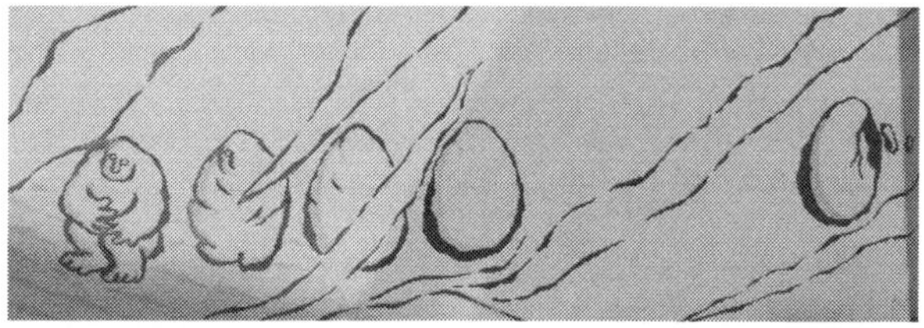

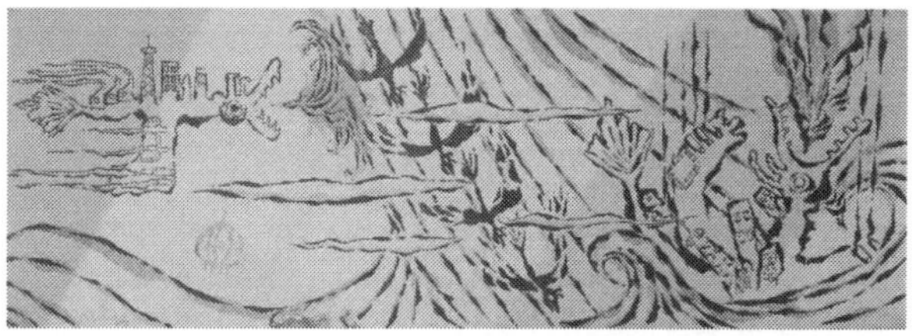

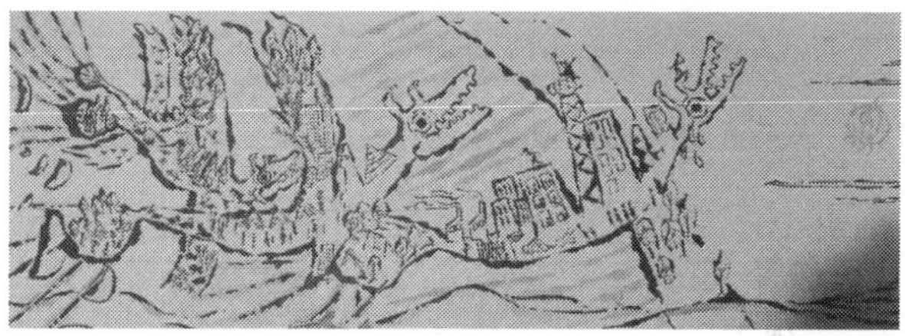

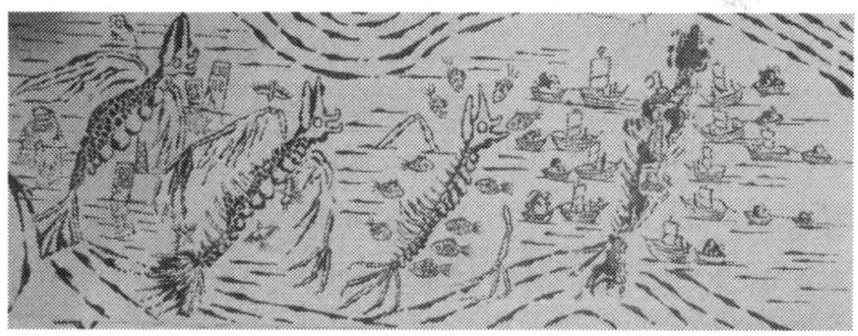

JS: This was exhibited in Switzerland?

YK: Yes, only in Switzerland. Not in Japan. For the exhibit of my drawings, I often wanted to include a story. So this is one of them.

JS: Nobody knows about it, except the Swiss?

YK: Yes, my Swiss friends. Really, I don't want to show too many people. But for you it's OK.

JS: Why don't you want to show people?

YK: It's my world, I don't need to show people.

JS: But it might make others feel happy.

YK: Really?

JS: Why is the time machine an onion?

YK: I don't know. This was drawn quite far in the past, during my wild Love-de-Lic days. It's not related to Onion Games. But for me, the onion is like an ancient creature, it's symbolic.

JS: What allows an onion to time travel? Does the peeling of skin send it through time?

YK: Actually, this is similar to an onion, but it's not an onion. <*looks through dictionary*> I'm very glad you're interested in this.

JS: It's a shame to keep it in a cupboard.

YK: Really? I don't know, when I drew these, I wanted to make it move, like a game. But at that moment it was not possible to make it move. Now maybe I could do it. <*finds word in dictionary*> Ah! It's a bulb!

JS: Like a tulip bulb?

YK: Yes, like a tulip bulb. A wild bulb can be a time machine because it grows underground in the same style as before - ancient bulbs were also underground. Maybe it's possible for the bulbs to see all of the eras of history, because it has existed from a long, long time ago. That's why I wanted to use them for a time machine, as a metaphor.

JS: That's deep.

YK: So when I'm not making games, I'm still making something. These kinds of things are not possible to sell. It's from the old room, before I moved house. Back then it was OK, but in the intervening six months insects have eaten it. I don't know why.

JS: Because it tastes good.

YK: <*laughs*> It must taste good - this special paper is expensive!

JS: What are your memories of working at Grasshopper. You joined with Wada-san?

YK: Actually, not with him. I didn't know Suda-san was gathering so many people, when Suda-san started to talk to me. Is that important? I have memories of Grasshopper. I was working there on *Shadows of the Damned*, and *Lollipop Chainsaw*, and I remember the good thing was that I met Massimo Guarini. He was an Italian guy who had been working in the games industry for a long time. He's a Japanese maniac who loves Japanese music and animation, and he is a really good guy. He speaks Italian, English, and Japanese. <*in an awed tone*> What an amazing person! I liked him, and now he is the boss of an indie game company, Ovosonico.

JS: Did you work with Tim Rogers?

YK: <*laughs*> Do you know Tim Rogers?

JS: And Brandon Sheffield.

YK: Yeah, yeah. They're wonderful. They loved *Chulip*. They came to ask about what I am doing, when I started to make *Little King's Story*, and I thought they would ask me about that. But no, they wanted to ask about why I made *Chulip*!

JS: *Chulip* was released in America.

YK: <*laughs*> I was surprised! We translated it from Japanese to Korean, first. After that I don't know what happened. When I joined Marvellous as a producer I asked them, and the Korean version was pending, while the American version was going ahead. "What? How can you localise it without Punchline?" Because at that time Punchline was already gone. Some very high level engineers reverse-engineered it, and they translated it into English, and Natsume sold it. In the end I was glad, because Love-de-Lic games didn't go overseas. But actually, mine often go around the world. <*laughs*> So I'm lucky. Really, I'm glad that someone in the US can play *Chulip*. But at the same time I wonder, "Do they understand what I was writing? No one asked me to read it, or asked, what is this?"

I remember during that era, if someone wanted to create a Japanese scene, the guys in America always wanted to make a Japanese person be a ninja. Either a ninja, or the Edo era. Maybe the Sengoku era too. Like samurai. But I wanted to express old Japanese towns, my old hometown in the 1960s, 1970s and 1980s. I wanted to show Japanese characters, but these characters exist in the real world, everywhere. Someone who drinks too much, the old woman, the younger girls gossiping, a man who owns an antique shop. Everywhere it's the same. *Chulip* is really filled with my soul. I want to recover the atmosphere of the *Chulip* era.

JS: If someone were to play only one Mr Kimura game, which would you recommend?

YK: It's up to the person. For those who love sub-cultures, I want them to play *Chulip*. But for the general public, I say *Little King's Story* is my maximum work, so please play it. <*laughs*> With *Little King's Story* I was still writing all the sentences by myself. Someone wrote it, but then I rewrote everything. <*laughs*> Even though I was a producer, the story parts, all of the text, I was writing it in Japanese first. And for the English version I read everything, so at that time my English ability really improved. The wonderful thing is, the other language versions, the French part, and Spanish part, I believe they worked well. Maybe these foreign language versions, for my later games, the quality comes from my experience working on *Rule of Rose*. I remembered the problems that can nearly happen when you don't control it well. So the English in my later games is good. I hope.

JS: *Rule of Rose* was a valuable life experience?

YK: At the end of the day, I can say so, yes. I knew what to be careful of. Now, suddenly, I've given up working as a producer, so I will never use these skills. For making multi-language versions I need to get some help, but it's not as a producer. I'm not writing the sentences for my next game. Because I don't want to translate them. I'm making games where it's not necessary to translate them. Minimal text.

JS: Fans might be willing to translate it.

YK: People say so. Do you think I have fans?

JS: You have lots of fans.

YK: This is maybe the difference between me and you. I don't have much faith in the world. Some people like my work, and some maybe still keep an eye on what I'm doing. That's why I'm very grateful. But at the same time, maybe my fan level is not as big as the big named creators, like Kojima-san, or Miyamoto-san, or Suda-san. They are very powerful. I'm more of a wanderer. No one can catch the wanderer, right? When I'm making games I feel good, when I cannot make my games I'm not feeling so good. From now I should concentrate on making my games, like *Potato Saga*. This *Potato Saga* does not need help from a lot of people. Maybe I do not want to work with a lot of people, and I do not want to care if people like me or not.

JS: It's easier to fulfil a vision with a small team?

YK: Not only a small team, but also maybe I'm jealous of other people who have a lot of fans. But at the same time, I do not want to hope that I will get a lot of fans. I do not want to think like this. Do you know what I'm saying?

JS: You want a small group who appreciate you?

YK: Yes, yes. Maybe after I complete my game with a small team, if I show my work I don't know how many people will notice it. This next step, if 100 people love my game, if 1'000, or even if it's just 10 people. The next step is if someone says they are happy to play my game, then these guys are my fans.

When I was at a publisher, and when I was the chief creative officer, maybe I was losing my way. And now I've run away from all of these responsibilities, and I've decided to go back to creating just one small thing. Now I'm recovering well. I want to know, what is my best creation? Really, I don't know if I can make these creatures again and again. If someone wants this I can make them. It's easy, by the way! It took seven days.

JS: It took one week to make *Potato Saga*?

YK: Not continuously seven days, but seven days over the course of two months. The last two days I had to work really hard. Plus I needed to prepare all of the parts before combining them. But I think you're wondering: So, what happens next? What is the next step for me? I do not know. I cannot live off this *Potato Saga* game; it can't sustain my life. If I want to survive I need to make money to eat food. I don't think my potato knights can pay the bills! *<laughs>*

JS: Perhaps you could try crowdfunding?

YK: Yeah, recently everybody has said so, but that's not my thinking.

JS: Actually, it's very stressful.

YK: Is it stressful?

JS: Very! Before I had one editor, now I have over 1'000 editors!

YK: I thought so! *<laughs>* Before everybody jumped on board with Kickstarter, I was thinking should I try it? Even though I don't have many fans. But while I was thinking about it, I thought, this is the same pressure as working as a producer! In which case, what's the point? Then Inafune-san was talking at TGS, and he seemed to have much less pressure than other producers, because a producer must think about the whole of a project: retail distribution, marketing, development, target audience, and so on. But with Kickstarter we must only take care of the audience. This is a good explanation, and after this, I was considering it, but still... I don't think I can stand in front of an audience of millions. *<laughs>* If I can succeed on Kickstarter with a new kissing game, then I will howl, and jump, and shout, and dance with happiness!

JS: About *Chulip*. The English manual was actually a guide which explained all the puzzles. Did they do the same for the Japanese manual?

YK: Is that really so? No, the Japanese manual is terrible. Really terrible. You cannot get the point of anything! Only the way of the controls. Really? The puzzles? Don't you guys want to find out the answers to the puzzles by yourselves?

JS: I do. But I think Natsume were worried that players couldn't solve them.

<Mr Kimura gets up to find the manual>

YK: They can do it. Because all the puzzles at that time were inspired by *Myst*. I really loved *Myst*, a lot.

JS: *Chulip* was influenced by *Myst*.

YK: *<laughs>* Yes, the puzzle parts. And I don't mind putting difficult puzzles in *Chulip*, because if people can play *Myst*, then it's OK. You do understand what this design is? *<shows Japanese Chulip manual>* This is a very famous style of Japanese notebook for children.

JS: *Boku no Natsuyasume* has a similar thing.

YK: Yes, yes! And we wrote only ridiculous things in it. This section is how to use the controls, and this is how to view the screen. It's very, very simple. Very short.

JS: Here's an image of an onion! A trend?

YK: It seems so, yes! I am only noticing this now. Here is a blank part for the player to write notes.

JS: It's completely different in the US manual. The writing is quite funny, in a whimsical style.

<shows a book - it's filled with detailed notes and screens, with some clever design ideas>

YK: This is a guide book for *Chulip*, how to complete the game, which we designed with Enterbrain. If you look through it, some of the sections are portrayed as newspaper clippings. A lot of the design weaves in explanations of how things happened. We tried to fill it with jokes, especially for explanations of things.

JS: A page with profiles. They had this in the English manual, but shrunk down.

YK: *<flipping the book to the back >* Usually we read from this direction, so if you flip the book to the back, the inside is a section of comics. Like Japan's *Shonen Jump*, or something. It's a small joke. <*laughs*>

JS: So, tell me about Onion Games.

YK: How do I explain Onion Games? In 2012 I went to GDC, and I saw the IGF, and I was so surprised and excited, because a lot of indie games were shown, and they displayed a style akin to wild nature. So I started to feel tears in my eyes. After that I made my company, but I could not start immediately, because there were no members and I need to work in order to eat. That's why Onion Games didn't move forward. After one year I started Onion Games, and the main members were Kurashima-san and Ikeda-san. But actually we are not three people, we were kind of the centre of my world - for example, we are not only making one game. We are working on at least four games.

JS: All for iOS?

YK: Yes. One guy is living in Fukuoka, who was an engineer on *Little King's Story*, and one guy is in another place, who is also an engineer. It's like we're creating a new relationship between the individual indie game developers, so maybe if my plan succeeds and I can show my game, then I want to go all over the world to sell and talk about my Onion Games story. But now, all I can say is, after *Potato Saga*, and after a lifetime of making games, my next step is to find a new way of making games and form a small team without company rules. I want to find a good marriage, like wine and food, between myself and the other teams. Since each one has a unique skill, or strong ability. For example one team has a strong programming ability, but they don't have art. If someone wants to make a game, but he cannot write code, then I want to put these two together. Through Onion Games, now at least, I wanted to try 10.

JS: Ten games?

YK: Ten teams. Of course for each one I want to provide an idea. How is this idea, how is that one? But now it's been reduced to four teams. So, what happened to the other six? Well, the six other teams... Making indie games is really hard on each person's life. I'm not a big publisher. What I can do is combine and tune, and maybe self-publish. They don't want to say, "We give up!" Naturally they are leaving the project without saying a word. Like fading out.

JS: People joined, then some left?

YK: I don't want to say I made 10 teams and suddenly 6 left. It happened slowly. One appeared, one vanished. Two appeared, one vanished. One still remains. Like this. Now I'm taking care of one, two, three, and this fourth part is pending by myself. Because I must work hard for this.

JS: So you've got four project at the moment? How far along, percentage wise, is each one?

YK: Ah... The projects, maybe 20%, 20%, all 20%. Not so much progress. Each one is working only one day a week like this. Yeah, of course, we are indies! We have to work for others when we're not making our games!

JS: Everyone has a day job, and Onion Games is a side project?

YK: Yes, of course! I must work for others too. For a proper job? I cannot say. This is contractual work. I can say for example that I want Kurashima-san to draw the character design, or I want Ikeda-san to make the game designs for other teams. <*laughs*> This is a part-time job of videogames.

JS: It sounds like a labour of love.

YK: Yeah, yeah. Also, I am living off this kind of part-time job, very much. <*laughs*> Maybe I should talk to publishers, but it still feels like it's not the time to talk. I will have a chance to discuss my plans. Maybe when you are publishing your book I will be ready to have discussions with publishers. But not now. I'm really concentrating on what is good, what I should make, and what is the next step. Even though I'm spending my individual bank account money a lot, I am thinking so what!

JS: I hope your projects go well.

YK: I also hope so. That's why, around me, there are very talented people. They are professionals, they are highly skilled as "real" videogame developers. They are ready to join if my project goes ahead with a publisher's backing. But I tell them, wait a little bit. We should be ready. First, we should invent a good idea, because once we start making this game we cannot go back. We cannot change the fundamental idea. So until we find out what that solid part is, we should not talk about money too much. That's why people around me are very understanding. They don't come asking for money. They are coming to discuss the game itself. You understand?

Of course they're concerned about the salary, but they're thinking about the game itself. It's a new atmosphere. I should take care of them, really. But at the moment I do not have a plan to take on the bigger world.

After the Tokyo Game Show I felt that a new world is on the horizon for indie developers. Sony and other publishers are ready for them.

JS: Are you interested in PC game publishers?

YK: Yes, of course. If I can make a game for them, it will be like *Chulip*, really. If I want to make something like *Chulip*, with a character living in a world, my world, I should use the PC first. When I was making *Chulip*,[46] the PC games market was very small in Japan. Very, very small. Now it is still small, but I feel something is coming. People are thinking that if gamers want to play real games, then the PC is good. Now we are watching Steam - only a few people in Japan are aware of its existence. I don't know why. Maybe people in Japan don't have an interest in downloading from an English web service? Really, it's things like *La Mulana* which influenced us to play indie games on PC.

JS: And *Doukutsu Monogatari*? (*Cave Story*)

YK: This is the pressure I feel. ZUN and Amaya appeared in front of me suddenly, after I came back from IGF. I asked, "How do indie Japanese developers do it?" Then suddenly Amaya-san's friend invited me to drink with Amaya-san. One year ago, I met with Amaya-san, and he's a really good guy! Very humble, and very eloquent when talking about games. He said to me, "It's OK. I spent many years working on just one game. But I don't know what I'll do next." But he makes very beautiful games. Then, next, ZUN appeared and said, "You don't need to think about the whole of the market. You should concentrate on the audience of the type of game you want to make." *<laughs>* These two guys suddenly appear and they start to talk about their philosophies. I was surprised, and their words encouraged me. *<adopts drone voice>* "Don't worry too much about the market, I spent five years, so what!" - "I'm only making shooting games, so what!" *<laughs>*

The games industry thinks in this manner: the smartphone market is like *this*, the smartphone users are like *this*, that's why we must make games like *this*. *<gestures with hands>* These are calculations by the market researchers. Not only market research, but a lot of things outside of development influences the creation of games. ZUN said to me, making games based on your impulses is OK.

JS: Please consider my book an open platform to say anything you like. Is there anything to add?

YK: The most important thing about it is Onion Games, really. Onion Games is my future, even though I'm trembling when speaking with companies. I don't know what is coming, I don't know what is good or what is bad, regarding Onion Games. But it is my future, so please write about Onion Games.

JS: Can you talk about any of your games?

YK: *<laughs>* I am thinking, first of all, we should complete our game without other people's money. Of course we will publish it, but it is difficult for us to sell it. But this is a very important step, to show that we made it. Once we succeed, I want to propose our new project, and then I can gather 10 or 15 people to make one game. They are like freelancers. So I want to start, not a triple-A title, but something middle-tier, of the same size and scope as *Chulip*. If I can find a good idea for something, other than *Chulip*. Now I am starting to think about this, in preparation for suggesting it to a publisher, but not now. Once I'm ready to publish the game, what I'm thinking is, I will try to sell it directly to the world. For example I might go to Mexico, and go to a cafe and have a small event with my friends or fans, maybe 10 or 20 I don't know, and in front of them I can make the game available on iOS in the region of Mexico. If I move to each country, and have an event that shows my new game, maybe explain it directly myself, in front of people, then it will be nice. So I want to go all over the world.

---

[46] Development started around 2000 or just before

~Appearing in a later volume~

Takashi TOKITA

Aziz HINOSHITA

If you enjoyed Mr Kimura's recollections of his time at **Square**, then check out later volumes of *The Untold History of Japanese Game Developers*, which will feature an interview with Takashi Tokita, the gentleman behind *Final Fantasy IV* and *Live-a-Live*. He reveals some fascinating points about Square's early days. And also Aziz Hinoshita, who played a key role in Square's localisation department, which included work on an unreleased game. Prior to this he worked at Athena, the company behind the *Dezaemon* series of shoot-em-up creation titles, as a pixel artist.

横田 幸次

YOKOTA, Kouji

DOB: 4 December 1963 / Birthplace: Sapporo, Hokkaido / Blood Type: A

~ Selected Portfolio ~

Nihon Telenet

Mugen Senshi Valis	- Famicom, 1987	(Graphic design)
Megami Tensei	- PC-88, 1987	(Graphic design)
Luxsor	- PC-88, 1987	(Graphic design)
XZR: Idols of Apostate	- PC-88, 1988	(Graphic design)

Nihon Falcom

Ys III	- Multiple computer versions, 1989	(Graphics design, maps)
Dragon Slayer: Eiyuu Densetsu	- PC-88, 1989	(Graphics design)
Dinosaur	- PC-88, 1990	(Graphics design)

Freelance (cross reference with work for Quintet and Shade)

Gaiares	- Mega Drive, 1990	(Game design and graphic design	- Telenet)
Dragon Quest V	- SFC, Sep 1992	(Graphics design, credited *Kouji Yokoya*	- Enix)
Emerald Dragon	- PC Engine, Jan 1994	(Uncredited	- Hudson)
Lunar: Eternal Blue	- Mega CD, Dec 1994	(Boss designer	- Game Arts)
Seiya Monogatari	- PC Engine, 1995	(Map graphics	- Hudson)

Quintet

Actraiser	- SNES, 1990	(Graphic design, localisation)
Soul Blazer	- SNES, 1992	(Graphic design)
Illusion of Gaia	- SNES, 1993	(Game designer and graphic design)
Robotrek	- SNES, 1994	(Character and monster designer)

Shade (incumbent)

Granstream Saga	- PlayStation, 1997	(Director, game design & systems)

Interview with Kouji Yokota - ***(contains Lunar: Eternal Blue ending SPOILERS)***
27 September & 10 October 2013, Shade company offices, Tokyo

When starting this project there were several names which readers repeatedly requested coverage on. One was Super Famicom-era developers Quintet, which spun off from Nihon Falcom. Another was Nihon Falcom itself, plus Nihon Telenet and Game Arts. Mr Yokota has worked for all four of these companies, in addition to being head of Shade, which itself spun off from Quintet. Originally I contacted a member of staff from Terranigma, via his brother on Twitter. The Terranigma developer said he could be interviewed and promised to put me in touch with a colleague. This plan fizzled out, but determined to get some Quintet coverage I contacted fellow writer Sorrel Tilley, who put me in touch with Mr Yokota, who in turn invited me to join him at the Sony Indies Stream party, which led to some valuable business card exchanges that ultimately saved the project when it was faced with sabotage by malcontents. In fact I interviewed Mr Yokota twice. There were difficulties with the material from the first interview, so it was worth visiting again. The two interviews have been edited into one - additionally, two fluent Japanese speakers gave the audio and text another pass. As a neat bonus I also met the developer of Popful Mail, Jun Nagashima. As it turned out, several former Falcom employees were now at Shade. Joining me on the day was Preservation Society President Joseph Redon, who brought with archive materials related to Mr Yokota's career. When we walked into the meeting room we spotted something special...

JS: There's a PC-88FH Black model[1] over there!

KY: *<laughs>* Yes, that's right.

JS: Boxes of floppies! Can you tell us about this?

KY: Actually, I tried to activate them and they still work. Would you like to see it?

JS: I'd love to. Can I shoot some video?[2]

<Mr Yokota moves over to the machine>

KY: I don't want any video to be linked with me. So whatever you shoot... If you post it somewhere, I don't want to be mentioned.

<the PC-88 comes to life, playing the classic opening track to Falcom's Ys III, loud and rich>

KY: You can turn down the volume.

JS: Was this your personal machine? Did you develop on it?

KY: This is the machine I used to use at work. More than 20 years ago.

JS: Do you still have your development materials?

KY: We needed a PC-9801 in addition to this, but I don't have that.

<JR explains Game Preservation Society>

JR: At the Game Preservation Society we're putting a lot of effort into preserving your work.

KY: I actually have a lot of these. *<refers to old development floppy disks>* But I don't have the hardware to play them.

JR: We have all the needed hardware at the Game Preservation Society. We have developed unique techniques to preserve old games.

KY: I have all the old games, but I'm not making any use of them. So maybe there's certain things I can donate.

JR: This would be very helpful, but on the contrary, we already have a huge archive of games, including yours. So in fact, if sometime you need your own work for anything, we would be happy to help ***you***.

KY: Thank you very much.

JS: What was the first game you saw?

KY: If you're talking about videogames, it was *Space Invaders*. And there used to be an upright driving game, I think that probably was the first game I was exposed to.

---

[1] A very rare model of PC-88 computer, obviously too old to be used for development; there were floppies nearby, and I wondered if these were development disks from Mr Yokota's early days. I saw the label later - they were official demo disks used in game shops

[2] I took video, but the screen scrolled

JS: When did you want to join the industry?

KY: I actually had my first computer at around the age of 20. So I was already interested in that kind of field. And I really like arcade games; *Space Harrier* by Sega I found very impressive, so I was very much attracted to the industry.

JS: Was your first job at Nihon Telenet?

KY: My first job, yes.

JS: Many answered wanted adverts when joining companies. How did you join Telenet?

KY: My friend was already working there and so he introduced me to the company.

JS: Who was your friend?

KY: Not really a friend, but someone who was senior in age.[3] We had a common friend from school, or acquaintance, through which I came to know that person, but he was older than me. So he wasn't really a friend of mine. He suggested there were some software houses I could try for an interview, so I decided to take some interviews. Back then, the titles of Nihon Telenet were quite attractive, so I chose that company as the first one I had an interview with. Then I was fortunate to be recruited.

JS: Nihon Telenet had a strong visual style.

KY: Yes, they did! *<laughs>*

JS: Which other companies did you apply for?

KY: Well, actually... Game Arts... There were some other candidates that I wanted to try, but Nihon Telenet was the first company I tried and I was hired, so I didn't get to.

JS: Nihon Telenet had a bit of a rivalry with Nihon Falcom and Zainsoft,[4] didn't it?

<We look through Comtiq magazine, at the Zainsoft spread, showing Jun Mukai and the CEO, Mr Miyamoto, learing over him>

KY: He's 16. Japanese regulations say you're not allowed to work too much. But he worked all the time! *<laughs>* He got Telenet into big trouble - the police visited the office!

JS: *<laughs>* Did you like Zainsoft's games?

KY: I liked *Tritorn*.[5] It's nice. But *Tritorn 2* was... Was *Tritorn 2* released?

JS: Yes, maybe in 1989?

KY: *<referring to Jun Mukai>* He left the company before *Tritorn 2* was completed. So I believe someone took over and finished it. After that I worked with him at Telenet.

JS: He joined Telenet? Zainsoft is interesting - I've heard rumours it was funded by yakuza...

KY: *<laughs>* Is that right? I didn't know that. But back then there were many companies who were founded by "them".

JS: *<refers to head of Zainsoft>* I also heard Miyamoto-san was difficult to work for because he was violent towards staff.

KY: I heard from him [Jun Mukai], yes. He was working without being allowed to leave the company office.

JS: Yes! I heard that! Miyamoto locked staff in!

KY: *<laughs>* He had to escape from Miyamoto-san's territory and relocate from Osaka to Tokyo so that Miyamoto-san would not chase after him. So that's how he joined the company and got the [Telenet] job. He was 16 then. So he was way over the legitimate allowed working hours stipulated by the law. There was a raid by the regulatory agency. The company, Nihon Telenet, was asked to show them his time card, as to how many hours he had logged in. Since he didn't have his own place when he joined Telenet, he rented a place from Telenet

---

[3] A sempai

[4] Zainsoft (aka: Sein Soft & Xainsoft) was an infamous computer game developer (both for its bizarrely amazing/awful games and its CEO physically beating staff); it's covered in a later book volume

[5] トリトーン; a side-scrolling action-RPG for Japanese computers, similar to *Xanadu* or *Legacy of the Wizard*

right next to the company office. He would either be working at the office or sleeping at his apartment. And I would also show up at the company, around 10 o'clock in the morning, working until midnight most evenings, and then leaving in order to catch the last train. So I was putting in, what, 14 or 15 hours a day? *<laughs>* Whereas he was putting in even longer hours than I was, because he was right next to the company!

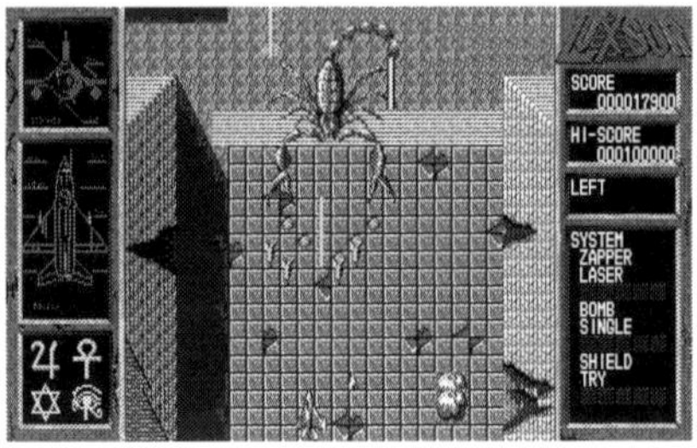

JS: Wow!

KY: Of course I had to, you know, spend the night at the company when the deadline for the software was coming up. We had to debug the software before completion, so we kind of stayed up all night to do that. Although we knew that the program was buggy, we weren't able to identify what the cause was. And since we were staying up all night it was not efficient, because we were very sleepy.

JS: Zainsoft games had so many bugs, many could be not be completed.

KY: That's right. I heard a rumour back then that they came up with this sneaky way to hide the bugs. *<laughs>* Supposedly they made the games so difficult it was impossible to get to the end, so the bugs would never be found! They did things like that because the company president would threaten them, saying: "Get this done by tomorrow, or I'll kill you." That kind of thing. In the past things were quite nasty.

When I was working for Nihon Telenet, I was in the middle of working on a particular game, but someone told me that they had seen my exact game already being sold in the computer shops! I was shocked. It wasn't even finished. But I guess the company had to deliver something or otherwise they wouldn't get paid. Ultimately several hundred of these [unfinished] copies were mixed in with the actual, final release, and we recalled and exchanged the unfinished versions. It happened over the course of about a week. Typically it would take a person about a week to complete a game, and so when some paying users complained about a bug or other problem after a few days, we exchanged their copies.

JS: Which game was this?

KY: *Luxsor.* [6] They were forced to release it before it was finished. Back then the launch dates were somewhat vague. The announced release date would be something like "the end of August" or "sometime during September", rather than a specific day. Since Nihon Telenet was financed or sponsored in part by a large electronics retail company called Yodobashi Denki,[7] Telenet had to release or deliver the products to Yodobashi in advance, before the general launch date. So I think they needed to meet the deadlines in order to receive money. So they had to launch the game prematurely, before it was actually complete, and then finish up the final version for the nationwide release. Since this was the early days, when the games industry was only first blossoming, or starting out, it was quite chaotic.

JS: I've heard that because magazines wanted adverts months in advance of the printing date, these would often contain screenshots which were entirely unrelated to the final product.

KY: Yes, yes, that's right. I think that the initial advertisement for *Ys*, by Falcom, only contained concept art and it did not actually show the content of the game at all. But that ended up being a trend among the game manufacturers - it would have a better impression on the prospective buyers. So they would just print a conceptual image to indicate the general idea of an upcoming title.

JS: A drawn image, rather than screenshot?

KY: Yes, just a drawing. That instance proved that we, the game makers, did not necessarily have to display the actual image of the game, but rather use a drawing instead.

---

[6] *Luxsor: Nights Over Egypt*, various Japanese computers; mix of overhead shooter & full 3D shooter, extremely difficult but with great music

[7] Yodobashi Camera, the famous electronics retailer that manages several gigantic, multi-story shops in key locations such as Shinjuku and Akihabara, as well as other major cities besides Tokyo

JS: *Luxsor* is regarded as a poor shooting game, but the sales were surprisingly strong. I think because of the graphics and music. How far were you involved with the graphics?

KY: I did the graphics for the title screen and visuals scenes; I can't remember which, but I created graphics either for the opening or ending visual scenes. The one with the air fighters in it.[8]

JS: The demo disk for game retailers was very important for the resulting sales?

KY: That's right. Because buyers would check the disk and decide how much they would stock. Some game titles can survive longer in the market, but in the case of Telenet titles the trend we saw was that they would show strong sales for a very short period of time, and then quickly they would end up in the resale market.

JS: You were in graphics. Did you study for this?

KY: I wasn't really trained, but I used to use computers of my own, so using my own computer I was drawing by myself.

JS: Something which impresses me about Nihon Telenet are the visuals. For example *XZR* makes excellent use of the limited 8 colour palette.

KY: Indeed!

JS: How did you learn techniques for pixel art?

KY: There are several techniques that you can use. For example together with colleagues, fellow designers, we tried different colours, or used dithering techniques to create additional colours, but there's no established technique that you can learn or study, you just develop your own way. First we were doing a technique called [dithering], to test various renders. You go through a trial and error process and try different colours, while looking at the screen. Computer graphics back then, the shape of the pixels wasn't really a proper square - it was a rectangle. So if you tried to draw a diagonal straight line, because of the rectangular shaped pixels it was quite difficult to have a very linear line.[9] But by changing the colours that constituted the line we wanted to draw, by overlapping the dots or pixels, we learned how to display clear lines. So that was really an outcome of trial and error.

JS: You drew hand sketches prior to pixel art?

KY: In order to get some ideas yes, I did sometimes draw sketches.

<shows folders full of sketches>

JS: Oh wow! Is this the original artwork?

KY: Yes, this is from *Ys III: Wanderers from Ys*. We did some boss monster designs.

JS: Can I take some photographs?

KY: *<laughs>* Ahh, these are not ours so...[10] *<flicks pages>* These are the sketches we did before hand. *Soul Blader*,[11] we have some sketches for that.

JS: Some sketches say *Soul Blader 2*. *(above)*

KY: We wanted to make *Soul Blader 2*, but actually instead we made *Illusion of Gaia*. This was not done by me, but by someone else. But based on these sketches I created pixel art. I made character graphics and boss designs. This is one of the boss monsters. These are made by professional designers, and then based on these I created graphics for different characters. So for each stage map this type of sketch was created, so there were multiple people involved in the process. We sort of shared the responsibilities.

[8] Most likely both; both contain air fighters and both have the exact same extremely beautiful art style

[9] The PC-88 screen resolution is 640x200 so the pixels are vertically stretched; it can differ on other systems

[10] Mr Yokota was saying his company, Shade, doesn't own the sketches, so he's nervous about them being in the book; presumably the copyright still belongs to Telenet, Falcom and Game Arts where applicable

[11] *Soul Blazer* in English; SNES RPG

JS: These colourful monster sketches are from?

KY: *Lunar 2: Eternal Blue*. (sketches not shown)

JS: When doing sketches to later reproduce on the PC-88, did they take into account the limited colour palette of the computer?

KY: Yes, that's right. Sometimes yes. However, if you start to think about the limitations of the colours, that would also limit the creativity of the designers. So we allowed the designers to draw freely, and then when we made them into pixel art we would try to arrange that.[12] We have to modify the shape of the sketches, because we have to make the characters move. So there was an understanding that we would be making some changes to the sketches.

<Mr Yokota steps out the room>

JR: So they were working like an arranger, similar to in music. Mr Yokota's job was akin to a "dot engineer", converting the sketch of an artist. *<referring to PC-88FH Black>* I think it was just used to test the final product. I think graphic design and programming were both done on PC-98. The disk he was showing was *Devil Dungeon*.[13] Usually it was used in game shops.

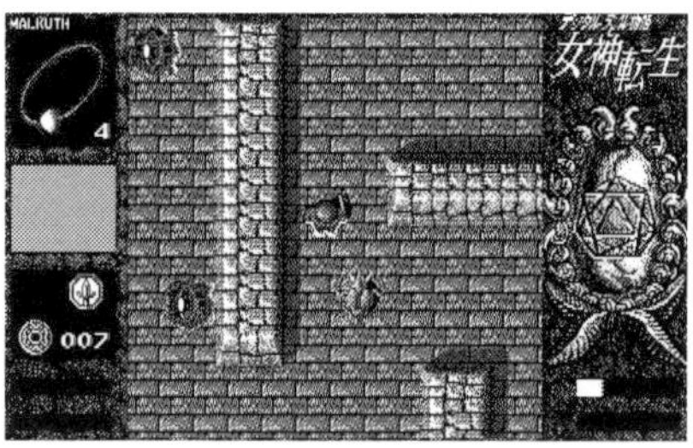

JS: Is that rare?

JR: Yes, pretty much. I have one for *YS II*, but it's the first time I've seen one for *Ys III*.

JS: He didn't want some sketches photographed.

JR: He said his company doesn't own those sketches. He didn't give any details, just "it's not ours". As I said, his work is pixel art. The sketches are work from designers before him.

<Mr Yokota returns>

JS: Was there any specific game that attracted you to Nihon Telenet?

[12] Mr Yokota used the important word "deformed", which is a technique to translate a normal drawing or picture into something formatted for computer graphics

[13] An official demo disk, very rare. Unlike some demo disks which are just copies, this was properly duplicated and has a full colour label

KY: *Valis*. For me, the visual design of that game was quite appealing, and also it has a very interesting story. So I was enticed by those things.

JS: You played this on PC-88?

KY: That's right. When I joined the company there was already the PC-88 version, and we were porting it to the PC-98, FM-7 and Sharp X1 computers. So we had the PC-88 as the core machine, and then we did adaptations.

JS: Speaking of the computers... You mentioned *Megami Tensei*[14] in email. For which computer?

KY: That's the one. *<gestures to PC-88FH>*[15] There's also a Famicom version, which was an entirely different game developed by Atlus.

JS: I'm interested to know your involvement.

KY: I was in charge of monster graphics for the PC-88 version by Nihon Telenet.

JS: Nihon Telenet and Atlus both worked on a version of *Megami Tensei*. How did Telenet get the license, and how come their game was different to Atlus' version?

KY: I had just joined the company at the time so I am not sure of the exact details, but I heard that when licenses to make game versions of the *Megami Tensei* novel were simultaneously acquired by Atlus (Famicom version) and Nihon Telenet (computer versions), the companies wanted to avoid the stereotypical genres of each system - action games on the Famicom, role-playing games on home computers. So they each ventured into the opposite genre. I don't know if this was because of instructions from the original author, or a voluntary staking out of territory by the two companies. Around this time, Atlus and Nihon Telenet were in contact with each other, and when Nihon Telenet later started developing

[14] Telenet version of *Megami Tensei,* for various computers such as MSX1 and PC-88 (1987), was radically different to the Atlus RPG on FC; the Telenet version was more like a *Gauntlet*-type shooter

[15] Therefore it was for the PC-8801mkIISR

for the Famicom, we received a brief orientation session from an Atlus employee.

JS: Could you sketch the layout of Telenet?

KY: I think our in-house designer drew a funny sketch of the Nihon Telenet development room, and it was published either in the manual for the home computer version of *Megami Tensei*, or in the official fan newsletter called the *User's Gallery*. It was a very good drawing as I recall. Maybe you could find a copy of the computer version of *Megami Tensei*? (shown below)

JS: According to the list you gave me, you worked on four games at Nihon Telenet.

KY: I was involved in other games as well, but for those games I was quite heavily involved. So my data was heavily used in those four games.

JS: I'd love to hear some Telenet stories. Especially regarding *XZR* on the PC-88.

KY: Well, back then when *XZR* was under development, the planner was quite fatigued and could not come up with any creative ideas. So he ended up adopting a very immoral, politically incorrect kind of idea involving Islam. Looking back I'm still surprised that Nihon Telenet actually went ahead and introduced that concept into the game, and were able actually to sell it and get it converted to other systems.

JS: The story involved a time-travelling Syrian assassin sent to kill the president of America...

KY: <*laughs*>

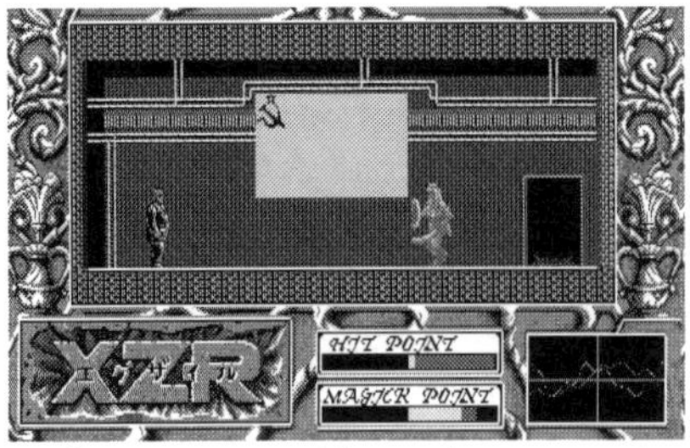

JS: ... and then kill the president of Russia too! (right)

KY: Yes, that's right! <*laughs*> It was quite dangerous actually! <*laughs*> The character would regain power by taking drugs, and if not the display quality would deteriorate. So now, I think that kind of game would not go through the censors, due to ethical criteria. I think the idea was more a fit for comics or manga. The original author of the game was saying it would be better fit to make it into a manga, rather than a game, because in terms of games you have to go through a very strict ratings system or censorship. So the author was saying that if somebody was able to translate this into manga, that would be better.

JS: I played all the conversions and wrote an article for HG101. I thought to myself, if the CIA is monitoring this, there are all these hot keywords, like cocaine, Middle East, "kill the president!" <*laughs*> We'll be arrested!

KY: <*laughs*> Yes! Back then it was a peaceful time where not many people were focusing on games. Now games are attracting a lot of attention from a large audience, but back then they were not so major. So we had the freedom to do whatever we wanted.

JS: Makes you miss those days of anything-goes.

KY: Yes, that's right. Well, yes, maybe there might be a little more freedom when it comes to indies games, but still, you have to kind of restrain yourself.

JS: Did you play through *XZR* to the end?

KY: Ahh, no, I left Nihon Telenet before seeing the completion of the game. Because it was originally decided that I was only to be involved with the opening of the game.

JS: Which version?[16]

KY: The first version on PC-88. I was in charge of the opening graphics for this.

JS: Only the sequel was released in English, for PC Engine and Mega Drive.

KY: Yes, so we created the original version and probably, I believe, it was ported.

JS: There was also an MSX2 version.

KY: Yes, that's right, I believe so. Normally at that the time the company would create the PC-88 version first, because it was the most popular, and then decide to port it to other hardware. I think that was the normal method they took.[17]

JS: Can you remember the porting to MSX2?

KY: After creating the opening for *XZR* I left the company. And I joined the *Wanders from Ys* team [at Falcom] right after that.

JS: This game was also converted to the MSX1? *<holds up the first Valis>*[18]

---

[16] The series started off as *XZR: Idols of Apostate,* with a katakana subtitle pronounced "exile"; what we know as *Exile* outside of Japan was actually *XZR II: When Trapped Between*. The third game in the series, *Phenomenon of Evil*, drops the *XZR* moniker and is known both in and outside of Japan as *Exile II*. See Hardcore Gaming 101 for a detailed article on them

[17] Games at Telenet at this time were first made for the PC-88 (mostly PC-8801mkIISR) and then ported to other platforms, including *XZR* and *Megami Tensei*

[18] Only a few games were ported to the MSX1. Other Nihon Telenet games were mostly ported to the MSX2. This is interesting because the MSX range has a low resolution and the pixels are perfectly square. So a port

KY: Yes!

JS: The MSX1 has very low graphics capabilities compared to the PC-88. Did you take part in the MSX version? How difficult was *Valis* to convert?

KY: We significantly had to simplify the graphics. Basically, you cannot scroll, so you have to have everything on one screen. We had to extensively modify the game design; instead of screen scrolling, you have to use screen flipping. So when the character is walking off the edge of the screen, you have to switch to the next screen, rather than scrolling it. There was a sprite function, so character movement was quite smooth. However, only one colour can be used. So in order to create colours, we had to overlap multiple sprites, because if you only have a single colour you can't tell what it is. So we tried to get at least three colours by overlapping the characters. So it's like character sprites for Famicom, you only have about three colours.[19] So we have to draw characters in a highly deformed, abstract way.

The MSX2 was a different story, because it has higher capabilities. The PC-88 had eight colours, but we were able to use 256 colours on MSX2, which was a big difference. As I said earlier, in order to give the impression of different colours we would put the pixels side-by-side to [simulate] more colours. But instead of that, with MSX2, we could just make the colours we wanted. I worked on the MSX2 version for this game. *<points to Ys III>* I redrew it and then gave it more, nicer colours, compared to the PC-88 original.

JS: You also did the graphics for *Valis* on the Famicom. How would you describe the technical differences working on the Famicom?

KY: That's a bit difficult... Because the hardware concept is completely different. [Something like the PC-88] is a personal computer, whereas the Famicom is specifically a games machine. But the biggest difference was that the memory capacity was limited. The Famicom had a smaller memory, so in order to create graphics we had to re-use the same sprites. So those were the limitations which cause the biggest challenge.

JS: Were the available Memory Mapper[20] chips also a concern?

KY: Yes, that's right. There's a limit to how many sprites you can use at any one time. So you have to reuse these sprites to create the stage map. For example... *<refers to Valis screens>*

Up: Valis, PC-88; down: Valis, Famicom

If you want to use original graphics you can only cover a quarter of the screen, but by mixing and matching all these original graphics tiles you can cover the whole stage. So the colour for the background would be a single colour blue, and then for the earth you would use just one tile, and place it side-by-side. This is another example. *<refers to screenshot, noting how a background building is comprised of the same sprites>* You take one tile and you line it up to create a building. See, it's a repetitive representation of the same image. So you have to be creative when designing the screen layout. If for example there's a symmetrical statue, or a sculpture, you would only draw the left or right half and then turn it around.

JS: Like a mirror image.

---

from MSX to Famicom is easy, but a port from PC-88 to MSX is hell - noting the word "deformed" used earlier, it becomes a deformation of a deformation!

[19] Character sprites in FC games usually use 3 colours and a "transparent" colour to show the background

[20] Chips inside FC/NES cartridges which improved graphical capabilities, such as multi-scrolling

KY: Yes, that's also a technique we used.

JS: On computer games, for example *Ys III*, Adol always holds his sword in his right hand, whether he faces left or right. It's accurate. But on Famicom games, characters switch hands because the sprite is mirrored.

KY: Yes, that was the case regarding the Famicom version. It might be that it was mirrored. You should have a sword on the right hand side, and a shield on the left - that rule was applied to the computer versions.

JS: As shown here, it's not mirrored. *<notes screens on back of the Ys III box for PC-88>*

KY: Yes, the shield is not mirrored. I think with the Famicom that was not possible.[21]

JS: Anything interesting to recall from *Valis*?

KY: With respect to *Valis*, at that time the Famicom's games only had either vertical or horizontal scrolling. So whereas the original *Valis* featured maps that could potentially scroll either way, you could not do this on the Famicom. We came across this issue, so we needed to add revisions and changes to the design. The computer version was purely an action game with story scenes only after the player completes each stage, but we introduced an exploration mode as part of the Famicom game. So now the player could enter houses and talk to people. We also made the maps more complex to deepen the gameplay. So we were forced to make changes, and take a different approach from the original *Valis* game.

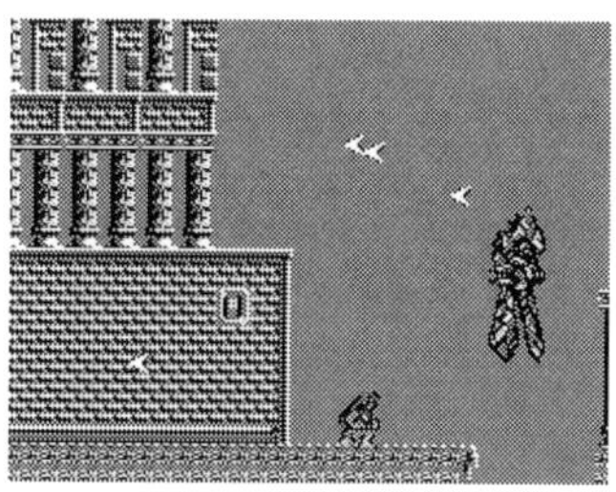

JS: It was like a remake, rather than port? *(right)*

KY: Yes, that's right.

JS: Why leave Nihon Telenet for Nihon Falcom?

KY: I left Nihon Telenet because I wanted to try new things. And also at the same time Nihon Falcom was recruiting a lot.

JS: Could you draw an office layout sketch of Falcom and Quintet?

KY: I'm not sure whether I can recall them. I can recall the Quintet office, because it was quite a simple layout. Falcom... *<laughs>* my memory is failing me!

JS: When you joined Falcom to work on *Ys III*, had you played the previous two games?

KY: Yes. It's not like I was a fan, but I was interested in the techniques they used. Because the scrolling was quite smooth, and the visual presentation, the speed, was quite fast. Nihon Telenet wasn't slow with regards to displaying visuals, but Nihon Falcom had the highest quality as far as I knew. So I had always been interested in finding out how they did it.

JS: How did you feel when you saw *Ys III* was a side-scrolling game?

KY: When I was joining the company I didn't know whether I was to be involved in *Ys III* or not. I was only told they were in the process of developing a side-scrolling action game - the *Ys* title had not been added yet. The project was simply referred to as "that side-scrolling action game". *Link's Adventure* on the Famicom inspired them to create the game. The main character wasn't important, so Adol was temporarily used, just for development. But that was not the final decision, it was just provisional when I was joining the company. Later it seems they let the designer create the character, and the designer submitted Adol - when the designer got involved he actually came back with Adol! He thought that because Adol was the provisional character, it meant he had to use him! *<laughs>* So they decided, oh well, we'll just use this character. So we were doing that for computers, and then in order to market the product we decided we had to make it *Ys III*.

JS: It was not even part of the *Ys* series?

KY: Yes, that's correct. At that time I didn't really think it was possible to have parallax or multi-scrolling on computers. So I remember I was quite surprised. Because when we distributed the demonstration disk you saw earlier, to retail stores, I remember that they were very surprised and there was a lot of

[21] You won't find many games where characters are not mirrored. *Sorcerian* by Nihon Falcom is famous as all monsters in the game were designed with a unique left and right facing sprite

reaction. We first created the action part, <*laughs*> and the story of *Ys* came later. So in that sense, the balance was not quite right. I think the company had the intention of making another *Ys* game when I was joining them - I was under that impression. I was mainly responsible for creating the map for the story in *Ys III*, and also the graphics for enemies and boss monsters.[22]

JS: Wait, they added the *Ys* name and Adol later?

KY: Yes. We first wanted to come up with an action game, so we came up with a demo version using Adol [as a placeholder]. But when the time came for us to actually launch the game, the management decided that it would be better to have the name *Ys* on it, which would sell better. So it was kind of like a spin-off from the *Ys* series. It was considered to be *Ys Gaiden* at the beginning, and they were originally thinking of coming up with *Ys III* separately. But because of the circumstances they decided to call the game *Ys III* instead of *Ys Gaiden*. I think, as you can see from the subtitle *Wanderers from Ys*, the original title they had in mind was going to be this. But at the last minute, the 11th hour, they changed the game name to *Ys III*. So since I was working there, I was part of the team, I knew this for a fact. With respect to the story, when I joined the company most of the parts were undecided, so the designers had the discretion to design whatever they wanted to, and came up with level layouts which were later compiled into a story. Most of the maps were non-existent, such as the stage maps for the town, so I did a lot of drawing which was added on to the game later on.

JS: The PC-88 version doesn't even have "*Ys III*" on the front cover! It's just *Wanderers from YS*.

KY: Yes, that's correct!

JS: When you say creating the map, do you mean structuring the layout, or just drawing it?

KY: I had to think about the layout. We knew that *Ys III* would have a story to it, so in the map there were already parts decided for the story, so we had to design it to accommodate those; I was designing the map while thinking about the layout in order to include the story in it. For example I would be asked to shape the map to have an event happen at a particular point - so I had the freedom to draw the map based on those story points. When the map was finished someone would add an event, so again I had to modify the map accordingly. So some scenes we were able to create freely, and some scenes we created under instructions from the designer. A check was implemented after the story was introduced. Then we would say we should extend the map for this part, to give more emotion to it. Or we changed the map, or we would direct the scene so that when the map starts, if the character moves a little the boss monster appears. So that kind of direction was given. So we had that in mind, as we designed the map.

[22] Various screenshots on this page taken from: **http://towerofretrogame.blog.fc2.com**

JS: Do you have any interesting stories from your time at Falcom?

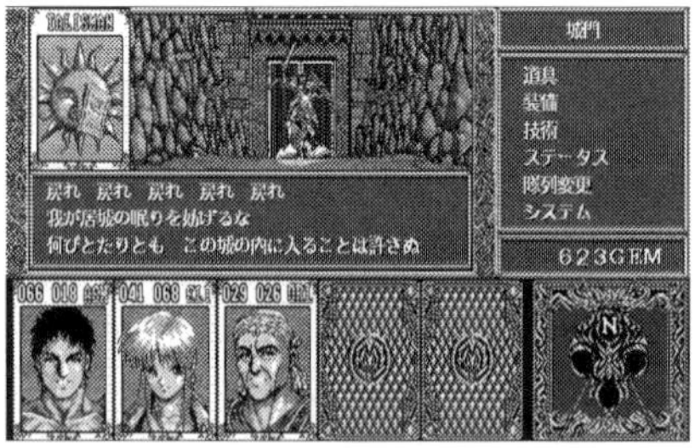

KY: Yes, one episode that I can recall from back then, when the development was going on, was that the Japanese calendar name changed from Showa to Heisei,[23] because the Showa emperor had passed away. This big funeral for the Showa emperor was held, but there was a huge discussion within the company whether there was going to be a day off for this special occasion. It turned out that we did not have a holiday! *<laughs>*

JS: Unfortunate! Much work went into *Ys III*.

KY: That's correct.

JS: I think the most advanced computer at this time was the Sharp X68000. Did you take part in the conversion of *Ys III* to this computer?

KY: Yes, I was involved. The X68000 had very powerful capabilities with advanced sprite graphics, meaning that the character would move very smoothly, so we used that in order to expand the action scenes. The MSX2's pixel shape was very similar to the X68000, it's very square. So we would convert from the MSX2 to the X68000, but the colours were much, much richer. So that's how we converted.

JS: When *Dinosaur*[24] was created, the market was slowly moving from PC-88 to PC-98. Were the graphics done on PC-98 then converted to the PC-88, or done on the PC-88 then upgraded?

KY: The PC-8801mkIISR version was the first, the original. But unlike other Nihon Falcom games the graphics were completely redrawn for the PC-98VM, which is 640x400 and has twice as many lines as the PC-88 version.[25] Then I was responsible for the graphics for the military guard. I wasn't that heavily involved in this, but I did help. I did the designing for the characters as well. Takahashi-san,[26] who currently works at Monolith, which is in the Nintendo group, he made *Xenogears* at Square, I think this was the first game that he was involved in creating. I think he was just one of the graphic designers, but I understand that he was very much a fully fledged member of the team in creating the world for this game. That's what I heard after I left the company.

JS: You only worked on three games at Falcom?

KY: *Legend of Heroes,* or *Eiyuu Densetsu* - I was involved in creating the ending graphics. I was helping on both *Eiyuu Densetsu* and *Dinosaur* with graphics, but I was more involved for *Ys III*, for PC-88, MSX2, and X68000. In terms of length of time, I was involved in *Ys III* longest. This magazine photo is from the time that I just joined the company - it was such a long time ago you may not recognise me. *<laughs>*

<shows magazine with Falcom company photo, showing Mr Yokota standing nearby Mr Kiya>

JS: Can I get a photo?

KY: Yes, I think so. This is Mr Kiya.

[23] The Heisei era started on 8 January, 1989

[24] *Dinosaur* is a 3D RPG much like *Wizardry* - you have to draw the map while playing. The graphics are gorgeous and all monsters are represented by tarot cards. But the biggest draw is the strong scenario and so called "serious" characters. For some fans it's one of the best Falcom games and the most unknown at the same time. Watch the introduction and you'll understand the dark and beautiful atmosphere

[25] For comparison, *Ys* on the PC-98 is 640x200 natively, or 640x400 with soft/black scanlines

[26] Tetsuya Takahashi, enormous RPG portfolio

Far left: Mr Kiya, (Legacy of the Wizard)
Far right: Mr Yokota (Illusion of Gaia)

JS: Did they send a copy of this magazine to all the staff, or did you buy it?

KY: Oh, I purchased a copy for myself.

JS: When you worked at the companies were you given a complimentary copy of every game?

KY: Yes, but not every time. For *Ys III* I was quite heavily involved, so I received a copy. But for those two titles [*Dinosaur* and *Eiyuu Densetsu*], I was only partially helping, so I didn't receive any copies.

JS: Did you purchase copies?

KY: Yes, but not every game I was involved in.

JS: Can you recall the year you left Falcom?

KY: We have our own way of describing time, it's currently called Heisei. It switched from the Showa to the Heisei era. So the first year of Heisei was 1989. I think I was with Falcom until around 1991...

JS: Perhaps you can solve a mystery for me. Apparently Quintet was founded in April 1989. Yet *Dragon Slayer IV* for the Famicom, in the credits screen, says: *July 1987, Quintet*.

KY: I think *Dragon Slayer IV* is about the members of the Drasle family.

JS: Indeed. What I'm trying to understand is, there seems to be discrepancy in the dates.

KY: It might have been that in 1987 Quintet was used not as the name of a company, but maybe for a certain group, or something like that. I vaguely remember that Quintet was a name for some group or a unit. And then later on maybe it became the official name of a company?

JS: It started as an internal development team?

KY: I'm not 100% sure. I'm just suggesting the possibility that the name was used for a team. [27]

JS: If you left Falcom in 1991, you must have been there when Masaya Hashimoto [28] and Tomoyoshi Miyazaki[29] left to form Quintet?

KY: Actually I wanted to leave with them. But you know, I had a family to look after, so I didn't take the adventure of leaving the company with them. So I stayed and they left before me. And then Yuzo Koshiro of Ancient left. But when those two people left, obviously the company didn't like that and there were some problems, with regards to them leaving. So I didn't want to leave with them, because I wanted to avoid having any trouble with the company. So I completed the original version of *Ys III*, and then after completion of that, Hashimoto-san and Miyazaki-san left the company. Then after they left we did the conversion of the original *Ys III*, and when we were working on this conversion they started Quintet.

JS: I actually interviewed Koshiro-san a few days ago. Did you work alongside him?

KY: I was good friends with Hashimoto-san; we'd go out for drinks and visit each other's homes, and so on. Koshiro-san and I were working for Falcom at different times, so I didn't know him at the office. But at Quintet I came to know him indirectly. He was freelancing by that time, so we contracted out to him the music in *ActRaiser*. Yuzo Koshiro was already in a family business and he was a contractor, so he was working at home when doing *ActRaiser*. So I

---

[27] The mystery was solved when interviewing Yoshio Kiya himself. The "quintet" refers to the 5 playable family members (mom, dad, son, daughter, dog) - according to him, there's zero connection to Quintet
[28] 橋本昌哉, director on the original *Ys: The Vanished Omens* at Falcom, co-founder of Quintet in 1989
[29] 宮崎友好, scenario writer for the original *Ys* at Falcom, and co-founder of Quintet with Mr Hashimoto

often visited him at his home and I saw him at the Quintet offices.

JS: Why were so many people leaving Falcom?

KY: Falcom was a conservative company, and games console were gaining momentum rather than computers. So we already had this desire to do console games even when we were still at Falcom, but the company said no. Nintendo's cartridge ROM business was considered high risk. So the company was reluctant to follow that. Having said that, maybe they were right in not doing it, because Falcom still exists. So maybe as a management decision, they made the right one. But as a creator, I was frustrated by the company's attitude. So for example, we wanted to make an action game for consoles that was similar to *Ys III*, but we couldn't do that. But later on we realised these desires with *ActRaiser*. So that's actually what happened.

JS: Listening to how you created graphics for *Ys III*, it seems graphic designers and programmers worked together closely. Did you work with Kiya-san?

KY: At that time, in Falcom, there were three teams. Kiya-san's team, which was doing *Dragon Slayer*. Hashimoto-san's team, which was responsible for *Ys*. Meanwhile *Dinosaur* and *Star Trader* were handled by Tomi-san. [30] So there were three teams in Falcom. Graphics designers tend to move around and work for different teams, but in my case I was almost always working on the conversions, so the majority of my work was for the *Ys* series. When I was asked to do something other than *Ys*, it was usually just helping with a small task. So I wasn't directly working together with Kiya-san in his team. Kiya-san had a very top-down style of working; he would decide everything and then instruct the team to follow his decision. Hashimoto-san would allow the team members to come up with different ideas, and then he would be willing to take on board good ideas. Tomi-san was in-between, he was in the middle. So each team had a different way of directing their work. That was the impression I had for each team. Actually, I personally felt I was fortunate to work for Hashimoto-san's team, considering my future career. So that's how I spent my years at Falcom.

JS: Today three of your employees are also formerly of Falcom.

KY: Yes, that's right.

JS: One of them worked on *Popful Mail*?

KY: Yes.

JS: The original PC-88 and PC-98 versions?

KY: I think the original versions. He was hired by Falcom after I joined the company, and he was making his own indie game,[31] which was similar I think, and then based on his indie game the design was refined and published under the Falcom brand. He didn't make that game for anyone else - he brought the game for the interview. He created it for himself and then brought it and presented it at the interview.

JS: *Popful Mail* started as a prototype?

KY: I think how it started was that everyone had a look and said, "Oh, this is quite well made!"

JS: Then they developed it into a full game?

KY: Back then, how the project was launched, it was not like there was a designated planner who came up with some kind of proposal. It was like if someone made something interesting, that would be presented to the president and he'd say, "Oh, this is interesting, maybe we can form a project." And that's how the projects were started. So it was quite a free environment. There was no sales or marketing plan. If the president liked it he would say you can start a project for it, and then we'd just make announcements to the media, saying the company is going to develop this kind of game. So that's what it was.

JS: Can I talk with Mr nagashima?

KY: Let me go fetch him. He should be on a break now.

---

[30] Kazunari Tomi. Apparently after leaving Falcom founded Studio Alex; involved with Game Arts and three *Lunar* titles (*Silver Star Story*, *Eternal Blue*, and *Samposuru Gakuen*). Filed a lawsuit against Game Arts in 2003, was countersued, and Studio Alex was bankrupted. ***(There are NO verified sources for this)***

[31] Jun Nagashima's interview is after this one - the actual events are slightly different

[I interviewed Mr Nagashima, see the next chapter, and he drew a map of Falcom's layout]

Jun Nagashima: There's more than one location I worked at, so I'm wondering which office...

JS: All of them!

JN: So this picture was taken at the Tomio building. *<Referring to photo in magazine>*

<Mr Yokota and his colleague converse extensively about Falcom>

KY: I only know the Tomio building. I remember the elevator was horribly slow. *<laughs>*

JS: Were they quite far from each other, the different buildings?

JN: When I was working at Nihon Falcom there was three locations. Not at the same time, we relocated twice. So the current Nihon Falcom building is the fourth location they've moved to. *<referring to photo>* This was the first building.

JS: With the stairway and logo above it.

JN: You'd go up the stairs and find the shop.

KY: A computer shop.

<Mr Yokota and his colleague converse>

KY: I remember the Tomio building layout.

JN: Yes, the Tomio building. Is this the one you want me to draw?

JS: Whichever you remember best.

JN: Can I take the notebook with me? Just the office layout?

JS: Yes, that would be fun to include in the book.

JN: OK, I'll try!

<Jun Nagashima returns with the layout sketch from Falcom>

JN: Is this OK?

JS: That's perfect! Thank you very much!

<Mr Nagashima returns to his desk>

JS: In 1991 you started freelancing, including on *Gaiares* for Telenet. For graphics?

KY: Graphics and game design.

JS: Please tell us about this.

KY: Sega was to launch the Mega Drive and they requested that Telenet come up with a game; Telenet staff were talking about creating a game for the system. After I left Falcom, one of my [former] programming colleagues who still worked at Telenet came to me saying that he had to work on this Mega Drive game, a shooting game, and the deadline was coming up, "So would you like to work with me?" So I said, "Oh, that sounds very interesting!" And that's how I got involved. It was a very small project, only involving a small number of people. We had a very good programmer for the game, and actually, initially there was only two of us. Myself and the programmer.

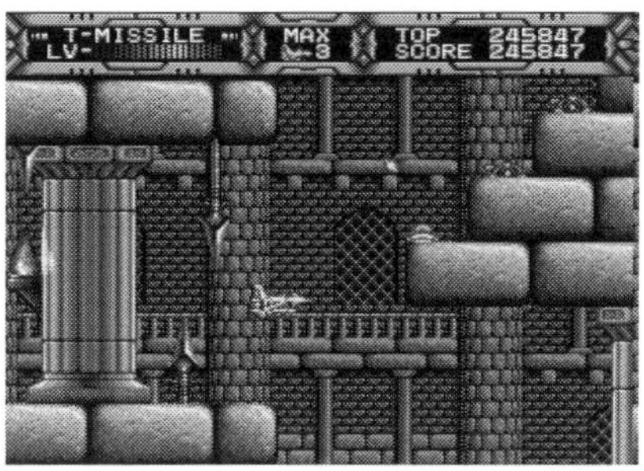

JS: Masayasu Yamamoto?[32]

KY: Yes, that's right.

JS: *Gaiares* was the first game you had direct, hands on control over the style and structure?

KY: Yes, that's correct. Initially we weren't focusing too much on the graphics, but the memory was size was doubled from 4 megabits to 8 megabits after we started the project, so we added the 4mb equivalent of story and visuals afterwards.[33] *<shows back of box screenshots with cut-scene graphics>* At that time we had a lot of freedom, where we could do whatever we wanted.

---

[32] Very large portfolio, including *Alundra 2*

[33] The intro alone is over 7 minutes of cut-scenes!

JS: It featured a genuinely unique weapons system.[34] Did you come up with it?

KY: Yes, yes. Indeed, it was a unique weapon in that it did not exist before - to capture from the enemies. Originally there was this dedicated weapon where you shoot an object like a ball at the power-up items, to collect it. But then we came up with this idea of adding an extra Option, and that lead to the idea of ramming enemies with the Option to capture weapons. We originally had the idea of switching items in real-time during gameplay, but then we also thought that it would be interesting if you can actually get the item from the enemy, so if you are trying to capture the item from the enemy you cannot attack them during that time. So we designed that as a sort of risk/reward mechanic for the player. Basically the idea was to evolve the behaviour and the way you used the Option from *R-Type*. This way, the Option itself transforms in various ways, and you apply the Option to an enemy to draw out or extract the individual characteristics of that enemy.

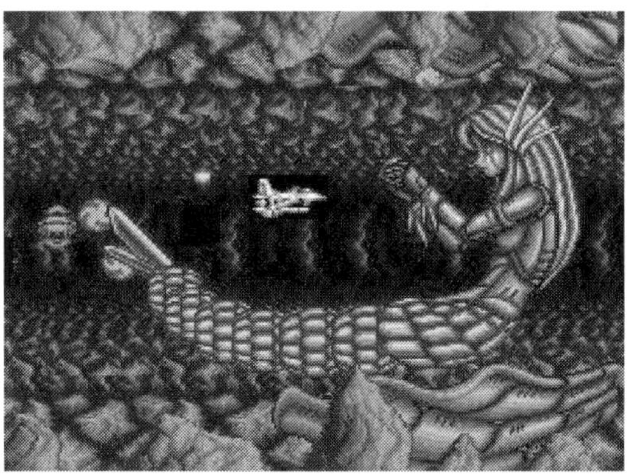

JS: This was released in 1990, and I recall later shooters adopting slightly different systems of salvaging weapons from enemies. Do you feel your creation influenced them?

KY: No, I don't know about that. *<laughs>* When it comes to shooting games the idea was of the essence; it can be said for *Gradius* games, *R-Type* games, or games which feature Options. So all the manufacturers were trying to come up with the best ideas in order to be more competitive than each other.

JS: It received high scores, but most said it was quite difficult to complete.

KY: Yamamoto-san, the programmer, was in charge of the game balance, but this game was originally intended for the overseas market, to begin with. But overseas, since there was a tendency for people to buy and play a game and then immediately sell it, as well as rental systems, the overseas publisher[35] had asked us to make the game more difficult so that it would not be rented and completed easily. So we went over to the overseas publisher to show them the demo, and then they said, "You should make it even more difficult!" We started getting concerned at this point, but we complied with their request. So ultimately the game became very difficult when it was released.

But I was only involved in the first 6 stages, and I was not involved in the 7th and 8th stages. So I don't know how difficult it ended up for those last two stages, because I was already moving on to the next job and by then my level of involvement was much lower. So I never beat the game either! *<laughs>* You can probably tell if you play the game, but there is a significant change in the bosses. Like I said, I was mainly in charge of designing the maps and boss monsters for the first 6 stages, whereas the 7th and 8th stage was mainly done by Yamamoto-san and a designer at Nihon Telenet, back then. It seems as though they recycled some of the monsters in the 7th and 8th stages, which was criticized and ultimately led to the game receiving lower review scores.

Originally they were going to use 4 megabits for the ROM cartridge memory, but then there was a request or desire to upgrade to 8 megabits. This resulted in a big change in the game's development schedule, and my own

[34] You had an "Option" module, like *R-Type*, but it could capture weapons from enemies

[35] Published by Renovation Products in the US

schedule prevented me from staying with the project all the way to the very end. It was rather unfortunate that I wasn't able to be with and finish this project to the end, because I had other assignments coming up already. As a result, apparently the people at Telenet did the work for the 7th and 8th stages in my place. In terms of visual scenes and story I was only in charge of coming up with the basic setting, and I was not involved with the characters at all. So I was rather surprised when I saw it later on.

JS: Speaking of the story, in English it's said the title is a combination of Gaia and Rescue. Is this what you intended?

KY: It's not quite... The *resu* (レス) part stands for El-Ee-Es-Es - or LESS - as in to lose.[36] So "*resu*" is "less", and Earth has been ruined, and humanity is trying to figure out what to do next and seeking out a possible solution. Actually, many of the parts of this game I don't understand in terms of story! <*laughs*> I would like to ask them why they came up with this kind of a story myself. Basically, I placed importance on ideas for the game itself, and I didn't think much about how the game would be ending, so for that portion I think the Telenet people did a great job in compensating or adding whatever needed to be added.

JS: So you invented the title itself, because the Earth is ruined?

KY: I came up with this title, yes. Perhaps it's because [the characters in the game] are reviving the Earth, so that's why everyone might have thought this "resu" stood for rescue, as opposed to "less".

JS: Telenet had many divisions. This box says Renovation. For the PC Engine there was Laser Soft? And at this time I think Wolf Team was a new company, but later merged with Laser Soft?

KY: Wolf Team became an independent company, a spin-off from Telenet. And Nihon Laser Soft was established to create titles for the PC Engine CD-ROM. Then the main Telenet company, branded as Renovation, was mainly creating software for computers. That was the general setup. There were different entities and later on they were all integrated. Telenet was very welcoming to different types of creators, and brought in talent such as people from the anime industry...[37] So nowadays if you look at the presidents of various companies and other top-level people, you'll discover that many of them were involved with some of Telenet's games in the past. Because we were very open to different creators. On the other hand, Falcom was not that kind of company. So whereas Telenet brought on well-known creators, including people who are still very famous today, Nihon Falcom was very closed, almost the polar opposite of Nihon Telenet. That's my impression at least.

JS: Did you see the US cover?

KY: *Gaiares* was changed significantly for the US release I think. I was really surprised at the American packaging - it made quite an impact.

JS: After freelancing for Telenet you joined Quintet. Do you know what happened to Mr Hashimoto and Mr Miyazaki?

KY: Did Koshiro-san tell you anything about them?

JS: Mr Koshiro explained Mr Hashimoto worked for Ancient a few years ago. He wasn't sure about Mr Miyazaki.

KY: There is a magazine called Famitsu, and they would organise a new year's party every year. About five years ago, at that party, I saw him and said hello, and greeted him, and that was the last time I saw him.[38] What I heard was that he was doing business with someone who is not related to the games industry. So I was under the impression he was no longer in the games industry, but I didn't get to ask further details.

---

[36] Katakana "re" and "su" symbols, pronounced "*resu*" or "res". According to this explanation, *Gaiares* means Earth-less, as in without the Earth

[37] Literally he says "animators", but in Japanese this referrs specifically to people from the anime industry, not general videogame animators such as sprite artists

[38] Mr Yokota didn't specify Hashimoto or Miyazaki - the contextual assumption is Mr Miyazaki

JS: There's a lot of rumours going around. One rumour is that one of them was arrested.

KY: <*laughs*>

JS: Another rumour is that one passed away.

KY: I have some contacts from those years, but the only information I can get is that we're not sure what happened to them. But had they been involved in some kind of trouble, I'm quite sure that would appear in the media, or it would be covered in newspapers or something. But the fact that we haven't come across any news about them, whether good or bad, means they are probably doing fine.

JS: Let's talk Quintet. Could you briefly tell me your role on *ActRaiser*, *Soul Blazer*, *Illusion of Gaia*, *Robotrek*, *Terranigma*, and I believe you were in charge of *Granstream Saga*?

KY: For *ActRaiser* I was involved in converting it for the international, overseas version. The localisation. For *Soul Blazer* my main responsibility was the map graphics. With *Illusion of Gaia* I was responsible for the characters and designing the world. For *Robotrek* I was doing the design for the robots.

JS: When you say robot designs, were you sketching them on pieces of paper?

KY: Yes. <*shows sketches*>

JS: I'd love to get a few photographs of you holding your work.

KY: <*laughs*> It's embarrassing!

JS: There will be a lot of happy readers.

KY: <*referring to robot designs*> The request was to design something quite retro, or old fashioned rather.

JS: Are you aware of the following Quintet has outside Japan?

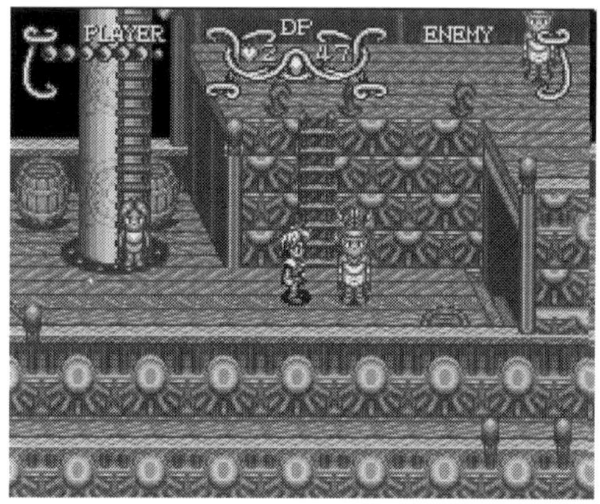

KY: I didn't know that.

JS: Your games are very much beloved.

KY: I mentioned this in the email, but in the past I was contacted by a writer from Retro Gamer magazine. I think it's a friend of yours?

JS: Yes, Sorrel Tilley.

KY: He requested Quintet information, which I shared with him.

JS: Mr Miyazaki wanted *Illusion of Gaia* (above) to be a direct sequel to *Soul Blazer*. But Enix wanted a stronger hook, so Moto Hagio[39] was brought in, along with Mariko Ohara[40] to write the story. Can you comment on the situation?

[39] Beloved *shoujo* manga artist; she's been prolific since 1969; character designer on *Illusion of Gaia*
[40] Award winning science-fiction writer

KY: The initial plan was to make *Soul Blazer 2*. But Enix wanted a hook, as you said, and wanted some celebrities for the game, so Moto Hagio and Mariko Ohara. Also don't forget Yasuhiro Kawasaki for the score, the music. [Ms Hagio, Ms Ohara, and Kawasaki-san came to meet with the development team and] were to be involved, and those were the instructions. Ms Ohara came up with the broad outline of the world and the story she wanted for the game. We got together for meetings with Miyazaki-san and discussed how to proceed. Miyazaki-san had some ideas that he wanted to implement [from the original *Soul Blazer 2* plans], so he would take the world created by Ms Ohara and try to realise his ideas within this world Ms Ohara created. The maps were created based on ancient ruins, and I had a lot of materials for that, so I supplied materials to design the stages.

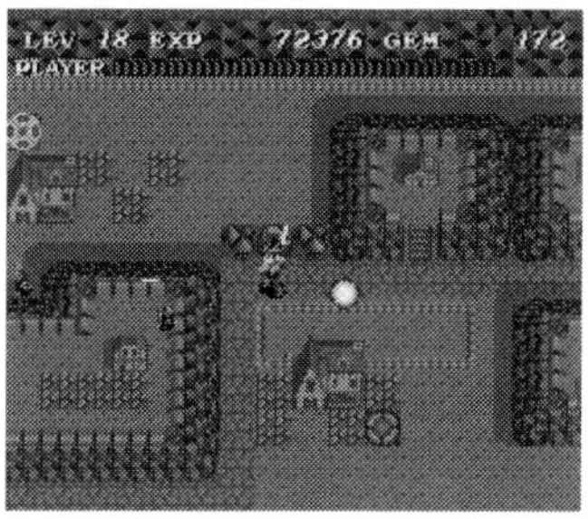

JS: What kind of materials?

KY: Visual materials of ancient ruins. Basically in *Soul Blazer* you have a town, and if you clear a certain scenario you can rebuild or reconstruct the town. For *Soul Blazer* even if you try to rebuild the town, we had only limited graphic data we could use, so we had to recycle the same graphics data. We had to create a foundation for the house, and we then had to create a house for

when you rebuild the town. So it was quite a challenging task for us to do that. In *Dragon Quest* if you enter a house and go up the stairs it switches the graphics, but when we worked on *Illusion of Gaia* the transition was smooth. We were able to have a smooth transition to the second floor from the first floor. We worked hard to create graphics that wouldn't look "cheap".

JS: Can I photograph your sketches which had "*Soul Blader II*" in it? This is a historical treasure.

<takes photos>

KY: This is for *Illusion of Gaia*, the normal boy turns into a warrior. It's not very clear, the lines are not very clear, but quite faint. There were many ideas and then there was the idea that he would transform three times. Initially the idea was similar to *The Corsican Brothers*.[41]

JS: *The Corsican Brothers*! Sorrel Tilley mentioned that.

KY: So there were twins, a boy and a girl, and based on [*The Corsican Brothers*] idea we thought maybe we can make a game.

JS: Twins, plus space- and time-travel!

KY: Yes, you would travel through time. Well, it just goes to show that we had different ideas for the game.

JS: Are these your sketches?

[41] French novella from 1844 about conjoined brothers who feel each other's pain even after being separated

KY: Yes.

JS: Can I get a shot of you holding it?

KY: <*laughs*> OK. You know, I'm very embarrassed.

JS: I think if you visited a game convention, a lot of people would want your signature.

KY: <*laughs*> I don't think so! I think you are exaggerating!

JS: Not at all! <*turns to Joseph*> Am I exaggerating, Joseph?

JR: No! <*laughs*>

JS: There was also the idea for Will's hair to move when near secrets. This was your idea?

KY: Yes, that's right. We thought it was quite interesting if the hair would move, because no one had done it; making the hair move was something new to try. So we thought, should we try it? We had the idea that the hair would move because of wind, and maybe we can apply that in a cave, and players could find the secrets because of the wind coming from holes or certain secret places, in caves; it would move the hair while in the caves. So by using the hair movement you could search these out.

JS: The US had a different boss in the Sky Garden area. In the Japanese version it was a giant bird; in the US it was a winged statue.

KY: I was not at all involved in the conversion for the American release [of *Illusion of Gaia*]. It happened to *ActRaiser* when it was converted, but what was pointed out was that for the Western version, we had to avoid using religious motifs. Especially the software for children, the younger users, the rules were very strict. The last bosses for *ActRaiser* were demons,[42] but they were rejected, so we had to change the design. [So for *Illusion of Gaia*], It may have had something to do with a religious reason, why we had to change the boss. When we had to change any design, it normally had specific reasons for that. Probably the overseas publisher[43] or directors saw certain motifs and then thought there might be some religious implications. So maybe they decided that they have to remove references to specific religions. Or perhaps it was related to the ratings, so they had to avoid it. So it might have been that they pointed out the design problems. For example, if there was a cross on the map, we were not allowed to show it, for the converted versions overseas.

[42] The 1st and 6th demon heads had their forward horns removed, the 4th was replaced with... lightning?
[43] Lit. says "buyer", but in Japanese this refers to a buyer in the import/export business, not end consumer

JS: America were the gatekeepers. First it came out in the US, and afterwards in Europe.

JR: It's also one of the reasons Japanese games could not sell as well all over the world, because America would first decide yes or no, and then sales in Europe were not as strong as expected.

JS: However, *Terranigma* came out in Europe but not America. There were exceptions.

KY: When Quintet came up with *Terranigma*, that is when Shade was established.

JS: That's why you were not involved with it?

KY: That's correct.

JS: *Terranigma* wasn't released in America...

KY: No, for some reason not in the United States. You emailed me saying that you were going to interview Mr Takeshi Tsuru; he was involved with *Terranigma*.

JS: Oh, yes! I got in touch with Mr Tsuru.

KY: Have you already interviewed him?

JS: He was going to contact a colleague and we were going to have a joint interview, but before I left for Japan I hadn't yet heard from him.

KY: Did you email him at his company address?

JS: Private email. His brother put me in contact.

KY: Oh, I see.

JS: Fans regard *Soul Blazer*, *Illusion of Gaia*, *Terranigma*, and *Granstream Saga*, as a loosely connected four-part saga.

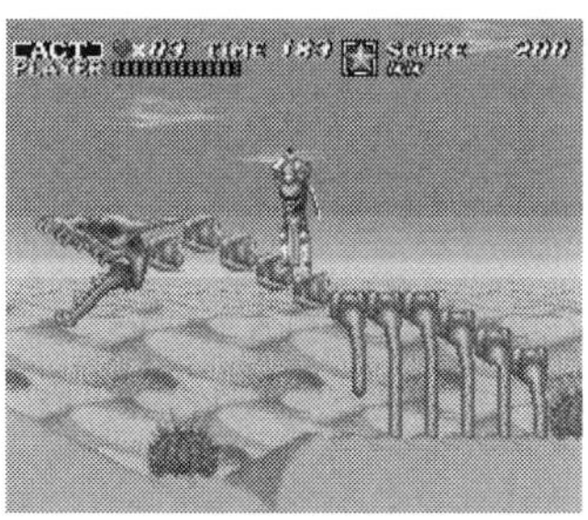

KY: Yes, I think there was a common custom or thread shared among the games, in terms of scenario writing, such as like the delivery of the dialogue, and so on. So in that effect I think there was some resemblance. Starting with *ActRaiser*, and followed by *Soul Blazer* and *Illusion of Gaia*, the games are definitely connected,[44] in Miyazaki-san's mind, at least. Whereas *Terranigma* and *Granstream Saga* are somewhat different. Because I was the one who came up with the basic idea for *Granstream Saga*. I don't know about *Terranigma* though.

JS: I suppose when someone likes all the games from a company, they want to draw connections.

KY: Yes. I can understand that, because as a fan it's exciting to discover connections or relationships between the characters and contents of the games.

JS: *ActRaiser* is part of a trilogy with *Soul Blazer* and *Illusion of Gaia*?

KY: Yes, I think like you said there are resemblances among the three games, because Miyazaki-san kind of liked the idea of having a god versus a demon, in which the main character is on the side of the god and battles the demon. That is the underlying concept that he likes to adopt, which unites those three games. He liked to grapple with the themes of creation and destruction, and he was good at entwining human existence within the context of creation and destruction in order to create drama. I think Miyazaki-san became very popular because he was able to come up with a convincing script, incorporating pathos, or a kind of sadness into it.

JS: In contrast, *Robotrek* was quite light-hearted. (left)

KY: Yes. The reason is because one of the planning staff was a woman, she used to belong to Falcom as well, and she was involved in a game called *Dinosaur*. Well, *Dinosaur* was quite dark, so she wanted to do something completely different and come up with something very fantastical and light, so that is why she came up with this new game, *Robotrek*. She intentionally made it light and happy with a pop sensibility. The game involves an inventor, but they didn't want it to be about cutting-edge technology. So

[44] Mr Yokota literally used the word for "contiguous land", as though the worlds of the games take place in adjacent countries or continents. But it's likely Mr Yokota was simply being metaphorical

they aimed for a more approachable and endearing, somewhat retro atmosphere, and outsourced the scenario and character design to us with that kind of world in mind. So I created the robot designs based on that.

JS: With a kind of an old fashioned feel.

KY: That's correct. <*brings out photo*> I found a couple of photographs of me and Miyazaki-san, from Quintet. This is the picture taken at the Quintet office back then.

JS: It's amazing! Can I photograph these?

KY: Yes, of course. We were both very young. [...] The office is not looking so clean or tidy.

JS: I think it looks great! It shows a working environment, which implies creativity. [...]

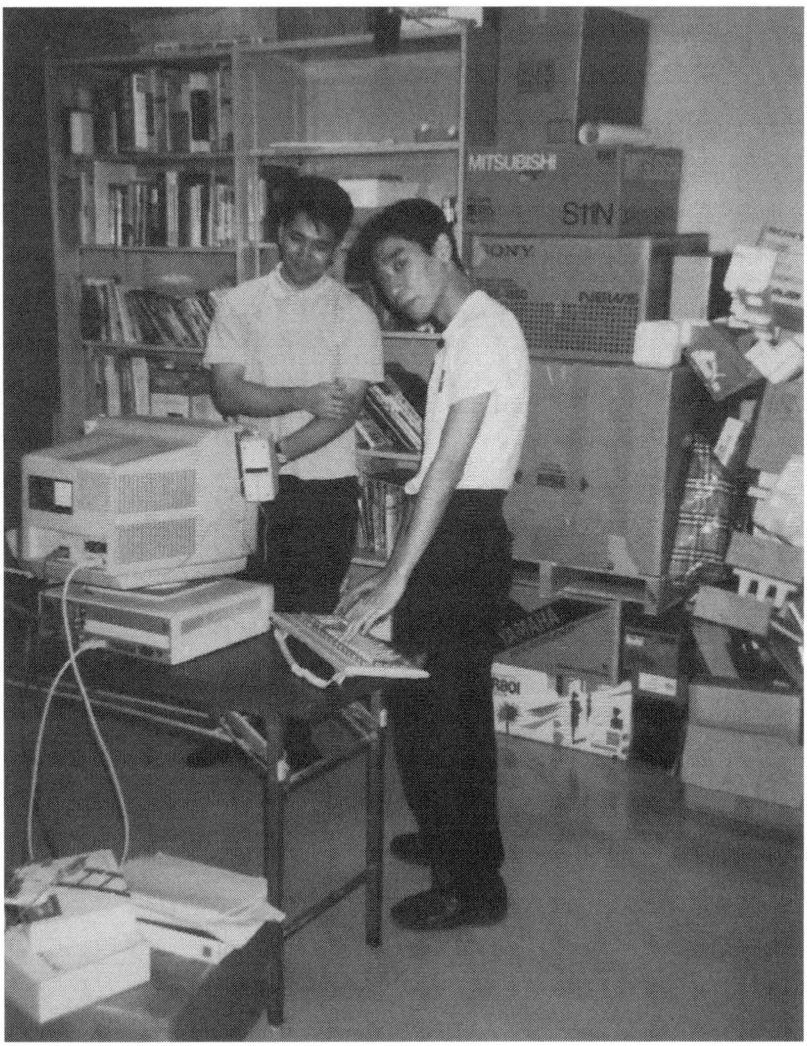

According to this list, after Quintet you freelanced on *Dragon Quest V*?

KY: Actually, the chronological order is wrong. [During] my career at Quintet I received a request from Chunsoft, asking me to help create the data for *Dragon Quest*. The data for graphics in the casino. Slot machines.

JS: Do you know anything about the Satellaview games Chunsoft worked on?

KY: Uh, no, I don't really know about that.

JS: After *Robotrek*, freelancing at Game Arts?

KY: Game Arts, yes.

JS: When freelancing, was this in their office? How did freelancing work at this time?

KY: It's a case by case thing. Basically I was working on my computer at home, creating graphics, and then putting them on floppy disks and posting them to the company. Or I would take them with me to the office when we had a physical meeting. So once a week, on a regular basis, I would go to the office and they would ask me or give me an assignment, to please complete this character by next week. So I would take that home, complete it and then come back before the deadline. For *Gaiares* the development work was done at a rented apartment, it wasn't in an office. I could go there and come home at any time. The programmer would actually just live there, always. So whenever I visited he was there. Sometimes I would stay there and do some work, or I was also allowed to take some work home and work at home. It was quite free.

JS: This apartment was rented by...?

KY: By Telenet, yes.

JS: Your worked on *Lunar: Eternal Blue* for Game Arts. I believe the dungeon designs were outsourced to a company called Vanguard?

KY: Vanguard was helping... It's either Vanguard who designed the dungeons, or we handled it in-house... Again, we split the work.

JS: It seems unusual that the company would outsource some sections to another company...

KY: Actually, there's a staff member of ours,[45] who was involved in the *Lunar 2* maps. So I can get him.

<Mr Yokota leaves; returns minutes later>

KY: I asked the person and it seems that Vanguard was involved, because there was a large workload at Game Arts, but Vanguard didn't do everything. Vanguard was largely involved, but not for graphic designing, rather level designing. So the in-house team at Game Arts also worked on that. It may be that all the basic parts and tiles of the dungeons were created at Game Arts by the main graphics designer, and following those designs Vanguard created the dungeon, using the parts. So in the end, even though it was outsourced the result was consistent. For example if you are to create a tower, you just create the ground floor of the tower, and to create the rest of the tower you simply re-use the parts from the ground floor. So that way they can still have a consistency in the image, but you can use an outsourced company. At Game Arts there was a main designer who was responsible for creating all the basic designs, and then that basic design was distributed to internal teams as well as external teams. So that's how I understand they worked back then.

<author picks up copy of Lunar 2 on MCD>

KY: Actually, I was very happy to see you brought in *Lunar 2* on Mega CD! *<smiles>* It's available on the PlayStation and Saturn, but they were different to the original, because the character that I put a lot of effort into was gone. It makes me very happy to see the original version of *Lunar 2*.

[Mr Yokota was visibly very pleased at the number of his old games we brought in]

KY: I used to have one. *<laughs>* I lent it to someone, but they never returned it. Sometimes I watch YouTube, because you can see the playing screens, and sometimes it makes me quite nostalgic. Sometimes it's an emulator, but I think the original version is the best.

[45] Sadao Kobayashi, now at Shade; graphic designer on *Terranigma*

JS: *Lunar 2: Eternal Blue* has special meaning for you. Please describe your involvement.

KY: Yes, so basically I was responsible for the boss monsters, but at that time nothing was set in stone as to how the bosses would be attacking, so I came up with the ideas and proposed them to the programmer, and worked on each of them, one by one. Some of the bosses hadn't been designed at all, so I came up with the designs from scratch. There was one key monster that was still only a rough idea, but the deadline was just around the corner, so I thought up almost the entire design myself and added a lot of details. Particularly, there's this character called the Star Dragon.[46] Although it's a dragon, it appears in the form of a human being. I was the one who actually came up with the idea and decided most of the details for this particular character. So those were the portions I was deeply involved with.

JS: You created the Star Dragon? Do you know why it was removed in the remake?

KY: I was not involved with the development so I have no idea why this happened. I also find it very disappointing.

JS: After the game ends there's a second quest with happier ending. Was this always intended, or was it added on request?

KY: Yes, I think it was intended from the onset. They explained the overall flow of the game to me, and I heard that my character the Star Dragon appears after the ending and becomes a crucial character. So I think that was the intention from the beginning. That was what I thought, and so I was assuming there was going to be a second ending.

[46] The Star Dragon is also known as the Phantom Sentry and later Star Sentry in the English SCD version, or Zeke/Sieg the Risen (ジーク-ザ-ライズン) in the JPN MCD original. Notable for carrying a pistol as a weapon. Pops up as a mid-boss, with a final encounter in the epilogue as an expert swordsman; in the Saturn and PlayStation remake he was removed, with the final encounter being against a literal "dragon" boss

JS: The reason I ask: the first ending isn't as happy. In other games, for example *Ico* on PlayStation 2, the second happier ending was only added at the request of the marketing team.

KY: Well, actually, I was working as a freelancer at that time, so I don't know what exactly the main people on the development team were actually intending to do. But when I joined this project it was already decided that the second ending would be the heroine going back to the moon, and for the second ending she would be reunited with the main character. Yes, I think they originally wanted the girl to be reunited with the main character, but maybe they were concerned about finishing the game in time. So maybe they decided to create the first ending as a potential stopping point, just in case there wasn't enough time in the development schedule to create the events that became the second ending.

In fact, they might have been planning to create a *Lunar 3*, but didn't know if they'd be able to do it. *Lunar 2* was a Mega Drive game,[47] and that system was nearing the end of its lifespan, and they knew the hardware would be retired soon, so they were trying to fit in as much as they possibly could.

This is just based upon my assumptions, but I knew they were behind schedule back then. They were originally supposed to release *Lunar 2* much earlier, but the game was delayed significantly, and ultimately became the final RPG released for the [Mega CD] hardware.[48] So this is just my assumption, but perhaps they took their plans for the unrealised *Lunar 3*, and inserted them into *Lunar 2* as the second ending.

JS: *Lunar 3* - wow!

KY: So, like I said, I don't really know their true intent, but having seen all the circumstances back then I assumed that they may have been intending a third game, but due to the delivery and schedule problems they kind of brought the third game's idea into the second ending and stopped there. But I don't want you to be writing about this, because I'm not sure for a fact.

[47] Accurate interpretation; MD was said in Japanese
[48] *Eternal Blue* was in fact the last Mega CD game of any genre that Game Arts made

There were two stage maps that were not inserted or included; those two stage maps were deleted. I'm not sure if they were re-used or resuscitated for the PlayStation version or the Saturn version. I never saw those updated versions, so I don't know for sure whether they reintroduced the stages that were originally cut. But for the [original] version at least, there were two stages, by which I mean continents [on the world map], that had to be cut because of schedule constraints. So had they been on schedule they may have been able to release the game earlier, in which case they may have come up with a third game. But this is just my assumption. So I think that's how things were back then.

JS: I love hearing stories about lost content.

KY: Yes, there's always a gap between the original planning and the actual schedule, because we come up with too many ideas and we have to remove them. So I think the stream, or the basic flow, against the original plan, was somewhat different. Yes, that's about it regarding *Lunar*.

JS: You mentioned the Mega Drive; did *Lunar 2* start on the Mega Drive? Because it was released on the Sega Mega CD.

KY: Yes, the Mega CD. Ah! I meant Mega CD when I said Mega Drive.

JS: Sometimes games start on one and shift to the other. *Phantasy Star IV* started on the Mega CD and was then changed to the Mega Drive.[49]

KY: Oh, alright.

JS: You mentioned your disappointment with the remake for Saturn and PlayStation, can you elaborate further?

KY: Well, I did not actually play the remake version myself, but I read through the strategy guide, and found out that there were changes made to the boss monsters in several of the stages. And I think I know the reason why they made some of those changes. I get the feeling that one particular character was based upon Kuidaore Ningyo,[50] which is found in Osaka. The original character was quite smart and cool looking, but they revised the character design to be more cute, or kawaii. Perhaps the change was made because of some copyright issues, or something. Yes, if you Google by punching in "Kuidaore Ningyo" I'm sure you can find some information about it - but I did notice the changes made to this boss character. Although I can understand why the character was changed, I was still disappointed.

[Top images from MCD, beneath is the PS1 remake, and left an actual photo. Notice the addition of cute hearts on the remake; the colours are also pastel]

JS: I looked up internet discussions on which version fans prefer, and there was lots of debate.

KY: With respect to sound, since the PlayStation is using CD streaming, the sound quality is better. And with respect to the animated movies, I think it depends on each individual's preference. For the original Mega CD version we couldn't use animated movies,[51] so we really struggled to come up with something that looked like an animated movie. Of course the PlayStation remake version has a smoother motion to the images, like proper animation, but personally I think

[49] Source: old magazines, such as *EGM*, had previews for the Mega CD version, with unique screens

[50] くいだおれ人形 - *kuidaore* is to eat oneself bankrupt, and *ningyo* is a doll. He's a robot clown mascot that stands outside the Kuidaore restaurant in Osaka. Photo taken from: **www.http://kuidaoretaro.com**

[51] This is true; while the game had cinemas, it wasn't actually full-motion video

the images are of higher quality on the Mega CD version. That is why I evaluate the Mega CD version higher than that of the remake version.

JS: How did you come to freelance for Game Arts? Did you work from home?

KY: I worked from home. Well, I think one of my friends came to me saying that Game Arts was looking for a game designer, and that's how I came to work for them as a freelancer. I went to the office for a meeting once a week.

JS: Do you know about *Lunar*'s localisation into English? Were you aware of fans outside Japan?

KY: No, I was not aware of that.

JS: Many say that *Lunar: Eternal Blue* is one of the reasons for owning a Mega CD.

KY: Wow. I came to know about that for the first time when I went to an exhibition, E3, and I noticed for the first time that the game had been localised into English, after having taken a look at the booth at the exhibition. The space area allotted for the booth was quite spacious, so I understood that it was quite popular.

JS: Did you go up and mention to people you worked on it, maybe sign some autographs?

KY: <*laughs*> No, no, I didn't do that.

JS: Had you played *Lunar: Silver Star Story* before working on *Eternal Blue*?

KY: No, I did not play it myself. But I saw people playing it.

JS: Let's discuss *Granstream Saga*. Some regard it as the final instalment of the Quintet series.

KY: Actually, as for *Granstream Saga*, I made a proposal for that. So the concept was slightly different from what was proposed by Miyazaki-san. So although there are some similarities it's different. However, when it came to the scenario, Miyazaki-san helped us in making the scenario, so therefore there is some colour of Miyazaki-san in the scenario.

JS: It was by Shade. Can you describe leaving Quintet and starting Shade?

KY: Quintet back then had business with Nintendo. We wanted to do business with other companies, but it was a tricky situation, and... <*pause*> Doing business with anyone other than Nintendo was difficult. So we decided to come up with a subsidiary which spun off from Quintet, so that we can start doing business with other companies as well. After I left Quintet they started receiving business offers and requests for game development, particularly from Sony Computer Entertainment, and also Sega, and so Hashimoto-san and Miyazaki-san thought that it would be a good idea to establish a new company so that they can dedicate software development to those companies. And they came to me asking if I was interested or not.

JS: Hashimoto-san and Miyazaki-san helped you set up Shade?

KY: That's correct. At first we had work outsourced from Quintet and were too busy to create our own projects, but eventually that work fell through, so we decided that we actually needed to sell ourselves proactively and make proposals to get a publishing deal. So that's how we ended up approaching Sony and Sega. But we knew that we had little chance of being accepted as an anonymous or not well known company. So we explained to Sega and Sony, saying that we spun off from Quintet to become an independent company, and since Miyazaki-san would be directing and overseeing the scenario [for *Granstream Saga*], it's going to be fine. So that's how we sold ourselves to those companies and that is why they decided to sign off on *Granstream Saga*.

Originally the company [Shade] started out as an outsource company for computer graphics (CG), so our initial business plan was to receive CG assignments from Quintet to be delivered back to Quintet. We were assuming that Quintet would be responsible for the programming, while we were in charge of the computer graphics. But things did not work out that way. The original setup was that Shade would produce the CG, and also interface with the publisher so that Nintendo wouldn't know about Quintet's involvement. Since Quintet had a relationship with Nintendo, Shade would deal with the other publishers, while Quintet would secretly handle the programming and scenario. But as I said, for some reason that did not work out. Most likely because another project was initiated within Quintet, so our work arrangement was cancelled. So we were compelled to look for a programmer as soon as possible and establish ourselves as a complete game development company. So that's how we started out.

JS: And your first game was *Granstream Saga*?

KY: We created two proposals for *Granstream Saga*, one for the Sega Saturn and one for the Sony PlayStation, and approached the publishers nearly simultaneously. At first we had a great response from Sega, we thought that they liked our idea, but it took them a long time before they came to a decision. Whereas Sony Computer Entertainment took only a week to accept our plans. So we went with Sony as our first platform. If Sega had made up their mind prior to Sony, we may no longer be in existence anymore! <*laughs*> Because the Sega Saturn was weak with regards to 3D functionality. Whereas the PlayStation was much better at 3D functionality. So had Sega chosen us before Sony, then we would have struggled big time. Actually, we were saved because of Sega's slow decision making process.

Much later, when we started experimenting with the Saturn development hardware, we found out that Sega was not so strong in 3D functionality. Actually, Sega showed us a 3D graphics demonstration almost around the same time, and we originally thought that the quality was quite good in terms of 3D functionality, but it turns out Sega were trying to make themselves look good by showing a pre-rendered movie. When the game itself was released it was almost entirely 2D rather than 3D.

JS: In English we say: "You dodged a bullet."

KY: Yes, that's it. We were really consumed with what we were doing.

JS: I liked the Saturn hardware in terms of the games that were eventually released. But as a journalist, I've heard incredible stories regarding Sega's business decision making and their internal politics. They seem internally conflicted.

KY: Yes, I actually had dinner with one of the Sega people last night, and he was also saying that the decision making that took place in Sega was not well thought out - or rather, reckless, such as in who they decided to hire. We were talking about the past, when those kinds of decisions were being made.

JS: There was almost a Saturn version! Any other unreleased games that you've seen?

KY: Are you asking about unreleased games that did not come to fruition before *Granstream Saga*?

JS: Yes, before. But also perhaps afterwards.

KY: There were quite a few plans that went into the ditch at the end of the day. But one of the good memories that I can recall is one of the first games that we brought to Sony. They had asked us to really challenge ourselves and come up with a genuinely unique and innovative game. At the time, Sony was doing things like buying up movie companies, so we suspected that Sony would be interested in movies, and we came up with this idea of a game in which you managed movies. We thought this would be a good idea for Sony, we thought they would like it, so we came up this idea of the user becoming a director and producer of a film, starting from a selection of actors and actresses, and formulating budgets, and actually shooting the action scenes. And if it gets a high score then the movie turns a good profit, which means they can make further investment to create even better quality movies. You know, assigning top notch actors and actresses. So we brought this idea to Sony and they flat-out refused it. They said, "There's no way you can make a movie on the PlayStation."

Which is a rather self-rejecting thing for Sony to say, <*laughs*> but that is what they said. They were contradicting themselves. Had we brought the idea now, when the PlayStation 3 and 4 are out, then they may have said yes. But back then it was PlayStation 1 and the graphics were not that high quality, so they thought that's not going to work.[52] On the other

[52] Funnily enough, there's a new PS3 game called *CV: Casting Voice*. You play a voiceover producer who

hand, *Granstream Saga* had an overhead view reminiscent of *Ys*, but with real-time 3D action. So we showed them our more conventional *Ys*-like proposal, and they said, "OK, that'll work."

JS: I think about six years ago there was a game exactly like that![53]

KY: Yes, since they had asked for a genuinely unique, new game, we came up with this idea and they didn't like it. So we went back to our original forte, which was a more conventional scenario and action game, and then they said that's OK, we'll go with that.

JS: That's a shame, I think you might have been on to a winner.

KY: Yes. So the Sony producers weren't actually looking for that far-fetched kind of a game. So the first producer for *Granstream Saga* was Mr Yamauchi. [54] But then he was replaced by somebody else because he needed to go work on a car game or something.[55]

JS: <*laughs*> A car game or something? You mean *Gran Turismo!*

KY: <*laughs*> Yes, *Gran Turismo*. So that is how we came to create *Granstream Saga*. The company that was in charge of the animated movies for *Granstream Saga* was a company called Production IG, which is now a major animation company. But back then they were just starting out, and approached Sony for work. At first they were working on some animation for a completely different game project by another developer, but that project fell through, so in order to fill in the gap in their work schedule, they switched over to *Granstream Saga*. The schedule was very tight, but they did an excellent job for us.

JS: Players were impressed with the animated cinemas, especially their high frequency.

KY: Yes, I agree with that. They came up with exactly what we were looking for. Quintet sent over [to Production IG] a scenario writer who worked together with us at Shade, under Miyazaki-san's overall supervision.

JS: Website IGN claims it was based on a manga called *Kros*?[56]

KY: What is related to the manga series *Kros*?

JS: *Granstream Saga*?

KY: <*talks to self, trying to recall*> No, I don't know anything about *Kros*. [...] We did not collaborate with anyone in that way for *Granstream Saga*.

JS: Is *Granstream Saga* the game you've had the most involvement with?

KY: Yes, that's right.

JS: *Granstream Saga* came after *Final Fantasy VII*. Did you feel a sense of competition?[57]

KY: <*laughs*> Yes... Well, *Final Fantasy VII* already had an established brand, whereas we were kind of new. It was our first original title, and was being supported and published by Sony itself. So we were exerting our utmost efforts in this. Our game was fairly orthodox in some ways, but then we heard the news and the new *Final Fantasy* came out, and we thought we needed to make our game more action-oriented. So we changed our policy midway through and decided to make the game even more action-like.

---

oversees the voice acting for anime, videogames, TV narration, and commercials. You're in charge of the voice casting and selecting the script. If you cast the right actors and give them the right guidance, you increase your standing as a producer and get access to higher-profile scripts and voice talent

[53] I was thinking of was *The Movies*, by Lionhead, first released on computers in 2005. As noted there's quite a few similarly themed games

[54] Kazunori Yamauchi, producer on *Gran Turismo*

[55] Although not noticeable in text, this sentence was extremely funny when delivered in person

[56] I don't know where IGN writer Jason Boor got this information, but not only is there no evidence for a connection, there is absolutely ***zero evidence*** that a manga titled "*Kros*" even exists. The closest thing I can find is an 8-volume manga series by Noriyoshi Inoue called *X* (クロス), pronounced "cross", from 1992. But it's apparently about an aspiring actor whose father is a mafia boss, and is not remotely related to *Granstream Saga*. Likely it's a fabrication!

[57] *FFVII* Jan 1997; *GS* Nov 1997

JS: The battle system is real-time, rather than turn-based. Was that a direct result to hearing about *Final Fantasy VII*? Were you originally considering turn-based battles?

KY: No, we originally had the intention of making it a real-time battle kind of game, but we were not really thinking about a high level of action, or a strategic element, to the battles. But as we worked on it we came up with all sorts of ideas. We started out simply as a conventional RPG, with the battles just a way to buy time, seeing the enemies as obstacles, but ultimately we decided to make the battles themselves more fun and enjoyable, and concentrated our efforts on the battle scenes. We didn't choose real-time battles because *Final Fantasy* was turn-based. We didn't think about adopting a turn-based system at all, we originally started out by incorporating real-time battles. We originally had the idea of characters alternating between guarding and attacking as the main game mechanic. At first we designed the enemies to fall after one or two hits, but over time we decided to deepen the battle system by making the fights longer and incorporating more blocking and dodging.

JS: The battle system is one of the highlights.

KY: After we had launched the game there were many comments coming from female players, saying that although the story itself was interesting, the battles were quite difficult for them to play, and so they gave up. So we kind of regretted that a little bit. And also there was a complaint from the users saying that they were not able to come across this secret weapon, called the "Onimaru", which is the most powerful weapon, and if the user can come across this weapon they can tear down the enemy with just one blow. So we prepared this secret, ultimate weapon for the player, but because of a mistake we made, the player only has one chance to acquire this weapon in the entire game.[58] That was one of the complaints we received. The user would have only one chance to come across this weapon, but it's hidden in one of the events, so unless they become aware of it they would never be able to use it. And so the way we hid the weapon was not so good. *<laughs>*

JS: From a technical point of view it's impressive. It runs almost constantly at 60 frames per second. Was this difficult on the original PlayStation?

KY: Back then fighting games such as *Virtua Fighter* were very popular. Those games influenced us, and we decided that we would minimize any performance issues, such as slowdown in the character motion, in our games. That was our policy in coming up with the data. But in order to do that we needed to simplify the characters' faces and make them less sophisticated. So as an RPG story it may have ended up looking a little bit cheap, which we also regret. So we had to omit faces on the 3D graphics, but if we used certain camera angles, or if the user took control of the camera and zoomed in, the user would easily notice the graphical shortcomings. From the top-down view, you would not notice that at all, however! But if you zoom in you can easily tell that they don't have any faces. So it was not so popular among the users, because the characters were lacking expressiveness. *<gestures to screenshot showing a character portrait in front, but that*

[58] After entering the secret church basement go south and face the west wall. Use Panther Eye to find metal, which can be restored to make Onimaru

same character in background> If you take a look at the character portraits up front they obviously do have faces, but if you take a look at the back, you don't see any expressions. And some users would of course only focus on the characters in the background. So if we wanted to be elaborate on the faces and the fingers, we would have had to compromise the 60 frames-per-second framerate.

JS: Personally, I like the omission. It gives it a distinct, stylised look.

KY: So in order to compensate for the characters faces in the background, we decided to make high-quality movies to enhance the storytelling.

JS: Faces are difficult to make look nice with the PlayStation 1. If you apply a texture map to the polygons they're very blocky. Omitting textures can hide the shortcomings of the hardware.

KY: Yes, that's a good point. I think you're exactly correct. Actually, we did attempt to render faces on the characters once, but due to the shortcomings of the PlayStation 1, and its limited number of polygons, the faces that we came up with ended up looking like masks, rather than faces. And so we had a character portrait in front, whereas we had a mask in the back, which looked weird. So we decided not to have a face on the character in the back.

JS: Do you have any screenshots of this prototype with masked faces?

KY: <*laughs*> No.

JS: Of all the games you've worked on, do you have a favourite?

KY: Yes, I would it say it would be *Granstream Saga*, because I was involved in it the most, and I had the most hands-on involvement on that. And I think that was the final game in which I was involved. Now I'm more on the producing side, although I do have opportunities to work hands on, here and there. But I was actually able to really put my strength into *Granstream Saga* the most. So I would say that it's my most favourite of all the titles.

JS: Does Shade still own the rights to the intellectual property? Could we see a sequel?

KY: No, Sony has the entire rights over *Granstream Saga* now. So we cannot create another game using the same name, *Granstream Saga*, anymore.

JS: That's unfortunate.

KY: Although we cannot use the name as it is, we can perhaps come up with a different name, but we're not sure whether we would be free to create a similar game. But that would be one option that we would like to pursue. I had many more ideas and stories to tell, which did not fit into this one particular game.

JS: Aha! My next question was: Did you have to leave stuff out?

KY: I had this idea of a self-contained, recurring world, like a world within a book. And the player character is actually the *maou*, or devil, [59] meaning that the player character or hero in the final world is actually a reincarnation of the *maou* from the very first world. In addition, some of the reincarnations along the way are key characters, and they transmigrate from their intermediate worlds to the final world. And these characters come together in the final world to face the end times. It's a little complicated, but as an example, among the sages in *Granstream Saga*, there was one sage who didn't appear in the game, and his backstory was that he died in a nuclear war between the Soviet Union and the United States, but then he was reincarnated and returned to this world.

There are multiple parallel worlds existing in which the world would go extinct a

---

[59] *Maou* or *maoh* (魔王) is one of the most prevalent and influential concepts in Japanese fantasy media. Originally an ancient Buddhist term, *maou* refers to the ultimate antagonist or archenemy, and has been variously translated as "demon king", "devil", "overlord", "dragonlord", and other names. In Christianity, the *maou* would be Satan. In videogames, *maou* almost always refers to the last boss, and the word itself is used to refer to major enemies in many Japanese games, such as *Chrono Trigger* (Magus), *Super Mario Brothers* (King Koopa), *The Legend of Zelda* (Ganondorf), *Shin Megami Tensei* (the Tyrants, specifically Mara), *NieR* (the Shadowlord), and *Dragon Quest* (various bosses). More recently, Japanese creators have been playfully deconstructing the term for comedic effect, as seen in the *Disgaea* series and the novel/anime franchise *Hataraku Maou-sama!* (*The Devil Is a Part-Timer!*), for example

number of times, and those who were involved in creating the cause of the extinction, or those who were unable to save the world, would reincarnate because of their remorse and regret over what they had done in their previous life. But as they fail, they become worse and worse, going over to the dark side. This main character, the original *maou*, decides that he wants to end this karmic cycle and bring that to an end. So that is what he does, but I wanted also to elaborate as to how each world had to end, because of these characters' karmic actions. Which I was not able to explain in this particular game, and I wanted to include that.

JS: Do you have it all written down?

KY: Yes, I have random notes written down here and there.

JS: If you like, I could have someone translate them into English, and put some of it in my book.

KY: *<laughs>* Well, if you were to look at my personal notes, you would see that I had a clear description of the various characters, and you would be able to get an idea of what I originally had in mind. But when you actually play the game, there's a lot of other information mixed in, and maybe the individual characters would become mixed up and somewhat vague. I actually wanted to articulate the characteristics of the characters to the users, which I was not able to do in this game.

JS: Was this due to deadlines, not enough space on the CD, or...?

KY: It had to do with the schedule. I had to focus on the adventure of the key character, which meant that the subplots and other elements were drastically simplified or removed.

JS: Masanori Hikichi worked on the music for *Granstream Saga*, and also for *Terranigma* and *Ys IV: Mask of the Sun* on SFC.

KY: That's correct. And he was also responsible for *Sonic the Hedgehog 2* and *3*.

JS: There were two versions of *Ys IV*, neither of which were by Falcom, because each was outsourced to a different company. Do you know anything about this?

KY: *<laughs>* I wasn't personally interested in *Ys IV* at all, so I cannot comment on that.

JS: Did you like the English packaging for *Granstream Saga*? *<shows the US boxart alongside the Japanese>*

KY: *<laughs>* Hmm... That's right, the THQ version. But the European version has this cover art. *<gestures to Japanese cover>*

JS: Shade developed WonderSwan Color games. Was the licensing better than at Nintendo?[60]

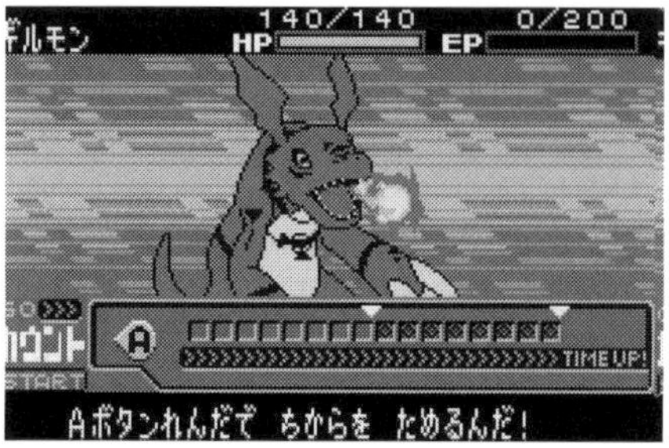

KY: Bandai was manufacturing the SwonderSwan. Bandai had the characters *Digimon*, which is like *Pokémon*, and they wanted to utilise that content. It wasn't because of the licensing, there wasn't any major problem with license agreements. I think the initial contact was... I don't know the exact background of it, but Bandai were looking for game developers for the WonderSwan, and we thought it sounded interesting. So I said we'll do that. Initially we were developing the monochrome version, in black and white, but during the process it was decided that the colour version [of WonderSwan] would be released, so I remember we changed to the colour version.

JS: You listed *Emerald Dragon* on PC Engine in the list of games you worked on?

KY: I think my name is not listed as part of the staff roll though.

JS: Did you work with a Mr Hiromasa Iwasaki?

KY: No, not together with him. They incorporated incomplete versions of my work

into *Emerald Dragon*. That is why my name was not on the staff roll. As a creator, I didn't want my name associated with half-finished work.

JS: What do you mean?

KY: Well, I sent them the final version of my artwork for the game, but they decided not to use it, and it was not included. And so I was furious, because perhaps I was young back then, and I didn't understand why that was the case.

JS: Wow, I had no idea about this! Can I print this story?

KY: *<laughs>* It's OK, go ahead. They apologised to me at the end. So that was OK, the case was closed.

JS: What was the data you provided?

KY: The overall map; the world map.

JS: Mr Hiromasa Iwasaki also worked on it, so maybe I'll ask him about the incomplete map.

KY: I don't think Iwasaki-san was so much involved in the game portion. It was a company called Alpha System, located in Kumamoto Prefecture on the island of Kyushu, who did the game portion. I was sending off data over one of the early online services using a personal computer. Since Kyushu is located far away I was unable to visit them once a week.

JS: You were using a dial-up modem?

KY: Yes, a modem.

JS: With baud speeds?

KY: Yes, 2800 baud speed.

<everyone laughs>

JS: Wow, slow!

KY: It took me about 2 hours just to upload this big of an image. *<Puts his forefinger and his thumb slightly apart - it's not very big>*

JS: Incredible...

KY: Yes, I'm really amazed by the internet today.

---

[60] Shade developed *Digimon Tamers: Digimon Medley* for WonderSwan Color, released July 2001

JS: Do you have any other unusual stories or secrets you'd like to share?

KY: <*long pause*> What kind of secrets...?

JS: Maybe secret is the wrong word. Something which everyone would enjoy hearing but doesn't know about.

KY: There's this one game, back there. <*points to wall with row of posters along it*> This is based upon a manga called *Project Arms.*[61] Actually, while we were creating this game, 9/11 took place. We were watching the television, while the World Trade Centre collapsed, that was during the evening. We originally wanted to set the final scene in New York, but that became impossible because of 9/11. We had redo the final map from scratch, so instead of introducing New York, we ended up introducing a scene which took place inside a dream world, in a kind of vast, empty dreamscape. We had originally imagined this battle against an enemy who turns into a gigantic monster and starts tearing down buildings and destroying the city, but... Our idea was a little too close to the reality of what had just happened, so we decided to change it.

We were better off compared to other developers. I heard that one of the game manufacturers completed a game, about an old building demolisher, but they couldn't release it because of 9/11. It was a puzzle action game where the players would set bombs to destroy buildings, but that was no good.

JS: I think there were a few such games.

KY: The one I'm thinking of was called *Biru Baku*.[62] I'm not sure what the title was overseas, but in Japan the game was called that.

JS: The one I played, with a similar idea, was *Bomber Hehhe* on Dreamcast.

[61] *Project Arms* for PS2, released March 2002

[62] By KAZE (PS2); katakana ビルバク, Romanised "Buile Baku"; eventually released in 2002 in Japan; saw a budget release in PAL territories under the new title of *Detonator*

KY: So, you know, some of the game companies had to give up releasing the products, whereas we were able to complete and sell ours. So we were quite fortunate.

JS: Yes, 9/11 affected everyone. Sega cancelled *Propeller Arena* on Dreamcast, because that had planes flying around buildings.

KY: I see.

JS: All the stories you've shared today I find utterly fascinating.

KY: <*laughs*> Well, I'm not a very famous creator or anything.

JS: You will be when I'm finished!

KY: I'm not sure whether my information would be of any help to you. <*laughs*>

JS: I'm not trying to flatter you, but you're a legendary creator. You've worked for a lot of famous companies. I think you'd be surprised.

KY: It's such a compliment, and it really inspires us to do a better job.

JS: Some of my favourite development companies have been Telenet, Falcom, Quintet, and Game Arts. You've worked for all of them, so I was keen to have this interview.

KY: Yes, I am grateful myself.

JS: Did you like what you saw back at the Sony Indies night?

KY: Yes, I think it was very sophisticated, both in terms of visual and sound quality, compared to, you know, the way it was in the past. Nowadays you can get high-quality visuals and sound inexpensively and conveniently in a professional manner, whereas back in the past it required manual labour, needing special techniques and equipment. So I think the quality in general has improved.

Now that you can easily obtain high quality visuals and sound, I would rather somebody come up with a brilliant idea, even though the visuals and sound might be mediocre.

JS: What about a game where you scare the users, or make them feel sad?

KY: Yes, of course. I think that's good for the people who want to play those types of games. Some people prefer violent or *Resident Evil* style games, which is a good thing, but you don't want to just abruptly throw *Resident Evil* into *Final Fantasy*.

JS: A lot of Quintet games have a feeling of sadness to them.

KY: Yes, yes. I agree with you. It's not something I really know about, because I only worked on little fragments of the games throughout the development, but the player experiences that feeling while proceeding through the full game. Ultimately, it was Miyazaki-san who was involved from the beginning to end in creating the games, and he knew how to enhance the games by accentuating certain things, and adding more detail in certain places. I think the users recognized and appreciated his work, and perhaps have a fuller understanding of its quality than I do.

JS: The skill to produce beautiful low-resolution artwork is disappearing. As someone who was involved in creating "dot art",[63] what are your thoughts on this loss?

KY: I think it cannot be helped. As the technology evolves the "dot art" and its artistry are destined to disappear I think. But at the same time I do miss those old days, when we had to create images using dot art. So I think it really is in an accordance with the history of game evolution - when games started to come out, we started out using manual labour. Then as time went by the games industry developed and we were able to put across great games. So dot art is part of the history, which I do miss.

JS: Are you working on a big project at the moment, at Shade?

KY: It's not a big project, but I'm working on a couple of medium sized projects.

JS: Do you have any final message you'd like to share with readers?

KY: I've been in this game development business for more than 25 years, but looking back I think the basic concept of game creation has not changed that much. Of course the platforms and the devices we use to express ourselves will continue to evolve, but I think it's very important for me always to look back to the basics, and not forget the basic concept - which is to offer joy to the users.

The things that go on top of that foundation will obviously continue to change, but as creators, we can't let ourselves be confused by that. It is a complex landscape, and we are bound to make mistakes, but the creator should always have this grounded intention of what they are trying to do, instead of being affected by the changes and evolution of the hardware and platforms themselves. So I would like to continue to engage in the game creation business, having that solid intention in place, and never to forget the basics, which is to offer joy to people.

[63] Pixel art is literally pronounced "dot art" in Japanese

~Appearing in a later volume~

ZAINSOFT

Now here's a mysterious developer, sometimes going under the name Sein Soft, Xainsoft and Zainsoft. The company specialised in action-RPGs, as something of a rival to Falcom. Based in Osaka, some have wondered if it was a front for certain "organisations" that cannot be named. Zainsoft was notorious for the brutal conditions staff worked under, suffering physical beatings and being locked inside until projects were complete. The games themselves, such as *DIOS*, were fascinating in their complexity and esoteric atmosphere. In this ***world exclusive*** interview the true story of Zainsoft is revealed by an employee who wishes to remain anonymous.

Yoshio Kiya

Legendary Falcom programmer, creator of one of Japan's earliest action-RPGs (*Panorama Toh*, pictured), and the man behind *Legacy of the Wizard*. In this exclusive English-language interview Mr Kiya reveals things about Falcom no one has ever known, detailing where the origins of *Ys* truly are, and what happened to him after leaving Falcom.

永嶋 純

NAGASHIMA, Jun

DOB: 19 June 1968 / Birthplace: Saitama / Blood Type: AB

~Selected Portfolio~

Everything from the Falcom era was published by Nihon Falcom. Subsequent games published by different companies. For rows **not marked** with an asterisk, Mr Nagashima was the main programmer.

Falcom

Ys III	- X68000, around1989 (※ tools, enemy characters)
Dinosaur	- PC-88 / PC-98, 1990 (※ helping out)
Popful Mail	- PC-8801 / PC-9801 / SFC, 1991
Ys V: Lost Kefin, Kingdom of Sand	- SFC, 1995
The Legend of Heroes 4: Akai Shizuku	- PC-9801, 1996 (※ Scenario programming)
Brandish 4	- Windows, 1998 (※ Programming)

Shade

Brightis / ブライティス	- PlayStation, 1999 (※enemy characters); awesome 3D action-RPG
Orphen: Scion of Sorcery	- PlayStation 2, 2000 (※ player control)
Mystic Heroes	- GameCube, 2002 (※ enemy characters)
Katekyou Hitman Reborn!	- PSP, 2010 (※ enemy characters)
Inazuma Eleven Strikers	- Wii, 2011
ColoQ	- Android
Danganronpa 1.2 Reload	- PS Vita

Interview with Jun Nagashima
10 October 2013, Tokyo

I first met Kouji Yokota at Sony's Indie Stream party in Tokyo; it was shortly after TGS and he invited me. Around us, young people were all showing off their PS Vita and smartphone apps, revelling in a rising wave of indie culture. Mr Yokota was surprised that I remembered the old games or that anyone still had an interest. I assured him that players still ardently adored the games of Quintet and Falcom. At that point he revealed that several employees of Shade were formerly at Falcom and Quintet. These were Yukio Takahashi; Sadao Kobayashi, graphic designer on Terranigma; and Jun Nagashima.

When I later visited Shade to interview Mr Yokota there was no time to interview these staff, though Mr Nagashima did sketch the Falcom layout. However, during my second interview with Mr Yokota, on 10 October, he brought in Jun Nagashima who was on a break. I did not realise he would be available, so everything is improvised.

JS: Please tell me about yourself before Falcom.

JN: While I was in elementary and middle school there was a comic called *Game Center Arashi*[1], which I loved and read frequently. An introductory guide to personal computers, featuring the main character of this comic, was then published, and once I acquired this book I started getting into computers. I learned BASIC on a Hitachi MB-6880 passed down to me from my uncle. In those days there was almost no concept of going out and buying software, as people mainly input program code listed in magazines. Unfortunately, there weren't many programs for the MB-6880, so I probably first learned how to program by porting and playing game programs written for different computer models. Later, I acquired a PC-8801mk2 by NEC, and was able to play retail games. Two titles from this period that impressed me were *Door Door*[2] and *Newtron*.[3] You may already know this, but the creator of these was Koichi Nakamura, now the chairman of Spike-Chunsoft. I loved the character design and gameplay, and played them a lot. Meanwhile, I was also writing programs, mostly in BASIC and assembler, and submitting them to game magazines. Before joining Falcom, three of my programs were published as type-in listings in magazines and awarded money, so I have many fond memories.

JS: When and how did you join Falcom?

JN: I remember joining as a fresh graduate in 1989. Since I had submitted several of my own games to magazines and had been published, I used them as a portfolio when applying for a job. I heard that, based on my work, Yoshio Kiya[4] recommended me for an interview with the company president at the time, Masayuki Kato. When I went to Falcom for an interview, copies of the magazines that published my games were lying on the desk, and Kato-san told me that Kiya-san had recommended me. My portfolio games were programmed to have BGM playing during the game, but since I didn't have the talent to compose my own music, I just used some sheet music I happened to find. Kato-san was rather particular about music, and I distinctly remember him grilling me hard about it, asking, "Where did you get this BGM?" But ultimately, he told me on the spot I was hired.

Back then, Falcom also ran a gift shop with Falcom-related goods in the company's office building, and new employees were placed there for about a month as general managers. Back then I was doing shop work and handling phone calls, and getting impatient wondering when they'd finally let me start making games.

JS: For *Popful Mail* I heard you came to Falcom with a demo and they requested it be expanded?

JN: No, that's not the case. I had created games while I was a student, which had nothing to do with *Popful Mail*. Those were sent to games magazines. There used to be a personal computer magazine called *LOGiN* back then, and they were offering openings for any amateur game creators, for their games to be featured in the magazine. So I sent the games that I had created while I

[1] By Mitsuru Sugaya, 1978~1984. Story about a boy obsessed with arcade games; very famous
[2] Trap enemies behind sliding doors
[3] Super obscure; collect fruit & kill caterpillars on a tree

[4] Creator of *Legacy of the Wizard*

was going to school, which were then featured in the magazine. Then I sent that game to Falcom and then they decided they wanted to hire me. What I had created, which was featured in *LOGiN*, and *Popful Mail*, have no connections whatsoever. The game entailed a frog character, sticking out its tongue to reach out and get things, which was unconnected to *Popful Mail*.

JS: Describe the start of the *Popful Mail* project. I heard it started on the PC-98?

JN: No, it was PC-88. After being assigned to game development, I was first involved with the development team for *Ys III*. At that time I was working together with Yokota-san, who is now the president of Shade. I don't know the reason why, but after development of *Ys III* ended, almost all of the associated staff quit Falcom - many key people including the [Shade] president, Yokota-san, left the company.

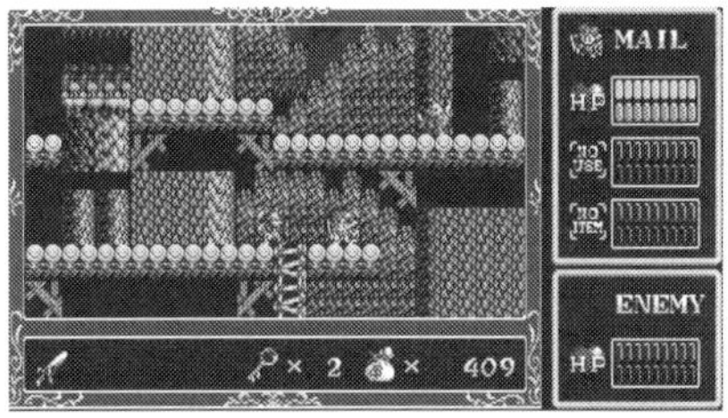

I remember being the only person left who had been involved with *Ys III*. A little while after that, Kiya-san instructed me to try to make a game for the PC-8801. So I was the only one from the team, alone, and the section manager said, "Since you're capable of programming, why not come up with something?" But I was the only programmer left on the team, and I had no graphic data to work with, so I was really at a loss as to what to do. But he said just, you know, fiddle around with whatever was already there at Falcom, and come up with something. So I was told to make a game, but I had no planner and no designer to help me. I simply focused on creating a sample prototype by reusing existing assets from games previously by Falcom.

I came up with a prototype which looked like a horizontally scrolling action game. Which in a way looked like *Popful Mail*, but it wasn't that, not quite. During this time, Kiya-san gave me a lot of advice, and I remember him as being a very generous and caring person. The sample from this period became the basis for *Popful Mail*. So, as I remember it, *Popful Mail* was not the result of consciously trying to make a game like that. It just happened to turn out the way it did.

JS: Kiya-san was legendary.

JN: When I was assigned to game development after joining Falcom, Kiya-san belonged to a separate team. He was a famous person in the game industry back then, and obviously I knew of him since before joining the company. To me, he was almost like a god, and I didn't have the courage to just go up and chat with him. Business seemed to be booming for Falcom during this period, and I got to go to Hawaii on an employee trip. We shared hotel rooms, and for some reason I was paired with Kiya-san. I don't remember what we talked about, but I remember being surprised about it, asking myself: why I was paired up with Kiya-san?!

It's very presumptuous of me to say it, but I thought Kiya-san was a genius who was able to come up with new technologies on his own. Reviewing the programs he made was extremely instructive, and I was very thankful that I joined Falcom. At the time, Kiya-san was Falcom's head of development, and he was effective in his role as a leader while also excelling as a programmer. He was someone I could really look up to and admire as a developer. Kiya-san left Falcom many years later, and I wondered what happened when he suddenly stopped coming in to work one day. When I heard that he had quit, I remember feeling uneasy about Falcom's future.

JS: Before *Popful Mail* you worked on *Ys III*. The main character, Mail, has red hair just like Adol...

JN: I was working on *Ys III* for the X68000. I don't think there was an influence on the main character, the red hair. As for *Popful Mail*, when the prototype started moving a graphics designer was assigned to the project, and this designer came up with this character all of sudden, and then we decided to call the main character Mail. And he also designed two additional characters as well.[5]

JS: What does ぽっぷる[6] mean? In English it's pronounced *Popful* and implies popping.

JN: The *Popful* name was thought out by somebody who belonged to the PR department.

[5] Probably Tatt the wizard and Gaw, the blue... thing

[6] Pronounced *poppuru*

it. But I was not involved in the development [of the MCD version] myself. I never knew there were many fans out there! *<laughs>*

Kouji Yokota: So the Super Famicom version sold overseas? Are they in Japanese?

JS: Only the Sega version, in America. I imported the SFC cartridge. It's a fantastic series of action-RPGs.

JN: *<laughs>* Thank you very much!

Although we also had a couple of ideas in our team - the codenames were thought out within our team as well. So the PR person came up with the *Popful Mail* name, he used hiragana characters for the "*Poppuru*" portion, and the *Mail* portion was written in katakana. *<writes it out>* But I knew it had to be written in alphabetical characters, so I came up with the English spelling myself.

JS: Can you recall any codenames?

JN: One codename that I still remember is *Scarlet Maid*.

JS: "*Maido*" as in maid?[7]

JN: Yes, but I can't recall the others. I think *Scarlet Maid* was one of the ideas because the characters were kind of cute. But then at the same time, there was an opinion that the name was hard to remember.

JS: Did you follow the game's conversions to other systems? As I mentioned to Yokota-san, *Eternal Blue* was one of the five reasons to own a Sega CD, and *Popful Mail* was another.[8]

JN: I heard these games are popular overseas for the first time only after you told me this! I know about the Super Famicom version because I developed it.[9] As for Mega CD, because there used to be a company called Sega-Falcom[10] in charge of developing that version, I knew about it.

JS: Japanese RPGs prior to *Dragon Quest* in 1986 seem more experimental. How would you describe the pre-*Dragon Quest* era?

JN: *Dragon Quest* was specifically designed to be completely user-friendly even to people who had never played an RPG before, whereas many prior games were mainly derived from computer RPGs, such as *Wizardry* and *Ultima*, and I feel that many of them might be called "user-unfriendly" or "tedious". Even so, I feel that with these tedious games, you were able to take your time more and enjoy them. I really enjoyed playing *The Black Onyx* by BPS and *Mugen no Shinzou* by Xtalsoft.[11] I would draw maps and other things on graph paper, and I think that building up your own record of the game like that was also part of the fun. Speaking of which, there's a series called *The Legend of Heroes* by Falcom, and when I joined the company the very first *Legend of Heroes* game was in mid-development. They seemed to be carefully studying *Dragon Quest* while making this game. Usually there was a monitor showing screens from *Dragon Quest* in one corner of the development room.

JS: Tell me about *Ys V* on SFC. It feels like an evolution of the series.

JN: *Popful Mail* was Falcom's first release on the Super Famicom, and for our second release, the president suggested making an *Ys* sequel. At the time a draft plot had already been prepared, titled "Lost Kefin, Kingdom of Sand". Our official

---

[7] Clarifying the correct pronunciation of メイド

[8] In truth I could name at least 20 games that made the Sega Mega CD worth owning, but my de facto top 5 list would be: *Silver Star Story*, *Eternal Blue*, *Popful Mail*, *Snatcher* and *Keio's Flying Squadron*

[9] Mr Nagashima did programming and scenario work

[10] Short alliance producing *Lord Monarch*, *Dragon Slayer: Eiyuu Densetsu* and its sequel on MD, and *Popful Mail* on MCD. A planned MCD version of *Super Brandish* and *Ys IV: Mask of the Sun* was cancelled

[11] Itself regarded as an influence of *Dragon Quest*

instructions were to use this draft plot as the basis for a new *Ys*. *Popful Mail* was our first time developing for the Super Famicom, and we learned a lot from our initial mistakes. For this reason, personally I was grateful for the chance to develop for the Super Famicom again. At the time *Ys* was known for its battle system of defeating enemies mainly by bumping into them, but implementing that system on the SFC felt a little bland, and so we experimented with various ideas by trial and error.

Meanwhile, a separate development team was working on *The Legend of Heroes 3*, and I did some playtesting for it. *The Legend of Heroes 3* retained an overhead view, but also introduced a concept of height. I thought this was highly original, and tried to incorporate this system into the new *Ys* to deepen the action. This was how *Ys V* came about. Around this time, home computer games were also flourishing, and so I did my best to present something which couldn't be done on a computer. Unfortunately, I personally feel that the result was of middling quality. During this same period, Square released *Final Fantasy 5* and *6*, and techniques such as their graphical effects were highly enlightening. Few staff members who had developed the previous titles in the *Ys* series were still at Falcom, so we enjoyed a fairly high degree of freedom in making the new game. I was also still quite young, so I worked deep into the night almost every day. We had an excellent development environment, but honestly, not many people were satisfied with the end product. I still regret not making a better game.

JS: Do you know anything about Studio Alex, and its founder Kazunari Tomi?[12]

JN: I am not familiar with Studio Alex, but when I joined Falcom, Tomi-san was already working as the main programmer in a different development team. As I said earlier, during the period when I was creating a sample prototype [for what became *Popful Mail*], there was a shortage of programmers, and so I helped Tomi-san a little on *Dinosaur*,[13] the game he was developing. I don't know the exact reason why, but after finishing development on the PC-9801 version of *Dinosaur*, Tomi-san quit the company, without even waiting until the game's release. At Falcom back then it was forbidden for programmers to insert staff credits into their games. However, Tomi-san broke this rule and inserted staff credits into *Dinosaur*. But since Tomi-san quit before the game's retail release, another programmer went in and deleted the credits. Tomi-san was friendly and easy to talk with. Many people quit Falcom around this time, and the people who left the company would often get together and go out for drinks or something. One time I was out with Tomi-san, and we had a conversation about how I was thinking of leaving Falcom. A few days later he phoned me at home, and introduced me to a game company he was acquainted with. In fact, this is how I ended up working at Shade...

JS: Why did you leave Falcom?

JN: Shortly after developing *Ys V*, I was instructed to create a game for the PlayStation, and was working on a sample prototype. Once the sample reached a certain point, the company told me to show it to the editor of a certain game magazine. The editor ruthlessly bashed the sample, and ultimately the project was scrapped. Around the same time, a senior programmer retired, and I became the most senior programmer within the company. My boss, the second-in-charge of Falcom, told me that he wanted me to oversee all development rather than continue working as a programmer.

I wanted to keep on making games as a programmer, and so I hesitated, realising that I wouldn't be able to create games anymore. At this point, a former Falcom colleague who had

[12] Tomi-san used to work at Falcom; Studio Alex is connected to the *Lunar* series by Game Arts

[13] Computer RPG blending Western and Japanese ideas

quit, and switched over to Shade, contacted me. I met with Kouji Yokota, the head of Shade, and ultimately ended up going there. Back then, Shade was composed of many former Falcom employees under Yokota-san's leadership, so that was probably a factor that helped me get a job there. I worked at Falcom for eight and a half years, but because of what happened, leaving was ultimately an easy decision to make.

JS: What are your plans for the future?

JN: It is the fate of the programmer, but regardless of whether it's game consoles or smartphones, the hardware specs keep getting upgraded, and times are difficult for developers with limited resources. Given the circumstances, as well as my own age and technical skills, continuing on as a programmer does not lead to a very bright future, so I am thinking that at some point it would be good to become involved with games in a different capacity, and not as a programmer. However, I still plan to keep on programming, even if it is only as a hobby.

JS: Can you draw a sketch of the Falcom offices?

JN: There's more than one location, so I'm wondering which office...

JS: All of them!

JN: This picture was taken at the Tomio building, the first building *<Refers to magazine photo>*

JS: With the stairway and logo above it.

JN: You go up the stairs and you'd find the shop.

KY: A computer shop.

<Mr Yokota and Mr Nagashima converse>

KY: I remember the Tomio building layout...

JS: Were the buildings far from each other?

JN: When I was working at Nihon Falcom, there was three locations. Not at the same time, we relocated twice. So the current Nihon Falcom building is the fourth location they've moved to.

JS: Whichever you remember best...

JN: OK, I'll try!

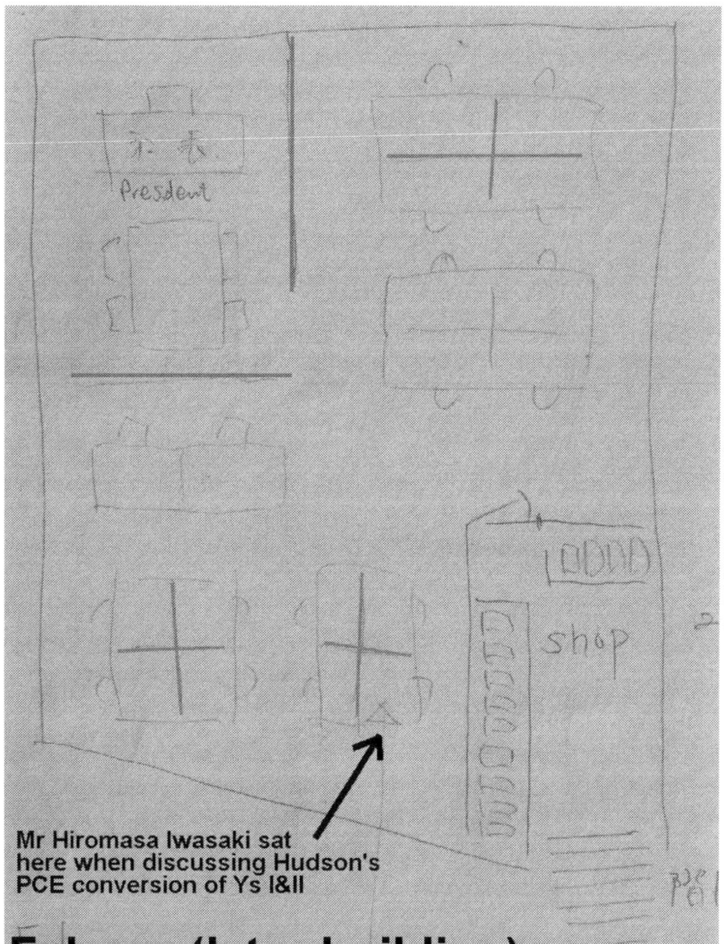

Falcom (later building)

<*Mr Nagashima sketches Falcom's later used* ***Kato Building***>

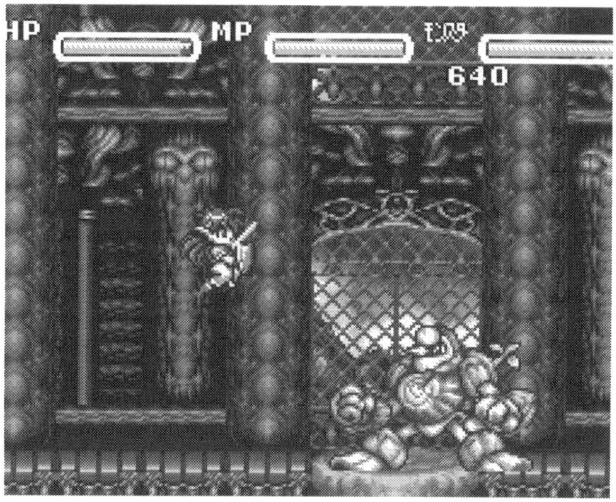

JS: I'm sorry to have taken up your break. Before we part, please sign my signature book.

<*everyone laughs*>

JN: Is it OK for me to sign? In kanji? Since I'm a programmer I don't think I can draw. Can I just write it alphabetically?

JS: Yokota-san is also in the signature book.

Kouji Yokota: That's right. I did sign it.

JS: Both of you having worked at Falcom, and now together at Shade.

KY: Yes. <*laughs*>

JS: Do you ever have nostalgic conversations about the old days?

KY: Yes, sometimes.

<*everyone laughs*>

JS: Is it OK if my cameraman, Nico, takes a photo of you for the book?

JN: I am afraid I would prefer it if there was no profile photo. I hope you understand. But I hope that my little anecdotes will be of some use.

JS: <*gives small gift*> For sacrificing your break, please accept this.

JN: Thank you very much.

~ Appearing in a later volume ~

Left: **Yasuo YOSHIKAWA**, creator of the simultaneously released, multi-system *DAIVA* series, and the overhead action-RPG, *Rune Worth*

If you enjoyed this coverage of Falcom, then be sure to check out later volumes of this book, which will have interviews with three major figures from T&E Soft, a developer that was something of a rival to Falcom over the years, especially in the action-RPG genre. Notably with titles like the *Hydlide* series, which sold massively and set several important precedents, plus *Rune Worth*. The *DAIVA* series meanwhile is a fascinating experiment in releasing multiple chapters of an epic SRPG saga across 7 different hardware platforms. Plus there's also coverage of an unreleased Super Famicom brawler.

Below left: **Tokihiro NAITO,** creator of the *Hydlide* series. RIGHT: **Tetsuya YAMAMOTO**, creator of *Undeadline* and an unreleased SFC game

古代 祐三

KOSHIRO, Yuzo

DOB: 12 December 1967 / Birthplace: Hino-shi, Tokyo / Blood Type: O

~ Selected Portfolio ~

<*Doujin* games - not a comprehensive list>

Graman Bee	- PC-88
Variant 7	- PC-88
Variant 7 - 2	- PC-88

<Musical work - in several instances, one of multiple composers>

Xanadu Scenario II	- 1986
Romancia	
Ys I: Ancient Ys Vanished	- 1987
Legacy of the Wizard	
Sorcerian	
Ys II: Ancient Ys Vanished	- 1988
The Scheme	
The Revenge of Shinobi	- 1989
Misty Blue	- 1990
ActRaiser	
The G.G. Shinobi	- 1991
Streets of Rage	
Sonic the Hedgehog (Master System, Game Gear)	
Super Adventure Island	-1992
Batman Returns (Game Gear/Master System)	
The G.G. Shinobi II: The Silent Fury	
Streets of Rage 2	
Slap Fight MD	- 1993
ActRaiser 2	
Streets of Rage 3	-1994
Robotrek	
Beyond Oasis	
Zork I: The Great Underground Empire	- 1996
The Legend of Oasis	
Shenmue	- 1999
Shenmue II	- 2001
Amazing Island	- 2004
Namco x Capcom	- 2005
Castlevania: Portrait of Ruin	- 2006
Etrian Odyssey	- 2007
Super Smash Bros. Brawl	- 2008
Etrian Odyssey II: Heroes of Lagaard	
7th Dragon	- 2009
Half-Minute Hero	
Etrian Odyssey III: The Drowned City	- 2010
Protect Me Knight	
Criminal Girls	
7th Dragon 2020	- 2011
Kid Icarus: Uprising	- 2012
Etrian Odyssey IV: Legends of the Titan	
7th Dragon 2020-II	- 2013
Etrian Odyssey Untold: The Millennium Girl	
Wangan Midnight Maximum Tune 5	- 2014
Momoiro Billionaire!	

Interview with Yuzo Koshiro
24 September 2013

I visited Yuzo Koshiro in Kino, which is a short train ride outside of Tokyo. I met Mr Koshiro outside the original company headquarters of Ancient, which is run by his mother. It was then a short car ride to Mr Koshiro's new office, which he had recently moved into because it provided better sound-proofing. We spent several hours discussing his career, seeing the doujin games he worked on, and enjoying lunch provided by his mother. Some of this day was filmed and can be found on the accompanying DVD.

JS: Can you recall the first game you played?

YK: The first game I played was probably when I was in elementary school. When I was in 4th grade, or 5th grade. It was a tennis game...

JS: *Pong*?

YK: *Pong*...? No, it wasn't *Pong*. I think it was an original game, made in Japan, and it was a tennis game. You would connect it to a TV and the screen would be black and white, and there were about 7 games you could play, that were tennis games. Around the same time Nintendo also published a similar tennis game, but that was in colour. I wanted that version, but I couldn't have it, so I played this other tennis game, which was black and white.

JS: Can you recall when you first had the feeling you wanted to work either in games or music?

YK: When I was 16, when I was in my first year of high school, my mother whom you just met, bought me a PC-88 to congratulate me on entering high school. At that time I just wanted to work on games, and I wasn't really thinking of working on music. The PC-88 did not have any sound features, and the reason I asked for one was I simply wanted to program games. That's why I asked my mother to buy me a PC-88. In terms of working on music, I only started thinking about that quite a while afterwards, when I was 18. At that time the PC-88SR[1] was released, and that had sound. I didn't have an SR at first, but one of my friends from high school had it, and when I went to his house to hang out, I'd use it. I really liked the music programming, and I thought I'd like to do something like that.

JS: In a previous interview you mentioned that you created *doujin* games which were never published. Can you tell me about these games?

YK: Sorry, could you give me a moment?
<Mr Koshiro leaves room, returns with items>

JS: Did you distribute these at Comiket?

YK: I'm not exactly sure which games you're referring to. I'm wondering if you're referring to *The Scheme*?

JS: I'll be asking about *The Scheme*. In the previous interview you mentioned programming several games which were not widely distributed.

YK: *<laughs>* Do you have the article? It's really not something that's worth describing.

JS: I think it's worth describing. Everyone has a beginning. *<quotes previous interview>* [2] *"I didn't have any titles that were published, but I did some work as an indie developer, games before Ancient. There was only one title that I released. That was a shooting game. It was kind of like an add-on game, not really a proper one... I have developed a lot of titles, but that was the only one I actually published or released. My friends in the doujin circle had games of their own as well, and I'd make music for their games. So my music was out there in the doujin scene."*

YK: I know now! I think there might have been some misunderstanding. First of all, the games that I programmed and were released, they were really just for fun. Actually, someone else did most of the programming. I was mostly doing the music. So those were the ones that were distributed at Comiket.

JS: Did you keep copies of these games?

YK: I have them, but I don't have all of them. *<laughs>* So I can't remember all the names. But I remember that there was one game called *Graman Bee,* and the name was a combination

---

[1] The initial model of PC-88 lacked proper sound; later models incorporated an FM synth card and more

[2] 1up.com: *Keeping the Classic Sound Alive: An Interview with Yuzo Koshiro*, Sep 2012

of two titles, *Twinbee* and *Gradius*, and that was released under my name.[3] Or rather that was a game that I made, but in terms of the other games, I belonged to a PC circle called "Harvest" and the other games were made by the members who belonged to that circle. They would do the programming, and they would do the art, and I would just provide the music to that.

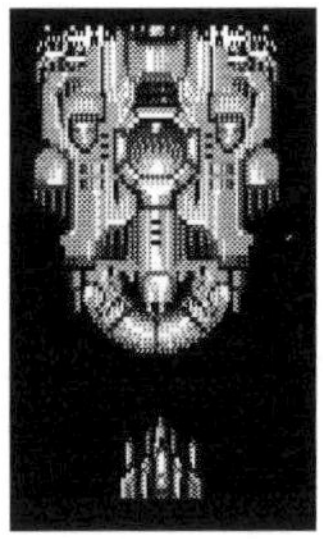

At that time there was something called the *100 Yen Disk*,[4] and those would be sold at Comiket. The reason why they were called *100 Yen Disks*, was that they were these floppy disks and each floppy disk contained several games, and they were sold for 100 yen. I think the interview is referring to those games, but I'm not sure. Perhaps I do have some with me. But I'd need to check. *<leaves room>* I'm looking for *100 Yen Disks* right now, so could you give me a moment? Oh, I found one! Could you come over here?

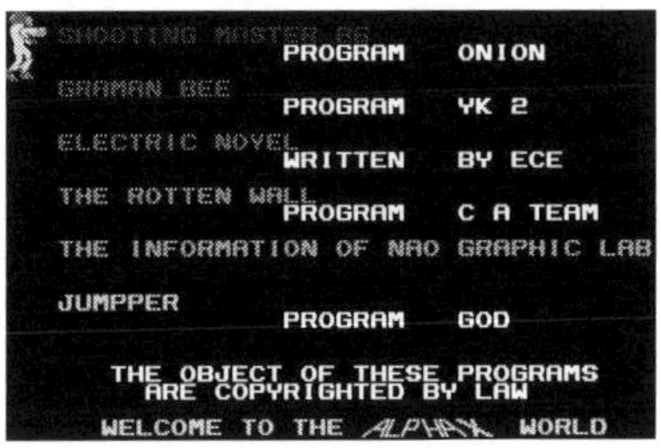

<we all move to the music booth in the next room>

JS: Is it OK to photograph?

YK: Sure, it's fine. *<music kicks in. Demonstration of Mr Koshiro's games - footage is available on the supplementary DVD>*

JS: Was this in 1989?

YK: In 1989, yes.

JS: How do you feel regarding these older games being emulated? There's controversy over emulation, because people download rather than buy the games.

YK: But this is not illegal. The software is something I made, so... *<laughs>*

JS: Let's say a fan of yours downloaded this old game. How would you feel?

YK: That's a difficult question! *<laughs>* It's a very difficult question to answer.

JS: With floppy disks for the PC-88 biodegrading, there might come a time when the only way to play them is emulation.

YK: I do have the disks. But the disks get old, and they become unreadable, so 7 or 8 years ago I had a friend convert the disks into data so that I could save them, even if the disks become unreadable.

JS: Can you describe the equipment in here?

YK: Yes, that's fine. But there may be some equipment that I can't reveal, but I can explain the other things.

<filming commences - first section is on his PC-88 game, Variant 7>[5]

JS: What is the name of this game?

YK: This is *Variant 7*. It's really difficult! I made this game but I never released it.

JS: We've got a world exclusive!

YK: Yes.

JS: Let's listen to the music.

<music is turned up>

YK: *<playing game - laughs>* It's really difficult! I'm going to put on some cheats. *<spaceship weapons increase>* This is a secret weapon - I'm cheating!

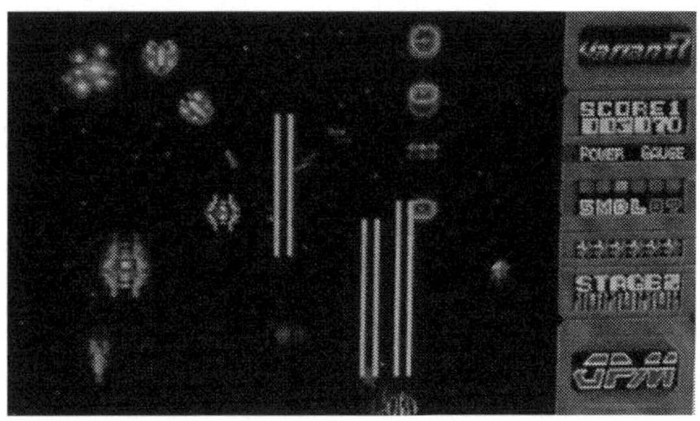

JS: *Daijoubudesu! (No problem!)*

YK: Then after this section we have some copyrighted music. *<laughs>* So I can't let you listen to that.

[3] Mr Koshiro's nickname on the disk was **YK 2**
[4] 7-part series with games, demos, and oddities; http://onitama.tv/museum/100yen.htm

[5] Due to space, the tour itself is not on the DVD

JS: Back then games would sometimes have music taken from commercial sources.[6]

YK: Yes, plus this was a *doujin* game. And also the manufacturers were not very strict at that time - but in this game we used some music from an actual shooting game. I never sold this game, so it was OK at that time.

JS: Your secret is safe with me!

YK: <*laughs*> But it's OK, because I don't have the music on right now.

JS: Let's discuss the equipment.

YK: Actually, before I begin, I'd like to note that I just moved into this office, and I just brought this equipment from the old office into the new one, so some of these devices are not actually working right now. But I can explain them.

This is a Portico 5042, as written here; this is a tape simulator. Below it is a reverb DP/4 parallel effects processor. Below that is a Neve 8816, which is a summing mixer. Below that is another mixer, and it's made by a company called Behringer, and it's called a Eurorack. If you take a picture you can see the names. We have a lot of British equipment. <*laughs*>

JS: Well, the British make a lot of good music.

YK: This piece of equipment... I don't know what it's called in English, but it's called AMEK in Japanese. This is a pre-amp for mics.

JS: Very modern. Do you ever still use a PC-88?

YK: No, I do not.

JS: You use Cubase[7] to simulate the sound?

YK: Oh yes, yes, right. OK, I will explain that a bit later. This is also a pre-amp for mics, it's an ISA Two. It's made by a company called Focusrite. This is a compressor, Universal Audio's 1176LN.

[6] *Olion* for PC-6001 had music from *Star Trek* and *Raiders of the Lost Ark*

[7] A sequencer, used with *Etrian Odyssey*

JS: This equipment on the right side here, for which game did you use it?

YK: <*laughs*> We don't have any games yet, with music created from this equipment.

JS: It's really brand new.

YK: This is actually a very rare piece of equipment. The company Neve, which made this, made this equipment decades ago,[8] and it's called the 2254 compressor. Over here I have an equaliser, made by a company called SPL, and as written here it's called Vitalizer. <*moves on*> This is where you get sound, it's kind of like a sound card, or sound board; it's called a Fireface UFX. On the far right we have synthesisers, but I only have two, or now three, in here at this moment. The one here is a Roland MKS-80. Beneath that is a Roland MPG-80.

JS: This equipment would give you a lot of freedom. Do you ever miss the old days, where you had to program the sound chip itself?

YK: Hmm... Do I feel nostalgic for those days? Not really. The reason being because I have Cubase, and as you said, that can emulate the sounds from the PC-88. I was going to talk about this later, but I have a game called *Sekaiju no Meikyuu*, and the English title is *Etrian Odyssey*. In that game I have sounds from the PC-88, so I still use sounds from the PC-88 quite a bit, so it's not really something that I need to feel nostalgic about.

JS: Thank you for tour. I'm happy that you invited me to your studio to see this.

<we return to the piano room, to find sandwiches waiting for us>

YK: If you are hungry, please feel free to have some sandwiches.

JS: *Arigatou gozaimashita.* [...] I've heard that you started working for Falcom as a part-time job while you were studying.

YK: First, to add to what I mentioned earlier, I was fiddling with the PC-88SR at my friend's house. I used the SR first to copy the music from a game called *Tower of Druaga*. So I was copying music from these games, and there was a magazine called the *Maicon BASIC Magazine*, and they had a sound contest. I sent the music that I had copied to this contest and it won. So that's how I started to work for them as a writer. At that time there was a column every month on videogame music, called *Videogame Music Corner*. So every month I would take the BGM from arcade games, and I would copy that on the PC-88SR, and I would post the program for it. So I was doing that every month, where I would copy music from other games, but one time I decided that I wanted to make some original music. I can't remember exactly how old I was, but I was working for *Maicon BASIC Magazine* immediately after I graduated high school. Then shortly after that I made a few original songs - I think I made like 5 or 6. This was separate from the music that I was copying, but I made some original music and I had it in stock. Also, there was a different magazine, called *LOGiN*, and this was published by ASCII. It was a magazine with computer information. They posted a job listing for Nihon Falcom, and it said that they were recruiting sound staff. So I decided to apply and I took some of my original songs, put them on a cassette tape, and I took it to Falcom. They happened to like my music, and decided to use it. So that's how I started working for them as part of the sound staff.

JS: You were a writer at *Maicon BASIC*?

YK: I was doing two things. One was that I was writing the column *Videogame Music Corner* for *Maicon BASIC Magazine*. Every month I would copy music from games and program it using the PC-88, and then it would be published. And then the second thing I was doing, was writing reviews for arcade games. So I would play these arcade games, then write a review for them.

JS: *Tower of Druaga* was quite challenging.

YK: <*laughs*> Yes, I think it was challenging. But I liked the game. The reason I liked the game was because the BGM was excellent. The game was difficult, but since the BGM was so good, I was able to play it until the end.

JS: Apparently it's easy to make a mistake at the end which sends you to the start.[9]

---

[8] Apparently the original Neve 2254 mono Limiter/Compressor was designed in 1969

[9] 1up.com: *Dru Hill: Chronicle of Druaga*, Oct 2004

YK: I don't remember if there was that kind of choice at the end... But one thing I can say, is there were manuals on how to play *Tower of Druaga*. It has floors from 1 to 60, and you solve riddles while proceeding through the floors. But when I played there was already a manual on it. There would be a sheet of paper and I would be looking at it to proceed. I was playing it while looking at hints. So it wasn't really that difficult for me. *<surfs internet on laptop>* But I'm looking it up right now!

JS: You can't do that - that's cheating!

YK: *<laughs>* It is cheating!

JS: I also looked for a guide online.

YK: *<surfing the net>* Ah, yes, yes, yes! *<quickly reads text in Japan>* I looked it up and I do remember now that there was a trap. It says if you make the wrong choice you get zapped, which I think means you get sent to the beginning. But I already had a guide that I could look at, so it wasn't that I was playing the game and had to solve the riddles. It was more that I was playing the game to listen to the music. So there was already a walkthrough that could guide me. So it wasn't really that difficult.

JS: Back in those days, in your opinion, which 3 games companies produced the best music?

YK: When interviewed I always say that there are 3 games that really made me want to make game music. One is *Tower of Druaga*, which we just talked about. The other two are Konami's *Gradius* and Sega's *Space Harrier*. I really liked the music for these games. Of course there were other games that had excellent music as well, but I think Namco, Konami and Sega were the 3 companies that had the best music at that time.

JS: At Falcom, were you in-house as a musician? *<shows Comptiq magazine with photos>*

YK: *<looks through magazine>* Your question is whether I worked at Falcom the company, or whether I worked at home? The answer to that is I worked at both. I believe that I worked half of the time at home, and then half of the time at the Falcom office. This was in 1987. *<holds Retro Gamer>* Do you write for this?

JS: Yes, I do.

YK: This is a question from me to you. But why did you decide to write a book on retro games?

JS: There needs to be more English interviews with those in the Japanese games industry. There's books covering America and Europe, but Japan is covered less due to the language barrier. This is me bringing balance to the universe.

YK: I see! *<looks through Retro Gamer>*

JS: Do you like *Akumajou Dracula* on the Super Famicom? I interviewed the director for this issue.

YK: Yes, I like it. Ahh, Ueno-san. Is he still in Konami now?

JS: No, he's in America, at a different developer.

YK: Ah, I see.

JS: Do you remember Mr Hashimoto and Mr Miyazaki from Falcom?

YK: Hmm, yes. *<looks over question sheet provided prior>* Some of these questions are difficult to answer! *<laughs>*

JS: If any make you uncomfortable, we can skip them. Some questions I might not ask.

YK: I'm glad you sent me these questions. I can think about how to answer them. So I appreciate you sharing these with me.

<After eating we all enjoy some iced coffee>

JS: With more recent titles, like the *Etrian Odyssey* series, you went back to the PC-88 style of sound. Is there something special about that style of sound, which you feel is timeless?

YK: I'm not sure how I should answer this. But first of all, I myself really like the PC-88 sound. I used it until the Mega Drive era, which is basically until *Bare Knuckle 2*, so I was using the PC-88 until then. After that I started to use a PC-98. But it was quite a long time for me, looking at my career. I used the PC-88 for about 4 years, so I feel it's a memorable sound from that perspective, for me. In terms of whether it can be used in today's world, the sound is really a chiptune sound, so it's a really simple sound. It's FM synthesis, so it's richer than beep or PSG, but being FM synthesis it's still a very simple sound. So I think in terms of today's world, it's rather limited music wise. So I don't think there's any reason to choose the PC-88 over something else. However, in terms of *Etrian Odyssey*, there was a clear reason why we used the PC-88. *Etrian Odyssey* was to be a revival of the RPGs you had back in the day. So we were looking for a sound that would match, and we looked at songs using rich synthesisers, and things like that. We tested a lot of songs, but in the end the director decided that the PC-88 sound matched the concept, so that's why we used it. So it was a sound which was really perfect for the concept of the game.

JS: You still do freelance work, right?

YK: Erm, no, I don't.

JS: You officially work for Ancient and other companies hire Ancient?

YK: I don't know if this answers your question, but for example, for Atlus, or *Etrian Odyssey* which is a game made by Atlus, I was asked by them to make music for it. So the communication was between Atlus and myself. But the contract was between Atlus and Ancient.

JS: I'm producing a DVD to go alongside my book. Would it be possible to officially commission you to produce some music?

YK: Oh, it's not using existing music?

JS: It can use older music, if you have the rights to license it. The important thing is that any music I use, I must be legally allowed to do so.

YK: In terms of existing songs, you can use my existing songs without any fee, for free.

JS: Wow! Thank you!

YK: However, in terms of the songs that I created during my days at Falcom, the company allows people to use their songs for free if it is not for commercial purposes. [10] But they are quite strict about that. So I would recommend that you do not use any songs from Falcom. But in terms of my existing songs, you can use them for free. As for creating a new song, it's not a matter of money. Rather it's a matter of time, and I'm quite busy right now, and I probably won't have much time until February or March of next year. My policy is not that I don't have any time, but if I am going to make music for someone, then I want to spend the time to make it well. I don't just want to make something really quickly, and then just hand it over. So when I'm busy, I tend to turn down requests for new songs, and that's really because of the time.

JS: That's a very commendable work ethic. It's also very generous of you. Of course I will credit you, and send you complimentary copies.

YK: Thank you, that would be no problem.

JS: You worked on *The Scheme* for Bothtec.[11] Did you visit the office? It's a bit like *Metroid*!

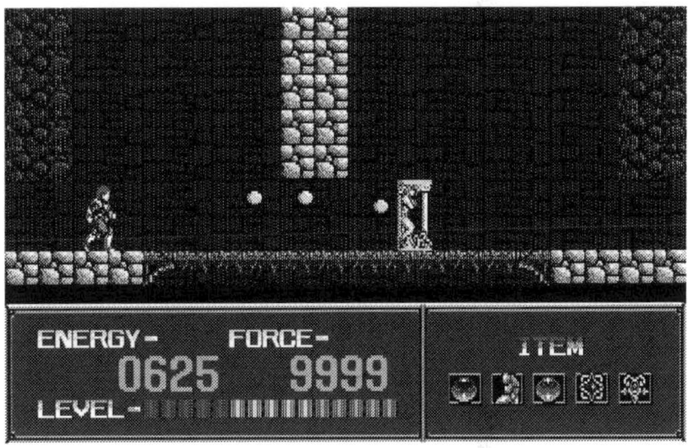

YK: You say *The Scheme* was very similar to *Metroid*. The programmer actually was heavily influenced by *Metroid* - so I think it's probably true that those two games are similar! I'd like to talk a little bit about Bothtec. I visited their office once or twice, for a meeting, but I never worked for them. In terms of *The Scheme*, Bothtec was holding a game programming contest, and *The Scheme* won an award in that contest. I think it might have been first place. So *The Scheme* was not exactly a game that Bothtec planned to make, it was a game that my friend, myself, and my sister - the three of us - all made. We entered the game programming contest and it won first place. So we got some award money, and we were also able to sell the game because it won.

JS: *The Scheme* is one of my favourite PC-88 games. Did your sister do the graphics?

[10] Check online - Falcom has an official charter allowing fans to use their back catalogue of music

[11] Bothtec eventually became Quest, best known for creating *Ogre Battle*

YK: It's a really difficult question! It's so long ago. For *The Scheme*, the three of us made it. The programmer was someone who I met through Harvest, the PC circle that I mentioned earlier. Harvest was a circle where we made *doujin* games, and the programmer's name was Hayashi-san.[12] He was also involved in making *100 Yen Disks*, so the game itself was kind of an extension of the games that we were making in the PC circle. And then the Bothtec contest came up. So we didn't really create this game from scratch. It was based on a bunch of programs that we created during our *doujin* era. This may sound really casual, but it was really just an extension of the *doujin* games, and it wasn't programmed from scratch. My sister was not really involved in Harvest, but she was working at Falcom as a graphic designer, at that time. Sometimes she would participate in the *100 Yen Disks*, part-time, or as a guest. So it was natural that she did the art for *The Scheme*.

JS: When playing *The Scheme*, the main character looks a little bit like Adol in *Ys*...

YK: <*laughs*> Right! You say the main character seems similar to the main character in *Ys*, called Adol, and the reason is because it was kind of a parody. In action games you see a lot of redheaded main characters, so it was kind of a joke. It was a parody. There wasn't really any deep meaning to it. Adol had red hair, so the main character of *The Scheme* also had red hair.

JS: Your sister, Ayano Koshiro, was involved in several games. Can you tell us about this?[13]

YK: In terms of my sister, I think she was influenced by me, and she also liked games - we both liked games. I liked to make music on the PC-88, but she liked to make dot graphics on the computer. There was an incident that really pushed her to pursue it, and it was also a contest. There was a company called Bullet Proof Software, and my sister and I both really liked a game they published called *The Black Onyx*, and BPS was planning to release a sequel called *Fire Crystal*. They had a pixel art contest for it, where people would send in their dot graphics of monsters. My sister applied for that and won an award. The art that she made was actually used in the game. So I think that really made her interested in the games industry. When I was working part-time at Falcom, I think I recommended her to Falcom, saying that she won this contest, and she has the skills, and she might be suitable to work there. Eventually my sister started working for Falcom, and she became the main graphic designer for *Ys I*. She mostly did the monster designs, and that's how she got her career started. So she won the contest and then she entered Falcom, so we really followed a similar path.

JS: I had no idea your sister's art was in *Fire Crystal*! Is your sister in this Comptiq photo?

YK: <*looks at old photos*> I don't think so. [...] No, she's not here.

JS: Can I print a family photo in the book? The Koshiro family has had a lot of influence.

YK: A photo? <*laughs*> I'm thankful that you said that about them. But they are both really reserved, and maybe it's just a Japanese tendency, but I feel slightly awkward about that too... <*laughs*>

JS: I believe you composed two different soundtracks for *The Scheme*. Why was this?

YK: The reason why there were two versions, was that first we had the PC-88 and that had three FM synthesis channels and three Programmable Sound Generators. So there was a total of six. After that the Sound Board 2 was released for the PC-88; it was a sound card extension, or upgrade. It had three additional FM synthesis channels, one ADPCM,[14] and one rhythm synthesiser.[15] But not everyone had this new sound card. Some people did, some people did not. *The Scheme* was well known for its rich music using Sound Board 2, however since not everyone had Sound Board 2, we also made a version using Normal 88 Mode, which had three FM synthesis channels, and three PSGs, as mentioned earlier. Hence two soundtracks.

JS: What was *Wanderers from Super Scheme*?

---

[12] Shinobu Hayashi; programmer on SMS and GG *Sonic The Hedghog*, developed at Ancient

[13] On the day I asked if Mrs Koshiro, head of Ancient, or Ayano Koshiro, were free to answer a couple of questions - unfortunately they were not

[14] Adaptive differential pulse-code modulation; it is used for sampling

[15] The advancement of audio in the PC-88 is complex. An excellent read is: *Lesser-known Video Game Soundtracks: The Scheme (PC-88)*, by Steve Lakawicz

YK: Yes! *<laughs>* I'd like to go and look for it, could you excuse me.

<we move to the sound booth with computer, to see Wanderers from Super Scheme>

YK: This is also a *doujin* game.

JS: *Wanderers from Super Scheme...*[16]

YK: *<laughs>* Let me play it a bit.

JS: That's amazing. What year was this?

YK: What year? I'm not sure which year, I think this came out shortly after *The Scheme.*

JS: I tried to look for information on this game, but it seems very rare.

YK: Yes. *<laughs>* Playing the game I just remembered, in the game you have cows and also UFOs, and at that time the concept of cattle mutilation was really popular - where people thought that these aliens would come to Earth in UFOs, and they would drain the blood from cattle. So there would be pictures of dead cattle with their blood drained, and people would say that this is the fault of aliens. So that kind of concept was really popular at that time, and the game was influenced by that.

JS: You left Falcom to go freelance, working for Quintet, which was founded by former Falcom staff. Why did you leave Falcom? Do you know how Quintet itself came about?

YK: *<laughs>* Yes, that was one of the questions I thought was difficult, when looking at the list! Hmm...

JS: OK. No problem at all.

YK: Quintet was established by Hashimoto-san, who was the programmer for *Ys*, and also Miyazaki-san, as you have in that photo there.[17] They were mainly developing games for Enix, which is now Square-Enix. When I joined them I had already left Falcom, so it had nothing to do with Falcom. But I knew them well, and they were looking for sound staff, so I decided to join. I first participated in developing *ActRaiser* with them, and I was of course in charge of the sound.

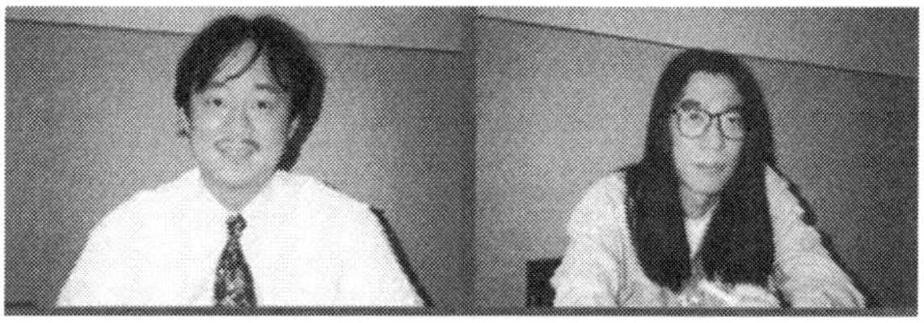

Masaya Hashimoto and Tomoyoshi Miyazaki

JS: Sources say Quintet was officially founded in April 1989, but the credits for *Dragon Slayer IV* say: Quintet, July 1987. Do you know why?[18]

YK: Really?! I think it's a coincidence. I really don't know why.

JS: Do you know any other mysteries in games?

YK: These things don't really come to you, when you think hard about them. You rather just come across them someday, suddenly. *<laughs>*

JS: A graphic designer at Westone said she hid portraits of her colleagues in a game's ROM.

YK: *<laughs>* I would like to share something with you, if I could think of something. But I'm not really coming up with anything. I think the story about *Fire Crystal* is rather unknown.

JS: What happened to Masaya Hashimoto and Tomiyoshi Miyazaki? I've heard wild rumours.

YK: What is a wild rumour?

JS: I heard that one had been arrested, another story involved a stabbing. It's all internet rumours. I'm trying to get to the truth.

YK: *<laughs>* I only know about it at a rumour level. So I think the information I have is basically the same as what you have. But I don't really think it's something that I would like to put in a book. I don't know if it's true or not. The company Quintet was shut down five years ago, and after that Hashimoto-san actually worked at Ancient for a while. But recently he left for his own reasons. In terms of Miyazaki-san, I really do not know what happened to him. I've heard rumours, but I don't know if they're true or not.

[16] Basically an extension and parody of *The Scheme*, using the same engine but with a funnier story
[17] From *GameFAN* magazine

[18] Japanese *Legacy of the Wizard* - Quintet message not in localised version

JS: After you left, Falcom sometimes released OSTs with your music, without crediting you.

YK: A difficult question! <*laughs*> Actually it's not sometimes but always the case that they don't credit me. But it's a really hard question to answer. I know that they don't credit me, but I don't know why. I don't know if it's because of some company reason. In terms of vinyl records or cassette tapes, or games, that were released when I was in Falcom, they did credit me. But after I left, any CDs or anything published, including games, whenever my music was used in those things, they never credited me. I don't really know why to be honest.

JS: Several Sega games state on the title or box: Music by Yuzo Koshiro. How did this happen?

YK: It was actually my mother's idea to have my name credited and displayed on the screen! <*laughs*> As I described earlier, there were some difficulties with Falcom, and I think my mother had that in mind as well, and she was also friends with the famous composer Joe Hisaishi,[19] and since they were close I think my mother always had the idea that the composer should have rights. I think she felt the same way for games, that composers should declare their rights for the music that they compose.

JS: Mr Hisaishi was a composer for Ghibli studios. He taught you music at a young age.

YK: Yes, yes, that's right. When I was in my second year of elementary school. So I believe I was 8 years old? Mr Hisaishi was a friend of my mother, and to be more precise, my mother was a piano teacher at that time, and one of her students was the wife of Mr Hisaishi. So that's how they got to know each other. At that time Mr Hisaishi was not as famous as he is now, he was not composing music for Ghibli, or rather Ghibli did not exist at that time. In terms of his work, he was a composer but he was also teaching how to compose. So that's how I was able to learn from him.

JS: Can you describe the founding of Ancient?

YK: I'd like to start from the reason why I had to establish Ancient. It was because Ancient created the Game Gear version of *Sonic the Hedgehog*, for Sega. But they said I would not be able to take on the work as an individual, however I could get the work if I set up my own company. But before that, I'd like to explain how I got to work with Sega. I started working with Sega through a game called *Super Shinobi*, which is on the Mega Drive. Through that game I became acquainted with a general manager called Takami-san.[20] He was the head of the consumer business, and he was the one who was overseeing Mega Drive and Game Gear. He was the one who offered me the work for *Sonic the Hedgehog*. So I founded the company and the first programmer we hired was Hayashi-san, who I worked together with on *The Scheme*. Ancient was basically made up of people that I knew through Harvest. My sister also joined, and my mother became the president. In terms of my family being involved in the company, it was really just a coincidence. It was really because Sega said that they would give me work if I set up my own company. So one thing led to another, and it was kind of a situation where I had no choice. In terms of who became the president, we just felt like only my mother could do that. So it was my relationship with Sega, and also the acquaintances I had with Harvest, which led me to set up Ancient.

JS: I thought the first game by Ancient was *Sonic the Hedgehog* for the Master System. But first you made *Sonic* for the Game Gear?[21]

YK: Hmm, yes, Game Gear. For the Game Gear.

JS: When was *Sonic* for the Master System?

YK: After the Game Gear.

JS: Ancient's first *Sonic* game was handheld?

YK: In terms of Sega hardware, the MkIII came before the Game Gear. We made the Game Gear version of *Sonic* in order to sell the Game Gear. But actually, the MkIII and Game Gear had very similar hardware, the system core. So it was very easy to replicate games that were created

[19] Composer, born Mamoru Fujisawa; numerous works, incl. *Valley of the Wind* and *Ni no Kuni*

[20] Likely Tomio Takami, creator of the MCD hardware

[21] I persist because of an anomaly: websites by Ancient and Sega state GG version was out 28 Dec 1991. Only date for SMS release is an unsourced date of 25 Oct 1991 on Wikipedia. There does not appear to be a Japanese release on MkIII, hence a lack of reliable release date

for the Game Gear, on to the MkIII. The MkIII was selling very well, even in other countries at that time,[22] while Game Gear was something that Sega wanted to start selling. MkIII already had more than 1'000'000 users, I believe, at that time. So Sega said to us, "You made a version for Game Gear, could you also make a version for the MkIII?" So it wasn't really something where we asked them for approval, it was rather something they offered to us.

JS: How did you get the license? Did Sega give Ancient freedom to develop it as they wanted?

YK: In terms of the license, getting the license, maybe we do things differently from the US and such. It was rather that I became acquainted with Sega, and I became acquainted with Takami-san, and he said, "So, we have a Mega Drive version of *Sonic*, do you want to make a Game Gear version?" So in that process I established my own company, and created the Game Gear version of *Sonic the Hedgehog*, but it wasn't really that I said that I wanted to make it. Rather it was that they proposed the idea to me, asking if I wanted to make it or not. I think for the first stage, we really kept in the mind the Mega Drive version of *Sonic*, and really focused on and took that into consideration. But for the second stage and third stage, it was planned by us and then it was checked by Sega. But they weren't very strict on what *Sonic* had to be. Of course we always kept in mind the original version, but Sega was not very strict about that.

JS: It's said that in 1999 you composed music for the unreleased *Bare Knuckle 4*?

YK: <*laughs*> I actually did not make the music for *Bare Knuckle 4* - the music for *Bare Knuckle 4* does not exist. However, the plan for the game did exist. At that time it was not Sega Saturn, but it was Dreamcast. *Bare Knuckle 4* was to be released on Dreamcast, and we created a prototype for it. It wasn't something where you could play the game, but rather it was something where it showed you how the game would look. So there was a choice between 2D or 3D, and we decided to go with 3D, and you could run around in the city and talk to people. So we created a prototype, but it was turned down for no good reason. We were the ones who brought in the plans, and they [Sega of Japan] were actually somewhat enthusiastic about it, but we were told that Sega of America had turned it down. [The reason why Sega of America had the ultimate decision-making authority was because] *Bare Knuckle* had been really popular in the US but it wasn't so popular in Japan, and we really could not expect it to sell well in Japan. But Sega of America decided to turn it down, because it was almost 10 years since *Bare Knuckle* was first released, and there was no one in Sega of America who could really understand the appeal of it. <*laughs*> So in other words, there was no one in Sega of America who could judge whether our version was good or not.

JS: Did Ancient keep the art assets and code?

YK: The graphic designer at that time is still with us, so if he has it, then we do. But if he doesn't then we don't. We don't have the program for it.

JS: Are there other unreleased games by Ancient?

YK: There are several games that were never released, but these are games that ended up not being good. So I want to forget about them. <*laughs*> But there is one game that I remember very well, it was for the PlayStation. I think you could picture it well if I describe it as a game similar to Nintendo's *Wii Fit*. But of course PlayStation did not have the hardware device that *Wii Fit* uses, so it was not the same in that respect. But you would do training according to a set menu, and you would try to lose weight. We brought a prototype to Sony, but I guess it was too early for that kind of game and it was rejected. So that was never released. Another game that was never released was the Sega Saturn version for *Kaiju no Shima*, which was a game released on Dreamcast.[23] The Saturn version was a completely different game, and it was never released. Meanwhile the Dreamcast version for *Kaiju no Shima* was released I believe in 2001, or 2002, I'm sure you can find out online. So the Saturn version was never released. The reason for that was pretty clear - it was because the Dreamcast hardware was released as we were developing it for the Saturn. So the Saturn became a device of the past, and that's why we had to cancel the development.

[22] Outside of Japan SMS did well in Europe and Brazil

[23] *Amazing Island* in English; came out on GameCube in 2004. Mr Koshiro clarified on Twitter that it started on Sega Saturn, and reached 90% on Dreamcast

JS: Whoever rejected the training idea at Sony must still regret it. *Wii Fit* sold millions!

YK: *<laughs>*

JS: Tell me about *Protect Me Knight*.

YK: We are currently making a sequel for the 3DS, and the release date is still to be decided. But the game itself is coming along, and will allow up to 4 players to connect their 3DS machines via a wireless network. So 4 players can play together at once.

JS: Did you want to comment on the original?

YK: The same thing can be said for the 3DS version. The programming, the graphics, and the game design, were all done by one of our staff members at Ancient, called Wada-san.[24] He's originally a graphic designer, but he did all of these things for this game. I only participated by providing the music. So he created the plans and everything, and I really just provided the sound for it, per his request. So in terms of the game, I can't really provide a detailed explanation on it, and the same goes for the Xbox Indies version.

JS: You had a unique sound in *Bare Knuckle 3*, alongside Motohiro Kawashima.[25] Some dubstep musicians say they're influenced by your work.[26]

YK: Really?! *<laughs>*

JS: One of the tunes in *BK 3* is called "dubslash".

YK: *<laughs>* I don't really know how to answer that! Is there really an artist who is saying he was influenced by *Bare Knuckle 3*? It was released around 1994, and meanwhile dubstep became popular around 2010 and onward. So it's a really new type of music, and there's 15 years or so in-between the two events. So I don't think that there is a direct connection between the two. However, *Bare Knuckle* was really popular overseas, and it was especially supported by fans in Europe and the US. Maybe children who listened to the *Bare Knuckle* music 15 years ago would be around their mid 20s now. If those people are deejays now, then there is a possibility that they listened to *Bare Knuckle* when they were young. I have heard that a certain deejay is my fan, but I've never talked to that person in real-life. So I don't really know the details. But if dubstep really was influenced by the sound that myself and Kawashima-san created, then I would be really honoured. But really I think it's just a coincidence. If the popularity of dubstep is somehow influenced by my music, or inspired by it, then I would feel very honoured.

JS: You produced music for *Sorcerian*. Have you ever heard of a game named *Sorceriman*? It's *doujin* - instead of 4 characters there's a giant.

YK: I've never heard of it, at all.

JS: Do you still play *Team Fortress*?

YK: I really like first-person shooters! But I don't have the time to play them anymore. I get really addicted to games, and then I play it for a really, really, long time. If I play an addictive game it affects my work, so I try not to play them anymore. When I was playing *Team Fortress*, I would eat dinner and then from 6 or 7pm, until 4 or 5am in the morning, I would play the game. Some days I would keep on playing throughout the whole day. It was really not good for my body, or my work. So although I really like first-person shooters, I don't play them anymore.

JS: Is there anything else you want to say?

YK: *<laughs>* I'm actually really bad at providing last comments, because I get lost at what to say. So I don't really have anything else to add, but I am interested in the other interviews you've conducted, John, and I'm interested in your book and I look forward to reading it. But in terms of my last comment, I really can't think of anything to say. I'm sorry.

[24] Unable to find his full name
[25] Composer, predominantly the *Bare Knuckle* series
[26] Wikipedia lists the following musicians with sources: Ikonika, BT, Labrinth, Joker, Darkstar, Childish Gambino, and Danger

~In memory of~

斉藤 智晴

SAITO, Tomoharu

17 November 1967 ~ 29 July 2006

~Selected Portfolio~

Shockman / Shubibinman 2	- PC Engine,	1992
Streets of Rage 2	- Mega Drive,	1993 (Designer)
Segagaga	- Dreamcast,	2001
Ketsui	- Arcades,	2003 (Character design)
Astro Boy: Omega Factor	- GBA,	2003 (Designer)
Culdcept Saga	- X360,	2008 (Illustration artist)

I worked with Saito-san on *Shubibinman* 2. He was a designer and an artist on this game. He was a really good guy and I respected him very much. He always had a passion for making games. He had a sense of humour. He was very kind to younger members on the team. When I visited his apartment, I saw a lot of the pictures he drew and his ideas for new games. I felt that he really wanted to make games a lot. I would like to say to him, "Thank you from bottom of my heart. I really enjoyed working with you. I learned passion for making games from you."
- ***Makoto Goto, colleague from developer Winds***

His name was "Lucky", and together with Nakai-san, was the soul of the Winds designer team. When he fell ill, and had to have his leg amputated, he went ahead with the surgery without hesitating. He said, "I don't need a leg to draw, my eyes and hands are plenty." He possessed the soul of a true artist. I'm sure he's still waving his brush around and challenging our ancestors in heaven. Godspeed Lucky! Make our ancestors stare in awe at your art!
- ***Masayuki Suzuki, colleague from developer Winds***

It's already been 8 years since he passed away. I can't believe it'll be 10 years soon. He was one of my dearest friends. We worked together so many times. I liked his artwork, and apparently he liked my artwork, too. We spurred each other on with the good friction of friendly competition. We were both stubborn, so we also got into arguments. <*laughs*> Once you become an adult, it's very hard to make close friends. I'm so glad I knew that great big fool! It's sad, having to use the past tense.
- ***Satoshi Nakai, colleague from developer Winds***

森田 真基

MORITA, Masamoto

DOB: *secret* / Birthplace: *secret* / Blood Type: *secret*

~ Portfolio ~

Columns 97 - Arcade / Sega Saturn, 1996 / 1997 (Director)

Die Hard Arcade - Arcade, 1997 (Special thanks)

Taisen Tanto-R SA-SHI-SU!! - Arcade, 1998 (Only sold in Japan and South Korea)

Sega Tetris - Arcade / Dreamcast, 1999 / 2000

Columns Crown - Game Boy Advance, 2001

Blood Will Tell: Tezuka Osamu's Dororo - PlayStation 2, 2004 (Main planner and scenario writer)

Interview with Masamoto Morita
26 October 2013, Tokyo

It's incredible how one thing leads to another. I contacted Mr Morita when researching Olion and its creator, Akira Takiguchi. Mr Morita had interviewed Mr Takiguchi some years previous for an online article and, as it turned out, now worked for him. I also discovered that he too had developed games, while at Sega. This fortuitous contact led to my spending the day at ASAHI Net in Tokyo, interviewing not one but four game developers, one of whom put me in contact with Kohei Ikeda, co-founder of Game Arts. Although hesitant with certain questions, Mr Morita gave a fascinating insight into Sega's transitional phase away from hardware and into a purely software role. For more background, check online for an English translation of the interview originally conducted by Mr Morita, with Mr Takiguchi, regarding Olion.

JS: Thank you for initiating today. It's amazing this all started with an email about contacting the creator of *Olion*, Mr Takiguchi.

MM: It was a happy surprise for me to receive your email, with interest in such an old Japanese computer game. Unfortunately, my web page *Olion Ultimania* [1] has not been updated since 2005. Takiguchi-san joined ASAHI Net, a Japanese internet provider, as one of the founding members in 1990. As for myself, I worked at Sega as a game development engineer between 1994 and 2005. *Olion Ultimania* is actually the web page that I built during those years, in my spare time. In 2006 I joined ASAHI Net too, and have been engaged in development of educational software with Takiguchi-san. Coincidentally, the history of computer games is my great interest too.[2] If there is anything I can help with, please let me know.

JS: I'm looking forward to discussing Sega.

MM: I can talk about myself, but I'm no longer part of Sega, so I would prefer not to put out too much information. I can talk about it, I can talk about what happened at Sega, but I need to get permission if it's going to be published.

JS: Don't feel obligated if you're uncomfortable. I can send you a PDF before publication.

MM: <*laughs*> So deleting stuff is OK!

JS: Obviously I want all your secrets, but...

MM: I belonged to the AM1 R&D division at Sega, which originally was the department to develop arcade games, but also started working on console games from around 2001. The games I developed at Sega are on the list I sent you. These are the products I created as the director or main planner. Much to my delight, I can still find *Columns 97* in some game arcades in Tokyo. This is actually the game I developed as the director for the first time.

JS: What was the first game you *played*?

[1] www4.airnet.ne.jp/mor/olion/

[2] Mr Morita brought in an expansive collection of original hardware and games, used as research

MM: That's a tough one... When I was a kid, this was before Nintendo's Family Computer came in, it was mainly arcade games. Even though those games were one play for 100 yen, that was expensive. It was a rare chance to play games. But I think Namco's old games are the main ones I played, like *Galaxian*, *Pac-Man*, and so on. And Taito's *Space Invaders*. It was the beginning of the videogame market, that kind of time. I was an elementary school student.

JS: What was the first computer you owned? Did you dabble in programming?

MM: It was extremely difficult! *<laughs>* I did not have a computer, but my brother had a PC-6001. I don't program games. *<laughs>*

JS: When did you feel you wanted to be involved in games?

MM: This is a difficult question too... I liked games, but it's not that I was ***really*** into it. When I tried to get my first job, I applied to Sega, Namco, and Konami, but those were the only game companies I applied to. What I really wanted to do was marketing, and I applied to other regular companies, and I also applied to foreign invested companies, like Apple and Hewlett-Packard. I got accepted at both HP and Sega. Then I saw *Virtua Fighter* at a game show. That's when I decided to join Sega! I liked computer graphics a lot. This was the era when computer graphics were rapidly developing.

JS: Due to 3D games.

MM: Yes. Also, for example, movies like *Tron* and *The Last Starfighter*, there was a lot of computer graphics starting to be used. I studied CG, computer graphics. If I had become a graphics designer, I could not draw anything I liked, there's going to be some rules. So I chose to be a director, rather than a designer. So I can decide what kind of product I want to make.

JS: You were given a choice when applying to Sega, to be either a graphics designer or a director? Could you choose your division?

MM: Before I entered Sega Corporation I could choose either to be a graphics designer, planner, or programmer. They had different types of tests to get into the company. I chose planner, and for my test I had to submit a page, or proposal, for a new game. I did not submit a proposal for a game though - it was not a computer game. *<laughs>* How can I put it? I submitted a proposal for a new type of sports game. A "new sport" in real life.

JS: Was this done at Sega's office or at home?

MM: I could write it at home. The instructions were so vague. The company just said write up a proposal, and that's it. So I wrote up a four page proposal, about four pages, filled with text and some pictures I drew.

JS: Of this new sport. Can you describe it?

MM: Yes. Do you know *Back to the Future*? The time machine, the DeLorian, I liked the DeLorian because... *<makes sound effect and gesture describing fire trails>*

JS: Oh yeah, fwooosh!

MM: So I watched the movie and got the idea from the DeLorian, and at that time rollerblading was popular. So I imagined that people who go rollerblading would be wearing strobe lights all over their body, and these lights would be flashing, and the people would travel so fast on rollerblades they could draw pictures with light. The strobe lights are controlled by computer, so for example the timing of the flashes would spell out a word. *<draws sketch to explain the idea>* It would appear as letters in the air.[3]

JS: Do you know anything on Ikegami Tsushinki?

MM: I don't know about this company at all. According to Wikipedia the company developed Sega's *Zaxxon* and Nintendo's *Donkey Kong*. And they produced Sega's *Congo Bongo*. But it was so long ago I don't know anything about this company.

JS: Could you draw the AM1 office layout?

MM: I was in the amusement R&D division 1, and there were divisions 1, 2 and 3. And also there were Consumer Divisions 1, 2 and 3. We were in the same company, but the culture of each division was so different. It was like completely different companies, but we were all together under one roof.

---

[3] The recent "Monkey Light Pro" is similar to this

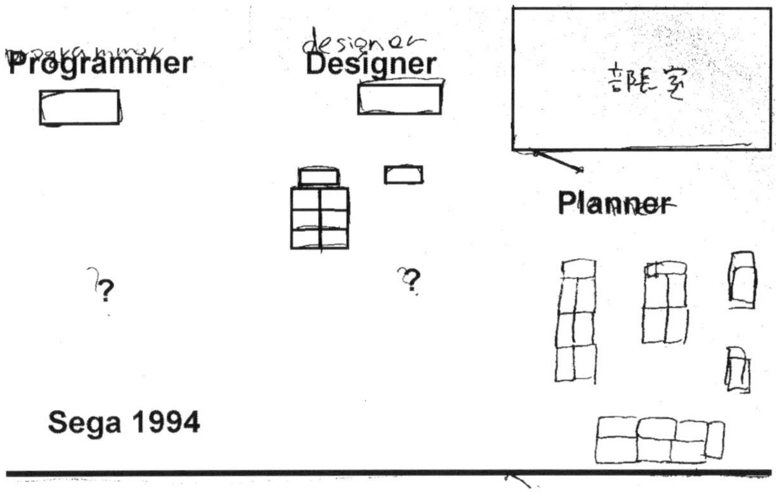

JS: So there was a lot of rivalry between R&D and Consumer Divisions.[4]

MM: Exactly! *<laughs>* That kind of thing happened almost all the time.

JS: Eventually R&D 1 made consumer games?

MM: Yes, but we still thought we were a different division. The consumer departments still made consumer games, even though we started to make some. And we were still like a separate company within Sega. And the layout of the offices was actually very different.

JS: What year is this layout sketch from?

MM: From 1994. It was laid out project by project, by division. The AM1 division had a planner section, art designer section, and programmer section.

JS: Was there a wall between sections?

MM: No, no wall. It was completely separated. You could not instantly tell who was involved with which project, because everyone was sitting. The programmers were seated all together, programmer, programmer... Then the art designers all together, and the planners all together. Sometimes programmers and designers sat very close, when they are involved in the same project, but basically we were all separated.

JS: 1994 is the year the Saturn was launched.

MM: Do you know ST-V?[5] In 1994 the ST-V arcade board was already developed.

JS: The Saturn was based on it?

MM: No it wasn't based on it, rather they were the same. ST-V was for arcades, and Saturn was for consumers. ST-V was a codename, Titan. The acronym stands for Sega Titan Videogame system. One of Saturn's moons is called Titan. In Sega's case they reused, or we shared the same hardware between consumer games and arcade games. The only difference is the volume of memory. Sega's consumer hardware used CDs and the memory was meagre, whereas in arcades it used ROM cartridges and memory...

JS: The Saturn had a slot for extra memory.

MM: The memory cartridge. Exactly.

JS: What was your first game at Sega? You were credited on *Dynamite Deka*.

MM: Yes. ST-V development was already taking place when I joined Sega, and a third-party was involved in this ST-V project. So Sega needed to check the programming of this.

[115 words removed. I asked if Mr Morita could recall the name of the third-party. Initially he thought it might have been Minato Giken, but upon later reflection he concluded it was not]

JS: What else did you work on?

MM: I helped with the release of many different games. One of them was *Die Hard Arcade*.[6] *<laughs> Die Hard Arcade* was a very interesting game. Uchida-san[7] developed it. Do you know *Golden Axe*? Uchida-san was the director of *Golden Axe*. Anyway, Uchida-san was my boss. He was assigned to develop a game in the US, at Sega of America. One of my colleagues who was a programmer worked with

[4] In Japan "consumer" refers to console/home games

[5] Sega arcade system - notable for *Radiant Silvergun*

[6] Mr Morita made a point of using the English name

[7] Makoto Uchida, 内田 誠

Uchida-san and helped him with the motion capture process and debugging. It came out in Japan first, but back then the title was completely different - it was *Dynamite Deka*. When Uchida-san produced the game in the US, he watched the movie *Die Hard*, and that's where he got the idea. But he couldn't use the name [in Japan] because of copyright.

JS: What can you tell me about the hardware?

MM: Hmm, that's difficult! <*laughs*> I don't think I should be telling you this! Our aim was to seek low-cost hardware. Do you know Model 2? Well, Model 1 was very expensive. ST-V was very inexpensive. So at Sega we wanted to line up a range of games, from low-cost games through to high-end games, or more expensive ones. The ST-V was more for the low-cost, less expensive games. For example car racing games would be Model 2. Puzzle games, shooting games, they would be on ST-V. That's how we distinguished between different arcade boards.

JS: Any stories about *Dynamite Deka*?

MM: Uchida-san, the director of *Die Hard Arcade*, he once said to me, "Make a game where the player has to tap a lot of buttons. The more times the player has to press the buttons, the more enjoyment the player will get out of the same 100 yen coin." <*taps table rapidly*> Having to press more buttons in a short amount of time is more exciting. An action game, with a kick button, a punch button... Uchida-san's games are fundamentally action games, so it's exciting to have to mash repeatedly on the kick button and punch button, or take damage and then tap-tap-tap to heal, because you're really fighting for it...

JS: You were in charge of developing *Taisen Tanto-R 'Sasissu!'*[8] is that right?

MM: I was the director.

JS: It was sold in South Korea. Did you have to make any special changes?

MM: That's right. <*laughs*> I shouldn't be talking about this too much!

JS: What's the harm?

MM: We didn't think about selling the game in the Korean market at first. We always decided to sell games in another country's market after the game has come out in Japan. This was the same for *'Sasissu!'*.

JS: What kind of changes were needed?

MM: The actual localisation was taken care of by another company. With videogames, it's not just translating words into Korean, but we had to be careful regarding expressions. The expression '*sasissu*' needed to be transformed, to be appreciated in the Korean market.[9] The captions had to be in Korean, and every single word needed to be changed into the Korean language.

JS: Can you recall the year that R&D Division 1 started making consumer games?

MM: Hmm... ST-V games could be transferred to the Saturn. The process of transferring was taken care of by another division. I think it was around 2000 when we started to produce consumer games from start to finish. Like Dreamcast games. Do you know NAOMI? The arcade/Dreamcast hardware, NAOMI. Sega wanted to use a female name for the boards. NAOMI as in Naomi Campbell. After that Hikaru. It started with Naomi.

JS: Did you ever speak with Isao Okawa?[10]

MM: He was too famous, too important, too high up! <*laughs*> I only saw him on one occasion. He gave a speech in front of all the development teams at Sega. That was the only time I saw him.

JS: I heard that before he passed away, he donated all his shares back to the company.

MM: I don't know much about those details, like what he gave back to Sega. But he certainly liked Sega, he treasured it.

JS: When the Dreamcast ended and Sega shifted to software only, how did you feel?

MM: I thought it was interesting! <*laughs*> I was hopeful about it. Because even if the

---

[8] 対戦タントアール サシっす; super obscure arcade title, Japan and South Korea only; final part in an action-puzzle minigame series

[9] The Japanese term mixes hiragana and katakana

[10] 大川 功; former Sega chairman, died March 2001

Dreamcast no longer existed, there was still NAOMI. For people developing games, new hardware is very interesting. Even if the hardware changed to PlayStation 2, or Game Boy Advance, it was very exciting for me.

JS: Let's talk about *Dororo* on PlayStation 2.

MM: I was the main planner. <*takes out a green book*> This is the script for *Dororo*.

JS: Did you have complete control over it?

MM: It's complicated, with regards to control of the project. The ultimate decision came from the main director, but the *Dororo* team - planner, artist, programmer - was very consolidated. We were close to the main director, so it was peaceful as a team.

JS: Was it always meant for PlayStation 2?

MM: Originally, yes.

JS: Were you a fan of Osamu Tezuka?[11]

MM: I think I am the chief expert of *Dororo* in Japan! <*laughs*>

JS: What were the increased risks or rewards in developing from a popular, pre-existing franchise?

MM: The biggest problem was that the author had already passed away. It was really difficult to discuss things with Tezuka Productions. I read all of the *Dororo* manga, and I came up with my own context, or understanding of the author's message. But there's no way to know the real message the author wanted to convey to the readers. The only thing we can do is ask Tezuka Productions and get their idea, or opinions on the message. The original manga was very grotesque,[12] and the characters are very explicit. Whenever they renew the print editions, what the characters say is altered or changed. What I wanted to convey is something based on the very first edition, but Tezuka Productions said no to that idea, and I couldn't use it.

JS: They censored the original manga! Conveying the *sekaikan* must have been difficult.

MM: There are very few people who can create *sekaikan*. It is something the designer already saw, somewhere, maybe unconsciously. Most designers create *sekaikan* which is similar to something they already know. They just change it a bit, from an already existing *sekaikan*. It could be pessimistic, but most examples of *sekaikan* are reinventions of existing things.

For me, *Xevious* was the first game that created an entire *sekaikan*, and brought it into the game world.

JS: What do you think of the *sekaikan* in Sega's *Panzer Dragoon*?

MM: Ahhh, *Panzer Dragoon*! *Panzer Dragoon II* is a nice game. The water surface is beautifully described. For *Panzer Dragoon*, Moebius did the cover. I love Moebius' *sekaikan*, it's original.

When I created *Dororo* for PS2, the designer Amemiya-san,[13] a famous creator in Japanese animation... Do you know *Mirai Ninja*?[14] I asked Amemiya-san to give me design ideas for *sekaikan*, but he brought me a design for rocks.

JS: Rocks?

MM: And other very small things, like a kimono, so it's the details. He said, "Place these things in your design, and this will make your *sekaikan*!" To share *sekaikan* is a very difficult thing, so there are many designers involved in game creation, so when outside designers are involved to create a game it's difficult to share the image of *sekaikan*.

Do you know *Gears of War*? The symbol of *Gears of War* is a gear with a skull. Place this gear mark everywhere and that will make your game conform to that *sekaikan*. <*laughs*> That's *sekaikan*! It's very easy, and effective, to develop *sekaikan*. Western games use that strategy everywhere. So you have to design a key component and place it everywhere, to give a game a proper and consistent *sekaikan*. That's an easy and effective way of implementing it when working with a lot of designers.

Akira Takiguchi: If you can develop a game by yourself, it's easy to develop consistent *sekaikan*. But now you have to hire a lot of people to make

[11] Hailed as the father of manga; died Feb 1989

[12] The story involves an unborn baby's organs being stolen by demons

[13] Keita Amemiya; 雨宮 慶太; character designs on *Hagane*, Super Famicom

[14] Both a Namco arcade game, and a film

a movie, or a game. The key component is most important when designing the games and animation. Morita-san mentioned his senpai, who was talking about how to create a much more Leiji Matsumoto[15] style of computers. Everyone recognises his designs for computers, with a circle screen.

MM: One thing I want mention about the *Dororo* episode. People play *Dororo* by themselves, it's a one player game, but if you connected another controller to the PS2, you can control the Dororo character. Player one controls Hyakkimaru, and player two controls Dororo. This was inspired by *Sonic 2*, and the ability to control Tails. I really liked *Sonic 2*. The director of *Sonic 2* was Mark Cerny, who worked on *Major Havoc*. Through *Major Havoc* Mark Cerny influenced *Theseus* and *Thexder*,[16] and through *Sonic 2* he influenced *Dororo*. *<laughs>* I wanted to imitate *Sonic 2*.

JS: I like that when you start the game, because he's missing his eye, everything is monochrome.

MM: That idea was from *Wizard of Oz*. I imitated the movie. *<laughs>*

JS: Was there resistance to this idea?

MM: When I created *Dororo*, Sega of America asked me to make changes. But I couldn't understand what Sega of America was requesting. Now, however, I understand why. They said let's make it like *Halo*! Make it save everywhere - wherever you are, the game saves automatically. Don't have meters or gauges on screen, and no health bar, and no map.

JS: It's tricky altering a game after it's made.

MM: Somebody has to decide about the game's balance, and there is no fixed proof that it is good. So it is a very difficult task and it could easily be ruined by the CEO's interfering.

JS: Do you like *Halo*?

MM: Hmm... Yes. I played *Halo* in about 2005, but I cannot enjoy any game when I am creating a new game. But after I quit Sega, I started to enjoy other games again. Now I've started to enjoy foreign games on the Xbox. I started to play *Halo*, but it was an old game by then. I was impressed. *Halo* was an amazing game - the first *Halo* was one of the best games.

JS: I personally don't like *Halo*...[17]

MM: Actually, I had hated *Halo* before playing it. But I played it after that long game creation period, and I found some interesting aspects to it. I finally understood the requests from Sega of America for *Dororo*, after playing *Halo*.

JS: I played the American version of *Dororo*, and it kept the map, and the health bar... Didn't it?

MM: Foreign games are approaching the quality of virtual reality. Whereas Japanese games are different. We do not try to approach reality. So we have things like life gauges. But we have no life gauges in ourselves! Sega of America asked me to erase the life gauge from the game.

JS: That would make it unnecessarily difficult; there would be no data feedback for the player.

MM: Another thing, Japanese games seem to share more with European games. The American games don't share anything directly. *<laughs>* In Japan we want others to "please understand me", without talking. We are rather implicit. But maybe with Europeans, to share ideas, we don't have to talk. We do not explicitly explain what we want. We think we can share the feelings. But with Americans, we have to give them explicit explanations.

JS: Any amusing anecdotes while at Sega?

MM: I brought this picture.

JS: IT'S SPIELBERG!

MM: And me! Steven Spielberg came to our office that day.

JS: Was this during development of *NiGHTS*?

MM: I think it's around that time. At the time many people visited Sega, like Michael Jackson. It was a really fun office.

JS: Can I photograph this photo?

---

[15] 松本 零士; creator of *Space Cruiser Yamamoto*

[16] *Theseus* was by Akira Takiguchi; *Thexder* was by Kohei Ikeda, and Game Arts' breakthrough game

[17] *System Shock 2* is more my kind of FPS

MM: Probably not a good idea...

JS: Perhaps I'll sketch it. Did he have his own private interpreter with him?

MM: I don't remember. He probably did, but I'm not sure.

JS: Why did you leave Sega?

MM: I could mention that *Dororo* was a very big project, and more than 70 people were involved in it. I kind of felt like I did everything I could do.

JS: Did you feel burned out? Lots of late nights?

MM: Not to that extent. <*laughs*>

AT: He stays up so late! He sleeps so little!

JS: What time do you get to sleep?

MM: Three... Three or four.

JS: What time do you get up in the morning?!

MM: Do you know Airfix? An English plastic model maker. My hobby is to build spitfires. Not Tamiya, [18] Airfix is very good. The design of Airfix plastic models, and the boxes, are designed to attract more people to enjoy model building. Young people. So it's easy to construct.

JS: So what time do you wake up?

MM: Six thirty.

AT: He's a three hour sleep kind of man. Like Napoleon! <*laughs*>

JS: How do you survive?!

<*everyone laughs*>

MM: Too much thinking keeps me awake. I'm working in my dreams!

JS: How did you join ASAHI Net?[19]

<Mr Morita converses with Mr Takiguchi - how long after the Olion interview>

AT: Perhaps six months after our interview?

MM: <*laughs*> Yes, that was because I met Takiguchi-san through the *Olion* webpage. I did apply for many other companies, but it was just so easy to go into a company where somebody I knew works. Also this company, ASAHI Net, had a lot of money, so if I wanted to start something new it's a good place work. <*laughs*> That's a very important point!

JS: Were you a fan of the AX series? When did you first play *Olion*?

MM: When I was around 12 years old; I was a 6th grader in elementary school.

JS: Would you say it's your favourite game?

MM: As a matter of the fact, *Olion* created by Takiguchi-san was my favourite. Around 2001, for the purpose of self-reflection, I analysed *Olion* again and made the *Olion Ultimana* web page. For me, what I want from a game is speed and excitement. In that sense, in *Olion* I could feel a lot of speed and it was exciting.

JS: You said you're not a collector, but buy older games to understand what others worked on?

MM: That's right. It's more that I want to know about the product rather than collect them. When I tried to come up with ideas for new games I often searched old arcade games, computer games for the Apple II or PC-6001, or game programs published in computer magazines. Have you heard of Japanese magazines *I/O* or *BASIC Magazine*? They appear so simple compared to recent games, but I could observe much ingenuity in them. So they became huge

---

[18] Extremely popular brand of Japanese plastic models

[19] I already knew that Mr Morita had known Mr Takiguchi after interviewing him for his website

inspirations for me. I was a game planner, I guess you would use the term "game designer" in English. I was neither a programmer nor a graphic designer. When I was in middle school, I read an article about Bernie DeKoven.[20] Back then, the programmer was equal to the designer, so he was introduced as a "weird" designer who only comes up with ideas or concepts of games, but does not or can not write programs. I never had a chance to play his games, but was definitely influenced by that article.

JS: <*refers to factory sealed copy of Illegas on MSX*> You never opened this one. Keeping it sealed prevents biodegrading?

AT: That *Battlefield Tank*, did you watch it when Morita-san displayed it on the projector?[21]

JS: Yes, based on *Battlezone*.

AT: He says that's one of only two cases where it's been able to work in emulators. So it's very rare to see it working, today.

JS: Really? It's difficult to emulate?

AT: No. Nobody has succeeded to run *Battlefield* on emulators, due to its difficulty of being read from the old tapes, which possibly have mould.

MM: There are not so many available old tapes, because that was *omake*.[22] If you didn't buy a joystick, you couldn't get it. There was no other way to get it. You had to buy a joystick. So there are few on the market.

AT: You had to buy a joystick to get the *Battlefield* game, there was no separate sales. So there are very, very few available on the market now.

JS: What about a tape images from the internet?

MM: Nothing was available on the internet about *Battlefield*, so I got the original tape and I read it.

JS: Did you see any unreleased games at Sega?

MM: <*laughs*> A lot of them!

JS: Can you tell me about any games? Can you give a rough estimate on the number?

MM: How can I put this? I'm proud that all the games I produced have been released, and I don't think there are many people who can say this. Because it is usual that many ideas for games come up, but they're turned down. That's normal. The only thing I can say is that all my games were released.

JS: But if you had to give a number, can you give a number of those others worked on? Maybe just a guess?

MM: Hmm, it depends on the time. When I first joined Sega one project lasted half a year, or a year. But *Dororo* took two years. Nowadays it's much shorter if it's a game for smartphones. So I cannot really make a rough estimate.

JS: Is there any message you want to say?

MM: I want to produce something beautifully structured. It can be anything, a game, or the project I'm working on now, Manaba,[23] or a website. My desire is to make something beautiful in structure. I believe that kind of beautiful product will last forever.

[20] Extensive career, including a book on game design: *The Well Played Game*

[21] This took place during Hiroshi Suzuki's interview, which preceded this interview with Mr Morita

[22] A bonus bundled with a game

[23] Cloud application service for educational institutions, run by ASAHI Net

~Appearing in a later volume~

If you enjoyed this slice of Sega coverage, then you'll really love later volumes of the book. I visited Arzest on my trip, and spoke to four major figures from Sega's history. Above, from left:

* **Naoto Ohshima** - creator of *Sonic*
* **Yoji Ishii** - creator of *Flicky* and *Fantasy Zone*
* **Manabu Kusunoki** - chara. design on *Panzer Dragoon*
* **Yutaka Sugano** - creator of the original *Shinobi*

One of the highlights of the day was when enjoying lunch with these four gentlemen; Mr Ishii took out his mobile phone and called up the creator of *Alex Kidd*, and right there arranges an interview. "Yes, this foreign journalist is in Japan, he wants to talk to you."

Left: Kotaro Hayashida
Seldom interviewed, Mr Hayashida created *Alex Kidd* and proposed the original *Phantasy Star*. Reluctant to reveal his identity (just yet), he asked that I use this cartoon image drawn by his daughter. Discover his true form in a later volume!

From the AX series to Game Arts

The AX series of games for the PC-6001 never left Japan. None of the titles were ported to any hardware sold outside Japan, and in all likelihood most people reading this book will never have heard of them. They are, however, extremely important, representing not only a shift in the dynamics of Japanese computer games, but also forming the philosophical ethos that would lead to the creation of Game Arts. The AX series, arguably, is Game Arts in a prototype form. During that nascent stage in computer evolution, before the days of the ubiquitous PC-88, the quality of game software was poor. Some games, if they could even be called that, were distributed on cassette tape with a photocopied sheet of instructions. The AX series aimed to change this, putting games on a level akin to books or films, with extremely high quality packaging and - most importantly - technically impressive software which was enjoyable and gave value for money. Each cassette tape contained multiple games, in addition to technical demos which showed what the hardware could do. The games themselves were also impressive, and included fast-paced first-person space shooters such as *Olion*, and first-person maze games like *Quest*.

A key figure in the AX series, and later co-founder of Game Arts, was Mitsuhiro Matsuda, who sadly passed away. Originally part of ASCII's 2nd publishing division, he wanted to improve Japanese computer games. His life is recalled on the adjacent memorial page and in the following interviews. Another key figure in Game Arts' history who passed away is Takeshi Miyaji, who is also recalled by colleagues.

The history of Game Arts is equally as interesting as what preceded it. The company formed from AX series creators to take advantage of the impending release of a new model of PC-88, and found great success with *Thexder*, which launched around the time of the new hardware. Game Arts rode a wave of new technology, producing technically masterful titles which would later be converted by Sierra Online for sale outside Japan. The company also embodies the shift away from computer titles towards consoles, which a lot of Japanese developers underwent. For those outside of Japan, Game Arts' most recognisable titles are probably its different RPG series for consoles, *Lunar* and *Grandia*. This is a recurring theme - Japan's computer history, forever intertwined with its console history, is almost unknown outside Japan, despite having a significant knock-on effect on the rest of the world. With the exception of Nintendo, and a few arcade specific developers, much of the bedrock for Japanese games is in computers.

After contacting Masamoto Morita and being put in touch with Akira Takiguchi, creator of *Olion*, he contacted two colleagues whom he developed games alongside: Hiroshi Suzuki and Masakuni Mitsuhashi. On 26 October, during a typhoon, I visited the ASAHI Net building and interviewed all of these gentlemen. It's somewhat melancholy to note that all of them, despite being witness to pivotal shifts in gaming history, are no longer in games, moving on to more serious professions. Mr Mitsuhashi in turn put me in contact with Game Arts co-founder Kohei Ikeda, and via a separate route I also interviewed Tomonori Sugiyama and Yutaka Isokawa, both of whom worked with Game Arts.

For more on the AX series, and Japanese computer history in general, I highly recommend the English translation of Masamoto Morita's interview with Akira Takiguchi, which is hosted on Gamasutra: **gamasutra.com/blogs/JohnSzczepaniak/20140304/212177/History_of_Japanese_computer_games.php**

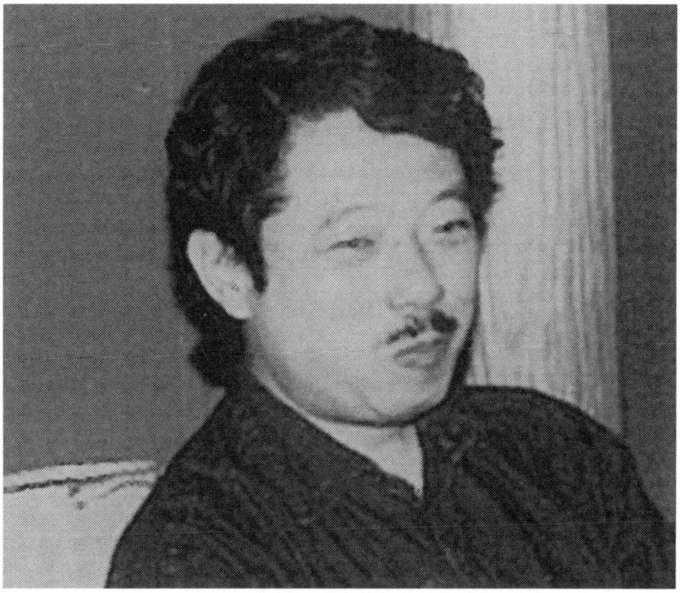

~*In memory of*~

松田 充弘

MATSUDA, Mitsuhiro

~Selected Portfolio~

Zeliard (1987) / *Veigues* (1988) / *Fire Hawk: Thexder 2* (1989) / *Lunar: The Silver Star* (1992) / *Silpheed* (1993) / *Gungriffon* (1996)

Matsuda-san was actually only a few years older than us, but he managed his team well in the company. Amazing! It was great to see that Game Arts did so well when following his advice, but sadly Matsuda-san's name has been forgotten in history, and he passed away rather lonely and too early. I'm happy to be able to give him proper credit this time... I miss him.
- ***Akira Takiguchi, AX series colleague***

Matsuda-san had an exceptional knowledge about games, and for all of us he was our teacher. It's very unfortunate that he passed away. He taught us a great many things about creating games. He was our *onshi*.[1] Even now when we're making games we're striving to create something that wouldn't make him angry. <*laughs*> I hope that he's kindly looking upon us from heaven.
- ***Kohei Ikeda, AX series and Game Arts colleague***

He used to manage the students, who were working part-time, which was very important. We were all so young and didn't know anything about business, having come from this computer club at university, and he kept us afloat. He was also a businessman and knew what he was doing. Because we were all fresh out of school we didn't really know much about the business world; whenever we broke the rules he was very kind and would explain why it wasn't OK, what was and was not acceptable. He was a very kind and generous person. We used to go out to restaurants as a team, not with Matsuda-san, then charge it to the company. Of course Matsuda-san would be surprised, but he would turn a blind eye to it. <*laughs*>
- ***Masakuni Mitsuhashi, AX series and Game Arts colleague***

---

[1] A teacher you owe a duty towards

滝口 彰

TAKIGUCHI, Akira

DOB: 5 July 1961 / Birthplace: *secret* / Blood Type: *secret*

~ Selected Portfolio ~

Dakara Ima Maicon	- October 1981, Shueisha	
MSX Official Handbook	- ASCII	
Nostromo	- CBM, unreleased	(sci-fi survival horror)
Ad Astra	- Apple II, unreleased,	(space convoy protection game)
Red and Blue	- Apple II, unreleased	(*Pac-man* style game)
AX-5: Olion	- PC-6001, 1981, ASCII	
AY-2: Olion80	- PC-8001, 1983, ASCII	
Battlefield	- PC-6001, 1983	(joystick "*omake*" game, akin to *Battle Zone*)
Illegus Ep. IV	- MSX, 1984, ASCII	(first-person maze game with day/night cycle)
Theseus	- MSX, 1984, ASCII	(incredible inertia platformer)

Interview with Akira Takiguchi *(aka: Akira Takeuchi)*
26 October 2013, Tokyo, ASAHI Net

Honorific titles, which change between Japanese and English style, are kept mostly as they were used during discussion. Masamoto Morita, colleague of Mr Takiguchi, conducted an interview with Mr Takiguchi several years ago for his OlionUltimania website. This interview was fascinating, so in about three places I've re-used interview answers from it. Any answer preceded by the symbol "&" is taken from this earlier interview. The full English translation can be found online by searching for it on Gamasutra. The rest of the interview was conducted in segments, both before and after interviewing Misters Suzuki and Mitsuhashi, so there will be some chronological anomalies.

JS: What was the first game you ever played?

Akira Takiguchi: *Space Invaders*. But I played some *Pong*, when I was in junior high. Or maybe elementary school? I saw *Pong*, and I played it in the kids' corner of the department store. I wasn't that interested. The real game that took my interest was *Space Invaders*, right?

JS: Many say either *Block Zushi* or *Invaders*.

AT: Yah, *Block Zushi* was earlier I think, but it wasn't a real grabber. It didn't grab my heart very much, but *Space Invaders* did! <*laughs*> And later *Star Fire*[1] was really good for me. I couldn't get high scores for *Space Invaders*, because there were many good players. But with *Star Fire*, by Exidy, I could. So when I came back from junior high, to my home, I dropped by the game centre nearby, and played several times a day. So it was a nice experience.

Writing a book is a major task if you have to collect information from various sources. When I was a university student I wrote several books, but the subject was simple. For example the *MSX Official Handbook* was just about MSX. So gathering information and writing was easy. But if you have to dig into the history and find interviewees, <*laughs*> that's tough work.

JS: Tell me more about the books you wrote.

AT: The first book I wrote, I was in Tokyo University microcomputer club, so it included Kei Yuasa and Atsushi Hiramatsu.[2] Kei created *American Football* for *AX-4*. I don't think Atsushi did anything in the AX series, though he was an excellent programmer.

We compiled a book, the title is *Dakara Ima maikon.*[3] This is a book for the newbies. Just those who want to play with a new microcomputer, like PET, Apple, and PC-6001. The first book was published by Shueisha, one of the major publishers, which still exists today. The second book was from the same publisher. But they're a general publisher. For the computer related publishers, like ASCII, I wrote the *MSX Official Handbook*.

JS: How did you come to write that? What year?

AT: I worked for the 2nd Publishing Division of ASCII, with Mitsuhiro Matsuda, but also for 1st Publishing Division, with Mr Miyazaki, as well as later on the 3rd Publishing Division, with Mr Yagi. I did the *Official MSX Handbook* with Mr Yagi at the 1st division in 1984, before the creation of the 3rd division. Sure, I used MSX a lot.

---

[1] 1978 arcade game, David Rolfe; resembles *Star Wars*

[2] 湯浅 敬 / 平松 淳

[3] *So it's time for microcomputers* - だからいまマイコン, Oct 1981, Shueisha, ASIN: B000J7SD6W

Because by then I did *Illegus* and *Theseus*. I worked with Mr Yagi later to write a couple of user manuals - the guidebook part - for NEC, including PC-98LT and PC-98H.

JS: Did you meet Kazuhiko Nishi, ASCII founder and creator of the MSX?

AT: Never in person, but I saw him at the office a couple of times.

JS: So ASCII provided you with Part 2, which is where the AX series for PC-6001 was made, but you also developed MSX software there, to be published by ASCII?

AT: That is correct.

JS: How old were you with your first book?

AT: I was 19, with *Dakara Ima Maicon*.

JS: That's quite young!

AT: Yah, but it was a developing industry, so those who knew computers, could write any books. <*laughs*>

JS: Many high school students started doing part-time jobs for computer software companies.

AT: Ahh, some of my friends did too.

JS: There weren't many who knew programming. So if you could program you had good prospects.

AT: One of my colleagues who built ASAHI Net was also such a guy, who started programming in junior high. Maybe he was the first person who won the Information Processing Skill test. He was the youngest who took the test and passed the test. Maybe he was 15, I think? In my case I didn't take any such test, I just wanted to make programs. Of course I couldn't... When I was maybe 16, microcomputers started to appear in department stores like Seibu. There was a microcomputer corner and they allowed us - anybody - to test programming. So whenever I could... <*laughs*> I left school and went to the Shibuya Seibu, and did some programming!

JS: There was a nickname for those who did not have a computer...

AT: Ahh, yes! The *naicon*.[4]

JS: Yes, the *naicon zoku*. Or tribe of people who didn't have one but used a computer at...

AT: ...at a department store or any electronic shop! *Nai* is no, so instead of *maicon*, it's *naicon*. <*laughs*> *Naicon* was the nickname I think for those who didn't have a computer but went anywhere to test programming. And of course there was no cassette tapes to save, so each time I visited Seibu I had to start again. So actually I didn't make large programs. I just played around. To do real programming I bought a TI-58. It's not a microcomputer, but a calculator with programming capabilities. So it's kind of an assembly language, but with Store and Recall, and some calculations. It displayed only numbers, of course. <*laughs*>

JS: A bit difficult to create games!

AT: Yah, but with clever usage of LEDs you could indicate, or you could do some...

JS: From limitation comes interesting ideas?

AT: Yah, severe limitation is the key, sometimes. So I made a *Star Wars* game. As I said in Morita-san's interview, *Star Wars* was a key for games, it was a big influence. Maybe I was 15 or 16. Do you remember when *Star Wars* was run in the states? Late 1970s I think.

JS: *Space Invaders* was 1978.

AT: If that was 1978... So I was a high school student. Maybe I was 16 when *Space Invaders* came out, and of course I spent a lot of *hyaku-en dama*, 100 yen coins!

JS: When you wrote your first book, were you credited under Akira Takiguchi?

AT: The book was actually authored under the name of Todai Maicon Club, so my name... I think it did appear as my real name. Because Akira ***Takeuchi***, which I used for the AX series, I created specifically for the AX series. So before that I never used it.

JS: I was curious about the pseudonym's origin.

---

[4] *Maicon* = personal computer; *Nai* = without

AT: <*laughs*> There was no big reason for that. At the time, nicknames were pretty popular. Just for fun, I think. Maybe I should have used my real name, but everybody in Todai Maicon Club used those nicknames, like Hirose-kun used Junpei Ryotsu.[5] And Mitsuhashi-san, he used Hiromi Ohba.[6]

JS: Did you ever have any other nicknames?

&AT: When I was in middle school, at some point my friends saw me sleeping in an "L" position on a school trip, and so they gave me that nickname. I went to a combined middle school and high school program, so I was called "L-kun" for a long time.

JS: There was a Naoto Ohshima in Todai Maicon Club, who used the nickname Mr Eccentrics.

AT: Eccentrics? Ahh, yah. But I never called him by that name. He was already employed by ASCII Publishing, so I think he's much older than the other Ohshima-san.

JS: There's three gentlemen named Naoto Ohshima working in games,[7] I've discovered. The one you knew, I think he worked on versions of *Wizardry* for ASCII.

AT: He's not a programmer, he was a designer. That's a possibility, but I've had no communication with him for a very long time.

JS: His kanji is 大嶋. The Sega gentleman's kanji is 大島. He made *Sonic the Hedgehog*.

AT: Maybe the most famous one! <*laughs*>

JS: The names are pronounced the same, but one kanji has a small yama symbol (山) in it. On some English websites the three gentlemen have become one person.

AT: Oh really? That's a rare case. OHSHIMA Naoto is not a common name.

JS: After the TI-58 what was the first proper...?

AT: ...personal computer I bought? When I entered Tokyo University, my parents bought me a typewriter. I actually asked them for a computer, but that was too expensive. <*laughs*> My parents were not rich, so I could only ask for an Olivetti's typewriter. Just to practise typing. I learned typing on that Olivetti, and wrote many things. And that ability certainly helped with programming fast.

JS: Yoshiro Kimura mentioned that because computers used the QWERTY keyboard, it was difficult for Japanese people to learn.

AT: Yes, that is true. Maybe I was a bit better than others with English - but my English has *deproved* since then! <*laughs*> My friends in Todai Microcomputer Club bought a PC-8001, and I didn't have one, so I just used the club's PET. It's a CBM.[8] Suzuki-san, who is coming at noon, made contact with Taito corporation, and they lent us a room and a few computers.

JS: A room in Taito's office building? Or was it where you programmed the AX series...?

AT: No, no. Close to the university in Komaba, they lent a small room - a one room *mansion*. It's different from Part 2.[9] It's a Taito matter, not ASCII. The Part 2 building was an ASCII thing. Back then it was difficult for a club to have a room in the university, because the *maikon* club was new and traditional clubs occupied all the available space. So Suzuki-san's contract with Taito, before I entered Todai, was very beneficial. There were some computers, I mostly used PET, and I wrote several programs in BASIC. Like the first version of *Nostromo*, before AX-2. I showed it to Taito. We had a contract that if we created a game and made a presentation, Taito would give us money. It was 100'000 yen[10] for a game. So that helped me buy an Apple II.

JS: Why wasn't Suzuki-san later involved with ASCII or the AX series?

AT: We talked to him, but he never wanted to. Probably because of his *I/O Magazine* connection. Actually, our club was also connected with another magazine, *RAM*. I did nothing for them though.

---

[5] Creator of *Steal Alien* (AX-2), *Car Race* (AX-4), and *Powered Knight* (AX-6)

[6] Works include demo programs in AX-1 to AX-4 and AX-6, *Nostromo* (AX-2), and *Quest* (AX-5)

[7] Slightly different Kanji; one at ASCII, another at Konami, and then the creator of *Sonic the Hedgehog*

[8] Commodore Business Machine

[9] Mansion is Japanese for small apartment; Part 2 was the building provided by ASCII for the AX series

[10] Roughly £300 / $440 in 1983 (fxtop.com)

JS: How popular was Apple in Japan?

AT: Apple II was pretty popular among computer hobbyists in Japan. Anyway, PC-8001 appeared only by September 1979. A teacher at my high school - the coach of Volleyball club I was playing in - bought an Apple II in 1978 for his statistic needs. It was expensive, I think around the range of 750k yen back then.[11] When I bought it, it had become a bit cheaper, maybe 480k yen. Several import shops existed, which also imported software. I bought my *Minotaur* package at Starcraft in Ikebukuro. Starcraft was a leading shop for Apple software, and they also connected Tony Suzuki to Broderband.[12]

JS: You were struggling to pay off the Apple II?

AT: Yes! I think it was in June that I bought the Apple II, and I had to pay 15'000 yen[13] a month, for a loan. Back then I didn't do any part-time jobs, just learning and just playing computers. So I didn't have a way to make money other than this Taito contract. My parents gave me 15'000 yen a month, and I had to pay 15'000 a month - so no money for eating! <*laughs*> But I lived with my parents, so eating was no problem. The money from Taito helped me a lot.

JS: What was this game for Taito?

AT: *Nostromo*, and then Taito asked... <*confers with others*> Taito asked me to create a game according to their specifications. That's the only time I recall where they gave us specifications. I created a game that was named *Red and Blue.* That was something in a *Pac-man* style. Red and blue circles chasing each other. I don't remember the exact details, but they gave us specifications and I used assembly language to make it work, and they gave us... <*confers*> 80'000 yen? <*confers again*> Ah, 180'000 yen![14]

JS: *Uchuu Yusou-sen Nostromo* (*Spaceship Nostromo*) is a sci-fi survival horror, where you avoid being detected by an alien while trying to escape the ship. I'm sensing an influence...

AT: I loved *Thunderbirds* during my childhood, that was a great influence on me. The next thing was *Star Wars* and *Alien*. The original one, ne.

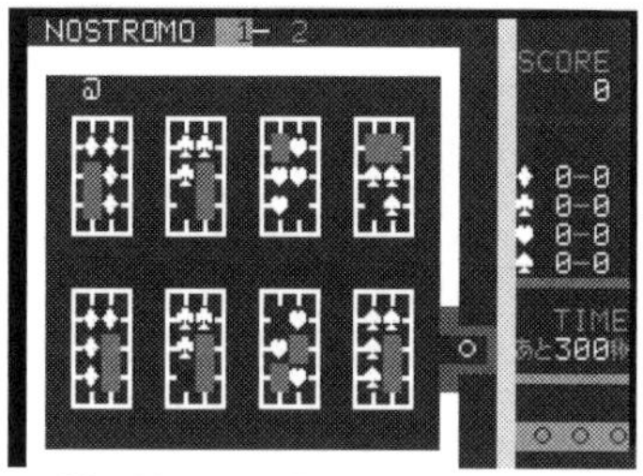

Collect the items needed to escape the ship while avoiding the sight of the alien

JS: Hence the name *Nostromo*. So everyone was making games in this room Taito provided...

AT: Yes.

JS: And then you'd show Taito the game, and then they'd give you money.

AT: Yes.

JS: But no one would do anything with the game, and it would never be published?

AT: Never published. But sometimes, like for *Nostromo*, I gave the idea to Mitsuhashi-san, and it was published eventually.[15] But other games were never published. I showed them a game, it was a space scrolling game. Like *Galaxian*, but there is a transport convoy in the centre, and you play a fighter to protect the convoy. The three freighters are partially secured by shields. That I created on the Apple II and showed it at Komaba Festival, the festival where Suzuki-san showed *Manbiki Shounen* to the public. That game was never published either.

JS: What happened to it? Do you still have it?

AT: No, sorry! <*laughs*> But I found many floppy disks, 5in Apple II floppies, yesterday. So maybe some of them still have data. But I cannot say for sure! <*laughs*>

JS: Is there anything on them?

AT: I still have an Apple II. And it works. And I have a PC-6001, of course. I have not had time to test them. They may, or may not work. I can pass them to the Game Preservation Society.

JS: Taito's deal was unrelated to the AX series?

AT: No, it had nothing to do with AX. This was a completely separate matter. Suzuki-san was

[11] Around £2'250 / $3'300

[12] geocities.jp/bochake2/apple_ii.html

[13] Roughly £45 / $65 in 1983 (fxtop.com)

[14] Roughly £500 / $750 in 1983 (fxtop.com)

[15] Mr Mitsuhashi remade *Nostromo* for AX-2 (top)

only connected with the Taito matter. Of course Mitsuhashi-san and I were in Taito's contract, but only Mitsuhashi-san and I were in contract with ASCII for the AX series.

JS: In hindsight, what do you think about the fact that Taito never published your games?

AT: If it was simply because the games weren't good enough - no complaints. What I remember I showed to them was:
1) *Nostromo* on a PET-2001
2) *Ad Astra* on Apple II
3) *Red and Blue* on Apple II
Ad Astra may have been further prototyped by Taito, because I remember - well it could have been a dream - that I saw one similar thing in a game show, but it never made it to arcades. The reason Taito asked me to create *Red and Blue* to their specification was because *Ad Astra* was a pretty good implementation.

JS: *Nostromo* was also inspired by Mr Suzuki's unreleased game, called *Dojin*?

AT: Yes, certainly. I created *Nostromo* on a PET CBM. Later Mitsuhashi-san ported it to PC-6001. My idea was different from *Dojin* - actually, *Dojin* was a very interesting and playable game. But the enemy was always viewable by the player. So because I loved [the film] *Alien*, as well as *Star Wars*, I wanted the enemy invisible to the player. Visible only when it ***is*** viewable by your character. So that's the idea of *Nostromo*.

JS: The *Nostromo* cover is amazing. Who painted the AX covers?

AT: Masashi Iwasaki. His site is on ASAHI net![16]

JS: So although never released, *Dojin* lived on?

AT: *<laughs>* You could say that! It's a pity that *Dojin* was never released to the public. Actually, did Suzuki-san talk about *Lupin III?*[17]

JS: He mentioned it, only briefly. It was an arcade title which Taito manufactured.

AT: Yes! Yes. But there was no actual money [changing hands] between Suzuki-san and Taito.

[16] asahi-net.or.jp/~xj9m-iwsk/
[17] Taito, 1980 on title; steal bags of gold and return them to your base; rudimentary AI without stealth

JS: Yes, he said he didn't receive any royalties.

AT: *<laughs>* No contract! But anyway...

JS: He says *Manbiki Shounen* inspired *Lupin III*.

AT: Yes, yes. It's pretty much the same. And I think *Manbiki Shounen* was better than *Lupin III*.

<Everyone laughs. Mr Takiguchi asks Mr Matsuhashi something, who confirms>

AT: *Manbiki Shoujo*, the sequel to *Manbiki Shounen*, was the first game to speak, but it was known only by inside people. So the first game with speech.

JS: The first game in the world?[18]

AT: Hmm, I don't know... The first computer game with speech could have been on the Apple.

<Mr Mitsuhashi suggests Castle Wolfenstein>

JS: *Wolfenstein* was 1981, after *Manbiki Shoujo*. So *Manbiki Shoujo* was never released?

AT: Never. Only privately shown to Taito and we played it, but...

JS: I want to clarify this: Taito would pay you to show them the games...

AT: Yes.

JS: Even if you did not give them the code?

AT: We did not give them ***any*** code.

JS: They just wanted to see them?

AT: Yes.

JS: Why do you think they did that?

AT: *<laughs>* That's a difficult question! Maybe they were recruiting? That's a possibility, but nobody ever joined Taito.

<laughter all round>

[18] Amazingly there's no consensus on the first game with synthesised speech. Some say *Berzerk*, others *Stratovox*; likely an arcade game from 1980; even less consensus on first home game; *Manbiki Shoujo* if released could indeed have become the first

JS: Let's discuss the AX series. It was quite important in those early days.

AT: I think so. That was the first book-style packaging in history, I think.

JS: So you moved on from Taito?

&AT: Taito's terms weren't all that bad, but it was work that didn't lead directly to a retail product, which is a bit weak in terms of motivating game development. That's when talk of ASCII came up. Yasuda-kun,[19] who was a member of UTMC[20] and who later created almost all of AX-1, worked part-time at ASCII. He was the one who proposed participating in a project for a series of PC-6001 software, which was conceived by Mitsuhiro Matsuda, the head of the 2nd Publishing Division. Matsuda-san felt indignant about the huge difference between games for the Apple II and Japanese-developed games. He believed there was no way that something possible on an Apple II wouldn't also be possible on a Japanese computer, and had a strong desire to provide quality games in a book-like packaging at a low cost. We were getting fed up of games being a cassette and some photocopied instructions, so I think most members agreed without hesitation. I think for each title in the AX series, a member said, "I'd like to do this," and that was accepted.

JS: Mr Matsuda wanted to show that Japanese games could compete with...

AT: *<laughs>* Ne! American games. But most American games used the same [style of] game package, though beautifully designed. What Matsuda-san wanted to do was publish games as books, I think. So it was designed to look like a book. The packages were fairly thick, and inside was a real book - a small booklet - and a cassette tape.

JS: I've not held an AX package yet. Was it similar to the big PC-88 boxes?

AT: It's just like a book. You should see one. Maybe Morita-san will bring it.

JS: How much did the AX titles sell?

&AT: In terms of market share, the PC-6001 fell far short of the PC-8001. Even the best-selling title in the AX series only sold about 40'000 to 50'000 copies. This was because NEC committed to that many copies from ASCII. I think the actual sales were more like 10'000 to 20'000. I don't know specifically, but the "naked cassette" games in those days only ranged from several hundred to several thousand copies, so compared to that we were a big hit.

JS: You mentioned at university the *maikon* club was new. Was there resistance from teachers? Did they see it as the future?

AT: Computers were part of the university system. Just big computers, not microcomputers.

JS: With a time-sharing system?

AT: Yes, a time-sharing system was very common. I never heard the teachers talking about it. My teachers were not so interested in microcomputers back then. But when I was in the fourth year, just before graduating, I had to write a paper. I made a small 3D CAD[21] system. My friend was working for a computer graphics company - very new in Japan. His name is Mr Ohta; he was a pioneer in computer graphics. We co-authored a book, *Applied Graphics.*[22] It included many contemporary techniques, like Z-buffer, ray tracing, and programs written in C language. I think that book was the first to show Z-buffer, A-buffer, ray tracing, and several mapping techniques. Of course *SIGGRAPH Conference Proceedings*[23] existed, but as a book I think ours was... *<laughs>*

JS: Which paid more, books or games?

AT: Interesting question. A book, yes. But *Olion* gave me more money, I think. They're not so different. Books took about, maybe four to six months to write, until publishing, and maybe it brought me 1 million yen? It's not much for six months work. *<laughs>* But for *Olion*, for three months work, I think it was a similar amount. So games were faster to produce. *<removes items from a bag>*

JS: Oh excellent! You have old *LOGiN* magazines.

---

[19] Goro Yasuda; *Arabian Rhapsody*, *Block Kuzushi*, and *High-speed Barricade* (AX-1), *Mastermind* (AX-6)

[20] University of Tokyo Microcomputer Club

[21] Computer Aided Design

[22] November 1987, ASCII

[23] Papers by the **S**pecial **I**nterest **G**roup on **GRAPH**ics

AT: I think Morita-san will bring in more, but I brought some. This is Issue Zero of *MSX Magazine.*[24] If you want it I can give it to you.

JS: Thank you! Old magazines have previews of games which were never released.

AT: But I don't remember so many "preview only" games. <*flicks through pages*> Actually, I wasn't so interested in others' games. <*laughs*>

JS: <*notices page*> This is Morita-san, of *Morita Shogi*, and *Alphos*.[25]

AT: He passed away recently, unfortunately.[26]

JS: Were you featured in any magazines?

<We look through various magazines, some including articles on Takiguchi-san, the AX series, and the Part 2 house owned by ASCII>

JS: Is this... you?

AT: Yah! <*laughs*> With different eyeglasses.

AT: There is another here. I wrote about *Shukan Asahi Weekly* and this was the extra issue from 1984. This was dedicated, the entire magazine, to new personal computers. My friend was working on other stuff, and he introduced me to... <*flicks through magazine to an advert*> Oh, it's Kouichi Nakamura-san, ne! My friend let the editor know that I was programming games, so he came... <*flicks through mag*> This is Part 2.

[24] Dated 6 October 1983; 200 yen; by ASCII
[25] Technically brilliant and famous *Xevious* clone for computers; an official license was granted by Namco
[26] July 2012, though news only became widespread a month prior to this interview

JS: The Part 2 apartment was owned by ASCII?

AT: It was lent by ASCII. That was a big house, a two story house. There was a Part 1, the external outside company room. And this was a second room for them, so this was called Part 2, I think.

JS: Several games were produced there.

AT: Yes! The entire AX series came out of this room. There was a two story... *<points to photograph of what at appears a bunk bed>*

JS: A three story bed!

AT: *<intense laughter>* Oh, three story! *<flicks page>* This is Nakamura-san. *<flicks to advert with Kouichi Nakamura>* I met him, maybe twice. In Akihabara, when he was just checking out PC shops. Before he became famous. He was, ne, much younger than I was, I think.

JS: You were saying your friend put you in touch with a magazine editor?

AT: So after this interview with the editor, I passed him the *MSX Official Handbook* that I published at the time. The next day the editor called me and asked, "Do you want to write for us?" So I wrote maybe 40 pages for this magazine. So I'm here, *<points to interview>* and here. *<flicks pages>* My wife was working for the magazine, so this was her creation.

JS: You met your wife through the magazine?

AT: Yes, she was working at the office, and I met her, we fell in love... *<laughs>* She graduated from Tama Art University, so she made this. *<points to article layout>*

JS: The art designer?

AT: Yes. So this game changed my life! *<referencing Olion>*

JS: Do you know about the unauthorised Korean port of Olion to the SPC-1000 in 1984?[27]

AT: To this day I had completely forgotten about it. My memory about this is very vague, so I don't think it appropriate to include my recollections, unless you get confirmation from a third party.

JS: *<photo of Part 2>* You're on the right?

AT: Yes, and this is Mitsuhashi-san.

JS: He went to work for Game Arts.

AT: Yes.

JS: And they asked you to join them?

AT: They suggested it, but not actually asked. Mmm... *<looks at article designed by wife>* So actually, to marry her, I wanted a stable job. So because of this connection... This *Shukan Asahi Weekly* was published by Asahi Shimbun, the second largest newspaper publisher in Japan, so the salary was good. *<laughs>* So I joined Asahi Shimbun, in the computer section.

JS: So everyone who worked on the AX series, they made their game here?

AT: Yes, everybody was working on a different project. There was very little cooperation between the programmers. Of course I got some help from Mitsuhashi-san, about music. That was removed from the emulation package[28] due to the copyright problem.

JS: Did you use music from other artists?

AT: Yes. *Olion* for PC-6001 used *Star Trek*'s music, and *Raiders of the Lost Ark*. So that was removed from the emulated games. So you'll just have to get the real ROM, to play it. *<laughs>*

JS: How do you feel about emulation today, of the AX series and older games? Some people say emulation is piracy.

AT: I don't think it's piracy! *<laughs>* That's already history.

JS: Would you say there's a statute of limitations - like if it's 20 years old and not being sold, it should be available?

---

[27] By developer Softmen, the port contains a full credit list in Korean. See Hardcore Gaming 101 for more

[28] The AX series was released as an emulated bundle

AT: It's a difficult question, and it depends on the author I think.

JS: The majority of old games are no longer available, it's not possible to buy them anymore.

AT: Right. But actual publication costs a lot of money, so that's inevitable. I'm very happy to see some people are still playing *Olion* and enjoying it. I never think of it as piracy because at that time copyright was much looser. If *Olion* has to be implemented today, the company must ask Sirius Software[29] to get a license first. Back then that wasn't done at all. I just mentioned the name of Larry Miller on *Olion*'s title screen. I think that was risky - if I did it today, I don't think... <*laughs*> No, no, I'd have to say no today. But that was a nice time. <*sighs*>

JS: Some of *Olion*'s enemy design were inspired by those in Larry Miller's games?

AT: Yes, but his designs were inspired by *Star Wars*. We never considered it seriously. First there was a dream, for myself to play a real *Star Wars* game. And I saw *Epoch*... I actually don't remember when I saw *Hadron*,[30] but anyway, *Epoch* inspired me to make *Olion*. Back then we didn't have to reverse engineer, I just looked at it and thought - I can do it! <*laughs*> So certainly that was a relaxed time.

JS: Today, as soon a company has a new idea, it takes a patent out. There was a lot of litigation regarding camera changes, with Sega.

AT: Do you know how, actually, those patents are used against each company? How they are actually used?

JS: Sega claimed it was the first to use camera changes. So they sued Nintendo and Sony, declaring they were the only company entitled to use them. But Nintendo made a counter claim, citing *Star Wars* on the X68000 as a precedent. One of my interviewees was a court witness - Sega threatened him to keep quiet.[31]

AT: Oh wow! That's terrible. But actually, Morita-san has a lot to talk about I think, because developers were recommended to file patents. I think Morita-san has a few patents under his name. Of course by Sega. Actually, patents are very hard to argue.

JS: Surely some ideas are universal? Regarding the camera change, when you watch a sports program they change camera angles.

AT: That's why we say *Egg of Columbus*![32] <*laughs*> The patent system is very simple. It does not act on emotions. If the invention has never been filed, and if it is new, they accept the patent. So whomever files a patent first, earlier, has the rights on it. We actually filed a few patents for the Manaba System. I created it with Morita-san. It's a service for universities, and it uses SMS for testing, issuing and collecting assignments, and distributing grades.

JS: *Theseus*[33] was an amazing platformer. It's also connected to *Thexder*.

AT: In Japanese, you call it *Thexder*. <*pronounces the TH as in "text"*> In English spelling you'd pronounce it your way, but in Japanese the proper pronunciation is *[Teguzda]*.

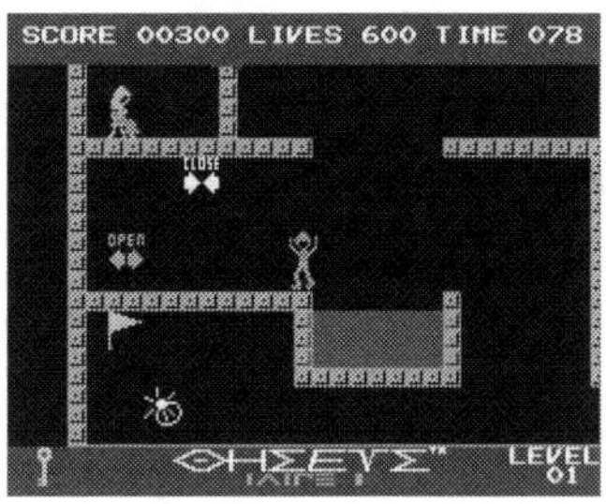

JS: And *Theseus* influenced *Thexder*?

AT: Yes, of course. The programmer Kohei Ikeda was part of the *Theseus* project. He did a smaller contribution, but he was a contributor. When Game Arts started, their first product was *Thexder*. I think Mitsuhashi-san helped. The main programmer I think was Satoshi Uesaka?

JS: You were the lead creator on *Theseus*?

AT: *Theseus*... Maybe we have to talk with Mitsuhashi-san about that. I think Mitsuhashi-san contributed 50%, and I did the other half.

JS: *Thexder* was a break out game in Japan.

AT: Yes! Certainly.

JS: Sierra Online brought it to America. It was based on *Theseus*, published by ASCII...

---

[29] Publisher of Larry Miller's *Epoch* for Apple II (1981), which inspired *Olion*

[30] Apple II, Larry Miller, Sirius Software, 1981

[31] Detailed in a later book volume

[32] A brilliant idea that seems easy after the fact

[33] MSX1, 1984, published by ASCII

AT: Actually, those who worked for the AX series: Matsuda-san was the leader, and the UTMC people, plus Mitsuhashi-san, 6 in total I think? And the Miyaji brothers[34] who joined later.

JS: Mr Matsuda passed away.

AT: Yes, he's the one who passed away several years ago. The Miyaji brothers, the younger brother also passed away.

JS: You were involved with *ILIGKS Ep IV?* Whose idea was it to name it that?

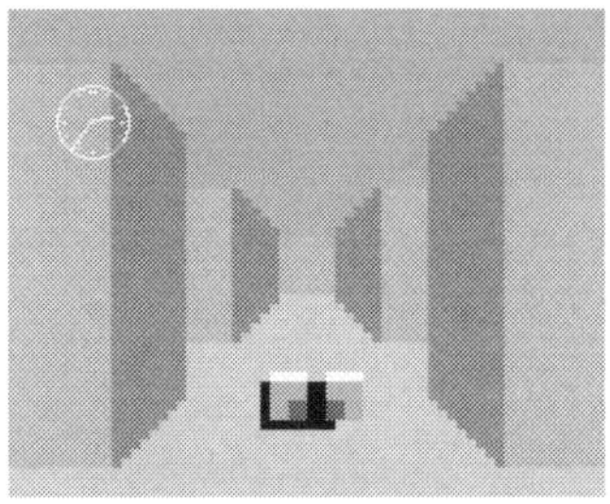

AT: Yes, I was. The code in both *Iligks* and *Theseus* is half attributed to Mitsuhashi-san and the rest to me. I wanted to name it in Greek, since at the time I was under the influence of *Minotaur*, and scanned a Greek dictionary to find *Iligks* (or Ι Λ Ι Γ Ξ). In reality, *Iligks Ep. IV* and *Theseus* share nothing with regards to setting.

JS: Why was the later released *Theseus* named "*ILIGKS Episode One - Theseus*"?

AT: Since *ILIGKS Episode IV* was a 3D game, I felt "episode one" was a suitable name for a 2D game, as if it was to go back in history. Of course, 2D is no way inferior to 3D!

JS: What happened to *ILIGKS Episode II* and *III*?

AT: No, there were no *Episodes II* and *III*. Nobody had clear images of what they'd like.

JS: Did you know the official English version of *Ep IV*, named *Illegus*, sold for over $400 on eBay?

AT: I never knew that there was such a version. Until now I never knew where the incorrect English title *Illegus* came from. This was it! The price is interesting, that much interest for these ancient games...

JS: When did you last meet Mr Mitsuhashi?

AT: Several years ago? But only a few times after graduation.

JS: So today is like a reunion!

AT: A reunion, right!

<Mr Takiguchi and Mr Mitsuhashi converse>

Mitsuhashi-san: Two or three years ago?

AT: Yes, Takeshi Miyaji had a big influence on many game programmers and directors, so a lot of people gathered at the funeral of Takeshi-kun, and the memorial party each year gathers many people. When our company went public, Takeshi Miyaji sent us flowers for celebration. In my name, not in the CEO's name, but I never, ever told him about it. I don't how he knew that our company went public.

JS: After *Theseus*, did you try developing a different type of game? I read something about wanting to make an RPG?

AT: Actually, never! *<laughs>* That comment, I think you are talking about the comment I made in an interview. Myself and Mitsuhashi-san were interviewed in *LOGiN*.[35] We said we wanted to create an RPG. What I wanted was a real-time 3D battle system. But maybe there was too little memory, and because I joined ASAHI Shimbun the plan faded out. *<laughs>*

JS: What was the first RPG you played?

AT: *Ultima I*. And I completed *Nethack*.

JS: Both Western RPGs.

AT: The reason I did not play any RPGs from Japan, is because the screen didn't interest me.

JS: It'd be interesting to see what you'd make.

AT: Interesting, perhaps, but that's *<laughs>* a parallel world!

JS: After *Dragon Quest*, all subsequent RPGs copied it. Whereas titles developed before it...

AT: ...have more variation.

JS: Exactly! Have you seen *Panorama-Toh*?[36]

---

[34] Youichi and Takeshi, co-founders of Game Arts

[35] According to an interview conducted by Morita-san, it was *LOGiN* magazine, April 1984

[36] Regarded as one of Japan's earliest RPGs; the first game by Yoshio Kiya, creator of *Legacy of the Wizard*

AT: He knows a lot. *<gestures to Morita-san>*

Morita-san: *Panorama-Toh* is a very difficult game. Maybe it's *kusoge*. *<everyone laughs>* It has a large dungeon, which the player must map. A magazine published a map of the dungeon, an enormous one, but there was a mistake. That confused players even more!

JS: The whole thing was programmed in BASIC.

[Mr Takiguchi shows me an MSX prototype, from the ASAHI Net archives. Footage can be found on the supplementary DVD]

JS: How did ASAHI Net come to own this?

AT: The ASAHI Net project started as a sub-project of Asahi Shimbun Computer Division. The computer division split off - as a very small company, 10 people, I was one of them - and became the original company, named ATSON. We brought these things over. This an MSX 1 prototype. This particular example was lent to Asahi Shimbun to make a book for the MSX.

JS: Lent to it by?

AT: I think it was Microsoft or ASCII, I do not know which.

JS: Does this belong to you now?

AT: No, no, this company. These are in the museum! *<laughs>*

JS: Have you tested it?

AT: Yes, with the *Theseus* ROM.

JS: How many prototypes were there?

AT: I don't know how many there were.

JS: Do you know when it was produced?

AT: Maybe 1983? When was the first MSX?

JS: In 1983. What else is in your archives?

AT: Not much, actually. *<laughs>* Maybe there is a TK-80, which was NEC's first microcomputer, before the PC-8001.

<shows AX game packaging>

JS: Were there any unreleased AX games?

AT: There were some, but none of the things we created.

JS: Worked on by other people?

AT: Mmm... *<confirms>*

JS: How were the numbers assigned? Did someone say, "My game is done!" Then it would be assigned the next number?

AT: Yes, that's the way the numbers worked.

JS: There's no missing AX numbers?

AT: It's sequential. Everything we started we completed and released, as long as they were good. *<looks over games>* This is Morita-san's collection, not mine.

JS: You met Mr Morita when he was starting his website, *OlionUltimania*?

AT: He was constructing the *Olion* fansite, and when it came near to completion he sent me an email for an interview.

JS: You're still active with programming?

AT: Actually, I'm losing more time recently. But the Manaba project started out six years ago, and I think it has now, about, 600'000 lines of code. We are an internet service provider, and there are many customers, about 500'000. We were established in 1990 and have been profitable for 23 years straight.

JS: Which programming language did you use?

AT: This was done in Perl. I moved from assembly 6502 MZ-80 to C. From 1988 to maybe 2000, I created most things in C and shell script. Today I write most things in Perl, and maybe JavaScript. <*laughs*>

JS: Could you program in assembly again?

AT: I don't think I could. <*laughs*> Occasionally I talk with Morita-san, and say we could make a new game. <*laughs*>

JS: For iOS systems!

AT: That could be fun. If it's not for business. <*laughs*> Do you play iPhone games?

JS: I don't have a modern phone. This iPhone is a loan. I don't like modern technology actually.

AT: <*laughs*> You are a strange person!

JS: I like the tactile feel of physical buttons.

AT: That's important. I prefer the feeling of old calculators. The feel of HP calculator buttons is the best, ne! It's interesting that we share the same feeling regarding physical objects. If we die, in the future nobody can explain how it worked. No one will know physical sensations. Unless someone like you, in the younger generations, comes up. Somebody must teach later generations, about the lost technologies we used.

JS: Do you miss your days as a game developer?

AT: I do miss it! Of course. And like I said earlier, if I could make a game with Morita-san that could be very interesting.

JS: What would you make?

AT: Morita-san would come up with the design, and I would work on the programming. It must be interesting to me, of course. I like an abstract style. Recent 3D games are too realistic. The real world is already here.

[Later I discussed Mr Takiguchi's hobby, which also involves the preservation of history]

JS: Tell me about your hobby.

AT: My hobby? Collecting photographs, from World War 2. Mostly German tanks and war records, books, manuals, documentation. Documents written by the divisions and military units. Just to learn what happened.

JS: I believe you've solved a couple of mysteries, by noticing discrepancies?

AT: <*laughs*> When you collect ***a lot***, when you interview a lot, you see subtle differences between things. So investigating photographs and documents, and finding discrepancies. There are markings on tanks and vehicles, they should have been properly recorded somewhere. But these documents are very hard to come by. Only photographic evidence can be found. So it is very hard to match the unit and the marking. So that's interesting to investigate.

JS: And you run a website with photos?

AT: Actually, it's not an active one. <*laughs*> It's easier for me to introduce myself to someone I do not know. For example when I buy photos on eBay, I say, please see this website.

JS: Do you buy a lot of photos on eBay?

AT: Yes. Currently my photo collection is pretty big. I never counted, but it's one room entirely dedicated to military photographs and books and documents. My wife complains, silently.

JS: <*laughs*> When did your interest start?

AT: That started in my junior high days. Every boy likes making model tanks. Then I started collecting books, because I needed more information. Then the internet came, and I could buy actual photographs from the period. So my main interest moved into that area. When looking at as many photographs as possible, you have to have very clear eyes to see what is there.

JS: As you say, there should be a record. You would think the military would have kept organised documents. It's similar to the games industry - no one really keeps a record, so information is lost. So you have to cross-reference everything.

AT: Yes! They should have kept everything. It's interesting but time consuming, and the problem is I do not have much time right now. I work from 7:30am to 8pm at night. Then I visit some restaurant to have dinner, then come home and sleep at 12 o'clock usually. Usually I wake up at about 6 o'clock, so six hours sleep.

JS: Working 12 and a half hours a day. You spend more time at work than anywhere else.

AT: *<laughs>* Yes. I want to spend more time on my hobby, but currently I cannot. So my collection is growing, but it's just growing. But I have to analyse it! I have to check more photographs to find new facts.

JS: What's the most exciting thing you've discovered?

AT: The most exciting thing is... There are many holes and rivets to create a tank. So there was a mysterious hole in the Tiger tank's front fender. The purpose was unknown, before I found it. I'll have to draw a picture.

<draws sketch>

AT: This is a side-view of a Tiger tank. This front fender has a reinforced hole, and its purpose was unknown. Some people said that this was used to put a pole in it and camouflage a Tiger tank with a tarpaulin. But you know how a tank works? There is a sprocket wheel to drive, which is directly connected to the engine, and moves the caterpillar tracks. This hole was actually to have a small crane, to change the sprocket wheel. Then, from an old German online book shop, I found a manual for Tiger tanks. There are so many manuals. But one of the manuals that handles the wheels. *<whispers>* And in that manual... I found a picture!

JS: And solved the mystery!

AT: The most exciting moment of my life! *<laughs>* And that's funny because German researchers should have found it earlier. But actually, no German researchers knew it. That's probably because there's so many different manuals. Or maybe there are no existing manuals in the library archives. That was strange: a Japanese, Far East researcher, finding it!

JS: These tanks were still in operation less than 70 years ago. It's not that long ago, and yet we're already losing the knowledge.

AT: Yes, so much knowledge is already lost. *<laughs>* It's easy to lose everything! Just put it in the dustbin. Actually, many German families put ***everything*** in the dustbin, because it's from the Nazi era. So collectors and military material dealers, they saved those things from the trash.

JS: Funny story about Sega. I know some people would regularly go through Sega's garbage to retrieve items - and they'd find hard-drives, prototype cartridges, and burned EPROMs of unreleased games. Some of this stuff was only saved because someone went bin diving.

<everyone laughs>

AT: Most people do not understand the value of old materials. Photographs, documents. Because there's a market, the military market, for photographs and documents. So if you properly evaluate it, maybe you could get 100'000 euro.

JS: It's the same with collectors. Like that MSX prototype, that would be priceless to a collector.

AT: Ahh, we have to be careful for it not to be stolen! *<laughs>* I have two PC-6001 computers at home, I have to get rid of them.

JS: Don't throw them away! Sell or donate them.

AT: I can donate it. But somebody has to receive it. We can sell it on Yahoo Auctions.

<conversation regarding auctions in Japanese>

JS: I know a guy in Saitama, who runs a warehouse with rare computers.

AT: I don't need money though. If I can give it to someone who really values it, that's better for me. That's the only reason why I still keep it. I have several things, for example. Not everything is my area of interest. So I want to get rid of it, but to somebody who really appreciates it. I have to find somebody. It's really difficult.

三橋 正邦

MITSUHASHI, Masakuni

DOB: 17 October 1961 / Birthplace: Toyama / Blood Type: O

~ Selected Portfolio ~

Activities published by ASCII (1981-1984)
AX-1: Demonstration / AX-2: Uchuu Yusou-sen Nostromo / AX-4 • AX-6: Demonstration / AX-5: Quest / AX-7: Demonstration - PC-6001, 1981, ASCII
Battlefield - PC-6001, 1983 (Main program, joystick "*omake*" game, akin to *Battle Zone*)
Illegus Ep. IV - MSX, 1984, ASCII (first-person maze game with day/night cycle)
Theseus - MSX, 1984, ASCII (incredible inertia platformer)

Activity in Game Arts (1985-1993)
Cuby Panic - PC-88SR, 1985 (BGM composer)
Silpheed - PC-88SR, 1987 (CSM speech synthesis, BGM composer)
Fire Hawk - PC-88SR, 1989 (BGM composer and music performance program)
Zeliard - PC-88SR, 1988 (Music performance program / CSM speech synthesis)
Silpheed 2 - Sega Mega CD, 1993 (Topography and asteroid automatic generation program)

Activities in companies and other organizations
Lunar: Eternal Blue - Sega Saturn, 1998, ESP (Play test management & system advice)
Game BASIC - Sega Saturn, 1998, ASCII / Bits Laboratory (Sample prog. specs advice)

Game-related books authored cooperation
Wizardry playing manual / Monster Manual 1-4 - M.I.A Agent 1986-1989
The road to the ground 4 Wizardry - Business ASCII 1989
MSX MAGAZINE eternal - ASCII 2002

Music CD / Composer
ORIGINAL SOUND OF SILPHEED - Apollo 1988
SILPHEED OFFICIAL GAME MUSIC SOUND - Toshiba EMI 1993
SILPHEED ~ PC SOUND of GAME ARTS ~ - Scitron digital content 2006
Game Arts Best Collection - WAVEMASTER 2012

Interview with Masakuni Mitsuhashi (aka: *Hiromi Ohba*)
26 October 2013, Tokyo, ASAHI Net

Mr Mitsuhashi was invited to the ASAHI Net offices by Mr Takiguchi, to talk about his work on the AX series and at Game Arts. As I discovered, he was also a lecturer at the Digital Entertainment Academy, a game design school run by Square-Enix, long since closed. Mr Mitsuhashi also represents the difficulty when researching names, since while his real name only yields a single entry on MobyGames, his pseudonym Hiromi Ohba brings up quite a few credits. He also had several uncredited roles, which are discussed. Some parts of the interview have been inserted from a later group conversation had over dinner.

JS: What is the first game you saw?

MM: The very first game videogame... Hmm... A tennis game, like *Pong*. Mid-to-late 1970s. Sometime around then, I remember seeing *Pong*.

JS: When did you decide to make your own?

MM: <*intense laughter*> In high school! You know programmable calculators? It wasn't a case of I saw *Pong* and immediately wanted to start making games, the feeling came a little later. This is a list of the games that I worked on. The AX series, *Cuby Panic*...

JS: And your first computer was...?

MM: NEC's PC-8001.

JS: Which computer did you use to program the AX series? Since they were PC-6001 games.

MM: Ahh! <*laughs*> For the AX series I was using the computers at the university.

JS: At ASCII's Part 2? Mr Takiguchi showed an article where you were both interviewed.

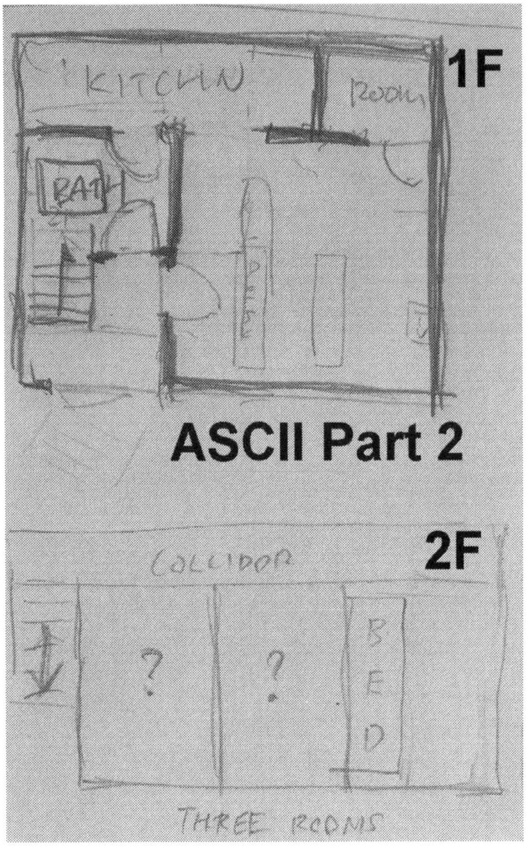

MM: Where was this? <*referring to map*>

AT: It's Part 2, obviously.

MM: Surely that's not it.

<*Mr Mitsuhashi and Mr Takiguchi discuss it*>

MM: OK, that is Part 2! How nostalgic! But this part here is wrong.

AT: <*laughs*> Sorry!

<*everyone laughs, Mr Mitsuhashi corrects it*>

AT: He studied architecture at the university.

JS: You studied architecture then made games?

MM: <*laughs*>

JS: It makes sense. In games you build worlds.

AT: It doesn't matter what you learned in university, most of his time he spent in TOTAI,[1] so it's not a university thing.

JS: How would you describe the AX series?

MM: That's a tough question! I feel like at that time, there were very good games being released and there were really bad games being released. The people who bought them were guessing to an extent. So sometimes you would pay 3'000 yen,[2] take the cassette home, and then you'd go, "Oh no! It's crap! And there's nothing I can do about it!" But with the AX series, I feel that from the start AX was a development where we put a lot of effort into quality, and developing a reputation for quality. One of the effects AX had on the industry is that it stopped a lot of these really bad games from being sold anymore, or being successful. Maybe it brought up the quality of the whole scene, as a result.

JS: Weren't there magazines with reviews?

MM: Hmm... Reviews like that, where they give a score and judgement, weren't really around at that point. It was much more, maybe informative than reviewing. So maybe the era of reviewing games as you know it, came a little bit later. <*flicks through a magazine*> This personal computer magazine, *I/O*, there's no actual reviews of games. It's much more informative, explaining how developers did things, type in listings. Hardware information, and so on.[3]

JS: Were you involved with the AY series?

MM: The AY series, eh? That was Takiguchi-kun.

JS: For AX-2 you converted Mr Takiguchi's *Nostromo* from CBM to PC-6001. Why was this?

MM: I liked it! It was extremely enjoyable.

AT: Oh, thank you very much! <*laughs*> I joined the AX project later than Mitsuhashi-san. He and Fujisawa-kun joined the AX series earlier than me. I later joined the team, but of course we were part of the UTMC, so we talked, and he

---

[1] Name of Taito's loaned room; prior to AX series
[2] Roughly £17 / $28 at that time
[3] Looking through the June 1984 issue of *I/O*, despite having 577 pages, and a lot of circuit schematics, there was nothing akin to "game reviews"

wanted to put *Nostromo* in the AX series. So I said, OK! Go ahead.

JS: And *Nostromo*, your original CBM version, that was inspired by Mr Suzuki's *Dojin*?

AT: Yes! And maybe by *Manbiki Shoujo*. But what I found lacking in the original *Manbiki Shoujo*, was that the manager could always be seen. So it's easy for the player to avoid the manager's movement. I wanted the manager to be invisible, unless he was actually visible to the character. That was the idea of *Nostromo*.

JS: When converting *Nostromo* to the PC-6001, did you have Mr Takiguchi's source code?

MM: *<laughs>*

AT: Of course he asked if I could give him the whole source code. But he didn't need it, he's a very good programmer, so he just made it.

JS: He just looked at it and replicated it?

AT: Yes, that's what we did in those days. We didn't copy source code. It's very tiresome to work with somebody else's code. We just wrote it to make the game look the same.

JS: Tell me more about *Nostromo*.

MM: There's a situation in *Nostromo*, where there is nothing to do except kill oneself to end the game. You have to collect certain items, but if there are none of that item left in the warehouse, your only choice is to be killed by getting caught by the alien. There is no way to end the game successfully, so you just have to kill yourself after losing certain resources that are necessary to exit the ship.

JS: *<gesturing to Battlefield on the list>* Is this *Battlefield* related to Morita-san's *Battlefield*?

MM: Ah, no, no, no. This is more like *Battlezone*, by Atari. It was inspired by it. You had to play it with a joystick and ASCII bundled it with one, and it was only available like that. It was an "*omake* game" that came with the joystick.

Mr Morita: So the joysticks would have buttons on the top, and you could move in four directions and... *<makes button clicking noise>*

MM: You would play with two of those joysticks.

JS: You also worked on *Theseus*?

MM: *Theseus*, and *Illegus*,[4] for the MSX. With Takiguchi-san. *<to Mr Takiguchi>* Did you talk about this already?

<Mr Mitsuhashi and Mr Takiguchi converse>

JS: Have you ever heard of a game called *3D Monster Maze* for the ZX81?[5]

MM: Ah! Yes, yes, yes.

<Mr Morita passes his sealed copy of Iriigasu>

Mr Morita: Please do not open it!

JS: Seeing all the incredible items you brought today, you're obviously a collector of rare items.

Mr Morita: It's less that I'm a collector of old games, and more that when I was making games, I wanted to know what other people had done. That's really where my collection comes from.

MM: Regarding *Theseus*, do you know *Major Havoc*? It's like *Major Havoc* for the MSX; it was inspired by it.

JS: Please describe your role on *Theseus*.

MM: Ah, main programmer! *<flicks to a magazine article>* This is an explanation of how the game works. This explains how it was programmed. The methods and the way we produced each effect, and so on.

JS: Programmed in assembly?

MM: Machine code.

---

[4] Sometimes Romanised as *Iligks*, *Iriigasu* and *Iriegas*; official UK release spelled *Illegus*
[5] Malcolm Evans (1982); avoid the T-Rex in a 3D maze

JS: *Thexder* was one of the major success stories for Japanese computers. It even reached America. This success was built on *Theseus*.

MM: I wish Ikeda-kun would say that to me. *Thexder*'s programmer was Kohei Ikeda.

JS: The title *Thexder* was derived from *Theseus*.

MM: Yes, that's right! *Theseus*, *EXOA*, and *Grobda*.[6] That's right. Please get in touch with Kohei Ikeda. *<writes down contact details>* When are you in Japan until?

JS: It'll be tight, my schedule is totally full.

Mr Morita: Have you heard of *Kai no Bouken*?

JS: No, which machine?

Mr Morita: Family Computer, by Namco. It came after *Tower of Druaga*. It was by Endou-san, creator of *Xevious*.

JS: So part of his *Gilgamesh* series.

Mr Morita: Yes, that's right! *<laughs> Kai no Bouken* came after *Tower of Druaga*, and it's very similar to *Theseus*. They were all kind of aiming for the feel of *Major Havoc*, and that's where they took their inspiration from, hence why the games are all quite similar.

JS: So *Major Havoc* is a prototype inspiration for *Theseus*, *Thexder*, and *Kai no Bouken*.

Mr Morita: *<laughs>* Yes, that's where the roots come from.

JS: Mr Mitsuhashi, I was going over your games and they're all credited to Hiromi Ohba.

MM: Yes, yes, yes, that's exactly right. Hiromi Ohta was a popular Japanese singer. And I'm a fan of her. *<shows photos of Hiromi Ohta with the AX series developers>*

JS: How come she was visiting you guys?

MM: Weekly Playboy ran an article about computer clubs, for promotion, and for that reason she visited and was photographed.[7]

JS: Did *3D Monster Maze* influence *Iriigasu*?[8]

MM: Yes, of course.

JS: How did you come across it, since it was for the ZX81 computer in England.

MM: Now, where did I see it... Through ASCII publishing? Maybe I never played it, but I would have seen computer magazine articles or screenshots. There were many, many computer games... Japanese magazines had content on software from other countries.

<Mr Mitsuhashi and Mr Morita converse>

MM: ASCII was the one that covered the international scene. Of course they covered hardware from abroad, such as the Apple II and the Apple III, and wrote about them alongside the domestic stuff. So we saw many, many games, from many other countries.

JS: *<looks through ASCII magazine>* Oh wow, they're covering an American fair here!

Article text reads: The People Living in the Personal Computer World.

MM: We saw many, many games from around the world. And so took inspiration when making our own games.

JS: You were at Game Arts for *Thexder*?

MM: That's right. The ASCII Part 2 members went independent. Some of the members were Youichi Miyaji, Game Arts co-founder, Takeshi Miyaji, and Mitsuhiro Matsuda.

JS: What year did you join Game Arts?

MM: I was working with them for a period without officially joining. It's hard to say when.

JS: What was your role on *Silpheed*?

MM: Sound technician, music composer, speech synthesis - or voice recording. *<Mr Mitsuhashi re-enacts the voice he did for the PC-88 version of Silpheed>* ***OMAIWA IWAKATTA!***

---

[6] See Kohei Ikeda interview for full explanation

[7] Due to copyright the photos cannot be shown

[8] There was another 3D maze game in 1982, titled *Monster Maze*, by Rob Schilling, for Atari computers. Also likely an influence, since it had items to collect

JS: You programmed the voice synthesis?

MM: Yes, yes.

<Mr Mitsuhashi gives me some shiny, silver foil Game Arts stickers>

JS: Oh fantastic! What year are these from?

MM: They were made when Game Arts first started, for promotion.

JS: Can you sketch the Game Arts office?

MM: Maybe Ikeda-kun could give you a good drawing. He'd be the one that knows it the best!

JS: Well, if you can remember it during the development of *Silpheed* on the Mega CD...

MM: They moved three times during development of the original *Silpheed*...

JS: And on Mega CD?

MM: That was in Ikebukuro... It was a boring office. I wasn't so involved in the Mega CD development. Mainly the original.

JS: Let's talk about that. Have you seen this picture from *Silpheed* (left) and *Starfox* (right)?

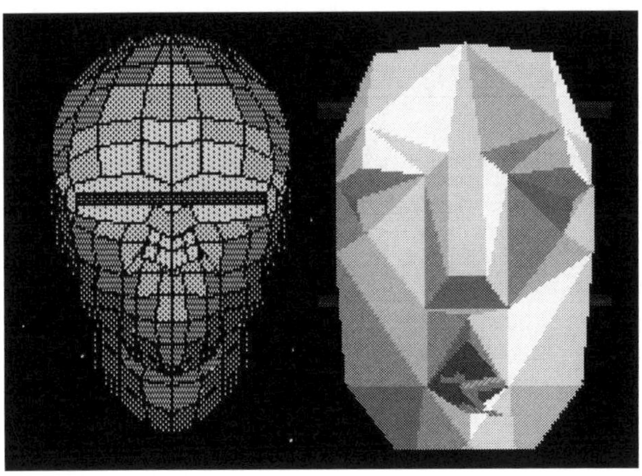

MM: I've played both of them.

JS: Do you think *Starfox* copied *Silpheed*?

MM: Yes, but you have to remember this was a time when everyone was copying everybody else.

JS: *Silpheed* came out in 1986, and *Starfox* came out in 1993, but the boss in *Starfox*, Andross, copied the *Silpheed* polygon face.

MM: *<laughs>* You mean *Silpheed*'s Xacalite. I did the voice for Xacalite, it's mine in the game: ***OMAIWA IWAKATTA!***

JS: Sierra brought *Silpheed* to America.

MM: Yes, yes. Tomoyuki Shimada, he passed away, he was the main programmer on *Silpheed*. He went to America, to Sierra. He had a lot of projects going on - when it comes to the changes between the two versions, I don't really know very much. He was really the only guy. Some Japanese developers from the original version did go over to America, to work on the American version as well, but I don't know who it was or how many went. I don't know where any [localisation] changes came from.

JS: In Silpheed, there were two hidden minigames. *Xacalite* and *Silpheed 2*.[9]

MM: *<laughs>* I remember that, *Silpheed 2*! And *Xacalite* was called *Xacalite Tza Tza Tza Tza... <makes sound effect>* I actually made both of those, and then hid them in the code. They were both BASIC games.

JS: I accessed them on PC-88. You had to switch disks then type: RUN "XACALITE" **or alternatively** RUN "SILPHEED2"

MM: Right, right!

JS: Developers often hid things in games. Are there any no one knows about?

MM: Unfortunately I think ***all of them*** were caught by magazines. So if you wanted to know what they were, you bought a magazine to find out. *Xacalite* was probably my favourite.

JS: I never understood *Xacalite*. You push any button, text scrolls up, and then it's game over.

MM: *<laughs>* Ahh, you had to hit the button just as the red text comes up.

JS: Oh, it's a timing game!

[9] *Silpheed 2* was a simple shooter with ASCII graphics

MM: <*intense laughter*> That's right!

JS: Were you involved in the FM-77AV port?

MM: I remember that one. No, I was not involved. I'm trying to think who did it...

JS: Sierra sub-licensed *Silpheed* to be converted to the CoCo I, II and III series of computers.[10] There was one floppy; one side was for the CoCo I/II and the other for the CoCo III.

MM: <*laughs*> Is that right? That's impressive.

JS: The CoCo adaptations are the worst ports ever. <*shows screens*> The company had a 16 year old work ludicrously long hours to make it.

MM: There was one version of *Silpheed*, that we were publishing for some system, that we rejected. Someone came saying, "We want to license it for this, here's the version we're ready to manufacture," but we rejected them. This was one time when we said we weren't having a version go out on that platform - but I don't know what platform it was.

JS: This CoCo version did come out, via Sierra. The CoCo I/II was so bad, the levels inside the space stations were just removed.

MM: <*laughs*>

JS: Any other *Silpheed* recollections you have?

MM: Delayed, delayed, delayed, delayed, delayed... Over and over again. The reason it was delayed, by us, over and over again, was because we felt we wanted to make a better game than we had at that point. So we kept delaying it so we could improve it.

JS: Did you leave anything out?

MM: When we were in the early stages of development, yes, we were cutting a lot of stuff. I don't know if I can remember it, but by the end we weren't really cutting stuff, we were just polishing. So within the weapons there was multi-direction bullets, and there was a feature we were thinking about where you could shoot in all four cardinal directions - you could even shoot behind you. But we cut it. So the "Cross Fire" function, where you shot like this, was cut from the game. The reason is, *Silpheed* doesn't ever have any reason for you to shoot behind. There's no enemies coming from the bottom of the screen, so we didn't need it. So instead of this, that's when we put in the Phalanx weapon, which shoots in lots of directions.

JS: What if enemies come down, you miss, they're below you, and you want to score?

MM: Yeah, it does happen obviously, but it's a rare case. <*laughs*>

JS: Any development secrets you can share?

MM: There were four composers on *Silpheed*. I did the opening, Kohei Ikeda did the music for the first stage, and there was Mecano Associates,[11] a music group. They found us through a magazine listing for part-time jobs. We got loads and loads of demo tapes. I would listen through them and say, this is no good, this one's no good, and so on. However, one tape was completely blank, no music, and it was their tape - Mecano Associates. The reason was an error in the recording. So the tape was blank. So I was going to throw it out, but then I called them, just in case, and said, "This is a blank tape. What was the title of your music going to be?" And all of the cassettes at that time had C-60 on them, because it was a 60 minute tape, so they said, "Yeah, the title's C-60, says it on the tape." And we thought that was a good joke. So because they were funny people, they were quite witty, we gave them another chance and they sent us the tape. The feeling was, these witty people could make a good soundtrack, so we gave them a chance.

JS: Who were the members?

MM: It was a pair of people. Kasatani and Aoyama were their names. Maybe Aoyama did the ending theme. While Kasatani did the other three tracks; the asteroid track, the fortress track, and the orbital track.

---

[10] Tandy, 1980; CoCo series (Colour Computer) was an evolution of the TRS-80

[11] As well as contributing to the first two *Silpheed* games, they also did the music for *Alisia Dragoon*

JS: Most shooters, getting hit meant game over. With *Silpheed* you had shields and when depleted would lose one weapon, then another, then die. You could still struggle to victory.

MM: Ah! He's passed away, but Takeshi Miyaji is the one who would have made that kind of decision! <*laughs*> One thing it could be is that, if you think about it, it's more natural if when blown up, you don't get to come back and try again. You've got one chance - you're the only hope. So giving players the weapons and then taking them away with damage, is more realistic.

JS: Genius! Rather than the usual three lives...

MM: Yes, that concept was definitely one of the design ideas.

JS: For *Zeliard*, were you the composer?

MM: Ah, *Zeliard*! The composers were Mecano Associates. But I programmed the music player routine, the music code, or functionality to have it in the game. What I did was, up until then anytime you wanted to put music in a game, one note would take up 2 bytes of memory. I made a compact sound driver that allowed one note per single byte.

JS: You doubled the capacity?

MM: We didn't double the amount of music, we took the music files and they required half the space. We were asked to fit the driver and the data into 3 kilobytes. It was very difficult.

JS: Such a different era back then.

MM: <*laughs*> The other thing that was a feature of that game, is that the music can change seamlessly. And that was something that I developed, and managed to pull off.

JS: Were you in the office with the rest of team?

MM: I went to the office from time to time, but I did most of my work from home. I created an 8086 sound driver, and Tomoyuki Shimada implemented that for the Z80 processor.

JS: Any anecdotes from *Zeliard*'s development?

MM: It was originally called *Fantasy Action*! <*laughs*> The original developmental code name. The game we developed after this was never released.

JS: *YOU MUST TELL ME EVERYTHING!*

MM: Mr Azumi [12] would be the number one person to ask. I don't know if either us would be able to contact him. <*laughs*>

JS: What can you remember?

MM: I remember everybody in the team working on it was very positive about it, looking forward to when it would be finished and released. But then it was just cancelled suddenly. I seem to remember it was a scrolling action game, a horizontal scrolling shooter. A bit like *Veigues*[13] maybe. That kind of style. It had big characters - you piloted a big ship.

JS: Were there any other unreleased games?

MM: No, I don't think so. Maybe just that one.

JS: You worked on *Silpheed* for the Sega CD?

MM: I worked on the polygon generator... How would you describe this, it "terraformed" or created the worlds. Data generating. The asteroids are polygons.

JS: Players ask how much was created in real-time by the hardware versus video streaming.

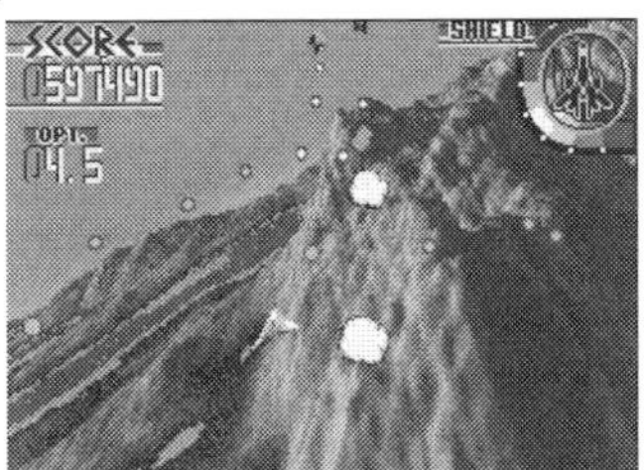

MM: ***Yeaaah, you've got it!*** Half and half, ne! The enemies are real-time, but the backgrounds are not real-time.

JS: What about the asteroids?

MM: No, no, no. Streamed.

JS: You could destroy some asteroids though.

MM: Yes, yes, yes. That's right. Some asteroids are real-time. The big battleship is not real-time. The big battleship is only a background, and streamed from the CD.

---

[12] Masatoshi Azumi; graph. designer & director at GA
[13] *Veigues: Tactical Gladiator*, PC-88 and PCE (1988)

JS: A very clever technique. It was seamless.

MM: This is not the sort of thing I'm an expert on, so I'm not sure how much I can explain.

JS: After the Mega CD version, did you keep an eye on further *Silpheed* sequels?

MM: No, I did not follow it. I quite like trying new things, so I'm not that interested in seeing stuff I did long go, how it changes.

JS: There was a PlayStation 2 version, an Xbox 360 version, and then an Android version.

MM: I've only played up to the Mega CD version. When we made the original we wanted to put in features that no one else had done, and maybe things that people thought were impossible to put into games.[14] But I think if you're making *Silpheed* to come out now, it's going to look generic. I think a lot of people copied things, and it became standard procedure for a lot of stuff.

JS: The X360 update was like you're sitting inside a cockpit, and could fly in any direction. It kept the name but was very different.

MM: I don't have a problem with that, them using the title. But I think people who played the original *Silpheed* might be confused by it. Asking, "Why are they doing this?" I can see how that might come up. What I wanted to do was make things where people would go, "Wow! I can't believe this has been made!" And I don't think the new *Silpheed* does that...

JS: Do you feel the Mega CD version of *Silpheed* is a remake of the first, or a sequel?

MM: Hm! I think it's an update, rather than a sequel to the original. The story is the next part of the storyline, but I think in terms of gameplay design and features it's in the same direction.

JS: Do you want to mention Mr Matsuda?

MM: I'd like to thank Matsuda-san. He greatly improved the team and our ability to work. Youichi Miyaji, the owner of Game Arts, he learnt a lot about business from Matsuda-san. He was a teacher for all of us, like a mentor.

JS: He helped with the formation of Game Arts.

MM: If Matsuda-san had not been around, Game Arts would never have existed. I have no doubt about that.

JS: Your most enduring memory of Game Arts?

MM: Everybody who worked there was obsessed with technology. They were tech maniacs. *<laughs>* Absolutely, it was passionate people who cared about technology. So the atmosphere of the office...

<Mr Mitsuhashi converses with Mr Takiguchi>

AT: It was fairly regular. The Game Arts start up office in Ikebukuro was very... ***Not*** normal. They were still students, they were still young. But by the time they moved to the main office, they were a real team in a normal office.

MM: It was definitely Matsuda-san. The reason a group of students could make a successful company was all down to Matsuda-san. It was absolutely his work, or his help, that allowed them to do that.

JS: You worked on *Lunar 2: Eternal Blue* for the Sega Saturn?

MM: Yes, yes. I was the "test play" manager.

JS: That version was developed by Vanguard?

MM: Right, right, right. Vanguard handled the programming for it.

JS: I interviewed the president of Vanguard recently.

MM: ESP was a company established by Miyaji-san, and other companies were managing the creation of games. I was not hired as an employee, rather somebody - nicknamed *Hikeshi no Natchan*[15] or something like that - at ESP asked me to test the game as a one-off job, so test management was my task. I spent a lot of time drafting design sheets related to controlling the difficulty of the game,

[14] The original *Silpheed* had a lot of firsts for 1986 - notably some impressive planet surface effects

[15] Lit. "Natchan the firefighter"

balancing, and I actually made graphs charting parameters like gold, XP, and so on. But Youichi Miyaji rejected it all. For example, in one case the XP reward was set to 12, but I decided that 8 XP would be better. But when somebody showed it to Miyaji-san, Youichi Miyaji, the elder brother of Takeshi Miyaji, he played it a bit and said, "This is too difficult, change it back!" <*laughs*> So my work was ruined. It was like a punch in the gut.[16] <*laughs*>

AT: But that happens often, in every industry! <*murmured agreement*>

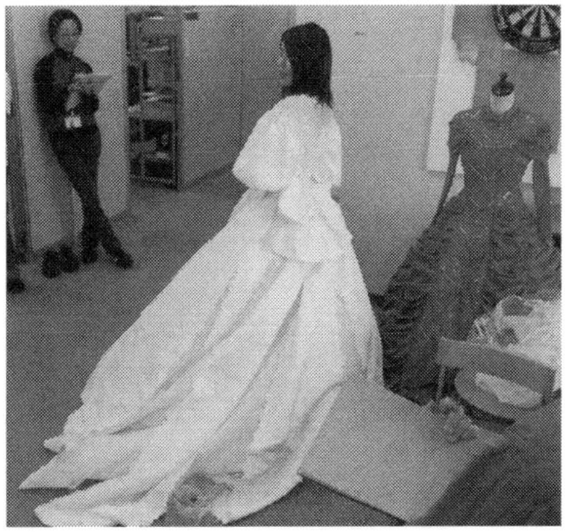

JS: Do you know Working Designs? They would license titles from Game Arts. They published four *Lunar* games. In *Lunar* on Mega CD you earn magic experience, to upgrade your magic powers, and you could save anywhere. But Working Designs thought this was too easy, so you had to spend your magic experience to save.

AT: That's... <*laughs*> Quite a fundamental change! It changes everything! Prior to this conversation, I talked with Morita-san about localisation. He had to change many things, to adapt it for different countries. [Regarding *Lunar*], it could have been different if a different publisher got the translation rights.

JS: <*noting Game BASIC, for Sega Saturn*> This says sample programmer?[17]

MM: Yes, sample programmer and general production adviser, on *Game BASIC*. It's a language, and I made sample BASIC programs and polygon character models.

JS: What did you do after Game Arts?

MM: I was teaching game planning at the Digital Entertainment Academy. It was by Square-Enix. The school is gone now. I did it for six years.

JS: When did you start?

MM: From 2001 until 2008. It was a school that practiced a specialised and practical type of education. At the same time it was a unique school. As the lecturers could set up the curriculum relatively freely, there were lessons which had their own unique character. When making games as a job, the other party is a virtual world. However, knowledge of the real world is demanded of the maker. I adopted lessons which showed not only photographs and materials, but also actual physical things.

In the photograph design seminar I made the students experience things like wearing a dress and feeling the way clothes move when the body does, and I called a dance teacher and got her to help the students experience body movements. Making games requires collaboration with other fields of study. It would be good if this kind of initiative spread into other schools which carry out game education. Your work involves a lot of imagination. So you must know reality - you must know about real things in order to create something imaginary.

AT: If a student thinks it's a new idea, it's probably already been invented by someone else.

MM: Yes, by someone else! But where in the world? For example, costume design. One assignment would be to design a costume never seen before. Some of the origins are amazing. <*shows photos*> From China, from India.

AT: Mitsuhashi-san's students invent things. But there are more real inventions already existing in the world. So for example, the assignment is to design strange architecture. And Mitsuhashi-san will bring in examples of strange architecture that already exists as reality. <*refers to photo*>

[16] Lit. "it made me throw up", used colloquially to refer to an unexpected and unpleasant shock

[17] The MSX version of *Theseus* is a hidden bonus

JS: This is all geared towards a good *sekaikan*?[18]

AT: *Sekaikan*, yes, that's right! So he has to teach *sekaikan*, and let students know about a lot of unknown designs.

JS: Where is this headrest from?

Mitsuhashi: Hmm... China. South-west China.

JS: To understand *sekaikan*, you need to have a wide knowledge of world culture. The usual translation is world view, but it's deeper than that. For example, to create good *sekaikan*, you should consider the language of the people in the game, or their politics, even if it's not shown.

AT: Everything is related, so you have to think about everything.

JS: Exactly! The unseen influences what is seen.

MM: *Sekaikan* must define what is right, what is correct, for the world. What is valued in the world? What is neglected? Define those values.

AT: Designing a language. We've already seen this with the Klingon language.

MM: The Klingon's costume and the Klingon world, it all represents "Might is Right".

AT: "Power is Right!"

MM: Klingon costume design, Klingon language design, Klingon world design...

AT: Vision is important for this.

<lots of Star Trek discussion>

JS: Do you consider yourselves *Star Trek* fans?

AT: I don't consider myself a fan, but I like it. I love it!

MM: Regarding *Star Trek*, with the Klingons, *Power is Right*. With the Ferengi, *Money is Right*. And for the Vulcans, *Logic is Right*. While for the Borg, what is it... *Fusion is Right*? *<laughs>*

JS: How would you describe humans?

MM: Humans... What would it be? Cooperation?

AT: In that sense, *Star Trek* has very well designed as *sekaikan*. *Star Trek* has the conflict of different *sekaikan*, so we have a lot of different, interesting stories.

JS: What are you involved in now?

MM: *<laughs>* Writing! *<speaks in Japanese>*

AT: *<explaining what Mitsuhashi-san said>* Stamps and rare items, those are the most important aspects of recent smartphone games. *<laughs>* Mitsuhashi-san does not work for the games industry now, because of the change in style of games which sell.

MM: It's run by Ferengi! The Ferengi ruined the games industry. Money is everything now!

(Below: design sketches for AX-5: Quest)

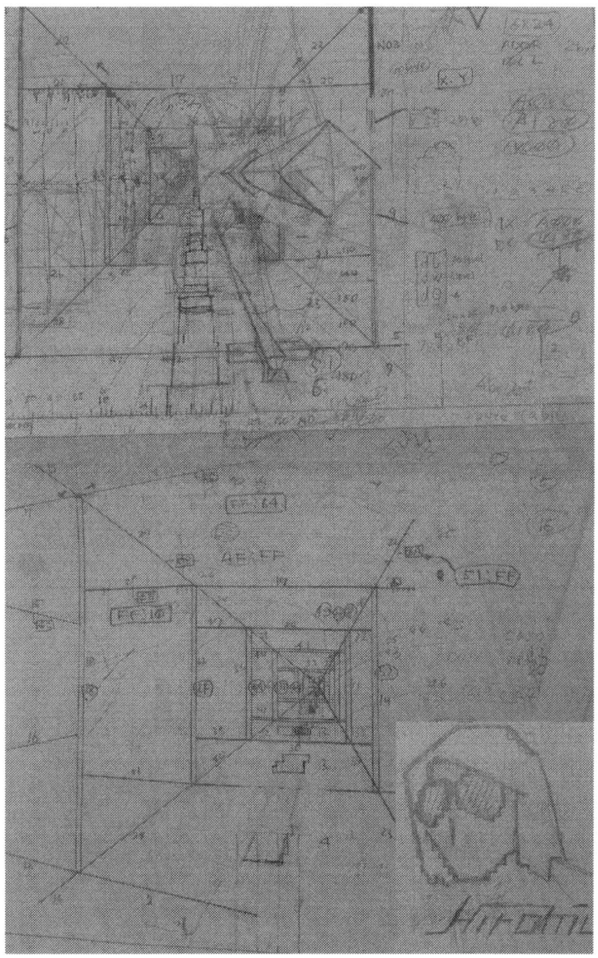

[18] Ethos behind the game world and its content

From left: Kanta Watanabe (Silpheed: Lost Planet director and programmer), ***Takeshi Miyaji*** *(centre), and Toshio Akashi (Lunar: Eternal Blue writer and director)*

~In memory of~

宮路 武

MIYAJI, Takeshi

December 1965 ~ July 2011

~Selected Portfolio~

AX-6: Space Enemy (1982) / *Thexder* (1985) / *Silpheed* (1986) / *Lunar: The Silver Star* (1992) / *Silpheed* (1993) / *Lunar 2: Eternal Blue* (1994) / *GunGriffon* (1996) / *Grandia* (1997) / *Grandia II* (2000)

Miyaji-kun was a very keen young guy in my memory. He had much confidence in what he was doing. He always pursued the best. And he knew respect. Thus after all these years he was loved by so many and it was a true shock when he died so young. He is also really missed.
- ***Akira Takiguchi, AX series colleague***

Miyaji Takeshi-san passed away at a really young age. He was I think 46 or 47, and he was the president of the company, so he had a lot of management work to do, but he really wanted to create games. Even up to the last moments of his life he was saying that he wanted to create games. Right now I think he's up in heaven, probably making games as much as he likes, now that he doesn't have employees to take care of. He was somebody whom everyone respected.
- ***Kohei Ikeda, AX series and Game Arts colleague***

At Game Arts he was the best programmer, but not so good at management or delegating work. He would take on all the work. He wouldn't delegate, maybe because the targets he wanted to reach were so high. When he was in G-Mode he became a better manager, and started to delegate.
- ***Masakuni Mitsuhashi, AX series and Game Arts colleague***

池田 公平

IKEDA, Kohei

DOB: 22 March 1963 / Birthplace: Osaka / Blood Type: B

~Selected Portfolio~

AX series 6, 7, 8	- PC-6001
SX series 1, 2	- PC-6001
Rise Out (ASCII)	- MSX
Theseus	- MSX
Star Command Σ	- MSX
Thexder	- PC-8801, early 1985
Thexder	- Famicom, late 1985
Silpheed	- PC-8801, 1986
Ragnarok Odyssey	- PS VITA

Interview with Kohei Ikeda *(aka: Hibiki Godai)*
4 November 2013, Tokyo

My interview with Mr Ikeda, co-founder of Game Arts and creator of Thexder, was a sudden arrangement. Mr Mitsuhashi, who I'd interviewed several days prior, arranged our meeting. Mr Ikeda gives a fascinating insight into the early, rocky history of Japanese computer games, their evolution and improvement through the AX series, the subsequent formation of Game Arts, and then the divergence between computer and console games in Japan. As Mr Ikeda revealed, Game Arts was born from the AX series, and was created to capitalise on the impending release of new computer hardware from NEC.

JS: What is the first game you ever recall seeing?

KI: You mean for work, or just for pleasure? For pleasure, table tennis.

JS: And the first model of computer you owned?

KI: A TK-80, by NEC.

JS: Did you program games on it?

KI: Yes, I did program, but also it was hand assembled by myself, the computer. I enjoyed the hardware, the assembly or construction part, as well as the software.

JS: Game Arts was not your first company...

KI: It was the second. The first company that I professionally worked at, for game development, was ASCII.

JS: Where you worked on the AX series.

KI: Yes, the AX series.

JS: How would you describe the AX series?

KI: At this time there were many low quality games in Japan. Some of them were a borderline scam. There were even "games" with 20 lines of BASIC code and a 3'000 - 5'000 yen price tag! The price of a computer at this time would be 100'000 or 200'000[1] yen, so it would be for rich people only to buy. There were so many terrible business practices. So Matsuda-san's goal in putting out this AX series was to produce a good quality game at a low price range, and to really push the industry to improve itself, basically. As a result of this effort, the quantity of bad games decreased significantly.

<shows game box - the front in Katakana says "Arabian Rhapsody">

KI: This was by Matsuda-san, and published by ASCII. It's the first one.

JS: Is the AX series how you met Masakuni Mitsuhashi and Akira Takiguchi?

KI: Yes. We played together, we went skiing together, we played mahjong together. They were friends, both Mitsuhashi and Takiguchi. In addition to these two gentlemen it was also, if you know the Miyaji brothers,[2] the very first gamers. The company had some kind

[1] Roughly £300 / $400 to £600 / $800 in 1983
[2] Yoichi and Takeshi Miyaji, co-founders of Game Arts

of a dormitory for the staff, so we wouldn't go home. We were all like family. Even now.

JS: The place you stayed and worked, it was called "Part 2" right? <*shows layout sketch*>

KI: Yes, ASCII Part 2. <*looks over sketch*> The kitchen, bathroom, living room, small room, and... I think it was two rooms. The corridor was quite wide actually, and there was a bed in the corridor as well. Seven beds in total; six here, and one in the corridor.

JS: It must have been quite cramped.

KI: Ah, well, it was bunk beds, but with three on top of each other.

JS: Can you tell me about the start of Game Arts? You were there from the beginning, right?

KI: Yes, I was there only the first four years, and then I was with my current company - Technical Arts. At some point, Game Arts started to concentrate on game consoles, because PC games didn't sell well. I wanted to work on computer software. That's why I moved out.

JS: Which year did you start and leave?

KI: The company was founded in February 1984, and I was the vice president, and Yoichi Miyaji was the president. In total there were eight people in the company. I left around 1988?

JS: Game Arts started working on the Mega Drive and Sega Mega CD?

KI: Yes, first it was the Mega Drive... It's certain I was still there in 1989 then...

JS: The first game you worked on was *Thexder*? <*pronounces "th" as in throw*> Or rather *Thexder*? <*pronounces it "texder"*>

KI: *Thexder.* <*pronounces it "tegzer"*>

JS: What was it like when Game Arts started?

KI: In ASCII, all of us were creating games, but we thought we wanted to go independent and create our own games. Of course it's also from a financial side, that there would be more returns on the work you perform; you'd get more profit. So, we thought "Why not give it a chance?"

JS: Was it difficult?

KI: Yes, it was really difficult. Normally when you start to make your own company, you go to a professional, you go to a lawyer and he prepares the documents for you. But for this, of course, you would need money. Therefore we did the documents all by ourselves instead. And of course we didn't know how to make them, so we went to city hall, submitted the papers, and they said no, this is not good. We went back, fixed it, again and again, about 10 times, until finally we got them right. Of course, because we did it all by ourselves, it cost next to nothing.

Also we had problems in terms of distribution. At that time, the average age of all the company employees was around 20 years old. When we went to a company to talk about distribution, they didn't take us seriously. So we had many failed attempts, and asked our acquaintances in ASCII. Only then we could finally put our work on the market. Also, the banks were really not taking us seriously. At that time in Japan, the term "venture" was still unfamiliar and not well understood.

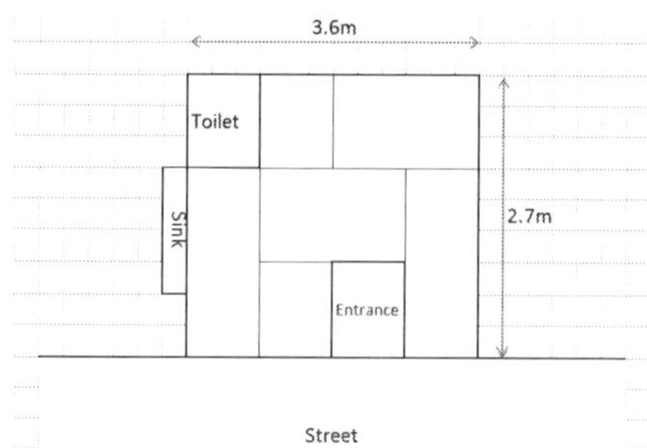

The first Game Arts office (9.72sqm), from Dec 1984 to Feb 1985. The founding members were Misters Matsuda, Y-Miyaji, Ikeda, Uchida, T-Miyaji, Uesaka, Shimada, Okabe, and Koyama. All worked in this office except Mr Matsuda. It was so small, the entrance way and toilet became a workspace

***

Also the office was very small - the office in which we worked. So because of this, for all the work not involving a computer we would just get a ride on the Yamanote Line.[3] You know the one that goes all the way around? So you'd buy one ticket for one station's distance, and then you'd just stay in the train and do the work. For example, the drafts for magazine adverts were done in the train, because they didn't involve

[3] Tokyo subway line that goes in a big circle

work on computers. Also we did some work, like this, in a *kissaten* (café). Like a tea or coffee shop. So yes, it was quite a difficult time.

The second office (right, 32sqm) was an apartment, where between 5-6 part-time staff plus eight of the founding members worked

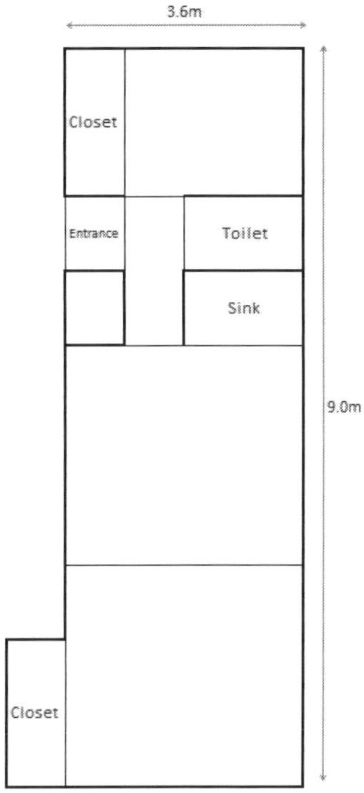

***

JS: The Yamanote Line was more comfortable?

KI: It was especially comfortable in the summer. We originally didn't have an air conditioner in the office, so the Yamanote line was really an easy work environment for us. Because there was air conditioning on the train.

JS: What if you got hungry?

KI: We ate cup noodles, basically junk food. The first year we really lived an unhealthy life.

JS: Tell me about your pseudonym, Hibiki Godai.

KI: There was a very popular manga at that time, and it had a character named Godai. I liked him and I decided to use that name. There's nothing deeply meaningful here. And also, Kohei Ikeda is such a mundane name in Japan and therefore difficult to remember. But Godai is a bit more uncommon and sounds more Japanese-ish, so people might remember it a bit easier.

JS: You worked with Mr Takiguchi on *Theseus*.[4] Was *Thexder* influenced by *Theseus*?

KI: *Thexder* was influenced by three games...

JS: <*interrupts*> *Theseus*, *Grobda*, and...

KI: <*interrupts*> Yeah, *Grobda*[5] by Namcot, and *EXOA*.[6] For the name, *Theseus* gave the TH, and *EXOA* gave the EX, while *Grobda* gave the DER. To combine the three games, it was pushing it a bit. But I thought that a made-up name would have more impact.

JS: It was an original, new word. *Theseus* was inspired by Atari's *Major Havoc*?

KI: Yes, yes. <*laughs*> Maybe we used about a million yen[7] in the game centres. Just on *Major Havoc*. Also Takiguchi-san and Mitsuhashi-san, we'd go there and play the whole day. Well, maybe a million is a bit exaggerated, but certainly more than half a million yen.

JS: *Thexder* was a best selling game.

KI: Yes, that's right. In that year, it was the biggest selling. At that time, in terms of action games, there were not many. Also, we used robots in the game. In Japan we had *Gundam* and *Macross*, and these were very popular. That probably helped with the popularity of the game.

JS: Sierra sold it in America. Were you involved?

KI: A little, only at the beginning. We had an acquaintance at Broderbund, and we tried to negotiate with those guys for a US release, but it didn't work out. Then somebody from Sierra approached us. At that time, I wasn't very familiar with what was going on in America, but as soon as we were approached we immediately said OK. We felt so honoured. We knew that the American market was much more advanced at that time. So we were very happy that an American company wanted to port our game.

JS: In Japan, on the same day as *Thexder*, *Cuby Panic*[8] was also released?

KI: Yes. There was a programmer whose name was a Sakai-san,[9] a friend of Mitsuhashi-san. He originally worked on it all by himself. Initially our plan was to release *Silpheed* at the same time with those two games. But the development of *Silpheed* ran into difficulties, and we had to delay its release. In the end, it was just these

[4] Maze platformer with inertia; Mr Takiguchi interview
[5] Arcade title, spin-off from *Xevious*
[6] Obscure computer game resembling *Xevious*; very different to *EXOA II*. Both published by ASCII

[7] about £2'600 / $4'000 in June 1983
[8] Action-puzzler; avoid being crushed by moving cubes
[9] Game Arts' Japanese website credits H.SAKAI,

two games, *Cuby Panic* and *Thexder*. *Cuby Panic* was a game of a new genre at the time. So it was a challenging thing to do, and it didn't really sell well. Probably, I'm thinking right now, that if we sold it today for smartphones *Cuby Panic* would sell much better. In those days, however, it was not received too well.

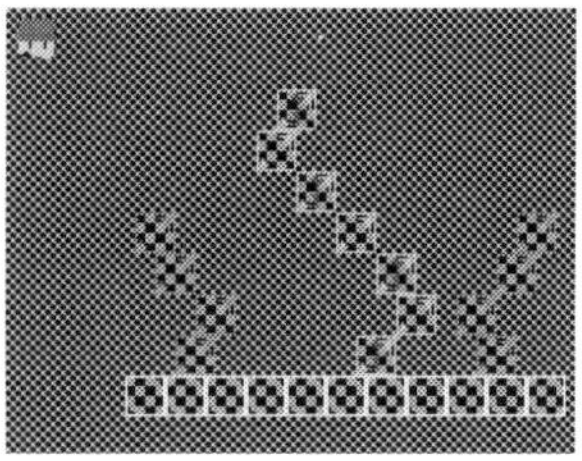

Cuby Panic (PC-88) really needs to be seen in motion to fully understand

JS: *Silpheed* was delayed until 1986.

KI: We just wanted to improve the quality. Takeshi Miyaji really felt that we should improve the quality, and since *Thexder* did really well, all of us at Game Arts wanted to make something that was even better. That's why it ended up taking more time.

JS: You also worked on the conversion of *Thexder* to the Famicom, right?

KI: We hired another company, Bits Laboratory,[10] for the conversion. Square published the Famicom version. They had a very low budget and time was also pretty limited, so in the end it came out as a rather low quality game.

JS: It had fewer levels than the PC-88 version.[11]

KI: That was because of small ROM capacity. But if you increased the ROM memory, that would increase the production costs significantly. So the policy of the publisher, Square, which is not a very good business model, was to go with a low a cost as possible in the production stage.

JS: *Thexder* influenced other games. *WiBArM*[12] from 1986 also had a transforming robot.

KI: I'm not personally familiar with that game. But yes, the second half of the 1980s, robot games became very popular. So there were many games with robots.

JS: Have you heard of *Alisia Dragoon* by Game Arts? It borrowed *Thexder*'s weapon mechanics.

KI: Sorry, I don't know.

JS: Do you have any interesting stories from the development of *Thexder* or *Silpheed*?

KI: <*takes out some material*> Have you seen this? <*shows photo on back of Thexder box*> We wanted to shoot this picture[13] with Mt Fuji in the background. But the weather was bad and it didn't work.

Another story is that with *Thexder*, it was initially for this new model of computer, PC-8801SR[14] from NEC, which was supposed to start selling in March 1985. We started development of *Thexder* in December 1984, but we didn't have the actual hardware to make it at the time. So we had to do the development on our own machines. We went to NEC and we asked them many times, "Oh, can't you give us a prototype to do this?" We tried to negotiate but they refused every time. And finally they said, "Alright then, only during the New Year's holiday, for about one week, we can rent it to you." So we got this prototype machine for one week, and we made the game on it. After the holiday we went to NEC to return the computer, and showed them a demonstration of what we did in that one week. They were so impressed they said that we can keep the prototype machine for longer. Thanks to this, we managed to release *Thexder* at around the same time as the release of this new model in March 1985. Because the hardware and this game came out at the same time, the game sold quite well.

That was how we intended to sell it from the very beginning, actually. We knew that the new model was coming out from the information we gathered when we were in ASCII,

---

[10] Not to be confused with UK's BITS Entertainment, which did outsource work for Japanese developers

[11] PC: 16 (Strategywiki) / FC: 5 that loop (GameFAQs)

[12] By the creator of *Thunderforce*, it had 3D sections

[13] Satoshi Uesaka (left) and Hibiki Godai

[14] Improvements include FM sound and the V2 Mode

and that's part of the reason we established Game Arts at that time; to release the game with this new model of computer. Same goes for *Cuby Panic*. Both of the games were designed to be released with this new model.

JS: During your dealings with NEC did you ever hear mention of a CD-ROM model of PC-88?

KI: It was sometime after that, I think it was the PC-88MC, and it was about two years later that it came out, right?

JS: There's not a lot of information on it. There were only a few CD games released.

KI: Yes. At the time, sales of PC-88 were going down, because the PC-98 model, the 16-bit one, was becoming the mainstream. So it was kind of like at the end of the PC-88 era. For game creators, basically, they'd stop making games for it. That's probably one of the reasons there were so few games for PC-88 on CD. Also, the CD-ROM drives [for PC-88MC] were made by Hudson in cooperation with NEC, and they had the technical information regarding the device, but they're a company in Hokkaido. Since game companies working in Tokyo couldn't get familiar with it, it was difficult to produce games for this platform. Also, at that time, for gaming, the X68000 by Sharp, and FM Towns by Fujitsu, were more popular models, and PC-88 wasn't doing very good against those. So maybe these are the reasons there are so few games.

JS: Mitsuhiro Matsuda and Takeshi Miyaji passed away, is there anything you'd like to say?

KI: <*silence...*> It was only two years ago that Miyaji-san passed away. <*takes out photos*>

JS: Who is this gentleman with the moustache?

KI: Matsuda-san. The second president of Game Arts, he passed away also.

JS: He was instrumental in the AX series.

KI: Yes, yes. <*shows outdoor photo*> On the far left is Tomoyuki Shimada of *Zeliard*,[15] and next to him is Takeshi Miyaji. And a woman from Sierra. <*referencing Shimada-san*> He also passed away, 10 years ago. Maybe 2004?

JS: Can I include this in the book?

KI: Sure, it's fine. It's a copy, please take it. I can also send you the file. <*referencing the photo and woman from Sierra*> This is Yosemite National Park. We went there for sightseeing, and she drove us.

JS: Was this when signing the deal for *Silpheed*, or *Zeliard*, or other games?

KI: It was during *Thexder*'s deal.

JS: Thank you for sharing it.

KI: Mr Shimada actually stayed there and helped with the game. I think we discussed *Silpheed* as well during the trip.

Zeliard was ported from PC-88 to DOS by Sierra Online. It's a side-scrolling action-RPG akin to Ys III by Falcom

JS: Were you involved with *Zeliard* at all?

KI: I helped a little bit, yes.

JS: All of Game Arts titles which came to America through Sierra are well regarded; *Thexder*, *Silpheed* and *Zeliard*.

KI: I'm very happy to hear that. I think there were not many games for the computer that went from Japan to America.

JS: A lot of console games, but only a few PC games - those from Game Arts, *Sorcerian*...

KI: Yes, that's right. We were very, very happy.

JS: You founded Technical Arts in 1988?

KI: There was overlap. It was actually in 1985.

JS: So you founded it before leaving Game Arts?

[15] A side-scrolling action RPG. Shimada-san is credited as programmer

KI: Yes, it was actually kind of like another brand within Game Arts. Then we just went our separate ways.

JS: Recently you were involved with games like *Ragnarok Odyssey* on PS Vita?

KI: Yes. I'm working with Yoichi Miyaji, in my old company, my old home.

JS: Please pass on my regards. The titles from Game Arts have a special meaning for my peers.

KI: I'm very happy to hear that.

JS: Do you have any final thoughts?

KI: Anything is OK, right? Technology has evolved a lot in the last 30 years, and computer games have changed a lot of course, but the people who create the games are still the same. The games right now, they don't seem to have a good balance, in my opinion. Of course they have great visuals, and the sound is amazing. The scale has gotten much bigger and the game lasts longer. You can have more than 1'000[16] characters in games now, like it's nothing special. Despite all this, it is my belief that the core of the game was better and much more fun in the old days.

So what I would like to do, is to once again make a game that is actually fun for young people to play, a game that you can enjoy. Right now many Japanese games are a pain to play. To improve your character you have to do the same, repetitive task over and over again. As if enduring is the game itself. That seems to be the playing style that's dominant right now. Whereas I believe that games should be more centred on the entertainment side, should be more fun. That probably is still the principal of a game. It would be great, say, if we could use today's technology to make good, entertaining games. Luckily, I'm still in the gaming industry and still producing games. So I'll keep doing my best to make good games.

JS: I think a lot of readers would agree with you. A lot of big developers are afraid to try something interesting.

KI: Right now it feels like the priority is going towards the business side. Make a game, sell it and make a profit. It feels like making an interesting game right now is being, let's say, passed on - it feels like it's given much lower priority and it's becoming second gear. Right now, I'm working with this new game in my company. What we're trying to do with it is to make it interesting for people who have never played games, people who think that playing games is a waste of money and a waste of time. We are hoping to make something revolutionary. We are now interviewing many kinds of people, including people who never played games, to create games that would be interesting to this segment of the population.

JS: I wish you the best of luck.

KI: Thank you.

Theseus for MSX, took inspiration from Atari's *Major Havoc* for arcades

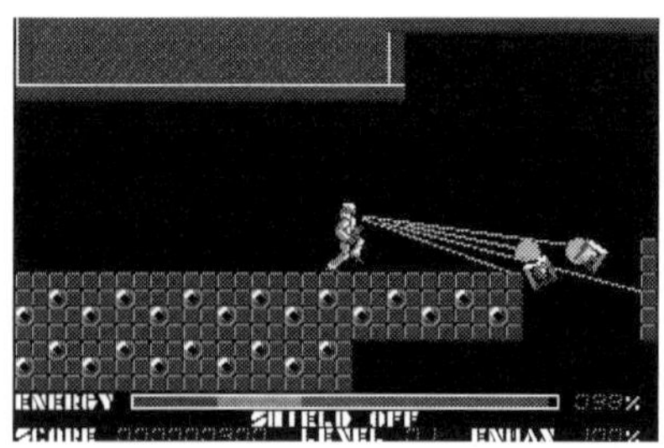

Thexder was influenced by Theseus and was a breakthrough release for Game Arts

[16] NPC characters, not kanji script characters

From left: Tomoyuki Shimada, Takeshi Miyaji, a Sierra representative, Kohei Ikeda; Yosemite National Park

~In memory of~

嶋田 智幸

SHIMADA, Tomoyuki

~Selected Portfolio~

Silpheed	- 1987	(Main programmer)
Zeliard	- 1987	(Lead Programming)
Alisia Dragoon	- 1992	(Music Programer)
Sonic the Hedgehog 2	- 1992	(Sound Programmer)
Silpheed	- 1993	(Sound Effects)

He was incredibly hardworking, and very serious about his work. No matter what you requested of him, no matter what you asked, he would do it. He was a very reliable person. I think all the Game Arts' programmers were like that, but he was a really good guy.
- ***Masakuni Mitsuhashi, Game Arts colleague***

Shimada-kun spent quite a long time fighting this illness he had, for almost 10 years. He had a very difficult time until the end. He was a person that really liked delicious food and wine, really enjoyed it, and had very strong tastes. We would often go out to have dinner. Also, he was my subordinate when I was working at ASCII. I taught him programming myself. Someone you teach dying ahead of you... It feels extremely regretful and sad.
- ***Kohei Ikeda, Game Arts colleague***

鈴木 浩

SUZUKI, Hiroshi

DOB: 1 March 1960 / Birthplace: Iwate Prefecture / Blood Type: A

~ Portfolio ~

万引少年 / *Manbiki Shounen (Shoplifting Boy)* - PET2001 (1979/11) / released in magazine *RAM* (1980/02)

ALIEN - PET2001 (1979/11), unreleased (only demonstrated in the university festival)

LANDING GAME - Basic Master Level 2 (1979/?), released on cassette tape by Hitachi Corporation

万引少女 / *Manbiki Shoujo* - PET2001 & PCG (1980/11), unreleased (demoed at the university festival)

土人 / *Dojin* - PET2001 & PCG (1980/11), unreleased (only demonstrated in the university festival)

F16 フライトシミュレータ / *F16 Flight Simulator* - Basic Master Level 3 (1981/?), cassette, by Hitachi Corp

ザ・コックピット / *The Cockpit* - BML 3 (1982/05), released in magazine *I/O* and cassette (1984/04)

ザ・コックピット / *The Cockpit* - PC-9801 port (1984/05), released on floppy disk by COMPAC

Interview with Hiroshi Suzuki
26 October 2013, Tokyo, ASAHI Net

This interview took place at ASAHI Net, after Mr Takiguchi's interview. Although Mr Suzuki was not involved with the AX series, he did work alongside Misters Takiguchi and Mitsuhashi, and reveals some very interesting facts regarding Taito. More significantly, Mr Suzuki details a now unimaginable era where computer users would create their own bespoke hardware from circuit boards, in order to use special controllers or features. With regards to the "Dojin" game covered in depth, we used various English words for its interpretation, some of which might have a negative subtext, but this does not reflect the game or the creator's original intentions. A more neutral word has replaced them throughout. In addition, the sketching of the game had a party-like atmosphere to it, so although quotes are attributed to specific people, they may not all be accurate.

JS: What was the first game you ever played? When did you want to make them?

HS: The first game I ever played was *Space Invaders*, the table-top version! I entered university in 1979, and that was around the time when *Space Invaders* was very popular. As for making them, I knew about type-in programs for the TK-80[1] appearing in a magazine called *I/O.*[2] Magazines all had the source code for games printed in them, including simulations of *Space Invaders*, but I wasn't at all familiar with computers or coding. These could also be made using microcomputers though, which motivated me to join a computer club in university. I was involved in this technology club; it was not a games club back then, because there were not enough games to warrant it. That's how I got interested. We looked at things like hardware, compilers, and LISP,[3] and so on. However, the computer club became a games club, <*laughs*> due to the wicked effects of myself and Mr Takiguchi! When I joined the club, I was one year above Mr Takiguchi in the university, and yes, it began as a very academic computer club, but we turned it into more of a... Maybe, a bit more of a casual games club. <*laughs*>

JS: Was there any resistance from members of staff? Or did they feel computers were the future?

HS: I majored in aeronautics. When I joined the university in 1979, we were still in the era where that was done using analogue computers. Obviously we're talking about the very first part of the first shift to more modern-style computers. So I think when I joined the university there wasn't a huge amount of awareness, and as a result I don't think many of the teachers had fully developed opinions on it. Obviously I used

[1] Stands for Training Kit, by NEC, 1976

[2] Apparently Japan's first computer magazine

[3] Higher level language first specified in 1958

what was considered, at that time, a very new machine to make a flight simulator. You know, a small one - an analogue computer simulation - but my professors thought that was an impressive thing. I felt they understood, they could see the potential and the fact that these were going to be the future. I do think they were positive towards that.

JS: Online there appears to be another Mr Hiroshi Suzuki, who developed games.[4]

HS: I didn't know that. But Hiroshi Suzuki is a fairly widespread name. I had no pseudonyms.

JS: Your first computer was a PET 2001?[5]

HS: I didn't buy one. The PET 2001 was very expensive and I was in university at the time, in 1979. What I used to do is, there was a showroom for the PET in Aoyama, where you could go and use them. There was also one in Akihabara. So that's what I did, in order to see the games. When I was visiting the showroom to use the computer, I pretty much spent all my free time there. I would go maybe not every day, but close to. What happened is, we worked on these games, and then at the university festival in November we would display them, and other students could play them. When Commodore PR was around, during the festivals, they would lend us the [PET] computers. So it was an opportunity for us to show our work and also to show off the potential of the hardware.

JS: I believe there was a nickname if you didn't have your own computer, pronounced *naicon*.[6]

HS: *<laughs>* I've never heard of it before! Is that right? I'm surprised.

JS: Mr Takiguchi told me about it.

HS: *<laughs>* I wasn't bullied by him, if that's what you're asking!

<everyone laughs>

JS: Did you sell your games at the festival, or was it just to show people?

HS: We didn't sell the games. But as a club we made a fortune telling program. This was in the autumn of 1979, and I was able to negotiate with the distributors to borrow several PET computers for this. It was done in BASIC. You could put in some details while at the festival, and it would print out a fortune for you - a bit like the ones at shrines in Japan, where you go in and find out how lucky you are. So we got money for that.

JS: A dot matrix printer with perforated paper?

HS: That's right, yes! *<makes sound effect of printing>* Very slow! *<laughs>* It used to take about three minutes to print a single page. It was 300 yen for a three minute viewing of a printer printing. At the festival I also exhibited *Manbiki Shounen*, which was later published as a BASIC type-in listing in the February 1980 issue of *RAM* magazine. And a game called *Alien*, which was only ever shown at the festival. In 1979 I also made something called *Landing Game*, for the Hitachi Basic Master Level 2. A plane would come in and you had to try to line it up on the runway. You only really controlled the height of the plane.

JS: This is another game which wasn't released?

HS: I displayed *Landing Game* at Hitachi's programming competition. It was also in BASIC. I have a feeling they may have sold it, on a cassette tape. Maybe, I don't think I got any royalties from it. Hitachi as a whole didn't have a great sales record back then. So maybe it wouldn't have sold many copies.

JS: Did you throw away your data disks?

HS: I'm not sure, I just don't have them anymore. They're lost somewhere.

JS: You learned programming through this club?

HS: Yes. Obviously there were no classes back then on it. It was really just me and my other friends in the club, and we had some magazines with information, but otherwise it was almost like research for us. We weren't being told anything, we had to find it out ourselves.

JS: Tell me about signing the contract with Taito.

---

[4] Check MobyGames, expansive portfolio

[5] Commodore Business Machine 2001 (PET); 1977

[6] *nai* = no, *con* = computer, rhymes with *maicon*

HS: It was actually back in 1979. Some Taito people came to the festival, and saw the games we had made, and that was when they sort of said to us, we want to make games together.

JS: So it's not a case of you visiting their office?

HS: Yes, that's right. I did not apply to them, they came to us.

JS: Did you ever visit the Taito building?

HS: Yes, I went a couple of times to do things like dealing with the contracts, and so on.

JS: Can you recall enough to sketch the office?

HS: *<laughs>* Ahh... It was called the Taito office, but really inside it was just a meeting room like this. I really don't remember any special features, or anything.

JS: Please describe working with Taito.

HS: It's hard to remember everything. We went to the Taito office and signed the contract within a month of getting the offer from Taito, after the festival, so it was pretty quick. While we were working in the university we would develop games. The terms of the deal were that Taito would provide a "club room" to develop these games, in addition to microcomputers to work on, PETs with Programmable Sound Generators. It was almost like an office for us to work in. And we had maybe two PET development computers that we could work with? Taito paid the rent and all the maintenance, like lights and so on.

JS: Taito encouraged you to present your games, and would pay you if they liked them?

Akira Takiguchi: Not if they liked them. If we made a presentation, Taito would pay.

HS: In exchange we would show the games we made to Taito and they would pay a one-time fee of... I think it was maybe somewhere between 50'000 and 150'000 yen,[7] depending on the game. They were also supposed to pay a separate royalty when the games were later commercialised. It's hard to recall.

JS: Even if the game was not good?

AT: So, so, so! *<laughs> (Right, right, right!)*

<everyone laughs>

HS: Basically there was a flat rate they would pay for any game, and then if they liked it you would get a little bit more.

JS: Did you work on the same games? Was there competition?

HS: We all worked on our own games, but there was no competition, there was no sort of rivalry. We didn't ever really make a game where we worked together on it. With the Taito contract everyone was working on their own game, and once it was finished you took it to Taito.

JS: Is this how *Manbiki Shounen* and *The Cockpit* came about?

HS: Ahh... *Manbiki Shounen* was made before the festival where Taito saw us...

AT: Suzuki-san's *Manbiki Shounen* was maybe stimulus to encourage Taito to give the contract.

HS: I made it between entering university and attending the festival, because I later showed it at the festival.

JS: You completed it in 1979?

HS: In Japan the university system starts in April, but at that time when I joined, I didn't have any knowledge about this, so I would say *Manbiki Shonen* was really developed in less than a month. Sometime leading up to the end of November, or middle of November, so I would say... Maybe it was made in October of 1979?

JS: It's a game where you're a shoplifter - where did the inspiration come from?

<everyone laughs>

HS: This was still a time when convenience stores were not yet all over the place; they were still kind of new to me, in a way. I remember there was a 7/11 near the university, and when I went there I was looking around, and I noticed that - maybe slightly different to the way they're laid out today - the shelves were stacked high and the walkways were so narrow, making it difficult to see. I just remember thinking to

[7] Circa 1980: £100 / $210 - £280 / $630 (fxtop)

myself, there's a game in this somewhere. I thought it was the kind of layout which may entice a shoplifter. So that's really the reason that *Manbiki Shonen*'s contents came about. *<laughs>* I don't have a terrible shoplifting history, or anything. *<opens a magazine[8] to an article on the game with type-in listing>* This is me, and this is the old style of 7/11 from the 1970s. *<laughs>* The pose I'm doing here, I'm pretending to shoplift.

JS: Did a few magazines cover it?

HS: Probably because the title "*Shoplifting Boy*" was provocative, a weekly magazine reported that a certain Parent Teacher Association was making accusations about the game...

JS: *<laughs>* The media always blames society's problems on videogames! Have you heard of *Castle Wolfenstein* for the Apple II?

AT: Ahh! *<recognises where this is going>*

HS: No, unfortunately I've never heard of it.

JS: *Castle Wolfenstein* is generally regarded as the first stealth game, along with *005* by Sega,[9] though *Manbiki Shonen* predates them.[10]

AT: Aha! *<laughs>*

HS: Oh, is that right? That's quite possibly true, I would say I didn't really pay any attention to other games that were being made at the time. I really got all of my inspiration from my trip to the convenience store.

JS: As far as I know there were no other stealth games in 1979. Yours could be the first example.

<everyone laughs>

HS: Hmm...

JS: If you made it in 1979, and *Castle Wolfenstein* was 1981, that's over a year apart.

HS: I didn't know that...

AT: What about *Heiankyo Alien*? [11] It was created by a computer club at Tokyo University.

HS: That game was maybe a chase game, which had some similarities. But maybe you couldn't call it a stealth game.

JS: It's not like you have to avoid the glare of the aliens, you just trap them in holes.

<We look at screenshots of Manbiki Shounen>

JS: Here you avoid the line-of-sight of the owner.

HS: That's the owner. He's like a security guy. I guess, maybe the inspiration that I took, or the thing that I used in the game, is I was quite taken with some other games which already had characters with moving parts, or moving sprites. A very comical, 1970s type of cartoon style. Sort of... Hmm, what was it. I think it had a balloon and spikes?

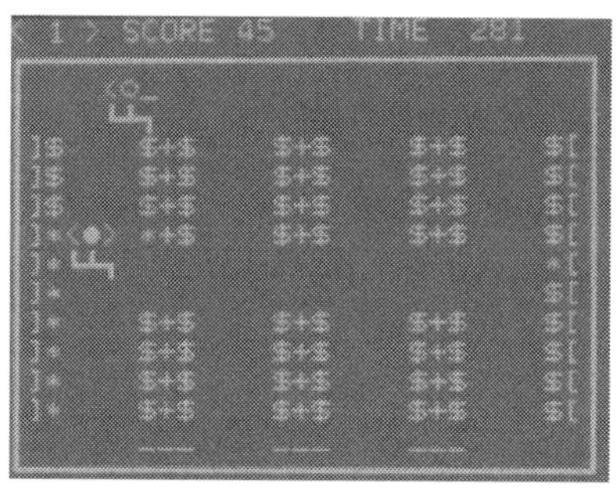

JS: *Crazy Balloon*, by Taito, from around 1980?

HS: I wanted to do something kind of like that. That's why I added characters like this, with arms and legs that can move. I wanted to make an original game with humorous movements. There was a story in the game. So this person would say 'AITETEYOKATTA'. *<refers to screenshot of game's opening sequence>*

AT: 7/11 bucked the trend in Japan of closing early, by staying open until about 11, so what he's saying here is, "Oh, I'm so glad it's still open. Good to see it open," that kind of thing.

---

[8] *RAM* magazine, Feb 1980

[9] *CW*, Silas Warner, 1981; *005*, Sega, 1981

[10] It also predates Namco's *Pac-man* (1981), another maze game about avoiding detection

[11] 1979, by Tokyo University's Theoretical Science Group - dig holes to capture aliens in a maze.

JS: Was the goal to steal a set amount, or simply go as long as you could?

HS: You did have to steal things, it wasn't simply for as long as you could... I can't remember how this timer worked. *<gestures to timer in screenshot>*

JS: This could be the first ever stealth game.

HS: Really? Thank you. *<laughs>*

AT: This is the boy version, *Shounen*. What Suzuki-san did next was make *Manbiki Shoujo*, *Shoplifting Girl*, in 1980, using a Programmable Character Generator, to make more realistic characters. The PCG was newly installed in our computers, so better graphics could be created.

HS: It also allowed more realistic movement of the characters. In addition, we used "*zero cross*".

AT: Zero cross is one method for generating sound on computers.

HS: *<draws on whiteboard>* This is a waveform of someone's voice. So zero (0) and cross (x), meaning on or off... No, that's not right. This is zero... Where did it go?

<everyone laughs>

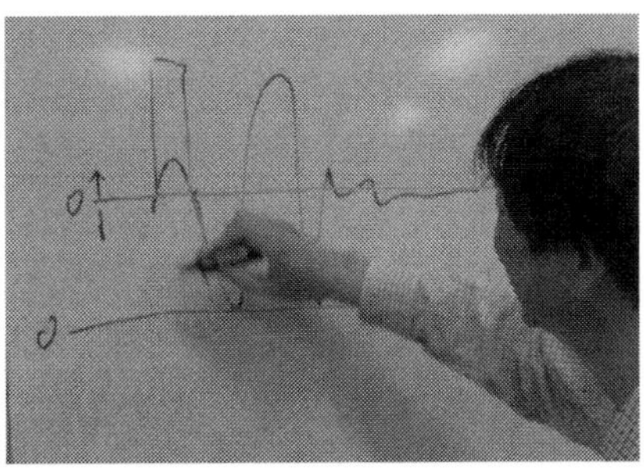

HS: Alright, on, off, on, off. *<finishes sketch>* We used the *zero cross* system to produce sounds that were like people's voices. So there was a sound element to *Manbiki Shoujo*. It spoke to you.

AT: It was a game that speaks!

JS: Real speaking?

HS: You could definitely understand it - it was language. And you could play it with a joystick controller as well. It was in 1980 that I made *Manbiki Shoujo*.

JS: That still predates *Castle Wolfenstein*. So you actually made the first two stealth games.

<everyone laughs>

JS: And then *Manbiki Shounen* was converted to the PC-6001 in July 1982?

HS: I'm not responsible for that port, somebody else did it. I never saw it in real life, but I've seen evidence of it. But it wasn't me who made it, and neither was it somebody from our circle at the university. I don't know who made it. My original BASIC code was put in magazines, as I showed you, so somebody could have easily reproduced it on a different machine. However, *Manbiki Shoujo* was written in machine code, assembly language, so it wasn't copyable in the same way.

JS: Do you still have the source code?

HS: I don't. *<laughs>* But it's printed in the magazine, so you can always make your own.

JS: But not *Manbiki Shoujo*. I'll check online, and see if there's anything on it.

AT: It wasn't on floppy disk, was it?

HS: Floppy... It was on cassette I think. Both *Manbiki Shoujo* and *Dojin* used the PCG. Those two were programmed in machine language.

AT: Eh, it was floppy, I'm sure.

<sketch of the room Taito provided>

AT: This was TOTAI, the room that Taito lent to us. A one room mansion. This was the desk, there were two computers, two PETs. And I think a television? I brought my Apple here. *<laughs>*

JS: Did you sleep in this room as well?

AT: This is Suzuki-san's residence. He *lived* here! And the next year, Mitsuhashi-san lived in here. *<laughs>*

JS: Was this an adjacent sleeping room?

HS: I didn't really live there. I did have another place to stay, but I ended up there so late all the time that I essentially lived there, is the way to put it.

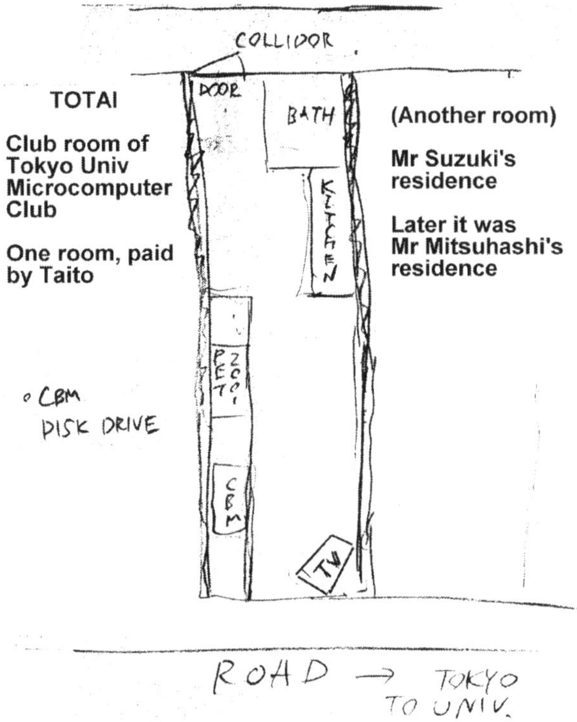

<looks over list of games worked on>

HS: This was a horoscope using the stars, as opposed to fortune telling. This is *Dojin*, not *doujin*, it's like a native.[12]

JS: What was that about?

HS: Sort of like a chase game... You were inside a forest, and there was a highway, with a car going along it. You were chased through the forest by natives, and then there were sort of roads going through the forest, and they were trying to get you to run through it so you'd be run over by another one who was driving a car.

JS: And these were... Savages?

HS: Not savages. More like...

AT: The original Japanese word "*dojin*" does not have a discriminating nature. It's about somebody who lives far away - so savages implies that their behaviour is savage, but the word *dojin* does not convey that.
<conversation in Japanese>

AT: But Suzuki-san's *Dojin* has the image of head hunting! *<laughs>* Which is maybe a little discriminatory...

JS: *<refers to paper with list of games>* So which of these games were sold by Taito?

HS: I definitely have a memory of Taito selling *Lupin III*. It was an arcade table. They definitely manufactured that. In the contract it stated that we would get royalties for PET games. *Lupin III* took a lot of its ideas from *Manbiki Shonen*, but I did not get any royalties for it.

JS: You programmed *Lupin III*?

HS: Taito developed *Lupin III* almost immediately after I presented *Manbiki Shounen* to them. So I think there are some parts that were derived from my work. For example:
- *Before the game starts, an animation of entering the building where the game takes place is displayed.*
- *After the game ends, an animation of being led away by the police is displayed.*
- *The object of the game is to steal the "$" symbols without being caught by the guards*

However, this is my conjecture, and not something Taito explicitly admitted. Also, I was not directly involved in the development. Although Taito sold the tabletop game *Lupin III*, they stressed that, "We only received inspiration from *Manbiki Shounen*, and did not turn it into a product." As such, they did not pay me any royalties. Basically, during the contract period, they did not pay any of the royalties that they would have had to pay if they did, in fact, turn *Manbiki Shounen* into a product.

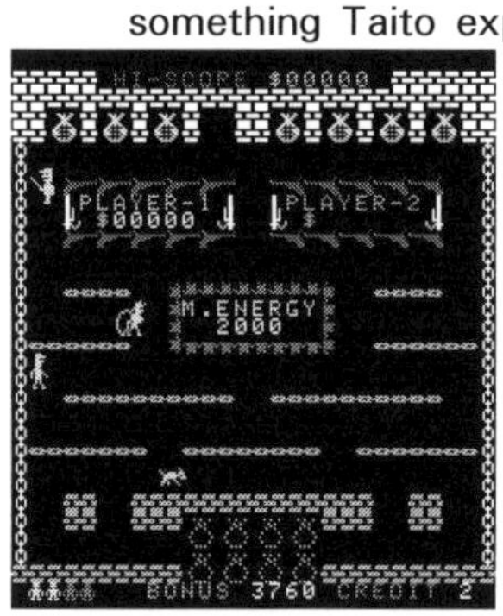

JS: Were you just paid a one-off fee?

HS: Yes, I got paid when I handed *Manbiki Shounen* over to them. I think it was around 1980, I'm not quite sure. The contract for all of the games that we took to Taito did have that clause that we would get royalties, but I don't ever remember getting royalties for any game that I made.

[12] The literal translation is native or aborigine (土人), though in the game there's no indication of locality

JS: The people you dealt with at Taito, were they producers?

HS: There were two who I dealt with.

JS: Can you remember their names?

HS: Ahh... The names... I seem to remember they were graduates of Tokyo University, my former seniors, and ***maybe*** they were developers, but I can't remember I'm afraid.

JS: Taito was running high on its success from *Space Invaders.* Were they arrogant?

HS: I didn't feel like they were arrogant at all. No, I feel like they were very kind, and it felt very much that from their perspective they were saying - if you can make games, that's great! Aside from maybe the royalties thing, they were very fair to us, they were very understandable, they were very good to us.[13]

[Masakuni Mitsuhashi joins us, introductions are made, some snacks are passed out. Mr Mitsuhashi shows a photo of the room Taito provided - he is to the right]

[13] In hindsight I think my questioning was a bit harsh - Taito did after all pay for the TOTAI office, supplied computers, and paid everyone for games which were never even officially commercialised

<We converse regarding the layout sketch, noting that the position of the window by the computers doesn't match up with the photo >

Masakuni Mitsuhashi: Maybe we moved the desks across the room a few times?

HS: *<laughs>* That part of the room smelled! It used to smell, so we moved the desks around so nobody had to sit over the smelly tatami.

MM: The drainage pipe from the air-conditioning went out that corner, and no-one wanted to sit near it. Very wet and so it rotted. Mushrooms!

HS: *<laughs>* Mushrooms.

JS: Right, tatami mats are made of straw.

HS: *<pointing to a different photo>* This was a *Space Invaders* game. I used to play it a lot, and would try to complete it without looking at the screen, or I'd try to play it with my feet. *<laughs>* Or try to do it just using the sounds from the game. *<laughs>*

JS: You must have gotten good at it.

HS: Yes, I could clear it with my feet, and I could finish the first screen without looking at it.

JS: These computer games, the ones after those displayed at the festival, they weren't actually published by Taito. How did you publish them?

HS: They were presented to Taito, and we received money for them, but they were never sold by Taito.

JS: So they're unreleased?

HS: Yes, I guess you could call them unreleased. I'm not exactly sure, if you mean unreleased as in sold, then yes they are unreleased. I also don't really have any memory of distributing them on my own, or anything. So maybe, yes.

JS: If I wanted to play *Dojin*, how could I?

HS: You can't. These games don't exist anymore.

JS: In which case you must tell me more! What you say now may become the only historical record of these creations.

HS: *<laughs>*

JS: Could you draw a sketch detailing *Dojin*?

<begins sketching - afterwards lots of fast discussion between all parties. Footage of this can be found on the supplementary DVD>

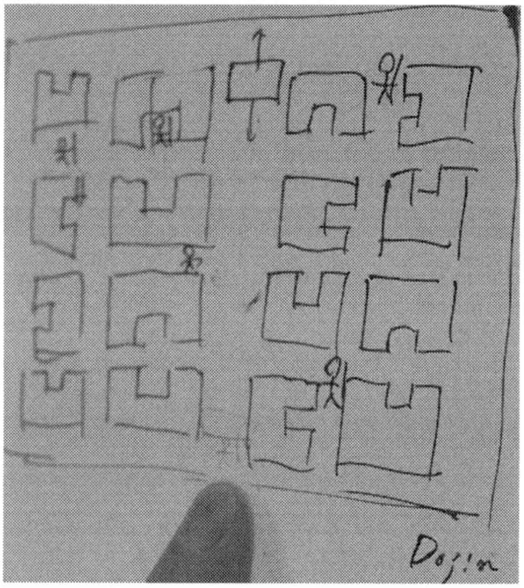

HS: These were the sort of things you'd hide around, they were generated at random. And then various natives would chase you, and there was a car, and like a highway here possibly. I'm not exactly sure what they were...

<Uninterpreted dialogue between Mr Mitsuhashi and Mr Suzuki>

HS: OK, I'm changing my answer from earlier, about what the goal of *Dojin* was. You were chased into a randomly generated forest, and there would be cars coming, possibly up and down the road, or just down the road, and if you could get the natives to cross the road at a point where the car would hit it, then it would be killed.

MM: There were walls on the outside, and he would be shoved along by the car and squashed into the wall. It wasn't a highway.

HS: Natives would be chasing you through a forest, or through these areas, and there would be a sort of...

MM: It had a piston action to it.

HS: Like a moving block, going up and down. If you could time it so a native was crossing this area, at the right time, it would push them into the north or south wall and squish them.

JS: Incredible. This game was never released?

MM: <*laughs*> I'd like to make that now!

JS: This was done in assembly. Is there the possibility that Taito has the source code?

HS: The truth is, really, we only just showed them the games. We did not even give them the code sometimes.

JS: Do you still have the code yourself?

<everyone laughs>

HS: No.

JS: Was this ever featured in a magazine?

HS: I don't think it was ever in a magazine.

JS: This means that this sketch is the only record on the face of the Earth!

<everyone laughs>

<Mr Mitsuhashi draws on whiteboard>

HS: <*laughs*> Actually, that is closer to what *Dojin* looked like!

JS: But I prefer this one! *<gestures to first sketch>* These red crosses are random?

MM: No, no, no. These are crushable walls. You could break through these to create paths, and then in the middle is like a piston, that would crush the characters...

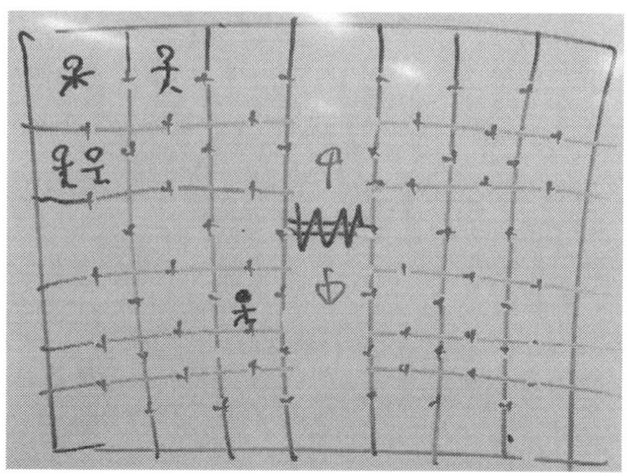

JS: Like a steam roller?

MM: Backwards and forwards, like a pendulum. The player can blast through the walls in one go, but the natives could not, it would take them some time to get through the walls.

JS: So you could create the maze as you went?

HS: The way the game progressed was, as you kept running away you would end up having to knock down more and more walls, or the natives would knock down more and more walls, so it became much harder to avoid them - because they were being held up by walls less and less. So if you could get every single one of the natives using that crushing machine, before they caught you, that was how you won the game.

JS: I would guess there isn't even any documentation on this in Japanese.

MM: No, this is absolutely just here.

JS: Looks like I have a world exclusive!

<everyone laughs>

AT: Maybe one or two Taito employees, or former Taito employees, might remember it, but...

JS: Mr Suzuki, what was the first computer you owned, for yourself?

HS: It was a Basic Master Level 3. I bought my first computer, the Level 3, in 1981. I was using the Level 2 in the showroom. I did make some games on the Basic Master Level 2, but that was before I contacted Taito, so it was unrelated.

JS: Was it quite an expensive computer?

HS: Yes, it was expensive. The price was 298'00 yen, which was too high, and it did not sell well. *<picks up a piece of paper>* This was a document that was distributed within Hitachi, it was an internal document.[14] This was a machine that never really knew what its target audience was, and whether it was for business or games. When I made games on the Master Level 2, in Japan there was a nationwide game developer's contest, and I won a prize there. I ended up talking to someone from Hitachi, which ran the competition, and I think the way that I afforded the Level 3 was because they knocked the price down for me, as a sort of congratulations. *<refers to photo in magazine>* Maybe these two won some sort of prize, and were made or asked to do this advertising, as part of their prize, as it were. Photographs of us... I don't have them now, but we were definitely featured in magazines like this.

JS: From a technical perspective did you feel the Master Level 3 was a powerful computer?

HS: The first point is it had a 6809 CPU.[15] It was 8-bit. Have you heard of it before? The computers I was used to, up until then, all had 8-bit processors. There was the Z80, and the 8080, both 8-bit and quite popular. The Apple II used the 6502 processor, so did the PET, also 8-bit. This one, the 6809, was the first in Japan ever to have a 16-bit register, which essentially means it had twice the capability, in terms of processing. This was around May 1980. At the time it was called the ultimate 8-bit processor. It was a little quicker than anything we'd seen before. That's definitely what stood out for me. It could handle a 640 x 200 pixel resolution, which at the time was considered high resolution! *<laughs>* That was also another big deal for me. This is maybe not so much game related, but it could display hiragana as well as katakana, whereas in the past you could only have katakana.[16] It couldn't do kanji at all though! Maybe those three things, the resolution, the processing capability, and the alphabet functionality, they were the special standout features of the Level 3.

JS: You mentioned the Z80 - I think it's still used.

HS: The Z80 certainly had a long lifetime. The 6809 had a relatively short lifespan. *<laughs>* This was kind of like a stop-gap between the

[14] It details the computer specs, like a sales brochure

[15] First introduced 1978

[16] Old Japanese computers had text in katakana; it's angular and easier to display, but is used for loanwords. Reading lots of text would be uncomfortable

8-bit and 16-bit processors. So although it was a 16-bit processor, the ones that came out after it, like the 68000,[17] were far better. This was very much... The prototype, maybe, of the 16-bit processor? Or one of the first, so it had its limitations and issues.

AT: I think it's the only CPU that has a "division" instruction. There was no multiplication or division in traditional 8-bit processors. Like the Z80, you could only add or subtract. It gave you more options; but it could have been slower.

HS: I never used that functionality when I coded for it.

JS: It must have felt like cutting edge technology.

HS: Yes, that's right. It was I think the strongest machine at the time, certainly in Japan, but obviously it didn't take long for Fujitsu and other computers to overtake it. When I bought it, I felt like this is the strongest machine out there. However, the amount of software was small since there was no development environment or tools, such as an assembler. When developing a game I specifically asked Hitachi for an assembler. Input/output devices were made on one's own, based on circuit diagrams published in magazines.

JS: What did you make with the Basic Level 3?

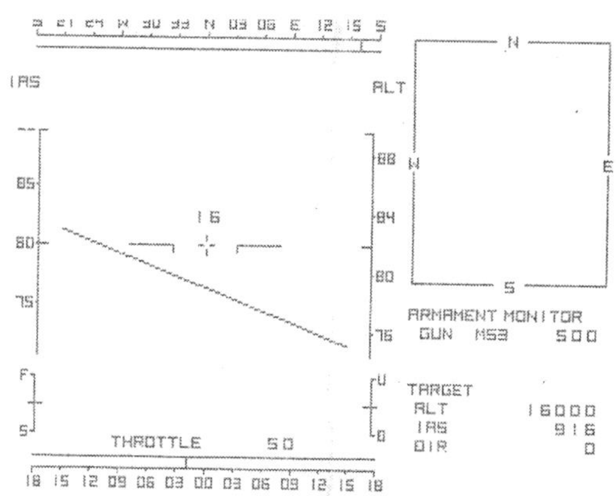

HS: For the 1981 spring festival, as an attraction for the aeronautics department, I worked on a game which showed the HUD from an F-16. Along with a friend from another faculty, we took the seat frame from a car and constructed a cockpit to go with this. Then we borrowed an analogue synthesizer from Mitsuhashi-san to reproduce the sound of jets. It was done in assembly and was even aired on an educational program by the NHK! The game that resulted, *F-16 Flight Simulator*, was released by Hitachi on cassette tape in 1981. This was like a prototype for *The Cockpit* in 1982.

JS: Was it tricky using the available hardware?

HS: I wanted to see how far you could push a microcomputer. I once saw a DC-8 simulator, by JAL, and thought I'd like to play one myself, and create a satisfying game. Since it's called a "flight sim", the simulated movement of the aeroplane must be carried out exactly. Moving in real-time is also important. For the screen refresh rate, at worst, I felt you'd need a minimum of 8 frames-per-second. To increase speed:
1) Drawing lines is slow - think of situations that can be represented by dots.
2) Improve calculation speeds - solve equations related to minor turbulence.
3) Optimisation at the machine language level - I wanted an algorithm with fewer CPU cycles.

As a result, a limited scenario covering "landing at night" was used. In May 1984 I ported it from the Basic Master Level 3 to the PC-9801, which had a 8086 processor. The computer was in the laboratory of my graduate school. It was published by COMPAC. I was told it would sell less than the Master Level 3 version, so I rushed through the porting that spring. It must have sold very well though - based on the royalties received, I'd estimate 100'000 copies! Later, others ported it to computers with a different CPU, like the 68000 and Z80. I suspect they were using the 6809 assembly list - which is rather impressive! Such enthusiasm.

JS: *The Cockpit* first came out in 1982. Where did the Taito connection come in?

HS: When I made *The Cockpit* I was no longer participating in club activities. Of course I didn't tell Taito that. I was very surprised to later discover Taito releasing an arcade game in 1987, which was exactly like *The Cockpit*![18] I had a talk with Taito and COMPAC, who had the sales rights for *The Cockpit*. However, I was

[17] First introduced 1979

[18] Although Mr Suzuki did not mention the arcade game, it's obviously Taito's *Midnight Landing*; which seems very suspicious, because a night-time flight-sim isn't exactly an obvious choice for an arcade game

disappointed with the attitude of Taito who, as usual, had no respect for the author, and so I decided to stop having anything to do with them. *<Mr Suzuki takes out various items>*

HS: This is for PC-9801. This is the original.

JS: This is a custom made circuit board?

HS: That's right, yes. Specifically for the PC-98, and was built for the purpose of using this large flight controller. (images top, middle) *<referring to a different circuit, bottom>* This is a sound board for the Level 3, and was built specifically for that. *<shows book>* [19] These are some of the articles published regarding *The Cockpit* software. This is a guide to creating the sound board (shown bottom). It's like a contents of what had been released.

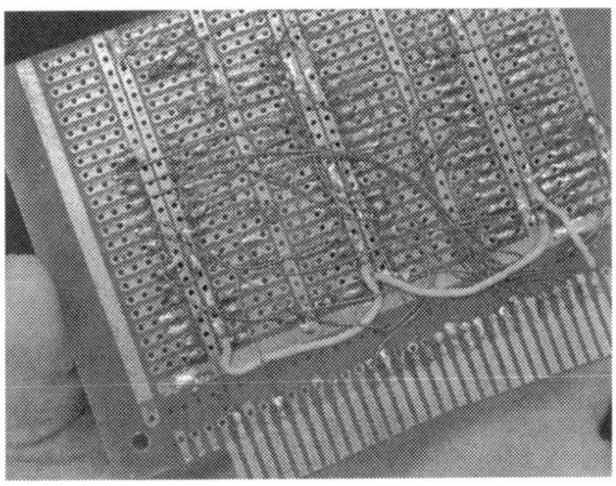

AT: This was for Basic Master Level 3?

HS: The original was for the Level 3, created for a contest.

AK: For *I/O* magazine?

HS: Yes, *I/O* was running a programming contest, I think maybe in Autumn 1983? This is a schematic for the sound board, a circuit board diagram. This was a particular circuit board schematic, a unique one, devised for the Level 3. It didn't have any sound capability, so if this card wasn't present it could only beep. It could not make any other sound. This was produced so that maybe people who weren't experts could make sense of it, and enjoy the games. *<laughs>*

JS: Was a user expected to construct their own sound card? Could you purchase this pre-made?

HS: No, not only did you have to construct it by yourself, but they also didn't sell packs of the required materials. *<laughs>* So you actually had to go to a hardware store and find the required parts, collect those yourself, and then assemble it. The board base is specifically for the Level 3, but these are all generic components, from any circuitry shop. These were not unique to the Level 3. This is the famous chip, AY38910. A Programmable Sound Generator. This is the SM76477, a noise generator, used to simulate the jet engines of an aeroplane.

JS: Would this sound board work on other games, or only *The Cockpit*?

HS: No, this sound card was specifically for this software. But you could produce software that would make other sounds, but you might need a card for that as well. *<laughs>* This was the only software made that used this sound card, so whether or not it could have wasn't the issue. It just didn't have anything else.

JS: A bespoke add-on just for *The Cockpit*?

HS: That's right, yes.

JS: How much did it cost to build such a card?

HS: Maybe about 7'000 yen[20] in the early 1980s?

JS: If you look at the back, you can see all the wires you had to solder together. I've modified consoles to increase the clock speed, but that's like four or five wires. There must be 50 wires here!

---

[19] Various books/magazines were shown, some with type-in listings, others with circuit board diagrams, showing how to build your own, thereby allowing audio on the Level 3 computer

[20] About £22 / $30 in 1984

<everyone laughs>

AT: Back in the 1980s plenty of people, the number of people who knew about or who could handle this sort of thing, was maybe higher than today. Educational knowledge about this sort of thing was much more common place. Everybody who was using computers at this point, they had sort of grown up on the radio, and back in those days the radios that were available, it was quite common to deal with these sort of things.

HS: Back in those days all computers, all these sorts of cards, would have their schematics available in magazines and so on. Learning about it was easily available, and learning about it was maybe not as archaic as it would be to learn about now. So definitely more people were aware of what this was.

JS: Were the schematics for this controller board also made available?

HS: This controller board was specifically made for the PC-98, so it was not in a magazine. So anything for the Level 3 would appear in this magazine, but then stuff that was made for the PC-98 specifically would not.

JS: If someone owned a PC-98 and bought *The Cockpit*, and wanted to use that controller, where would they go for this information? Did PC-98 magazines carry it?

HS: Not at all!

<everyone laughs>

HS: But it's an extremely simple board... For the Level 3 there was no sound output, or a joystick for that matter. But for the PC-98 there were various peripherals, controllers, and so on.

JS Could this be bought as a set?

HS: No, you could not buy a set, but...

AK: If you read this manual, *<gestures to The Cockpit>* there are only keyboard controls mentioned in here.

HS: This kind of flight stick, or joystick controller, was put out as a peripheral for the PC-98 and so on, but getting it working, getting hold of the board for it and so on, would be a case of reading up on the subject. It wasn't ever sold as a pack, it was very much up to the user to research and find out what they needed, to make it work with the game.

JS: Can you sign my two signature books?

HS: *<laughs>* I've never given my signature like this before.

JS: As the gentleman who created the first stealth game, I must have it. Is there anything else you wanted to add? Please consider my book an open platform.

HS: It was an era where... Certainly the stuff we've been talking about today, comes from an era where if you didn't have an understanding of the computers and the games, you simply couldn't enjoy them. Even if you wanted to use a controller, with a flight simulator, you had to have an understanding of circuit boards and computers. Whereas today people don't have that - if you want to play a game, you just pay for it, and that's how games exist today. I think if you are willing, the people who are reading this book, if you are willing to put in the effort and the time required to learn code, and to learn the fundamentals behind it, it is an incredibly fun experience. It's maybe more rewarding than simply being a consumer. So please try it.

JS: Thank you very much. Please look forward to receiving the book next year. Hopefully it will correct some misinformation in the West.

HS: Well, developers themselves forget their own games, so it's not always the researcher's fault!

~ *In memory of* ~

三辻富 貴朗

MITSUJI, Fukio

Aka: MTJ

1960 ~ 2008

~ Selected Portfolio ~

Bubble Bobble	- Arcade, 1986 (Game Design, Character Design)
Rainbow Islands	- Arcade, 1987 (Story and Game Design, Character Design)
Syvalion	- Arcade, 1988
Darius II	- Arcade, 1989 (Game Designer)
Volfied	- Arcade, 1989 (Game Design, Character Design)

When discussing Taito there's a few games you can't ignore. The most obvious is *Space Invaders*, but another would be *Bubble Bobble*, by the late Fukio Mitsuji. Designed to encourage two player cooperation, which thereby allows access to a special ending, the game was adored by all, ported to numerous systems, and saw multiple sequels and spin-offs right up to the present day. It's an iconic part of gaming's history, with a delightfully whimsical setting and tricky secrets. The sequel, *Rainbow Islands*, is equally as beloved.

In addition to creating these timeless classics, Mr Mitsuji was involved in teaching game design, notably with the *MTJ Game Designer's School*, where he also had a regular column. Sadly the website with information is now accessible only through the Wayback archives.

It's worth watching the interview Mr Mitsuji did for the *Taito Classics* compilation, where the above image is taken from. He was a games developer with much to teach the next generation.

杉山 智則

SUGIYAMA, Tomonori

DOB: 19 September 1969 / Birthplace: Shizuoka Prefecture / Blood Type: A

Interview with Tomonori Sugiyama
30 September 2013, Tokyo

I was put in touch with Tomonori Sugiyama after speaking with his colleague Yutaka Isokawa, who suggested I could interview both of them. We enjoyed a meal at an incredible tofu restaurant, before walking to the Vanguard offices. What fascinated me about the company is the number of projects it has worked on as an outside contractor. Vanguard did a lot of work with Game Arts, notably on the Lunar series and later Grandia, and it was also involved with some unusual Saturn hardware add-ons. The company also took Chou Aniki in interesting new directions and handled Falcom's Eiyuu Densetsu Yume no Kiseki brand. More than all this, Mr Sugiyama conveys some of the complexities inherent in the Japanese games industry. The single company name you see on a box isn't always the whole story.

JS: Can you recall the first videogame you saw?

TS: The first videogame that I played was *Space Invaders*. I was an elementary school student back then, and I had to ask my mother to take me to a department store in order to play them. But the department store was not in the town where I used to live, so it was a long trip to visit. So *Space Invaders* left a strong impression on me, and I really wanted to play as often as possible. But I couldn't do so because it was not located in my neighbourhood.

JS: When did you get into games development?

TS: When I entered high school I encountered the personal computer. One of my seniors at school had an Apple II at his home, where he let me play *Wizardry*. I really enjoyed it. So I would commute to his house and stay overnight, just playing games, until the morning! <*laughs*> This was my first encounter with games which made up my mind that I would like to be involved with game development.

JS: I'm surprised he had an Apple, not a PC-88.

TS: Yes, so I think it was fortunate that my friend had an Apple II. Immediately afterwards I asked my parents to buy me a PC-88, which they did, and then I started playing *The Black Onyx*, which was by BPS. I played that quite a lot.[1] And BPS was just around the corner, in our neighbourhood. <*laughs*> It was right there, in the next block.

JS: Maybe I'll try to photograph the building.

TS: Unfortunately the BPS office is no longer there! <*laughs*> The head of the company, Henk Rogers, now lives in Hawaii. He made a fortune on *Tetris*. Henk is a friend of mine.

JS: I'm interviewing Henk over Skype when I get home. *Black Onyx* was an early RPG in Japan.

TS: Please tell him Sugiyama sends his regards! <*laughs*> Anyway, I became really interested in RPGs after having played so much of *Black Onyx*. I really fell in love with it. Then when I was in the 3rd year of my high school I created an RPG with one of my friends. Then we submitted it to one of the competitions being held by Enix, which much later produced *Dragon Quest*. We won one of the awards, although it was not one of the top awards. So that's how I got started in the games industry.

JS: Did you have your photo on the box?[2]

TS: Well actually, instead of Enix, our game was published by Koei, which produces the *Nobunaga* strategy games.

---

[1] Mr Sugiyama used the word やり込み (*yarikomi*): this Japanese gaming term means doing anything beyond simply playing a game from start to finish. It can refer to speedrunning, but the meaning is much broader, and also encompasses 100% completion, secret optional bosses, max level, score attack, no-damage/no-miss runs, and various other specialised playthroughs, such as low-level or solo runs in JRPGs, and pacifist or no-bomb runs in shmups. Xbox achievements and PS trophies can also be considered *yarikomi*. Often, Japanese game reviews will judge a game on its やりこみ要素, meaning how many secret/optional elements are included, or how much a game allows for deeper, more advanced play. Games with a high *yarikomi* potential include the older *Final Fantasies*, *Disgaea*, *Monster Hunter*, arcade shmups, Bethesda games, *Dark Souls*, and *Pokémon*. In a more casual sense, as used here, *yarikomi* can simply mean playing the heck out of a game

[2] Enix comp. winners had a profile on the box back

JS: What was the name of your game? I know someone with a big PC-88 collection.

TS: It did not sell at all! But the name of the game was *Axiom*.[3] I don't think he would have it! <*laughs*> We were not the top winners, but we were awarded one of the prizes.

JS: How come Koei published it instead of Enix?

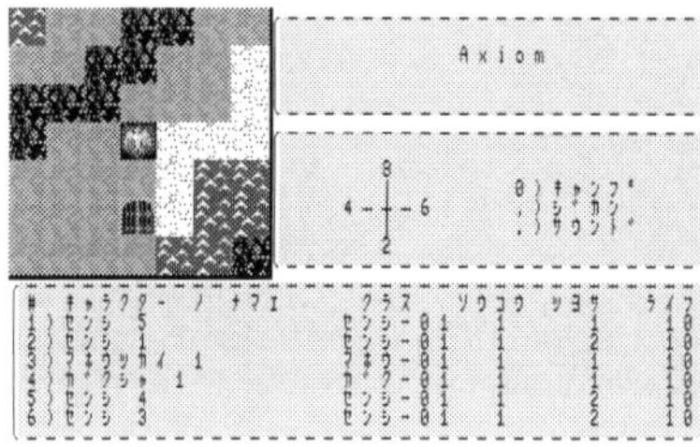

TS: It was a business decision made between Koei and Enix. We had nothing to do with why it ended up being published by Koei. This is just my assumption, but back then I believe Enix was not so strong on RPGs, whereas Koei was strong on RPGs and simulations, and they were working on an RPG called *Dungeon*. It's my assumption that Enix asked Koei to release our game on their behalf. Enix developed a strong reputation for RPGs only after they released *Dragon Quest*.

JS: Japanese RPGs prior to *Dragon Quest* have a unique style. As an RPG developer how would you describe the pre-*Dragon Quest* era?

TS: It's well known that *Dragon Quest* was inspired by the classic RPGs *Wizardry* and *Ultima*. *Final Fantasy* was then inspired by *Dragon Quest*. Together, these two titles defined the trajectory of the Japanese RPG. There were some excellent titles before then, but the gameplay was not always polished, so they didn't become hits. I think that RPGs before *Dragon Quest* understood the appeal of the RPG, but maybe it was a time of exploration, trying to find that Japanese style of the genre. In that sense, I think those titles were a valuable experiment.

You know, I was so into games that I failed one of the entrance exams for university! <*laughs*> So I decided I needed to concentrate on my studying, and forget about games for at least a year. After I was successfully admitted to university I was so relieved, I went to Enix once again, saying I would like to help, and asked if they had any part-time openings. The first job given to me was debugging for *Dragon Quest 1*.

JS: Really? Wow, the original!

TS: <*laughs*> Yes, yes! That's correct! The original version. I was very impressed with that, so it really motivated me, and then I really became determined to create games like this while I was still going to university.

JS: The debugging was at Chunsoft?

TS: No, I was doing the debugging at Enix. Chunsoft was the developer, whereas the publisher was Enix. I was part of the debugging team of the publishing part of Enix.

JS: Can you recall any differences between the debug version and the commercial version?

TS: I believe they were basically the same. The way Enix operated back then was totally different compared to today. They used to carry many freelance creators on board, and the producer of Enix would round them up. I thought I would be able to create games much faster, but it took so much time. <*laughs*> But I was able to accumulate a lot of technical experience along the way. When I was in the first year of my doctorate programme, I founded Vanguard [4] together with my colleagues, as well as my subordinates from university.

JS: Could you draw the Enix offices?

TS: Hmm, that's difficult. I first met Isokawa when we both joined Enix. So maybe he remembers. Every year Enix got bigger and bigger! So perhaps I don't remember! <*laughs*>

JS: After debugging *Dragon Quest*, and before forming Vanguard, did you work on any games?

TS: I was involved with the production of some original games for home computers. I created and released two titles. [5] The reason why I founded Vanguard was because I wanted to retain the excellent talent in a fantastic team. If we were just working on a project on a freelance basis, we would have to end and disband the team upon completion, and then we would lose all the talent because they would be moving on to the next project. Even if the project is ongoing,

---

[3] アクシオム, PC-88 (1985); romaji subtitle is *Vessel of Pensance Bait Hides the Hook*. An overworld map with 3D first-person dungeons and random battles

[4] **www.vgd.co.jp** - contains detailed history pages

[5] *Reichsritter* and *Gunyuu Sangokushi*, both PC-98, discussed in Yutaka Isokawa's interview

since they're freelance they would have to be looking out for the next project after finishing the current job. So they'd have another job waiting.

Another reason is if you're working on a freelance basis, even if you come up with brilliant games, you cannot actually maintain your high reputation. Because once the project is over, the team will be dissolved. So the game may remain, but the members go their separate ways, and the same level of achievement and prestige is not maintained. Whereas if you have a company, you can retain not only the excellent talent, but also accumulate experience over time. Even if a particular developer or creator leaves the company, the reputation for quality is still accumulated and associated with that company. So we decided that the way to make great games was to assemble a great team, and create a company that would serve as a symbol of quality reflecting the team's achievements.

JS: In earlier interviews[6] you mentioned making Famicom software, and a colleague, Akatsuki Miyazaki, encouraged you to found Vanguard?

TS: Yes, that's true. Regarding Miyazaki-san, it's not Akatsuki, but rather Akira. The kanji itself reads Akatsuki, but his name is Akira Miyazaki.[7]

JS: Was there also a Satoru Miyazaki?[8]

TS: Ah, you're right! His name is *Satoru*, not Akira. I think it's the same person. Let me check one more time to be sure. *<uses phone>* It's the same, identical Miyazaki-san. There was only one involved. His name is difficult to pronounce correctly. His first name is written using the *akatsuki* (暁) character. As a first name, this character is typically read as "Akira", but his name uses the less common reading of "Satoru".[9] *<shows photo>* This is him.

JS: Mr Miyazaki is head of Bits Laboratory?

TS: Yes. He's still head of the company. I was starting to feel that I needed to form a company and I was discussing this with Miyazaki-san to get advice. And he told me, "Well then, do it!" He was the one who convinced me. I was consulting with him while in the process of forming Vanguard. Usually when you establish a company, you don't have any clients or work to do at first, but I was lucky because Miyazaki-san contracted out some work with me immediately, upon completion of founding the company. So the first year we already had work in progress. The first product that we worked on was *SD Gundam*,[10] followed by *Ai Cho Aniki*.[11]

JS: What were the FC games before Vanguard?

TS: I think that the name was *SD Gundam Gachapon Senshi 5: Battle of Universal Century*. I think that was the name of it! *<laughs>* That was the title for the final instalment of the *SD Gundam Gachapon* series on Famicom.[12]

JS: Bits Laboratory did adaptations of *Bokosuka Wars, Thexder, Darius*, and other games.[13]

TS: Yes, that's right. They've been around from the onset of the industry, and they were very well versed in programming. But unfortunately they spun off and turned into two different entities. But neither are working well. So they have downsized quite a bit. But they were an excellent developer back then, with high programming skills. But I cannot tell you more about what was being made! *<laughs>* We just helped them out a little, so I only know about the bits we actually worked on. *<laughs>*

JS: They were involved in many interesting titles.

TS: Yes, indeed! They're all conversions. Since they were highly adept with programming, they did an excellent job on the conversions.

---

[6] **www.gpara.com/contents/creator/bn_214.htm** (dead)
[7] Akira Miyazaki is not listed under either name on MobyGames, but Bits Laboratory's games are - notably the *Thexder* port to Famicom, several other conversions, and development of *Ai Chou Aniki* for PCE-CD. MobyGames state: "*Founded as an association of freelancing developers. In its earliest days it seems to have gone by the name Workss* [sic]." Not to be confused with UK dev BITS Entertainment, which also did outsourcing for Japanese companies
[8] Above games have a Satoru Miyazaki credited
[9] As a word, 暁 is pronounced akatsuki, meaning dawn, daybreak. When used as the Kanji character for a person's name, it's pronounced Akira or Aki, and in rare cases like this one, Satoru

[10] On Vanguard's website: *SD Gundam Gachapon Senshi 5: Battle of Universal Century* for FC (Dec 1992)
[11] Sequel to *Cho Aniki*, PCE-CD (1995). Wikipedia says dev. by Masaya and pub. by NCS, MobyGames says pub. by Masaya and dev. by Bits Laboratory
[12] The interpreter got confused and gave the wrong question. I specifically wanted to know the FC games before the formation of Vanguard, mentioned in the GPara interview, rather than the first by Vanguard
[13] *BW* and *T* were for FC; two *Darius* titles for PCE

JS: FC hardware made conversions difficult.

TS: Yes, exactly.

JS: Let's discuss *Ai Chou Aniki*. It involved Bits Laboratory, Vanguard, Masaya, and Nippon Computer Systems. It seems complicated.

TS: It is. NCS is the same Masaya.

JS: Masaya was the games division for NCS.

TS: Basically, NCS and Masaya are the exact same entity. They just released games under the name of Masaya whenever they launched a title. Regarding *Ai Chou Aniki*... Actually, when this offer came from NCS, we were just starting out our company, and the size of the business was very small. So we were able to be involved thanks to Bits Laboratory vouching for us, because they were an already established company. So Bits came to us, saying, "Why not work on this project together?" Bits took care of most of the project development, whereas Vanguard was responsible for the planning and the graphics of the project.

JS: NCS initiated the idea for a *Cho Aniki* sequel, then Bits and Vanguard made it together?[14]

TS: Yes, so the directing was done by Bits Laboratory. The programming was done by Bits Laboratory. Whereas Vanguard did the graphics and planning.

JS: Can you recall a graphics designer called Satoshi Nakai, who produced art for *Cho Aniki*?

TS: Actually I've never met Mr Nakai before. There was this first version, called *Chou Aniki*, which was followed by *Ai Chou Aniki*. But the instructions we were given was just to work on it as freely as we wanted, based upon the original version. We had the discretion to come up with a new version while working from general ideas supplied by NCS. Of course the editing and checks were done by the designers, which were sent off to NCS. I assume Mr Nakai did his work at NCS, but unfortunately I had no opportunity to meet him; I don't know for sure.

JS: Were you directly involved with the design?

TS: Do you mean involved with the graphics design, or game design?

JS: An excellent question![15] **Either. Were you hands on, or more in a managerial position?**

TS: Yes, we were basically cooperating on the planning portion of the project, whereas Bits Laboratory acted as the game director. Basically we were responsible for coming up with the plans for what kind of stages would be involved in the game, and how the game would proceed. How the levels would be expressed.

JS: Did you personally draw stage layouts?

TS: For the most part I was acting as the manager, or team leader, giving out instructions to the staff. Although I did draw some of the layouts and so on. There was a very cooperative team atmosphere within our group, because that was important for us, to come up with nice visuals, particularly for *Ai Chou Aniki*. The atmosphere of the game was very important, and it really turned out well. We tried to maintain that kind of cooperation in order to promote ideas coming from the entire staff. So we all encouraged each other to come up with great ideas, and if they were good we would go with it. If they were not so great, we would reconsider and come up with a better one.

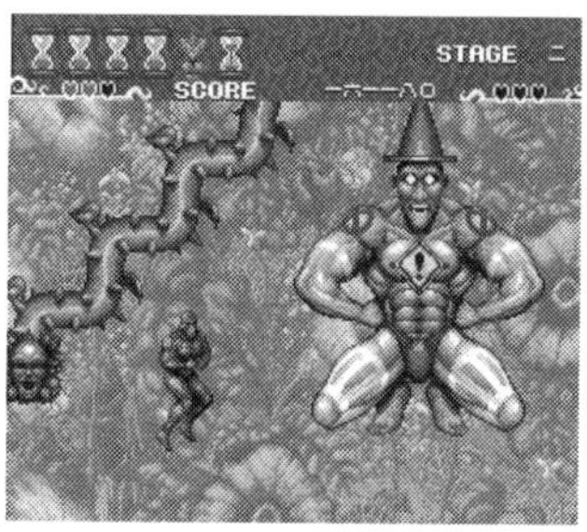

JS: *Ai Chou Aniki* has a unique control system: the position of your character is vertical, and the player enters different button combinations to attack. How did these ideas came about?

TS: I think it was during the planning meetings. We were brainstorming how to create a worthy successor and improve on the first game.

JS: Outside of Japan the series is mainly attributed to Masaya, but Vanguard left a lasting creative mark. How do you feel about it?

[14] What's interesting is that the *Cho Aniki* sequel took a different direction to the original; mechanically innovative and thematically much more bizarre

[15] In English a designer creates level layouts, whereas in Japan the designer creates pixel art; the person who devises the mechanics is usually called a *planner*

TS: Well, yes, I can say that *Cho Aniki* can boast excellent visuals, but I think that rather than making a major contribution, we had the honour of taking a small part in the development. I think the reason *Cho Aniki* is so long-lived is because of all the effort exerted by all the relevant parties, including Masaya, Bits Laboratory and us.[16]

JS: I want to document that Vanguard played a key role in the series' early formation.

TS: <*laughs*> Thank you very much.

JS: Vanguard's website mentions prototypes for the Sega Saturn. A video phone system,[17] and a network mall, for online shopping?[18]

TS: Ah, yes we did!

JS: With NTT?[19]

TS: Yes. Together with NTT and Victor.[20]

JS: This was never released?

TS: No. Well, accurately speaking it was commercialised. But it was short lived and the service was discontinued.

JS: Please tell me about these.

TS: Basically it's the same online shopping service that is provided by businesses such as Rakuten,[21] for example. So I think back then this was a very forward looking service. The biggest difference between Rakuten and this service was the marketing, or the sales abilities. Rakuten combines a huge number of affiliate shops, whereas our service lacked that. Since people from NTT and Victor were mostly system developers, they were not well versed with how to market or sell the service.

JS: Vanguard's website says 1994 for those two. Were you given prototypes for Saturn hardware?

TS: I don't think so. I think those projects came after the Saturn's release. On the other hand, that pattern [of developing on pre-release prototype hardware] was the case for *Lunar* maybe, and *Grandia*.

JS: Vanguard made a version of *Tetris*. Is that how you met Henk Rogers?

TS: Yes. <*goes to shelf to pick up Tetris for WonderSwan Color*> For this version of *Tetris* we worked together. <*points to Blue Lava Wireless leaflet on nearby shelf*> The Blue Lava Wireless [22] CEO is Henk Rogers. Mr Rogers' parents' business was jewels. That's why gem names were used for the names of his games: *Black Onyx*, *Fire Crystal*, and *Moonstone*.

JS: You first met when Vanguard made *Tetris*?

TS: Well, back then BPS' office was just around the corner, and Mr Rogers' wife, Akemi-san, was one of the managerial people at BPS. She may have been an executive, or company president, I forgot. But that is how I became acquainted with them. Since I knew Akemi-san, I eventually got to know Mr Rogers, and so I went to him saying we wanted to work on *Tetris* for WonderSwan.

JS: Why develop on WonderSwan, rather than other handheld devices? Was the Bandai licensing agreement easier than Nintendo's?

TS: You're right on, basically. That's exactly right. *Tetris* used to require a different license agreement for each platform. Nobody had made a WonderSwan version yet, so we approached them [Bandai] and asked, "Why not let us do it?" Since we had already worked on Bandai's *Gundam* for the WonderSwan platform, we already had a relationship with Bandai. So through our negotiations, or our network

---

[16] This sentence was rich with the flavour of Japanese humility - Mr Sugiyama's feeling is less "pride of authorship", and more a sense of privilege and honour in providing assistance

[17] セガ・サターンを用いたテレビ電話システムの試作開発 - *Prototype development of video phone system for use with Sega Saturn* (NTT)

[18] セガ・サターンを用いたネットワークモール（オンラインショップ）システムの試作開発 - *Prototype development of network mall (online shopping) system for use with Sega Saturn* (NTT / Victor)

[19] Nippon Telegraph and Telephone Corporation

[20] Victor Company of Japan, more commonly JVC; produced the laser drives for most Sega Saturns, and also a branded model of Saturn (segaretro.org)

[21] Rakuten is a huge Japanese online shopping portal similar to Amazon. Rakuten allows affiliates to sell their wares through the Rakuten site, so customers can transparently browse combined product listings from many small vendors on the same web page

[22] Blue Lava Wireless developed mobile phone games; sold by Henk Rogers in 2005

connection with Bandai, we went over to them saying we would also like to work on *Tetris*.[23]

JS: Vanguard also developed for Nintendo's GBA. Could you describe the differences between working with Bandai and Nintendo?

TS: It was simple. It was just up to Bandai's discretion which platform they wanted to use for their *Gundam* game. When Bandai opted for WonderSwan, we worked with WonderSwan. When they moved to Nintendo, then we got involved with the Game Boy Advance.

JS: So they took care of all the logistics?

TS: Well, to elaborate further, first there was the WonderSwan project, which was a type of game hardware by Bandai. But that did not sell well. So Bandai decided to discontinue the platform and instead entered into Nintendo's GBA. So that is why they asked us to continue working on it, and why we switched over from WonderSwan to GBA.

JS: When you develop for Nintendo, they charge a high percentage for each cartridge?

TS: That's correct.

JS: *Lunar* was partially developed by Vanguard. How did you come to work with Game Arts?

TS: The Miyazaki-san who I mentioned earlier, he was good friends with Miyaji-san, the then president of Game Arts. So it was Miyazaki-san who introduced me to Miyaji-san. So for the first *Lunar*,[24] which was for the Mega Drive in Japan, we started working on the debugging for that.

JS: You mean the Mega CD, right?

TS: The Mega CD. <*nods*> Our first job assigned by them [Game Arts] was the debugging for the first *Lunar*, and then they decided to come up with *Lunar 2*,[25] and for that we were responsible for just a tiny portion of the graphics and planning.

JS: Dungeon planning?

TS: Yes, that's right.

JS: You first said the Mega Drive, which used cartridges. The Mega CD was CD. Did *The Silver Star* start on cartridge, and then change to CD?

TS: The first *Lunar* came out on cartridge.

JS: It came out on CD. Did Game Arts start with cartridges and then upgrade to CD?

TS: Let me Google it. <*takes out smartphone*> Since I was just assisting for a short period of time, I was not involved for the entirety of development with the first *Lunar*. So I may be mistaken - that's why I want to recheck this.

JS: Maybe we've discovered and solved another mystery. Perhaps it changed formats?

TS: That may have been the case. They may have upgraded to the CD version midway through, meaning they may have started out intending it for cartridges.

JS: I heard Sega started *Phantasy Star IV* on the Mega CD, and then downgraded it to cartridge.

TS: Yes, that can happen. <*looks at phone*> Sorry, I made a mistake. Yes, it did come out on CD, not cartridge.

JS: During debugging, it was a CD version?

TS: Yes, that would be the case.

JS: When doing graphics and level design for *Lunar 2*, how did you provide the data to Game Arts? Floppy disks delivered in person?

TS: <*laughs*> Yes, I brought over the floppy disks. Once a week I would deliver the floppy disks to Game Arts, for their review. Once it was signed off I handed them all over.

JS: Floppy disks for NEC's PC-98 computer?

TS: Yes, that's right!

JS: Do you have any anecdotes? Were you shown the work Game Arts was producing, in order for Vanguard's to match stylistically?

[23] From the sound of it, the decision to work on the WonderSwan was not so much a consideration of the hardware, but rather because Vanguard had a good relationship with Bandai from the beginning
[24] *Lunar: The Silver Star*, Mega CD (Jun 1992)
[25] *Lunar: Eternal Blue*, Mega CD (Dec 1994)

TS: Yes, I was very impressed by the volume of work that [Game Arts and Vanguard] respectively produced. Yes, this was quite extraordinary, in that this was the first attempt to present animated cutscenes by reading data while it's being displayed on the screen. Of course it's nothing new nowadays, but back then *Lunar* was one of the first titles to implement animated cutscenes. So everybody was so ambitious and excited about working on this, they came up with too much content. More than could be recorded on the CD. <*laughs*> So they had to edit it, and drop some portions of the game.

Meanwhile, the Sega Saturn was already being planned. I remember there was a very heated debate, as to whether they were going to go ahead and launch Saturn, or not, and ultimately yes, it did come out in Japan.[26]

JS: What kind of content was cut?

TS: Oh, I don't know about that.

JS: Vanguard also worked on *Lunar: Silver Star Story* for the Saturn: game system design, dungeon design, battle design, and combat data.

TS: Yes, so since we had experience assisting on the original *Lunar 1* and *2*, [Game Arts] came to us saying please help us develop *Silver Star Story*. This was quite a memorable assignment, because when *Silver Star Story* came to us, to be worked on, [Game Arts] said that they were already almost ready for launch. But when we actually went over to them, nothing was under progress. So since I had no plans on that particular day, they kept me there at their office, and they asked me to help them out - on the spot! I ended up working there for a month without going back [to Vanguard]. I was retained by them.

JS: By Game Arts?

TS: Of course this was a request by Game Arts, but the main developer for this project was Japan Art Media. Or JAM as an abbreviation. So I just went there for a visit as an observer, but they kept me for a month.

JS: When working on *Lunar 2* for the Saturn, did you have direct contact with Game Arts?

TS: Of course, yes. We did our best when we were brought on board at the last minute for *Silver Star Story*, and the way we helped wrap everything up was highly evaluated. So when they decided to release *Lunar 2*, Vanguard took the main role in the development. So therefore Vanguard was assigned to work on *Lunar 2* for the Saturn.

JS: When Vanguard was given the *Eternal Blue* project for the Saturn, did you have the freedom to make changes?

TS: Well, basically we started out from scratch. It was practically a brand new title. Of course the main story was basically the same, but all of the details were updated.

JS: In the Mega CD version of *Lunar 2* there was a boss with many names (Phantom Sentry, Star Sentry, Star Dragon, Zeke the Risen). Do you know why it was removed in the update?

TS: I don't know.

JS: Of the four discussed *Lunar* games, which did Vanguard influence the most?

TS: Of course the last one. The Saturn version of *Lunar 2*.

JS: Do you have any anecdotes to share?

TS: Hmm, let me think... Well, one thing I can say is that the animation is brilliant. Yes, the animation was very attractive, and we were really particular on the animation during the development of *Lunar 2*. For the animated scenes, the lead character designer was called Toshiyuki Kubooka,[27] and he always did a great job in managing all the staff to come up with excellent animation and characters. The movie *Berserk*[28] came out recently, and he was actually the director of that movie.

---

26 Mr Sugiyama is referring to the Sega Saturn hardware, rather than a Saturn version of *Lunar.* The hardware launched 22 Nov 1994 in Japan. *Lunar: Eternal Blue* for SCD launched 22 Dec 1994 in Japan

27 窪岡俊之; illustrator, other notable works include the *Giant Robo* anime

28 *Berserk: Golden Age Arc III: The Descent*, Feb 2013

JS: You worked on the PlayStation adaptation?

TS: That's correct.

JS: Do you know a company called Working Designs translated that into English, for America?

TS: Yes, I knew that. Working Designs was really in love with *Lunar*, and they would go out of their way to do whatever they could, to help the *Lunar* games out. So I have good stories to tell. But at the same time, bad stories to tell too.

JS: Could you share these?

TS: The good story is that they were very passionate and showed a genuine love of the *Lunar* games. And I have two bad stories to tell, actually. *<laughs>* So the [English] staff assigned to the *Lunar* project were so much in love, that they tended to leak information - they would talk about *Lunar* on the fansites. So the president of Working Designs called us up, saying, "I found this information on the fansites, did you leak it?" And we were flabbergasted! Because we didn't know what he was talking about.[29] So that was one incident. Another story is that [***21 words REDACTED***].

JS: Victor Ireland was head of Working Designs... He was passionate about his work.

TS: Yes, he was the one [***REDACTED***]! The president of Game Arts, Miyaji-san, was infuriated about that.

JS: I had no idea. Victor Ireland is legendary among English fans of Japanese games.

TS: *<laughs>* Well, I would like to hear what you know about Victor.

JS: Victor often interacts with consumers. One story I heard was when WD sent review copies for *Alundra*, it contained a line of dialogue that reviewers phoned him asking about. Victor was pleased they played to the end of the game, but SCEA made WD remove it before production.[30]

TS: *<laughs>* Yes, I believe he would have to do that. If you get into a fight with the Japanese contents holder, it would be difficult for you to release good, valuable titles, so staying in business becomes more and more difficult.

JS: I know Vic had a lot of difficulties with Sony and the PlayStation 2, because they would not allow him to release *Goemon*. Which seemed to be the end of Working Designs.

TS: Could be.

JS: Do you know Studio Alex and its founder Kazunari Tomi?[31] He used to work for Falcom.

TS They were making a spinoff to the *Lunar* series called *Mahou Gakuen LUNAR!*,[32] but there was some trouble, and a different production studio took over. I don't think Tomi-san made any more games after that.

JS: Can you describe Vanguard's involvement with *Grandia*? I was surprised to discover Vanguard did the dungeon designs.

TS: Oh yes, yes. We really put our efforts into *Grandia*, and I think it was a very interesting title. What I remember most about this game is that the users are viewing the game world from above at an angle, looking down, and there's a

---

[29] The leaker was one or more persons working on the *Lunar* localisation, who shared confidential information without the consent of Vanguard or Victor Ireland

[30] Taken from a thread on NeoGAF, where user *Vireland* posted screenshots. The puzzle involved standing on character Meia's head, after which she says: *"You're lucky I give good head, loverboy! Most girls would ask that you cough up a ring first!"*

[31] Wikipedia says Studio Alex developed three *Lunar* titles with Game Arts as co-developer. In 2003 filed lawsuit against Game Arts over secondary creator copyrights to *The Silver Star*. Was sued over *Magic School Lunar* animation and bankrupted **(no sources!)**

[32] A side-story. Originally *Sanpo-suru Gakuen* for Game Gear; updated as *Mahou Gakuen LUNAR!* on Saturn

turn command, and if you use the command you can rotate the world significantly. So by taking advantage of [the camera angle], we were able to hide things like treasure chests. And I remember, very well, having a heated discussion, or debate, with the person in charge of *Grandia*[33] - he was saying this would be too difficult for the users to follow along with, whereas I counter argued, telling him that it would have to be this complicated or else it would not be fun.

JS: Was Vanguard involved with the mechanics of the battle system?

TS: No, we were not involved with the battle system in *Grandia*.

JS: What was the reason for Game Arts bringing Vanguard on board? Was it due to the workload?

TS: I think one of the reasons why they invited us was because they recognised us to be a growing company - they recognized and appreciated our accomplishments, such as *Lunar* and so on. And another reason is what you mentioned, there was a lot of work to be done physically on *Grandia*. I believe those two are the main reasons why Game Arts called us in.

JS: Did Vanguard do all the dungeons in *Grandia*?

TS: No, that would not be possible. Just several percent of the dungeons.

JS: Vanguard recently developed *Eiyuu Densetsu Yume no Kiseki*,[34] do you have a close relationship with Falcom?

TS: I've known Kato-san[35] the chairman of Falcom for a few years now. Actually, yes, when I mentioned around the office that I know Kato-san the chairman of Falcom, one of the Vanguard employees who is a big fan of the *Eiyuu Densetsu* series, specifically the *Kiseki* series,[36] came to me saying, "Let's work on it!" *<laughs>* That particular employee was a director, so I asked him to come up with a proposal, and once he had completed it I accompanied him to visit Falcom, to give an impassioned speech to the person in charge there. *<laughs>* We ended up talking with them for four hours, on all sorts of topics, but mainly on how much we love *Eiyuu Densetsu*. So since they saw who we were, and they trusted us, they said, "OK, you go ahead and work on it." So that is how we got permission to go ahead. This was released only two or three months ago for Japanese smartphones.

JS: Unfortunately, so many smartphone games never leave Japan.

TS: Well, this is basically a card battle game, though we use the characters from the *Kiseki* series. So maybe the fans who are really into RPG games might find it not to be what they expected. It would be great if we could release this title overseas. But it seems like they would not like it unless it's available as an Apple iOS application. Whereas this one is a "web type" application.[37] So for the foreseeable future we don't see any opportunities for releasing it.

JS: There seems to be a division between America and Europe, and then Japan, in terms of mobile content and the preferred format.

TS: Yes, you're exactly right.

JS: Takeshi Miyaji of Game Arts passed away. Would you like to say anything?

TS: Yoichi-san was the older one, and Takeshi-san was younger brother. I was meeting quite frequently with the older brother, Yoichi-san. I did not get to meet Takeshi-san so often. But I remember very well that Takeshi-san was always saying that *games are love*. I think he meant it in various ways. I don't remember his remarks accurately, so most of it is my assumption. But I think he meant it to mean that if you pour your heart into creating games that you love, the customers will recognize that and love them too. In that sense, I think he genuinely loved making games, and I think he always had customers and users in mind when creating games.

JS: Vanguard has been involved with *Chou Aniki, Lunar, Grandia, Trauma Centre, Gundam, Legend of Heroes,* many games which have a long lineage. What is the future for Vanguard?

---

[33] This person was never named, it could be any number of people

[34] 英雄伝説:夢の軌跡, smartphones, Jul 2013

[35] Masayuki Kato, founder, March 1981

[36] Specifically the *Trails in the Sky* sub-series, which started with *Legend of Heroes VI* in 2004

[37] Presumably a browser game made for smartphones

TS: We're mainly focusing on smartphones for the future. Up until now there had been huge restrictions on us, that we could only deliver content to our domestic users. But with the advent of smartphones, now we can actually contact and approach our customers or users globally, in order to deliver our products. Which is a brilliant thing. I think this is a wonderful situation for us. Up until now we had to involve platform holders, distributors, and localisation people, in order for us to be able to deliver our contents to our overseas game users. But thanks to companies like Google and Apple, some things have been simplified significantly, and now we actually deliver games to our global users directly. Which is fantastic.

JS: In your personal history, what was the title you're proudest of being involved in?

TS: Most proud of?

JS: That you have the warmest feelings of.

TS: I would say the number one is *GNO*.[38] This was directed by Mr Isokawa. This was Vanguard's first online game. And since online games obviously are quite different from regular videogames or console games, we had a lot of difficulties that we had to overcome, in order to release this. So the good part about online or network games is that we can obtain user's comments directly from them, over the internet. Right now *GNO2* and *GNO3* are also active, and this game has already been played for more than 10 years online. Which is great. We were really proud of being able to come up with a game of such longevity.

JS: That's excellent.

TS: If I were to mention one more... I would say it would be *Lunar*! We had a lot of headaches to overcome, and we had a lot of problems that we needed to address. <*laughs*> We really struggled along the way, but at the end of the day, I think we came up with a brilliant game. So it's very difficult for me to choose one over the other. *Lunar* or *Gundam*. I would say both!

JS: Can you recall any unreleased games from over the years?

[38] *Gundam Network Operation*, an online series based on the famous mecha brand

TS: Yes, there are some, but almost none.

JS: Any you worked on for Game Arts?

TS: No, none for Game Arts. There was one with Bandai. <*signs book*> Thank you very much!

JS: It's been an honour. Is there anything else you'd like to mention?

TS: I think we covered just about everything.

JS: We didn't talk about Vanguard's range of table-talk RPGs![39]

TS: Ah! Yes, we were working on table-talk, and I think Isokawa-san can talk about that! <*laughs*> Well actually, I came to know Isokawa-san through a club activity during college, a circle activity. The name of the circle, or club, was Keio HQ. So this circle was mainly to play board games, or table-talk RPGs. Don't forget to mention it to him, about Keio HQ later!

[39] "Table-talk" is the Japanese term for pen & paper or tabletop RPGs. According to its website Vanguard produced three in 1994, all related to the *Bell Foul Magic School* series

~Appearing in a later volume~

Hidenori Shibao

Continuing our coverage of Enix and the world of Japanese RPGs, Mr Shibao discusses his two *Lennus* projects, the first of which is known as *Paladin's Quest* outside of Japan. In addition, he was a scenario writer on the PlayStation 2 FMV horror game, *The Fear*. Mr Shibao also provides a fascinating insight into the world of Japanese games journalism, strategy guides, and creating a high quality *sekaikan* in games.

Henk Rogers

Following on from what Mr Sugiyama said in his interview, a later volume will feature an in-depth interview with Henk Rogers, formerly of Bullet Proof Software. One of Japan's earliest RPGs was *The Black Onyx* by BPS, which influenced a generation. Mr Rogers also reveals something never said before, on the difficulties of bringing it to market.

磯川 豊

ISOKAWA, Yutaka

DOB: 1969 / Birthplace: Kawasaki City, Kanagawa Prefecture / Blood Type: B

~ Selected Portfolio ~

PITMAN	- MZ-700, 1985	(Sole programmer, *Oh!MZ* type-in)
PITMAN+	- MZ-700, 1985	(Sole programmer, *Oh!MZ* type-in)
Catrap	- Game Boy, 1990	
Puzzle Dai Meikyuu (パズル大迷宮)	- Sharp Electronic Notebook, 1990	**- PICTURED BELOW**
Reichsritter	- PC-98/X68000, 1990	
Gunyuu Sangokushi (群雄三国志)	- PC-98, 1991	
Yu Yu Hakusho (幽遊白書)	- Super Famicom, 1993	
Yu Yu Hakusho - Tokubetsu Hen (特別篇)	- Super Famicom, 1994	
NeGcon controller	- 1995, part of the design team	
J-League Soccer Primegoal EX	- Arcade / PlayStation, 1995	
Lunar 2: Eternal Blue	- Saturn/PlayStation, 1998/1999	
Kidou Senshi Gundam: Giren no Yabou Kouryaku Shirei-sho	- Sat, 1999	
Tetris	- WonderSwan Color, 2002	
Gundam Network Operation	- Windows, 2002	
Gundam Network Operation 2	- Windows, 2004	
PITMANIA	- i-mode, 2005	
GNOi	- i-mode, 2005	
Pro Soccer Club Wo Tsukurou! ONLINE	- Windows, 2007	

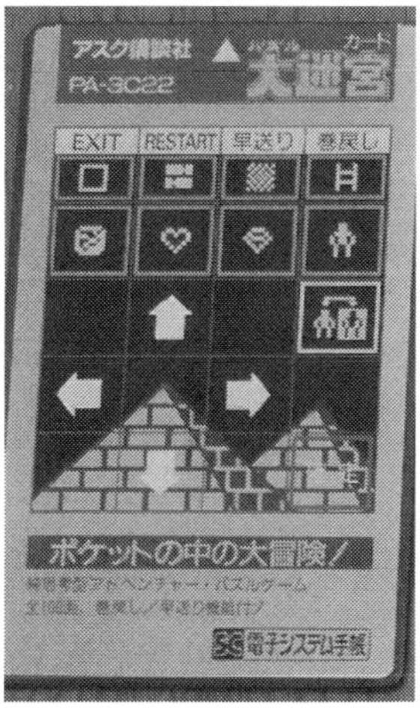

Interview with Yutaka Isokawa
30 September 2013, Tokyo

After interviewing Mr Sugiyama, in the Vanguard offices, I walked to Mr Isokawa's home, which was nearby, and enjoyed a meal while conducting the interview. Mrs Isokawa started at 09:00am that morning preparing food, using the finest ingredients from around Japan. We drank a little sake and I presented Mr Isokawa with a gift: the magazine containing his original source code for the first Pitman game; he'd lost his original copy. The supplementary DVD contains a lot of footage from this interview, since Mr Isokawa took apart Namco's NeGcon controller and explained the inner workings, in addition to describing an unreleased game the company was working on.

[At train station, where we met]

YI: I saw your itinerary and all the dates are booked with so many scheduled interviews. <*laughs*> But on the other hand, it's good that you have so many interview appointments.

JS: I'm looking forward to discussing Vanguard with Mr Sugiyama, because I believe you worked on some prototype Sega Saturn devices.

YI: Yes, we also produced RPG games such as *Lunar* for the Sega Saturn, and some of the games do not even appear on the company's list.

JS: We can discuss programming techniques, from the 1980s.

YI: <*laughs*> Yes! I'm looking forward to that.

[Later, at Mr Isokawa's home]

<Mr and Mrs Isokawa give me gifts of music CDs and material with Japanese artwork on it>

JS: Thank you for these wonderful items.

Mrs Isokawa: This music is from one of my friends. She's a musician and plays the Irish accordion. This is her CD.[1] She's been involved with sound production for games in the past. This is music on sakura cherry blossoms. It's a memoir for you, that you've been in Japan, and since sakura is the national flower.

JS: Thank you very much.

Mrs Isokawa: This material has an *ukiyo-e* picture of a cat, depicted by a famous artist called Kuniyoshi-san. This was the archetype of what became Japanese manga. So I thought this would be a good memory for you to keep. Please use it as a towel, or however you need, while on your travels.

JS: Oh, it's too special to use simply as a towel!

<everyone laughs>

[...]

JS: Your first game was *PITMAN* for the MZ-700 computer system?[2]

YI: Yes, that's right.

JS: A colleague of mine in Germany, Samuel, and myself, have had a strong interest in *PITMAN* and its history. I wrote a feature on it.

YI: The article you uploaded to the Hardcore Gaming 101 website?

JS: Yes, that's the one.[3]

YI: I've read that.

JS: We compared all the different versions.

YI: I learned that my program was translated and published in France[4] - I found out about that for the first time when I read your website. Well, I couldn't understand all of it, I just got a brief picture of what was written. <*laughs*>

JS: If you have any questions, let me know.

---

[1] The music has a Ghibli Studios feel to it

[2] Programmed in HuBASIC; published in *Oh!MZ* magazine Aug 1985; source-code labelled 1985.3

[3] **hardcoregaming101.net/catrap/catrap.htm**

[4] Sylvain Bizoirre, president (1982-1986) of the French Sharp User Club, the Sharpentiers, and editor of the club's magazine *La Revue des Sharpentiers*, converted the Japanese original to S.BASIC, publishing it in issue #15 (Nov 1985)

YI: *<laughs>* That's OK. Perhaps I should explain from before *PITMAN* came about?

JS: Definitely. I like to know who makes the games I play, and discovering interesting stories. So when I heard you lost your original copy of the magazine with your first program...

<At this point I take out the copy of Oh!MZ which Samuel had given me>

YI: *<laughs>* Why do you have that?!

Mrs Isokawa: Oh! Why in the world do you have that?

JS: To return it to its owner.

YI: *<laughs>* Are you serious?

JS: When researching *PITMAN*, we wanted to see the original. So we had a friend in Japan buy it on *Yahoo! Auctions* and send it to us in Europe. Now I've brought it back to Japan. This is a gift from myself and my colleague Samuel.

YI: *<laughs>* Seriously? That's amazing! Thank you very much!

JS: *Douitashimashite! (You're welcome!)*

YI: This was the only one that I was missing! Thank you so much! I am so surprised! *<laughs>* Wow! Can I open it?

JS: Yes, please.

<everyone laughs>

YI: I really did not have the original anymore. As a result, I did not have the source code when there was a discussion about converting it to Japanese mobile phones. So I had to go all the way to the Diet Library to make photocopies of these pages.

Mrs Isokawa: Wow, that looks great! *<laughs>* Our daughter was asking us, do you really not have it? We had to answer no, we do not.

JS: You mentioned this was the only one you lacked. Did other magazines have your games?

YI: Well, there was *PITMAN+*, an extended version of the original which was released afterwards. Let me see if I have the photocopies... *<searches in box of items>* It may not be here...

JS: Did you also make *PITGAL*, listed in the November 1985 issue of *Oh!MZ* magazine?[5]

YI: No, I did not. *<searches elsewhere>* *PITMAN+* is not in here either... After this [original] was published, another article was published which extended and updated the rules for the game. *<looking through items>* Oh, here it is, *PITMAN+*. This version incorporated a few different elements, such as gold nuggets which do not fall downward. This updated version was the underlying basis for the Game Boy version of *Pitman*.

JS: In the Nov 1985 issue of *Oh!MZ* there was *PITGAL*. It seems someone copied your game. Do you know anything about it?

YI: Well, yes, there is a reference to *PITGAL* here, in this particular article. I think it came out in this same issue, with *PITMAN+*. But I was not the developer of it. And also, somebody else was responsible for converting the original *PITMAN* to the MZ-2000.

JS: What was the first videogame you saw?

YI: Well, the very, very first game that I saw was a table tennis game. Like *Pong*, with a paddle on each side. If you're talking about the real videogame stuff, then my first exposure to that kind of game was *Space Invaders*.

JS: Around 1978?

YI: That's right, 1978. That was when I was 9 or 10 years old? Because I was born in 1969.

JS: So you were about 16 when you made the first *PITMAN*?

YI: Yes!

JS: Tell me about the years leading up to 1985.

[5] While unable to source a copy of *PITGAL*, it seems to be a derivative work featuring a female character

YI: I have to begin by telling you that the first time I had free access to a computer, was when I was 14 years old. Or when I was in eighth grade of middle school. So that is when I started programming, and I developed a couple of programs using that computer.

JS: Which computer model?

YI: It was the same computer used for *PITMAN*, an MZ-700. I'm sure you know, but my friend used to own an Apple IIc computer. Well, his Apple had much better graphics than mine, of course! *<laughs>* So most of my middle school days were spent visiting his home to play games on his computer. One of the games was called *Lode Runner*. I really liked *Lode Runner*, very much, and I thought that I'd like to come up with a similar game myself. But my computer, the MZ-700, only allowed a text [ASCII] display, so trying to reproduce *Lode Runner* on it was very difficult. So it took me quite a long time to come up with a game - I came up with one that would only display the panel portion of *Lode Runner*. Although it took a while I was successful. *<laughs>* I attempted to recreate just the puzzle aspect of *Lode Runner*, and eventually succeeded. I spent a lot of time working on that! *<laughs>* My computer back then was so slow! On top of that, since I tended to spend every waking moment in front of the computer, my parents told me I could only use the computer on Sundays! *<laughs>*

[In English] Sunday only!

<laughs - reverts to Japanese> So what I did was, I would write out the programs on a piece of paper on weekdays, and then I would type them into the computer and try to run it on Sunday! *<laughs>* I believe it took me about a year and a half to complete this game. So this is how I came to create *PITMAN*.

JS: The magazine paid for every program they printed, correct?

YI: Yes, back then, whenever you contributed an article to these kinds of magazines, the author would be paid 10'000 yen per page.[6]

JS: That's good money! I'm a freelance writer and right now the average rate is 10'000 yen per page. In 1985 that was worth more.

YI: Indeed.

JS: Is it true you added a lot of comments to the code, to make it appear longer?

YI: *<intense laughter>* That's true! Yes, I think I was able to add another page or so! How did you find out about that?!

<everyone laughs>

JS: I think I saw it on your website.

YI: *<laughs>* Well, it was me! Yes, it is true.

JS: I think it's an ingenious idea.

YI: The way it worked back then, and *PITMAN* was no exception, if you contributed a program to a magazine, anybody could take your code and port it to a different type of computer without asking permission. It was not illegal or anything like that. So that's why I do not remember much about *PITGAL*.

JS: Did you create any other games before *PITMAN*? Perhaps small ones?

YI: Yes, I did. I created a game, much shorter than this one, with less code, and I sent it off to a publication called *Maicon BASIC Magazine*, which was quite famous among computer users. But it never made it to print.

JS: *PITMAN* was in HuBASIC?

YI: There were two types... *<leafs through magazine>* Yes, it was HuBASIC.

JS: *PITMAN* arrived in France because the head of an MZ fan club would receive this magazine, and convert some programs to S.BASIC.

YI: Well, not until yesterday, when I read your article about the conversion, did I even know about this! *<laughs>*

JS: Sylvain Bizoirre was president of the French Sharp User's Club. *<explains background>*[7]

YI: Thank you for researching all that. Amazing.

JS: We're a bit obsessed - we're *PITMANIACS!*

---

[6] At today's rates, about £65 / $100; in 1985, around £33 / $39 (source: fxtop)

[7] **hardcoregaming101.net/history/history4.htm**

<everyone laughs>

YI: Please send my regards to Samuel.

JS: What happened after *PITMAN+*?

YI: Other than the fee for my article, nothing happened after that. I was paid the fee and that was it. I remember having purchased some English study materials, by using part of my pay, which was 70'000 yen altogether. But regardless, my English ability is only about this level. *<laughs>* I was informed that *PITMAN* was going to be ported to the Game Boy while I was at university. But until then I had no idea that all these people were taking an interest in my program.

JS: There's five years between then. What did you study at university?

YI: This was when I was in 12th grade in high school, and then the following year I had to study for the entrance exam for college. The following year I went to college, and as Sugiyama-san explained to you earlier, while I was attending college I joined a board game circle called HQ.[8] In our circle, we also played computer games, as well as board games. I can't remember exactly, but I think that around this time while I was working on *PITMAN* [for GB], I also started making computer games for Enix.

JS: Was this *Reichsritter*?[9]

YI: It's German. Maybe Sugiyama-san explained this earlier, but Enix used to hold competitions. Well, Enix is now called Square-Enix. But just like magazine competitions, Enix would solicit submissions from prospective applicants, and for those who were awarded prizes, their creations would be commercialised.

JS: With a little photo on the back of the box.

YI: Yes, that may have been the case. So by holding contests and selecting winners, Enix would discover new talent. Enix would then approach the contest winners and ask them if they wanted to keep making games for the company. Then that person would be able to assemble their own project team to create a new game, and if successfully developed, Enix would publish it. Sugiyama-san approached a couple of members from our circle, from college, asking whether we'd be interested in joining his project.

JS: What did you study?

YI: Mechanical engineering.

JS: *<holds NeGcon>* Oh, which must have been useful for this...?

YI: *<laughs>* Well, it didn't really help much for that project. I was actually studying computer graphics, although I belonged to the mechanical engineering department! Because nobody else understood computer graphics.

JS: Pixel art?

YI: No, not pixel art. It's kind of difficult to explain. I don't know how much detail I should go into, but basically it was simulations on a computer. It dealt with electrical and heat conductivity. Inside water there are very fine particles. If you heat them up they start circulating. You find out by applying a magnetic force to see what happens to those particles in the water. Once you collect all the data, it would be summarised into a nice looking computer graphics display. I was in charge of the computer graphics portion of that analysis. *<laughs>*

JS: Sounds complicated.

YI: *<laughs>* Indeed! I got a bit sidetracked.

JS: *Puzzle Daimeikyuu* (*Puzzle Labyrinth*) is listed on your website, did you develop this?[10]

YI: Well, the original idea for *PITMAN* came from myself. But the person who actually designed and developed this game to become a product for the Game Boy and Sharp systems, was Michitaka Tsuruta. ASK-Kodansha, one of the famous publishers in Japan, came to me saying that they wanted to port *PITMAN*. So from that request I loaded up and played the original again.

[8] In Japanese a "circle" (サークル) is a recreational club focused on a particular activity. Circles are particularly popular on college campuses, but they can exist anywhere. *Doujin* groups are also referred to as circles

[9] Strategy game with medieval European setting

[10] Sharp's *Denshi System Techou* (電子システム手帳), basically an electronic organiser which used interchangeable cards and could play games. According to Mr Isokawa 5'000 units shipped

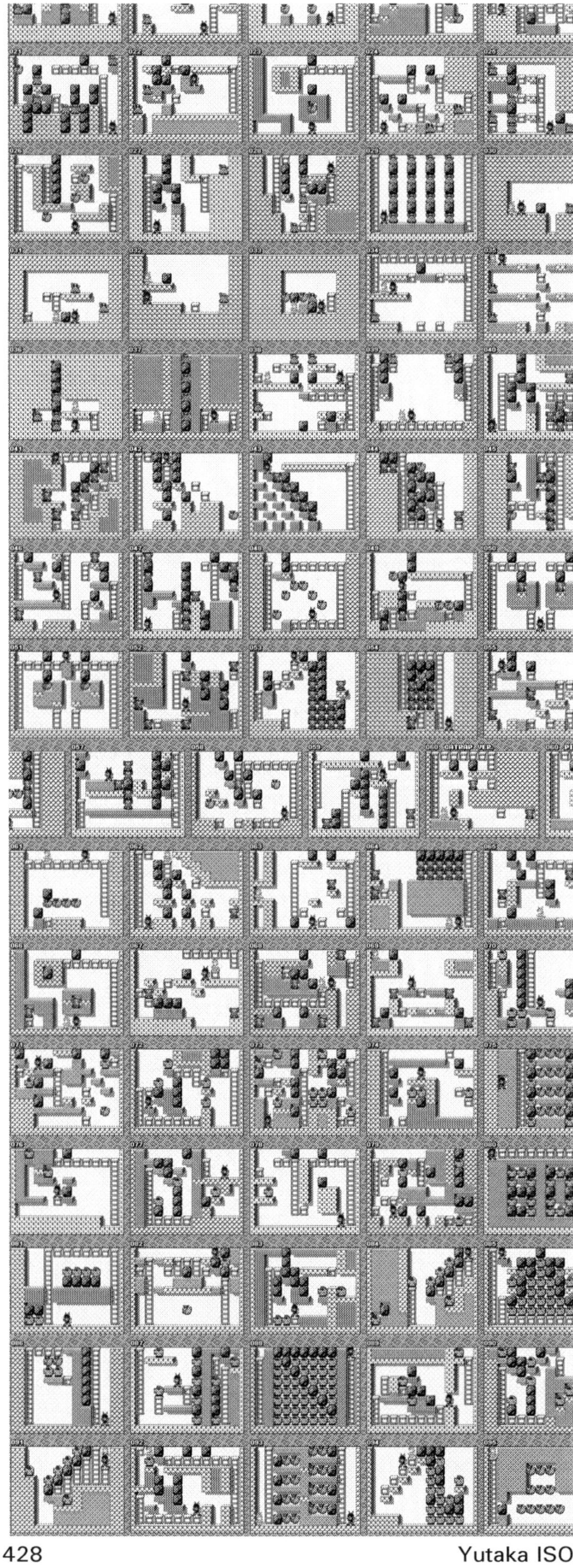

YI: The original version only allowed one character to be manipulated on the screen, but when I received that request I went back and came up with a new idea involving two characters being controlled within the same screen. So I programmed a new version of the game and brought that idea to the publisher. So back then, the games would only be displayed on computers or television screens, so I recorded my computer screen showing the new version, *<laughs>* and brought the video tape to the publisher, and suggested, why not do this?

JS: Do you still have this video?

YI: Ah, no, I'm sorry I do not! So basically they bought the idea. Coincidentally, they had already created two characters, Pitboy and Pitgirl, that they were planning to use. So they incorporated my new idea, enabling the player to alternately switch between these two characters on screen.

JS: This was for the Game Boy. Which developer did you deal with?

YI: ASK-Kodansha. I think their current company is just ASK.[11]

JS: *<showing print out of every Catrap level>* Someone nicknamed MP83 made this.

YI: That's amazing! *<counts the levels>* One hundred and one?

JS: There's only a hundred levels, [12] but interestingly, level 60 is different between the Japanese and American versions.[13]

YI: Oh, really? I did not know that! It's difficult for me now, when I play *PITMAN*. It's always, "Oh, oh no!" *<gestures in frustration>* Some levels I edited randomly, and then I would play it myself to see if it could be cleared. So some were not designed, they were really random.

---

[11] Acc. to MobyGames ASK-Kodansha was a subsidiary of Kodansha, founded in 1981, and in 1998 became independent of Kodansha, named ASK. Co. Ltd. The companies ASK, Sumitomo, and Kodansha founded Asmik. The Japanese GB and Sharp releases have ASK-Kodansha on the box, while the American GB release has Asmik. There are few reliable sources. Note: Wikipedia incorrectly references an unrelated Californian software company called ASK Group

[12] Actually there's 103; bonus 3 are only via password

[13] US version's level seems easier than the Japanese

JS: Wow, randomly made!

YI: Like this one.[14] So the first time I played it, I did not know if it was possible or impossible.

JS: That's incredible. I think one of these levels is based on the MZ computer?

YI: Ah, yes, yes! Which one...

JS: It's round 77.[15] Why did the GB version make the characters into cat people?

YI: *<laughs>* Well, that was designed by Michitaka Tsuruta-san, I was not involved with the character design.

JS: Looking back on it, how do you feel about this decision? All the modern releases of *PITMAN* have reverted to the stick-man design.

YI: *<laughs>* Yes, you're right. I personally very much like Tsuruta-san's idea of updating it into cat people. [As for it reverting to stick people for phone releases], there were two reasons for that. One was that it was very difficult to reproduce the image of the cat people, because the pixels used on mobile phones are very small, so it would blur the image. The second reason was they wanted to differentiate themselves from other games, and add a retro or classic feel to it.

Mrs Isokawa: Would you prefer beer, or sake?

JS: Sake sounds very good.

<everyone laughs>

Mrs Isokawa: The bacon in this dish was the same variety served at the G8 summit, and comes from Hokkaido. Would you like some?

JS: Thank you very much.

Mrs Isokawa: If there's anything you cannot eat, please just leave it.

JS: It looks lovely. *Itadakimasu!*

<everyone says kanpai together - we enjoy the gourmet meal>

JS: A little sake means the best answers will come out. In about an hour, I'll ask for all the company secrets.

YI: *<laughs>* We bought these plates at the Ghibli Museum. If our apartment was a little more spacious, I would have asked you to stay with us this evening.

JS: Thank you very much. Though tomorrow morning I'm catching the early train to Kobe.

[...]

JS: For *Reichsritter*, what programming language did you use?

YI: C language.

JS: When did you first learn C?

YI: I just studied it on my own, during college.

JS: Describe to me how you became programmer on *Reichsritter*.

YI: Sugiyama-san was the designer. He was looking for programmers, so he called in three people, including myself, to create this game. But since we were newcomers, we had a lot of difficulties moving forward. Back then the development environment was not so friendly for those who wanted to work on computer games. So we had to start out by creating the tools to use the computer. So it took us a lot of time.

JS: It's an RPG?

YI: That's right. It's a combination of an RPG and a strategy game, so it was similar to something like *Fire Emblem*.

JS: Were you fans of *Fire Emblem*?

YI: *<laughs>* I wasn't particularly a fan. But both Sugiyama-san and myself were thinking that we wanted to come up with something gigantic, an RPG or a strategy game, on our own. So that is why we went ahead and challenged ourselves with it.

JS: There were other programmers?

YI: There was the main programmer, the sub-programmer, and myself.

---

[14] I never made a note of the level he pointed to, but I *think* it was maybe level 88

[15] The breakable floor is an enormous M, while the permanent bricks are a tiny Z

JS: To go from *PITMAN* in BASIC, to this in C, sounds like a big jump to make.

YI: Yes, so back then, depending on the hardware, they had different specifications for the BASIC language. So it was very difficult to port from one hardware to another. But it was being rumoured that C language, on the other hand, would enable you to create cross-platform programs. The reality didn't quite live up to that promise, <*laughs*> but we really felt that C was the future.

JS: Did you ever use assembly language?

YI: Yes, I did. We used assembly language partially for coming up with this game as well.

JS: Then after *Reichsritter*, you worked on *Gunyuu Sangokushi*?[16]

YI: Do you know *Sangokushi*? It's part of ancient Chinese history. It's a popular theme in Japan.

JS: It's not related to *Reichsritter*?

YI: No, they're unrelated, totally different. For this game I was in charge of the game design, and I also did the programming myself.

JS: Do you have any interesting stories regarding the game design?

YI: There were a lot of challenges. There was this game called *Dungeon Master*,[17] I don't know if you know it. Basically you were able to freely manipulate objects in front of you on the game screen. We were very influenced by that particular game. And usually with strategy games, you have military units represented by numbers, but we decided to make it more like a board game, and allow the player to pick up these units, move them around, and place them on the field. Another game called *Sangokushi* had been released, by another company called Koei, which is a very popular series in Japan. Since I belonged to the game circle where we used to play strategy games quite often, I was really interested in and liked them a lot. But from a board game player's perspective, it [Koei's *Sangokushi*] was rather uninteresting, because everything is simply expressed as numbers. So we decided to replace the numbers with objects instead, to make it more interesting.

JS: After *Gunyuu Sangokushi* Mr Sugiyama left Enix to found Vanguard. You went to Namco?

YI: That's correct.

JS: There seems to be a gap from 1991 until 1993 in your portfolio. What happened in 1992?

YI: There was another game we were going to work on at Enix, in 1992, but it did not come to fruition. That year I had to graduate from college, and then I had to get a job, so the game project fell through along the way. The way Enix's computer game development projects worked, was that only after the game started selling, would the creators, or authors, start receiving royalties. But other than that, we were paid nothing. So it was very difficult for me to continue working on it after I had graduated from college. Of course Enix released *Dragon Quest* during the same time frame, but they had formed a different project team for that.

JS: You worked on two RPG/simulations while studying. How did you find the time?

YI: Well, instead of spending only four years at college, it took me six years to graduate! <*laughs*>

JS: I see!

YI: <*intense laughter*> My studies at college were my side-business.

JS: This unreleased game at Enix. Can you tell me about it, or any other unreleased games?

YI: My games? I do not know about projects started by others that later went down the drain. But with respect to my own ideas, yes, I drafted some design plans for potential games, but I had difficulties collecting enough staff so that I could actually realise the plan. So that is why the projects fell through. Hmm... <*laughs*> I'm not sure what else I could say about them!

JS: What was the name of the Enix game?

[16] Loosely: *Rival Warlords of the Three Kingdoms*; it deals with a similar theme to Koei's *Romance of the Three Kingdoms* series

[17] First-person dungeon crawler, 1987

YI: I don't even remember. We didn't come up with the name when the project is initiated. But I remember trying to come up with an RPG.

JS: Can you recall anything else about it?

YI: Well, since it did not become a product, I don't remember too well. <*laughs*> I apologise.

JS: Mr Sugiyama mentioned games at Vanguard that were not released. Including one for Bandai. Were you involved?

YI: Yes, I was involved with most of the games produced by Vanguard. So, yes, I was involved. There were some for Bandai, and there were projects for others too, of course.

JS: Describe joining Namco.

YI: Japanese college students go through a normal process where they take examinations for companies before they are accepted. So I just went through the normal procedures, took the test, and got accepted by Namco. I was exposed to Namco's videogames as a child, for example *Xevious*, which was quite impressive. So I was always thinking that I wanted to join Namco, because they produce such great games.

I was involved with the programming for these types of games, <*refers to RPG boxes on table*> while I was a college student. But upon entering Namco I was assigned as a planner, or game designer. Not as a programmer. While I was working for Enix as a part-timer, I had the opportunity to witness many high-level, legendary programmers there. And I thought it would be impossible for me to establish my career as a programmer. But after joining Namco I found that there were all sorts of people. Even some of my colleagues who joined Namco in the same year, who were employed as programmers, had never actually done any programming before. But they were hired as programmers anyway.

JS: I spoke with Professor Kishimoto,[18] who said Namco would hire people with no programming experience then train them on the job.

YI: Yes, that's right.

JS: You worked on two *Yu Yu Hakusho* titles. Then you joined the NeGcon team?

YI: The NeGcon team, yes. Actually no, there weren't any separate teams per game, per say. We belonged to the segment or the division which was called the "consumer game team" - where all of us were involved with the NeGcon. So after I joined the company I created this. <*refers to Yu Yu Hakusho*> There was a lead designer for this game called Hideo Yoshizawa.[19] He came up with the *Klonoa* series.[20] He also made *Mighty Bombjack*, together with Michitaka Tsuruta, when he belonged to Tecmo. So I was assigned to Yoshizawa-san's team upon entering Namco. I was really surprised to learn that he used to work with Tsuruta-san in the past.

JS: And then Mr Tusuruta worked on *PITMAN* for the Game Boy.

YI: Yes, exactly.

JS: Lots of connections between games.

YI: Yes! The Japanese game industry is a very small world, actually. So at work you would run into a friend who knows this person, or knows that person, who had worked on a particular game before. And so on.

JS: Did you have any interesting stories regarding these two *Yu Yu Hakusho* games?

YI: Well, I didn't program these. I joined the company in April, and this game was released at the end of October. Usually, back then, they would spend about a year to come up with this kind of game. However, they wanted to shorten the time to market, so the company decided to throw in 20 more staff to create it, which was quite a lot of people for a game back then. So in August and September we used to actually stay overnight at the company, trying to rush through so that we could meet the deadline. We were basically living at the company for two months. The game was completed at the end of October, and was then launched in December. So we had quite a long, very enjoyable vacation in December! <*laughs*> We were able to take a lot of time off.

JS: These crunch times, where you stayed at the company, were you married at the time?

---

[18] Yoshihiro Kishimoto, creator of *Pac-Land*

[19] Also writer & director on several *Ninja Gaiden* games

[20] Starting on PS1 *Klonoa* was a light-hearted 2.5D platformer; highly recommended

YI: *<laughs>* No, not yet!

JS: Crunch times happen a lot in games.

YI: Yes. Back then, particularly in Japan, Christmas season was the peak time for sales in the game industry.

JS: Earlier, when we weren't recording, you told me a wonderful story about the NeGcon's inspiration coming from someone at Namco seeing a female colleague playing a racing game on the Super Famicom, and moving the controller in time with the vehicle. Which led to the project's start. Could you retell me that story?

YI: Yes, Ms Okawa[21] would shake the controller sideways, to the left and right, when she was playing a racing game for the Super Famicom.[22] She would physically move the Super Famicom controller from side to side, like this. *<gestures with whole body>* Ms Okawa was the one who created *Valkyrie no Densetsu*,[23] which was a very popular game produced by Namco. For arcades. Let me get it up on Google.

Mrs Isokawa: Can I serve you the curry? My daughter's English teacher, who used to study abroad in the UK, told us that if you're having a visitor from England, you must serve them this particular brand of curry. Which is called Vermont Curry.

YI: *<referring to computer with YouTube video> Legend of Valkyrie*. Do you know it?

JS: Yes! *Legend of Valkyrie*. Ms Okawa inadvertently inspired the creation of the NeGcon.

YI: That's correct. But there was a creator called Kuriyama-san.[24] He was observing the way she played the game.

JS: Could I have their full names?

YI: Hm... I don't remember their first names. One moment... No, I don't know. We don't usually go by our first names in Japan. Otherwise yes, Kuriyama-san was inspired by the way Ms Okawa moved, so he thought about the concept of twisting the controller, which could result in different [in-game] movements. The members of the consumer [console game] team back then, had this idea that if you come up with a different type of controller, something different from the regular game pad bundled with the game console, then you might be able to come up with a totally new type of game. So the NeGcon name, the first part of the name stands for *nejiru* and means to twist, which was the whole idea behind it. That's how they were inspired by Ms Okawa's movements with a controller.

JS: Was it specifically racing games in mind?

YI: For racing games we had a steering wheel in mind. So we thought about how we could reproduce steering movements. The end result was the idea of twisting the controller, like this. *<gestures>*

<we take a break to eat>

Mrs Isokawa: Many animation fans find that this brand of Vermont Curry ends up in a lot of anime available in the UK. We were worried you would be concerned about what you ate, because of the Fukushima incident. So all the vegetables and the ingredients were produced either in Hokkaido or in Kyushu.

JS: It's delicious! When I came to Japan, I did not have fear for myself. The people of Japan have to live with this every day. So I want to press on without fear.

YI: Thank you very much!

Mrs Isokawa: And this sake produced before the event took place!

<everyone laughs>

[...]

JS: You were talking about the NeGcon.

YI: Have you got the video set-up?

<parts of the following section are available on the supplementary DVD>

JS: Yes, it's good.

---

[21] First name unknown; arcade-history.com says the only credits on the *Valkyria no Densetsu* arcade game are: Spanky Usukura, Nam Nam, WanWan, Astron Ishii
[22] Racing title never ascertained
[23] Namco, arcades, 1989
[24] Satoru Kuriyama; production manager on *Ridge Racer*, also listed in Namco controller patents

YI: So this is how you normally manipulate a steering wheel. <*gestures*> Instead of just holding it at the same level, we decided to kind of twist and turn the wheel instead, at the same time. Then we have the accelerator and the break equivalent buttons here, on the right hand side. What we wanted to do was to level the height here, for both buttons. But we also wanted players to be able to keep the button pushed down. So that's why made a recess here, by the buttons. And we came up with many prototypes, before reaching this final design. We came up with different prototypes having a different depth and height for buttons. Finally we ended up with this design, or form.

JS: Were there any prototypes which had a drastically different shape to that one?

YI: Well, it was our first time to twist the controller in that way. <*laughs*> It may have been better if we had elongated these parts at the end, in a curved shape, then it would be easier for the users to hold on to. There was one prototype having a longer end. But other than that... Having four buttons was always a given. But we debated about whether we should make all four buttons analogue, things like that, so we created many prototype versions experimenting with different combinations of circuit boards. I think those were the prototypes we tested.

JS: Was Ms Okawa involved with the NeGcon?

YI: I don't know if my memory is accurate or not, but by the time this NeGcon development came into play, Okawa-san was no longer with Namco. I think I remember that she had left the company the same year that I joined the company.[25]

JS: Mr Kuriyama-san's idea was long after seeing her using the Super Famicom controller?

YI: The NeGcon was the result of a long-term project at Namco to develop a new type of controller. The idea was there, but it took a very long time to actually design and build a physical model. This controller project was already in motion when we first started talking about developing for the PlayStation, maybe even earlier than that. I heard people talking about it back then. Since I was just a new entrant to the company I had no access to the company secrets yet! <*laughs*> But I did hear that this idea had been in place for a long period of time, even before I joined the company. Around this time, other companies like Sega and Sony were producing their own game hardware, and so Namco naturally had this desire to create their own hardware too. So maybe it [NeGcon] was just a part of it.

JS: Namco wanted to come up with hardware, do you mean a home console or peripherals?

YI: No, not a controller, I meant a home console. There wasn't a concrete project in place, but I think Namco did want to create their own hardware [game console] like Nintendo, Sega, or Sony had.

JS: Unbelievable!

YI: So Namco had seen Sega as their main rival, or competitor. <*laughs*> Since Sega already had their own console hardware, Namco really wanted some hardware of its own too. But on the other hand, when Nintendo released their Family Computer system, Namco contributed tremendously by offering all kinds of software for it. So the company was called the "king manufacturer" so to speak. <*laughs*> Namco also contributed to the growth of the PlayStation, because we offered so much software for the system. But aside from supplying software to other companies, Namco had always wanted to provide hardware of its own, as well.

JS: Both Konami and Taito worked on developing a home console. It seems every arcade developer wanted to make their own.

YI: Yes, that's right.

JS: So when was the last time you saw the inside of the NeGcon?

YI: I think the last time I saw the inside was when the prototype was completed, during the development phase.

JS: When would that have been?

YI: My memory is a bit sketchy... <*laughs*> I believe an electronics company called Alps Denki was responsible for the actual manufacturing of the NeGcon controller. I think they brought us the final manufacturing prototype for our

[25] April 1993

approval before going ahead with mass production.[26] But I don't remember when exactly that was.

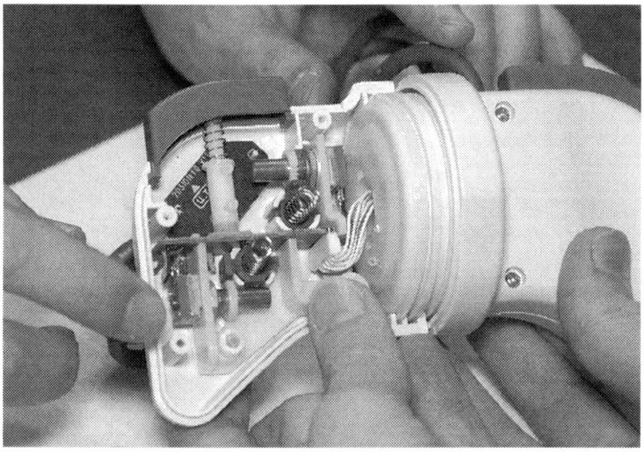

JS: <*places screwdrivers on table*> We might never be able to put this back together.

<everyone laughs for a while - Mr Isokawa begins unscrewing the NeGcon>

JS: Talk us through it.

YI: I don't know if I can... This is the switch to hold down. Here and here we have the volume switches.[27] Where by pushing the button here, this volume cylinder inside is activated and it rotates. Like this.

JS: As this button goes in it turns the cylinder.

YI: Yes, it rotates.

JS: To produce an analogue input.

YI: Yes, that's right, this and this. And I believe a similar mechanism was included either in here [central plastic compartment], or in this side as well. And I think the volume control mechanism for this central portion, was installed in this left side. Or it may have been in here...

JS: There's a bit of oil on this central mechanism, obviously to keep it lubricated.

YI: Yes.

JS: Let's see if we can put this side back together. <*struggles to put it together*> Was it tricky like this with the prototype?

YI: *<laughs>* I don't remember!

JS: I bought this as Akihabara.

YI: Wow.

JS: I think it was only 400 yen.

YI: Oh, really? It's a clean one.

JS: <*unable to put it back together*> I think I destroyed it. I'm sorry for destroying your work.

YI: It's very difficult to put back together.

JS: Let's try putting it together a different way...

YI: No, I think that way is more difficult... *<laughs>* Let me try.

JS: Ah, I've just got the buttons back in place.

YI: *<tries to assemble it>*

JS: Ah, so close! This version has different shaped shoulder buttons to the one you have.

YI: Yes, you're right.

JS: But they both have the model number 101.

YI: That's quite mysterious. This one, *<refers to personal controller>* I think this was the first, real original one. Plus the way the buttons are pushed in...

JS: Does it bring back memories?

YI: *<laughs>* Hmm, it does indeed! I didn't play the key role in creating this though. You might want to talk to others about how it. I was just taking part. Kazumi Mizuno[28] was instrumental in development of most of the NeGcon. He was the manager of graphic planning and development in the consumer disvision of Namco at that time. I think he manages Windream now.[29]

[26] Namco finalised the design specs and took them to Alps, who then manufactured a production sample to show Namco what the end product would look like. After reviewing this final sample, Namco greenlit the actual mass production by Alps

[27] Apparently also called a "potentiometer" - these are the cylinders adjacent the springs in the photo

[28] Supervisor on *Ridge* and *Rage Racer*

[29] http://windream.co.jp/index.html

JS: You fixed it, great!

YI: Wow, yours is much cleaner than mine.

JS: Would you like to trade? <*starts opening the other side*>

YI: Should I help there?

JS: Sure, but you'll have to give a commentary.

YI: Like what?

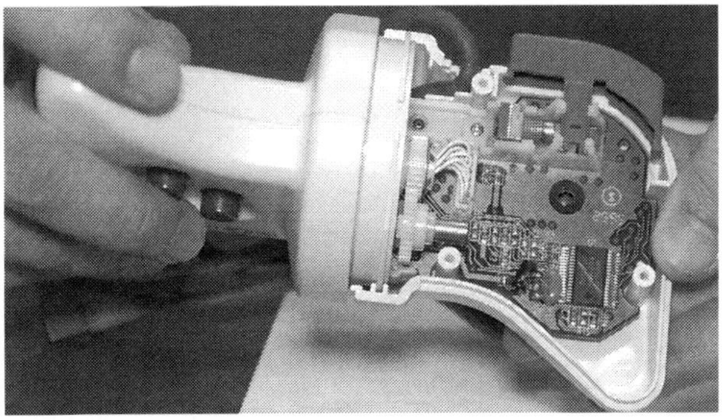

JS: Describe your recollections of the time.

YI: I remember that we were very much concerned about the strength of this bit here, in-between the two sections. Because we thought this place would be vulnerable to breakage. [Anyone] who actually tested the controller, <*with emphasis*> tended to be really aggressive and turn the controller quite... <*laughs - gestures aggressively*>

JS: This left side, housing the d-pad, has a much simpler set-up.

YI: This one, <*points to volume dial*> is the only volume switch on this side, in the left shoulder button. So this right shoulder button does not have a volume switch, only on the left side is one used. <*points to central mechanism casing*> And the volume controller is inside here, on this side, on the back of this plastic casing. In this compartment.

JS: As you twist it, you can see it turning the cog. So there's a volume control for the left shoulder button, but not the right one.

YI: That's correct.

JS: There's no analogue input on the right, it's digital, but it has a spring to give the illusion of being analogue?

YI: Correct, this right side shoulder button is not analogue. It's digital. The reason why is because we designed it with the idea of controlling an automobile in mind. You have an accelerator, a brake, and a clutch on a manual automobile. So we wanted to insert three different volume controller switches. But looking back, I think if you had another volume controller in the right-hand shoulder button, it could have been more diverse in terms of game variety.

<*looking more closely inside*>

JS: It's got a Namco branded microchip.

YI: Yes. It says Namcot. So Namco had two different brands. One was Namco, and the other was Namcot. During the Super Famicom era there was a limitation as to how many titles one company could release. So to solve that issue Namco came up with two different brands, so that they could increase their number of products or titles. I think this [the name on the chip] is a remainder from that practice.

JS: <*holds two NeGcon controllers side-by-side*> Almost identical apart from the shape of the shoulder buttons.

YI: Yes, it looks that way. After this model came out, I think one of the variations had a black colour on this portion.[30]

JS: Like a limited edition?

YI: Is it a limited version? I think the form on both sides became much more simple, than this one. As far as I can recall.

<*we struggle to put the left side together* >

JS: I think it was designed this way, once you open it you can never close it...

YI: <*laughs*> Yes, to start with it, I think we really struggled in coming up with a design, because we wanted to put as many volume mechanisms in as possible, into this small space.

[30] There is a revised model of NeGcon in black

JS: There was a game on the PlayStation where you could wash windows, and then squeeze your cloth by twisting the NeGcon.[31]

YI: *<intense laughter>* Well, actually, before I left Namco I was working on a golf game using the NeGcon! But it didn't come into production.

JS: Let's film a demonstration of this unreleased golf game.

<this section is on the supplementary DVD>

YI: *<stands, holding controller>* You'd stand like this, and then you'd hit the ball like this. So while you swing your arms, you twist the NeGcon. *<moves arms in a swinging motion>*

JS: So in a way, it was like a precursor to Nintendo's Wii.

YI: *<intense laughter>* Well, this project fell through for two reasons. Firstly, most of the golf players back then were rich and powerful, upper management type people. So we were afraid that they would look at our game and say, "That's not how you swing a golf club!" *<laughs>* We were also notified that you do not twist your clubs when you swing. Secondly... Sony released *Minna no Golf*,[32] which became quite a famous, long running series. If we were to commercialise our idea, we would have been competing against Sony's *Minna no Golf*, so we decided not to finish this as a product.

JS: Awesome, we've discovered an unreleased game that used the NeGcon to play golf with!

YI: *<laughs>* Well, it was really fun for us trying out the prototype of the game, using the NeGcon! We had a great time with that title.

JS: I spoke to quite a few people, and they said they really liked it for racing games. Fans are disappointed that you can't plug it into a PS3.

YI: Yes, I know about that.

JS: It should still work on a PS2 though.

YI: Yes, it does work on PS2, I believe.

JS: Since my controller is still white, would you like to have it as part of your collection?

YI: Yes, that would be wonderful.

JS: *<offers controller as a gift>*

YI: Thank you very much for all your gifts!

JS: It's not really a gift. Since you worked on the NeGcon, and you wrote the article for the magazine, really I'm just giving them back to their creator.

YI: I'm very happy, thank you.

JS: *<referring to two controllers sitting side-by-side>* He now has a friend!

<everyone laughs>

JS: Thank you for your hospitality, and the incredible food. I believe you started at 9:00 this morning preparing it?

YI: She was nervous. *<laughs>*

Mrs Isokawa: If you had more free time during your trip, we would have loved to invite you over again. When you're back in Japan again, please come visit us.

JS: Thank you for such a wonderful offer.

YI: This is a Japanese sweet. It's just a block of sugar, really.

Mrs Isokawa: Children don't like this, but once you grow up, you start to like them.

JS: Really, children don't like them? I'm surprised. *<wryly>* Don't trust kids. They're fussy with everything.

[...]

JS: I met a student the other day, who put me in touch with a former Namco employee, who is now a professor.

YI: You mean Kishimoto-sensei?

JS: Yes!

---

[31] This was *Studio P* - please see the Takaki Kobayashi interview for more

[32] aka: *Everybody's Golf*, PS1, 1997

YI: When I joined Namco, he also belonged to the consumer games division. I think he was a section manager, or something like that.

JS: Yes, he drew the sketch of Namco's layout, in my book.

YI: The one you showed me. Yes, the game industry is not a big industry, so we tend to know each other.

Mrs Isokawa: I often have the opportunity to listen to my husband and his colleagues talk about games, and it's really interesting, the conversations they have.

[...]

JS: <*referring to magazine*> Please don't lose this again.

YI: <*laughs*> I promise you! <*leafs through magazine*> This was published in 1985. Wow. That's 28 years ago.

JS: Who owns the rights to *PITMAN*? The GB version was re-released on 3DS as a download. Yet Vanguard releases it on mobile phones.

YI: It's going to be complicated to discuss that topic. I would have to talk about copyrights related to the game. So there's a copyright on the visuals of the game, to start with. So for the visual copyright for *PITMAN*, the holder would be Tsuruta-san, or ASK-Kodansha. In principle, copyright law does not protect the idea of the game itself. But on the other hand, this is a puzzle game, so there is a copyrightable design of the levels in the game. Or in other words, the puzzle portions themselves. But since they belong to the original idea, the copyright for this portion belongs to me. So you may have heard about the *Pac-man* litigation? The copyrights over games become very complicated. So the idea of the game is not protected by copyright law, but the expressive visual elements are protected. So there's two different copyrights, for the visual portion as well as the puzzle portion, or the levels portion. So for the 3DS re-release, the copyrights, or the royalties, are paid both to Tsuruta-san and myself.

JS: A complicated situation.

YI: But I myself did not think to assert my rights aggressively. As I said earlier, back then, with games it was the norm for everyone to copy each other's work and make something new out of it. This would happen over and over, and the games would develop and spread that way. *PITMAN* was from that era when this activity was commonplace. Just like the example you gave [of the Sharpentiers] in France. So if anything I was happy that people were using my ideas. But nowadays they kind of take advantage of the lack of protection, which is quite often seen in China. They come up with, maybe you could call them bad or malicious copies, such as pirate versions and practically identical clones.

Ideally people would use the original version as a framework, or reference point, so that they can add new ideas on to the original, to make the original even better, as a way of showing respect to the original work. But that is not often the case nowadays.

JS: Let's discuss *Lunar 2: Eternal Blue*. What was your involvement in the Saturn and PlayStation versions?

YI: I was involved as a programmer for *Lunar 2: Eternal Blue*. I was responsible for the system menus for controlling the game, such as the configuration menu, as well as the battle portion of the RPG.

JS: Had you played the original on Mega CD?

YI: Yes. I was looking around my house for it so that I could show you, but I could not find it. I'm sorry.

JS: The Mega CD version was in Mr Sugiyama's meeting room.

YI: Maybe, yes.

JS: I believe Vanguard worked on the original two titles, for Mega CD, and then on the updated versions for Sega Saturn.

YI: That's right. My involvement with *Lunar 2: Eternal Blue* began with the project to port the original Mega CD version over to the Sega Saturn. As far as I know, I think Vanguard was also involved in the original Mega CD version for *Lunar 1* and *2*. But since I wasn't working at Vanguard during that time, I don't know much about that.

JS: What astounds me is that the *Lunar* games are so popular in the West, and yet few know Vanguard was involved.

YI: <*laughs*> Yes, that is astounding. Well, what I mean is, it's astounding to find out that *Lunar* is so popular overseas.

JS: Working Designs localised the games, allowing a lot of people to enjoy them.

YI: Around the time of porting the Sega Saturn version to the Sony PlayStation, we learned that the PlayStation version was also going to be released in English, and one of the persons involved with the English localisation overseas came to work at the Vanguard office briefly. So this person showed up at our office in Shin-Yokohama one day, and he was carrying an entire desktop computer on his back! He said it was his game development PC. <*laughs*> We spent the next few days giving him lectures on how we developed our games. <*laughs*> Then he flew back to America. <*laughs*>

JS: Was this Victor Ireland?

YI: Ah! Yes, it may have been him. I think that name sounds familiar, that could be him.

JS: Victor was legendary. In the Mega CD version of *Lunar 2* there was a boss with many names (Phantom Sentry, Star Sentry, Star Dragon, Zeke the Risen). Do you know why it was removed in the update?

YI: I'm afraid I don't know.

JS: Do you know Studio Alex and its founder Kazunari Tomi, I believe it was involved with *Lunar*?

YI: I don't know about this either. I'm sorry that I'm unable to you with those questions.

[Noting the time]

JS: Thank you for inviting me in to your home to answer all my questions, and the many gifts, and for taking a day off work to facilitate this.

YI: I don't think I was able to answer all your questions, so any further questions you can email me. I'll try to answer them to the best of my abilities.

JS: Yes, there's much to discuss.

YI: Well, there is 30 years of history. If after returning from Kobe, if you have time, you're welcome to stop by again. It's not far from Shin-Yokohama station.

JS: Thank you very much.

Below: Mr Isokawa was turned into a manga character for a GNO related comic by Bandai

~Appearing in a later volume~

Professor Yoshihiro Kishimoto

There's even more Namco discoveries from the creator of *Pac-Land* and *Baraduke*, including a rather amusing story on the practical jokes the divisions played on each other. In addition, Professor Kishimoto was the programmer on Namco's *Star Wars* game for the Famicom, the one where Darth Vader turns into a scorpion, and he reveals the entire story. Most significantly though, will be the world exclusive publication of detailed credit listings for all of Namco's early arcade games. Until now we've never known who made them...

Michitaka Tsuruta

The creator of *Bombjack, Solomon's Key* and *Fire & Ice* discusses a lifetime of game development, starting at Tecmo (formerly Tehkan), and then beyond. While best known for his expertly designed puzzle-action platformers, Mr Tsuruta also worked on an anime-themed adventure/RPG hybrid for the PlayStation (*Imadoki no Vampire: Bloody Bride*), and a football series. He also discusses the update for Mr Isokawa's *PITMAN* on GB, and shares some sketchbooks filled with concept art.

Visiting Hokkaido

7 ~ 8 October 2013

4am. There is never a good way to deal with such an early rise. But I wanted to visit the northern island of Hokkaido, and I had been invited to interview three gentlemen from dB-SOFT: composer Yasuhito Saito, and programmers Takaki Kobayashi and Keita Abe. In addition, Mr Saito spent time at Data West, and could give the inside story on the unreleased *Bounty Arms*. Meanwhile Misters Kobayashi and Abe were later involved with Agenda, a company hired by Hudson to produce games for the PC Engine, and now Smileboom, which is doing some interesting things on the 3DS. Myself and Nico Datiche spent the preceding night at Joseph Redon's place, in order to brave an early morning car ride to the airport and our flights. Joseph's apartment was a place of - quite literally - wall to wall and floor to ceiling games.

Other plans for the Hokkaido included visiting ZOOM in Sapporo, creators of the *Genocide* mecha games, *Lagoon* RPG for X68k (later ported to SNES), plus *Mister Mosquito* for PlayStation 2. Unfortunately while an interview was planned, the head of the company mentioned that he was currently involved in some business that might make this unfeasible. It's unfortunate, but ultimately I was unable to visit ZOOM.

Fortuitously, during my interview with Mr Kobayashi, he mentioned that he was still in contact with Takeshi Takebe in Sapporo, the 6th official employee of Hudson. He took out his phone and made an impromptu phone call - we would be meeting him the next day! All the secrets of Hudson's formation would be revealed, including the funky PC-88 adaptation of *Super Mario Bros*. My interpreter on the first day was a language professor, and she was the best interpreter of the trip.

I also visited the abandoned Hudson Laboratory, on the outskirts of Sapporo. It was recommended by my Hokkaido guide, Matthew Fitsko, who sent me links to the realtor website offering it for lease. I'd met Mr Fitsko online some years previous, when researching an article on Japanese computers. A professional translator, and extremely knowledgeable on games, he would prove to be an invaluable pillar for the book. We caught a bus and then walked through the woods to find the lab, lonely and hidden amidst hills and pinewood. The perimeter was marked by yellow tape, warning outsiders not to cross.

I crossed the yellow line, wandered around, and pressed up against the office windows, noting an empty sticky-tape dispenser with what appeared to be some former staff's name on the front. What looked like a trashed floppy drive lay in a waste paper basket. There were some filing cabinets, but the labels were too far away to read. With some excitement I took hi-res shots with my camera, then used the zoom function on the display, hoping to read, *"Unreleased Games Be Yonder!"* The labels read, "Timing Charts" and "Office Supplies". There were no magical discoveries at the lab, just lots of overgrown foliage, which makes sense given its abandonment. But it was a poignant reminder of how fragile the eco-system of the games industry is. At one time NEC and Hudson led the vanguard for the CD medium in games, and produced a multitude of hardware variations, such as the PC Engine, its CD add-on, several varieties of combined system, US variations, a handheld PCE, plus later the PC-FX. In Japan the PC Engine held a strong position. The cataclysmic fall from power for Hudson, later to be absorbed and forgotten within Konami is tragic, and it can happen to any hardware manufacturer. The poignancy was heightened for me when later in the trip I attended the Hudson Memorial Night in Shinjuku, Tokyo. Although Hudson staff moved on, they still get together to give informal talks to an enrapt crowd. Two floors underground in a repurposed club, eating *Takahashi Meijin* dumplings (a speciality specifically for Hudson Night), and listening to the Hudson gang talk about the old days, with slides and photos projected on a wall.

Before leaving the lab, to attend the interviews in Sapporo, I noticed two gentleman by an upper floor window, eyeing me suspiciously as I took photographs. I suggested to my compatriots that we reveal ourselves to be foreign investors wanting to lease the property, so as to get a tour inside. Unfortunately the buses had a schedule to keep, and so did we. Onwards!

After my interview with Mr Takebe the next day I spent some time sightseeing in the popular town of Otaru. This included sampling local cuisine, visiting an Ainu crafts store, and having coffee inside an enormous warehouse illuminated only by candlelight from a thousand tiny flames.

I liked Hokkaido. It's cool, as in frosty winters with heavy snow and buildings made of brick. They also really like potatoes, as I discovered when eating out. There's a rambunctious, earthy, flavourful feeling walking the streets. According to Mr Redon there's also a lot of game collectors in Hokkaido, "Because the winters are so cold there's nothing to do but stay indoors and play videogames all day."

The supplementary DVD contains plenty of footage of this visit to the Hudson lab, a night drive around Sapporo, footage from the inside of a capsule hotel, and an unreleased Hudson PCE game.

~Appearing in a later volume~

The distant and more recent pasts of **Hudson Soft** come together, revealing things never before known outside of Japan. Office maps, company secrets, and long lost forgotten games are uncovered.

Takashi Takebe
The 6th employee of Hudson discusses the company's start, how they allied with Nintendo, the creation of Famicom BASIC, his helming of the *Super Mario Bros.* remake for PC-88, plus an unknown Hudson Soft vending machine project!

Hiromasa Iwasaki
Details the later years of Hudson, including his involvement with *Ys Books I&II* for PC Engine, and an initiation the company had for new programmers. As a games journalist he knows secrets that few others do.

dB-SOFT Gaming 101

None of dB-SOFT's games officially left Japan. They are however very interesting, either for setting precedents, or simply for pure controversy. Here's a crash course on a few discussed during interviews.

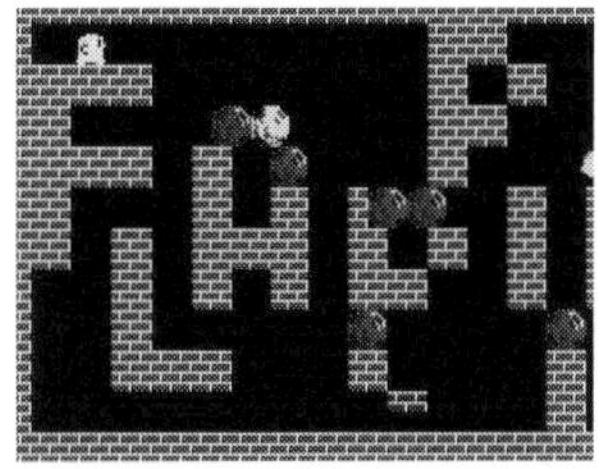

Flappy - **PC-6001, FM-7, MSX, NES, PC-88, X1 & others (first released 1983) :** *Sokoban* variant with gravity: push a stone to the goal while crushing enemies or putting them to sleep with mushrooms. *Flappy* could be dB-SOFT's most successful game, being ported to multiple systems and receiving sequels until after the millennium. Each of the ports had distinct levels based on the hardware. Although it looks cute, it's brutally difficult.

Layla - **Famicom (1986) :** Probably dB-SOFT's best known game outside of Japan by virtue of easy access through NES emulation. Control one or two sci-fi anime babes (simultaneous 2P!) through a series action-packed platforming levels. Has an early NES-era charm.

Cross Blaim - **MSX (1986) :** Basically *Metroid* for the MSX, with RPG elements like a currency system. It was originally going to be a 3-player game, much bigger, with even more *Metroid* flourishes, but was severely cut back before release. Even in its truncated form it is highly recommend.

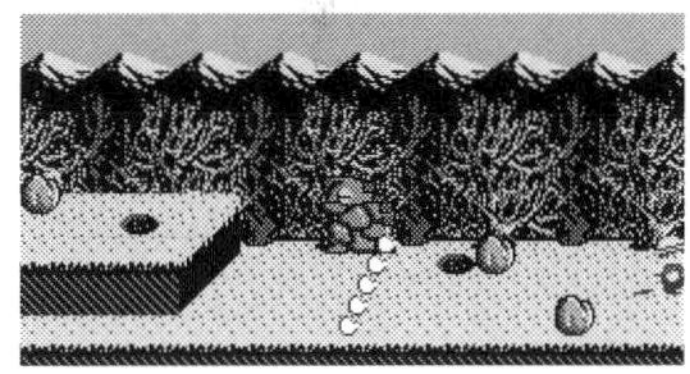

Woody Poco - **PC-88, PC-98, MSX2, FM77AV, Famicom (first 1986) :** Amazing action-RPG predating but similar to *Mystical Ninja*. Equip one hand with a weapon, the other with a passive tool (ie: lamp for dark areas). Eat to stop hunger, energy recharges based on food level. It features in-game time with day/night cycles, and four distinct seasons with colour changes. Buy gear, sleep at hotels, gamble, bribe NPCs, you can even steal from shops - which gets you labelled as a thief for the rest of the game.

177 - **Sharp X1, PC-88, X68000 (first 1986) :** Japan's equivalent of *Custer's Revenge* (the name is the criminal code for sexual assault). It ignited a furore that went all the way to the government. A woman runs left while the player gives chase, leaping over obstacles. There's an area map at the top; leaping and touching road signs suspended in the air cause the girl to take a different route. Players must leap over animals which appear from the right, then dash to the left when the girl leaps over them. When close players hit space bar to remove clothing (top, skirt, bra, briefs). Doing this five times starts Act 2, which is coitus in the form of a QTE without prompts. The correct direction key raises "desire"; the wrong button depletes it. If desire is raised before "power" depletes, the game concludes, whereupon the couple marry.

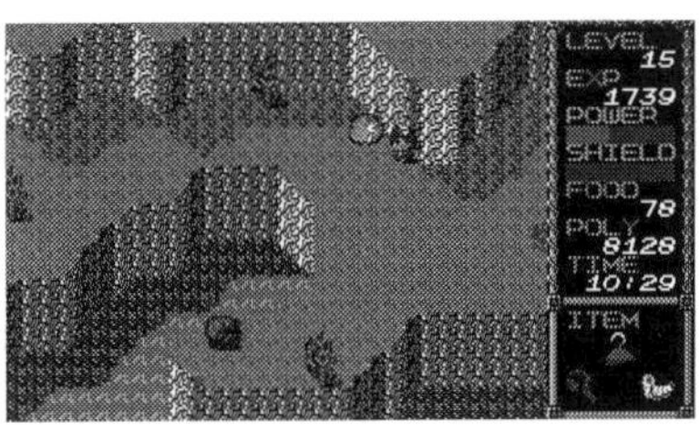

The Story of Melroon - **PC-88, PC-98 (1989) :** An incredible action-RPG no one outside of Japan has heard of. Predating *A Link to the Past* by nearly 2 years, this is a far richer game, with extremely smooth scrolling. There's a time system with day/night cycles, XP levelling, and three styles of play (overhead map, side-on towns, and side-on puzzle levels like *Flappy*). Like *Woody Poco* you eat to avert hunger, and your health recharges based on this. You can also have an animal companion for combat, a variety of weapons and items, you learn words for NPC dialogue, and there's a selection of crazy hats with special abilities!

Studio P - **PlayStation (1996) :** Not developed at dB-SOFT, but rather Agenda, this was helmed by Takaki Kobayashi. The simplest way to describe it is as a warped equivalent to *Mario Paint*, albeit with a lot more minigames and everything else. It's mouse compatible and also works with Namco's NeGcon controller - you can twist the pad in a minigame to wring the water out of a wash cloth, and also use it as a musical instrument. There's standard drawing and music creating tools, in addition to the ability to make 3D polygon models with textures, plus sequencing options for these. You can create a small 3D environment, then place objects inside and have them move around like in a movie, backed by music. While not tested, online videos also imply there's even a vocaloid tool built-in. It really is as wacky as it sounds!

斉藤 康仁

SAITO, Yasuhito

DOB: 15 March 1967 / Birthplace: Sapporo, Hokkaido / Blood Type: B+

(B:95 W:58 H:98)

~ Selected Portfolio ~

In charge of music composing and arranging, unless otherwise stated

dB-SOFT

Volguard - PC-6001mkII/PC-6601, 1984 (Programmer)
Volguard II - Famicom, 1985 (Also wrote song lyrics!)
Zunou Senkan Garu - Famicom, 1985
Layla - Famicom, 1986
Cross Blaim - MSX1, 1986
Woody Poco - PC-88 / X1 / Famicom, first 1986
177 - PC-88 / X1, first 1986 (Programmer - **Under Macadamia Soft label)**
Produce - PC-88 / X1, 1987
Tetsudou-Oh - Famicom, 1987

Data West

** Psychic Detective Series Vol.1 ~ 6* - FM Towns (For #1 only the main theme)
Subtitles: *Invitation, Memories, AYA, Orgel, Nightmare, SOLITUDE*
** The 4th Unit Series Vol.1 ~ 7* - FM Towns (For #1 & 2 only arrangement)
Subtitles: *Linkage, Dual Targets, Zero, D-Again, Merrygoround, Wyatt*
Misty - FM Towns, 1989
RAYXANBER I - FM Towns, 1990
RAYXANBER II & III - PC Engine, 1991 & 1992
Vajra - LaserActive, 1993 in USA
Gulclight TDF2 - FM Towns (**Published by Pack-in-Video**)

Enterbrain/ASCII

RPG Tsukuru 4 - PlayStation, 2000 (Sample music)
Music Tsukuru DX - Windows (Sample music)

Interview with Yasuhito Saito
7 October 2013, Sapporo, Hokkaido

After arriving in Hokkaido our first order of business was visiting the abandoned Hudson laboratory on the outskirts of Sapporo, after which we rendezvoused with Mr Saito in a coffee shop. Joining him was a friend, Taku Kuroda, who is an indie movie producer and is incredibly knowledgeable on games. Matt Fitsko also joined the interview, bringing his technical knowledge of Japanese computers. Mr Saito's meishi, or business card, was a CD with his contact details printed on the front, and a selection of musical tracks on the disc itself. Quite ingenious I thought! Our discussion focused on Mr Saito's time at dB-SOFT and later Data West, with some fascinating insight on some controversial titles, and the unreleased Bounty Arms. The interview was split into two halves, the second being at Smileboom, after the joint interview with Takaki Kobayashi and Keita Abe. Questions and answers are not chronological.

<shows old copy of Comptiq, which had a feature on dB-SOFT - pictured previous page>

Yasuhito Saito: It's such fun just looking through old magazines. Ah, Square and Enix side-by-side!

JS: Your photo is in here - do you have this issue?

YS: No, I do not.

Taku Kuroda: But I do!

<everyone laughs>

YS: *<leafing through magazine>* Oh, Kogado![1] The president of Kogado is still a friend of mine.

Matt Fitsko: They're still in operation actually. They still make computer games.

YS: They're still making the *POWER DoLLS* series.[2] *<flips magazines>* Ah, BPS!

JS: I'm interviewing Henk Rogers next month.

YS: Cross Media, I don't know this company.

TK: It's related to Victor.

YS: Are you so knowledgeable?

<everyone laughs>

YS: Everyone in this magazine looks so young! Ah, Hummingbird, Thinking Rabbit, I feel nostalgic seeing these names. Wow, PSK! They made *ecchi*. *<to author>* H-games![3]

TK: It is the eternal theme!

JS: Everyone knows hentai!

TK: *<looking at magazine>* Riverhill Soft, they were banned.

YS: Really?

TK: Yes, it was.

YS: But when I was with dB-SOFT, I wasn't friends with people who worked for other software makers, so much. Only after I moved to Data West,[4] when I moved to Osaka, I made many friends in the business. After working at Data West - they made *Rayxanber* - I became acquainted with other people who worked for game developers, and started talking with them. Some of them are still my friends and we communicate through Facebook. *<takes out Rayxanber III>* This is not from dB-SOFT! But I brought *Rayxanber* to look at.

JS: I played it on an NEC Duo-R system!

YS: This is the only one I still have - I couldn't find anything else.

JS: My favourite of the trilogy. Great music.

YS: Thank you very much.

---

[1] 工画堂スタジオ / Kogado Studio; famous for the 2nd *Cosmic Soldier* and the original *Miracle Warriors*

[2] Long-running strategy RPG series featuring sexy all-female squadrons of mecha pilots; an English version was published by MegaTech for DOS around 1995

[3] Ecchi, mildly erotic or kinky; H-games, as in hentai, a stronger variety

[4] According to company website, established May 1984, founded May 1986, in Osaka; best known for the *Rayxanber* shmups and the unreleased *Bounty Arms* on the original PlayStation

JS: Data West was in Osaka. How would you describe the difference in work environments between the Kansai region and Hokkaido?

YS: Firstly, it's too hot in Kansai! The working environment itself is not so different in Sapporo or Kansai, but Osaka is much closer to Tokyo and I can just hop on the Shinkansen train and head to Tokyo, or Nagoya, if I wanted to. Sapporo is isolated, compared to Osaka or Tokyo. But for me the working environment includes culture, and humidity, and temperature too. As for inter-personal relationships, it was difficult. It was tough in Osaka. For me, anyway.

JS: Why was that?

YS: We always said, "Yeah, we understand!" But people in Osaka stick their nose into other people's affairs, compared to people in Sapporo.

JS: I brought a small gift for each of you. <*passes them over*> Thank you for coming out today to be interviewed.

YS: Thank you very much for coming all the way to Japan - to Sapporo, it's not close to anywhere!

JS: I flew from Tokyo this morning. [...] Can you recall the first videogame you ever saw?

YS: Ahh... *Galaxian*. I think it was *Galaxian* and it was at a game centre. That's what I remember.

JS: Please describe how you first became interested in music.[5]

YS: The very first time I became interested in music, I think was when I was 5 or 6 years old, and I heard *The Ventures* on the car stereo, my father's car stereo. I think it was tracks like *Pipeline* and *Diamond Head*. I really liked that kind of music.

JS: How did you join a games company?

YS: <*laughs*> Actually I didn't enter dB-SOFT specifically because I wanted to be there, but rather as a result of my job hunting. When I was a senior high school student I had to start job hunting and my first choice was Xerox, but I failed the screening there. Then I went to Fujitsu, which was my second choice, and I failed. And so on, and so on. Until finally I went to dB-SOFT, but I wasn't thinking of becoming a game developer or anything. I just wanted a job.

JS: According to your website, they wanted someone who could make game music, and although you did not have any experience, you said that you did?

YS: <*laughs*> Exactly, yes.

JS: How did the interview go?

YS: Actually, while I was doing job hunting, I was rejected so many times by other companies I was kind of giving up, finding a proper job. Actually, the person who introduced me to dB-SOFT was my high school teacher, and he suddenly said one day, "You should go to dB-SOFT after school, and just meet someone there." So I went, without expecting very much, and then a middle-aged man answered the door. Because I was not expecting much I was very candid and had a kind of teasing attitude - I was not serious at all in answering his questions. The old man then asked what are my hobbies, and I said music. He said that music will become a kind of focus for the games industry in the future. I said something like "Uh-huh" and did not really take him seriously. The entire interview went by without any serious or sincere attitude from me, and at the end of the interview that middle-aged man gave me his business card, and I found out then - only then - that he was the Executive Vice President of the company. And then I thought, "Oh no! Now I'm dead! I will never be hired." So I went home without expecting much, sort of giving up.

JS: Whoa...

YS: Then suddenly I was hired! But I was not hired as part of the music related staff. I was hired as a programmer, even though I said I'm good at music.

JS: <*looking in Comptiq*> Is the gentleman who interviewed you in any of these photos?

YS: No, he's not in any of these photos. He was the vice president but he's not here, these are other executives.

---

[5] Although not mentioned in his answer, Saito-san's online biography states he grew up in a house with a music organ, which he played

JS: It's interesting you were hired as a programmer. You helped with general coding?

YS: Yes, I was creating programs.

JS: What was your first computer?

YS: It was a Macintosh. I didn't own my own computer until I quit Data West and came back to Sapporo. That was the time when I bought myself a Macintosh.

JS: Let's go through the games listed on your website. Your first game was *Volguard*?[6]

YS: Yes. I can recall that. I don't know if you know about *Volguard* or not, but it's a shooting game, and I worked on the PC-6001mkII version. My role as a programmer was to create the movement of the enemies, or opponents. Then, later, someone said, "Oh, by the way, you can make the music too." So I said yes, and from that moment I was put in charge of the music for all the products.[7]

JS: The game data came on an cassette, but the music had to be generated by the computer.

YS: Yes, exactly!

JS: Which computer did you do the programming on, and what language did you use?

YS: The programming language was assembler, for the Z80 and 6509 microprocessor. The computer model was...

JS: Did you code using the PC-6001 itself?

YS: I think I did it on the Sharp X1? There was an original dB-SOFT Operating System for the X1. It wasn't for sale, but was used for developing things. I can't remember clearly. Also I was using an ICE.[8] We removed a CPU from the computer and replaced it with an IC Emulator. It was a Hewlett-Packard 64000.

JS: A lot of programmers used an HP 64000, which could emulate other processors.

YS: Yes, that's right. There were so many of them at dB-SOFT.

JS: How does the HP 64000 relate to the Sharp X1 mentioned earlier?

YS: I can't remember so well... They were different, independent systems. Some people used this and others used that.

JS: Did you also help with programming on *Volguard II*, *Zunou Senkan Garu*,[9] *Testsudo-Oh*,[10] and *Layla*?[11]

YS: For Famicom games I did not help with programming at all, I just worked on the music for the games.

JS: For *Layla* you only worked on music?

YS: That's right.

JS: Can you recall the development of *Layla*?

YS: I cannot remember who was in charge of developing *Layla*...

JS: The character designs changed a lot through development. In the manual they look different to in the game...[12]

TK: <*with recognition*> Yes, yes! That's it!

JS: ...which looked different to the box, and early magazine previews showed them differently again. Was *Layla* always changing?

TK: Ah, yes! The initial characters shown in magazine previews had more realistic proportions.

YS: Really? Sorry, I can't remember at all!

JS: Can you recall any anecdote from *Layla*?

---

6 Simple hori-shmup for various computers, PC-6001mkII, PC-6601, PC-88, X1, FM-7, MSX (1984)
7 There aren't many YouTube videos for *Volguard*, those that exist tend to be conversions and lack music; NicoNico has the PC-6601 version with great music
8 In-Circuit Emulator

9 頭脳戦艦ガル - vertical shmup for FC (1985); amusingly, dB-SOFT labelled it as a "scroll RPG"
10 Railway-themed board game for FC (1987)
11 Action-platformer for FC (1986)
12 **http://laylairis.web.fc2.com/pad.html** is a great fansite detailing the changes to the design

YS: I think I named the game *Layla* (right).

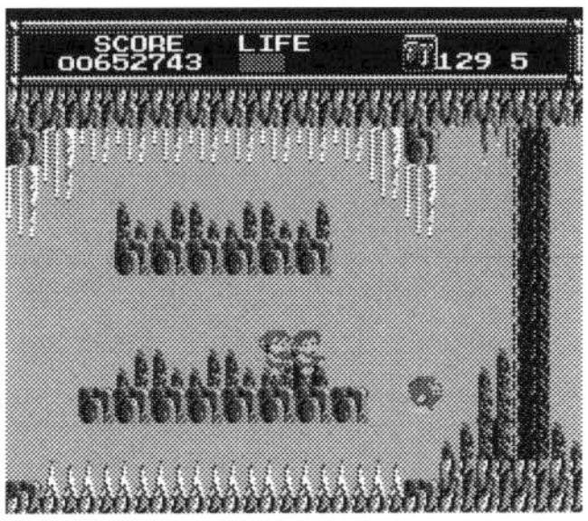

JS: Really?!

<everyone laughs>

JS: The world shall know this!

YS: Thank you very much.

JS: How did you come up with it?

YS: Eric Clapton![13]

<raucous laughter>

JS: Once published it'll be all over Wikipedia.[14]

YS: *<laughs>*

JS: Were there plans for a *Layla* sequel?

YS: I don't think there was any plan like that. I think the ending for the original could go both ways. It's open ended. So maybe if we wanted to make a sequel, we could.

JS: It was released for the Famicom. When composing music for it, was any other hardware version being considered? For example the MSX?

YS: No there wasn't. When we were making Famicom software, it was usually only for that. There were other games which were originally for personal computers, like *Woody Poco*, which were later converted to Famicom. But that wasn't the case with *Layla*.

JS: You came up with lyrics for *Volguard II*? Was it in the manual, or just for personal enjoyment?

YS: Yes. In a way you could say it was for my personal amusement, but for *Volguard II*, when I was creating the music the lyrics came at the same time, because I had to note the rhythm of the words, for example, "*BAR-RI-ER*" or "*RAY-ZAH*" or "*HACHIOGO*",[15] so each word has its own rhythm. So I really needed to create it with the music. I was only asked to create the music, but I voluntarily wrote the lyrics too.

JS: Do you want to sing them for us?

YS: What?! *<laughs>* No thanks.

JS: Perhaps after a few drinks.

YS: Yes... Maybe!

JS: Did you enjoy programming, or did you prefer focusing on music?

YS: I did not enjoy doing the programming. My main purpose was music, and I really enjoyed it. Programming was a job. It was not fun!

JS: This leads me to *Cross Blaim,*[16] which you did the music for. I believe the game was originally for three players...

TK: Yes!

YS: *<laughs with recognition>*

JS: ... and it was going to be much bigger, and even more similar to *Metroid* than it was. Why did the final product turn out differently?

YS: Yes, originally there was a plan of making it bigger, but I didn't remember it until Kuroda-san reminded me just now. This person, *<points to photo in Comptiq>* Hasegawa-san,[17] he was in charge of developing *Cross Blaim*. I don't know where he is now. But I think he's the one who decided to shrink the game, make it smaller in scale.

JS: Can you recall any details about the original version? What you can recall now, could become the only record history ever has.

YS: Ahh... *<jokingly>* Hasegawa-san was kind of a selfish guy!

---

[13] Referring to the same-named Eric Clapton and Jim Gordon song (1970) - the signature riff is mesmerising

[14] I ***think*** Mr Saito may have been joking, actually

[15] It means "8 directions"

[16] An extremely impressive *Metroid* clone for the original MSX (1986), with various RPG elements

[17] Credited in *Cross Blaim* as Takami Hasegawa; few records online

The Cross Blaim (MSX) team. Mr Saito seated far left, Mr Nishimura behind him, Mr Takadono behind the screen, Mr Hasegawa on the far right

<everyone laughs>

YS: A good guy, but maybe a bit selfish.

MF: Did you ever have some sort of prototype?

YS: My only involvement in *Cross Blaim* was making the music, and I was not involved in character creation or planning at all. Sorry I can't remember. *<going through magazine photo>* Hasegawa-san was the leader, and he was deciding everything by himself. Nishimura-san was the programmer.[18] Takadono-san was the graphic designer.[19] But I just did the music.

JS: When the game was reduced, were any of your music tracks removed?

YS: No, I think all the pieces I composed went into the shrunken version.

JS: I'm always interested in unreleased material.

YS: Everything I composed was released, sorry. Anything that was rejected was deleted, so I don't have it anymore. I won't keep them. Anything that was not used in the game, those which were rejected, I would delete them.

JS: You would destroy your own work?

YS: Yes.

JS: Wow! That's a bit sad.

YS: Then I will try to keep them next time. *<laughs>*

JS: It's always sad to destroy someone's creative output. Even if it is rejected. People in the future might enjoy experiencing it.

YS: I never thought that way, the way you said, because that piece even if it was rejected was the only thing I created at that time, for that particular project. *Wabisabi*.[20] *<laughs>*

Interpreter: *<laughs> Wabisabi* is a sort of Japanese humble mentality.

YS: *Ichigoichi*.[21] It's only for that particular occasion. *<laughs>* It will be useless for others.

JS: Just because some manager rejects it, all that means is that individual, at that time, did not like it. But his view is not universal.

YS: Exactly. However, actually, I reject them myself. Whatever I submitted was mostly accepted. Just like a pottery artist destroys his own pottery before exhibiting.

JS: You eventually made music for CD-ROM, but prior to this you programmed the music, for systems such as the PC-6001, Famicom, MSX,

---

[18] Akihiro Nishimura
[19] Osamu Takadono

[20] 詫び寂び / *humble simplicity*
[21] 一期一会 / *A once-in-a-lifetime encounter, hence should be cherished as such*

PC-88, X1, and also FM Towns. Did you have a hardware preference?

YS: This is a borderline, because after the FM Towns we didn't actually have to program, you could just put digital audio on a CD-ROM. But among these systems, the Famicom, MSX and so on, my favourite was the Sharp X1. It had an optional FM music card, and that was my favourite, if you ask me. I also wrote my own music drivers for this optional FM card.

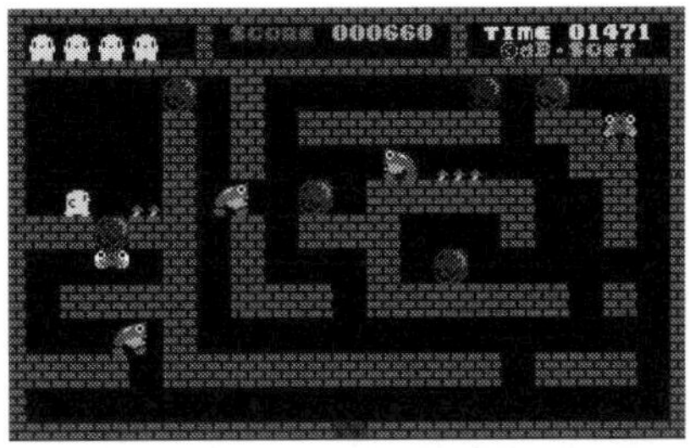

JS: You said dB-SOFT had their own OS. Did they have a name for this OS?

YS: It was called IDOS.

JS: Do you know anything about dB-SOFT's early days? They started as a game store...

YS: I only know that the company used to be a game store, but I don't know anything other than that.

TK: I knew the store, because I sometimes went there and bought some games. dB-SOFT started as Hokkaido Computer Land, and after that the company founded a computer game development department called Seven Turkey.

JS: Yes, I've heard that.

TK: Seven Turkey released some games, the main platform being NEC's 8-bit computers, like PC-8001, or PC-8801. Most of the games only had ASCII graphics.

YS: Oh, I didn't know that! Seven Turkey?

JS: It's ironic, because the word "turkey" in English is used if something is of poor quality.

<everyone laughs>

TK: That image... Those games were ***so bad***.

YS: *<jokingly to Kuroda-san>* You could say anything, because I wasn't there.

JS: One of dB-SOFT's best selling games was *Flappy*, across multiple platforms.

YS: My wife stamped the completion certificate for *Flappy*. People would beat *Flappy*, and they could mail in a little form to dB-SOFT, and then my wife would stamp the little certificates for beating the game, for finishing *Flappy*. (left)

JS: Please tell us more! Do you know anything about *Flappy*?

YS: I'm not that familiar with it. Because it was already complete when I joined.

JS: Was your wife involved with *Flappy*?

YS: Not much, in detail. I wasn't involved with *Flappy* at all, and when I entered it was already completed, and my wife was working in the planning section, and when I joined the company I wasn't really like a subordinate to her, but kind of a helper, an assistant. I sometimes also stamped the certificates with her.

JS: You met your wife through dB-SOFT?

YS: That's right.

JS: What a nice story.

YS: *<in a English>* A nice story!
<in Japanese> Of course.

JS: Is she still involved in games?

YS: No. [...] This *[Flappy]* looks like a cute game, but actually it isn't at all. It's a difficult game when you start playing it. Probably I'm the one who copied all the floppy disks, for this one. I was doing every kind of chore and work.

JS: How did you and Mr Kuroda become friends?

TK: Because Saito-san is now a musical producer - I had the opportunity to make a music video, for one of those indie music groups in Sapporo. That's how we knew each other. I've worked with him a long time, not just games, but also live events or film making.

JS: Saito-san's music is incredible.

TK: Yes, and his music is really emotional. That's why I love it, especially *Rayxanber II* and *Rayxanber III*! It's a masterpiece of his work.

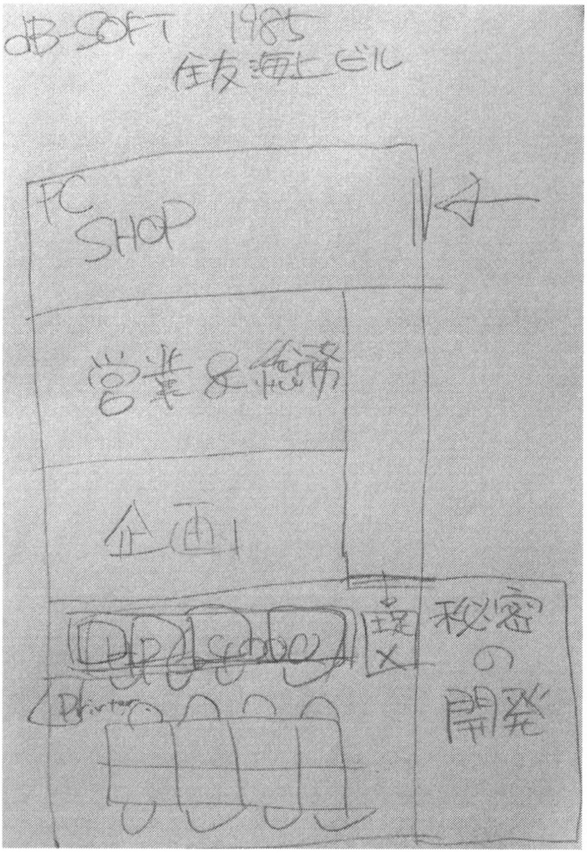

JS: Can you draw the office layout at dB-SOFT?

YS: The layout? OK!

<shows previous sketches>

TK: Westone!

YS: And Irem! The Sony layout looks so simple for such a huge company.

<discussion regarding sketch by Saito-san>

YS: In the front of the building there was just a general computer shop, where they sold not just dB-SOFT titles, but also hardware and software from other companies (top). You had a general administration and sales division here, in front (2nd down). Then a planning division here (3rd down). Then you'd kind of step down here (central door with X), here you would take off your shoes, in a kind of Japanese style, and then you'd have the work area here (bottom). It was a kind of Japanese styled work office, where all the desks are together, no cubicles or anything. And then this is the "secret development room" where they would work on the top secret projects (right side). Things that other people wouldn't know about - no information could be leaked out.

JS: Did they all smoke in the office?

YS: There was smoking area, separate from the rest of the office.

JS: I've heard that quite a few developers in the 1980s allowed smoking in the office.

YS: I think people in the sales section were smoking there, but the development section had a separate smoking area. We could not smoke in the working area, in order to protect the Hewlett-Packard machines... Because they were so expensive and we didn't want to ruin them with smoke.

JS: Can you recall the price?

YS: No, I cannot. But I heard they were very expensive.

JS: Someone once told me the HP 64000 was in the region of $25'000. Astronomically expensive.

YS: If this was the price abroad, then probably it was double or more in Japan. Like maybe 5 or 6 million yen?

JS: Did the harddrive take up a lot of space?

YS: Yes, yes.

JS: Was the room air-conditioned?

YS: Yes, that's right.

JS: You coded in assembler, did you pick it up when joining dB-SOFT?

YS: Only after I entered dB-SOFT.

JS: That must have been difficult...

YS: No, not at all. There weren't many commands for assembler, it was quite simple. So it was easy. After I entered dB-SOFT I didn't even know how to connect the personal computers on their back sides.

JS: Did you play a lot of games at the time?

YS: After I entered dB-SOFT I had to do testing, when creating or developing the games. I did play games, but not much apart from work. Before dB-SOFT I only really played *Xevious.*

JS: At game centres or on the Famicom?

YS: Ah! It was before the Famicom *Xevious* was released, so it was at game centres.

JS: I wanted to ask about *177*. It was rather controversial. What was the atmosphere like at dB-SOFT? Were people concerned about it?

YS: <*laughs*> There were no concerns at all, in the company. Especially people in the sales section were so happy when it became a topic in the Japanese diet,[22] because they thought it would really sell well. And it did sell, not just well, but greatly. As the main programmer, I was so happy too.

JS: You were the main programmer?! I thought you only did the music. How did the project start?

YS: Hmm... There was a proposal or plan to make adult software, and before *177* there was a software called *Macadam*,[23] which was adult software, and which sold quite well. The feeling was, let's make another game, a new version, for the Macadamia Soft label. There was an *ojii-san* at dB-SOFT, a middle-aged man, specialising in adult themed software, who used to be a taxi driver. <*laughs*> He proposed the plan for *177*, and I was designated as the main programmer, and the graphic designer was a woman, whose name I don't think I should mention. And I was of course also in charge of music.

JS: The graphics designer on *177* was a woman! It has an infamous reputation. How did she feel about the game, while working on it?

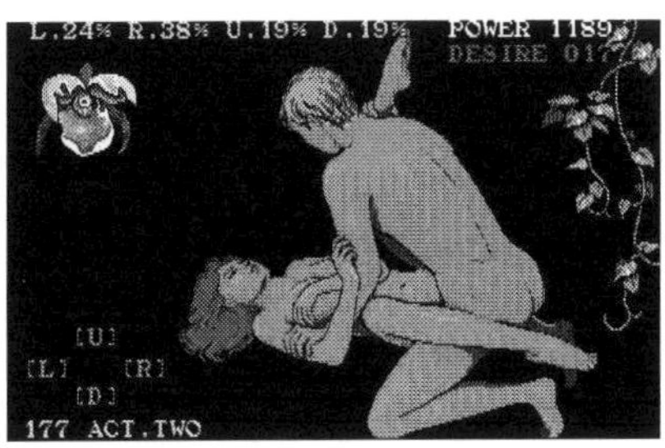

YS: We didn't think we were making something bad. <*laughs*> It just happened to become the topic at the diet. But of course none of us were able to tell that to our parents, and even now my parents don't know that I was involved in creating *177*.

JS: Is it OK to document it in my book?

YS: Of course, it's fine. That information should be online, so there's no problem about that.

MF: What I always thought was interesting, about *177*, is the ending...

YS: <*laughs*>

MF: In the ending you actually get married. During the game you're chasing and assaulting this woman, but in the ending you get married... Was it the taxi driver who came up with that?

YS: Yes, it was the taxi driver!

MF: It's interesting because you're trying to get the girl, but then it's almost like you lose the game by getting married at the end. It's Game Over both when you win and lose.

YS: Right, the taxi driver was a weirdo!

<*everyone laughs*>

JS: How did the taxi driver come to work for dB-SOFT?

YS: <*laughs*> I have no idea, he was already there when I joined!

JS: Sounds like a colourful atmosphere at the time.

YS: It was a fun place to work.

JS: *177* was released...

YS: <*interrupts - tone of incredulity*> You're asking me about that again?!

[22] Parliamentary assembly; deals with laws

[23] Various computers (1985); *Macadam: Futari Yogari* (二人愛戯 lit. *Foreplay for two*) tasked you with stimulating a woman's body using various tools (a vibrator, melting candle, a mouth, feather, and whip); *Macadam* was developed by dB-Soft but published under the Macadamia Soft adult label; two other titles were published, *177* and *Don Juan*

JS: We should probably discuss it, given its infamy. You coded the PC-88 and X1 versions?

YS: I used X1 at the beginning, then I transferred it... Originally I made it using the X1 but later it was converted to PC-88 and other computers, and that was by somebody else.[24]

JS: Can you explain the brand name Macadamia Soft? This was like a subsection of dB-SOFT.

YS: Yes, it was like a sub-brand. It was a brand specialising in *hentai* games. So when we created adult software we used the brand name Macadamia Soft.

MF: It was fairly common then, Koei did it too.

JS: They were worried about their reputation?

MF: Not necessarily. Just to have a unified brand with specific consumer expectations - Macadamia Soft produces this sort of software.

YS: Yes, exactly.

JS: My colleague says the *177* cover art was beautiful - do you know who painted it?

YS: The cover art, who was the artist? Probably, I think Mr Moriai was the designer at that time.

JS: Can you remember his name?

YS: I can only remember his family name.[25]

JS: Were you credited under any nicknames when working at games companies?

YS: When I was composing for adult games I created different names each time.

JS: What were they?

YS: Hmm... No, I can't remember. *<laughs>*

JS: How did you invent the nicknames?

YS: Because I can't remember what the names were, I can't remember how I came up with them! *<laughs>*

TK: I saw in a games magazine, the nickname *Macadam Saito*.

YS: *Macadam Saito*?! I don't remember that!

TK: *<laughs>*

YS: That's too obvious!

JS: How many adult games did you work on?

YS: I was programmer only on *177*, and for music, maybe 4 or 5 games?

JS: What was your involvement in *Woody Poco*?

YS: I only did the music for *Woody Poco*.

JS: Which other games in this list were you involved in the game programming side?

YS: Only *Volguard* and *177*.

JS: Why did you leave dB-SOFT for Data West?

YS: It's simple. Because dB-SOFT no longer let me do the music, and Data West said I would be able to work on music.

JS: dB-SOFT wanted you to do more programming?

YS: No, that's not it. They wanted me to work on user support and sales.

JS: That doesn't sound like fun.

YS: No, not at all! *<in English>* ***Terrible!***

JS: At Data West you made music for the FM Towns...

MF: The FM Towns was a very advanced system for its time. As a composer, did you feel a greater sense of freedom working with the FM Towns and sound hardware it provided?

YS: That's right. There was a great sense of freedom at the beginning, using CDDA for the music. It provided me with unprecedented freedom as a composer, and because there was no longer the limitations of a sound chip, I was happy to start with. But then I realised they were using the same CD for data, and when the data reading started then I had to stop the music. So

---

[24] There appears to be an X68000 version with improved keyboard controls

[25] MobyGames has a Paul Moriai credited under "special thanks" on *Layla*, also by dB-SOFT

later on I found it was not as free as I thought it would be.

MF: Data West is famous for its DAPS system.[26] Did that help at all, did it allow more freedom to play the music you wanted while the game was being loaded?

YS: It wasn't like that actually. With DAPS, movie data was always being read from the CD, So there was even less room to read or play CD music in between. So that's why I had to go back to using the FM Towns sound chip. And I thought, "Oh great, a sound chip again."

MF: *<laughs>* Yes, the FM Towns had a pretty slow CD-ROM drive, and so Data West used this DAPS system to stream and play smooth video during games, and they used that for almost all of their games. So whereas before Saito-san could use the CD for digital audio, when using the DAPS system he had to go back to the sound chip and use synthesised music instead of digital. DAPS was a video compression system that enabled multimedia to be efficiently streamed from a CD-ROM disc. Before the adoption of coding formats such as AVI and MPEG, digital video playback was taxing for the average computer, and the slow read rates of early CD-ROM drives could barely keep up with the constant stream of data. DAPS allowed for smooth, interactive playback of digitized video and animation, and was used extensively in Data West games for the FM Towns, such as The *4th Unit* series and the *Psychic Detective* series.[27] By utilizing DAPS, Data West became an early forerunner of the multimedia and FMV fads of the mid-1990s, beating the rest of the market by 2-3 years.

JS: *<picking up Rayxanber III>* You mentioned this is all you could find. Were you given copies of every game you worked on?

YS: I did not own them originally, even at the beginning.

JS: The company did not give you a complimentary copy?

YS: Actually, I had to buy this copy. If I had asked, the company would have given it, but I was so busy I didn't think I would have time to play them at home. So I didn't ask. It would be too much to ask - "Give me everything I worked on" - when I decided to leave the company, so I did not ask for them. So I bought it later.

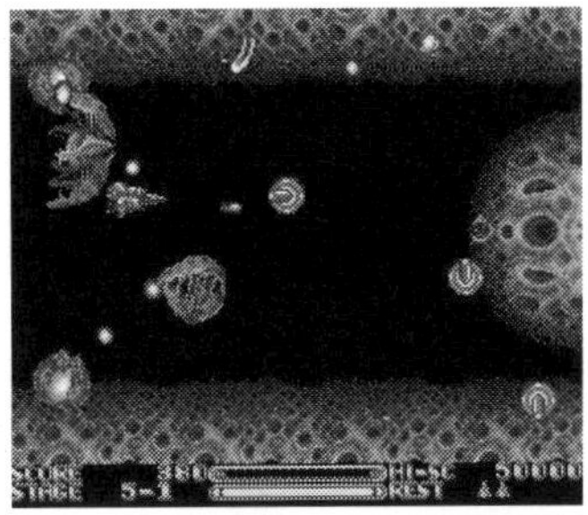

JS: Did you play *Rayxanber III*? (left)

YS: Not with this copy, but I did play while I was developing the music. Using the *invincibility* mode! It was a very difficult game to play!

JS: The first and second I thought were almost impossible to complete. But I managed to complete the third game without cheats.

YS: Yes, that's right. *Rayxanber II* (below) was extremely difficult. This [number *III*] was a little bit easier, but still too difficult for me.

JS: Did you have a favourite of the three games?

YS: Hard to say, but I liked *II* and *III* for playing.

JS: I very much liked the soundtrack for *II* and especially *III*. It has a kind of jazzy sound to it. Do you have anecdotes from composing the music?

YS: Probably it was whatever I wanted to create at that time. As for *Rayxanber*, because it's a shooting game, and there are different stages, each stage has its own theme music - Stage 1 music, Stage 2 music, and so on. Of course there is a storyline for the entirety of each *Rayxanber* game, but I was looking at the background graphics for each stage, and whatever inspired me from there was the source of creation. So I wasn't really thinking of jazzy, or anything.

JS: Did a game's designers give you a theme they wanted to convey?

[26] Data West Active Picture System

[27] *Psychic Detective* by Data West - not be confused with the same-named FMV game on PlayStation

YS: I don't know about other musicians or composers, but in my case I always look at the storyboard, kind of the visual design drawings, to learn what the story for the game is.[28] Then I will have a discussion with the story writer, and ask what kind of music the story writer wants and in which scenes. Then I would just rely on the storyboard and use my imagination to write music. But I'm kind of a twisted composer, *<laughs>* so I don't really want to create the music typically used for games. So even if it's a shooting game, I did not want to write music that sounded typically like shooting scene music. Not something like brave or heroic music. I wanted to twist it a bit, I wanted to create music unlike game music when people heard it. That was the same even when I was creating for dB-SOFT too. So the short answer is: relying on the storyboard and using my imagination. The producer did not tell me what to create, I was able to create whatever I wanted to.

JS: Are you aware of your fans outside of Japan?

YS: No, I was not.

JS: Some fans have uploaded your soundtracks to YouTube. How do you feel about this?

YS: Yes, I am happy about that.

JS: Presumably it's not commercially available anymore, the older soundtracks?

YS: I'm happy regardless of whether it's available commercially or not. Because I'm not the one who owns the rights anyway.

JS: Out of your very large portfolio, do you have a favourite project or piece of work?

YS: Yes, my favourite project was *Rayxanber*, and *Psychic Detective Series Vol.5 Nightmare*, for FM Towns.

JS: Why are these your favourites?

YS: They contain the music that I objectively think were good pieces.

[28] Most of Mr Saito's work at Data West was for adventure games, with a heavy focus on story - so this answer applies mainly to them, rather than *Rayxanber*

JS: If anyone wanted to discover your music for the first time, the tracks from these games represent you at your best?

YS: Yes, that's right.

JS: Can you tell me about *Bounty Arms*?

YS: *<in English, feigning unawareness> Bounty Arms?! What is this?! <laughs>*

JS: It was an unreleased PlayStation action game at Data West. It looked amazing. They released a playable demo of the first level.

YS: Hmm-mm!

JS: A video of a large snake boss by a waterfall.

YS: Mmm! *<gestures a wavy pattern like the boss would move>*

TK: Yeah! *<repeats the gesture>*

JS: *<laughing>* You guys know what I'm talking about!

YS: It wasn't released though, yes.

JS: There's very little about *Bounty Arms* online, anything you can recall is historically important.

YS: There should be a video on NicoNico Douga. I wonder why they decided to stop developing it. Because I brought a sample version to Tokyo, carrying it from Osaka, to introduce it to the editor of a magazine. Then I returned to Osaka after that, then it was already decided to stop development. So I had to call up Sony and apologise. And Sony was surprised. They weren't upset, but they were surprised, and all the sections at Sony started calling me to ask, "Why is it cancelled?"

JS: Did you know the reason?

YS: Not at all.

JS: Did you play it?

YS: Yes.

JS: What percentage was complete?

YS: Sixty percent. Already they had decided how many copies to produce for the first shipment.

JS: How many units?

YS: I don't remember the details, but probably 30'000 or 40'000 units.

JS: Do you still have that demo disc?

YS: No.

JS: Can you describe it? I've only seen the first level. What came after? Can you draw sketches?

YS: Hm? Levels? *<laughs>* I can't draw, and I don't remember much. I can't draw the characters or anything. The only thing I remember is doing this, *<gestures>* with your arm, which would extend. That's all I remember.

JS: Can you recall the second stage? It starts in a jungle, then there's a waterfall boss.

YS: Ahhh...

TK: It could be played on some demo disc, for the PlayStation.[29] I own the demo. But I don't know what comes after that stage.[30]

<Mr Saito and Mr Kuroda confer regarding the demo - at length>

[29] kidfenris.blogspot.com/2009/09/bounty-arms-demo.html

[30] The demo is just the first jungle stage and boss

JS: The reason I ask is, when the world ends and aliens visit the rubble, and all humans are dead, this book with our interview will be the only record of what was in the game.

YS: *<laughs>* Why do think this book will remain on the ruined Earth?!

JS: Well, this book and other books.

<everyone laughs>

YS: The only thing I remember is that Sony, all the sections in Sony, rushed to call me, asking why, why, why. Another thing I just remembered, was that when I was visiting Tokyo, to visit different magazine publishers, I just happened to stop at Sony to introduce this, then Sony staff locked me in... I know this is not what you want to hear, I know that what you want is content of the game, but maybe this is another episode to events. Sony's staff locked me in a meeting room and told me that I should check the advert for *Bounty Arms*, so they said, "Don't leave before you finish checking the advert!" I had to complete this advert then return to Osaka. Then when I returned, I was surprised to find it was gone - cancelled.

JS: The game was well on its way to release - at least in Sony's mind.

YS: Yes.[31]

JS: This list here of your games, this *Vajra* game, is this *Kishin Douji Zenki* for the PC-FX?

[31] *Bounty Arms* was an overhead action game for PlayStation with 2 selectable characters, gorgeous graphics, and a mechanised whip weapon

YS: That one wasn't me; the one on the list was for Pioneer's LaserActive system.[32]

JS: There was also a song for *Cross Blaim*?

YS: *<sings a little bit>* This is my handwriting. *<gestures to Comptiq magazine>* These are the lyrics printed here.

JS: Do you know there was a large article mentioning the song, in *GAMESIDE* magazine?[33]

YS: Yes, this was in *Action GAMESIDE*.

JS: A friend of mine wrote it - could I trouble you to sign his copy of *Cross Blaim*?

YS: Whooaaaah! Can I take a look at this?

JS: Sure.

YS: Probably I myself packed this, *<picks up leaflet>* into this paper bag, or put the game's cassette into the packaging. Maybe I even assembled the cassette!

JS: dB-SOFT staff assembled the games?

YS: All the staff did this. I remember using a screwdriver to assemble the cassettes, yes. Plus I blew into this paper bag, to inflate it, to put these items into it.[34]

JS: It might have DNA in it!

YS: So my DNA will remain on the Earth even after the aliens attack!

TK: We can make clones!

<everyone laughs>

YS: *<Signing Cross Blaim>* Aahhh, this is so nostalgic. This is my current signature. I can't remember how to write my old style one. *"Thank you very much, Komabayashi-san!"*

<discussion about signature, which pen to use, my two signature books, etc.>

TK: I have a magazine article with information of the *Cross Blaim* prototype. It completely describes the game.

JS: *<taking signature book from Mr Saito>* Oh, there's a second book to sign.

YS: Do you want the same signature?

JS: Feel free to put anything you like.

YS: Anything I like? Even curry rice?

TK: *<Noticing Mr Nishizawa of Westone's signature>* Is there any mention of his unreleased *Aquario* game?

JS: Yes! But he said it's top secret.

TK: Recently he was tweeting about raising funds for it. He found the master data for it.

JS: Yes, he has everything except the sound data, I believe. Almost everything is complete.

TK: But the soundtrack was released separately.

JS: True. I think it's just the coding for it they don't have.

[...]

JS: Do you know about any other unreleased games, perhaps from dB-SOFT?

YS: Nothing like that, as far as I know. Only *Bounty Arms*.

JS: *<hands details form>* Can I have your first and family names in kanji and romaji? Plus a postal address. These are optional: date of birth, place of birth, and blood type.

MF: Plus three sizes!

YS: Three sizes?

---

[32] An interesting oddity. For NEC's PC-FX there was *Kishin Douji Zenki FX: Vajra Fight* (developed by Hudson, 1995). For the LaserActive system (created by Pioneer, with NEC designed add-ons which could also play PCE CD-ROM games), there was another game called *Vajra* (developed by Data West) using the NEC-specific LD-ROM^2 format. According to the LaserActive Preservation Project, *Vajra* was a 1993 launch title for the NEC PAC-N10 in North America

[33] This was written by Takayuki Komabayashi from BEEP SHOP in Saitama - see supplemental DVD

[34] The *Cross Blaim* packaging, like most computer packaging of the time, was full of neat items. Various leaflets and the manual were stored inside a dB-Soft branded envelope, or "paper bag"

JS: No Matt, that's what the taxi driver would ask for!

<*everyone laughs*>

YS: OK. <*writes stuff down*>

TK: About unreleased games, I know a hardware game developer in Sapporo. Do you know a development company called Data East? Do you know an arcade shooter called *Darwin 4078?*[35] It uses an "evolutionary" power-up system. One of the music composers developed it. He also has many stories about the games of Data East. His name is Tomo Furukawa. He also developed the sequel, *Super Real Darwin*, which was converted to Genesis as *Darwin 4081*. The prototype of *Super Real Darwin* was a completely different game developed by another team. After the old team retired, he re-designed the game system and all of the characters in only in two weeks.

JS: We're in Sapporo tomorrow as well. We leave in the evening.

TK: I can give you some information I heard.

JS: Do you have his contact details? I'm worried I won't have time tomorrow. Maybe you can phone him and mention we're in Sapporo.

YS: Here you go. <*hands form back*> With three sizes.

JS: I hope you're happy now Matt!

<*everyone laughs*>

JS: Why did you leave Data West?

YS: That's something I can't really talk about openly. Not to the public, yet, anyway.

JS: That's OK. Not if it makes you uncomfortable. How did you come to do work for Pack-in-Video?

YS: How I came to compose for Pack-in-Video titles? This *Gulclight TDF2*[36] was another title from Data West. Pack-in-Video was just responsible for the publishing, but it was actually developed by Data West.

[35] Data East, 1986
[36] Turn-based strategy title, sequel to *T.D.F.* - also available on PCE CD-ROM

JS: You composed samples for *RPG Tsukuru 4*,[37] and *Music Tsukuru DX*. Was there any additional challenge, composing for products that allow users to compose themselves?

YS: Not at all. Whatever I'm told to do, I will do. It's not difficult. Whatever the situation, I compose music suited for it.

JS: Are you still involved with game music?

YS: I'm not doing it now, but if somebody wants me to, then I might do it. It's not like I quit. Probably Kuroda-san will start creating games.

JS: Mr Kuroda, are you a *doujin* game creator?

TK: Ahh, yes... Yes! Because my hobby is game programming. So now I'm making a really small game. I'm paying respect to the early videogames of the 1980s. So I offered Saito-san the opportunity to make music, and he made some for me!

JS: What is your game's name?

TK: It's *Nyam Nyam Snakey*. It has a primitive videogame style. It's a platformer. Do you know Universal? It's an arcade game maker. *Mr Do*, and other things. Something like that.

JS: And Mr Saito composed all of the music?

TK: Yes, there are two composers for this game. Half of the music is his.

[These were questions asked later, while at the Smileboom offices, alongside Mr Kobayashi]

JS: Mr Saito, can you name your favourite music from other companies? A top 3?

YS: Number 3... Game Arts.

JS: *Silpheed*!

YS: Yes, yes! Number 2... System Sacom.[38] [The company's musician was] Manabu Saito.[39] He passed away, but I was very close to him as a musician. He was very talented.

[37] Known as the *RPG Maker* series in English
[38] *Marchen Veil, Mansion of Hidden Souls*, plus others
[39] Composer on *Euphory* (X1) at System Sacom

JS: I'm sorry to hear that.

YS: And number 1... Yuzo Koshiro! *<laughs>* I don't want to say this, but I have to admit... Yeah, Yuzo Koshiro. I can't help mentioning it, but he is good. *<laughs>*

JS: Is there anything else you'd like to add?

YS: I've told you quite a lot! So I don't think I have any more. I just wanted to say it was fun at the time to work and take these kinds of silly pictures. *<points to magazine with photo of Mr Kobayashi - see subsequent interview>*

Takaki Kobayashi: I don't know why we were able to create something like that, looking back. Probably that was a time when there was lots of money everywhere.

YS: Because it was during the economic bubble years. I remember that we were laughing while we were creating.

Mr Kobayashi: We never heard about sales or profits, we just made things for enjoyment.

YS: *<reading from Cross Blaim advert adjacent Mr Kobayashi's photo in an old magazine>* This quote is from a fan named Sasaki, who used to live in Tokuroda. He was 14 years old and he said, "*Tooo[...]otemo omoshiroi!*"[40]

<everyone laughs>

Mr Kobayashi: That must be have been from one of the consumers.

YS: Probably it's an excerpt from the user questionnaire postcard, or something. That came with *Cross Blaim*. I was telling John that probably I was the one who assembled *Cross Blaim*, because everyone was working on that. Either myself or Kobayashi-san's DNA is in that paper envelope.

<everyone laughs>

JS: Is there any message you wanted to convey?

YS: I myself never imagined or realised that my work was followed by overseas fans, and to hear that makes me feel very, very glad. To those people, please check my website or homepage regularly.[41] And if I release something, please purchase it! Although the website is Japanese only, please do your best to read it.

JS: The web address is interesting. It's 3, 1... I can't remember it all.

YS: *<in English>* Three, one, one, oh, one. (31103)

Interpreter: Ah! That's a Japanese phonetic play on words. Three in Japanese is *san*, so *Sa*. And one is *ichi*, or the *i*. Then the 1 and 0 is ten, which can be pronounced *juu* or *toh*. So *Sa-i-to*. Then three at the end is *san*.

YS: *SA-I-TOH-SAN.*

Below: The map of Data West, in Osaka, while Mr Saito worked there

[40] Ree[...]eeeally fun!

[41] www.31103.com

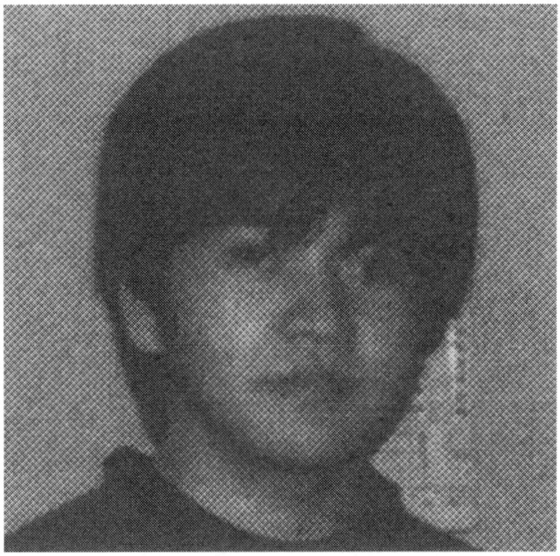

~ *In memory of* ~

斉藤 学

SAITO, Manabu

1970 ~ 1992

~ Selected Portfolio ~

Music composed while at System Sacom

Euphory	- Sharp X1, 1987 (Fantastic action-RPG with great music)
Fire Rock	- Famicom Disk System, 1988
Chátty	- PC-88, 1988
Void of 380'000 Kilometers	- Sharp X68000, 1989
Darkness of Kin	- Sharp X68000, 1990
Darkness of Kin: The Final Chapter	- Sharp X68000, 1990
Smart Ball	- SNES, 1991
Darkness of Kin	- PCE CD-ROM, 1993

He passed away, but I was very close to him as a musician. He was very talented. Manabu Saito... *380'000 Kilo no Kokuu*.[1] That's the distance to the moon. It was one of the games he composed for. That was my favourite of his music. We often talked about having a live event, a concert, for fans of Data West and System Sacom. Two musicians named Saito getting together to have this concert. But we just talked about it. We wanted to do that kind of event, but after that we didn't meet each other for a long time. Then I heard that he passed away one day, and I felt very lonely.
Yasuhito Saito - Data West composer

[1] Part of a long running System Sacom visual novel series; 38 万キロの虚空; literally "A void of 380'000km"

小林 貴樹

KOBAYASHI, Takaki

DOB: 1 April 1967 / Birthplace: Yubari, Hokkaido / Blood Type: B

~ Selected Portfolios ~

~ Takaki Kobayashi ~

Woody Poco	- PC-88, 1986 (later ported)	
Konyamo Asama de Powerful Mahjong	- Various	
Melroon	- PC-88, 1989	
Prince of Persia	- PCE CD-ROM, 1989	(Compression)
Dragon Slayer Gaiden	- Game Boy, 1992	(Program)
World Heroes 2	- PCE CD-ROM, 1993	(Tool programming)
Fatal Fury 2	- PCE CD-ROM, 1994	(Tool programming)
Studio P	- PlayStation, 1996	

Currently head of SmileBoom - developer of *SmileBASIC / Petitcom* for the NDS and 3DS, and also *Action Game Maker / Indie Game Maker* for PC.

~ Keita Abe ~

Konyamo Asama de Powerful Mahjong	- Various	
Melroon	- PC-88, 1989	
Prince of Persia	- PCE CD-ROM, 1989	(Main Programming)
Crest of Wolf / Riot Zone	- PCE CD-ROM, 1993	(Main Programming)
World Heroes 2	- PCE CD-ROM, 1993	(Main Programming)
Studio P	- PlayStation, 1996	

阿部 啓太

ABE, Keita

DOB: 8 February 1969 / Birthplace: Sapporo, Hokkaido / Blood Type: A

Interview with Takaki Kobayashi and Keita Abe (dB-SOFT)
7 October 2013, Sapporo, Hokkaido

After our initial interview with Mr Saito in a Sapporo coffee shop, we walked to the SmileBoom offices nearby, to conduct interviews with Takaki Kobayashi and Keita Abe, which had been arranged for us by Mr Saito. All three gentlemen had known each other at dB-SOFT, so this was something of a reunion. The atmosphere was jovial and nostalgic. For much of their careers Misters Kobayashi and Abe worked alongside each other, so there is much overlap for their questions.

JS: Gentlemen, can you recall the first time you ever saw a videogame?

TK: I think I was in junior high school, so it must have been when I was 12 years old or so. It was *Block Kuzushi*, or *Pong*.

KA: It was when I was 10 years old, or so. I was in elementary school, and at that time at the game centres we were able to pay 10 yen for a game - *Space Invaders* and *Block Kuzushi*.[1]

<we take out a magazine with a photo of Mr Kobayashi>[2]

TK: *<wild laughing>* I'm so embarrassed! It's so humiliating!

JS: Could you hold it up so we can get a photo?

TK: But it's humiliating!

<everyone laughs intensely - Mr Saito walks over to look, making jokes about it>

TK: It's harder than a mug shot!

JS: The book will detail your life and career, this is really interesting!

TK: It's so disappointing to remember that I was doing something like this. *<laughs>*

JS: Were designers promoted as celebrities?

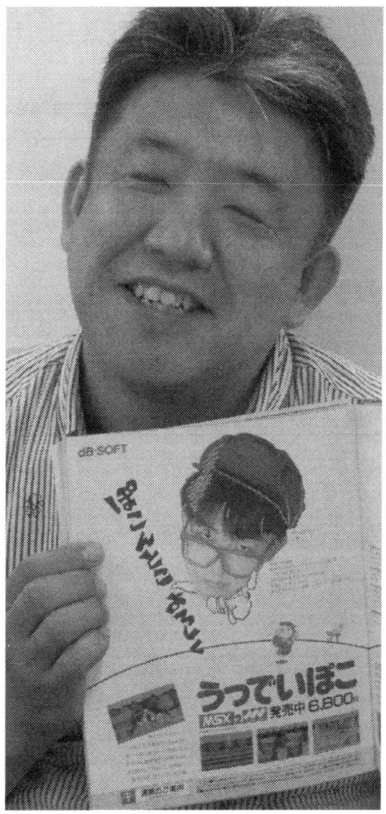

TK: *<laughs>* These types of photos were popular at the time, during the economic bubble in Japan. There was so much money in many companies, in dB-SOFT too. There was a boom surrounding people calling themselves *meijin* or "master" to advertise their company, such as Takahashi Meijin[3] or Hashimoto Meijin.[4] Basically whoever was considered to be really good at playing games - but actually they weren't so good! *<everyone laughs>* I think I'm mimicking those *meijin* in this photo.

MF: He doesn't think Takahashi Meijin is all that good. So there's a nice bit of juicy scandal there! You can interview Takahashi Meijin...

JS: ...And ask about his rival in Hokkaido! What was the first computer each of you owned?

TK: My first computer was a Casio FP-1100.

KA: Mine was a Sharp MZ-700, with the money I earned from a newspaper round. I bought it when I was in middle school.

<Nico returns and we discuss where to take photos>

JS: How about the CEO's office?

TK: There's no CEO office or anything. *<laughs>* We're all in the same office, we're that kind of company. The CEO and staff are all in the same office.

[1] *Block Kuzushi* = *Break Out* (Atari) or clones of it
[2] The magazine ad was for *Woody Poco* on MSX2, and shows a photo of Mr Kobayashi's head with a small caricatured body; the text beside the face says "Game designer Kobayashi"; below it is a mini-biography
[3] Toshiyuki Takahashi; Hudson's frontman for *Adventure Island* series, famous for high shmup skill
[4] Shinji Hashimoto, now producer at Square-Enix; AKA *Hashimoto Meijin* during the *Famicom Meijin Boom*; wore iconic red glasses identical to those in the advert

JS: It sounds like a warm atmosphere.

TK: There's a restricted area in the back of the room, with confidential machines. So you can only photograph from a certain limited angle.

<Nico and interviewees leave for photos>

JS: Regarding both of your careers, I know the games you worked on at dB-SOFT. They were *Woody Poco*, *Konya no Asa Made Powerful Mahjong*, and *The Story of Melroon*.

KA: *Woody Poco* was completed before I joined.

JS: Can you describe how you joined dB-SOFT?

TK: I was doing a job search when in senior high school, and I found an ad from dB-SOFT, so I went to an interview and I was hired.

JS: Which year was this?

TK: In 1985. I was a programmer.

YS: We entered in the same year; myself and Mr Kobayashi, and another staff entered dB-SOFT in the same year.

KA: I graduated from the same senior high school as Kobayashi-san, and every year either or both Hudson and dB-SOFT recruited new staff. But it happened that on that specific year, when I was going to graduate, Hudson was not recruiting anyone. Since I wanted to be involved in the game industry in Sapporo, dB-SOFT was my choice. It would have been in 1987, two years junior to Kobayashi-san. The dB-SOFT company was in the techno park in Sapporo. They used to own the building, with a tennis court, squash court, and showers. But they're obviously no longer there. [Years later] I happened to be hired, or commissioned for work, by another company which purchased that building, which dB-SOFT used to use. That round shaped building had so much dead space. The architect of the building must have been rather dumb to design that kind of building. *<laughs>*

JS: When you joined the company, I believe the mascot "*Bakkun*"[5] was already in place? Do you know who created it? Why was it called *Bakkun*?

TK: *Bakkun*! *<laughs - whispers with Mr Abe>* It's the shape of a stag beetle... I don't know.

JS: Is it a portmanteau of the words "bug" and "kid", as in computer bug?

TK: Hmm... It's a mystery!

JS: So it was inspired by stag beetles?

TK: We also thought that was a stag beetle.

JS: Do you know why *Bakkun* is crying?

<everyone laughs>

TK: It could be from the term computer bug. I wonder why it's crying!

JS: Was the president of dB-SOFT directly involved with game development?

TK: No.

JS: Did he play games by dB-SOFT?

TK: The dB-SOFT president? No, he wasn't playing anything.

JS: Mr Saito was programmer on *177*, can you remember that time at the company?

TK: The structure at the time at dB-SOFT was three teams: the word processor team, the game team, and the adult software team. Those teams were not making only word processors, games or adult software. They made all types of games. Therefore all the teams worked together in the same room. There was a rotation schedule, the staff members were not fixed. So sometimes they rotated or sometimes if a particular team wanted more staff, they would borrow from other teams. *<laughs>* We weren't really thinking that we were creating a game, but rather that we were programming something. Combining program code and graphics and sound. So that's how we regarded our work, as assembling something. So even female staff were debugging *177*, and she would just do it without any particular emotion. She wasn't

[5] バッくん; resembles a golden stag beetle, sort of similar to the FDS mascot

embarrassed, and [during debugging] would say, "Why can't I take her clothes?" <*laughs*>

JS: Did female staff comment on the game?

TK: No, not at all. It was no different than other regular games. It was what they did, and even the package was created by a female member of staff in the advertising section.

JS: Mr Saito thought it was a Mr Moriai.

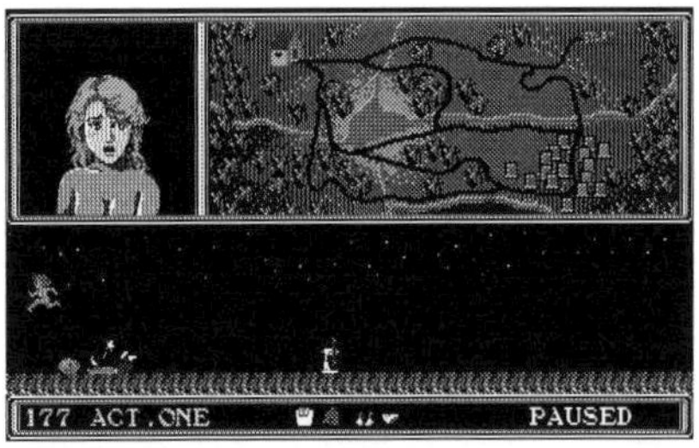

TK: Ah, Moriai-san! It's nostalgic hearing that name. <*chats with Mr Saito sitting nearby*> Female students from an art university, specialising in painting, came in - maybe 5 of them, or sometimes 10 of them - and drew all the female bodies for the adult software. Because they were studying art, it was somewhat artistic compared to the erotic game software of the time. Not just for *177*, but *Macadam*[6] too.

JS: They were drawing pixel art on the computer?

TK: Yes, only the dot artwork.

JS: Women from the art university came and used computers at dB-SOFT to create erotic art?

TK: Yes, exactly. They were using the Sharp X1 Turbo computer.

JS: *177* was considered a national problem. Is this why dB-SOFT stopped creating erotic games?

TK: <*laughs*> Probably, yes! In a way, that is correct.

KA: This mahjong[7] title we worked on also contains some erotic content.

TK: But that was mild eroticism. Within dB-SOFT there was not a borderline between erotic and regular games... Games were games.

JS: There was no impact because of the outcry?

TK: Other than it [*177*] sold well! <*laughs*>

YS: dB-SOFT was happy, rather than considering it a problem.

JS: Tell me about *Woody Poco*.[8] Was it already decided when you joined the company, or did you launch it?

TK: No, it wasn't started yet. I launched the project myself.

JS: Did you program all the versions, or were the conversions handled by others?

TK: Yes, actually for the PC-8801 series I was the programmer, but there was already a more senior programmer than myself. That person programmed all of them, and I was sort of the assistant.

JS: Do you remember anything about the FM77AV version?[9]

TK: <*converses with Mr Abe and Mr Saito*> Did we use 4'096 colours for *Woody Poco?* Probably it was converted by Inada-san, but we can't remember whether he was promised employment or not. Maybe he joined the company later.

JS: Can you recall his first name?

TK: What was Inada-san's name? ...Sorry, I cannot remember!

JS: You also designed *Woody Poco*, right?

TK: Yes, I did the programming and the overall design, the game's rules, and I also designed some of the characters.

JS: Many say *Woody Poco* is the best game from dB-SOFT. It's impressive for a first game.

TK: <*laughs*> Thank you, but I'm embarrassed to be complemented like that! It's so unexpected!

JS: It's original because it uses time, a day/night cycle, and also changing seasons.

---

[6] See preceding chapter for *Macadam* description

[7] The game on the table was *Konyamo Asama de Powerful Mahjong* - Mr Abe is holding it in his photo

[8] See opening pages for description

[9] FM-77AV was superior to older models of the FM-7 computer. Catch copy for 77AV was *So-Tennen-Shoku* (総天然色) meaning "All natural colour", since it could use 4'096 colours. The subsequent FM-77AV40 model apparently had 262'144 available colours

TK: There was a function called "palette" where you could change the colours, and it was in the hardware. I wanted to use that function, so for example I was able to change from blue to black. During programming I thought that the time of day or the seasons would be a good framework for doing this. That was the time when the PC-8801mkIISR was released, and that new type had more colours to use.[10] So I wanted to use them in order to express something, so came up with that concept of changing times, day and night, and the changing seasons. I invented that for the game just to use the palette function. So it was simple.

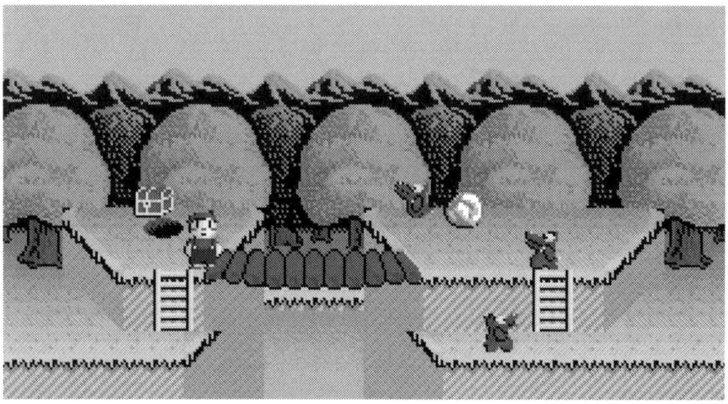

The FM-77AV version of Woody Poco

JS: The eponymous *Flappy*[11] appears in Stage 5. Was that your idea or were you asked to add him to *Woody Poco*?

TK: *<intense laughter>* Probably I used him without any permission!

JS: Was the character still popular at dB-SOFT?

TK: Yes, that's right. He was continuously popular. Even when we were doing this, *Flappy* was popular internally at the company.

JS: The ability to steal shop items in *Woody Poco* predates *Zelda* on Game Boy by 7 years.[12] I think Nintendo might have copied your idea...

TK: I think we just happened to come first. I doubt they copied us! *Woody Poco* was simply the result of us putting ideas that we could implement into the game. I don't think it was important enough to be copied. *<laughs>*

JS: Last question about *Woody Poco*. Do you remember any medicine to turn into a human?

TK: *<wild laughter>* It's not stored in our memory...

YS: ...but you guys remember all of this stuff!

<everyone laughs wildly>

JS: Well, we try our best.

TK: The reason I'm laughing is we've forgotten so much, but you guys remember so much!

JS: I know there was this "medicine" called *ningen ni naru kusuri*,[13] but there's little information on it. So I'm hoping you can remember what it was.

TK: *<laughs>* I remember it was not used in the end.

JS: Wasn't it something players received after completing the game? You write in to dB-SOFT with a password, and then you get the medicine.[14] Was it just a memento?

TK: Whoever cleared the game had to take a photograph of the screen - which would have to be taken using an old conventional camera, of the time, and then develop the film. They'd have to stick it to a postcard and send it to dB-SOFT. Then the company would send a sachet with the words *ningen ni naru kusuri* on it - *medicine to become a human is inside*. We were supposed to put it in an envelope and send it back. But actually, what's inside will probably disappoint some of the people who kept it, if they even did. It was seeds. I can't remember what flower, but it was seeds for flowers. Maybe five or six seeds in one sachet. But we didn't think anybody would really use it, by sprinkling it on the ground. Because we thought players would store them, as a treasured memento. So nobody really tried, I don't think.

---

[10] SR model introduced the V2 mode, which allowed up to 8 colours from an increased palette of 512

[11] A sort of mascot character for dB-SOFT

[12] Steal an item and you're branded a thief, complete with appearance change; shops no longer sell to you

[13] 人間に成る薬; lit. *medicine to become human*; because the eponymous Woody is a wooden puppet

[14] Quite a few companies did write-in promotions to receive something after completing a game

JS: What's the relation between medicine to become human, and flower seeds?

TK: *<laughs>* You guys! There was a female member of staff in the PR section, different from those drawing the female bodies, but she was making many different kinds of goods, and designing those paper things,[15] and she is the one who came up with the idea. But I don't know what's the relationship between the seeds and the medicine.

JS: Can you recall her name?

TK: *<converses with Mr Saito to confirm>* Megumi Yoshida.

JR: I was not expecting that, regarding the seeds. Were you the one who came up with the hidden secrets in *Woody Poco*?

TK: *<laughs>* Secrets?!

YS: I'm Googling it now!

<everyone laughs>

JR: John, let's give him a clue... Bikini!

TK: *<laughs - then realisation>* That's for the Famicom version!

JS: If it was for the converted version, then it was not your idea?

TK: No, it was my idea. The publisher of the game's guide book was upset because I didn't tell them this hidden secret. *<holds book>* This is a strategy guide for *Woody Poco*. But I didn't tell the secret to the publisher, rather I told the secret to some elementary school kids, then one of them took a photo and spread the information. So in the end the publisher was very upset. *<laughs>* That's what I remember.

JS: Can you describe the secret?

YS: I think you already know and are just testing Kobayashi-san!

<everyone laughs>

[15] Paper things = manual, calendar and *Woody Poco*'s adventure diary; basically like *omake*

TK: Probably Google knows better. *<laughs>* There is a shop in the summer themed stage and probably - I can't remember clearly - if you wait in front of the shop's cashier, just wait there for a certain period, then the woman at the register, her clothes will fall off and she is wearing a bikini. *<laughs>*

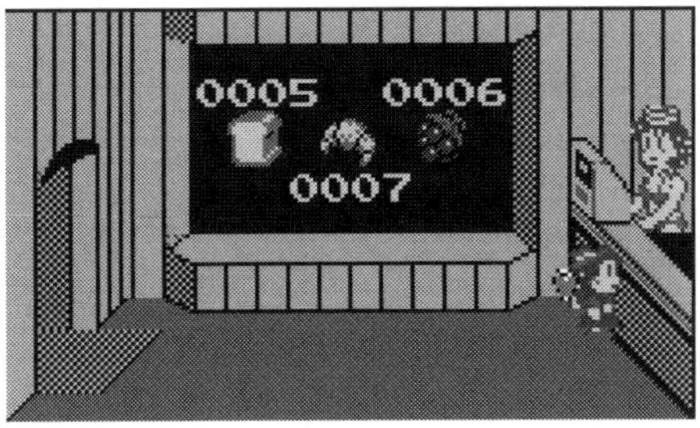

JR: I think you had to push a button 200 times to do that.

TK: *<laughs>* Really?! Is that right?

JS: You worked together on *Konyamo Asama de Powerful Mahjong*?[16]

TK: There was also a design team, we were the programmers.

JS: I believe the game had strong sales. It's different from other mahjong games, and has a lot of features, including an "easy mode" and secrets based on the in-game timer.

TK: First of all, there wasn't any pre-defined concept. At that time, not only with this game, but dB-SOFT's tendency was to include everything; we wanted to include and put everything we had into whatever we were making at that particular time.

JS: Ideas?

TK: Not just ideas, but everything we had. The only fixed idea was that it would be mahjong. If it's just a simple mahjong game, then it wouldn't be good enough. So we came up with "*Poco Mahjong*" which is inspired by "*Ponjan*"[17] - we weren't stingy at all with the ideas or materials. We didn't hold anything back.

MF: If they came up with something they put it in the game, to make the fullest game they could.

TK: *Ponjan* mode was simple, compared to regular mahjong, so even children could play it. Then we thought not just mahjong, but let's put a character and scenario, or story in it. Then the

[16] 今夜も朝までパワフルまあじゃん

[17] *Ponjan* (ポンジャン), also known as *Donjara*, is *mahjong* for children with simple rules

other idea was why don't we also put erotic content into it too? So everything went into this one game.[18]

JS: So if I understand this correctly, it's a mahjong game with a child-friendly *ponjan* mode, and also an erotic scenario for adults?

TK: No, it's probably not suitable for children! <*laughs*> But mahjong is somewhat difficult, because of the complex rules. This mode was so simple that even children could play. But obviously children did not play, because it contained adult material - the clothes of your opponent would come off! <*laughs*>

JS: *Ponjan* mode was more for beginners... I've heard a rumour that the original title was: *Ultra Miracle Super Wonder Powerful Excite Mahjong*.

<*both TK and KA laugh intensely*>

TK: This rumour is correct! It was originally titled like that. The reason we changed it, was that it was too long.

JS: Did you feel that yourself, or did the boss say it was too long?

TK: <*laughs*> My boss pointed it out, and I also thought it would be too long. All the staff said that was too long!

JS: You were talking about the rewards for people who finished your games, and also the postcards. Did you have a lot of contact with your fans - those who bought your software?

TK: I myself replied 100% not only to fans but also to the [customer feedback] postcards; whoever was angry or upset about certain aspects of the game. When they wrote to me with the claim postcards then I wrote back asking about what upset them, or what their complaint was, in a very polite way. Then that person would write back again. Those answers would be very useful for creating the next game, as a kind of hint. We are still doing the same thing today, using Twitter. If we explained and answered in a sincere way they would understand, and would not be upset anymore.

JS: Regarding the kanji in your name, I looked online and found a Takaki Kobayashi credited for *Tengai Makyou*, *Ys I&II*, and *Dragon Slayer*, is that you or someone with a similar name?

TK: This must be a different person, I was not involved in those first two games. Though I was involved with *Dragon Slayer Gaiden* for Game Boy, from Epoch.

JS: With *Dragon Slayer Gaiden*, were you shown the source code from Falcom's original version, or did you program from scratch?

TK: We developed it ourselves from scratch, and ended up with a breezy game that didn't feel like *Dragon Slayer* at all. It was my first time programming for the Game Boy, so I have fond memories of it.

KA: I wasn't involved with the *Dragon Slayer* project, but I remember that we did all the programming ourselves.

JS: You brought your own copy of *Woody Poco* for the PC-88. Did you keep copies of all the games you made?

TK: No, this is the only one I have. Maybe somewhere I have others, but I can't find them.

JS: I'd like to ask about a game which probably was not released, called *Black Wing*. Do you know anything about it?[19]

KA: I helped a little with that game, but it was Nakajima-san's project. It was a fighting game.

TK: What machine? Wasn't it for the Sharp X1, or was it PC-8801?

KA: It was something like *Final Fight*. I don't think that was released. I just helped, but... I can't recall Nakajima-san's full name.

JS: Do you know why it was not released?

KA: Probably because before this fighting game was fully completed, the game section within dB-SOFT became two different, independent sections. It became two different companies, outside of dB-SOFT.

---

[18] *Woody Poco* himself is a character

[19] ブラックウィング; the name is mentioned in online lists, but there is no other information

JS: Can you recall the company names?

KA: One was Agenda, and the other was Aro System I believe.

TK: The game section within dB-SOFT split, and became two independent companies, one was called Agenda, and that company still exists here in Sapporo. The other became a subsidiary of a company called ICM, which was making peripheral equipment for personal computers in Osaka. This subsidiary was called Aro System. So that's why *Black Wing* disappeared.

JS: Was it a decision from dB-SOFT to stop making games, or did the people within dB-SOFT want to leave the company?

KA: Probably the later reason! *<laughs>*

JS: May I ask why the staff wanted to leave?

<both TK and KA laugh intensely>

TK: Well, I wonder why they wanted to become independent... Hmm! *<laughs>*

YS: I was already away in Osaka at that time!

TK: That's right! To put it in a simple way, the top management spent too much money.

JS: Do you know what was more profitable at this time, games or utilities?[20]

TK: Utilities.

JS: There was a game by dB-SOFT, *Cross Blaim* for the MSX. It was a 3-player game, and much bigger. Then it was changed. Do you know why?

<TK and YS converse>

YS: I told John that it was because Hasegawa-san was selfish and he wanted to stop.

TK: What I can recall now is probably there was a graduate from Tokyo University - which is the best or most prestigious university in Japan, while Kyoto University is the second best. Either that was a student doing a part-time job, or maybe a graduate from there. But anyway, he started saying, "I can do it!" Then there was a setback and he failed, and he couldn't continue anymore. So that game had to be shrunk down. But I'm not sure either.

JS: *Konyamo Asama de Powerful Mahjong* had a sequel, was it made by you two gentlemen?

KA: Yes, both of us worked on it.

<we check how much time we have left>

TK: Are you leaving tonight, or are you here tomorrow? Would you like me to introduce you to other developers?

JS: I wanted to visit ZOOM but they were unavailable. Who would you recommend?

TK: There is Takebe-san, from Hudson, who made *Princess Tomato in the Salad Kingdom*, and *Family BASIC*, so if you want to interview him tomorrow, I can make a phone call. But Nakamoto-san, who made *Dezeni Land*, is a bit difficult. Since he gets angry when we meet him without asking about his schedule. I have to leave now, but if you can stay longer I can come back later and maybe we can all have dinner together. Do you have any plans after this?

JS: Sounds fantastic!

<Mr Kobayashi leaves for a moment>

[We converse casually while enjoying snacks - the recorder was off until a humorous anecdote]

MF: Mr Abe was saying there used to be a little, like... You know, Yoshinoya is a little restaurant with a pot sticker, you know gyouza, and the pot sticker would say "All you can eat" - so they would go down there while they were making the boxes, putting together the boxes, and he'd have his garlicky breath, with the leaks and everything from the gyouza, and then go

[20] As mentioned, dB-SOFT also produced office software, such as word processors

"HAAAAA" into the paper bag. <*laughs*> The customer would open it up and... <*sniffs*> It smells like gyouza!

JS: What was the average age of the staff?

YS: The former taxi driver was the real old one. The others were around 22.

JS: Mr Abe, the taxi driver would have been there when you joined?

KA: Ah, Shibata-san! He made *Macadam*. I can't remember his first name.

YS: I did not mention his name! I simply referred to him as the former taxi driver![21]

<*everyone laughs*>

JS: Don't worry, the record will show Mr Abe disclosed it.

KA: I don't have anything to do with him now, so it's OK.

JS: dB-SOFT was your first job in game development. Where did you go after dB-SOFT?

KA: I joined Agenda, one of the companies which became independent of dB-SOFT.

JS: Can you tell me more about the move?

KA: From dB-SOFT five people moved to Agenda, including myself and Kobayashi-san. There was also Fumiya Matsui, who used to be the director, or section chief, of the development or technical section. Another person was Kazuhiro Iga, he used to be section chief for the sales department. There was another person from outside dB-SOFT, a Goto-san. But I can't remember his first name. These five established Agenda.

YS: Wasn't Goto-san's first name Kazuhiro as well, albeit using different kanji?[22]

JS: Which games did you work on?

KA: After we became independent and established Agenda - I can't remember how long but it probably took about 6 months for one game - we were making games for the PC Engine, for Hudson. Three of them, including *Prince of Persia*, *Crest of Wolf*,[23] and *World Heroes 2*.

JS: What else were you involved in?

KA: *Doraemon* for the Game Boy. *Doraemon 2: Animal Wakusei Densetsu*. It's too old and difficult to remember now. <*laughs*>

JS: And you joined SmileBoom recently?

KA: Last week! After Agenda I was involved in the PlayStation's *Douga de Puzzle da! Puppukupuu*, a puzzle game involving video footage.[24] That was with Kobayashi-san, he planned it, and I was the programmer. Then that was followed by *Studio P*. Then a billiards game, *Carom Shot*.[25] And after that I quit Agenda before Kobayashi-san did, and I started up a company called LET, and became a CEO. For about 10 years I was making *conventional* mobile phone games.

JS: Conventional?

KA: Dumb phones!

MF: Not smart phones. They're called Galapagos phones in Japan.[26] The kind of built up Japanese phone culture that existed in the late 1990s until the early 2000s. So those mobile games, from that era.

JS: Yes, there's been some interest on English forums about this "lost world" of Japanese phone games which never left the country.

<*Mr Saito mentions something*>

KA: Although I was the CEO of LET, I wasn't involved in this particular project that Saito-san

---

[21] There was a humorous, slightly awkward moment because the name had been inadvertently disclosed

[22] This is correct - *Crest of Wolf* credits a "Kazuhiro Gotoh" as one of the managers

[23] aka: *Riot Zone* on Turbo Duo

[24] 動画でパズルだ！プップクプー ; The English subtitle is "*A digital movie puzzle game*" - screenshots look like a cross between *Mario Paint* and *Kinetic Connections*

[25] The sequel was localised as *Backstreet Billiards*

[26] *Garake*, meaning *Garapagosu Keitai*, or Galapagos Phones, denoting their isolated evolution in the world market; Japan Today has a good online article

just mentioned. It was a project for a very popular local TV programme, called *Suiyou Doudeshou*.[27] The company was making CD-ROMs for that, and I was involved just a little bit, but not really.

JS: Did you keep any materials from dB-SOFT?

KA: I don't have anything.

JS: Were you involved in the production of the data disk for the mahjong game?

KA: Ahh! Yes, I was!

JS: Why did dB-SOFT sell this data disk through the Takeru vending machine?[28]

KA: <*laughs*> I don't know, I didn't hear why.

YS: I was already out of dB-SOFT. When I was there, I wasn't told why.

JS: The data disk is called *Volume 1*, but there was no *Volume 2*. Why wasn't it continued - were the sales not good?

KA: Probably the reason that there is only *Volume 1*, is that before we started thinking about *Volume 2*, we started developing *The Story of Melroon*, which was the last game from dB-SOFT. So we couldn't do a *Volume 2*.

JR: For the mahjong sequel there's an interesting feature where the game would change based on the real-life calendar. If it's New Year the design changes to reflect this. This could be a first, a precedent.[29]

KA: This was Kobayashi-san's idea. I didn't realise it was the first!

JR: This was February of 1989.

JS: There were no other games that used the computer's internal clock?

JR: It's difficult to say. Maybe there was something on Macintosh, or Apple II. But definitely for the Japanese market it was something new.

KA: I didn't know that!

JS: Do you know of any other special dates you included in the game?

KA: Christmas and New Year's day...

JS: Leap years?

KA: No event for leap years... I can't even remember if there were birthday dates! Sorry, I can't recall! I remember making one for New Year, and I remember I probably put Christmas in too. But I can't recall anything else.

JS: *The Story of Melroon*, an action-RPG, had interesting features. For example there's a quiz, and NPCs say different things depending on whether it's day or night. It feels like an evolution of *Woody Poco*.

KA: At that time home computer games made by Nihon Falcom were said to be the highest in terms of technology or quality, for example *Ys I*, and *II*, and *III*. We wanted to make something equivalent to what they made. Kobayashi-san and myself discussed the possibility and then we were able to do parallax scrolling.[30] So the two of us were working on it, but Kobayashi-san's taste was for fantasy, so it became a fantasy type of game. <*laughs*>

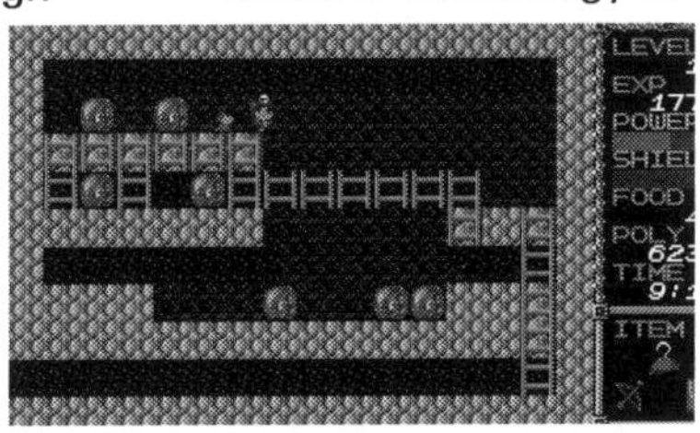

TK: *Melroon* is less a sequel to *Woody Poco*, and more a culmination of game ideas we wanted to use. Prior to development, while on a lunch break I tried to jump over the fence between the

[27] 水曜どうでしょう; *How do you like Wednesday?* A variety show produced in Hokkaido

[28] Loosely analogous to FDS vending machines. From MobyGames: "*Takeru was a software label by Brother Industries. Takeru did not sell software over the counter, instead it used vending machines placed in computer shops.*" Sadly a lot of vending machine exclusive titles are feared lost forever after Takeru closed the service. Vending catalogues detailing these lost games are now possibly our only record

[29] The significance is that in terms of Japanese games, this might be the first instance of real-world dates augmenting a game - at least the X68000 version

[30] In Japanese *tajuu*, lit. multiple scrolling

company parking lot and a grass field, fell on my head, and lost my memory. This was the inspiration for the system of remembering keywords from conversations, and erasing your memory by dropping a 16t weight at the church. Back then, our development style was to make what other companies weren't, so we didn't refer to software from other companies - although we did study other games for technology insights, such as methods of displaying graphics.

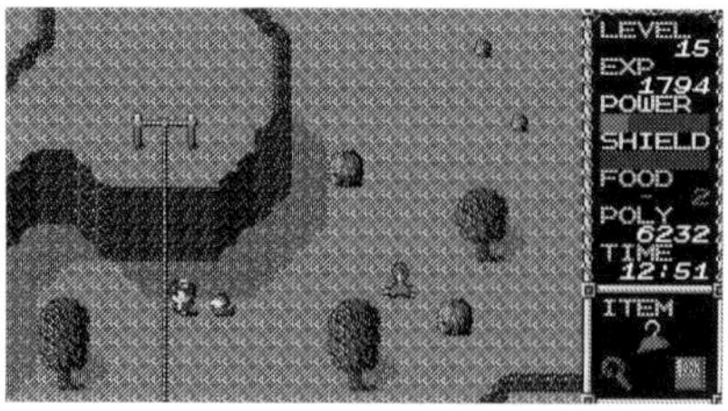

JS: Regarding your PC Engine games, did Agenda create the full games?

KA: The entire thing.

JS: *Prince of Persia* and *World Heroes 2* were conversions, but *Crest of Wolf* was a sequel to an arcade game by Westone...

KA: *Crest of Wolf* was a sort-of "semi-remake" - not a remake, more like a half-a-remake. Because there was an original arcade version, but we changed some of the characters or stages. So we used some of the original designs and characters, but we added and changed some characters or designs.

JS: Did you work with Westone, when developing *Crest of Wolf*?

KA: Yes, that's right. At that time their game was only available in game centres in the Osaka area, so I went all the way to Osaka just to see it being played, in the game centre. I saw it, learned a lot, and then came back.

JS: Were you shown *Riot City*'s arcade source code when creating *Crest of Wolf* for PC Engine?

KA: For *Crest of Wolf*, we borrowed the arcade PCB, and programmed the game from scratch while playing the arcade version for reference.

TK: I'm sorry but I wasn't involved as a programmer so I am unsure of the details, but the CPU was very different, so I think it probably amounted to just glancing at the source code. Alternatively, we may have ported the code by converting all the CPU instructions with the use of macros...

JS: The credits mention Akafuku Ieiri and Moro Okamora from Red Company Corporation.[31] Did you meet them? How was Red involved?

KA: The development of *Crest of Wolf* was subcontracted to us from Hudson. Since Hudson created the graphics for us, and since we did not have direct contact with Red Company, I don't know the details regarding Red's involvement.

TK: I'm sorry, but I don't know about Red's involvement. As it was subcontracted work from Hudson, maybe they were participating in some way on the design side of things?

JS: In Japan it was *Crest of Wolf*, while in America is was *Riot Zone*.[32]

KA: Yes, I remember that they changed the name when it was sold abroad.

JS: Do you know anything about the politics? I spoke with Mr Nishizawa of Westone, and the way I understand it, Sega ended up owning the characters in the original *Riot City*, which is why it had to be "half remade" with new characters.

KA: I did not know that detail. But I knew there was politics involved. At that time Agenda was not making the graphics for this game, so we were told, "Please change it to this."

JS: To what degree did Agenda work with Westone? Did Mr Nishizawa visit Agenda's office? Or did you liaise only with Hudson?

KA: No, Westone dealt directly with Hudson, and I, myself, only once went properly to Osaka to greet Mr Nishizawa, but that was the extent of it.

[31] As visual director and character design respectively

[32] In Japanese arcades the prequel was *Riot City*

JS: But Mr Nishizawa, Westone, is in Tokyo?

KA: Hmm... I can't remember now if it was Tokyo or Osaka! But I remember that I went to Westone to give greetings to Mr Nishizawa.[33]

JS: You travelled from Hokkaido.

KA: Yes, all the way from Hokkaido.

JS: Otherwise Agenda handled all other aspects?

KA: Everything to do with programming, yes.

JS: Did you send update reports, game portions?

KA: Yes, something like that happened between Hudson and Agenda. We did not know whether Hudson was showing it to Westone or not.

JS: I don't recall Mr Nishizawa mentioning Agenda when discussing *Crest of Wolf*.

KA: My involvement with Westone was small, just visiting the office and saying hello quickly, and then leaving.

JS: Is Agenda credited in the game?

KA: Probably not, I think.[34] There was nothing in the work done for Hudson.

JS: You also worked on *Prince of Persia*...

KA: Yes.

JR: Perhaps I have something wrong in my database, but *Prince of Persia* was not published by Hudson, but rather Riverhillsoft...[35]

KA: <*laughs*> Actually that was done by Agenda and Hudson, but probably Hudson wanted to show the name Riverhillsoft, just to show that many software houses were involved. But didn't mention Agenda.

MF: So Hudson was developing lots and lots of games by sub-contracting through places like Agenda. Then they would negotiate with other companies, like Riverhillsoft, for the sale and promotion. So you have many games that Hudson was developing, but it would appear that it was multiple companies publishing them.

JR: Just to show that many companies were developing for the PC Engine, so they can encourage others to join them.

KA: Yes, exactly, so Hudson didn't want the consumers to think that Hudson was the only company, and rather many companies were making games for it. So it's a major thing.

JS: So they funded development, and then paid other companies to publish them?

MF: Not necessarily paid, but negotiated with other companies to handle the sales.

JS: Creating a false front to show that everyone loves the PC Engine...

MF: <*laughs*> I don't know, it's interesting to think about how sinister it might seem, but actually that was fairly common back then. You'd contract out to other publishers.

JR: This was unexpected!

KA: But this is not what I heard directly from the executives. That's only what I think.

JS: What was it like working for SNK on *World Heroes 2*? Did SNK visit Hokkaido? Did you visit them in Osaka?

TK: Unfortunately we didn't have any direct dealings with SNK.

KA: I did not directly meet with SNK itself. Before development started, I travelled with a Hudson representative to an arcade where they were performing a location test. I observed and played the game there. After that, I remember that we developed the game while referring to the arcade PCB, and did not have any meetings or other contact with anyone other than Hudson. On PC Engine, with *Garou Densetsu*[36] and *World*

---

[33] In which case it seems the arcade game itself would have been in the Tokyo area only

[34] While Mr Abe and others are named in the credits, there's no mention of Agenda, only Westone & Hudson

[35] Perhaps best known for the *J.B. Harold Murder Club* series; later *Doctor Hauzer* (3DO) and *OverBlood* (PS1)

[36] Referring to *Fatal Fury 2*, circa 1994

Heroes 2, development started at around the same time. Hudson was really, really pleased with the work, and how quickly we were able to produce such high quality stuff.

JS: Did SNK give you source code?

TK: The source code was provided.

KA: But as mentioned with *Crest of Wolf*, we borrowed the PCB and used that for reference while programming the game from scratch.

JS: What other games did Agenda do? Not those you worked on, but any games.[37]

KA: *Douga de Puzzle da! Puppukupuu*, and *Studio P*, and *Ore no Ryouri*, all on PlayStation. And *Gacharoku*, which was for PlayStation 2. But that was around the time I left Agenda, so I don't know any further.

JS: So those four games were fully designed and developed by Agenda?

KA: Exactly. Everything. Designed and developed.

JR: I would say that *Studio P* is one of my favourite games.

JS: Can you share any stories regarding *Studio P*? I would like to introduce it to English readers.

TK: That was another title filled with game ideas we wanted to try out. The NeGcon was released together with *Ridge Racer*, and in trying to come up with a funny way to use this peripheral, I created the towel-wringing minigame. Also, if you complete all of the puzzles, a musical instrument played using the NeGcon, called the "*hegimona*", becomes available.[38] I also received a compliment from the inventor of the NeGcon from Namco, who told me, "I thought of towel-wringing, but I didn't think of actually putting that in a game." I also think *Studio P* may be one of the only console games that allows the player to do 3D modelling and walk around a 3D space.[39] Since we were making all this odd software, someone from SCE became interested in our work, and that led to development of *Ore no Ryouri*[40] and *Gacharoku*.

KA: Basically *Studio P* was initially music creation software, and also because we created *Douga de Puzzle*, in a way *Studio P* is the second version of that. But there's also puzzle game elements, as a kind of *omake*, or bonus. There's 3D modelling, and it uses the NeGcon controller, which can twist. Kobayashi-san wondered what we could make using the functionality of the NeGcon. So we came up with the idea of a flute, and also *hegimona*, and we were able to create this kind of "instrument", which was able to create analogue sound. Then another idea we came up with, using the NeGcon, was to squeeze the water out from a dirty cloth [in a cleaning minigame], called *Zoukin-Shibori*. So we were able to input everything. Many different ideas.

JR: So you would put anything in the game. In the end the balance was quite good, and it was really enjoyable. I remember I played it for days and days. Even though I had no skills regarding music, it was fun to play with *Studio P*.

JS: How did the market react to the game, and were the sales good?

KA: Hmm, I don't recall it sold well. Not that much. The "core fans" really liked it, a lot! And they sent in the questionnaire postcards with very positive comments. But the sales weren't that good.

JS: It sounds like it was ahead of its time. Did you lose money on it?

KA: The billiard game, *Carom Shot*, sold well. <*laughs*> We didn't really lose money with *Studio P*. (left)

---

[37] *Game Developer Research Institute* has an excellent online list covering Agenda and its games

[38] Note: *hegimona* （ヘギモナ） is a fictional instrument

[39] *Mario Artist: Polygon Studio* for Nintendo's 64DD (1999) also allowed players to create 3D models

[40] Awesome/popular cooking & restuarant management game for PS1, with cult following outside of Japan

Above from left: the author, and project assistants Joseph Redon and Matt Fitsko, at the dB-SOFT interview in Sapporo

YS: That billiards, *Carom Shot*, game sold well worldwide.

JS: Was it the first game from them that was sold worldwide?

KA: Yes, I think it was the first product that we released for consumers abroad.

JR: John, I strongly encourage you to introduce *Studio P*, it's unknown but very interesting!

JS: Do you have any materials left from *Studio P*?

KA: *<laughs>* Most of the ideas came from Mr Kobayashi, who would suddenly come up with an idea. So it wasn't really mine.

JS: SmileBoom developed *Space Milkman*. How would you describe working on XBLIG?

TK: I am very grateful to Microsoft for creating an environment that allows a small, unknown development company to make their work available all over the world. *Space Milkman* was developed using the *Action Game Maker* (*Action Game Tsukuru / Indie Game Maker*) software,[41] which we also developed. We were able to establish a system that allows game creators to run and sell games created with this tool on a console system. It's all thanks to XNA and the Xbox 360. I have no doubt that this helped spark the current indie game boom.

<Kobayashi-san shows us SmileBoom's latest 3DS product - Petitcom, or SmileBASIC>

MF: This is their new software, it's actually the third instalment, and it's the BASIC language; it's a BASIC interpreter that you can run on the Nintendo DS. So you can actually write BASIC programs and run them.

JS: This is by SmileBoom?

MF: Yes, this is what they're currently working on. This is their new release.

JS: Is this out already, or a prototype?

TK: It's coming out next year.

MF: So this is actually the third version. I remember a couple of years ago when they released the first one.

JS: Awesome. You program simple games on it?

[41] *Action Game Maker* is part of the *Tsukuru* or *Tkool* (ツクール) series of game creation software currently published by Enterbrain (a brand of Kadokawa). The most famous of these is *RPG Maker*, which has existed in various forms since the early 1990s

MF: Uh-huh. Yeah. It's a full feature BASIC.

<Kobayashi-san shows their prototype on 3DS, lines of code shown on the screen>

TK: *<laughs>* It doesn't really work too well with the 3D currently.
<lots of Japanese conversation about the prototype - including Tiny Xevious>

JS: So if we ran this code, what is it?

TK: This is just a test program, because we're still implementing all the BASIC commands. With this version, for 3DS, you could probably run... The 3DS is twice as fast as the DS, so you could probably create a game with the quality level of a SNES title, or even a 2D PlayStation game. You could actually program the game with this version of BASIC.

JS: So a simpler Famicom style of game would be super easy?

TK: Yes!

MF: Yes, I remember an advertisement for them, a couple of years ago.

JR: SmileBoom were at Tokyo Game Show.

JS: I didn't see the booth - my apologies.

TK: It was the "Hokkaido Booth".

JS: I was doing interviews all day long.

MF: They sold about 20-30 thousand copies in the United States and Europe, for previous versions of this BASIC language. There's a lot of nostalgic people.

TK: The first one was not 3DS, it was DSi, it was one of the downloadable titles for DSiware.

JS: Is it possible to share programs?

JR: You have to go to a convenience store, like 7/11, you put a code in, it prints out a page with QR codes, and then you read the QR codes with your DSi camera, and then you get the program. I did it for *Tiny Xevious*.

JS: 2014 is the 50th anniversary of the BASIC language. Both dB-SOFT and SmileBoom produced their own variants of BASIC. Would you like to comment?

TK: Many developers in Japan and the rest of the world, including myself, learned how to program by creating games in BASIC on computers with limited expressive power. I have the job I do now because I was using BASIC in my youth. Nowadays, computing devices designed for touch panels from the ground up are readily available in homes, along with a huge number of free apps. Computers have become just tools for running apps. It is my hope that by bringing back BASIC, we can regain that sense of a person being in complete control of the computer, and increase the number of children - and adults - who are interested in using a computer to make things.

JS: Would you like to add anything about SmileBoom's DS BASIC, or your future plans?

TK: Currently, we are developing a new *Petitcom*, *SmileBASIC*, for the 3DS. This software allows you easily to implement the stereoscopic camera, touch panel, and sensors with BASIC commands, making it possible to create 2D games in BASIC that are on the level of a Super Famicom or PlayStation game. I believe that if there's an environment allowing you to make games easily, there will be young people who will show us new ideas that no one's ever seen before. It is our hope that young people will create something we never could have imagined.

JS: Do you have any final messages?

MF: Was Takahashi Meijin really not that good at videogames?

KA: Well, everybody knows that Takahashi Meijin isn't *that* good. <*laughs*>

TK: SmileBoom is taking on new members and steadily growing in scale. We will continue to make friendships with people around the world who want to turn interesting ideas into something concrete, and continue to create products filled with joy and delight rather than violence and savagery. We work for a day when everyone around the world has a smile on their face. If you're ever interested in our little company, please give us a call! <*smiles*>

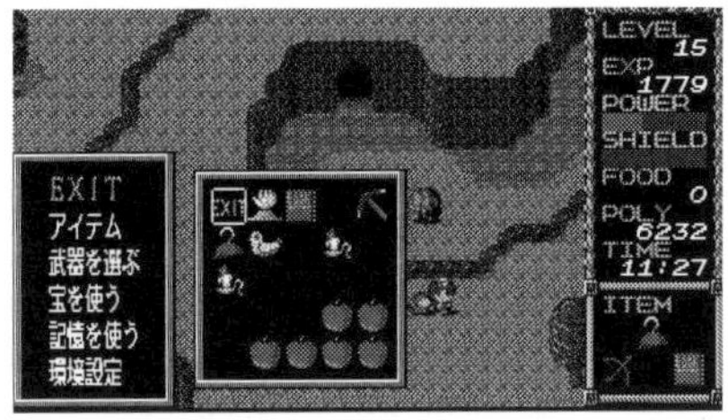

<*author prepares to leave*>

JS: Thank you for giving of your time so generously today.

MF: And thank you for making such great games!

TK: <*laughs*> Oh, it's just part of the job!

Dinner interview with Takaki Kobayashi and Keita Abe

This conversation took place during an evening meal with the president of SmileBoom, Takaki Kobayashi, and his colleague Keita Abe, plus Matt Fitsko, Joseph Redon and Nico Datiche. There were no planned questions, but I recorded the conversation anyway, and it yielded some fascinating snippets. Since it was unscheduled there was no official interpreter, though Matt Fitsko, our guide for the Hudson laboratory and Sapporo in general, kindly joined us and filled in. In instances where the Japanese speaker was unknown, ambiguous or multiple people, I've attributed it to MF who interpreted. Where I could clearly recognise the original speaker, I've used their initials instead. The information here should be taken in the context it was provided - a casual evening of merriment. In a journey filled with difficulty, this enjoyable night out in Sapporo was a blessing.

<everyone laughing wildly>

MF: The person who made "dB-BASIC" was the main programmer for *Woody Poco*.

<brief technical clarification on what ICE stands for: In-Circuit Emulator> You'd use the probe to access the circuit directly and emulate different computer systems.

So they were saying, the way that you could make the scrolling and everything move faster on the PC-88, was by making a smaller horizontal band on the screen. You could cover up the top and bottom and then the remaining screen area you could scroll it very quickly.

JS: Because there was less to process?

MF: Yes, it was just the way the video memory was arranged.

JS: Was it related to the way the PC-88 refreshed the monitor?

MF: I'm not sure it had to do with the monitor so much, rather the way the graphics sub-system of the PC-88 worked. They [dB-SOFT] kind of looked at *Ys* by Falcom, and saw that's how you could do the scrolling and make it so smooth.

<Joseph converses with Kobayashi-san and Abe-san while author has Nico take photos - lots of laughing; more conversation about life in Hokkaido and dB-SOFT>

MF: They were saying the dB in dB-SOFT stood for decibel. I always thought it was database, as in database software.

TK: In the CEO's office he had a huge speaker!

JS: I'll go over this recording carefully later.

Everybody shouts into microphone:
"WOODY POCO WAHEY!!!"

<wild laughter all round>

TK: The guys who made *Flappy* were a pair of planners named Oikawa and Obata. I wasn't really sure whether they were employees or what. They were already gone by the time I joined, but they would still show up from time to time. They would come around, wearing like a hood, and they'd hand me this plan, or scenario document, for the games. They'd just say, "Well, make this. Make *Laptick*," or whatever it was.

JS: And everyone had to take turns making erotic games, for dB-SOFT's alternative Macadamia Soft[1] brand?

TK: Yeah, but it was more like if this team needed somebody, you could pull them from another division. People would just kind of switch around as needed.

JS: What I found fascinating was that the erotic artwork was done by female art students. Did dB-SOFT train them in using the art programs?

<Discussion between JR and TK regarding female staff doing the erotic pixel art - branches off into other topics, such as game packaging>

MF: So the packaging for *177* was made by mostly women, in the sales and planning division.

<MF translates question about art programs>

TK: First there was a girl who was good with computers and she knew how to draw pixel art.

KA: And a [male] student came in and was also drawing stuff.

TK: Then he brought in more female students, and he kind of trained them on how to convert the art, or just how to create pixel art. *<laughs>* He did the naughty bits!

<everyone laughs>

JR: You've got to see the original packaging for *177*, it's gorgeous, with embossed gold letters, and as Kobayashi-san just told me, it cost a lot of money to make it.[2]

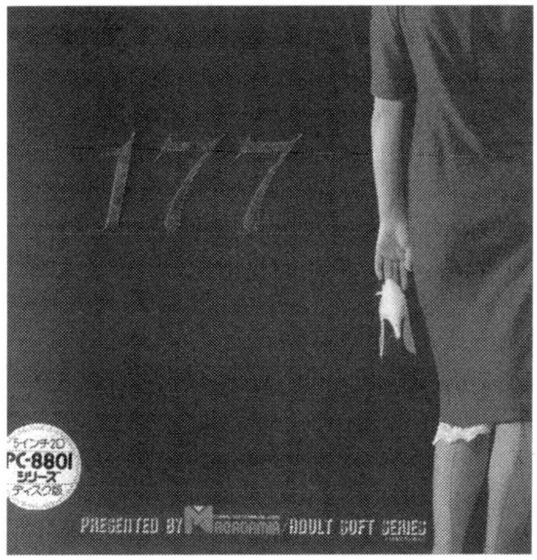

<Discussion on concerns whether they would get in trouble>

MF: They didn't really think that *177* would be involved in that kind of... You know, there just was not that sort of impetus to restrict [game developers]. So they could just kind of make whatever they wanted to.

JS: The ending was interesting. If you catch the girl, you end up marrying her.

MF: Right, right. So you're trying to have your way with her, but then if you get her, you kind of... It's really this sort of sexist thing, that you can turn rape into a running game. But then at the end, you marry the girl. Then the guy kinda gives you this sheepish look at the end, like, "Whoops, I fell in love."

JS: Would you describe the gameplay as being an "infinite runner" almost?

MF: Well, no, there's an ending. Because you have to chase her across the screen and she throws debris at you. And there's stuff in the park, like the... *<to Joseph>* What else is there in it? There's the dogs, and rocks, and you have to jump over them.

JR: And a mole, various types of rubbish...

MF: So you have to make it across the game.

---

[1] マカダミアソフト; for publishing *eroge*

[2] *177* lettering is shiny gold foil embossed on the paper. It's not clear in b/w, but the woman is holding a shoe

JR: Chase the girl, catch the girl, and *do it*.

MF: Yes, catch her before she gets away.

<lots of conversation in Japanese - regarding who came up with game's shocking premise>

TK: It was Mr Shibata, he thought up the game's idea! *<laughs>* He was in charge of all the Macadamia Soft stuff.

MF: He was the taxi driver mentioned in the earlier interview.

<Japanese conversation regarding the ending>

MF: So yeah, they weren't really thinking it through too much. You know, the guy takes responsibility for himself, [chasing the girl and then marrying her].

<talk about Tiny Xevious, Naoki Horii>

JR: He knows about Mr Horii,[3] who is very, very famous I think today, around retro gaming and emulation. He's like the sensei of emulation. It's crazy what he did for *Fantasy Zone 2*, because it's not emulation. He started programming it on the real hardware, Sega hardware. I mean the PCB. After that they made a conversion to the PlayStation 2. They did not develop it directly for PlayStation 2. So you can run it in arcade mode, 15kHz. I think it's the only PlayStation game running in 15kHz. So you really have to try to get an interview with Mr Horii.

JS: I sent him the email, with a list of my last 10 days available, but never had a reply. We need to email him again and say we're running out of slots. Now there's only five left!

JR: I think he's so busy that he probably missed your email. Send him a reminder.

<conversation about Kobayashi-san's Studio P on PS1, and eating - fatty pork with grated daikon radish>

JR: I think I finally understand why *Studio P* was so interesting.

<laughter all around>

[3] Naoki Horii, head of M2

TK: I didn't have much of a policy[4] when making games back then. I just tossed in everything that seemed interesting and fun.

MF: Mr Kobayashi's philosophy was just to put everything into the game.

JR: [Games like *Studio P* were] a total mess, all over the place, but somehow formed a whole.

TK: Hey! We all worked pretty hard on that stuff! *<laughs>*

<lots of laughter regarding the game - discussion regarding Namco's NeGcon controller and its use in a musical minigame>

JR: About the only game that used the NeGcon was *[inaudible - sounds like racing games]*, so *Studio P* piqued my interest when I saw "NeGcon compatible" on the box. What's going on here? It's a music game, but it supports the NeGcon? That's odd; I'm gonna buy it.

MF: That's one thing I really like. I collect a lot of PlayStation games, but I like the experimental nature of how a lot of developers were doing new things. It is really kind of a precursor to the Wii style of control.

<Japanese conversation regarding NeGcon - lot's of laughter>

MF: Apparently the Namco guys were really impressed by Kobayashi-san's towel wringing simulation game that they made for *Studio P*!

JR: *Studio P*, it's addictive! *<laughs>*

<very lengthy conversation between author and MF on visual novels, while JR converses in Japanese with TK and KA>

JS: I don't think any dB-SOFT games were officially released outside of Japan? Does Kobayashi-san know if dB-SOFT was ever in talks with someone about releasing something?

JR: We asked this same question to NCS, and Mr Suzuki's answer was they thought they did not have the power themselves, to do overseas

[4] The English word "policy" has entered the Japanese lexicon and evolved somewhat. It can refer to a plan of action, but also connotes a set of personal convictions or rules unique to an individual

marketing. So they were waiting for someone to buy their license and do it for them. I think this never happened for dB-SOFT because they were in Hokkaido, and they were mostly releasing games on computers. They did produce some Famicom games, but I don't think they had a chance to bring them overseas. Hudson, which was also in Hokkaido, was different because the founder of Hudson went to America. He saw what was going on in America, and said, "This will happen in Japan too." So he came back to Japan, founded Hudson, and started reselling computer games and software. The same as Softbank. Hudson and Softbank are similar.

MF: Yes, they really are! Softbank never invented, they were only publishers.

JR: Not sales, distribution. From the beginning they said, "We'll only do distribution." And they did well, because they had 70% or 80% of the distribution market in Japan.

MF: The guy who started Softbank, he was a real shark. Softbank is hugely successful now, you know they brought the iPhone over to Japan and things like that. [...] The CEO of Softbank, he's kind of like the Japanese Bill Gates. He's a really sharp businessman. Softbank, now they're mostly about mobile phones, but they're called "software bank" because they were originally this big seller of computer software.

<TK and KA and mentions something related to floppy disk production - intense laughter>

JS: Did you develop the copy protection for dB-SOFT's computer games?

TK: That's something we all did. In fact, there was a company called Tokyo Denca [5] that manufactured floppy disks, and they generally decided where to [intentionally damage part of the disk for copy protection purposes].

JS: So you would create a master disk, and take that to Tokyo Denca for mass production? Or did you give them the source code?

TK: The data was already written to the floppy disk, so we would tell them that we created this type of mechanism, so only read these sectors, and so on.

JR: The Japanese Game Preservation Society developed technology able to make a complete copy of the disk's surface while leaving the copy protection intact. So we can preserve an exact copy of the software.

TK: *<Incredulous>* Wow, that's... *<laughs>* What are you people doing? *WHAT ARE YOU PEOPLE DOING?!*

JR: Do you disapprove?

TK: You're crazy! *<laughs>* All this talk about floppy disks and technical stuff...

JR: We're just a bunch of weirdos.

TK: How did you even get involved with all that kind of stuff?

JR: I just can't help it.

TK: *<laughs>* No, it's great. Admirable. Good luck with that. *<laughs>*

MF: *<laughs>* He says you're just a couple of weirdos - he says thank you, thank you for all these extremely obscure observations about all of their old stuff.

<conversation about local area>

TK: There are a lot of *bishoujo* and *ero* game developers based in Sapporo. Many of them have been in business for a long time. There are at least 12 companies, because they make a calendar every year, and each company is in charge of one month.

<discussion about sea urchin, how the best in Japan is in Otaru, and a sea-urchin festival>

JR: Tomorrow you're interviewing Takeshi Takebe. He was in Hudson Soft from the beginning, so he knows everything about how the company started, and what happened between *Dezeni Land*[6] and their first game on the MZ-80K system.

---

[5] 東京電化, officially romanized as Tokyo Denca (www.denca.co.jp). Apparently they were one of the largest cassette tape/floppy disk duplicators (a company contracted by a software studio to produce the actual retail copies of computer game media)

[6] www.hardcoregaming101.net/dezeniland/dezeniland.htm

<*confirms with Kobayashi-san the time and meeting tomorrow*>

JR: You really have to concentrate on the beginning and even before the beginning of Hudson. Because Hudson started in the USA. I think there is little to ask after *Salad Kingdom*.[7] Because we know everything after this game. But before, I think we have no one to ask.

JS: Did *Family BASIC* come after it?

JR: OK, *Family BASIC*, of course. You will also have Iwasaki-san, who started with Hudson in Tokyo, with development of PC Engine games. So he doesn't know about the old stuff of Hudson's, he doesn't know about the PC-88 or Sharp X1. Actually... He does know, because he asked a lot of people, and he compiled all the stories in his *doujin* magazines, of course. But I cannot remember if he wrote anything regarding Hudson prior to 1984. So you have to concentrate on this period.

JS: Would this Mr Takebe know about *Cannon Ball*, for the PC-6001?

JR: It's not a rare game. I have it.

JS: It's basically what *Pang* was based on. I wonder if he knows how Mitchell Corporation got hold of the license.

JR: If you have time, why not. But definitely concentrate maybe not on games, but on the company and people. Just grab names, dates, and places. Stuff like that. I have questions, but they will just be questions I think regarding *Dezeni Land*, and *Salad Kingdom*. Just make sure the readers understand they're very important games. It's just 90 minutes, then afterwards we have to pick you up.

TK: Would you like something else to drink?

JS: Could I have another of these?[8]

TK: No, go ahead!

<*everyone laughs*>

MF: He's going to order you a different flavour.

JR: So Nico will take photos at the end, because time is precious at the beginning.

MF: Personally, I'd like to know more about all the different hardware they were involved in. Like how they met up with Sharp to make the operating system for the X1.

JR: I need to leave to write some questions. Can you coordinate with Kobayashi-san to meet at the right place tomorrow? I will send the questions to your phone. OK, John, see you tomorrow after the meeting.

<*Joseph departs with Nico*>

JS: Did you envision yourself here?

MF: <*laughs*> I envisioned maybe a quiet evening...

<*lots of laughter and discussion*>

<*waiter brings new variety of sake - as ordered by Kobayashi-san; brief discussion, reconfirmation of the type he ordered*>

Waiter: Your sake, sir.

TK: This is the shinigami brand of sake?

Waiter: Yes sir, the *shinigami* brand of sake. That's correct.

<*everyone laughs*>

MF: <*laughing*> He said it's not a very strong sake, but it's just called... *THE GOD OF DEATH!*[9]

[7] *Princess Tomato in the Salad Kingdom*, first released 1984 on computers as *Salad no Kuni no Tomato-hime*

[8] A local variety of speciality sake

<wild laughter>

MF: Not strong at all, it's actually quite mild! *<laughs>*

JS: The name is just there to deceive you...

MF: He's putting down the *GOD OF DEATH!* Maybe it's like the Death character in *Discworld*? Sort of friendly.

<smartphone camera comes out>

MF: He's going to take a before and after picture.

TK: Will it go down OK? *<laughs>*

[Author's note: the sake is served in a tall glass sitting inside a tiny bowl, the glass being filled to overflowing, the liquid's tension then forms a slight dome above the rim]

JS: The challenge now is to drink without spilling.

<tastes sake>

JS: That's fantastic. *Kanpai!*

<everyone says kanpai!>

TK: *<laughs>* You might not wake up tomorrow morning.

MF: We're staying at a Sapporo capsule inn.

TK: What are you doing after you leave Hokkaido?

JS: Returning to Tokyo tomorrow. I've got one day off then more interviews.

TK: Ah, that's great!

JS: Then after that I'm going to Osaka to interview someone from Zainsoft.

<Matt talks with Kobayashi-san and Abe-san>

MF: Mr Abe, he joined dB-SOFT because he really wanted to make games. Not like Mr Saito who just accidentally fell into it.

JS: Then ends up programming one of the most controversial games in Japan!

MF: *<laughs>* Yeah! Also, it turns out Mr Abe and Mr Kobayashi both went to same high school together.

KA: So Kobayashi-san joined dB-SOFT, and since we were from the same high school, and since Kobayashi-san was doing a really good job, thanks to that [the guys in charge] said, "Well, you're Kobayashi-san's friend," and then they brought me on board too.

TK: *<laughs>* I wanted to play games on the computer, but I didn't have the money to buy the games, so you have to make your own. In England are there similar movements going on to preserve the early British software scene?

JS: Lot's of people preserve games, hardware, magazines, everything. Almost everything related to the ZX Spectrum is preserved. In England people still make new games for these old machines.

TK: Eh! New games for old computers?

JS: Programmers like the challenge.

TK: *<Jokingly>* Weirdos!

<everyone laughs>

TK: Unbelievable!

KA: The challenge is how can we overcome the limitations of these machines, and create something enjoyable.

JS: Make the machine do things not thought of.

<conversation in regarding computers>

[9] Lit. 死神

MF: He was just saying, now it's sort of... Not censorship, but I mean, the restrictions that Nintendo places on software, and also for PlayStation and Vita, what you can make...

JS: In terms of content?

MF: Yes, in terms of content. What types of things you can put into a game. Even today it can still be quite strict, about what kind of content can be put into a game. Of course with the old computers you could basically just do whatever you wanted.

JS: You couldn't put "H content" in.[10] H games which are ported from PC to Xbox 360 or PS3 have the erotic content removed.

TK: Do you come to Japan often?

JS: The first time I came was 13 years ago.

TK: The PlayStation 2 had just come out then.

JS: The second time was 12 years ago.

TK: There's a place in Hokkaido where the waves are really tall. It kind of makes these cliffs. It's kind of like the English coast! *<laughs>*

JS: This is my first time on the island of Hokkaido, so I can finally say I've been here.

TK: Hokkaido is easy to visit for an Englishman, because the weather is mild, or cooler than Tokyo is.

[... ... ...]

JS: When joining dB-SOFT, was Mr Shibata there?

TK: He was already there. He was kind of running his own little coffee shop before. *<laughs>* Then he got some kind of construction license to operate construction vehicles, bulldozers and things, then he changed his mind and said, "No, I want to make software for a living!" *<laughs>* So he came to dB-SOFT and made *Macadam*. The last game he made - he made another game after *177,* since *177* was so big - *<laughs>* but it was terrible! The title was *"Oooku"*, from the Edo period.[11]

MF: *Oooku*, which is kind of this medieval Japanese, sort of like the matrons of the house.[12] There was a TV series based on it. It's kind of like the women who ran things back in medieval Japan. They would run the household, so presumably the game was based on that, if the title was *Oooku*.

TK: You had all these Japanese style doors,[13] and they would open like this, *<makes sound effect> Ba! Ba! Ba! Ba! Ba! <laughs>* Then inside, you see a woman in a kimono, and she turns around, and she pulls up her kimono. *<laughs>* So you could see her derriere, basically, and then it's like *Space Invaders...*

<everyone is laughing wildly by this point>

TK: Her butt just kind of wiggled back and forth, and the player has this sort of bamboo pole, and you just kind of had to stick her in the butt.

JS: Sounds like *Donkey Kong 3* to me!

<everyone laughs even harder>

TK: Yes. So that game didn't make it at all, as a product. They killed that one quickly. They put that one out of its misery. That was his idea, but they killed it, and said, "Yeah, this is definitely not marketable!"

JS: If *177* got the government upset, can you imagine what that would have done?

TK: *<jokingly>* In a certain sense Mr Shibata was a genius, a certain type of genius...

JS: Don't they say there's a fine line between genius and madness?

<Matt explains the phrase - everyone laughs>

TK: But I actually owe a lot to that man, just for... You know, just kind of learning a lot of things about the industry. I was kind of under his wing for a little bit, so he probably influenced me as a developer. It's nostalgic discussing these old times. Back in the old days we were just able to make whatever we wanted, we never really

---

[10] Adult or hentai material
[11] 大奥 / おおおく

[12] Wikipedia: The harem of Edo Castle, where the women connected to the reigning Shogun resided, including the shougun's mother, wife, and concubines
[13] *Fusuma*, sliding door-like room partitions in Japanese architecture. Similar to paper-based *shouji*, but opaque

thought about, how much is this going to sell? Is there a market for this? It was just, sort of, an environment of free creation.

JS: A wild, untamed frontier for games.

TK: <*laughs*> The world is just a smaller place now. You know, now you can come across the ocean and keep in contact with us online, and talk about this old stuff.

KA: I'm really grateful that people all the way over in England would play our games and appreciate them. I'm really happy to hear that.

JS: A common story I hear is that developers in Japan don't realise how many people love their games outside of Japan.

TK: It's a nice experience for me too, because you bring back all these memories and things which you've kind of forgotten about. You think to yourself, "Yeah, I did do this..."

JS: Like medicine to turn you into a human being?

TK: <*intense laughter*> We loved giving little gifts and prizes to the fans.

JS: That's why the games are remembered.

TK: Yes, dB-SOFT had a company slogan, and it was: "From Sapporo to the World." So that was kind of the... You know, the company had that sort of mentality. At SmileBoom we're kind of inheriting that ethos - we want to give something to the world, with what we create.

JS: Did Kobayashi-san work on *Crest of Wolf*,[14] or was that only Abe-san?

MF: That was by Agenda, wasn't it?

JS: I'm sure both Abe-san and Kobayashi-san went to Agenda.

<*interprets question*>

KA: Yes, I did all the programming.

TK: And I manipulated the graphics data, to squeeze it all down, consolidate it. I made this tool, "Tsumetsume-kun".[15] <*makes compressing sound effect*> To compress it to something that would fit on the CD. I did the same thing for *World Heroes 2*, I was in charge of putting together the graphics data. The first time I did this was for *Prince of Persia* on PC Engine. I had to put the player character, the prince, into these little boxes of 128 pixels by 128 pixels. <*intense laughter*> So the turban was also kind of the pants! We just reversed the pants and used that![16]

JS: I never noticed - I'll have to check!

<*everyone laughs*>

TK: I'm not sure that it was actually the pants and the turban, but I had to fit all of the images for player animation into 128x128 pixel areas, so I cut down on the character data by reusing portions that were even slightly similar. I think there were other minor parts that were reused, but I've completely forgotten. Sorry about that.

KA: On PC Engine, with *Garou Densetsu*[17] and *World Heroes 2*, development started at around the same time. Hudson was really, really pleased with the work, and how quickly we were able to produce such high quality stuff.

TK: Ahhh... I have a simple love for programming games.

KA: Back then, Kobayashi-san's theme was, "how to waste technology".

TK: How to waste technology?

KA: How to waste technology making the stupidest sort of game we could possibly create!

<*everyone laughs*>

MF: Something that is technically excellent, and then kind of worthless artistically.

JS: Well, as long as you liked it, you can't say it's artistically worthless.

<*discussion and laughter*>

---

[14] Japanese name of *Riot Zone* on PC Engine CD-ROM (1992); sequel to arcade *Riot City*

[15] From 詰める (*tsumeru*): to squeeze, cram in, pack tightly

[16] I think perhaps they're referring to graphics which were re-used in a cut-scene

[17] He's referring specifically to *Fatal Fury 2* on PC Engine, circa 1994

[176 words redacted, relating to a game I made, involving a vicar who turns into a lawnmower]

<everyone laughs, followed by brief conversation in Japanese>

TK: Shibata was on a totally different level. There's no way I could live up to him.

KA: To me he was just some weird old guy. *<laughs>*

JS: I wonder where he is. He must be 70 now?

TK: I've no idea. Maybe around 60 years old. He wasn't that much older than us. He might even still be in his 50s actually. There's a dB-SOFT game called *Produce*, do you know it? Shibata-san came up with the concept for that game too.

[Author's note: Produce deserves more than a footnote. While Oooko was offensively trashy, Produce for Japanese home computers is staggeringly ingenious. It plays like a prototype for Tecmo's Deception - you place monsters in a maze to scare one of your three friends to death. Mechanically, the game displays three animated, first-person dungeon crawling POVs from all three friends simultaneously as they walk around, stumbling into monsters until they die of a heart attack. I nearly had a heart attack myself when discovering that a Makoto Shibata was designer on Tecmo's Deception. Could they be the same person? Probably not, since YouTube credits for Produce list Shoichi Shibata as the director... Unless he used a fake first name?]

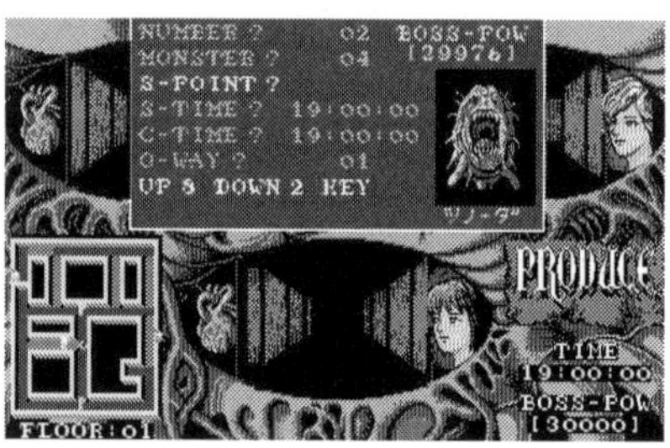

TK: It was kind of like this monster house, and there's these three characters who are trying to escape. The characters are actually controlled by the computer, while they're trying to escape from the house. Then there's ghosts or monsters which appear along the path. *<laughs>* The ghosts that pop out scare the characters, and so then their heart rate goes up. Then if it goes up too much the heart bursts - BAM!

JS: Did you enjoy today?

KA: I never thought I'd be reliving all these memories with a guy from England! I'm glad I had so much fun making games 20 years ago.

TK: *[Not quite audible, but it sounds like Mr Kobayashi is teasing Mr Abe for implying that his current job isn't as fun as it was 20 years ago]*

TK: At times like these, I think of how much fun it would be if I could speak English. *<laughs>* It's so frustrating!

JS: When the book is out, people who can't speak Japanese will hear both of your stories.

TK: *<laughs>* I didn't have very much important stuff to say! We had fun this entire time, just making games. The past was a lot more fun, now we kind of look back and remember how fun it was.

JS: You're fortunate to have lived in that era.

MF: They said if they would have known, they would have been more careful about keeping a record, and preserving things for posterity. *<laughs>* They had people who basically lived at the office, for up to a month, just sleeping there and working through every day.

JS: Under the desk in a sleeping bag?

MF: Yes, just lay out a futon under the desk.

KA: *<laughs>* I would just work until I sort of passed out, then just lie down, wake up, then get back to work again.

JS: Because it's Hokkaido, what was the heating situation like in the winter?

TK: The computers were hot! We didn't need the heating, because the computers generated it.

JS: I was speaking with someone from Masaya, and they said because the boss didn't want to pay for heating, when they slept in the office they wrapped themselves in newspaper.

TK: That's not going to cut it in Hokkaido, you can't keep warm with just newspaper when it gets cold here! *<laughs>*

~ Appearing in a later volume ~

Three Human Entertainment alumni return to reflect on a life in games. Above, from left: **Masatoshi Mitori** discusses how he helped create ocean-survival title *Septentrion* when just a student. **Hifumi Kouno** talks about his *Clock Tower* series of horror titles, running Nudemaker, plus a couple of games you probably don't realise he worked on. **Masaki Higuchi** taks two unreleased games from Human Entertainment, including a *Space Harrier* clone for Virtual Boy. **Ryouji Amano** rounds out our coverage by explaining how the Human Creative School came about, before discussing his series of popular sports titles.

稲船 敬二

INAFUNE, Keiji

DOB: 8 May 1965 / Birthplace: Kishiwada, Osaka / Blood Type: *secret*

~ Selected Portfolio ~

Street Fighter	- Arcade, 1987 (Graphic designer)
DuckTales	- NES, 1989 (Graphic designer)
Chip 'n Dale Rescue Rangers (**pictured**)	- NES, 1990 (Graphic designer)
Yo! Noid (aka: *Kamen no Ninja Hanamaru*)	- NES, 1990 (Character design, illustrations)
Breath of Fire	- SNES, 1993 (Character design, illustrations)
Mega Man 1 ~ 7	- NES/SNES, 1987 ~ 1995 (Various designer roles)
Mega Man 8	- PS1/SAT, 1996 (Producer)
Mega Man 9 ~ 10	- PS3/X360, 2008 ~ 2010 (Producer; design role on *9*)
Mega Man X 1 ~ 3	- SNES/PS1/SAT, 1993 ~ 1995 (Character designer)
Mega Man X4	- PS1/SAT/Win, 1997 (Producer)
Mega Man Legends	- PS1/N64/Win/PSP, 1997 (Producer)
The Misadventures of Tron Bonne	- PS1, 1999 (Game concept, producer)
Mega Man Legends 2	- PS1/Win/PSP, 2000 (Producer)
Legend of Zelda: Minish Cap	- GBA, 2004 (Producer)
Lost Planet: Extreme Condition	- PS3/X360/Win, 2006 (Producer, original story)
Dead Rising	- X360, 2006 (Producer)
Street Fighter IV	- Arcade, 2008 (Executive producer)
Lost Planet 2	- PS3/X360/Win, 2010 (Executive producer)
Dead Rising 2	- PS3/X360/Win, 2010 (Executive producer)
Asura's Wrath	- PS3/X360, 2012 (Executive producer)
Dragon's Dogma	- PS3/X360, 2012 (Executive producer, uncredited)
Resident Evil series	- Various
Onimusha series	- Various
Hyperdimension Neptunia Mk2 & Victory	- Cameo appearances
Zombrex: Dead Rising Sun	- Director

Mighty No. 9 - **www.mightyno9.com**

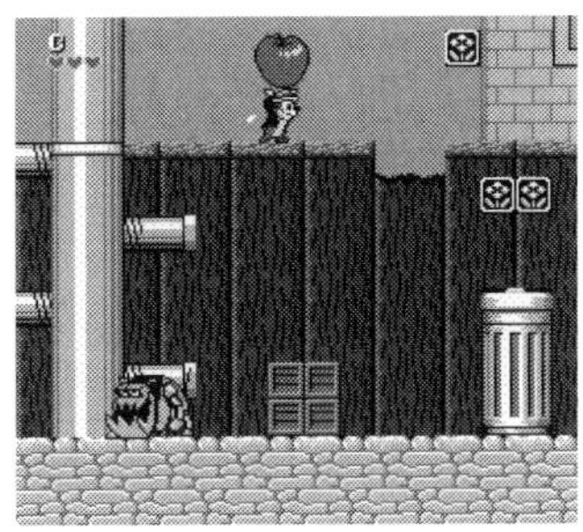

© Capcom

Interview with Keiji Inafune (aka: INAFKING)
29 October 2013, Tokyo

Due to our limited time of 90 minutes I was unable to cover all the topics planned, notably Mr Inafune's work on popular cartoon licensed games, and also an interesting YouTube video where someone successfully simultaneously completed four different Mega Man games (3-6) using a single controller input. When discussing with a colleague a proposed question related to the YouTube video, he gave me a worried look, "You can't ask him that! They're going to find me unconscious on the street and the newspapers will be saying: 'Foreign journalist mysteriously disappears in Tokyo.'" Though I had some difficult questions, Mr Inafune was extremely eloquent and diplomatic throughout. A true gentleman.

JS: What was the first game you ever played?

KI: Perhaps Nintendo's *Block Kuzushi*. It came out before the Famicom. It was a games machine, but there was no cartridge functionality. Whatever games were in there, they were the only ones available. They were things like maybe a *Pong* or tennis game, or a *Breakout* type of game. It was the one before the Famicom and it was a big success for Nintendo. This was around about when I was in primary school, or just starting middle school.

JS: I've seen them at conventions.

KI: I thought games were amazing, it was the era of *Space Invaders*. Back then there was a game centre and I really wanted to go, but in those days there would be older people who would threaten you for your money, or say, "Hand over the cash!" So my school had a rule that you were not allowed to go to the game centres. But I really wanted to go, and that's when Nintendo brought out their first machine. Eventually I got hold of one these systems. In the arcades they had *Space Invaders*, which is what I really wanted to play, but unfortunately the Nintendo machine did not have that. There were two versions, one with 6 games, and one with 12. The one I had came with 6 games.

JS: With the bright orange casing?

KI: <*looks up image on smartphone*> That's the one. You had to twist this dial.

JS: When did you want to create games?

KI: Actually, when I was growing up and going to school, games were nice for me, but I was not super invested in them. What I really wanted to do was be an artist, and draw and produce artwork. I actually got my first job at Capcom through my artistic desire, through art related job hunting. It wasn't until *Mega Man* was done and I had worked on it, that I really became interested in game development and creating games. Certainly, my interest when I was growing up was art.

JS: When you joined the *Mega Man* team, the Rockman character[1] was partially designed?

KI: When I joined the *Mega Man* team his outline existed, his basic pixel art was done. Not even pixel art, rather his pixel structure was done. Kind of the skeleton, if you will. Things like his final look, as well as things like his jumping animation and so on, still had to be completed. He existed as a single sprite when I joined, no animations existed, no poses existed, and they had not been designed when I joined the team.

JS: Your mentor, Akira Kitamura, he created that rough outline? Was he in charge of the team?

KI: He was the leader of the team for *Mega Man* and *Mega Man 2* - nowadays you would call this role "the director".

JS: What was it like working for him?

KI: <*laughs*> He was an incredibly strict person! He was strict but it was because he had a real love for games. He was always in the office, slept at his desk, and he was always researching or working on the games. He taught me about the required strictness of game development. You can't slack off. You have to do your best all the time. That's sort of the message, of what I learned from him. Kitamura-san would sleep through the night, at his desk, and then the next morning he would do the checks for the content that I had produced the day before. Obviously he didn't sleep so well, and since he was a very, very strict person, often some of the stuff that was good - the stuff that we had all worked on - he would say, "This is no good, and this is no good," and so on. You could say he was a perfectionist. He was incredibly hard to please, with incredibly high standards, and his rules towards character development were so obsessively careful, true perfectionism. That bled over into his approach to game development as a whole. My team in particular really bore the brunt of his drive I guess, his demand for perfection, and we were directly under him. So it was... Yes, we had his full attention. He taught me about the concept of getting exactly what you want for the character on to paper and into the game, not settling merely for something close to your design. It's about getting exactly what you want in the game. He taught me that. I would say that I think the way he taught me, that very strict way, is what kept me interested, and kept me going. Even after he stopped, and I worked on the games without him, I do believe his influence and his approach, which I now believe in, shines through all the products I've worked on, and all the *Mega Man* games. So even though he was not involved in some of them, I do believe that they are games produced under his methods, even if not by him.

JS: Would you describe yourself as a strict team leader, for *Mighty No. 9*?

KI: <*laughs*> I think when it comes to the development of games, and my titles, I think that strictness for perfection of the content is absolutely necessary. Even now. But, I think if I

[1] In Japan Mega Man is called Rockman, we alternated names throughout the interview

was to treat my team now in the way I was treated back when I was working on those early games, they would quit. You have to think about the environment, you have to think about the way you talk, you have to think about the way you treat people, and I think that has changed. So although the strictness is required with the product, I like to think that the way I interact with my team is different.

JS: This strictness, how does it relate to allowing the public to create content for *Mighty No. 9*?[2] Online someone said you've assembled a talented team, but are diluting their skill by allowing amateurs to be involved.

KI: <*laughs*> Actually I've been doing that all along, since *Rockman* and *Rockman 2*. I put in user designs that children had drawn. It was just something I naturally wanted to do. Now, about whether the quality of the boss designs declined after *Rockman 2*, I do not think that's true. I did all of the boss designs. People don't contribute a fully designed boss, they don't contribute a personally drawn sprite, or anything like that. They will send in their basic design and I will take the fundamentals of their idea and produce the boss from that. So if for example the user design features a boss with a cross on his head, I would keep the cross and design the rest. I would take the fundamental characteristics of a user design, add my personal touch, and create a likeness with those characteristics, like a portrait sketch artist. That way, the fans would see the final result and think, "That's my design!" But this way the quality is still maintained. In fact, even fans without much artistic skill could still contribute. Obviously if we just put straight in what they made, it would probably make the game less entertaining for other fans. So by doing this we think we can both protect the quality of the game, and make sure it feels right, and feels coherently a part of the game. But also that Kickstarter backer's idea, their personality, can be put into the game.

Shinsaku Ohara: So the idea behind the Kickstarter project is that you get ideas from backers, which is something that's been going on even from *Mega Man* - after *Mega Man 2*. It's not something new that we started, with this Kickstarter, having people pitch in their ideas. It's something that he [Inafune-san] has been doing since back then. So it's just along the same lines of what he's always been doing.

JS: Tell me more.

KI: From *Mega Man 2* onwards. The first game was the only one which didn't have any influence, and then from the second one onwards Kitamura-san said, "I want to get some ideas from players and put them in."

JS: As far back as the 1980s this interaction existed. How was it facilitated, back then?

KI: Well actually, the concept of crowd sourcing if you will, or getting ideas from the public, is not that rare in Japan. Even back then. In the 1980s, many Sentai anime or manga like *Kinnikuman*, *Kamen Rider*, *kaiju* entertainment,[3] and others, would use magazines to conduct fan submission campaigns and solicit new monster designs from many different children and so on. I did that when I was kid - I saw those things being run and I even sent a few of my own ideas in. It was something that Japanese kids were all familiar with and participated in. We didn't invent the system, we didn't pioneer this idea. We simply took that as a hint, as an idea for something that we wanted to do with *Mega Man*, and our aim was to have characters and bosses that we ourselves would have enjoyed as children. We wanted to get back to that sense of childlike excitement and wonder.

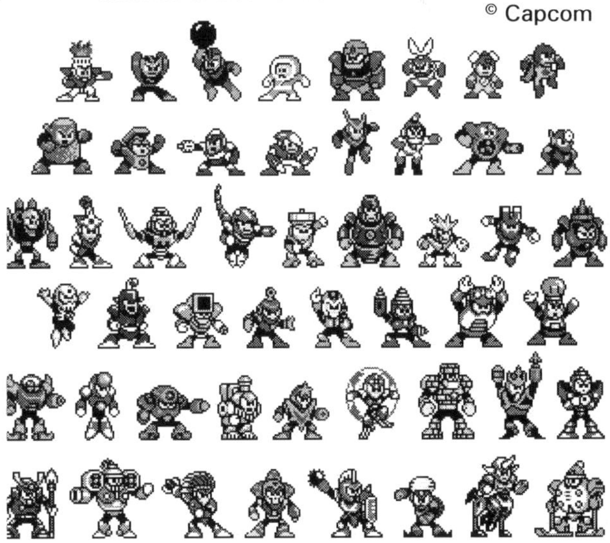

Selection of bosses from Mega Man 1~6

[2] Some higher level tiers allow public participation

[3] Lit. "strange creature" - basically monster films *et al*

JS: Did you get piles of postcards and letters?

KI: I think the most we ever saw was about... We used to get over 100'000 ideas, I think. That was around about the time of *Mega Man 5* or so. That kind of time. I'm not quite sure. But it was a lot! We got a lot of ideas.

JS: *Mega Man* was made blue due to the 56 colours of the Famicom. With an unlimited palette would you have used a different colour?

KI: The Famicom limit was the reason, and from the very first pixel sprite design by Kitamura-san it was done using that palette, so he was very limited. There were reds, but they were very garish reds. Also at that time there was Mario, and he's red! Also, if you look at things like *Power Rangers*, and superhero groups, the red is always the leader, right? For some reason the leader always wears red, while blue is usually the support character's colour. So maybe some people thought, "Why is he blue?" when they saw him. But that was the way the Famicom worked. I think if we had not had the limits of the Famicom, perhaps he would have been a different colour. Perhaps red.

JS: Of course when you created the Zero character, for *Rockman X* on the Super Famicom, you made him red.

KI: Yes, you're right. When we were first developing *Rockman X*, Kitamura-san was already gone, so I took the lead. I wanted to take the opportunity to design a character I really liked, and make him the lead character. That character was Zero. I wanted a character who was Han Solo rather than Luke Skywalker. But if you make Han Solo, Luke still has to be the main character, right? So *Rockman X* had to be the main character, but I gave Zero all the cool traits. Designing *Rockman X* was supposed to be my responsibility, because he's the lead character. But I gave that job to my subordinate so I could focus on Zero.

JS: Did you want to make Zero the lead character at that time?

KI: I knew I couldn't do that. But I could make Zero seem like he could have been. He was my personal main character, and I designed him that way. I made him red, a hero's colour.

© Capcom

JS: I thought Zero's design was excellent.

KI: Thank you!

JS: Today there are no colour restrictions. But *Mighty No. 9*'s character design uses a lot of blue.[4] Do you feel you're restricted by the popularity of *Mega Man*?

KI: I think it's fair to think of this as a spiritual successor to the *Mega Man* series, and so obviously if you look at his shape, at first glance you will think of *Mega Man*. I think of *Mega Man* when I first glance at him, so I think everybody does. And that's fine. But the thing to remember is that *Mighty No. 9* is a transforming character. The way it works is, he's number 9, right, and there are 8 other robot friends, a team if you will. In *Mega Man* when you beat a boss you would steal their special ability, but in this game, you go and help or rescue the other 8 members of the robot team, and in exchange you transfer their data to yourself and become able to transform. Mighty is actually grey, he's not blue, and as you use their skills the parts of his armour will change to different colours. When we did the Kickstarter the panels of the armour were blue, but [Mighty] is not blue - he's not blue because of *Mega Man*. It's just one of his different armour colours. Since I am involved in the design, obviously I carry that *Mega Man* influence forward, but even though Mighty may look like *Mega Man* at first glance, we deliberately designed him to be unlike *Mega Man*. But I would say, to answer the question word for word, I don't feel limited by the designs of the past games.

Shinsaku Ohara: I think your question was, why is *Mighty* reminiscent of the original *Mega Man* character. The design of *Mighty No. 9* is rather simple, and it stays true. Because he's got his other brothers, other robots you could say, his

[4] This observation was based on the very earliest promotional materials for the Kickstarter

design is neutral, as a base. Once you rescue the others, he transforms. I'm not talking just about colours. His shape is very neutral, but it will change as he transforms.

KI: He's grey the whole way through, but when you want to use a particular skill you will change your shape and your colour to a specific type.

JS: Tell me more about the transformations.

KI: It's not just a weapon change, it's not just a colour code change, it's a full transformation of the whole body.

JS: I noticed the Intercept logo next to the Comcept logo. How are they related?

KI: The way they were developed, they're basically the same company. But for legal reasons it was beneficial to have both existing, and the way it started was that Comcept would be the designers, or the planners of the project, and then Intercept would be the actual coding and putting stuff on paper in development. But I think it's better just to think of them as one company, or one name, really, in terms of what we're doing.

JS: There was another logo in the entrance, for Ding. Are they related too?

KI: Ding is also part of us, and it's the department that deals with the development of social games, and cellphone games, and things like that. With regards to Ding, in the same way as Intercept, it's really best to think of it all as one big entity. That was also because of legal reasons, we needed to have that legal separation of the two. But it's all one big group, if you will.

JS: *Mighty No. 9* is seen as the highest profile Japanese crowdfunding project to date. What initiated it? Did other projects inspire you?

KI: The reason we went with Kickstarter, is we obviously needed money to produce the game. We had a target of about ninety-million yen (90'000'000), or $900'000, but if we'd just used Japanese crowdfunding[5] we probably could have gotten to about 5-10% of that. It would not have been realistic to produce a game on that budget. So once we decided we needed fundraising which included an international audience, there's not really much else besides Kickstarter. So that's why we chose it. In terms of you asking about were we inspired by other Kickstarter projects, I think they acted as a proof for us that it could work. But I don't think there's a particular project, prior to our Kickstarter, that made me decide to do it.

JS: For a lot of developers Tim Schafer's adventure game was the catalyst.

KI: It was not the only reason we chose to do the Kickstarter, but certainly the success of DoubleFine reinforced in us the belief that Kickstarter could work. If we were only to use Japanese crowdfunding, I believe the absolute best we could have hoped for is 5'000'000 yen.[6] That's my prediction. But DoubleFine had raised considerably more than that, so that's why we decided to go for Kickstarter, and this was our target - the 90'000'000 yen.

JS: You actually beat DoubleFine. In the end it was $3.8 million for *Mighty No. 9* compared to $3.3 million for DoubleFine.

KI: Yes, though we did not beat them, we simply raised more than them.

JS: A noble viewpoint! All the funds raised are public knowledge - do you feel there are risks in having your finances publicly known?

KI: No, I don't think there's really any risks, or negative elements. I actually think having people know... Having a target tells people that we know how much money we need to produce this game. When we hit that target it tells people the game will happen. It's something they can believe in. I think openness in development, and openness in relations with your fans, is a good thing. So no, I don't think there's a risk. I think there's merits to it, rather than negatives.

JS: If outside entities know how much money you have, it might affect the quality of services and quotes they provide. Perhaps license fees to develop on certain platforms?

[5] There are a couple of bespoke Japanese analogues to Kickstarter, though the goals reached don't compare anywhere near to Kickstarter's massive amounts

[6] £33'300 / $50'000

KI: The license fee is set, so it is not affected by the amount we raise. What I'd like to make very clear is that the ratio of income share between us and the company that would own the hardware platform, is fixed. It won't affect the way we use the funds, it won't affect the way we interact with that hardware maker. It will be handled in a way that is standardised, or professional for the industry. So it's not a case of we're taking advantage of the funds we've raised, or that the hardware developers would take advantage of the fact we raised that much.

JS: More funds also means higher expectations.

KI: No. I mean, I think it doesn't matter if you're just on your goal, or if you're ten times that, the expectations from the users are always high. Because they've donated their money - they obviously believe in our ability, and they demand that we use our ability to the best, to produce the best game we can. I think within the functionality of Kickstarter there are the stretch goals which allow us to add more things in, but even if we could not do that, the expectations of the users are high. Obviously there's a pressure that comes from that, there's a pressure to perform, to produce, but the amount of money that's written on the website does not change that. I believe that regardless of the amount of money we raise, and regardless of the number of people who pledged, the demand for quality and the demand for us to perform to our best is always there.

JS: How would you say the Japanese games industry has changed since you joined Capcom, with regards to creative freedom?

KI: Speaking about the way the games industry has changed, its approach and that sort of thing... Actually when I began working on games it was relatively free, because games didn't take so long to develop. And they didn't really cost very much to develop. The first *Rockman* had a team of 6 people, and we did it in about 4 months. Which means that relatively speaking there wasn't really that much of an investment from the company. If it had not come out, if it had been cancelled, it wouldn't have been the end of the world. Maybe for the first two-thirds of my career, I was operating under that sort of style. Obviously there was pressure, and maybe pace was the pressure, we were a little bit hurried by the company, perhaps. But the only pressure we had at that time, really, was from our users to make good games. Then maybe, and it's hard to say exactly when, but maybe about 10 years ago there was a sort of... slump in the Japanese games industry. Maybe there were some complaints about the quality, and that's when the business side of the companies we worked for - all companies in Japan - that's when they put a lot more financial pressure and business pressure on us as developers. All of a sudden we were working under pressure from the users, and pressure from the business side and financial elements of our companies. I felt it was the sort of thing which could not be avoided. I did not feel particularly angry towards the business side, it was just something that came to be. So seeing Kickstarter, and seeing the opportunity to make a game exclusively funded by the users, exclusively funded by people who care about games, for me it felt a little bit like we were going back to the old way of doing things. I think yes, there's pressure there, but the pressure comes exclusively from people who will play the game and are interested in the game. We get a break away from that financial pressure to perform.

JS: You're entering a brave new world with a completely new type of publishing model.

KI: I like going into methods, I like the challenge of doing things that people say can't be done. For example, we developed titles in Japan with a focus on the West. *Dead Rising* and *Lost Planet* for example are two games which sold better in the West and were aimed at the West. They were developed at a time, when in Japan people were saying you can't do that, as a Japanese developer you cannot develop for the West. People would say: "You don't understand how foreigners think, you don't understand what they want, you don't understand how to make a game for them." And I thought to myself, how ridiculous. I'm going to do that. This is something that people say I can't do, well I want to do it. With *Street Fighter IV* as well, that was another game where it was designed or developed with a foreign market in mind. If you look at foreigners who are interested in Japanese games, if you ask someone who says they like Japanese games, "What do you like?" They always say games from the past. The classics, like *Mega Man*, and titles like that. If you look at the modern Japanese game market, it's not really the same. The people from the West who say they like Japanese games, and they always come out with an old title, they never come up with a modern Japanese title, it's always a classic, and I feel kind of sorry for those people. Because the Japanese game market has moved on from there, and is not what it used to be. So I wanted to take the past, and what I worked on in the past, but I wanted to move it forward into the future. I didn't want to recreate old games, I wanted to take elements of the past that foreigners who like Japanese games have obviously got into, and I wanted to make that part of the future.

JS: Perhaps you've just been asking the wrong people? I love Japanese games. I would probably mention *Valkyria Chronicles*, *Demon's Souls* and *Bayonetta* as Japanese games the West could never hope to replicate.[7] There's quite a few.

KI: I'm not saying there are no good games in the modern Japanese industry, I'm not saying that at all. You mentioned *Bayonetta*, and that's fine, but I think when people from the West think about the Japanese games industry, they imagine the classics, rather than modern titles. If you looked at all the top 10 selling games around the world, 15 or 20 years ago, maybe 8 or 9 of them would be Japanese. But if you look at them now, probably none of them are going to be Japanese. If you look at the top 50 now, you might see 2 or 3 titles from Nintendo, but other than that, I think foreigners would recognise the older games better, as it were.

JS: Is there anything you think current Japanese developers could learn from Western companies?

KI: I think it's entirely things they need to learn from the West, actually, and I think back in the day it was the Western development teams learning from the Japanese. But now I think it's swapped around, and now it's the Japanese who need to learn from the Westerners. I think those in the West who learned something, have gone on to use what they've learned - maybe modern Japanese developers need to learn it back, as it were, to bring it back.

JS: Why do you think Japanese games were so successful in the West, in the past? Related to that, foreign games had a bad reputation in Japan. I've heard the phrase "*yoge kusoge*" mentioned.[8] Your thoughts on these contrasts?

KI: I think it's to do with the limitations of hardware. Back with *Mega Man* you were working with such a tiny, such a strict, such a difficult set of parameters, a set of limitations on colour, on memory and so on. I think the Japanese were better at looking at the limitations, and figuring out how to get past them, or how to use them to the best of their ability. For example, we only had 6 people working on *Mega Man* - what was our solution, because we had such a small team? We just worked all the time, we worked 24 hours a day, and slept at the office. In the West you would not have been able to do that, and now in Japan you can't do that anymore either. But in those days you could. I think, to use the car industry as an analogy, nowadays American and European cars, they can be massive and they can throw in loads and loads of technology, and that's great. But if you want to get a car which is very, very small, but you still have to fit 4 people in it, or you've still got to fit hybrid technology in it, Japan is where people are good at looking at those limitations and working out how to marry those limitations with their goals. I believe that's where the difference in the industry and the difference in the thought processes are. So whereas with Western games they sort of saw everything as a limit and as a problem, maybe even as an excuse for less quality games, in Japan we embraced that and accepted the situation we had. And we made the best possible games we could. I think for example with *Mega Man*, we looked at the colours and we said, "OK, what does this colour limitation mean for our character? How can we make the best character from this limitation?" Whereas my image with maybe some Western developers is that they drew a picture of a character's design, and they said to their programmers or whoever, "Right, now put this in the game." And the programmers would have gone, "Oh my, there's no way we can do this." Maybe the head developers and so on in the West would have replied, "No, you must, that's just the way it is." Whereas in Japan it was much more that we would look at the options we had available, and work from them.

---

[7] I wish I'd had time to list more - from the PS3, X360, Wii, DS and PSP generation, there are easily more than 100 astounding Japanese games

[8] *yoge kusoge* = Western games, crappy games

JS: Fellow journalists were pondering - is there a risk of Capcom suing Comcept? This is not in any way related to characters in your game, or their similarity to anything else, but rather the fact that you were on the board of directors at Capcom, and so had access to privileged information including other Capcom staff.

KI: Of course I cannot say there is zero chance of that ever happening, but I don't think it will happen. I mean, we are not doing anything, I am not planning to do anything that I believe in any way would infringe on or in any way lead to infringement. For example with *Dead Rising* and the film *Dawn of the Dead*, they are both creations where you have zombies in a shopping mall. That's the basic concept. But the story is different, the way the game is played is different [to what characters do in the film], you could make a hundred different games with the basic concept of zombies in a mall. In the same way with *Mighty No. 9*, if Capcom were to sue every game that had a robot in it, or every game that had a character that's blue in it, that would be ridiculous. There are similarities, but I don't see how they could build a case on that. It's for them to decide, and it's out of my hands, but I have not heard anything from them about it, and I do not believe there is any risk, or any possibility of that happening. The games have similarities, but they're not the same thing.

Shinsaku Ohara: To add to that, by asking these sort of questions, perhaps the way that you write it, or perhaps the way someone else writes it, could be seen as deliberately trying to bring Capcom down, or make them angry. If an article came up like that, with the intention that management at Capcom might see it... The media is creating a rivalry that does not exist.

KI: Honestly, one thing I would like people to understand, for you to understand, is that the reason I'm doing this interview is for people who are interested in game history and so on. I'm not trying to, I don't want to inflame or provoke Capcom in any way. Obviously when I talk about my past, when I walk about my history there, I do incur a certain risk in that, but I want it to be clear that the point of this interview, and the point of this process, is for the interest of the readers. I want people to understand that I have no intention of being aggressive towards Capcom, or anything like that. That's very important for me to say.

JS: You have many followers. I want to convey your thoughts accurately in the correct context. Do you have any parting thoughts?

KI: My desire, my goal, is for the games of Japan to command the same amount of respect and the same amount of sway as they did in the golden era. I don't want people to think we're going back, we're not going back, it's not a case of trying to be again what we were as developers back then. It's about taking what was good from that era, taking the part of it that made it so successful, made it so popular, and made those games so good, and moving forward with it. I hope that people can enjoy once more, or find in these games that we are making, once more what first drew them to the titles we made in the past.

JS: Thank you very much. *Ganbatte kudasai*.

<everyone laughs>

~Appearing in a later volume~

The future of Japanese games, in the hands of modern developers

Taka Kawasaki

Shinsaku Ohara

A lot of veteran developers such as Keiji Inafune are helping to shape the future of Japanese games. **Taka Kawasaki** first discovered games when translating the English rules for *Dungeons & Dragons* into Japanese; today he handles the Unreal Engine for Epic Games Japan, and reveals the intricacies of Japanese developers who license pre-made game engines. **Shinsaku Ohara** started by working for Capcom, on *Dino Crisis 2*, and in later years after working on games like *Resident Evil 4* and *Dead Rising 2* joined COMCEPT as one of the starting members to help lift the company off the ground. He discusses working with Nudemaker during *Steel Battalion*'s development, and describes an unreleased aerial game by Capcom for the GameCube...

ROZNER, Stephen & William

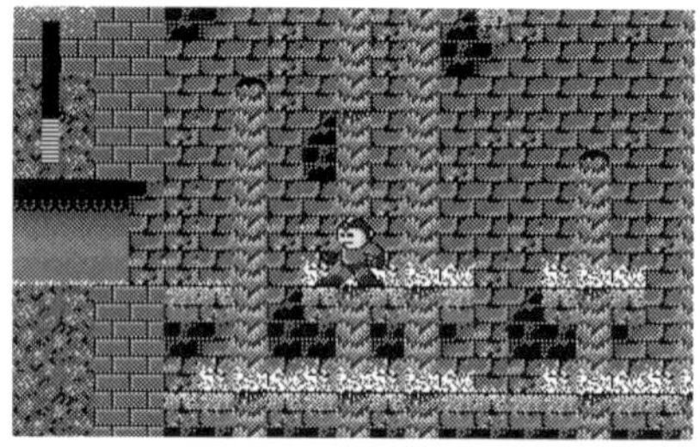

After editing the Keiji Inafune interview, and reading his recollections on the *MM* boss designs, it suddenly occurred to me: no one has ever researched the origin of the two DOS games, developed by Rozner Labs, published by Hi-Tech Expressions, and with the approval of Capcom USA. Finding answers should be easy, I thought, since only one person was responsible for the design, programming, graphics and sound on the first title: **Stephen J. Rozner**. On the second game, *MM3*, he again took on all roles, albeit with graphics handled by a **William Rozner**. A little searching led me to **http://www.twistory.com**. I'd heard about the DOS games, but never put any time into them. But they intrigued me, because they were not conventional console ports to PC, in the same way something like Konami's *Metal Gear* was. They were radical reinterpretations of the NES titles; wholly original games!

The games, sadly, have a negative reputation among fans. Some fansites openly refuse to acknowledge them, encouraging further misinformation and misunderstanding. After 30 minutes of play my initial reaction was that *MM3*'s maze-like levels were too confusing, while *MM1* was a fun though simple platformer. Only three bosses are selectable and a few hours later I'd completed Sonicman and Dynaman's stages. In the context of 1990, being a one-man effort, *MM1* is honestly not the poor game fans accuse it of being. If anything, given its brevity, it's more like a shareware title or highly polished fan effort. I had fun, especially with Sonicman's level. For comparison I then played *MM3* on an actual NES (not emulation). It hit me like a brick in the face: there was **zero** vertical scrolling. The NES titles are purely horizontal affairs - climbing or descending results in the game pausing, and the screen flipping over. Obviously this is a limitation of the memory mapper chips Capcom used, and the flick of the screen is perhaps the game bank switching, similar to how *Metroid* did with elevators. Conversely, the DOS games featured smooth full-screen multidirectional scrolling throughout all the levels. Astounding.

This caused me to re-evaluate *MM3* and put time into completing a few levels. Most are actually ingeniously structured, notably the Shark Man, Oil Man and Wave Man stages. The game also allows the eponymous blue robot to swim, a first in the series![1] Emulated through DOSBox, in conjunction with JoyToKey, the controls are tight and precise, the action smooth once you've found the right number of emulation cycles. The VGA graphics have less colours than some might expect in 1992, but *MM3* is a legitimately fun game, interesting, and with a gratifying sense of exploration. In *MM3* if you destroy enemies, lose a life and restart, those enemies are still absent from the stage. It's a fully persistent game world! Combat is more satisfying than the NES games, where enemies constantly respawn (they also respawn in *MM1* for DOS). Apart from the VGA colours, *MM3* is a technical marvel which would have been impossible to replicate within the capacity of the NES games. Multidirectional scrolling would have required more advanced mapper chips, while the aforementioned lack of enemy respawns is probably beyond the NES' capabilities. My only complaint is a lack of any music. It leaves the levels feeling empty.

I'm not sure if this interview will change anyone's misconceptions of the games. But I'm pleased to document the story behind them. I hope that at least a few players will try *Mega Man 3* for DOS, with an open mind and a sense of curiosity. It's not Keiji Inafune's *Mega Man*, but it was never meant to be.

[1] In the later released *MM8* there is also swimming

Interview with Stephen & William Rozner
Via email

JS: Stephen, I believe you worked on the *Mega Man* games for computers?

SR: Yes, I am the culprit behind the PC versions of *Mega Man*. I can definitely give you information on the how and why for the creation of these games. I created some C64 Capcom games which led me to work at Capcom USA. Some of this started at that point, and I continued to make many PC games for Capcom after going on my own. I should be able to answer most of your questions. I will try to cover those pertinent to the DOS games. Some of these may be rabbit holes and would probably require a bit more thought and discussion. There have been a few occasions where people have tried to contact me about the *Mega Man* games, but it is obviously easier nowadays. I am also working with my brother William again here at Twistory, as history tends to repeat.

JS: Have you ever been interviewed before?

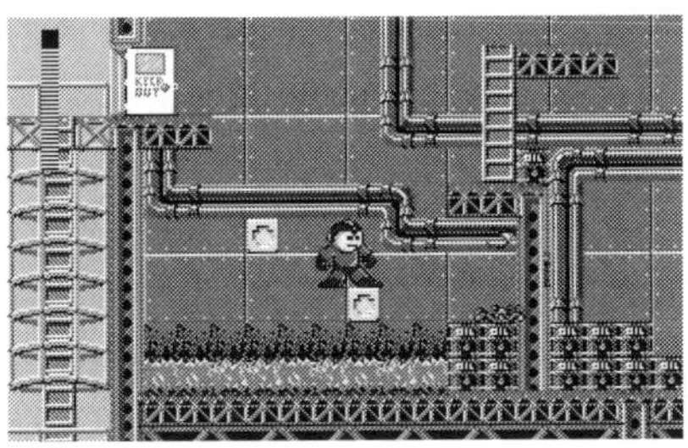

SR: I was contacted maybe once or twice by people who did love the PC games and had webpages about them. But at some of the companies I worked at I wasn't sure I wanted to discuss anything outside the current job. Big corporations don't seem to like publicity they don't control and I have signed a lot of NDAs and waivers over the years.

JS: Please describe your backgrounds.

SR: I had been programming for years, originally on a friend's old S-100 bus computer [1] exactly like the one in *WarGames*.[2] We had to use raw machine code poked from BASIC, and I think I ported *Berzerk* on it. I messed around with school Apple IIs, TRS-80s and VIC-20s until my dad got me a C64, spending $600 on the computer and another $600 for the disk drive when they first came out.

I was going to junior college and working at Hughes Aircraft writing administration software when I got a weird break. Friends that owned a pizza delivery joint got a card from a Pacific Dataworks [3] delivery asking about programmers. I was working on a *Kung Fu* port on the C64 I showed them, and since they needed someone to do *Street Fighter* it was a perfect fit. I learned a lot about multiplying sprites and burning ROM debug applications to C64 cartridges. I even made a connector between my PC parallel port and the C64 which allowed it to use my PC harddrive as if it was a C64 disk drive. Great for development which was done on the PC and sent to the C64!

WR: Unlike Steve I didn't really go in for the programming side of computers. I did play around with some BASIC coding and graphics on the VIC-20 and our C64. For me it was BASIC code and C64 sprite animations. Steve had been working with computer code for years in a number of locations. While I was getting my Bachelor of Architecture from the Southern California Institute of Architecture, Steve asked it I could help generate some art for him, maybe around 1991. I didn't have a computer so I did the art on his Amiga. This was after he left Capcom and he finished *MM1*. Steve's background and knowledge in computer graphics helped me out a lot. I could draw - but doing so on paper is one thing, execution of the same skill in a different media is another! So from then on, before we formed RLSG, I did side work for a few games.

JS: When you say you worked on C64 games, Stephen, do you mean *Pocket Rockets*?[4]

SR: My first professional game job was at Pacific Dataworks. There I made the C64 *Street Fighter*, **(below & adjacent page)** a port of the very first arcade version. It's worth noting there was a UK version that I don't think was as good. I could not get Sagat in my version of the game, so it's missing one opponent, because he was too big for the sprite multiplying we were doing, and making a short version of him just didn't look or

---

[1] Early computer bus (1974), part of the Altair 8800
[2] 1983 film, Matthew Broderick is a computer hacker

[3] Pacific Dataworks International (originally Lyndon & Associates); founded in Jan 1987 by Troy Lyndon
[4] Stephen Rozner is credited on various C64 websites

feel right. The US version has much better defined characters with full black outlines. I also helped work on C64 versions of *Bionic Commando*, *Strider*, a hockey game and a few others - not sure how many were published. I also made an NES version of *Street Fighter* that never made it out.[5] **(below is the C64 version)**

JS: How did Rozner Labs form?

SR: From Pacific Dataworks I went to Riggs International (I think) with one of its founders, after around a year. There we made *Pocket Rockets*, just me, an artist and the boss. After about another year the three of us were brought into Capcom USA. I just became an employee and my boss, Chris Riggs, was supposed to start an internal US development team. That never materialized at Capcom USA, so I was managing outside development including lots of UK work. During this time we had a C64 WWI game that was shelved and then I just started to make the *Mega Man* PC game by myself. I left Capcom USA and they agreed to publish it in the US when I completed it. It was just me doing the programming, art, audio - the works! I went back to working with Chris Riggs at a few different companies including Radiance Software. Eventually I moved back to Thousand Oaks and started Rozner Labs with my brother William and another friend. The name comes from the name friends gave our house, since we had every tool imaginable to work on cars, build furniture and whatever else. For years I said I would start a company named Rozner Labs, and eventually I did. The acronym RLSG means Rozner Labs Software Group.

WR: After my graduation in 1993 I helped Steve move back to Thousand Oaks. Shortly after that we decided to form Rozner Labs (RLSG). We didn't start the company with the idea or hope to do an actual *Mega Man* title. Though Steve's contact at Hi-Tech Expressions, via Capcom USA, opened the door for us to develop PC ports of many of their console games. There were three of us that started RLSG. For about a year we three, plus around 8-10 other employees, worked out of a small two bedroom condo. Steve and I shared a bedroom that also had three desks for employees to work at during the day. The living room housed the other desks for everyone else. Things got better once we had enough funding to move into an actual office.

JS: What was the relationship with Hi-Tech?

SR: Hi-Tech was distributing just about all the C64 and other non-Nintendo games Capcom USA sold. It was through my relationship with Capcom USA that I was connected with them. A lot of the Rozner Labs games were published through Hi-Tech Expressions and all our Capcom USA work certainly was. I think this is also where we started working with Col Stone, who eventual went to work at Acclaim.

WR: I can say that without them on our side, as a publisher, our early days would have been much harder.

JS: How did the Capcom deal for *MM* come about? Did you deal with Capcom Japan?

SR: Capcom Japan seemed to have little to do with the titles Capcom USA did, outside Nintendo and arcades. As said earlier, *MM1* was just me starting a project that my boss Joe Morici decided they could publish. When we did *Mega Man X* and *Super Street Fighter II* we actually got the block graphics and audio from Capcom Japan, and in the case of *Super Street Fighter II* we also had long conversations before they gave me SNES assembly code. I told them it was the best way to get the timing right, so I wrote a converter from SNES assembly to PC assembly, so I could match the game almost exactly. There was a UK version (may have been *Turbo* but I am not sure), but again I think the US version was better because I had the exact SNES timing for the controls. Capcom USA bundled 6 button joysticks to make it easy to play *Mega Man X* and *Super Street Fighter II*.

JS: There were no stipulations from Capcom?

SR: For the first *Mega Man* PC I just made whatever I wanted since I loved the *Mega Man*

[5] A port of the original arcade title; named on a few "coming soon" lists in old magazines; unreleased!

NES games so much. There are only three levels and the boss level because I had to do literally everything myself.

JS: How long did development take? Did Capcom supply source code, art, free games?

SR: Until *MMX* and *SSFII* there was nothing we got from Capcom Japan or USA. Generally you played the arcade or NES/SNES game and converted it. For *Mega Man X* we still had to play the game and produce code from scratch to get the same gameplay. It wasn't easy! All the PC games were maybe 6-9 months to port, including the *Mega Man* PC games since it was just me, and later just me and William. We also had to do some screen captures and art cleanup of it; William can tell you how painful that was.

WR: For *MMX* and *SSFII* we did receive some asset files for characters. They were in a format that broke the sprites into 8x8 blocks. For *SSFII*, I think we also received the backgrounds in this same format. Aside from these graphical assets we got some text documents and nothing else. Some of these documents gave us information about what weapon did what to whom, and diagrammed some of the bosses' special movements, but not much else.

Before I could start working on the graphics Steve had to create some code that would rebuild the sprites from these disordered 8x8 blocks. To my recollection we did not receive background tiles for *MMX*, so they had to be done from scratch using screen captures and playing the game to get reference information. We had one game published by Hi-Tech, *We're Back*, where we received no art assets and had to do everything from screen captures and in-game reference, including all animations. I believe the main character, the T-Rex had over 120 frames of animation alone.

Once Steve developed the code to parse the 8x8 blocks for the two Capcom games we got started. For *MMX* we had to rework all of the character graphics since we were going from a rectangular pixel platform to a square pixel platform. What you started with are sprites that were all thin, so a round tire would look more like an oval not a circle. It was better than nothing, though. For *MMX* and *SSFII* I had some of my artists take the lead on reworking the sprites and I would then approve the final. For the *MMX* levels, I created the majority of the tile sets. I had some of the other artists help create the levels in our editing tool that Steve built. He kept updating and revamping this tool throughout the history of RLSG. It was great!

JS: What I like is that the *MM* games are wildly different reinterpretations of traditional *MM*.

SR: For *MM1* it was just me because I loved the NES games so much. I don't think Capcom Japan would allow a port to PC, so I had to make my own. Joe Morici was great support in this after I left Capcom USA. For *MM3* it was more odd. William and I created a game design called *Eco Man*, in which you turned mutated enemies back into original form as you went through levels. If you look at the levels you can tell its origin, with mutated plants and animals, and things like oil and nuclear waste containers. We were told they would publish it if we turned it into a *Mega Man* title. We had the same basic gameplay and bosses as [the first] *MM*, so it was easy to back port. Plus our character in a hazmat suit was about the same size.

JS: Can you describe the creative process when coming up with original new bosses and layouts?

SR: You can see the layouts were much more open and organic since it was not a *MM* game to start. We wanted players to wander around the oil rig, boat and the rest in a much less linear way. You'd have to think and backtrack occasionally. We thought linear *MM* levels were too predictable.

WR: Yes, the game that became *MM3* started out as *Eco Man*. We developed a whole world around him without any notion of *MM* level structure. While developing *Eco Man* we wanted the option for a player to explore more of a level by placing power-ups and other bonus item in out of the way locations. This would give them a reason not to just power through the levels. Steve's initial work an *MM1* gave me a base for the character animation for *Eco Man.* That may have been a reason why Hi-Tech decided they would publish if we reskinned it as *MM3*, since they had the rights for that title and we had a game that was finished. They gave us a contract and a few months to make the modification to turn it into *MM3*.

JS: It looks like *MM3* used some sprites from the NES, for boss portraits?

SR: I am not sure the sequel used too much art from the NES. I think the bosses themselves were still our own creations, and the enemies were not really changed from the *Eco Man* design. I would have to look again to see if any menu graphics or even an enemy or two were taken from the NES.

WR: For *MM3* we created everything, including the bosses from scratch. We did get some style sheets for *MM* from Capcom through Hi-Tech. We did use the latest NES *MM* as reference, but that was all. All of the weapon stats, which one was better for killing a boss, was all on our side.

JS: How come it jumps from *MM1* to *MM3*?

SR: This is really funny, but Capcom USA reused the *MM* NES box art for *MM* PC, so they wouldn't need new art. *MM3* on NES may have been recent, so it was used for the second PC game's box art. I think the *MM3* NES box boss may have looked reasonably close to one of our bosses.[6] There never was or would be a *Mega Man 2* for PC.

JS: *MM* being able to swim was a brilliant idea.

SR: I remember people at Capcom USA thought it was very cool. I can't recall if anything like this ever made it into the Japanese NES/SNES games, or if Capcom Japan ever commented. We knew you would have to get from the oil rig to the oil tanker and then to shore for the oil refinery. It took a long while to get a good, playable swimming physics model, but it worked well. I think it was a rather new and interesting thing for the time.

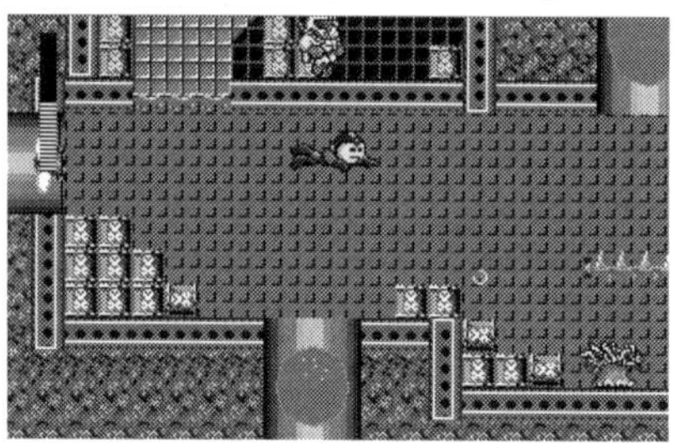

WR: Another bi-product of *Eco Man.* It was awesome once we got the *MM* animations and physics working. I think it is the only time *Mega Man* has swam in game. Capcom didn't hate it otherwise we would have had to change it out.

JS: The multidirectional scrolling in the *MM* games is impressive, especially in *MM3*!

SR: I think that the NES/SNES might better handle the true *MM*-style of scrolling, going in one direction at a time. This would be better for the block/tile based way the consoles build levels. It likely also saves memory rather than having open and large levels. Console cartridge prices were based on memory size, so any memory savings helped. On the PC you are freer with memory, but not completely free. It was difficult to use more than the approximately 500kB or so available in early PCs without extra memory hardware and paging tricks. But on the PC the [graphics card at that time] was very slow with only bit-by-bit access. So all the block/tile work was done in software with a renderer to push them onto the screen line by line.

Everything up until the mid-1990s, and *MMX* and *SSFII*, was done in assembly language, very low-level coding. From that time, more and more was done in C or C++. But for many years you still needed to build the graphics rendering in assembly for speed.

JS: The games are not well documented. Can you remember any secrets hidden within?

SR: I probably still have some code or notes laying around, but I would have to dig data up. *MM* PC may not have had much, but *MM3* PC should have had more cheats. There were some special areas where walls were not solid, so you could get into them if you kept poking around. I know we had codes to get the weapons automatically, or recharges, but I can't recall them off hand. I'm a bit older now and maybe losing my memory.

WR: I may have some papers on this as well but I'm not totally sure. I tossed out a lot of old papers in my last big move in 2006.

JS: Did you work on any unreleased games?

SR: I think I had over 50% of the games I worked on published. That was a super high number back then. A few unreleased games are *Street Fighter* on NES, the WWI C64 game, a bunch of cool SNES games at Rozner Labs which I am not sure I can give more detail on. It is tough to remember now.

WR: We had a SNES game titled "*NFL Heroes*" that never came out. You travelled through time,

[6] *MM3* has identical box art for NES and DOS, apart from a single background enemy is removed on DOS

like in the film *Time Bandits*, as a boy or girl, and were helped out along the way by NFL mascots that each had a different power to aid you. A port for *Crash Test Dummies* never made it out, though the game was basically done. We had one or two titles for THQ that never saw the light of day either. There are a few others but I just cannot recall them right now.

JS: What happened after the DOS *MM* games?

SR: I did a *Ninja Gaiden* PC game just after *MM* PC. I don't recall too much else around that time now. I worked on some of the worst NES games, like one of the *Where's Waldo*. But you create what you get paid for. There were a few others around that time. I worked on an *Alien 3* SNES game, and a *Darkwing Duck* for... NeoGeo or TurboGrafx-16, I'm not sure. At Tahoe Software I also worked on a Mountain Sports game that never made it, while we were talking with 3DO. There was also a brush with a basketball game before Rozner Labs. We then did a lot of PC ports. I met Greg Thomas of Visual Concepts for the basketball project, and we did a PC port of the *We're Back* SNES game. I really liked the game and the port. We also did a few *Beethoven* games, based on the movies with the St Bernard dog. This is where we did some really cool SNES games that never made it out.

Soon after *D* with Acclaim, and both *MMX* and *SSFII* for Capcom, we closed shop at Rozner Labs to go work with Static Online. Here William and I met Brian Morrison, whom we work with now. They were making a telephone / modem game service which quickly became an internet game service. I did a lot of the underlying Windows device work to allow many games to share one connection to our service. We were years ahead of our time, but things don't always work out. I ported *Wipeout XL* to our network service, which actually made it into arcades and a huge motion simulator platform. Also through Sony / Psygnosis I ported *Formula One 97* from Bizarre Creations to our network. This was fun and I got to work in Liverpool with the team for a few weeks.

Some time later I was in Cardiff, Wales, at a company working on a motion simulator for the *Formula One 97* game. This made it into arcades and could connect up to 8 simulators in one race. It was sweet spending two weeks in a prototype simulator getting the motions right. William, Brian and I struck off on our own to complete work on a customizable MMORPG server when Static Online changed names and started doing just audio and video serving. The timing was not great, the internet bubble burst, so we split ways I ended up at EA Sports Tiburon in Florida. I worked on the networking for all the sports titles, *Madden*, *NCAA* and *NASCAR*. Over the next 6 years I lead teams to update and make the networking more reusable across titles. I worked a lot with EAC in Vancouver to this end. After the new networking needed for the last *NASCAR* X360 title I left EA. I had a short stint in Massachusetts at Play Hard (or Quick Hit) working on a web football game. This was a short winter, after which I moved back to Florida before I married and moved to London with my wife.

I found a job at a small Xbox studio in London working on a Sky TV app for the X360. I lead a team to build a similar TV and pay-per-view app for Canal TV in France. This eventually became the basis for many of the TV apps on the US X360. [...] Eventually I got the call from Twistory. Myself, Brian and William would be back together making games with Brian's brother who started making comics and wanted to branch into games. So here we are with *Belle's War* and the hit *Ouch! Couch*.

WR: From RLSG, Steve and I went to work at a company called Static. They were into the development of multiplayer games and that is where we wanted to be. There I headed up the art department, GUI development, and a few other things including internal game development.

After leaving Static I moved into web development, flash animation and moonlighted in the early mobile games market. The game companies I worked for during this period were more fly-by-night and not worth mentioning. I settled into a full time web development position for a friend of mine for about 8 years. Steve, Brian, Mink and I wanted to get together to develop games and that finally came to pass. Now we have *Belle's War* and *Ouch! Couch* on multiple platforms.

後藤 誠

GOTO, Makoto

DOB: *secret* / Birthplace: *secret* / Blood Type: A

Winds Co., Ltd. employee

Shockman / Shubibinman 2 - PC Engine, 1991 (Game and AI programmer)
Vixen 357 - Mega Drive, 1992 (Battle programmer)
Unnamed RPG (NDA) - PC Engine, 1992 (Sub-prog., events production, minigames)
Sengoku Denshou[1] - Super Famicom, 1992 (System and map programmer)
Doraemon ~Nobita to Maigo no Kyouryuu~ - Sega Pico, 1993 (Main programmer)
KeroKero Keroppi - Sega Pico, 1993 (Objects and system prog.)

Independent Contractor

Don Quixote: A Dream of Seven Crystals[2] - LaserActive Mega LD, 1994 (Main prog., developed LD control library, battle system & enemy check tool)
Hyaku Monogatari - PCE CD-ROM, 1995 (Main prog., dev. animation engine & tools, streaming movie engine & tools, original script sys., managed budget, organised team of 10)
Zoku Hatsukoi Monogatari ~Shuugaku Ryokou~ - PC-FX/SAT/PS1, 1997~98 (Same as above)
Digital Angel -Cyber Angel SS~ - Sega Saturn, 1997 (Same as above)
Initial D - PlayStation, 1998 (Main prog., dev. events sys & script tools, trained 2 progs.)
Fishing Teacher 2 - GBC, 1999 (Main prog., anim. tools, directed team of 2 prog & 3 designers)
Burn Out - PlayStation, 2000 (Main programmer, map tools)
Boku Doraemon - Dreamcast, 2000 (Chief prog., original script sys., director, organised team of 5)
ESPN GOG Bass 2002 - GBA, 2002 (Director, chief prog., planning docs., animation tools)

Square-Enix Co., Ltd. employee

Front Mission 4 - PlayStation 2, 2003 (Events prog., script tool for events and cut-scenes)
Front Mission Online - PS2/Win, 2005 (Events & server prog., orig. script system for events)
Crystal Tools - Common dev engine and tools, internal use, 2006~2008, Developed Cut-Editor tool for making cut scene events.
Final Fantasy XIII - PS3, 2008 (Tools & events prog., extended functions for Cut-Editor)
Dragon Quest X - Wii, 2009 (Same as above)

Silicon Studio Corporation / Matchlock Corporation

Effects tools (NDA) - confidential, 2010~2011 (Developed 2 particle effect tools for new hardware as a team leader. Directed a project team of 3 foreign staff members using English. Negotiated with clients on production schedules to promote efficient work flow)

Matchlock Corporation

BISHAMON Evangelist & Tools & Middleware Division Director - Present day

---

[1] A scrolling fighter by SNK
[2] A fascinating laserdisc game for the Sega Mega Drive add-on for Pioneer's LaserActive system. According to the LaserActive Preservation Project it's an epic RPG with maps, equipment and random battles, spanning 30 hours; not to be confused with the arcade laserdisc game *Super Don Quix-ote* from 1984. For more visit: **http://laseractive.wordpress.com** and their YouTube page **www.youtube.com/user/LAPProject**

Interview with Makoto Goto
21 October 2013, Tokyo

I met Makoto Goto for coffee one afternoon, since he was one of my Ask a Question backers. It turns out he worked on some rather interesting retro games, and was in charge of several high-profile projects in later years, so I had some questions. This was unplanned, so it's more of a casual conversation. Goto-san is also the gentleman who asked Phil Fish that famous question... We spent around an hour chatting about the past, present and future of Japanese games. What I found especially interesting was Goto-san's involvement with development studio Winds, which was used as an outsource company by a lot of other developers, producing parts of games through to entire titles.

JS: Mr Goto, you're a programmer?

MG: Yes, I'm a programmer.

JS: You first started working in games when you were 19?

MG: Yes, when I was 19 years old.

JS: That's very young.

MG: Yes. <*laughs*>

JS: So you were an assistant programmer?

MG: I was a sub-programmer and worked on *Shubibinman 2*.[1]

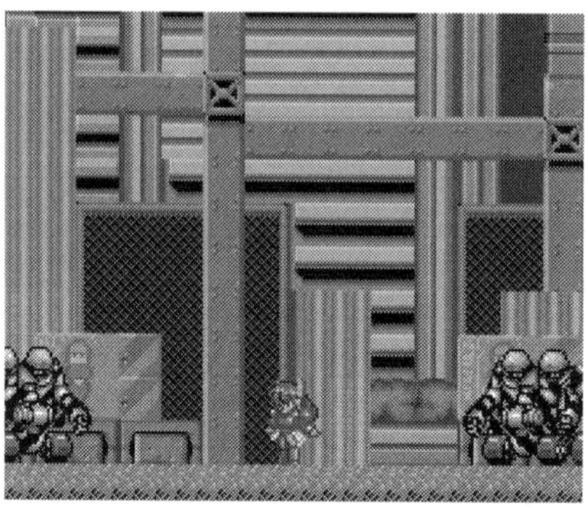

JS: Your first job?

MG: Yes, this was my first job, and the first title I worked on.

JS: What was the first game you had as a child?

MG: Ahh... I liked playing side-scrolling action games. For example, do you know *Contra*, by Konami? And *Mega Man*, and *Castlevania*. This was my favourite game! But the first videogame was... *Super Mario Bros*.

JS: For the Famicom?

MG: Yes, but that was a videogame. Do you know *Game & Watch*? This was by Nintendo, very small, and this came before the Famicom. I liked *Game & Watch*. When I was a junior high school student I bought the Famicom and played *Super Mario*.

JS: What was your first *Game & Watch*?

MG: Do you know *Octopus*? It was my first.

JS: Mine as well!

MG: I enjoyed playing it a great deal - I'd sometimes fight with my brother for my turn to play the *Game & Watch*. "Next it's my turn!" - "No, no! You've played it for too long already!"

<*everyone laughs*>

JS: When did you want to make games?

MG: Oh, yes! The first year of senior high school. When I was a senior high school student I wanted to make a game. I liked making programs. Some programming magazines contained type-in listings. These were BASIC programs, the BASIC language. I typed up some of these programs, and I studied them. How to play and how to control things on-screen. I learned how to program some games by studying these type-in listings in magazines. When I was a high school student I also worked with assembly language - I learned it specifically to make a game. I continued with programming after I graduated.

JS: *Shubibinman 2* for PC Engine was assembly.

MG: Only assembly language! I enjoyed learning assembly language, it was very exciting! I was really excited to work with it because before that the BASIC language was slow. Very slow. But in contrast, assembly language was almost too fast! <*laughs*> We could draw characters and control characters with a lot of speed.

[1] Four part series of platformers on PC Engine and SFC; second title released in USA as *Shockman* for TG-16

JS: Good for action games.

MG: Yes! I think the English word is... prep school? I wanted to go to university, but the timing was... Well, I missed it.

JS: You missed the entrance exam?

MG: Yes, I missed it.

JS: So your first experience on consoles was for the PC Engine?

MG: Yes, the PC Engine. *<shows English word>* Preparatory school for university. When I was a student at the prep-school for university, I needed to earn money through part-time jobs. I was looking for a job, an *arubaito*, and I found out about this programming job. This was for making *Shubibinman 2*. For the first time I met Toshirou Tsuchida,[2] and also Satoshi Nakai.[3] I met them at this time and was allowed to join the team working on the *Shubibinman 2* project. The point is, I was able to make programs using the assembly language.

JS: You worked on the AI and the 2D shooting sections, right?

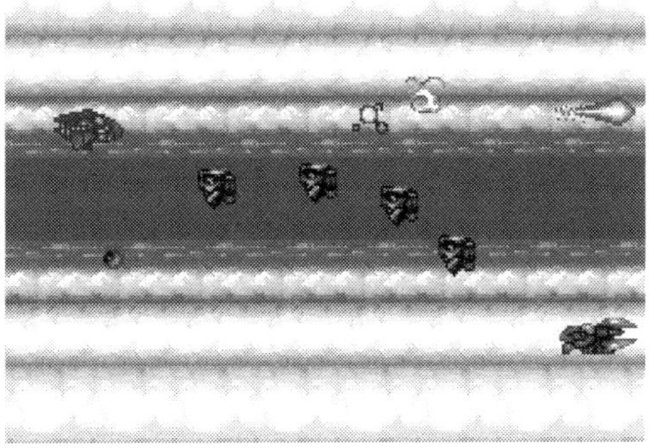

MG: Yes, the shooting stages - for those, all the programming was done by me. Plus some of the AI for the boss characters, some stages, and a lot of characters... I made the AI programming for quite a few smaller characters.

JS: For the *zako* enemies?

MG: *Zako*! Yes, yes, small enemies. Plus I worked on the level designs with the game's designer and artist.[4]

JS: Tomoharo Saitou. He passed away in 2006. I am including memorial pages in my book.

MG: Oh! That's nice! Is it also possible to add a mention for "Suu Urabe" in the book? Suu Urabe, real name Hiroaki Suzuki, was a character artist on *Shubibinman 2*. He passed away in 2001. Thank you for deciding to include memorial pages for Saitou-san and Urabe-san, your book will be my treasure.

JS: Do you have a photograph with Urabe-san, which I can print?

MG: I don't have a good picture unfortunately. I will email you a picture that was in an article in *PC Engine Magazine* (*MaruKatsu PC Engine*) from 1990. I'll scan it. I was so young in that picture! *<laughs>*

JS: How many people were there on the *Shubibinman 2* team?

MG: Only 4 or 5 people? A very small team.

JS: Mr Nakai mentioned Winds, an outsource company. He produced graphics for Winds, which would pass it on to a developer.

MG: Ahh yes, that's right. I feel nostalgic discussing all this.

JS: What kind of company was WINDS?

MG: It was a small company. This is the company's URL. *<writes it down>* [5]

JS: Did they specialise in outsourcing?

MG: Yes, they did.

JS: What kind of relationship did Winds have with Masaya?

MG: Some members who quit NCS established and founded Winds. Satoshi Nakai and Tomoharu Saitou were members of the establishing founders, in 1989. I joined the company the next year, in 1990.[6]

---

[2] 土田俊郎; producer on *Shubibinman 2* and *Cybernator*, perhaps best known for *Front Mission*

[3] 仲井覚; amazing artist, worked on *Cybernator*, *Culdscept*, *Code Veronica*, many others

[4] Tomoharo Saitou; he also did character designs for *Streets of Rage 2*; passed away in 2006

[5] www.winds-net.co.jp

[6] Earliest work by Winds, according to their website, is character design & pixel graphics for the original *Shubibinman* on PC Engine in 1989, while more recently the company worked on the 3D computer graphics backgrounds in *MGS V: Ground Zeroes*.

JS: How many people worked at Winds?

MG: When I joined the company, about 10 people were working there including me.

From left, some of the Shubibinman 2 team: Suu Urabe, character artist and known comic creator in Japan. Tomoharo Saitou (seated), artist and character designer. Norihiko Yonesaka, assistant producer. Toshiro Tsuchida (seated), producer, and in later years producer on Arc the Lad for PlayStation. Koji Hayama, musician, in later years for Half-Minute Hero. On the far right, Makoto Goto when he was 19 years old.

JS: Did Winds work on any unreleased games?

MG: When I was there, they were no unreleased games.

JS: I looked at MobyGames, an English website. It doesn't list all the games you worked on. What did you work on after *Shubibinman 2*?

MG: Afterwards it was... Do you know *Vixen 357* by Masaya?[7] After *Shubibinman 2* I joined this project. This is a Mega Drive game.

JS: I've not heard of it. *<looks it up online>* Looks like a strategy game.

MG: Yes, exactly! This one! *<gestures>* This opening scene, I made it! *<laughs>*

JS: There was not a lot of memory on cartridges.

MG: Yes, very small memory. After *Vixen 357*... I have a resume I can show you. I want to work at an overseas company. My wife graduated from an American university, plus I want to experience working at an American company.

JS: I've heard that life at American game companies, like EA, can be very difficult.

MG: Difficult? Ahh... It's a very tough job.

JS: Your resume mentions an unnamed "character action-RPG" for PC Engine, from 1992. Can you reveal the name or some info?

MG: This was going to be an RPG using a character from a certain famous action game. I joined the project partway through as an event system programmer. However, the project was cancelled several months later. I was very disappointed. *<takes out laptop>* This is my business PC.

JS: Top secret stuff in there?

MG: Yes! *<laughs>*

JS: Can I have a copy of your resume?

MG: No problem. Is it OK to email you a project list of things I worked on?

JS: Sure. *<notices sticker on outside of laptop>* You were at CEDEC 2013?[8] Kenji Eno posthumously won an award there.

MG: Yes, he received an award. I was also a speaker at CEDEC.

JS: What did you speak about?

MG: About game jams.[9] How to drive motivation in a game jam. That was my session.[10]

JS: Do you miss these old days?

MG: Oh yes. *<gestures to screen - Front Mission: Online>* I worked on this one.

JS: Ah yes, I spoke with Aziz Hinoshita, about *Front Mission: Online*.[11] They closed it down.

---

[7] Mecha strategy game for Mega Drive, 1992

[8] Computer Entertainment Developers Conference; an annual event with awards - http://cedec.cesa.or.jp

[9] When a group of developers come together to create games over a short time period

[10] It was an hour long presentation on August 22

[11] To be printed in a later volume

MG: I know him. I worked with him for *Front Mission Online*. Unfortunately, This game's service was closed now. Hmm... My first title was *Shubibinman 2*, then *Vixen*, then *Sengoku Denshou* (pictured right).[12] Then... Do you know *Doraemon*?

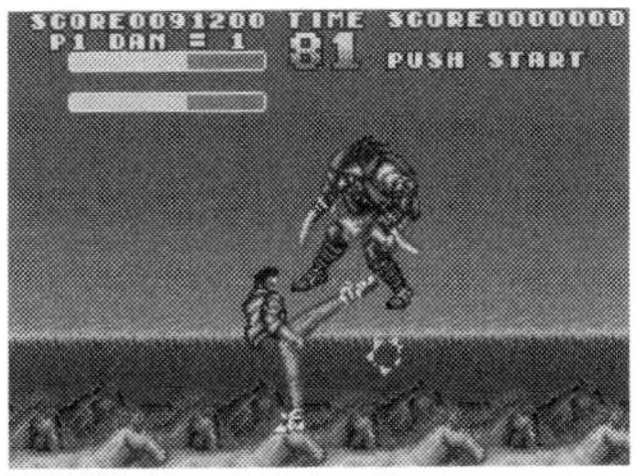

JS: Yes, the little *neko* robot.

MG: *Neko* robot, <*laughs*> yes! This was educational software for the Sega Pico. That makes it a unique game, don't you think? Next was this, a horror novel game.[13] And then a visual novel game.[14]

JS: Tell me about working on the Sega Pico.

MG: The Sega Pico was sold as an educational toy for young children. On the inside, it was a Mega Drive. It was an educational game console that added books, a touch pen, and a tablet to the Mega Drive hardware. The games were specially designed books with ROM inside, and could be played by inserting the book into the Pico. As you turn the pages, the same pictures as in the book would be displayed on a TV screen. By turning the pages of the book and touching the pages with the touch pen, children were able see things change on the TV. They could also use the tablet to write or draw pictures. Many educational games for children were released.

JS: <*looks at resume*> Then more *Doraemon*?

MG: Ah, yes. I worked on more *Doraemon*. <*laughs*>

JS: Does this mean confidential?

MG: Yes, I worked at Square-Enix, and worked on a confidential project. I also worked on *Front Mission 4*, *Online*, and *Final Fantasy XIII*, and *Dragon Quest X*. I made the cut-scene system for the game. It was similar to real-time events. The next job was Silicon Studio, where I created a particle effects engine and tools. My current job is at Matchlock Corporation, a middleware company. I make 3D particle tools for other game developers.

JS: Sounds complicated.

MG: <*laughs*> Very complicated. Do you want to see my current job? This is the product I'm working on. This is a particle tool.

JS: Used in an action game, for explosions?

MG: Ah, yes! Explosions, smoke, and as a generator of various magical effects. Some effects designers and artists will find it easy to create effects using this tool.

JS: Games involve so many people now.

MG: Ah, yes. Now the development environment is very complicated, and development teams are a much higher level, creating really complex programs. That's why we need middleware. For example Unity, or Unreal Engine. This, the particle effects engine, is an independently functioning engine. It's not dependent on another game engine to work.

JS: You can use it any game?

MG: Oh yes! Any game where you can adjust the game engine. This is a GPU-based particle engine, and this is a magic effect. <*gives demonstration of various visual effects*>

JS: Do you find mathematics easy?

MG: Mathematics... You need to know 3D mathematics. This is an artist's authoring tool, so it's very easy to make some effects. Very easy effects - these are fireworks.

JS: How many people on this project? Just you?

MG: No, 8 people now. Since Square-Enix, my job has been making environmental tools. <*goes through resume*> This was for cut-scenes; I made an event system, or a cut-scene tool. At my previous company I made two effects tools. Now my job is making effects tools. Now, however, I feel that I want to make some action games. <*laughs*>

[12] *Sengoku Denshou* (戦国伝承), lit. *Legacy of the Warring States*; originally a scrolling fighter by SNK; Goto-san was programmer on the SFC port (1993)
[13] *Hyaku Monogatari: Honto ni Atta Kowai Hanashi*, PC Engine CD-ROM (1995)
[14] *Zoku Hatsukoi Monogatari: Shuugaku Ryokou*, PC-FX (1997)

JS: Maybe you should consider indie games? *<long monologue on indie games>*

MG: Yes, and we can release it independently! It's a really, really good environment. I want to make games in an environment like the one I remember from *Shubibinman 2*. With a very small team. I want to make a game abroad, in the future maybe. Are you available this Thursday night?

JS: Let me check. The 24th, I'm free that evening. But I have interviews the next day.

MG: Near Nakameguro station, I'm going to drink with various people in the games industry. This is an "*Ootaru Drinking Party*". It's very much in the Japanese style, in a traditional restaurant. There are a lot of foreigners from the games industry at this party. I go there sometimes each month, to exercise my English. <*laughs*> You could maybe make some connections? I think you'd have a chance to interview other people.

JS: Can anyone attend? Do you need a ticket?

MG: Ah, no ticket, and no reservation.

JS: Thank you! I'll see if I can make it.[15]

MG: I'll send some details.

JS: For *Shubibinman 2* did you work from home?

MG: I worked at the office to make the game.

JS: The office of Winds?

MG: Yes, Winds! It was a very small office. This was a condominium, or rather one of the rooms in a condominium. Very small! Like an apartment.

JS: What do you think of digital games?

MG: Recently I bought some games via Steam, on download. Do you know *La Mulana*? I bought the updated version. I played *La Mulana* until the end. And I played *Fez*!

JS: *<jokingly>* No! You shouldn't play *Fez*!

MG: <*laughs*>

JS: *Fez* is by Phil Fish!

MG: Yes, but you misunderstand him. He's a very pure and honest person, I think. Did you see *Indie Game The Movie*?

JS: I saw a trailer, but I've not watched it yet.

MG: I strongly recommend everyone watch this movie. Because you can understand the environment of making indie games.

JS: Yes, there was Phil Fish, Jonathan Blow, and Team Meat. Have you played *Braid*?

MG: I bought it, but I haven't played it yet. Recently my favourite game is *They Bleed Pixels*. This game, <*laughs*> it's a lot of fun!

JS: *<looking over Steam list>* Oh, *Faster Than Light*. Have you played that?

MG: No. I've never played it. I only bought it.

JS: It's like *Star Trek*. You should play it.

MG: Like *Star Trek*? I like *Star Trek* so much. I'm a trekkie!

JS: So am I! Is it popular in Japan.

MG: Yes, it's very famous. I liked *Voyager* the most. The *Voyager* series is very good, and also *The Next Generation* too.

JS: What's the translation like in Japan?

MG: Everything is translated into Japanese. Dialogue, and subtitles. I try to read the subtitles while listening to the English to improve my English speaking.

JS: But *Star Trek* uses very strange words.

MG: <*laughs*> Yes, I think so!

JS: You'll learn stuff like *magnetic phase coils!*

MG: <*laughs*> Oh yeah. My wife says the same thing to me. This is not good English! <*laughs*> My wife strongly recommends *Friends*, for conversation. But I prefer things like *Star Trek* and *X-Men*. <*laughs*>

JS: Tell me about working on *Don Quixote*.

[15] Unfortunately I could not make it - I had 2 interviews on 25 October, and 4 interviews the day after that

MG: What I most remember about the development is going to Pioneer's factory where they were developing the LaserActive. I saw a gigantic machine used to burn (press) LaserDiscs. There were very few LaserActive games, so it was a very rare and valuable experience to be involved with the development. The LaserActive was a very unusual device. It had two interchangeable hardware modules supporting the Mega Drive and the PC Engine, and also enabled users to play both Mega CD games and PC Engine CD-ROM2 games. *Don Quixote* was an unusual combination of a Mega Drive + LaserDisc game. I developed it on a LaserActive development kit connected to Mega Drive hardware. The program, naturally, was a Mega Drive program. The most surprising thing was how it took up to a week to burn a LaserDisc, at cost of around 100'000 yen.[16] My supervisor was very angry with me when the game wouldn't launch because of a programming error!

JS: How did you join the project?

MG: At the time, I was going to university classes in the evenings. I heard about the game at the company where I was working part-time during the day, and ended up joining the project. It was a busy time for me, with game development during the day, and university classes at night.

JS: Could you describe the game?

MG: In *Don Quixote*, specific animated video on the LaserDisc would play as the game progressed. The game itself was an RPG. The player would walk through a forest, encounter and fight enemies, gain experience, and level up. As the game progressed, bosses would appear at specific locations, and couldn't be defeated unless the player had fought their way up to a certain level. The player won the game by defeating the final boss. Also, the in-game graphics were entirely animated video. The animation was split up into short clips, which would be joined together and displayed by random access of the LaserDisc. If you were to play back this game on an ordinary LaserDisc player, you'd simply see a nonsensical series of short clips. But when played as a game, the short video clips are correctly joined together to present the game screen.

The key point was how to make the random access of the LaserDisc as fast and accurate as possible in order to play back the correct video. Control of the LaserDisc had to be built into the program, in the same way as the control routines for the Mega CD. The major difference versus the Mega CD was that LaserDiscs had inferior random access compared to CDs. Since LaserDiscs were so large, there was a big difference in angular velocity between the outer and inner edges of the disc. As a result, getting the LaserDisc head to move to the correct position (sector) and read out data from the target sector was difficult, and rarely successful on the first attempt. If the wrong sector was read, a neighbouring animation clip would be played back. I had a lot of trouble with this issue.

JS: This was for Premier International, right?

MG: Premier International was a very famous company in the Japanese film industry, so I was able to hear some very interesting stories about the entertainment industry and celebrities. I can't share these stories, but I remember being surprised at how the mindset and culture differed wildly from the game industry.

JS: Did Premier International give you source code examples to make programming easier?

MG: I did not receive any program source code, but they did give me all of the animated video that was going to be burned onto the LaserDisc.

JS: Do you have any final message?

MG: I developed the very first Pico game. It was released simultaneously with the hardware, so I was under immense pressure, and poured a lot of work into that game. On the other hand, it was also the first game where I worked as the lead programmer. That experience led to my current interest in serious games. I want to apply the power of games to a variety of fields such as education, medicine, and tourism, and not just games as entertainment. I hear that there are an extremely large number of such serious games in the US, France, and the Netherlands. Through the Pico, I had the rare and valuable experience of creating educational games over 20 years ago. So now I would like to use current technology to leave behind some wonderful games for the children born in the future.

[16] Around £630 / $900 in 1994

~In memory of~

うらべ・すぅ

URABE, Suu

Passed away 7 October 2001

~Selected Portfolio~

Kaizou Choujin Shubibinman	- PC Engine, 1989	(Character design)
Sol Bianca	- PCE CD-ROM, 1990	(NPC design)
Shubibinman 2 / Shockman	- PC Engine, 1991	(Scenario writer, graphic designer)

Unfortunately an English Wikipedia page doesn't exist for him. He passed away in 2001. In addition to working on games, he was also a famous indie comic artist in Japan. He was a really good guy and very kind to people.
- ***Makoto Goto, colleague from Winds***

He was working as a freelance talent for NCS since before the formation of Winds. I first met him in a subcontracting interview. I was amazed when I saw his work. One of these days, my time will come too. On that day... Suu-san, you better let me read the rest of your unfinished comic. <*laughs*> This time you have plenty of time until the deadline! Saying "Sorry, it's not ready yet... by next week..." won't work anymore. Get it done! What? Statute of limitation? No way. There's no way I'm going to forget about it and let you off easy. After all, I'm your fan.
- ***Masayuki Suzuki, colleague from Winds***

He was my superior at work. We were pretty close in age, but he had previously done work with Masaya. Even though his artwork was dainty and cute, he was a powerful person, full of vitality. He was the first person among my friends to pass away... It's already been about 20 years maybe? He was a great singer, with a pair of lungs like an opera singer! When we went out for karaoke, we'd be like, "You sure don't need a microphone!" <*laughs*>
- ***Satoshi Nakai, colleague from Winds***

~Appearing in a later volume~

Continuing our look at Winds there's an interview with **Satoshi Nakai** (left), legendary artist who created the mecha designs for *Cybernator*, and the bosses in both *Gynoug* and *Resident Evil: Code Veronica*. On the same day, **Takato Yoshinari** (upper right) of Success was interviewed, along with **Ken Ogura** (*Operation Darkness*) and **Masahiro Fukuda** (*Cotton*). While at Success I also interviewed **Masayuki Suzuki** (below right), mastermind behind *Langrisser* and *Shubibinman 3*.

~*Ask a Question*~

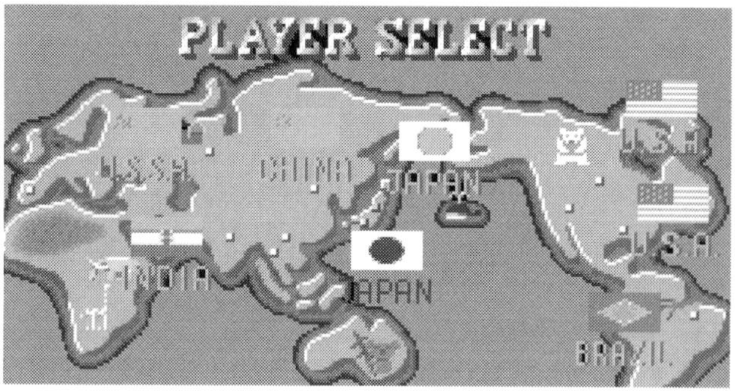

The *Ask a Question* tier evolved over time. Initially it allowed one question for a specific interviewee, but with the expansion of the Guest Editor tier, this tier expanded to allow up to 3 questions for interviewees, assuming there was time during the interview. Of the 13 *AaQ* backers, two were not contactable during the project at all, so I am unsure of their profile details and postal addresses. But I wish to thank them for their support: **Masao Watanabe** and **Rune Knytling**. I tried contacting them outside of Kickstarter, but as yet have been unable. **Makoto Goto** was also an *Ask a Question* backer, but given his history in the games industry I also decided to conduct an interview - with fascinating results!

Anthony Marandola

DOB: *secret*
Location: New Jersey
Blood: O
Favourite Game:
Mega Man X (SNES)
Message:
It's not X you should worry about - it's me! ~Zero

*****

Artemio

DOB: 21 January 1976
Location: Mexico
Blood: O
Favourite Game:
Strider (Arcade)
Message:
Keep old games and hardware alive.

*****

Chris Sevigny

DOB: 20 June 1985
Location: Vancouver, Canada
Blood: O
Favourite Game:
Takeshi's Challenge (Famicom)
Message:
Sometimes a card, other times a cad.

*****

Garrett O'Boyle

DOB: 22 November 1990
Location: Colorado
Blood: AB
Favourite Game:
Shadow Tower Abyss (PS2)

*****

George Mori

DOB: 19 March 1979
Location: Miami, FL
Blood: *secret*
Favourite Game:
Shenmue
Message:
I miss the glory days of Japanese development. At least Falcom still lives.

Jose Zagal

DOB: 12 May
Location: Chile
Blood: O
Favourite Game:
Advance Wars (GBA)
Message:
Videogames are the cultural art form of the 21st century, so lets not forget their history!

Shane Gill

DOB: 24 April 1989
Location: Sheffield, UK
Blood: A
Favourite Game:
Dragon Quest
Message:
Thanks for having me! I'd like to give a shout-out to my friends at NormalBoots.

*****

Shinogu

DOB: 26 January
Location: Brooklyn
Blood: A
Favourite Game:
Metal Gear Solid 2: SoL
(PlayStation 2)
Message:
70% of my body is *MGS2*, which I guess explains my skinniness.

*****

Manuel Sagra

DOB: 8 September 1979
Location: Madrid, Spain
Blood: O
Favourite Game:
Streets of Rage 2 (MD)
Message:
The legend will never die.

*****

Oh Young Wook

DOB: *secret*
Location: South Korea
Blood: *secret*
Favourite Game:
The Legend of Heroes II: Prophecy of the Moonlight Witch (PC)
Message:
We must dig up gaming history before it is forgotten.

~ *Guest Editors* ~

The Guest Editor tier, the highest tier besides the signature book, also evolved. Initially it allowed up to 3 questions and a choice of chapter topic. It quickly became apparent that certain topics could not be covered, for example *Fire Emblem*, so a few Guest Editors changed their topics, and one downgraded to the *Ask a Question* tier. Once the topics were set though, I decided to allow an unlimited number of questions - or at least as many as I could fit into the allotted time.

Chris Walden

DOB: 18 March 1990
Location: Basingstoke, UK
Blood: *secret*
Favourite Game:
Final Fantasy IX (PlayStation)
Message:
Is *The Last Guardian* out yet?

Jared Neal

DOB: 3 July 1986
Location: California
Blood: B
Favourite Game:
Suikoden 2 (PlayStation)
Message:
Hi!

Yoshimasa KUSAKA

DOB: 31 May 1976
Location: Tokyo, Japan
Blood: A
Favourite Game:
Metal Gear 2: Solid Snake (MSX2)
Message:
I like the MSX series, its simplicity.

Matt Sephton

DOB: 16 December 1976
Location: St Ives, Cornwall
Blood: O
Favourite Game:
MaBoShi (Wii/DS)

Visual Novels USA

DOB: 3 August 1990
Location: Peoria IL
Blood: A
Favourite Game:
Umineko When They Cry (PC)
Message:
You should pick up and play a good visual novel, yes you.

~ Backers ~

2 Player Productions
A Crane
Aaron Clark
Aaron Corff
Aaron Costello
Aaron Kaluszka
Aaron Rieger
Aaron Stelmaszek
Abdulhamid Khan
Abdullah Bin Abdullah
Abhilash Sarhadi
Abilash Pulicken
Abouani Anais
Adam Kempa
Adam Koziolkiewicz
Adam M Schoolcraft
Adam Nelson
Adam Norton
Adam Rippon
Adam Squire
Adam Stevens
Adam Szpakowski
Adam Wenzel
Adrian Gordon
Adrian Purser
Adrian Schmettau
Adrian Stutz
Aiman Ahmed
Aki Savolainen
Alan Bell
Alan Kleiman
Alan Zabaro
Albert Kaaman
Aldo Quispel
Alecry
Alejandro Balderas
Alessandro Calabrese
Alex Aplin
Alex Baker
Alex Brem
Alex Evans
Alex Kuo-Jeng Tsai
Alex Reid
Alexalyne Cosas
Alexander Lee
Alexander Moon
Alexander Napoli
Alexander Smith
Alexander Steers
Alexandre d'Helt
Alistair Carroll
Allan Mills
ALLEN KWAN
Alois Wittwer
Alp Aziz Torun
Amanda C Slaughter
Amber Ulmer
Amna Hashmi
Amy Sutedja
Anders Bengtsson
Andre Kishimoto
Andreas Hedman
Andreas Hoppler
Andreas Jansheden
Andreas Kessissoglou
Andreas Svedlund
Andrew "Chouster" Chou
Andrew Atkinson
Andrew Baillie
Andrew Beecroft
Andrew Burmeister
Andrew Calvin
Andrew Crawshaw
Andrew Dang
Andrew Dean
Andrew Fisher
Andrew Hayward
Andrew Janke
Andrew Kenny
Andrew Ogier
Andrew Parker
Andrew Smyth
Andrew Vestal
Andy Davis
Andy De Wilde
ANDY KITKOWSKI
Andy Logan
Anglionin Louis
Anthony A Miller
Anthony Hall
Anthony Hanson
Anthony Herana
Anthony Heugh
Anthony Marandola
Anthony Nemoff
Antoine CHAUVIN
Anton Nilsson
Antti Manninen
April Urso
Ari Gibson
Arjan Bakker
Armen Ashekian
Armindo Schimith Correia
Arne Beer
Aron Williamson
Artemio Urbina Garcia
Arthur Gould
Arttu Multanen
Arttu Ponka
Arturo Holguin Fernandez
Ashleigh Tai
Ashley Day
Aske Trankjaer Furunes
Atley Joseph
Augustine Tay Zhong Yuan
Aya Ishida
Bagel Mckhoury
barnaby chambers
Barrie L Davis
Bastiaan van Rooden
Ben Stevens
Ben Wilkinson
Benjamin ARNAULT
Benjamin Gallardo
Bia Paige
Bjoern Boye Skjoldhammer
Blake Wilhelm
Blanchet Ludovic
BoB Morgan
Bobby Barton
Bobby Schweizer
Bodenand Xavier
Boris Agee
BOURDON Nicolas
Brad
Brad Crawford
Brad Welch
Bran Handley
Brandon Boyer
Brandon Enta
Brandon McDaniel
Brenda Romero
Brent Poynton
Brett Camper
Brett Kaplan
Brian Bizier
Brian Connolly
Brian Elliott
Brian Gan
Brian Golding
Brian Hardison
Brian LeBlanc
Brian Ngov
Brian R. Santos
Brian S Lang
Brian Smith
Brooks Sligh
Brunon Bobrowski
Bryan Baraoidan
Bryan Beck
Bryce Newbury
Budd Lam
Burkhard Franke
C. Caleb Jewett
C. Sevigny
Cabel Sasser
Caitlin Riley
Caleb Branson
Can Gemicioglu
cancian stephane
Candice Johnson
Carl Salbacka
Carla Magrelli
Carlo M
Carlo Savorelli
Carlos Escalante
Carlos Gutierrez Valerio
Carlos Pinto
Carlos R. Monarrez
Caroline Choong
Carsten Prag
Casey Cane
Casey Loe
Cass Holgate
Cera Youngson
Chang En Kai
Charles K Manila
Charles Wong
Chase Mixon
Chaunce Butterfield
Chelsea Quinn Baker
Chiuan Lyu
Chloe Bradley
Chris Bidwell
Chris Collette
Chris Drzewiecki
Chris Ellis
Chris Faylor
Chris Halvorson
Chris Lord
Chris Marshall
Chris Plewes
Chris Schofield
Chris Walden
Christian Arzate Cruz
Christian Bell
Christian Geiger
Christian Kessler
Christian Peralta Roque
Christian Ruiz
Christian Topnik
Christian Tschanz
Christiano Weirich
Christopher Deliz
Christopher Drouin
Christopher Duenas
Christopher Hall
Christopher Harvigsson
Christopher Hippe
Christopher Leong
Christopher Motter
Christopher Munn
Christopher Petersson
Christopher Pioli
Christopher Ramdeen
Christopher Supino
Chun Wah Kong
Clara Fernandez-Vara
Cody Guillory
Cody Martin
Cody Quest
Cole Wardell
Colin Bessell
Conall McMahon
Conner Hill
Coquereau Brice
Cori Gehring
Coues Ludovic
Coulange mathias
Craig Lupienski
Craig Smuda
Craig Venz
CT Huang
DAISAKU IKEJIRI
Daisuke Oyama
Dale Markey
Dale Taylor
Damian Butt
Dana H Damron II
Daniel
Daniel Adamic
Daniel Bishop
Daniel Cleaton
Daniel Crenna
Daniel Daddario
Daniel Dames
Daniel Dussault
Daniel Heslop
Daniel Hinman
Daniel Rider
Daniel Walder
Daniel Wong Palacios
Daniel Zhang
Danielle Allum
Danny Baxter
Danny Hogan
Danny Jameson
Danny Schmidt
Danton Farmer
Daria Varfolomeeva
Darlinda Casso
Darran Jones
Darren Michaud
Darrin Devito
Darryl Pineda
Darwin Pek
Dave Soloway
Dave Voyles
David Anderson
David Burk
David C Thompson
David Chang
David Crookes
David Ellingsen
David Estrella
David Gonzales
David Green
David Hankin
David Hudson
David Hunt
David Isherwood
David Kapp
David Korth
David Kudrev
David Lerat
DAVID LUECKE
David Lyons
David Marrott
David McIntyre
David McKie
David Northover
David Petchey
David Petyt
David Quina
David Sillitoe, Product Madness
David Teo Yi Jie
David Thomas
David Thompson
David Thomson
David Tran Quang Ty
David Turner
David Voswinkel
David W. Weaver
David Wolinsky
David Wragg
Davis T Vu
Dawn Oshima
Deborah Hare
Debra

DELGOFFE Antoine
dennis de vos
Dennis Rubinshteyn
Dereck Welch
Derek Bender
Derek Chow
Derek Yu
Derrick Smith
Devendra Mahendran
Devin Monnens
Diep Thai
Dietmar Uschkoreit
Dimitrios Samaras
Dolan Scherfel
Dominic Ferrer
Dominik Lampke
Don Hogan
Dotan Dvir
Douglas Trapp
Dr Martine
Dr. Kimberly Voll
Dugan Jackson
Dustin Burnett
Dustin Williams
Dyllon Ashton
Earl Garcia
E.B.D. Holland
Ec Carlos
Ed Descault
Eddy S Tandya
Edmund Ching
Eduardo Garabito
Edward Mah
Edward Tran
Edward Welsby
Eero Pihkala
Eirik Suhrke
Elijah Ritchie
Ellen Kaye-Cheveldayoff
Elton Borges Mesquita
Emily Tuten
Enrico Di Franco
Er Lern Loh
Erasmus Brosdau
Eric Boghos
Eric "ShouTime" Chung
Eric Freeman
Eric Killen
Eric Moede
Eric Nagler
Eric Owens
Eric Regelman
Erik Elgerot
Erik Gallup
Erik Pede
Erik Sundqvist
Erik van Antwerpen
Erik Voskuil
Erin Spencer
Esteban Conejeros
Ethyn Connors
Eugenio Berardi
EUILLOT Jonathan
Evan Brownfield
Evan Gowan
Ezra Hanson-White
Fabien Grossekemper
F. Vispo
Fabio Leporelli
Fabio Santana
Fabio Vitali
Farhad Mustafa
Farrokh Parang
Felix Martin Arrieta
Felix.Wassmer
Filipe Carvalho
Fiona Milne
Flemming Dupont
Florent Poiraud
Florian Bussmann
Florian Mihola
Fly Shearn
Forrest Ryan
Francesc Xavier Blasco
Francisco Alberto Serrano Acosta
Frank Cifaldi
Franklin Hamilton
Frans Antonissen
Frantz Louis-Jacques Jr.
Fredrik Hauger Olsen
Fritz Mills
FROMENTIN Simon
Fukuda Takuya
Fumihiro Kanaya
GamesYouLoved
Gareth Lough
Garrett O'Boyle
Gary Kilby
Gavin Fitzgerald
George Bray
George Mori
George Selembo
Gerard Antoine Remy Bastien Arce
Gil Megidish
Glenn Dalby
Glenn Ignacio
Gokhan Bag
Gonzalo Salgado Gamboa
Gorges Florent
Gorm Lai
Graham Banting
Graham Bowman
Greg Cobb
Greg Hackmann
Greg Hartman
Gregg Turek
Gregor Kartsios
GREGORY CALAY
Gregory Shefler
Gregory Wier
Guadalupe Alvarez Gil
Guilherme Saba
Guillaume DAVID
Guillaume Lebigot
Guillaume Verdin
Guillermo Banuls Aizpiri
Gunnar Hogberg
Guy dawson
Hakim Boukellif
Halil H Ra
Han Yip
Hanae CHINO
Hannu Korhonen
Hans Winterhalter
Harley Gresham
Harmik Khoronian
Harry Bournazos
Hector Ascencio
Heejae Chang
Heidi Liesman
Heidi Luecke
Heidi Sosinski
Heinrich Pinardo
Helena Szczepaniak
Hendrik Lesser
Henri Toivonen
Henrik Flink
Henry Gilbert
Henry Phillips
Henry W Schubert
Heremans David
Herve Anne-Solene
Hideaki Kominami
Hidenori Shibao
Hirokazu Kashio
Hiromasa Iwasaki
Hiroshi Arai
Hiroshi Iwanaga
Hiroyuki Matsumoto
Honfei Li
Hourdin Vincent
Hugh Briant
Hurel Matthieu
Iain Riley
Ian Glynn
Ian Horswill
Ian L. Glidewell
Ignacio Esains
Igor Doslov
Ijke Botman
Iker Del Campo Saiz
Ioannis Psaroudas
Isaac Ahern
Isaac Bardis
Israel Rodriguez Nava
Ivan Adame
Ivan Diaz A‌lvarez
Iwan van Blerk
Jaakko Hakulinen
Jack Waghorn
Jacki Rountree
Jacob Gordon
Jacob Saunders
Jake Smith
Jala Prendes
James Agnew
James Austin
James Barry
James Briscoe
James E Phillips III
James Greenhalgh
James James
James Kay
James Kehoe
James McCawley
James Monkman
James Oikawa
James Pope II
James Rutherford
James Scott
James Tudhope
James Woodward
James Wragg
Jamie Aczel
Jamie Gregory
Jammar Prince
Jan Bielecki
Jan Sperling
Jan-Arne Sobania
Jani Klingberg
Jared Neal
Jared Shaver
Jared Zane Chickoree
Jarrod Anderson
Jason Aubain
Jason Batten-Carew
Jason Breti
Jason Butkans
Jason Cipriano
Jason Fletcher
Jason Li
Jason Miles
Jason Neifeld
Jason Ramke
Jason Rebelo
Jason Schreier
Jason Scott
Jason Scotti
Jason Smith
Jay Cooprider
Jay Garcia
Jay Portelli
Jayme Watson
Jean ALLOIN
Jean-Marc El Baki
Jeff deSolla
Jeff Gilbert
Jeff Lambert
Jeff Rivera
Jeffrey Lewis
Jeffrey Melichar
Jenny Rouse
Jens Habermann
Jens Marut
Jeremiah Wood
Jeremy Huntink
Jeremy Neiman
Jeremy Nissen
Jeremy Read
Jeremy Steffen
Jesse McGatha
Jesse Watson
Jessica K. Wong
Jessica Ying
Jim Bulmer
Jim O'Connor
Jimmy A Guerrero
Joachim Hesse
Joao Batista Reis
Joe Kanuritch
Joe Saint
Joel Catalan
Joel Forth
Joel Kreutzwieser
Joey Hwang
Johan Hallstan
John Andersen
John Arnone
John Bruce
John DiSanto
John Ellis
John Ford
John Henderson
John Kaminar
John Kane
John L. Gehron
John Leen
John Peter McGrath
John Pickering
John Raymond C. Lim
Johnnie Hamn
Jon John
Jon Redshaw
Jon Shafer
Jonatan Lofgren
Jonathan Agno
Jonathan Barrett
Jonathan Benefiel
Jonathan Choi
Jonathan Leung
Jonathan Lumb
Jonathan Smith
Joni Laurila
Jonic Linley
Jordan Atkins
Jordan Cognard
Jorge Pedrero Reyna
Jose Angel Lara Sanchez
Jose Antonio Barroso
Jose Jorge Enriquez Rodriguez
Jose Juan Munoz Moreno
Jose Luis Equiza
Jose Luis Espinoza Cuevas
Jose Luis Tur Santolaria
Jose Manuel Marquez Rodriguez
Jose P. Zagal
Joseph Cortese
Joseph K. Garrahan
Joseph Rard
Joseph Re
Josh Fairhurst
Josh Hall-Bachner
Josh Rudis
Josh Schonstal
Josh Sparks
Joshua Castor
Joshua DeGagne
Joshua Thompson
Jouhaine Aljobair
Juan Jose Ibanez Amat
Juan Ortiz
Julian Garnier
Julie Jurgens
Julien MARIEZ
Jun Mukai
Jun Yoshino
Jung-Sheng Lin
Juno Jin
Jurie Horneman

Justin Chen
Justin Chow
Justin Harvey
Justin Jones
Justin Lombardi
Justin Ng
Justin Scott
Justin Stallone
Karim Hadj-Ahmed
Karim Masri
Kari-Pekka Ahola
Karl-Johan Nilsson
Kastel
Kate Branner
Kathleen Abbott
Kathleen French
Kathleen Kuo
Kathryn Montgomery
Kazuhiro TAKAHASHI
Keane Ng
Keith G Hayward
Keith Hladik
Kelly Horan
Kelly Ziemski
Ken Nim
Kenichi Matsuo
Kenmiller
Kenneth Nida
Kevin A Swartz, MD
Kevin Bachus
Kevin Brand
Kevin Christman
Kevin Giguere
Kevin Grasso
Kevin Linden
Kevin Melin
Kevin Ng
Kevin Oke
Kevin Robinson
Kevin Savetz
Khaled Naser Al Koudmani
Khoi Phan
Ki-Hyun Cho
Kim Hyungjin
Kim Pedersen
Kimmo Rostedt
Kin Chung Yu
Kin Lok LEUNG
Kinnon Yee
Koh Ming Yi James
Koichi Kimura
Konstantin Kirch
Kristian Handberg
Krystyna Jan Bobrowscy
Krzysztof Bobrowski
Kuniaki Watanabe
Kurt Adam
Kurt Kalata
Kurt Van Ristell
Kush Patel
kyle a snyder
Kyle Bolton
Kyle Ito
Kyle Lester
Kyle Mackaravitz
Kyle Robertson
Kyle Soward
Kyrre Havik Eriksen
Label Sak
Laszlo Benyi
Laurent Mazouer
Lawrence Clark
Leandro Cid
Lech Lozny
leclerc yohan
Lee Jackson
Lee Taylor
Leif Hedly Birkeland
Thorbjornsen
Leon Bobrowski
Leon Byford
Leon Hilu
Leonard Toy
Leong Mun Kew
Leslie Law
Liam Allen-Miller
Liam O'Shaughnessy
Lik Chan
Lila Papiernik
Lionel Marechal
Lisbeth Nilsen
Logan 'Logie' James
LOH TING
Lorenzo Ceccotti
Louie Kamarinos
Ludwig Oetker
Luis Alis Ferrer
Luis Coelho
Luis H. Garcia
Luis Levy
Luiz Gilberto de Barros Filho
Lukas Marti
Lukas Mathis
Lukas Schaffner
Luke Edgington-Brown
Luke haugh
Luke McCarthy
Luke Orphanides
Lutz Ohl
M Hanlon
M. Rule
M.H. Epere
Mads Stald
Makoto Goto
Manuel castellano corral
Manuel Sagra de Diego
Marc Heitler
Marc Paimblanc
Marc Rollan Serrano
Marcelo Reis Pinto
Marco Lazzeri
Marc-Olivier Chauvin
Marcus Devlin
Marcus Evans
Marcus Lindberg
Marcus Persson
Marcus Rangell
Maria Guadalupe Vlcek
Marius Beyermann
Mark Cook
Mark Elliott
Mark Holland
Mark Paterson
Mark Pidal
Mark Reick
Mark Taormino
Mark Ting
Mark Wheatley
Markus Autio
Marshall Ward
Marten Bruggemann
Martin Boecking
Martin Henrik
Martin Picard
Martin Tremon
Marty Chinn
Mary Williamson
Masakazu, Taniguchi
Masao Watanabe
Mat Allen
Mat Corne
Matheus Fraguas
Mathew Stevens
Mathieu Hebert
Matt Allen
Matt Clemson
Matt Leone
Matt Sephton
Matt Shores
Matt Wilkinson
Matthew Alpert
Matthew Austin
Matthew Barr
Matthew Borgard
Matthew Campbell
Matthew Deeprose
Matthew Earney
Matthew Hill
Matthew Hodgson
Matthew Howell
Matthew Humphries
Matthew Keller
Matthew Kenyon
Matthew La France
Matthew Lagan
Matthew Licata
Matthew Mayatt
Matthew Ng
Matthew Recenello
Matthew Reis
Matthew Tipton
Matthew Vose
Matthew Walkden
Matthias Ziller
Matti Rantanen
Mattias Dahlberg
Max Mielecki
Max Symmes
Max Wawer
Maximilian Olbers
Maximilian Rehkopf
Melanie Mauch
Melanie Nazelrod
Melissa Louie
Micah Keawe-Dunaway
Micah McFarland
Micha Savelsbergh
Michael Baraniecki
Michael Boon
Michael C Maroon
Michael Conkin
Michael Damiani
Michael Danquah
Michael Do
Michael Dougherty
Michael Dragone
Michael Falkensteiner
Michael Frisch
Michael Geyre
Michael Green
Michael Hallard
Michael Ivan Miley
Michael Martignetti
Michael Nelson
Michael Pianta
Michael Quandt
Michael Raison
Michael Reichelt
Michael Richardson
Michael Scuderi
Michael Stadler
Michael Stearns
Michael Tedder
Michael Tervoort
Michael Tobin
Michael Walton
Michele Zaltron
Michiel Koning
Miguel Angel Rodriguez
Mendez
Miguel Herranz
Mike Falkingham
Mike Jones
Mike Meltzer
Mike Shewan
Mike Stedman
Mikhail Tatyanin
Miles Aurbeck
Minoru TODA
Miodrag Kovacevic
Mitchell Healey
MIYACHI SATORU
Mohammad Hanif Jhaveri
Mohammed A Ali
Mohibur 'NurBoy' Rahman
Moise Breton
Molongo Christophe
MORAUX Benoit
Morin Guillaume
Moritz Sommet
Moshe
Mr C Mckinlay
Mr Justin Palmer
Munechika Nishida
Munly Leong
N R CORY
Nabeel M. Al-Haider
Nami Kusumoto
Naseer Alkhouri
Natasha Yellowlees
Nathan Fouts
Nathan Treichel
Nathaniel Donley
Nathaniel J. Huston
Naveau Julius
Neil Atkinson
Neil Evans
Neil Kenny
Nicholas Basile
Nicholas Chaimov
Nicholas Custer
Nick Atkins
Nick Dominguez
Nick Emmerich
Nick Evans
Nick London
N. McVroom-Amoakohene
Nick Nillo
Nick Porcino
Nico Assinck
Nicolas Allgaeuer
Nicolas BOULIN
Nicolas Cailleaud
Nicolas Sallin
Nicolas Torres
Niels van Rongen
Nigel Chee
Nikita Kozyrenko
Nikolay Kryuchkov
Nikos Constant
Nils-Henrik Lundquist
Nina Khosla
Noah Bacon
Nobuyuki Hirashima
Norihiro Sawada
Nuno Antunes
OH YOUNG WOOK
Ola Bismo Klashaugen
Oliver Bermoy
Oliver Clarke Smith
Oliver Feldwick
Olivier Crepin
Olivier Hustin
Olivier Lejade
Olivier Riedo
Olivier Vigneresse
Ondrej Omar Martinek
Owen Baron
Owen Searfoss
Pablo Tourino
Parthipan Pathmanapan
Pascal Sygnet
Pat Randell
Patrice Dupont
Patrick Alfonsi
Patrick Benfield
Patrick Bregger
Patrick Griffin
Patrick Harmon
Patrick van der Ende
Patrick Yeung
Patrik Paarnio
Paul Blair
Paul Brownlee
Paul Darbyshire
Paul Egan
Paul Evans
Paul Hachmann
Paul Hodgeson
Paul Knights
Paul Martin
Paul Mcgee,

Paul Schmalenberg
Paul Trautrim
Pauli Nykanen
Pavels Trifonovs
Pedro Vaz de Mello de Medeiros
Per Kristian Brastad
Pere Lluis Vidal
Pete Muller
Peter Cintula
Peter O'Dell
Peter Smith
Peter Tomatz
Petter Bjelm
Phil Williams
Philip Falco
Philip 'MrPhil' Ludington
Philip Pryce
Philip Wagner
Phillip Wong
Pier Paolo Guillen Hernandez
Pierre Gosselin
Pierre Hayeur
Pierre-Luc Lapointe
Pietro Recchi
Pit Thommes
Quinton Klabon
R Hunter Gough
Rade Martinovic
Rafael Blasco Rozas
Rafael Borges Ventura
Rafael San Miguel Thurn
Raffael Zaghet
Rakesh Singh
Ramon Gamaliel Gonzalez Acero
RAMON MERCHAN SANZANO
Ramon Verlinden
Randall Hailer
Raphael Gouin
Raux Corentin
Ravinder Ruprai
Raydere
Remy Lavoie
Renya Iizuka
Renzo Adler
Rhys Lewis
Richard Burton
Richard Davey
Richard Gilmore
Richard White
Rick Felice
Rick Lindeman
Rishi Alwani
Robbie Byrne
Robert Arlauskas
Robert Hazelby
Robert Khoe
Robert Love
Robert M Fenner
Robert Mertling-Blake
Robert Sobaszek
Robert Wolf
Robert Zupko
Robin Furr
Rocky Khasow
Rodrigo Maximo Menezes de Lima
Rolando Cedillo
Ron Dippold
Rory Solley
Rosatti Vincent
Ross Foubister
Ross Ingram
Ross Main
Ross Rosenberg
Rowan Carmichael
rucar patrice
Ruda Moreira
Rune Knytling
Rune Vendler
Russell Johnson
Ryan Burton
Ryan Dodds
Ryan Elis
Ryan Evans
Ryan Finkler-Pfeffer
Ryan Gan
Ryan Murphy
Ryan Pas
Ryan Schlegel
Ryan Seney
Ryan Suwarsa
Ryan VanMeter
Ryan Vissers
Ryosuke Nagao
Sagi Abutbul
Salvador Mora
Sam Bushman
Sam Moseley
Sam Parwar
Sami Hangaslammi
Samuel Cho
Samuel Constantino
Samuel Engel
Samuel Derboo
Samuel Schmid
Samuel Thomas
Samuel Vines-Stancill
Samuli Jaaskelainen
Santiago Orozco
Santiago Romero
Sara Sim
Satoshi Asaka
Saugat Manandhar
Scott Fintel
Scott Tsai
Scrybo.com
Sean Korzdorfer
Sean O'Brien
Sean Owczarek
Sean R. Renshaw
Sean Schatzman
Sebastian Donnerstag
Sebastian Matyas
Sebastien BERAT
Sebastien Perier
Sebastien Valencia
Segundo Nallatan Jr
Sergey Akimov
Seth Gingo
Seung Chan Lim
Seungback Shin
Shad Ali
Shams Ben Amor
Shane Cibuls
Shane Gill
Shane Starkey
Shane Sweeney
Shaun Hughes
Shaun Inman
Shawn Collier
Shen Lu
Shigeru UCHIYAMA
Shiva Allari
Sho Ito
Siddhartha Chatterjee
Simon Borgenvall
Simon Chapuis
Simon Christensen
Simon Revell
Simonetta Paolella
Sjur Sorli
Soren Lauridsen
Sorrel Tilley
Spc Damon English
squidamus
Srikar Nalluri
Stefan Herzog
Stefan Voswinkel
Stephan Rozendaal
Stephan Weis
Stephanie Woor
Stephen Bruce
Stephen Green
Stephen Kitt
Stephen Swan
Stephen Swift
Stephen W. Chen
Steve Baines
Steve Lockett
Steven Anthony P Brown
Steven Kaltenbach
Steven Martin
Steven Maruszak
Steven Piozet
Steven Popoff
Steven Pritchett
Steven Stadnicki
Steven Staton
Stuart McAlpine
Stuart Peake
Sukrit Siripun
Sven Schmalfuss
TAKAHIRO OKI
Takashi Kawano
Takeshi NAKAMURA
Tan Chia Ren
TAN YANG YANG
Taylor Aidan
Taylor Johnson
Taylor Logelin
Taylor Morris
Terufumi Ochi
Tetsuya Ishibashi
The Index
Theo Satoshi Tanaka
Thibaut Saumade
Thierry Bazillon
Thomas Edmister
Thomas Frohlich
Thomas Gooddy
Thomas Hood
Thomas Lewis
Thomas Liebert
Thomas Nickel
Thomas Planques
Thomas S. Ciolek
Thomas Taimre
Thomas Zimmermann
Thomson Reuters
Tiarnan McNulty
Tieg Zaharia
Tim
Tim Fischer
Tim Suter
Timo Soilamaa
Timothy and Jacquie Millman
Timothy Banas
Timothy Chappell
Timothy Werner
Tobias Bjarneby
Todd Crockett
Todd Johnson
Todd Little
Todd Showalter
Tom Dawson
Tom Hinkle
Tom Robertshaw
Tom Rojas
Tom Voros
Tomas Gradin
Tomasz Finc
Tomer Gilron
Tomm Hulett
Toni Kurki
Toni Makinen
Tony Martinez
Tormod Tjaberg
Toru Yamada
Toshiyuki Hashitani
Toyotaka Fukushi
Travis Canady
Trevor Ali
Trevor Paulson
Trevor Williams
Trey Smith
Troy Fox
Ty Cottingham
Tyler Martin
Tyler Robertson
Tyler Sill
Tyron Wain
Vanessa Lambert
Varenne olivier
Vicky Lee
Viktoras
Ville Hahtonen
Vincent Baidoo
Vincent Diamante
Vincent Lefevre
Vincent LEVY
vincent Riley
Vinicius Braga de Andrade
Vittorio Giorgi
Vizzacchero Sebastien
Vogelchan.I.A.
VRC-7
Wade-Hahn Chan
Wai Ming Chow
Wassim IBEN
Wataru Ishigame
Wen Hsuan Chung
Wes Ehrlichman
Wesley Fok
Will Carlough
Will Swannack
William Anderson
William James Matthews
William Reisdorff
William T. Voss
WILSON BILKOVICH
Wing-Pui Chung
Wouter de Hoogd
Wyatt Epp
Yakov Grinberg
Yann Best
Yaw Glover
Yin Khwin Oo
Yolanda Bentancourt
Yoshihiro Shingu
Yoshimasa KUSAKA
Yuji Suzuki
Yu-Ling Wong
Yury Ilinskiy
Yusuke Misawa
Zach Gage
Zach Mcdowell
Zachary C Koeneke
Zhiming Chen
Zoe Tsang
Zoya

INDEX

Other great game books

*****

By Hardcore Gaming 101

Please visit:

http://www.hardcoregaming101.net/books.htm

HG101 Presents: Castlevania

Welcome to the hell house! *Hardcore Gaming 101 Presents: Castlevania* includes 158 pages with full reviews of over thirty *Castlevania* titles - starting from the 1987 Nintendo original up to the 2014 *Lords of Shadow 2* - plus reviews of clone games, soundtracks, books, trivia, and more!

HG101 Presents: Sega Arcade Classics Vol. 1

Get ready to enter the world of Sega! *Hardcore Gaming 101: Sega Arcade Classics Vol. 1* includes 168 pages of extensive reviews of over seventy classic games originating from the 1980s and 90s arcade scene. Covered series include *Space Harrier, After Burner, OutRun, Fantasy Zone, Wonder Boy/Monster World, Alex Kidd*, and more!

HG101 Presents: The Guide to Classic Graphic Adventures

In 1984, Roberta Williams of Sierra On-Line designed *King's Quest*, the world's first graphic adventure. A huge step beyond the text-oriented games that preceded it, the genre took the world by storm, and proved immensely popular with computers over the next decade. A combination of storytelling and puzzle solving, they provided the ability to explore a world and experience a narrative without the need for twitchy reflexes demanded of arcade games. This nearly comprehensive book includes reviews for over 250 games from the golden age of the graphic adventure genre, running from 1984 to roughly 2000, focusing on prominent publishers such as LucasArts, Sierra On-Line, Legend, and several other popular and not-so-popular series and games. Also includes interviews with several adventure game developers, including Al Lowe (creator of *Leisure Suit Larry*), Corey Cole (creator of *Quest for Glory*), Bob Bates (founder of Legend Entertainment) and Josh Mandel (writer and designer for Sierra).

*****

By Sorrel Tilley

Monochromatica: Tales of Original Game Boy Development

Celebrate the Game Boy's 25th anniversary with *Monochromatica: Tales of Original Game Boy Development*, a book compiling dozens of brand new behind-the-scenes interviews with the people responsible for *Pokémon, Monster Max, Donkey Kong Land*, and many more! Coming in 2014. Like it on Facebook for updates.

32541161R00296

Made in the USA
Charleston, SC
18 August 2014